State of New York to Elijah Hunter Dr.

To Four Years & Four Months Pay as Captain allowed me for Secret Services perform'd by me for the United States from the 1 Novr 1778 to 1 March 1783 @ 40 Dolls ⅌ Month — £ 832 — —

I do hereby Certify that during the late war, Captain Elijah Hunter of Bedford in West Chester County was, on the Recommendation of Mr John Jay, then President of Congress, and of Major General McDougall employed on some secret services, which he performed, as far as came to my knowledge with Integrity and to my satisfaction.

Given under my Hand
this 1st Day of December 1783

Go Washington

GENERAL WASHINGTON'S CERTIFICATE TO THE CHARACTER OF A SCOUT.

New York in the Revolution as Colony and State

These Records Were Discovered,
Arranged and Classified
by

James A. Roberts

Comptroller
in
1897

HERITAGE BOOKS
2012

HERITAGE BOOKS
AN IMPRINT OF HERITAGE BOOKS, INC.

Books, CDs, and more—Worldwide

For our listing of thousands of titles see our website
at
www.HeritageBooks.com

A Facsimile Reprint
Published 2012 by
HERITAGE BOOKS, INC.
Publishing Division
100 Railroad Ave. #104
Westminster, Maryland 21157

Originally published:
Albany, New York
1897

— Publisher's Notice —
In reprints such as this, it is often not possible to remove blemishes from the original. We feel the contents of this book warrant its reissue despite these blemishes and hope you will agree and read it with pleasure.

International Standard Book Numbers
Paperbound: 978-0-7884-2284-3
Clothbound: 978-0-7884-9347-8

ARCHIVES

OF THE

COLONY AND STATE OF NEW YORK

IN THE

REVOLUTION.

DURING my first term of office as comptroller, the work of putting the old records of the comptroller's department in systematic order for purposes of easy reference was undertaken. This work in its progress brought to light quantities of forgotten papers relating to the services performed by New York in the Revolutionary war. These papers, long since detached from their original file packages, were promiscuously scattered through great masses of old vouchers and files. I realized at once their great value and importance, and my impression has been most amply confirmed by the judgment of Col. F. C. Ainsworth, whose great work in arranging for the United States government the contributions of men made in the various wars by the separate states and colonies, is well known. Competent men were, therefore, set at work searching out and arranging these papers, and this task, though slow and laborious, is believed to have been thoroughly and intelligently done. The success of this work is very largely due to the earnest and intelligent interest taken in it by Col. Charles O. Shepard, and his efforts were greatly assisted by the efficient work of Mr. William B. Wemple of this office.

These papers contain the muster and pay rolls of different organizations, and the historic value and importance of the papers is clearly proved by the fact that they alone show New York to have furnished nearly one and a half times the number of troops with which she is usually credited, and adding to these the names obtained from other reliable sources, the aggregate is more than twice the number usually credited. General Knox, first secretary of war, in his report to Congress of the number of troops furnished by each colony, gave New York credit for but 17,781 men, and this report, copied into our histories, very naturally has ever since been accepted as correct. We now find positive proof of the service of 41,633 men. I therefore submit the following pages containing the names, rank and organization of these 41,633 men, whose services can be shown beyond any question, with the greater satisfaction for believing that a great historical injustice, reflecting in many minds on New York's patriotic spirit in the revolutionary struggle, will hereby be rectified, and she take her place, second only to Massachusetts in number of troops furnished, and, under the circumstances surrounding her, second to none in lofty patriotism.

It is true that lists of names of New York's revolutionary soldiers have been heretofore published, but these were derived almost entirely from other than original sources, the state treasurer's books of account being the chief source, and their accuracy, for this reason, has been a matter of grave doubt, and therefore the results could not be accepted in historical works. All the names published in this volume are derived from that highest of sources, the original muster and pay-rolls, and thus the services of the individual and the aggregate are conclusively shown. Several thousands of the names, particularly of those belonging to the regiments of the "Line," were obtained from rolls on file in the War Department at Washington, through the courtesy of Hon. Daniel S. Lamont, Secretary of War. And here it may not be inappropriate to say that Col. Ainsworth, after personal examination of the records of service found in the comptroller's office, was so well satisfied of their accuracy and value, that he has had the same transcribed and placed in the records of the War Department, and the 41,633 names found here will now appear to the credit of New York in the government's record of the revolutionary war, soon to be published.

Nor do the names contained in this volume in all probability comprise all of those from New York who performed service in that great struggle. Cases exist in which records of a full quota of field, staff and line officers for a regiment have been found, but no enlisted men. This state of things was proof positive, to any one with knowledge of military affairs, that a deplorable deficiency in the records existed. It was not uncommon, as I am credibly informed, for the officer commanding an organization to retain all the records relating to his command. Indeed, the records from which the names of the men in Colonel Gansevort's regiment, Third New York Line, were obtained, are still in the possession of the descendants of Colonel Gansevort, and the only original record of Alexander Hamilton's artillery company is in the possession of the New York Historical Society, to which body we are indebted for its appearance here. Had New York, as several of the colonies did, published the record of its revolutionary service, while the records were still all existing and their location, and the facts connected with them, were within the memory of living men, a far more accurate result would have been reached. As it is, there can be little reasonable doubt that in some cases records of service have been lost, and that New York can never show the full number of troops furnished by her in the struggle. This is almost conclusively shown by the fact that the papers relating to pensions granted by the state for injuries received while in service in the Revolutionary War disclose many names which do not appear upon any roster in our possession.

In any consideration of what was contributed by the separate colonies to the success of the war, it is proper that the situation in each colony should be taken into account. New York, more than any other colony, was the battle-ground of the war, as indeed, from its position, it always will be in any conflict with Great Britain. The first forts captured from the English in the war were Ticonderoga and Crown Point, May 10th and 12th, 1775; and the first attempt to construct an American navy was made by Arnold on Lake Champlain in June, 1775. Johnson's last raid through the Mohawk valley, in which the battle of Johnstown and various smaller encounters were fought, took place in 1781. Between those dates were the expedition from New York into Canada, resulting in the siege and capture of the fort at St. John's, September 25th, 1775, followed by the capture of Montreal, and ending in the disaster at Quebec; the expedition to Johnstown, resulting in the surrender of three hundred armed Scotch Highlanders, January 19th, 1776; battle of Long Island, August 27th, 1776; battle of Harlem Plains, September 16th, 1776; battle of White Plains, October 28th, 1776; attack upon and capture of Fort Washington, November 16th, 1776; naval battles on Lake Champlain, October 11th and 13th, 1776; the various manœuvres of the eventful year 1777, which preceded the famous battles of that year; the battle of Bennington, fought on October 16th, 1777, on New York soil, but largely by Vermont boys, and which prevented the British from receiving needed supplies; the successful defence and sortie from Fort Schuyler, and the bloody battle of Oriskany, August 6th, 1777, which prevented the junction of St. Leger with Burgoyne, and made the latter's surrender inevitable; the glorious battles of Saratoga, September 19th and October 7th, 1777, leading to Burgoyne's surrender, October 17th, 1777; the destructive expedition up the Hudson under Sir Henry Clinton, October, 1777; Johnson's Indian raid through the Mohawk, Schoharie and Susquehanna valleys, 1778; Sir Henry Clinton's second expedition up the Hudson, May, 1779; Mad Anthony's capture of Stony Point with 543 prisoners, July 15th, 1779; the expeditions under Colonels Willett and Van Schaick against Onondagas, and the horrible retaliatory raids made by the Indians, 1779; Sullivan's expedition against the Indians in 1779, and the battle near the present site of Elmira; Johnson's raid into the Mohawk valley, 1780, and Governor Clinton's pursuit; the destruction of the Canajoharie and Fort Plain settlements by Brant, August, 1780; the extended raid of Sir John Johnson, Brant and Cornplanter, in the autumn of 1780, with the battle near Stone Arabia, and Carleton's raid on the upper Hudson, 1780. The surrender of Cornwallis in 1781 was the practical end of the conflict, and the foregoing list of military movements shows that every year during the conflict New York was the scene of very active service.

The extensive fighting done within our borders brought into active and honorable service branches of military which in colonies where no fighting was done were relieved. Our militia were the heroes of many hotly contested fields. The battle of Oriskany, in its percentages of killed and wounded, the bloodiest battle of the war, was won by the militia, and Burgoyne's surrender thereby made sure. The militia bore a highly honorable part in the ever memorable battles of Saratoga. But many men undoubtedly performed splendid service in the emergencies which called out the militia and then retired quietly to their homes, leaving no record of their service which can now be found.

Again, the portions of New York occupied by the whites were surrounded on almost all sides by tribes of hostile Indians, who were incited and led by still more savage whites. Brant was sometimes humane, but Butler never. The Hurons had inherited from many preceding generations the disposition to make hostile raids upon the territory of their ancient foes, the Iroquois. At the breaking out of the war the influence of Sir William Johnson over the tribes of the Iroquois was almost boundless. His position as Indian agent had brought him into close relations with these tribes, and this position he seems to have honorably used and to have succeeded in convincing them that he was their friend. His mantle, at his death, fell upon his son, Sir John, and his son-in-law, Col. Guy Johnson, and that they used their influence to the fullest extent to stir up Indian hostility to the patriotic citizens west of Albany is a sad page in the history of the war. The course pursued by Johnson in his raid of 1780, which is shown on a map which follows, and which was carefully prepared, and the account of the raid which has been compiled for this purpose, show the wide range of territory which was covered by this raid. Bear in mind that this was but one of several, and the condition of frontier New York during the war can be imagined. It required something more or less than patriotism to induce the frontiersman to leave his family with the prospect before them of that most horrible of frontier experiences, an Indian raid.

In the summer of 1776 the control of New York city, of Long Island and Staten Island and a part of Westchester county passed into the hands of the British, there to remain until after the treaty of peace, the evacuation taking place November 25, 1783. Fully one-tenth of the state's population, from which men could be drawn to recruit the armies, were thus locked up. The population of New York state in 1790 was 340,120, and of New York city alone, 33,131.

The influence of the Johnson family in the Mohawk and Schoharie valleys was predominant, not only with the Indians but with the whites as well. Sir William Johnson was the man to whom they all looked up; capable, occupying high positions and owning large tracts of land and having almost boundless control of the Indians. It is not strange that his influence should have been so great with the whites, and to that cause may be attributed the fact that many followed his successor, Sir John, in his defection.

These facts, briefly stated, show New York's trying position in the Revolutionary War, and confirm what was said at the outset, that in lofty patriotic endeavor, New York was second to none of the thirteen colonies.

The military forces of the Colony and State during the revolutionary struggle, were divided into three classes.

The Line; which regiments were in the United States service under General Washington. There were also regiments of artillery and an organization of "Green Mountain Boys" in the Line.

The Levies; which were drafts from the different militia regiments, and from the people direct as well, and which could be called upon to serve outside the State during their entire term.

The Militia; which then, as now, could only be called out of the State for three months at a time.

Records are found of four privateers in the service and pay of the State — the schooner "General Putnam," the sloop "Montgomery," the sloop "Schuyler," and the frigate "Congress." These armed vessels took many prizes, and records are found of the division of the spoils.

Of the **Line**, 9 organizations.

Of **Levies**, 7 organizations.

Of **Militia**, 68 organizations are traced by these records.

In all 84.

Associated Exempts were a unique class and were authorized by an act of April 3, 1778. They comprised: "All persons under the age of sixty who have held civil or military commissions and are not or shall not be re-appointed to their respective proper ranks of office, and all persons between the ages of fifty and sixty."

They could only be called out "in time of invasion or incursion of the enemy."

The militia regiments were designated, first by their colonel's names and next by their counties, as "Fisher's Regiment, of Tryon County."

Instances crop up, here and there, in which a number was given to a regiment; as, for instance, "The Sixth Albany County," but it is a moot question if such was the general practice. Be that as it may, the name of the colonel is found to be quite sufficient for full identification.

The Militia was called out when wanted; kept as long as wanted, and the soldiers then sent to their homes. Sometimes a regiment or a part of a regiment would be called out half a dozen times in the course of a year, and for half a dozen days at a time, and again it might not be needed in the entire year.

Officers and men seem to have served in different organizations almost indiscriminately. At one call, they were in one regiment or company, and at another call, in another regiment or company.

It is, therefore, very difficult to keep trace of them on the different pay-rolls or "pay-books," as they were sometimes called.

Nepotism, or family influence, was most marked, and some regiments contained as many as five and seven officers of the same family. (See Colonel Brinkerhoff's regiment, and the Millers', in Colonel Thomas' regiment.)

Counties were divided into districts, and the colonel of the regiment in each district was given almost unlimited jurisdiction in military matters. He was required to see that every male between the ages of sixteen and fifty was enrolled. Later, the age limit was extended to sixty.

If an able bodied man, he must serve when "warned" under penalty of fine and imprisonment; but if incapacitated, he must contribute toward furnishing and equipping another man — any person furnishing a substitute being exempt for the time that substitute served. Quakers, Moravians and United Brethren were enrolled, but exempted from service upon payment of money, which varied in amount as the war progressed until, in 1780, they were obliged to pay £160 per year.

One miller to each grist mill, three powder makers to each powder mill, five men to each furnace, three journeymen in each printing office, and one ferryman to each public ferry, were also exempt. Each soldier must present himself armed, and with a blanket, a powder-horn and a flint, and sometimes even a tomahawk was required.

All officers in the cities of New York, Albany and Schenectady were ordered to wear their swords during divine service under a penalty of twenty shillings.

Rum, sugar and tea were regular rations, and the amount was gauged by the rank. A major-general was deemed to require, and was allowed each month, four gallons of rum, six pounds of sugar, and half a pound of tea. A brigadier-general, three gallons of rum, four pounds of sugar, and six ounces of tea. A colonel, a lieutenant-colonel, and a major, two and one-half gallons of rum, and the same amount of sugar and tea. A chaplain, ditto as to sugar and tea, but only two gallons of rum.

The scale was continued until a non-commissioned officer and a private received one pound of sugar, two ounces of tea, and one pound of tobacco; but no rum.

A colonel's pay was $75 per month, or one York £ per day.

A lieutenant-colonel's pay was $60 per month.

A major's pay was $50 per month.

A captain's pay was $40 per month.

An adjutant's pay was $40 per month.

A lieutenant's pay was $26⅔ per month.

An ensign's pay was $20 per month.

A sergeant's pay was $8 per month.

A corporal's pay was $7⅓ per month.

A private's pay was $6⅔ per month.

Nor was this, by any means, always in money. It was sometimes in State notes and sometimes in authority to "impress" articles or animals under supervision of some designated officer, who should give a receipt, in the name of the State, to the impressee.

As late as 1784, the large majority of the soldiers were still unpaid for their services in 1776-7-8-9-80-81-82.

On April 27th of 1784, the legislature passed "An act for the settlement of the pay of the Levies and Militia for their services in the late war."

This statute provided that abstracts and pay-rolls of the different regiments and separate commands should be certified by the State auditor; he deducting for advances made to officers or privates by "impressing" or otherwise, and an allowance be made for the depreciation of the pay of such as had been in captivity, for the time they were in captivity.

Upon receipt of these accounts from the auditor, the treasurer of the State was required to issue to persons, to whom pay should appear to be due, or to their legal representatives, certificates of indebtedness bearing five per cent interest, and such certificates should be receivable for purchases of forfeited estates, or in payment for waste or "unappropriated lands," taxes, etc.

Officers could not "throw up or quit" their commissions until they had served fifteen years.

All slaves killed in the service were to be paid for.

In time of invasion, any slave, not in the military service, found one mile from his master's abode, without a certificate from his master showing his business, might be "shot or otherwise destroyed without fear of censure, impeachment or prosecution for the same."

In 1781, it was provided that any slave who should enlist and serve "for three years, or until discharged," should be declared a freeman of the State.

In the same year, a bounty of "Land Rights"—so-called—(a "Right" being 500 acres) was offered to officers and men for two regiments then to be raised, for the defense of the State.

To a colonel, lieutenant-colonel and major, four Rights. To a captain and a surgeon, three Rights. To a lieutenant, ensign or surgeon's mate, two Rights, and to a non-commissioned officer or a private, one Right.

Any master or mistress who should deliver an able-bodied slave to serve, one Right.

By an act of April 1st, 1778, each Militia regiment was divided into "classes" of fifteen men each. When soldiers were needed to recruit the line regiments, each class must, within nine days, furnish a man fully armed and equipped. In case they neglected so to do, the designated officer proceeded, at once, to draft one of the number by lot.

By an act of March 11th, 1780, every regiment was again divided into "classes;" this time of thirty-five men each, and when soldiers were required as before, these "classes" were also called upon to furnish a man as before, and in case of failure so to do within fifteen days, were fined a sum equal to double the amount of the highest bounty which had then been given. This fine was collected by distress and sale of goods and chattels of those refusing to pay, or, if not possessed of property, they were committed to jail "without bail or mainprize" until the sum was paid.

If a "class" furnished a man as the law required, it received a money bounty, sometimes as much as £80.

As the war progressed, and the needs of the government became more pressing, land "Rights" were added to the money bounty, and on March 23d, 1782, an act was passed providing that any "class" or any person who furnished an able-bodied man to serve "for three years, or during the war," should be entitled to 600 acres; or 350 acres for a two years' enlistment; and any person or "class" who should deliver a man within twenty days from the time of notification, 200 acres extra.

The meaning of Militia is—"The military force of a nation."

In this connection it may not be out of place nor uninteresting to trace this branch of the public service from its inception to the commencement of the Revolutionary war.

The militia of this continent had its origin in a law promulgated in 1664 by James, Duke of York and Albany; the owner, by a grant from Charles the Second, of a large territory, which included the territory which is now eastern and southern New York. "The Duke's Laws," as they are still called, covered numerous subjects and were most paternal and creditable.

As to militia, they provided that: "All males above the age of sixteen shall be enrolled and be subject to military duty. Each person must provide himself with a good, serviceable gun to be kept in constant fitness, with a good sword, bandoleer and horn, a wormer, a scourer, a priming wire, a shot bag, a charger, one pound of good powder, four pounds of pistol bullets and twenty-four bullets fitted for the gun, four fathoms of serviceable match for match lock gun and four good flints for the fire lock gun."

Four local and one general training days per year were prescribed for each "Ryding" and once in two years, a general training day "for all the soldiers within the government."

The militia were to be taught "in the comely handling and ready use of the arms, and in all postures of war and in all words of command."

In case of failure of anyone to appear for duty, he was to be fined, and the fines were to be divided; one-third going to the commanding general and the remaining two-thirds to be divided amongst the other officers. Ample power was given the general for collecting the fines.

This code seems to have held, in most of its features, until 1702, when Queen Anne modified and amended it. She ordered that all males between the ages of sixteen and fifty be liable for military duty and, in case of an invasion, all between fifteen and sixty. She generously allowed, even ordered, each captain to furnish drums, bugles and colors for his company, and emphasized the order by a fine of £2 for each month he was in default.

This was also provided: "Every soldier belonging to a troop of horse shall appear twice a year for a drill and muster, provided with a good, serviceable horse, not less than fourteen hands high, covered with a good saddle, housings, breast-plate and crupper, a case of good pistols, a good sword or hanger, one half a pound of good powder and twelve sizable bullets, a pair of boots and suitable spurs, and a carbine well fixed with a belt, swivel and a blanket, under penalty of ten shillings for the want of a sizable horse, and ten shillings for want of each or either of the other articles." "New York County Horse" must have blue coats and breeches and scarlet waistcoats, and their hats laced with gold. "Albany County Horse" must have blue coats, but their hats laced with silver.

"Every foot soldier must provide himself, and appear and muster with a good, well fixed musket or fuzee, a good sword, belt and cartridge box, six cartridges of powder, a horn and six sizable bullets. At home, he must always have on hand one pound of good gunpowder and three pounds of sizable bullets." For want of these articles a fine of twenty shillings, and prison charges until the fine were paid, was imposed.

At his discretion, the captain was allowed and authorized to levy upon and sell the delinquent's goods.

"In case the offender be unable or refuse to pay, and he have no goods to distress, he shall ride the wooden horse, or be laid by the neck and heels in a public place for not to exceed an hour."

For seventy-three years, or until 1775, nearly the same law was re-enacted each year, the title almost invariably being:

"An act for settling the militia of this Province, and the making of it useful for the security and defense thereof."

No mention of compensation for military service was ever made, and when the number of articles which each soldier must furnish are taken into consideration, it will be seen that the tax was, by no means, an inconsiderable one.

This was the condition of the militia when the cloud of the Revolutionary War threw its shadow over the land.

JAMES A. ROBERTS,
Comptroller.

No. 42,629

I DO HEREBY CERTIFY, That Henry Chalick, priv.

or his Assigns, are entitled to receive out of the Treasury of the State of New-York, the Sum of One Pound Six Shilling & One Penny

Current Lawful Money of the said State, with the Interest at Five per Cent. per Annum, from the Eighteenth Day of June One thousand seven hundred and Seventy-nine pursuant to the Directions of a Law, entitled, "An Act "for the Settlement of the Pay of the Levies and Militia, for their Services in the late War; and "for other Purposes therein mentioned," passed the 27th Day of April, 1784.

£. 1. 6. 1. Gerard Bancker Treasurer.

"TREASURER'S CERTIFICATE."

The currency in which a grateful but impecunious country settled with its defenders.

TOUCHING THE OWNERSHIP OF A SLAVE.

TABLE OF MILITIA PAY.

RAID OF

SIR JOHN JOHNSON

ON THE

SCHOHARIE AND MOHAWK VALLEYS, IN OCTOBER, 1780.

The following description of the devastation of the Schoharie and Mohawk valleys, by Johnson, Butler and Brant, in October, 1780, is made from original manuscripts in the "Clinton Papers;" "The Northern Invasion," by Franklin B. Hough (1866), published by the Bradford Club, and of which seventy-five copies only were issued; and notes prepared by Prof. Rufus A. Grider, of Canajoharie, N. Y.

THE invasion and destruction of the Schoharie and Mohawk valleys by Sir John Johnson, in October, 1780, had for its object the cutting off of the supplies of wheat, rye, cattle, etc., which aided in supporting General Washington's army, and also the depopulation of those districts by destroying the resources of those who fed the enemies of King George. The raid was executed in a masterly manner. He accomplished all he intended doing, except the destruction of the three forts in the Schoharie valley.

The army was collected at Lachine, near Montreal, and proceeded up the St. Lawrence into Lake Ontario, through the Oswego river to Lake Oneida, and up Chittenango creek, where their boats were concealed and left; thence south-east, overland, crossing the head-waters of the Unadilla river, to a point about ten or fifteen miles south of Otsego lake, on the Susquehanna river, where the Indians, and seven companies of regulars, who came up the Susquehanna from Tioga Point, joined Sir John; thence east to about four miles from the Schoharie river.

The approach of the enemy had been conducted with as much secrecy as possible, but two Oneida Indians, having deserted, brought in the intelligence of their movements. It had been expected that the first attack would be made upon the upper fort.*

Early in the morning, on the 17th of October, the enemy were discovered passing at some distance from the upper fort. A signal gun was fired to notify the posts below of

* This fort stood about five miles west of south from Middleburg, and was completed in 1778.

this movement, and their garrisons hastened to make such preparations for defense as their situation allowed. No attempt was made by the enemy to molest the upper fort; but finding themselves discovered, and secrecy no longer possible, they began at once their work of devastation, by setting fire to buildings, barns and stacks of grain.

Soon after the first alarm, a party of nineteen volunteers was sent out from the middle fort,* to ascertain its cause, but soon returned, having narrowly escaped being surrounded and cut off. The enemy soon appeared before the fort, and some skirmishing ensued between their advance forces and small parties of the garrison, but without loss on either side.

Colonel Johnson then brought up a small mortar and a brass three-pounder field piece, and fired for some time upon the fort, but without material effect. An officer and two men were then sent, bearing a white flag, but as they approached the fort, they were fired upon. This checked their advance, and they returned. The flag advanced a second and a third time, but was each time stopped by a rifle shot from the fort, when, finding further attempt at parley impossible, the firing was resumed. The work of devastation having been completed, and the spirit of the garrison appearing to defy an assault, the invaders, about three o'clock in the afternoon, desisted from further hostilities, and continued their march down the valley.

But two persons were mortally wounded in the middle fort, while the loss of the enemy is believed to have been greater. The little garrison had expended most of their ammunition when the enemy retired.

Several scouts sent out from the lower fort† to learn the progress of events up the valley, returned, pursued by the enemy, who appeared about four o'clock in the afternoon, and passed this fort upon both sides. Several sharp-shooters were stationed in the tower of the church, who were prepared for effective service, and the enemy, after firing a few cannon shot, two of which lodged in the timbers of the roof, and burning several buildings in the neighborhood, continued their march without attempting further hostilities at this place, and encamped for the night a few miles below.‡

Intelligence of the presence of the enemy at Schoharie reached Governor Clinton at Albany by noon on the 17th, and Lieutenant-Colonel Veeder sent another messenger with a full account of the destruction of the settlements as soon as the enemy had passed the lower fort. Orders were at once sent to General Robert Van Rensselaer, and measures were immediately taken to rally a force of militia sufficient for pursuit. The general arrived at Schenectady towards evening, on the 18th, while the horizon in the direction of Schoharie was still glowing with the fires set by the enemy the day before, and lost no time in consulting upon measures for hastening the march of his troops in pursuit of the enemy.

* Situated within the limits of the present village of Middleburg, and built in 1777.

† It stood a mile north of Schoharie court-house; was built in 1778, and at the time of the raid was commanded by Lieutenant-Colonel Volkert Veeder of Caughnawaga.

‡ Near the present village of Sloansville.

He also sent word to Lieutenant-Colonel Veeder, directing him to send such troops as could be spared from the Schoharie forts, to hang upon the rear of the enemy, but to avoid an engagement until he could come up. This order was faithfully executed. His force at that time was about seven hundred men, but more were expected during the night. A few head of cattle, intended for Fort Schuyler, were slaughtered, and all the ovens in town were put in requisition to supply the troops with bread.

During the evening General Van Rensselaer called a meeting of the principal citizens to consult upon means for hastening his march, and it was proposed to use wagons for transporting them a part of the way; but a sufficient number could not be collected during the night, and this plan was abandoned. The troops were bivouacked in the suburbs of the town, and as soon as they could receive their rations in the morning they began their march up the south side of the river. Governor Clinton, who was then at Albany, took measures for assembling at once such remaining troops and supplies as the country could afford, with the view of following the expedition and sustaining its movements.

About 8 o'clock on the morning of the 18th the enemy resumed their march down the Schoharie valley, and leaving Fort Hunter,* half a mile to their right, continued up on the south bank of the Mohawk, to a place now known as Willow Basin, a short distance below the Nose, where they encamped for the night. Their route was marked by a general pillage and burning, with the exception of a few houses owned by persons supposed to be of loyal sympathies. Most of the inhabitants were alarmed of the coming danger in time to escape into the fields and woods, where they witnessed the plunder and destruction of their property. A detachment under Captain Duncan crossed to the north bank and destroyed what had escaped the invasion of Sir John, in May previous, excepting a stone church at Caughnawaga† that had been built under the patronage of Sir William Johnson a few years before the war.

On the morning of the 19th, having forded the Mohawk with his main body at Keator's Rift, near the present village of Sprakers, they continued their course up the north side of the valley, as the south, having already been ravaged in August by Brant, had but little left to invite destruction, for two miles, to Homestead creek (now known as Nellis Glen), and headed northward to destroy fruitful Stone Arabia district.

General Van Rensselaer continued his march during the day with as much expedition as the state of the roads would admit, and about six o'clock at night on the 18th had arrived opposite the former residence of Sir William Johnson, nearly twenty miles above Schenectady.

A council was called by the general as soon as the troops could be properly disposed, consisting of a number of field officers, and the General suggested to them the necessity of taking measures to procure intelligence of the enemy's route. It was agreed to send out a party to make discoveries, which was accordingly done. As the road was closely

* Built in 1712, at the junction of the Mohawk river and Schoharie creek.

† Now Fonda, Montgomery county.

wooded, and it being very dark, the council agreed that it would be imprudent and dangerous to march over the hill until moonrise. They accordingly waited for the moon, which appeared at ten o'clock, when the march was resumed, but the road over the hill was very miry and deep, which impeded the march. They arrived at Fort Hunter about midnight and crossed the Schoharie instantly, in a scow and on wagons, and proceeded in their march, without delay, to Van Epps'.* where they arrived about four o'clock, and halted not more than an hour. Here letters were written to Col. Dubois, at Fort Rensselaer, and Col. Brown, at Stone Arabia, advising them of his situation and his intentions to pursue the enemy closely and to attack them by break of day. Intelligence was here received that the enemy were encamped at Anthony's Nose, on both sides of the river.

About three miles north of the Mohawk at Palantine Bridge, was Fort Paris, which consisted of a farm house and outbuildings, a store, barracks for over one hundred soldiers, all enclosed by pickets, with a blockhouse on its western side. The commandant was Colonel John Brown, an officer of undoubted ability and tried courage, who had under him a force of about one hundred and thirty men of the Massachusetts levies.

About three-fourths of a mile south of Fort Paris was a one-story stone farm house, owned by Johannes Kayser. Its walls were pierced on both its gable ends; on its front and rear oak timbers topped its walls, which had openings for defense by riflemen. It also had a garrison of enlisted soldiers, and was known as Fort Kayser.

It is not certainly known whether Colonel Brown received the message of General Van Rensselaer, or whether his movements were occasioned by the rumors he received of the enemy's approach, and his own sense of duty under the circumstances. He, however, formed his command in line of battle, on the morning of the 19th, except a few left to guard the fort, and marched down the road leading southward towards the Mohawk. He met the enemy on the slopes of the valley, about a mile from the present village of Palatine Bridge, when a battle ensued that continued to be fought with bravery, until himself and thirty-nine of his men were killed, and two captured. The remainder of his troops broke and fled towards Fort Rensselaer,† about three miles distant, on the south bank of the river.

The loss of the enemy on this occasion is not known.

Forts Kayser and Paris, at Stone Arabia, were at this time crowded with families, and capable of but feeble resistance. The enemy had, however, no time to waste in attacking them, and after the defeat of Colonel Brown, they dispersed over a wide extent of country, setting fire to everything combustible in the settlement.

When General Van Rensselaer arrived at the Nose, on the 19th, where the enemy had camped, they had left hours before and had crossed the Mohawk a short distance west of the Nose. He did not wish to cross there, fearing an ambuscade, and did not know what route Sir John was going to take, nor did he deem it prudent to get in front of the enemy's

* Present village of Fultonville.

† It stood about half a mile west of the present village of Fort Plain.

line of march. His advance informed him that they heard the conflict with Colonel Brown, and had learned of the latter's defeat and death, through fugitives who came to the river.

The next rift is Frey's, opposite Canajoharie. (The present village did not then exist.) General Van Rensselaer tried to cross the river there, but found it impracticable, so he marched to a fording place about one and a half miles below Fort Rensselaer.

Orders were given for the troops to cross to the north bank as soon as possible. They were exhausted with fatigue, the river was too deep to ford, and the means of crossing were limited to a rude bridge made by placing wagons in the stream, along which the men could climb with difficulty, from one to another. Several hours elapsed before they were all over and had joined the levies and Indians under Colonel Dubois, who had crossed at Walrath's ferry about a mile above.

Several miles above Garoga creek is the stone farm house of Adam Klock, built in 1750. Its walls were loop-holed, as can yet be seen. The public road whereon both armies advanced was along the river, on the south front of the dwelling, where now the New York Central railroad is located. On the east side was a good-sized apple orchard, on the west a stone wall running north, and a kitchen garden; on the east a stone wall running up to a field; in fact, the divisions of fields, orchard, and even the pig and cattle yards were fenced with stone, three feet high.

Sir John, unable to avoid his enemy, decided to meet him at a place south of the public road. From the flat a peninsula (now an island), jutted out into the river, and on it were placed Regulars; his right could not be turned, as the water was deep and the current rapid. On the lowland also were Regulars. Sir John's line extended up the hill, whether on the west or east of the house, or on both, is not known. The destroyers, the Mohawk Indians, were in ambush on the hill to the left. His army faced east.

General Van Rensselaer placed Colonel Cuyler with the militia at the left on the lowland, next the Mohawk; in the center Colonel Whiting; on the extreme right was Colonel Dubois with his fresh troops from Fort Plain, or Rensselaer. Firing began by the pursuers when five or six hundred yards from the enemy, who were protected by stone walls. The left wing was in disorder all the time. Colonel Dubois marched on till he gained the flank of the enemy's main body, pursuant to the general's order. It began to grow dusk, and he perceived that his front had got into the enemy's rear; he faced his men about, marched, undiscovered, down to the enemy, firing platoons from right to left, when the enemy broke and ran, and the whole line would have been doubled up, and a complete and decisive victory won, had daylight lasted a little while longer. But it was then so dark that persons ten feet distant could not be recognized. Colonel Dubois and his men, being mistaken for the enemy, owing to the darkness, were fired on by friends in front, and lest the men should kill each other, the firing was ordered to cease. Sir John fled from the field with the Indians and Yagers, doubtless supposing all was lost. General Van Rensselaer, being unacquainted, consulted Colonel Dubois where a suitable place to camp could be found. Colonel Dubois selected a place one mile from the battle-field, where they could not be surprised during the night, and where the wagons with provisions could reach the troops.

There the night of the 19th was spent. The general ordered his officers to be ready to continue the pursuit by daybreak next morning.

Colonels Clyde and Benschoten, with the forces, by order of the General, occupied the battle-field during the night, and protected the booty which the enemy abandoned, consisting of baggage, two field pieces, wagons, hundreds of cattle, and about fifty horses, many of which were afterward claimed and returned to Schoharie. During the night Johnson's army crossed to the south side of the Mohawk at various places above, the greater number at Christie's Rift, now Upper St. Johnsville. The pursuit was resumed at sunrise on the morning of the 20th. At one o'clock the troops had reached Fork Herkimer, having marched eighteen miles. There Governor Clinton overtook the army and pursued to within fifteen miles of Oneida. They could go no further, the provisions, which had to be carried on pack-horses, being exhausted, the country uninhabited, and the soldiers worn out. They found the remains of their last night's encampment, but the enemy were beyond reach of pursuit, and they returned to Fort Herkimer.

Was General Van Rensselaer to blame because he failed in demolishing Johnson's army? The evidence of those who participated in the pursuit, and the verdict of the Court of Inquiry, unanimously acquitted him, saying: "The whole of General Van Rensselaer's conduct, both before and after, as well as in the action of the 19th of October last, was not only unexceptionable, but such as became a good, active, faithful, prudent and spirited officer, and that the public clamors raised to his prejudice on that account, are without the least foundation.

(Signed) JACOBUS SWARTWOUT,

President."

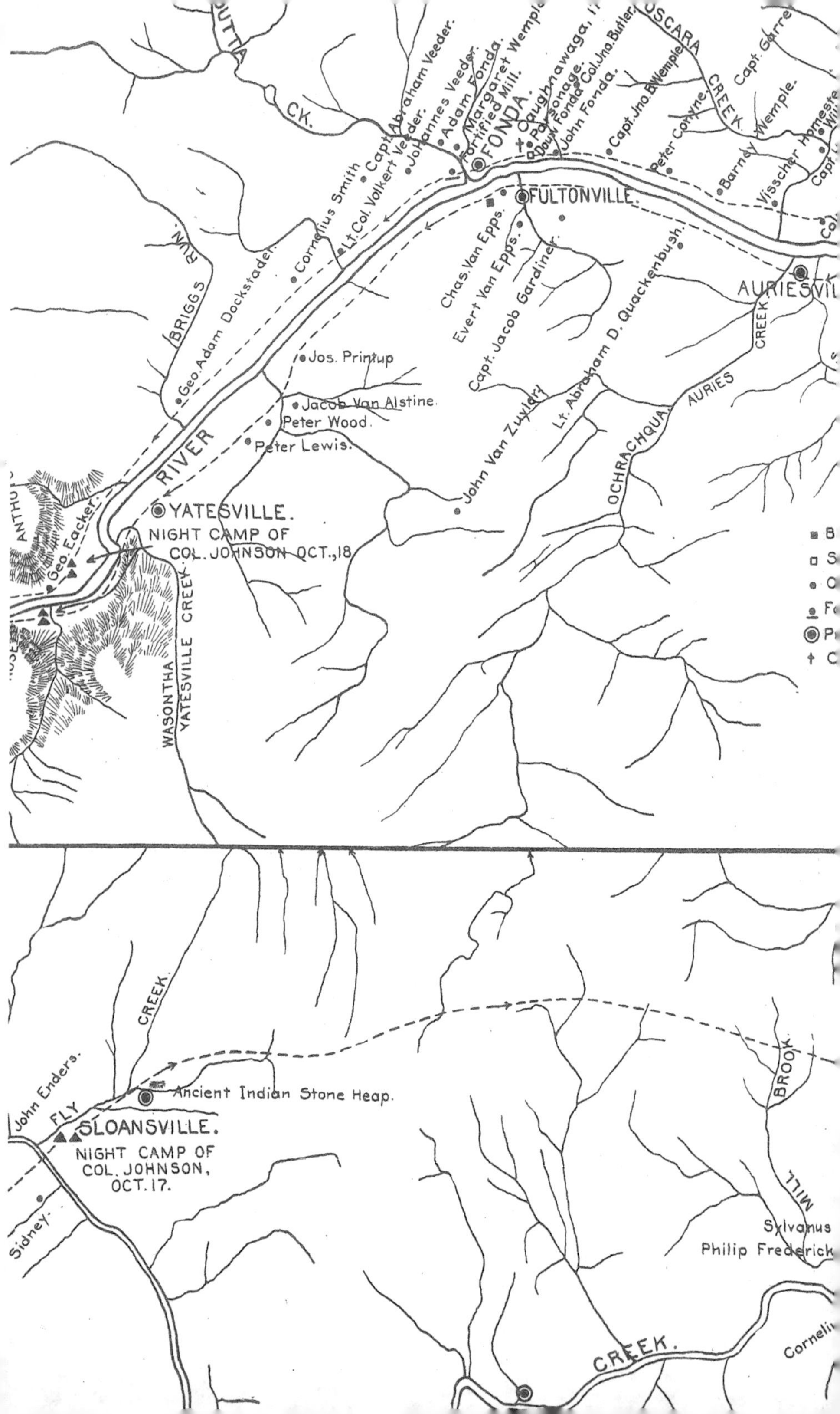

CK.
Capt. Abraham Veeder.
Johannes Veeder.
Adam Fonda.
Margaret Wemple.
Fortified Mill.
FONDA.
Caughnawaga,
Parsonage.
Dow Fonda
Col. Jno. Butler.
John Fonda.
Capt. Jno. B. Wemple.
Peter Conyne.
CREEK.
Capt. Garret
Barney Wemple.
Visscher Homestead.
Cornelius Smith
Lt. Col. Volkert Veeder.
FULTONVILLE.
AURIESVILLE
Chas. Van Epps.
Evert Van Epps.
Capt. Jacob Gardiner.
Lt. Abraham D. Quackenbush.
BRIGGS RUN.
Geo. Adam Dockstader.
Jos. Printup
Jacob Van Alstine.
Peter Wood.
Peter Lewis.
John Van Zuyler.
OCHRACHQUA
AURIES
CREEK
RIVER
YATESVILLE.
NIGHT CAMP OF
COL. JOHNSON OCT., 18
Geo. Eacker.
WASONTHA
YATESVILLE CREEK
CREEK.
John Enders.
FLY
SLOANSVILLE.
NIGHT CAMP OF
COL. JOHNSON,
OCT. 17.
Ancient Indian Stone Heap.
Sidney.
BROOK
MILL
Sylvanus
Philip Frederick
CREEK.

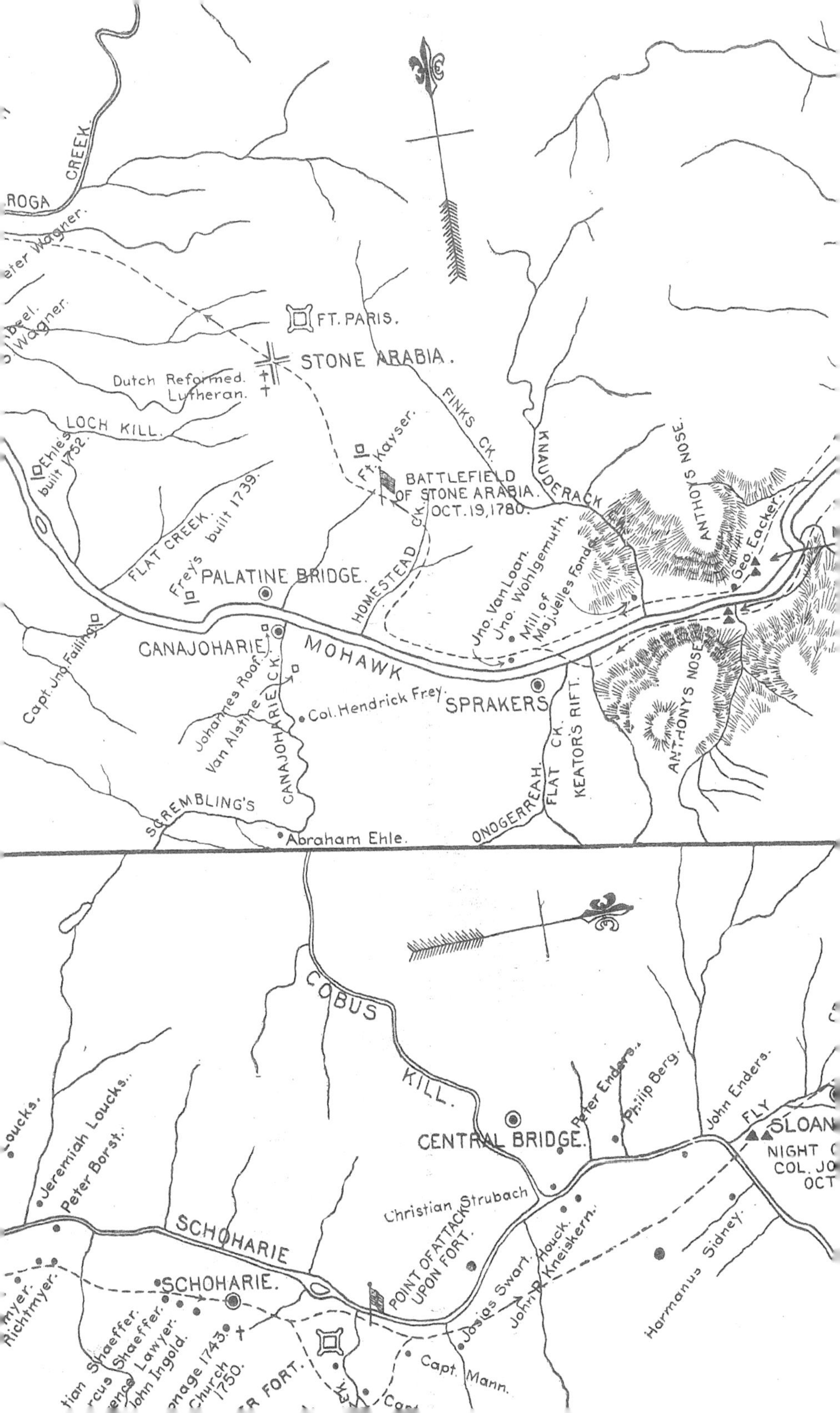

CREEK.
ROGA
Peter Wagner.
beel.
Wagner.
FT. PARIS.
STONE ARABIA.
Dutch Reformed.
Lutheran.
LOCH KILL.
Ehle's built 1752.
FINKS CK.
Ft. Kayser.
BATTLEFIELD OF STONE ARABIA. OCT. 19, 1780.
KNAUDERACK
ANTHOYS NOSE.
Geo. Eacker.
FLAT CREEK.
Frey's built 1739.
PALATINE BRIDGE.
HOMESTEAD CK.
Jno. Van Loan.
Jno. Wohlgemuth.
Mill of Maj. Jelles Fonda.
Capt. Jno. Failing.
CANAJOHARIE.
MOHAWK
Johannes Roof.
Van Alstine.
CANAJOHARIE CK.
Col. Hendrick Frey.
SPRAKERS
ONOGERREAH.
FLAT CK.
KEATOR'S RIFT.
ANTHONYS NOSE
ANTHONYS NOSE
SCREMBLING'S
Abraham Ehle.
COBUS KILL.
Loucks.
Jeremiah Loucks.
Peter Borst.
CENTRAL BRIDGE.
Peter Enders.
Philip Berg.
John Enders.
FLY
SLOAN
NIGHT
COL. JO
OCT
Christian Strubach
SCHOHARIE
POINT OF ATTACK UPON FORT.
Josias Swart.
Houck.
John P. Kneiskern.
Harmanus Sidney.
myer.
Richtmyer.
SCHOHARIE.
tian Shaeffer.
rcus Shaeffer.
ence Lawyer.
John Ingold.
onage 1743.
Church 1750.
R FORT.
Capt. Mann.
EK.
Con

EXPLANATIONS.

No rank below ensign is given in this volume.

Detailed information will be found on the manuscripts themselves. The index indicates only the volume, folio and page where a name may be found.

It is a matter for regret that these records do not present a complete roster of all the men from New York engaged in the Revolutionary War. Many rolls are missing, and many are defective, but such names as could be found are given. In some cases no enlisted men appear; only the officers of the organization.

The spelling of names is erratic and unreliable. Many of the soldiers could not write, and the spelling of a name depended upon the whim of the scribe.

" Deserter " written after a name must not be taken too seriously. Frequently the men absented themselves to gather crops, to attend a sick wife, or to bury a child, but it is found that the soldier generally returned, and was again taken up on the rolls.

A PAROLE.

ACCOUNT CURRENT WITH MAJOR GENERAL ALEXANDER MC DOUGAL AND SUITE.

NEW YORK COLONY AND STATE

IN THE

REVOLUTION.

THE LINE.

1st Regiment.

COLONEL GOOSE VAN SCHAICK
LIEUTENANT COLONEL CORNELIUS VAN DYCK
MAJOR BENJAMIN LEDYARD
MAJOR JOSEPH McCRACKEN
ADJUTANT JOHN BRODGDEN
ADJUTANT JOHN L. HARDENBERGH
ADJUTANT PETER BENJAMIN TEARSE
ADJUTANT (CAPT.) JOHN H. WENDELL
QUARTER MASTER HENRY VAN WOERT
PAY MASTER ABRAHAM TEN EYCK
PAY MASTER JEREMIAH VAN RENSSELAER
CHAPLAIN SOLOMON FRELIGH
SURGEON DANIEL BUDD
SURGEON WILLIAM MEAD
SURGEON DANIEL MENEMA

Capt. Leonard Bleeker
" William Brown
" Jacob Cheesman
" John Copp
" Robert Edmonston
" Andrew Finck, Jr.
" William Goforth
" John Graham
" James Grigg (Gregg)
" Benjamin Hicks
" Cornelius T. Jansen

Capt. John Johnson
" David Lyon
" Moses Martin
" Daniel Mills
" Robert McKean
" Charles Parsons
" John Quackenbos
" George Sytvis
" Henry Teabout
" John C. Ten Broeck
" Richard Varick

CAPT. DAVID VAN NESS
" JAMES VAN RENSSELAER
" NICHOLAS VAN RENSSELAER
" ABRAHAM A. VAN WYCK
" JOHN WANDLE
" JOHN WILEY
" JOB WRIGHT
" GUY YOUNG
LIEUT. AARON AORSON
" BENJAMIN BOGARDUS
" JOSIAH BAGLEY
" ABRAHAM B. BANCKER
" JOHN BARNS
" GERAURD BECKMAN
" VICTOR BICKER
" WILLIAM BLOODGOOD
" ABRAHAM E. BRASHER
" JAMES CLARK
" JOB COOK
" HENRY DEFFENDORFF
" DANIEL DENNESTON
" JOHN DENNEY
" HOLTON DUNHAM
" WILLIAM A. FORBES
" JOHN FURMAN
" DANIEL GAUS
" BENJAMIN GILBERT
" ABRAHAM HARDENBERGH
" NATHANIEL HENRY
" EBENEZER HILLS
" JOHN HOOGHKIRK
" JOHN HOUSTON
" SAMUEL LEWIS
" PETER MAGEE
" CHRISTOPHER MILLER (MULLER)
" WILLIAM MOULTON
" RANALD T. MCDOUGALL
" EDWARD NICOLS
" DIGBY ODLUM
" JAMES WILLIAM PAYNE
" BENJAMIN PELTON
" JONATHAN PIERCY
" MICHAEL RYAN
" WILHELM RYCKMAN

LIEUT. BARENT STAATS SALSBURY
" WILLIAM SCUDDER
" ADIEL SHERWOOD
" EPHRAIM SNOW
" HENRY SWARTWOUT
" SAMUEL THORN
" PETER VERGEREAN
" PETER ISAAC VOSBURGH
" PETER VAN BUNSCHOTEN
" NANNING VAN DERHIDEN
" CORNELIUS VAN DYCK
" ARONDT VAN HOOK
" JOHN VAN NESS
" TOBIAS VAN VEGHTEN
" BARTHOLOMEW J. VAN VALKENBURGH
" GOER'T H. VONWAGNER
" ISAAC VAN WERT
" JOHN WILLIAM WATKINS
ENSIGN LUTHER BISSEL
" JONATHAN BROWN
" WILLIAM W. DEPEYSTER
" JAMES FAIRLY
" DOUW J. FONDA
" JOHN FONDA
" DOUW FONDEY
" THEADOSIA FOWLER
" THOMAS HAIGHT
" BENJAMIN HERRING
" THOMAS HICKS
" NICHOLAS KETTLE
" JACOB I. KLOCK
" GILBERT R. LIVINGSTON
" JOHN MARSH
" JAMES MOORE
" JEREMIAH C. MULLER
" JOHN MCCLUNG
" ELIAS PALMER
" GEORGE PALMER
" JOSEPH PUTMAN
" CORNELIUS C. ROOSEVELT
" ADAM TEN BROECK
" JOHN WALDRON
" JOHN PERKINS WENDELL
" SAMUEL YOUNG

ENLISTED MEN.

Abbee Samuel
Abenather Jiles
Able Hendrick
Able John
Acker Albert
Acker Conrad
Ackerson Jacob
Ackinson James
Ackland Francis
Ackler John
Ackley Joel
Acklin Francis

Adaar Alexander
Adams Emanuel
Adams James
Adams John
Adams Matthew
Adams Samuel
Adams Thomas
Adams William
Adamy Henry
Addams Albertus
Adier Alexander
Africa Cask

Agard Joseph
Agard Judah
Agard Noah
Aim George
Aitkins Andrew
Akens Moses
Algoyer Bastian
Alhiser George
Alkinkrack John
Allen Amissy
Allen John
Allen Jonathan

Allen Richard
Allen Samuel
Althiser George
Altiser Jeremiah
Amarr John
Amerman Jam
Ammermain Obadiah
Amory John
Anderson Cornelius
Anderson David
Anderson Durias
Anderson Samuel

Anderson William P
Anson Lockward
Anthony John
Anthony Peter
Appart John
Arlow John
Armstrong Adam
Armstrong Archibald
Armstrong John
Armstrong Thomas
Artwick Cristian
Artwick Lawrence
Ash Henry
Atkinson James
Auston Lockward
Babbat Reuben
Babbitt John
Babcock Elias
Babtist John
Bacchus George
Bacchus John
Backer Christopher
Backhorn Jacob
Bacon Thomson
Badger Joshua
Badinger Philip
Baechus George
Baechus John
Bagley David
Bailey John
Bailis Elias
Baily Joseph
Baise James
Baker Benjamin
Baker Christopher
Baker Elnathan
Baker Hendrick
Baker Henry
Baker Ichabod
Baker John
Baker Joseph
Baldwin Cornelius
Baldwin David
Ball Joseph
Ball Robert
Ballantine William
Ballard Benone
Baman Trueman
Bambridge Charles
Bangle John
Banks Benjamin
Bannon Edward
Baptiste John
Barclay John
Bardeen Robert
Barker Stephen
Barman Ebenezer
Barnes Henry
Barnes Patrick
Barnhart John
Barret John
Barrett Walter
Barrit James
Barron John
Barry John
Barse Isaiah
Bartholomew Daniel
Bartow Lasha
Basharow John
Basiel Michael
Bass Henry
Bassaroon John
Bassell Richard
Bates Conrad
Bates Justice
Batis Conradt
Battersby Robert
Battis John
Bauman Lemuel
Bawn Samuel
Baxter Lockwood
Baxter William
Baylis John
Beadle Moses
Bealor Jacob
Bealor Joseph
Beard Jam
Bears David
Beckweth Jedediah
Beddinger Phillip
Bedner Johan Christian
Beeby Ezra
Beedle John
Beedle Moses
Beekman John
Beidell Thomas
Bell John
Bell Robert
Beneway Ezekiel
Benford George
Beng William
Benham James
Bennet Charles
Bennet Henry
Bennett William
Bennitt James
Bermingham James
Berrnerd Samuel
Berryhill John
Berve Jacob
Berwist John
Bevans Benjamin
Bevie Jacob
Bevins Jacob
Bice Henry
Bice Peter
Biggraft George
Biller Michael
Billington Elias
Bingham Abisha
Bishop James
Bishop John
Blaar Jacob
Black Archibald
Black David
Black John
Black Peter
Blair Kelso
Blanch James
Blanchard Ephraim
Blancher Ephraim
Blanck Cornelius
Blatner John
Blayer John
Blie Daniel
Blie John C.
Bliss Samuel
Bloom Albert
Bloom John
Blom Albart
Blowers Ephraim
Blue Daniel
Blum Albert
Bogardus Hendrick
Bogart Gilbert
Bogart John
Boice James
Boice John
Bolton James
Bolton John
Bolton Matthew
Bolton William Livingston
Bombreys George
Bonnell Nathaniel
Bonnell Simeon
Booker John
Boom Frederick
Boom John
Boom Nicholas
Borgordes David
Bornhart John
Boss Joseph
Bouch William
Bourguin John James
Bourk John
Bourns John
Bouse Henry
Bouse James
Bouse Peter
Bouy William
Bovie Jacob
Bovie Mathew
Bowen John
Bowen Wessel
Bower George
Bowman Albert
Boyce James
Boyce John
Boyd George
Boyd Jonah
Boyd Jonathen
Boyd William
Boyer Godlep
Boyle Philip
Brader Andrew
Brading John
Bradley James
Bradshaw William
Bradt James
Brady Thomas
Bragin John
Braidey Richard
Brand Henry
Brand Isaac
Brandoes George
Brant Christian
Brasher Henry
Brass Abraham
Brass John
Bray Thomas
Breadinbaker Baltes
Brend Isaac
Brewton Bartholomew
Briggs John
Brighton John
Britlingar Frederick
Broadbrook Edward
Bromagham Thomas
Bromley John
Bromley William
Broughton Bartholomew
Brown Charles F.
Brown David
Brown Elisha
Brown Evert
Brown Francis
Brown George
Brown Isaac
Brown James
Brown James, 2d
Brown John
Brown Joseph
Brown Nathaniel
Brown Nicholas
Brown Thomas
Brown Thomas B.
Brownan Samuel
Browne Nicholas
Bruce Benjamin
Bruch David
Bruin Moses
Brumbly John

Brumbly William
Brumley John
Brumley Simon
Brumley William
Brunck Casper
Bruster Benjamin
Bruter Arthur
Bruton Bartholomew
Bryan John
Bryan Paul O
Buckett John
Buckhout James
Buel Abel
Buel Ezra
Buis James
Bulger John
Bullack Archibald
Bullion William
Burch Isaiah
Burch Philip
Burch Samuel
Burck Edmund
Burgess Michael
Burk John
Burk Patrick
Burkdoff John
Burkstaff Peter
Burnes Barney
Burnes Henry
Burnham William
Burn Daniel
Burn David
Burns Frederick
Burns Robert
Burr William
Burrough Nathan
Burrough Thomas
Burve Matthew
Burvis Thomas
Bush John
Bushland Patrick
Butler John
Buttler Thomas
Button Thomas
Buyford Henry
Buys James
Buzer Petter
Byerd Godfrey
Byington David
Cable Jacob
Cable Zabulon
Cahel Robert
Cahill Cornelius
Cahill John
Cain Abel
Cain Henry
Caldwell Mathew
Caldwell Philip
Callichan John
Cambell Robert
Camell George
Cameron Daniel
Cameron Hugh
Campbell Archibald
Campbell Burdee
Campbell Canute
Campbell Duncan
Campbell George
Campbell Hugh
Campbell James
Campbell John
Campble Burdock
Campble Kenneth
Canada John
Canal John
Cane Henry
Canely Patrick
Canfield Dennis
Canfield Thomas
Cannon Thomas
Canter Jonas
Carmack William
Carman Abraham
Carman Hendrick
Carman Joseph
Carman Samuel
Carman Thomas
Carman Willet
Carmichael John
Carr Dan
Carr William
Carter Jeremiah
Carter Rubin
Case Joseph
Casey James
Casey John
Casey Robert
Cassedy Edward
Casselman Christian
Castelman Christophal
Casterline Hiram
Catch John
Catline Bradley
Cator William
Catterling Matthias
Causton John
Celia John
Chace Robert
Chadwine Lewis
Chambers Leonard
Chanels John
Chapey Stephen
Charles Christian
Charlsworth John M.
Charters James
Chase Jacob
Chase John
Chasey Stephen
Chasley Peter
Chatfield David
Chatfield Samuel
Chatnell Christopher
Chatterton Joseph
Chattin William
Chilner Christopher
Christainsa Peter
Christian Charles
Christian Zachariah
Churchill Stephen
Cidney Rodolph
Clapper Peter
Clark Benjamin
Clark John
Clark Ransome
Clark William
Clarke Anthony
Clement Nicholas
Clements Jacob
Clopper Peter
Clough Benjamin
Cockley John
Cogden John
Collard Edward
Condo William
Connelly John
Conoway William
Cook John, Jr.
Cooper Thomas
Copeland William
Copernoll Adam
Cornelius Hendrick
Cotter James
Countz Adam
Cox Charles
Craig John
Cranck John
Crandle Godfrey
Crantz Mark
Cronkhite John
Cronkhite Patrick
Crosson Samuel
Crowder Anthony
Crowfoot Samuel
Cummins Cornelius
Cummins John
Curry Thomas
Daily Nathan
Dalton Benjamin
Dalton John
Daniel George
Daniels Henry
Daniels Thomas
Darling Ephraim
Darling Moses
Daugherty William
Davenport James
David Isaac
Davidson William
Davis Cornelius
Davis Daniel
Davis David
Davis Evan
Davis John
Davis Richard
Dawson Daniel
Day Aaron
Day William
Dean Henry
Dean James
Dean Samuel
Dean William
Debbedy Brent
Debois John
Debois Lewis
Debrouce John
De Camp Matthias
De Clark Abraham
Decker John
Deforest Abraham
Defrance John H.
Defreest Abraham
De Freest Henry
Degrushe Elias
Delamater John
Delong Daniel
Delong Ezekiel
Demount Henjost
Demont Joseph
Dennis John
Dennison Daniel (see Denniston)
De Roshea Anthony
Derotter George
De Statsmarn Jean
De Vaults Peter
Devenport Daniel
Devenport John
Devinport Thomas
Dewit Aaron
Deyo Hugh
Dickens William
Dickson James
Dickson John
Dingman Abraham
Dingman Adam
Dingman Gerrardus
Dingman John
Dobbs William
Dodge Alexander
Doghorthy Mark
Doleway Andrew
Dolton Frederick

Donaghy Patrick
Donnelly James
Donoven John
Dority Francis
Dorn John
Dorrity William
Dorson Daniel
Dorum Stephen
Doty Isaac
Dougall Thomas
Doughaty John
Dougherty Charles
Dougherty William
Doughty Elias
Doughty John
Douglass George
Douglass James
Douglass Jonas
Douglass William
Dowler George
Downing Andrew
Downing Richard
Downs Patrick
D Pew John
Drincks Andrew
Drum Jacob
Duboise Lewis
Duff David
Dulhagin Frederick
Duncan George
Duncan James
Duncan John
Duncomb Dennis
Dunford Wells
Dunham Andres
Dunham Stephen
Dunham Sylvanus
Dunhom Iseral
Dunlap James
Dunlap John
Dunn Joseph
Dunnavin Daniel
Dunning Jacob
Dunning Jesse
Dunning Michael
Dunnivan John
Dunscomb Edward
Durgen Patrick
Durham Stephen
Durkir Mathew
Dutcher Benjamin
Dutcher Bernard
Dutcher David
Dutcher Derrick
Dutcher Henry
Dyckman Joseph
Dyke John
Dyke Joseph
Eagins Joshua
Earnestpier John
Earvin James
Easterly Thomas
Easton Henry
Eaton George
Echler John
Ecker Lambart
Ecklar John
Edds Joseph
Edgerly John
Edmans Matthew
Eggens Joshua
Eggs Samuel
Eison Aaron
Ekons Samuel
Eldridge Jonathan
Eldridge Joseph
Eligon Abraham
Eligon John
Elliott Francis
Elliott John
Ellis Benjamin
Ellis Daniel
Ellis William
Elliss Thomas
Elverston Edward
Elviston William
Elwiston Edward
Elwiston William
Emingway Samuel
Emrich Hendrick
Ennis Henry
Erven James
Erwin Andrew
Erwin James
Essmond John
Euerhite John
Evans Joseph
Evans Patrick
Everan Martin
Evenlts Stephen D.
Ewing Benjamin
Eyres William
Fairchild Jesse
Falter Augustus
Fargerson James
Farguson William
Farrel Garret
Farrol John
Fauck Jacob
Fealay John
Feishler George
Felly Augustus
Felte Augustus
Ferguson Israel
Ferguson James
Ferguson Robert
Ferguson William
Ferrell John
Ferris John
Ferry John
Fichter George
Field Patrick
Filty Augustus
Finch Jonathan
Finn Thomas
Finney John
Fisher George
Fitch Caleb
Fitzgerald John
Fitzgibbons William
Fleming Michael
Fletcher James
Flick Martin
Fling Henry
Fling Thomas
Flinn Andrew
Flinn John
Flint Jonathan
Flood Francis
Floods Alexander
Florince Thomas
Flyhearty Stephen
Flynn John
Fonna Anthony
Foor John C.
Forbes Alexander
Forbush Alexander
Forbush Bartholomew
Forbush Jacob
Force David
Ford John
Ford Timothy
Foreman Christian
Forgason Hazekiel
Forguson James
Forneyea John
Foster James
Foster John
Foster William
Fothergill Hugh
Fothingill Hugh
Foulks Robert
Foulstrow Henry (see Fowlstroh)
Foushee Pedro
Fowler James
Fox Philip
Foy David
Foy Edmond
Foy Edward
Foy Patrick
Fradenbergh Petter
France Conrad
Franck Jacob
Fravel Henry
Frazer Duncan
Frazer Jeremy
Frazer John
Frazier Jeremiah
Frazier Simeon
Frederick John
Fredinburgh Isaac
Fredinburgh Matthew
Fredinburgh Peter
Fredrick John
Freehart Lewis
Freeland John
Freeman Elisha
Freeman Obadiah
Freeman Stephen
Freeman Thomas
French Jacob
French Joseph
Freyenschiner George
Friday Conrad
Friensiner George
Frilick Joseph
Frinck Elisha
Frisbee Edward
Frost Edmund
Frost Samuel
Fry Christopher
Frye Peter
Fullen Michael
Fullerton John
Fulmer George
Fulton Francis
Furman Gabriel
Gadge John
Gaites Michael
Galaspy William
Galbreath Richard
Gallaway James
Gallaway John
Gamble Thomas
Gankins Philip
Ganoshow Peter
Gantly Peter
Gardener Andrew
Gardenier Samuel
Gardineer Gilbert
Gardineer Peter
Gardner Jacob
Gardner Levy
Gardner Peter
Gardner Thomas
Gardner William
Garrat Samuel
Garret James
Garrison Abraham
Garrison Hartshorn
Garrison Peter

Garter Henry
Gasper Peter
Gates Michael
Geabs Addem
Geers Benjamin
Genung Benjamin
Geonovoly Samuel
George Robert
Germain Isaac
Gibbs Eliakim
Gibbs Simeon
Gibson Thomas
Gifford William
Gilbert John C.
Gilbert Samuel
Gill James
Gilmor William
Ginnings Solomon
Ginnis Peter
Glasbey William
Gleeson Thomas
Glen Robert
Glenney William
Godington William
Godwin William
Goff Isaac
Goff Joseph
Goldar, William
Goodale Benjamin
Goodcourage John
Goodwin William
Goolsmith Jeremiah
Gordenear John
Gorman Patrick
Gorman Richard
Gouss Jacob
Grace James
Grady Thomas
Graham Robert
Grant Allen
Grant Benone
Grant Jacob
Graw James
Gray Eliphalet
Gray James
Gray John
Gray Philip
Green Boswart
Green Charles
Green Peter
Green Timothy
Green Silas
Gregg Thomas
Griffiths Barney
Grimes Samuel
Grimseley William
Grite William
Groote William
Gross John
Grote William
Groundhart George
Guilleeo John
Gundellow John
Guth John G.
Guthrie Abram
Gutlich Christian Ernest
Haburn William
Hadger Robert
Hadley Bishop
Hadlock James
Hagarty John
Hagerman Nicholas
Haily John
Haise Thomas
Hait Joseph
Hale John
Halinbeck Aaron
Halinbeck Casper
Hall Charles
Hall James
Hall Simon
Hall William
Hallebrant John
Halmer Lenord
Haman John F.
Hamilton James
Hamilton William
Hamlet Richard
Hamleton George
Hammon Daniel (see Hammond)
Hand David
Handell John
Handerson Samuel
Handley Thomas
Hanford Obadiah
Hanion Ede
Hankey John
Hanley John
Hannawell John
Harman Jacob
Harpear William
Harrious Hendrick
Harris David
Harris George
Harris Hendrick
Harris Michael
Harris Thomas
Harris William
Harris Zachariah
Harrison Levi
Harrison Philip
Harriss Richard
Hart Thomas
Harter Adam
Hartigh John
Harvey William
Harway John
Hasan John
Hattis Thomas
Hauff John
Haven John
Havens Joseph
Hawel Aaron
Hawes Joseph
Hawke John Wain
Hawkins Isaac
Hawkins John
Haycock John
Haydon Hosea
Hayes Thomas
Haynes Thomas
Hays Stephen
Hays William
Hazard Raymond
Heard David
Heathcrock David
Heavens Joseph
Hedgers Dayton
Height Stephen
Heller Nicholas
Helmer Anyost
Helmer John
Helmer John, jr.
Helmer John Dedrick
Helmer John Jost
Helmer Philip
Helmer Richard
Hemingway Samuel
Hemminway Isaac
Hender Frederick
Henderson Elisha
Henderson Patrick
Henderson Samuel
Henderson William
Hendrickson Cornelius
Hendry David
Henford Obadiah
Henkey John
Henly David
Henning John C.
Herd Joseph
Herter Adam
Hervey William
Hews James
Hicklin William
Hiddy James
Hide Thomas
Hier Jacob
Higbey Samuel
Higby John
Higgins Archibald
Higgins Samuel
Higgins Thomas
Hildredth Elijah
Hill Ebenezer
Hill Henry
Hill John
Hill Nicholas
Hill Samuel
Hilton William
Hilts Frederick
Hines Thomas
Hines William
Hipe Jacob
Hitchcock James
Hoaksly James
Hoareford Jesse
Hodge Abraham
Hodge David
Hodge James
Hodge Stephen
Hodges David
Hofman Aaron
Hofman Andrew
Hogan Patrick
Hogan Roger
Hogle John
Holbert Aaron
Hollay Samuel
Holley Benjamin
Holms David
Honeywell John
Hooper Jacob R.
Hope Thomas
Hopkins Samuel
Hopkins William
Hopp Abraham
Hoppell John
Hopping Ebraham
Hoppole John
Horner George
Horsford Jesse
Horsmer George
Horton Thomas
Hosford Ithamer
Hosier Thomas
Hoskins Thomas
Houff John
Hous John
House Christian
House Jacob
House John
Howard Randal
Howard William
Howell Aaron
Hoyt Thomas
Hubbard Adam
Hubbard Caleb
Hubbell Isaac
Hudson Bernard
Hudson John

Hudson William
Huff Abraham
Huff John
Huff William
Huffman Aaron
Huffman Andrew
Huffsteder Christian
Hufnegal Christian
Huges James
Hughes John
Hughes Joseph
Hughes Michael
Hughes Thomas
Hulbert Aaron
Hull David
Hull William
Humphreys David
Hungerford Daniel
Hunter Jonathan
Hurd Elijah
Hurley Anthony
Hurligh John
Hurtock John
Huston John
Huston Silvenis
Hutcheons Edward
Hutchins Jedidiah
Hutchins John
Hutt John
Hutton Andrew
Hutton Robert
Hyatt Abraham
Hyde Thomas
Hyer Alexander
Hyer Jacob
Hyme Conradt
Hynes Thomas
Hyre Jacob
Indian Stepny
Ingersol John
Ingoson John
Isaacs Isaac
Jackson Archibald
Jacobus John
Jamison Alexander
Jarvice Joseph
Jenks Thomas
Jennings Luke
Jennings Solomon
John Francis
John Jeremiah
Johnson Abraham
Johnson David
Johnson Josiah
Johnson Shubael
Johnson William
Johnston John
Johson Nicholas
Jolly Richard
Jolly William
Jones David
Jones Edward
Jones Evan
Jones Ezra
Jones Jacob
Jones James
Jones Thomas
Jones William
Jonsons William
Jonston Edward
Jonston James
Jordan Robert
Jordon Thomas
Joseph Peter
Joseph Reuben
Juell John
Kablem Reuben
Kady John
Kallam Reuben
Kanely Patrick
Karnes George
Karr Mark
Kater James
Kater Wilhelmus
Keady Daniel
Kearish Frederick
Keef Arthur
Keef William
Keelen Icabud
Keeler John
Kefelty Felte
Kelch John
Kelch Nicholas
Keller John
Keller Nicholas
Kelly David
Kelly Hugh
Kelly Patrick
Kelly Philip
Kelme Lemuel Jones
Kelsh John
Kelsh Nicholas
Keltz Nicholas
Kendrick Thomas
Kener Christian
Kennedy Robert
Kent Jacob
Kepple John
Kerby Thomas
Kerfer Henry
Kerk George
Kerr Abner
Kerr Anthony
Kerr Henry
Kerr James
Ketch John
Kett Richard
Keyser Henry
Keyser John
Kidd Alexander
Kiddy James
Kiddy John
Kilburn Zacheus
Killer John
Killer Nicholas
Killip Alexander
Kils John
Kilts Conradt
Kimon Robert
Kincaid William
King John
King William
Kingsland Nathaniel
Kinler Nicholas
Kinter Nicholas
Kirby Thomas
Kirk George
Kirkland William
Kitchel Matthew
Kller John
Knap Aaron
Knap Mathew
Knight John
Korl George
Korl Saverines
Krak Godlip
Kronkhite John
Kronkhite Patrick
Kunnian Benjamin
Kyser Henry
Lackey Hugh
Ladd Joseph
Lafferty John
La Lancit John
Lamb Joseph
Lambert Abraham
Lambert John
Lambson Thomas
Lampier Francis
Lander Edward
Landon Benjamin
Lane Thomas
Lang James
Lanpher John
Lansing Gerrit
Lasher Jacob
Latemore Roger
Lathers Ezekiel
Laughlin Barnard
Loverty John
Lavey John
Lawell Abraham
Lawn George
Lawrence Isaac
Lawrence Jacob
Lawrence Mathew
Laybagh Abraham
Leaplink John
Leather Ezekiel
Lecky Hugh
Lee Daniel
Lee David
Lee Robert
Lees Martin
Lemon Alexander
Lenny Philip
Lent Hercules
Lent Moses
Leonard Robert
Leonard Thomas
Leroy Henry
Lestor Thomas
Lestrange Samuel
Letahers Ezekiel
Lewee John
Lewes Lockert
Lewey John
Lewis Henry
Lewis James
Lewis Joseph
Lewis Lockard
Lewis Peter
Lewis William
Lewman Peter
Lewy John
Light James
Light Lemuel
Lighthall Abraham
Lighthall James
Lighthall John
Lighthall Lancaster
Lighthart Daniel
Limbaker John
Linch Owen
Linch William (see Lynch)
Lindsey Abraham
Linegar John
Liniger John
Link Henry
Linn Aaron
Linsey Abraham
Lint Philip
List John
Littlejone John
Lock Philip
Lockhart Hugh
Locksul John
Logan Thomas
Loik Philip
Loman Peter
Long Andrew
Long Elias D.

Longley John
Lonkes Nicholas
Loosie Jacob
Louckas Petter
Loucks Andrew
Loucks John
Loucks Jost
Loucks Matthew
Loudon William
Loughren Hugh
Louis John
Loux Hendrick
Love Davis
Lovejoy John
Low James
Low John
Lower Henry
Lower Jacob
Lowman Peter
Lucherd Fredirick
Lucum John
Ludlow David
Ludlow Samuel
Lugar Christ
Luse Robert
Lusk Michel
Luthar John
Lyby John
Lynch James
Lynch Michael
Lynch Owen
Lynch William
Lyney John
Lyon Ebenezer
Lyon Joseph
Lyons James
Lysle John
Lytle William
Mackarell Joseph
Mackay Alexander
Mackey John A.
Madison Samuel
Mafit John
Mahan Patrick
Mahon John
Maitor John
Maker Solomon
Mallad Andrew
Malone John
Manchester Elias
Manes Isaac
Mansey Nathan
Manuel Andrew
Mapes Phineas
Mara Patrick
Marche Anthony
Marcle Henry
Marines George
Marjason Frederick
Markee John
Marony Alexander
Marony Florence
Marricle Anthony
Marricle Henry
Marricle Samuel
Marsden Humphrey
Marselis Garret
Marsh Ephraim
Marsh John
Marshal Simeon
Marshall Robert
Marshall Thomas
Marstes Jonathan
Martin John
Martler Peter
Marull Henry
Masden Humphrey
Mash Ephraim
Mason George
Masters Jonathan
Mastor George Peter
Mathews James
Matrat Fransis
Matrat Gidion
Maxwell Cornelius
May Henry
Mazure Christian
Mead John
Measal Peter
Medcalf William
Meeker Solomon
Meeker Uzel
Megarr James
Meggs Seth
Mellon Charles
Melony John
Mennen Robert
Meradeth Peter
Merral John
Merricle Henry
Merrill John
Merrit Stephen
Merselus Garret
Messenger Uriah
Michells Thomas
Mike John
Miles John
Millar John
Millard Daniel
Miller Alexander
Miller Casper
Miller Daniel
Miller David
Miller Henry
Miller Nicholas
Miller Peter
Millner Thomas
Mills Alexander
Mills John
Mineck Henry
Miner Moses
Ming Edward
Mingas Morris
Minick Barnhart
Mipe John
Mitchel Ensign
Mitchel Joseph
Mitchell Edward
Mitchell George
Mitchell Hugh
Mitchell James
Mitchell Penant
Mitchell Vinant
Molay John
Momenday David
Monday William
Money Ambisct
Monger Benjamin
Monger Bouten
Montgomery James
Mooney William
Moore Abraham
Moore Frederick
Moore John
Moore Marcus
Moore Philip
Moore Pliny
Moore Richard
Moore Robert
Moore Thomas
Moore William
Moorewise Daniel
More Jacob
More Martin
More Thomas
Morey Thomas
Morgan James
Morgan John
Moroney Florence
Morrell William
Morris Edmund
Morris Harvey M.
Morris Isaac
Morris James
Morrison Edward
Morrison Hugh
Morrisson Richard
Morrow Andrew
Mosher Hezekiah
Mosher Nicholas
Moss Daniel
Moss Ebenezer
Moss Isaac
Moss Stephen
Mott Samuel
Mott Thomas
Mountanye Jacobus
Mounts Richard
Muche Johannis
Mulford Ezekiel
Mulholland James
Mullen John
Muller Peter
Mulligen Philip
Mulony William
Multer Peter
Mumford James
Muncey Nathaniel
Munday David
Munroe Alexander
Munrose Elijah
Munsey Nathaniel
Murey Bartley
Murphey Daniel
Murphy Edward
Murray Bartly
Murray George
Murray James
Murray William
Musta Mathew
Mutry James
Mutter Peter
Myers Frederick
Myers Henry
Myres Jacob
McAlpin William
McArthur Duncan
McArthur John
McCally Hugh
McCann Mich
McCarrol Joseph
McCarthy Daniel
McCarty Dennis
McCauley James
McCawley Hugh
McCevers James
McChesnay William
McChesney John
McClane Daniel
McClaughlin Bernard
McClean Anthony
McClean John
McCloud Daniel
McClough Joseph
McClure Moses
McCollough Andrew
McColly Hugh
McColm Samuel
McColum Ruben
McComin John
McConnel Hugh
McConnel William

McConnoly Hugh
McCormac Bryan
McCormic John
McCormick James
McCoy Alexander
McCoy George
McCoy James
McCoy William
McCracken William
McCullom Samuel
McDaniel Daniel
McDaniel Michael
McDavitt Henry
McDonald Hugh
McDonald James
McDonald John
McDonald Michael
McDonald William
McDonnell James
McDormet Cornelius
McDormot Henry
McDougall James
McDougall John
McDowal Ben
McDugle William
McElroy James
McEntosch John
McFall Paul
McFarland Hosea
McFarlin Hosser
McFarlin John
McFarling Thomas
McGaryhee Edward
McGauchee Edward
McGee James
McGerrihe Edward
McGinis Daniel
McGinly James
McGinnis John
McGinnis Stephen
McGlaughlin John
McGraw John
McGreggor Daniel
McGriger John
McGuigan Michael
McIntire Bernard
McIntire Phinias
McIntire Thomas
McIntosh John
McKay Alexander
McKay John A. A.
McKay William
McKeel Michael
McKellop Alexander
McKenney John
McKenny James
McKenzie Malcom
McKewn James
McKinley Archibald
McKneal John
McKown James
McLain Anthony
McLane John
McLaughlin Bernard
McLaughlin John
McMaham Michael
McManes Hugh
McManus William
McMasters Alexander
McMickell John
McNeal John
McQuarter William
McQuin Philip
McRannels Owen
McWilliam James
Nafee Garret
Nagle Fradrick
Narley Mathus
Neal Jeremiah
Nebby Michael
Nellson Allen
Nelme Lemuel Jones
Nelson John
Nesbit Joseph
Newman William
Newtown Jonathan
Nicholls George
Nickason Eliphas
Niel John
Niel Thomas
Norse Goorope
Northon Henry
Northwear George
Norton George
Norton Henry
Norton John
Nott Samuel
Nottingham Thomas
Notz Jacob
Nutter William
Oar William
O'Brian Andrew
Obrine Cornelius
O'Bryan John
O'Bryan Thomas
O'Cain Jeremiah
Odle Joshua
Odle Richard
O'Donaghy Patrick
O'Farrel Michael
Ogden Daniel
Olen Henry G.
Olendorf Leonard
Oliphant William
Olmsted Nehemiah
O'Neil Charles
O'Neil James
Onele John
Ootesohoudt Peter P.
Orr Baltis
Orr William
Osburn Aaron
Osmur John
Osterhout Isaac
Ostrander Peter Wm.
Otter Isaac
Oudeskirk Myndert
Owens Daniel
Owens Terence
Owens Uriah
Paddock John
Padrow Dennis
Painter Edward
Painter Frederick
Palmer Jabish
Palmeteer Isaac
Pangborn Beeby
Pangborn Noah
Pangborn Samuel
Pangburn Jonathan
Park Timothy
Parker Edward
Parker Elisha
Parker Isaac
Parker James
Parker John
Parker Nathaniel
Parker Richard
Parkhoof Frederick
Parks John
Parry Richard
Paterson James
Paterson Thomas
Pathen Ebenezer
Patrick Robert
Pattan Edward
Patterson Edward
Patterson James
Patterson John
Patterson Joseph
Patterson William
Paul Arthur
Paul William
Payne Richard
Peak William
Pearse John
Peas Nathaniel
Pease Conrad
Pease Hanyost
Peck William
Peers John
Pell John
Perau John
Perigo Usal
Perkins James
Perkins Joseph
Perry William
Perse John
Peters John
Petry Jacob
Pettit Samuel
Phelps Israel
Phelps Jonathan
Phillip Wouter
Phillips William
Philpsa Christian
Pickering Rich'd
Pier John Ernest
Piggle Henry
Pilgrett Henry
Pinkney Jonathan
Piper Lewis
Pippinger Abraham
Pitter William
Platner John
Platto Thomas
Plimley Henry
Plough Dennis
Plowman Christopher
Poff George
Porter Elisha
Porter Nathaniel
Potter Samuel
Poulson Michael
Povey Joseph
Pratt Charles
Preble Samuel
Preston Benjamin
Preston Jonathan
Preston Othniel
Prett Jacob
Price Adam
Price James
Prime Michael
Primley Henry
Prindle Jotham
Prine William
Proctor Robert
Proper Frederick
Prossor Philip
Prouth Degory
Pudney Thorn
Pudny Francis
Putman David
Quackenbos Cornelius
Quackenbush Jacob
Quackenbush John
Quain Peter
Queen Christopher
Quin Patrick
Quinn William
Race Charles

Radenbergh Peter
Ragan William
Rains John
Rair John
Raljie David
Raljie John
Ramsey Adam
Rancier John
Randell Henry
Randle Thomas
Randolph Christopher
Rankens James
Rankins Daniel
Rankins Thomas
Ransier John
Ransur William
Rappolt George
Ravelia Lewis
Ray James
Ray Michael
Read James
Reany David
Rear John
Rearden Thimothy
Redding Frances
Reece Martin
Reed James
Reed John
Reed Joseph
Reed Nathaniel
Reed Thomas
Reemer George
Rees Martinis
Reily Thomas
Relay Lewis
Rendolf Nathaniel
Rennix William
Reonalds Isaac
Requig Jacob
Retchey Charles
Revelea Eselea L.
Revelea Lewis
Rex James
Reyning Jacob
Reynolds Abijah
Richards Peter
Richards Samuel
Richards Simon
Richardson Isaac
Richardson Robert
Rickhow Abraham
Ricmond Semion
Rider George
Ridout David
Riemer Johan George
Riley James
Rinder Christian
Risdall William
Ritcherds Simon
Ritchie Charles
Ritter Moses
Rivers Joseph
Rivet Samuel
Robennire Christian
Robert Jacob
Roberts Thomas
Robertson Richard
Robertson William
Robins Aaron
Robins John
Robinson James
Robinson John
Robisson Robert
Rochery James
Rockwell Simeon
Rodman Joseph
Rogers Allen
Role Samuel
Rood William
Rooker Joseph
Roomer William
Roppolt George
Rose Albert
Rose Andrew
Rose John
Rose Samuel
Rositer Charles
Rosman Coenraedt
Rosman Frederick
Rosman Philip
Ross Simeon
Rossiter Charles
Rotchery James
Rourk Mathew
Row Anthony
Row James
Row Stephen
Rowland Daniel
Rowley Timothy
Ruckerstice John
Rudolph Christian
Ruland Thomas
Rumpass George
Runals James
Runnions Benjamin
Russell James
Russell John
Russell Joseph
Ryan Daniel
Ryan Dennis
Ryan Robert
Ryan Thomas
Ryder George
Rynax William
Rynder Christian
Rynders James
Rynders John
Rynhart George
Ryring Jacob
Sager John
Sager Stotts
Sailer Zacheus
Sailor Jacob
Salisbury Gasper
Salisbury John
Salisbury Joseph
Salley Andrew
Salmond William
Salsbery Joseph
Salsbury Cornelius V.
Saltsman Jane D.
Saltsman John
Saltsman Peter
Salyer Zacheus
Sanders Robert
Sangh Peter
Santford John
Saultas Solomon
Saunders Robert
Savage Richard
Saxberry William
Sayer Robert
Schellenbergh George
Schoolcraft John
Schoolcreft Lawrence
Schreeder John J.
Schriner Lodewick
Schriver Peter
Schryver Christyan
Scott Edward
Scovill Silvenus
Screeder John J.
Scrivenor Zadock
Seabrin Frederick
Seager John
Seager Staats
Seager Thomas
Seamore Henry
Seandlin James
Seeger John
Seely Ephraim
Seevey Joseph
Seggar John
Selfridge John
Selfridge William
Selyea Lewis
Semore Henry
Service Philip
Servis Daniel
Sessinger Nicolas
Setler Andrew
Sevain Thomas
Sevey Joseph
Sexbury William
Shade John
Shankland Andrew
Shannon Thomas
Sharer James
Sharerer Lodewak
Sharlock John
Sharon John
Sharp Cornelius
Sharp John
Sharp Lewis
Sharp Thomas
Shaver Henry
Shearman Jesse
Shearman Peter
Sheely John
Sheft George
Sheldon Joseph
Shelenbergh George
Shell Christopher
Shell Elisha
Shell George
Shell William
Shelly Cyrus
Shely John
Shepherd True
Sheppard Henry
Sheppard Thomas
Sherdeur Abraham
Sherlocke John
Sherman John
Sherman Peter
Sherriden James
Sherriden Richard
Sherwood Samuel
Shields Daniel
Shiffington John
Shilly Cyrus
Shipman John
Shirts Henry
Shirts Nathis
Shirts Peter
Showers Adam
Shrum Jacob
Shuetts John
Shufelt George
Shultze John
Shurtz Henry
Shuts John
Shutts Peter
Sickel John
Sickels Abraham
Sickels Zackariah
Sidsor Michael
Siles Christopher
Simmons John
Simmons Philip
Simmons Polter
Simpkins Gideon

Simpson James
Sinclair William
Sinnet John
Skeehan Jeremiah
Skiffington John
Slate William
Slater Nicholas
Slighter Nicholas
Slingerlandt Peter
Sloane Hugh
Sluiter Jonas
Sluiter Nicholas
Slump Martin
Sluyter Jacob
Slyter James
Small George
Smalley Timothy
Smith Archibald
Smith Conraedt
Smith David
Smith Duncan
Smith Elihu
Smith George
Smith Isaac
Smith Jacob
Smith James
Smith John
Smith Joseph
Smith Robert
Smith Stephen
Smith Thomas
Smith William
Snell Zeley
Snyder Jacob
Solyer Zaccheus
Soper John
Soper Richerd
Sorning Adam
Souls Thomas
Sox Jacob
Spaperd Didimew
Sparick Christian
Spear Henry Frederick
Spears Jonathan
Speigler Henry
Sperick Christian
Spinne Daniel
Spray John
Spring Benjamin
Spur John
Squire Jonathan
Srader Christian
Staal Gorlegh
Stader Christian
Stagg Jasper
Stagg John
Stalker Malcome
Stall Charles
Stall Garlock
Stalsman John D.
Stanly Daniel
Stansbury William
Stanton Elijah
Stanton John
Starling Levi
Starr George
Stauder Christian
Steed Johannes
Steen William
Steinly John
Stephens Abraham
Stephens William
Stephenson John
Stering Adam
Stevens Abraham
Stewart Charles
Stewart Joshua
Stiles Moses
Stiller John
Stilt David
Stivers Caleb
St. Lawrence George
Stock Charles
Stock George
Stockham Isaac
Stoddard Ichabud
Stokes John
Stone John
Storing Adam
Storm James
Stout John
Stoutenger George
Stover George
Stover Nechi
Stratton Husey
Strawder Christian
Strobridge James
Stryker Elias
Stump John
Sturdivant Samuel
Sturgess Isaa
Stymeson Robert
Sudder Benjamin
Sudlow Samuel
Sulfridge William
Sullivan Cornelius
Sutherland Daniel
Sutton Benjamin
Sutton James
Swales John Commens
Swan Joshua
Swaney Daniel
Swartwout Cornelius
Swartwout Simon
Swayer Lambart
Swigar Paul
Syle Christopher
Tably Jacob
Tabor Edward
Tagget Robert
Talbot William
Talmadg John
Tare Godfry
Tarrey Nathaniel
Taylor Edmund
Taylor George
Taylor William
Temple Joseph
Tenneray Zopher
Tepperwine Christian
Terry Nathaniel
Tharp David
Tharp Peter
Tharp Thomas
Thomas Edmund
Thomas Ezekiel
Thomas John
Thompson Alexander
Thompson Andrew
Thompson James
Thompson John
Thompson John (2)
Thompson William
Thorn Peter
Thorp Richard
Thurner William
Tiercy John
Tilsey John
Tipperwine Christian
Titsworth Thomas
Titus John
Tobin Edward
Tobley Jacob
Tolbard William
Tombs John
Tombs Stephen
Tomkins Abraham
Tomkins Edward
Tomkins Israel
Tool John
Toorel Roger
Torbin Edward
Totton Samuel
Townley Joshua
Trigleth Richard
Tully Samuel
Turnbull William
Turner John
Turner Samuel
Tuttle Joel
Uens William
Uthest John
Utter Gilbert
Valence William
Valentine William
Varian John
Veal Jeremiah
Vedder Aaron
Very George
Viele Andrew G.
Viesell Nicholas
Vinegar Samuel
Vonck Peter
Vonck William
Vradenbergh Isaac
Vradenburgh William
Vredenbergh Matthew
Vredenburgh Peter
Van Alstin Abraham
Van Amborough Abraham
Van Atler Joseph
Van Atta John
Van Atta Joseph
Van Benthuysen Martin
Van Beuren George
Van Blarcum Jacobus
Van Blarcum James
Van Bluck John
Van Bonhagel John C. B.
Van Buran George
Van Cleef Lawrence
Van Debal Jacob
Van De Bogart Gysbert
Van Debogert James
Van Denbergh Daniel
Vanderboc Jacob
Vanderbogart Nicholas
Van Derbow Jacob
Van Derhoof Cornelius
Vanderhyden Ad'm
Vanderhyden Derrick
Vanderhyden Gersham
Vanderwerker Jacob
Van Derwerker James
Van Derwerkin Martin
Van Desbider Adam
Van Deusen Abraham
Van Devore John
Vande Water Cornelius
Vandueus William
Van Dyck Peter
Van Dyck Peter T.
Van Etten John
Van Etten Joseph
Van Everin Martin
Vangothnet Joseph
Van Hauren Cornelius
Van Hoaft John
Van Hook Isaac I.
Van Houton John
Van Kleeck Henry
Van Kleeck James

Van Loan Nicholas
Van Ness Cornelius
Van Netten Joseph
Van Orden Albert
Van Order Charles
Van Salisbury Cornelius
Van Size John
Vansly Martin
Van Slyck Martin
Van Snell John
Vantassel Cornelius
Van Teveren Martin
Van Tine John
Van Valkinburg Lambert
Van Vleit Abraham
Van Vorst Christian
Van Vorst John
Van Winkel Symon
Van Zile William
W—— Rubin
Waddle William
Wadkins Thomas
Waggerman Emanuel
Waggerman George
Wagoner Frederick
Walch Thomas
Waldron Barent
Wale Patrick
Walker Matthew
Wall Patrick
Wallace Daniel
Wallace William
Wallacer Christian
Wallis James
Walsh Edward
Walsh John
Walter Jacob
Walter Martin
Walters David
Walton Jacob
Walton John
Wan Thomas
Wandell Jacob
Wandell John
Ward Daniel
Ward David
Ward Jesse
Ward John
Ward Josia
Warder Thomas
Waring Benjamin
Waring Michael
Warmoed Christian
Warmood Mathias
Warmoth Christian
Warner Christian
Warner Michael
Warren Edward
Wart Benjamin
Waters Sterling
Waters William
Watkins Benjamin
Watson Joseph
Watson Major
Watson Thomas
Waugh Samuel
Way John
Weasell Nicholas
Weatherstine John
Weaver Adam
Weaver Christian
Weaver George
Weaver Henry
Weaver Michael
Weaver Nicholas
Webb Samuel
Webber Adam
Webber George
Webber William
Webbers James
Wederick Michael
Wederwax William
Wedge Stephen
Weed Abijah
Weed Ezra
Weekes Abraham
Weeks Jacob
Weeks Micajah
Weeler Robert
Weghan Conrad
Wegman John
Weighlien Mathias
Weiscover Jacob
Weiss Lewis
Weken Conrad
Welch Henry
Welch John
Welch Nicholas
Welch Richard
Welch Thomas
Weldon Jeremiah
Wells John
Welsh Joseph
Welsh William
Wemp Barent (see Wemple)
Wemple Barent (see Wemp)
Wendell Jacob
Wendell John
Wendle Addem
Wesels Evert
Wessell Nicholas
West Stephen
West Williston
Westfield Andrew
Weston James
Wetherick George
Wetberick Michael
Weyland Mathew
Wezil Nicholas
Whalen Richard
Whaler John
Whaley Michael
Whalin Walter
Whay John
Whealen Richard
Whealon Walter
Wheeler Henry
Wheeler Isaac
Wheeler John
Wheeler Robert
Wheeler Samuel
Whiswick George
White Ely
White James
White Joseph
Whiteside William
Whitley John
Whitley William
Wibert John
Wichland Mathias
Wick James
Wifenbach Henry
Wiggins William
Wilcox Abner
Wiley Alexander
Wilkenson Thomas
Wilkinson James
Wilkinson Robert
Wilks John
Willagan David
Willet John
Williams Charles
Williams John
Williams Robert
Williams Solomon
Williams Uriah
Williams William
Williamson John
Willice John
Willis James
Wilmot Leonard
Wilmoth Francis
Wilsey William
Wilson James
Wilson John
Wilson Josia
Wilson Michael
Wilson Robert
Wilson Samuel
Wilson William
Winblow Edward
Windeler Mathew
Windford Henry
Windsor John
Winn Joseph
Winn Peter
Winne Killijan
Wisenbeck Henry
Witham William
Witherick George
Witherick Michael
Wolf Michael
Wolkens Benjamin
Wood James
Wood Peter
Wood Samuel
Woodcock Peter
Wooderd Titus
Woodroff Ephrim
Woodroff Matthias
Woodroff William
Woodruff Daniel
Woodworth Reuben
Wooley Abraham
Worden Nathan
Worder Thomas
Wormley Jacob
Wormoet Christian
Wormwood Christian
Wrather Thomas
Wright Benjamin
Wright Edward
Wright John
Wright Robert
Wright Samuel
Wuine William
Wyatt John
Wybert Frederick
Wychaline Matthew
Yengling John F.
Yeomans Isaac
Younkins George
Young Christopher
Young Ebenezer
Young John
Zeager Thomas
Zeaster Michael
Zundell George
Zyranius Christopher

Rochester 21 [illegible] 1779 —

Pay to Robert Provoost Esqr. the Bearer [illegible] of One Hundred and Eighty Pounds [illegible] of the Subscribers which by a Law of this State passed the 13th Ultimo entitled "An Act for the payment of the Salaries of the several Officers of Government and for other purposes therein mentioned" is granted to us severally and his Receipt shall be a discharge from us —

Philip Cortlandt Col.
Fred. Weissenfels Lt. Col.
Nich. Fish Major
Chas. Graham Capt.
John F. Pell Capt.
Jacob Wright Capt.
J. Hallett Capt.
[illegible] Lieut.
Wm. Glenny Lieut.
John Burnett Ensign
[illegible] Lieut.
[illegible]
Wm. Munday Lieut.
Jn. L. Hardenbergh Lieut.
Isaac Vanwoert Lieut.
Christopher Codwise Lt.
[illegible] Lieut.

Th. Nukerck Capt. Lt.
Tunis V. Wagenen Lieut.
Rob. Provoost Jun. Ensn. & Pay Mastr.
Danl. Menema Surgn.
Abm. French Capt.
Wm. [illegible] Lieut.

To Gerard Bancker Esqr.
Treasurer of the State N. York

SIGNATURES OF OFFICERS OF THE 2D LINE.

State of New York
ss.

At a Council of Appointment
held at Kingston the 15th day of June 1780.

Present

His Excellency George Clinton Esquire, President.

The Honorable { Rynier Myndertse, Levi Pawling, Isaac Roosevelt } Esquires, Members.

Resolved that the Reverend Johann Daniel Gros be, and he is hereby appointed Chaplain to the Levies raised for the Defence of the Frontiers of this State.

By Order — Extract from the Minutes Robt. Harpur Clk of Council

APPOINTMENT OF CHAPLAIN GROS.

Dr State of New York in Accot Current with Nicholas Fish Cr

Dr		Cr	
To my Pay as Major from 1st Aug 1780 to 31 Dec 1780 is 5 Months [illegible]	£ 100 —	[illegible] in the Year 1780 [illegible]	£ 150 —
[illegible]	32.5.4		
[illegible]	4.12 —		
[illegible]	3.14.4		
[illegible]	4.9.4		
	£ 150.0.0		150.0 —

ACCOUNT CURRENT WITH MAJOR NICHOLAS FISH.

2d Regiment.

COLONEL PHILIP VAN CORTLAND
LIEUTENANT COLONEL ROBERT COCHRAN
LIEUTENANT COLONEL PETER REGNIER
LIEUTENANT COLONEL FREDERICK WEISSENFELS
MAJOR NICHOLAS FISH
MAJOR PETER SCHUYLER
ADJUTANT JOHN L. HARDENBERGH
QUARTER MASTER WILLIAM COLBREATH
QUARTER MASTER LEVI DE WITT
PAY MASTER (CAPT.) MICHAEL CONNOLLY
PAY MASTER ROBERT PROVOOST, JR
CHAPLAIN ISRAEL EVANS
SURGEON EBENEZER HAVILAND
SURGEON DANIEL MENEMA

CAPT. HEZEKIAH BALDWIN
" SAMUEL T. BELL
" ELISHA BENEDICT
" JAMES BLEADEY
" HENRY DUBOIS
" THEODOSIUS FOWLER
" ABNER FRENCH
" ABRAHAM FRENCH
" CHARLES GRAHAM
" JOHN GRAHAM
" JONATHAN HALLETT
" JOHN F. HAMTRAMCK
" JAMES JOHNSTON
" EDWARD LOUNSBERY
" ELIHU MARSHALL
" DANIEL MILLS
" CHARLES NUKERK
" HENRY PAWLING
" SAMUEL PELL
" BENJAMIN PELTON
" JOEL PRATT
" ABRAHAM RICKAR
" ISRAEL SMITH
" BARENT TENEYCK
" HENRY VANDERBURGH
" BENJAMIN WALKER
" ANDREW WHITE
" GEORGE WHITE
" JACOB WRIGHT
" CHRISTOPHER P. YATES
LIEUT. JACOB BAMPER
" ROSWELL BEEBE
LIEUT. FREDERICK BEEKMAN
" TJERCK BEEKMAN
" BENJAMIN CHITTENDEN
" MATTHIAS CLARK
" JEREMIAH CLARKE
" CHRISTOPHER CODWISE
" DANIEL DENISTON
" SAMUEL DODGE, JR.
" JAMES FAIRLIE
" ANDREW FINCK, JR.
" JOSEPH FRELICK
" WILLIAM GLENNY
" ELEAZER GRANT
" DORICK HANSEN
" THOMAS HUNT
" CHRISTOPHER HUTTON
" GEORGE JOHNSON
" JAMES JOHNSON
" JOHN KEYSER, JR.
" GIDEON KING
" JOHN G. LANSINGH
" GILBERT J. LIVINGSTONE
" WILLIAM MOULTON
" JARVES MUDGE
" WILLIAM MUNDAY
" JOHN MCCLAUGHRY
" WILLIAM MCCUNE
" WILLIAM NOTTINGHAM
" BARNABUS OWENS
" CHARLES PARSONS
" NATHANIEL ROWLEY
" ISAAC SHERWOOD

LIEUT. ISRAEL SPENCER
" SAMUEL TALMADGE
" RUDOLPH VAN HOWENBARGH (HOVENBERGH)
" NICHOLAS VAN RANSELEAR
" TUNIS VAN WAGENEN
" ISAAC VAN WOERT
" CHARLES F. WEISSENFELS
" ANDREW WHELEY
" ROBERT WOOD
ENSIGN JOHN BROWN
" NEHEMIAH CARPENTER
ENSIGN SAMUEL DODGE
" PETER DOLSON
" STEPHEN GRIFFIN
" THOMAS HAIGHT
" JOSEPH HARPER
" LEWIS R. MORRIS
" RICHARD MOUNT
" WILLIAM PETERS
" DIRCK SCHUYLER
" BARNABUS SWARTWOUT
" BARTHOLOMEW VAN DERBURGH
" EPHRAIM WOODRUFF

ENLISTED MEN.

Ackey Adnijah
Ackley Jacob
Ackley James
Acurman William (see Ocurman)
Adams Noah
Adams Peleg
Adamy Henry
Adkin Andrew
Aimes Hugh
Ainsworth Henry
Albright Jacob
Albright John
Alexander Jonathan
Alger George
Allen William
Allison John
Allison Robert
Alport John
Amerman Derrick
Ames Ashel
Ames Levi
Ammerman James
Ammermon Cornelius
Anderson Alexander
Anderson Samuel
Andress Thomas
Andrews Isaac
Anthony John Francis
Arkenburgh Henry
Armstrong Archibald
Armstrong Benjamin
Armstrong John
Arnold Oliver
Ashly Aaron
Asquith John
Asten Benjamin
Asten Holmes
Asten Jeremiah
Asten Martin
Astin John
Avary Nicholas
Ayer Nathaniel
Babcock Garsham
Bacon Penial;
Badleis John
Bagle Silas
Bailey James
Bailey Joseph
Baily Ebenezer
Baker Benjamin
Baker Elijah
Baker Judah
Baker Pearce
Baker Samuel
Baldon Zuriel
Ball Shadrick
Bangel John
Banks Benjamin
Baragar Walter
Barans Glean
Barber Benjamin
Barber John
Barber Stephen
Barber William
Bardeen Robert
Bare Jacob
Barker Jonathan
Barkin William
Barlow Joseph
Barnam Samuel
Barnes Richard
Barnheart David
Barns Abijah
Barns Elisha
Barns James
Barrager Walter
Barren John
Barrett Michael
Barrett Peter
Barrian John
Barrit Bartholamy
Barrit Ephram
Barritt Oliver
Bartholemee John
Bartlet Lemuel
Bartoe Jonas
Bartoe Morres
Basamer Jacobus
Basan Daniel
Basemer Michael
Basemore John
Bason Daniel
Batersby Robert
Bates Zephaniah
Baxter Lockwood
Bay John
Bayles James
Baylie Ebenezer
Baylis John
Bayson Daniel
Beach Amos
Beach Asa
Beagle Silas
Beaker Judah
Beatch Amos
Beats Zepheniah
Becannon Samuel
Becker Henry
Beebe Burnagus
Beebe Rodrick
Beech Amos
Beely Joseph
Beets James
Beevins Christ
Beggs Jonathan
Begraft Thomas
Bell James
Bell Matthew
Belnap Asa
Benedick Ambris
Benjaman Jonathan
Benjamen Samuel
Benjamin Ebenezer
Benn Daniel
Bennedict Caleb
Bennet Jabin
Bennett Jacob
Bennett James
Bennett Samuel
Bennit Joshua
Bennitt Jeremiah
Bennitt John
Bennitt Timothy
Benson Thomas
Benson William
Benten Arthur
Bently George
Berlow Joseph
Berrian John
Berry William
Besemer Jacobus
Betts James
Bettys William
Bevens Christopher
Bevens John
Biddle William
Bigham James
Bill Ezariah
Bingham Abijah
Birch John
Bismer Michael
Black Jacob
Blackney John
Blake Felove
Blakely John
Blinn Simeon
Bloose John
Blossome Peter
Boardman Ephraim
Bockers Jacob
Bodley Andrew
Bogardas Peter
Bogardis Abraham
Bogardus David
Bogge John
Boice Jeremiah
Boice Peter
Boice Simon
Boldrige Daniel
Bolen Michael
Boleton George
Bolton Jonatha
Boman Albart
Boman Luke
Bonett Joseph

By His Excellency
GEORGE WASHINGTON, Esq;
General and Commander in Chief of the Forces of the
United States of America.

THESE are to CERTIFY that the Bearer hereof John Cooper — Soldier — in the first New York — Regiment, having faithfully served the United States six years — and being inlisted for the War only, is hereby Discharged from the American Army.

GIVEN at Head-Quarters the 8th June 1783

G. Washington

By His Excellency's
Command,

[illegible]

REGISTERED in the Books
of the Regiment,

[illegible] Adjutant.

THE above John Cooper —
has been honored with the Badge of Merit for six
Years faithful Service.

[illegible]

A DISCHARGE FROM GENERAL WASHINGTON.

HEAD-QUARTERS, June 8th 1783.

THE within CERTIFICATE shall not avail the Bearer as a Discharge, until the Ratification of the definitive Treaty of Peace; previous to which Time, and until Proclamation thereof shall be made, He is to be considered as being on Furlough.

GEORGE WASHINGTON

REVERSE SIDE OF DISCHARGE.

Bonus James
Booker John
Bordman Andrew
Borrill Zachariah
Bose Peter
Boswick Edward
Bostwith James
Boswith William
Bovie John
Bowan Charles
Bowman Lewis
Boyd George
Boyles James
Bradain John
Bradner Andrew
Bradner Benoni
Brady Lewis
Braett Andrew
Brandt John
Brann Samuel
Bream Baltus
Bredinbaker Baltis
Brett James
Brewer Jeremiah
Brewer Samuel
Brewton Arthur
Briant John
Briant Thomas
Bridges James
Brigs Jonathan
Brinck Cornelius
Brinton David
Britt James
Broadt Andrew
Brockway Russell
Brooke Thomas
Brooker Walter
Brooks Joseph
Brooks Thomas
Brotherton John
Brott Andrew
Brower William
Brown Benjamin
Brown David
Brown Joel
Brown John
Brown Jonas
Brown Joseph
Brown Justice
Brown Samuel
Brown Thomas
Browne Frances
Bruhard Nathaniel
Brush Eliakim
Brush Selah
Brust Martin
Brutan Arthur
Buck Enoch

Buckanon Samuel
Buckhoud William
Buckhout John
Budine Francis
Bunce Abraham
Bunce Daniel
Bunt Lodwick
Bunting Thomas
Burch John
Burchard Nathaniel
Burdick Elisha
Burdick Gideon
Burdick Henry
Burdick Moses
Burge Michael
Burges Archibald
Burke John
Burke Thomas
Burket John
Burline Lewis
Burn Henry
Burnett Ebenezer
Burnett John
Burnham William
Burns James
Burns Michael
Burns Robert
Burrows Thomas
Burwell Zechariah
Busby William
Busen John
Bush John
Bussing John
Cabalson Michael
Cable George
Cady John
Cady Lemuel
Cady Palmer
Cahoone Hyman
Cahoone Joseph
Cairley Joseph
Calkin Simon
Callegan John
Cambee James
Cambell Andrew
Cambell William
Cammoran Daniel
Camp Asa
Camp Elias
Campbell William
Campble John
Cane William
Canfield Samuel
Canklin Daniel
Cargel Isaac
Carll David
Carly Joseph
Carman John

Carrigan William
Carrill David
Carson James
Carter James
Carter John
Cartwright Henry Arbraham
Casady Edward
Casaday Peter
Casselman Richard
Castor Adam
Catherling Matthew
Caviner Moses
Cazard Richard
Certain James
Certer Philip
Chainny Ware
Chalenor Christopher
Chamberlin Girdon
Chamberlin Wyatt
Champlain James
Champlan Edward
Chapman Asa
Chapman Charles
Chapman Joseph
Chapman Josiah
Chapple Benjamin
Charlesworth John M
Charters James
Chase Caleb
Chase Jacob
Chase Lott
Chatfield David
Chelson Beriah
Cherrey John
Cherwood Nemiah
Chesshier Neamiah
Christeen Peter
Christian John
Christman Nicholas
Christoper Andries
Christy John
Church David
Church Reuben
Clark Abijah
Clark David
Clark John
Clarwater Martin
Claxton George
Cleark John
Cleveland Josiah
Cleveland Jonas
Clewater Martin
Cliff Joseph
Cline Jacob
Close Samuel
Closser Christopher
Clumpha William

Coal David
Cobler Conrad
Cockle George
Coe Philip
Coefield James
Cogdon John
Cohoon Himan
Cokely John
Coldwell William
Cole Abraham
Cole Frances
Cole Henry
Cole Moses
Cole Philip
Cole Samuel
Cole Tunis
Collings Alber
Collings John
Collins Edward
Collins John
Collins William
Combs John
Commons Patrick
Conaway John
Concklin John
Concklin Joseph
Condon David
Conkling Daniel
Conn William
Conner Daniel
Conner Patrick
Conner William
Connite Conrod
Connolly James
Connor Edward
Connor James
Constable Garrett
Contryman John F.
Conway Cornelius
Cook George
Cook Sapines
Cooke Hyman
Cooke Nicholas
Cool George
Cool Rufe
Coombs Peter
Coon Jacob
Coon Timothy
Coony George
Cooper John
Copelin William
Corkins Simon
Cornel Joseph
Cornelison John
Corter John
Cortney Francis
Cortor Philip
Corwin George

Corwine Gersham
Cosier Hezekiah
Costeloe James
Costerhoudt Peter
Costerly James
Cottrill Richard
Countriman Jacobus
Courter Philip
Covel Philip
Cowen Thomas
Cox Charles
Cox John
Cox Robert
Cox Simon
Cozard Richard
Craft Jacob
Craft Nathaniel
Craigen Peter
Crain William
Crandle Henry
Crandle Willson
Crandle Wright
Crane John
Crankhite Abraham
Craton Thomas
Crawfoot Zachariah
Crighoof John
Crisple Abraham
Cristenon Benjamin
Crofoot Samuel
Croft James
Crofts Jacob
Crook William
Crosman Daniel
Cross John
Crowin Silas
Crugor William
Crum William
Crumb Christopher
Crumb John
Culbertson William
Cully Charles
Cummin Benjamin
Cummings John
Cummins Ebenezer
Cummins John
Cuningham James
Cuningham Shubal
Cunningham Archibald
Cunningham Henry
Currin Samuel
Curry James
Curtes Caleb
Curvain Edward
Curwin Gersham
Curwine Edward
Cushan John
Dailey Israel
Dalton Frederick
Danford Prince
Danford Wells
Danielson Isaac
Danielson Thomas
Dannils George
Darby Asa
Darby Charles
Darrow Christopher
Darrow George
Darrow Jedediah
Daton Ezekiel
Daugherty John
Davee Isaac
Davee John
Davenport Humphrey
Davenport John
David Isaac
David Jonathan
Davie Isaac
Davie John
Davie Oliver
Davis Anderson
Davis Andrus
Davis Benjamin
Davis Chapman
Davis David
Davis Ezra
Davis Herman
Davis Hugh
Davis John
Davis Joshua
Davis Patrick
Davis Peter
Davis Samuel
Davison Andrew
Daviss Richard
Davisson James
Davisson John
Day Aron
Dayton Bennit
Dean Benjamin
Dean James
Deane Isaac
Decker Christopher
Decker Martin
Decker Michael
Deen Henry
Deffendorff Henry
Defoe George
Defoe John
Degrusen Elias
Deharsh Philip
Dekerson Abraham
Demerist Nicholas
Deming Simeon
Demitt Joseph
Demond Moses
Demond William
Denney Peter
Dennis John
Dennis Mydert
Denniston Thomas
Denton Preston
Depew Abraham
Depew Cornelius
Depew Francis
Depew Henry
Depew John
De Pont Bostion
Dermott Richard
Derry James
Derusia Anthony
Devanport Jonathan
Devore Abraham
Dewey Elisha
Dewitt Benjamin
DeWitt John
DeWitt Peter, Jr.
DeWitt Peter, Sr.
Dexter Jonathan
Dickerson David
Dickeson Abraham
Dickins Peter
Dickins Thomas
Dickinson James
Dickinson Varsil
Dickson Robert
Dimmick Perius
Dimminick Samuel
Dimmis John
Dimmuck Benjamin
Dimon Moses
Dimond William
Dobson John
Dodge Richard
Dolloway Jeremiah
Dolph Moses
Dolton Thomas
Donalds George
Donnalds John
Dounaldson Peter
Dority William
Doty John
Doty Samuel
Doughty Elias
Doughty Peter
Douglas George
Douglass James
Douly Elias
Dow Vulker
Downing Andrew
Doxey Stephen
Drake Asel
Drennin Hamilton
Drew George
Drew Oliver
Drummond David
Drummond Griger
Dubois John
Dudley Simon
Duguid John
Dunbar William
Duncan Thomas
Dunivan John
Dunlap Andrew
Dunlap James
Dunn Alexander
Duran Francis
Dutcher Barnett
Dutcher Barrick
Dwyre, Thomas
Dybol Hezekiah
Dybol Zachariah
Eagleston John
Eaglestone James
Earl William
Easterly Thomas
Eastwood Daniel
Eavens John
Edwards William
Edwords Edward
Eggbert Daniel
Eggers Elijah
Egleston Eli
Elder Joseph
Eliot Henry
Eliott Archabald
Elkingburgh Peter
Elliott John
Ellis Jacob
Ellis John
Elsworth John
Elvingstone Edward
Ennest Peter
Ennis Peter
Enris David
Epton Benjamin
Ergenbrech John
Erwin John
Esmond John
Evans Thomas
Evins John
Evins Moses
Factor John
Fairchild Abner
Fairchilds Ephraim
Fall Robert
Fanford Obadiah
Farrel Garret
Farrington Robert
Fashee David
Fellows Moses
Felt Solomon

Felton Lewis
Fenton Amos
Ferdon John
Ferguson Samuel
Ferris John
Ferris John, Junr
Ferry Charles
Fetherly John
Fetherly Thomas
Fields Philip
Fiero Abram
Finch Jonathan
Finck Hanjost
Fine Andrew
Finel Edward
Finton Amos
Fish Caleb
Fish Moses
Fish Sebra
Fishee David
Fits Gerral Thomas
Fitzgerald Michael
Fitzjearls William
Flagg Ebenezer
Flansbury Daniel
Fleming Jacob
Fleming William
Fling Thomas
Flint Nathan
Flood Francis
Flummin Francis
Follerd John
Foot Joseph
Forbush Nicholas
Force Timothy
Ford Benjamin
Ford George
Ford Timothy
Forganson James
Forgerson Samuel
Forster Nathaniel
Forster William
Fosburgh Jacob
Foster Benoni
Foster John
Foster Nathaniel
Fouler Cornelius
Fowler George
Fowler Michael
Foy Patrick
Foyer Thomas
Fradenbourgh Mathew
Framer Michael
Francis John
Francisco Henry
Francisco John
Frank Henry
Franks Michal

Frazier John
Frear Peter
Frebush Mathew
Fredrick Johannes
Freeland John
Freeman Nathaniel
Freer Peter
Fremain Jonathan
Fretter John
Frimiah Mitch
Frimier John
Frost Edmond
Froth James
Fuller Daniel
Fuller Josiah
Fulton Alexander
Fulton John
Fulvia Thomas
Gabine John
Gage Richard
Gall John
Garbine John
Gardener John
Gardner Andrew
Gardner Benoni
Gardner Jacob
Gardner James
Gardner Jesse
Gardnier Clark
Gareheart Matthew
Garmin James
Garrison Abraham
Garrison Hartshorn
Garrison John
Garrison William
Garvey Francis
Gaudt Benjamin
Gay Edward
Gee David
Gee Ezekiel
Gee John
Gee Moses
George Joshua
Gerard Benjamin
Germin James
Gibbons John
Gibson John
Gilaspie James
Gilbert John
Gilbert Seth
Gilbert William
Gilchrist William
Gilder Ebenezer
Gildersleeve Joseph
Gilderslivis Joseph
Giles Richard
Gimblet Peter
Ginnings John

Girle Thomas
Glaspy James
Glexton George
Glover Thomas
Goff Ashbel
Goff Oliver
Gold John
Golding Thomas
Goldsmith Ezra
Goodall James
Goodfellow Moses
Goodin George
Goodwin Abraham
Gordon Abraham
Gorham Jabus
Gorman Patrick
Got William
Gould Asa
Gould John
Graham John
Grahams Andrew
Grahams Moses
Granger John
Graves Jedediah
Graves Joseph
Graves Lewis
Gray John, Jr.
Gready Thomas
Green Beriah
Green Clark
Green John
Green Peter
Green Silas
Greenwood John
Gregg David
Greswill Miles
Grey Nicholas
Grey Silas
Grey Thomas
Griffen Hezekiah
Griffeth Abraham
Griffeth Jeremiah
Griffin Aron
Griffin Benjamin
Griffin James
Griffin John
Griffin Joseph
Griffin Joshua
Griffitts Samuel
Griggs Jeremiah
Grill Thomas
Grisal Jabus
Grograin John
Guile Joseph
Guillion John
Hackley Ezekial
Hadley Joseph
Hadlock James

Haight Ceasor
Haight Thomas K.
Hall David
Hall Israel
Hall John
Hall Lynos
Hall William
Hallack Jeffera
Hallett Richard
Hallick Jeffery
Halnbeck Henry
Halsapel Zachariah
Halsey Abraham
Halsey Thomas
Hambleton William
Hamilton Patrick
Hammer William
Hamon John
Handley James
Hanes John
Hanford Jeremiah
Hanley James
Hanyon Garret
Harding Henry
Haris Moses
Harmanse Edward
Harper James
Harper William
Harrington Anthony
Harrington Ebenezer
Harrington James
Harris Cato
Harris David
Harris George
Harris Henry
Harris Richard
Harrison Joseph
Hart Daniel
Harty Christopher
Hasbrook George
Hasbrouck David
Hatchins William
Havens Isaac
Havens William
Hawk George
Hawkey Henry
Hawkey Richard
Hawkins John
Hawkins Zopher
Hawley Benjamin
Hawley Samuel
Hawley Zadock
Hay James
Hayes John
Hays John
Hays Nathaniel
Hazerd James
Heath Josiah

Heavens Peter
Heavlish Michael
Hebmore John
Helmer John
Henderson Samuel
Henderson William
Henjericklick Johan
Henneysee John
Henry Wells
Henson Nathaniel
Heppel Adam
Herington Isaac
Hermans Edward
Herring Jacob
Herrington Benjamin
Hessum John
Hewet Benjamin
Hewett Edmond
Hewit Arthur
Hibbard James
Hibbirdt John
Hicks Jacob
Hicks Lewis
Hiet Henry
Higby Samuel
Higgins Archibald
Higgins Jonathan
Higgins Thomas
Higher Alexander
Higley Rozel
Higley Seth
Hill Aza
Hill Elijiah
Hill Solomon
Hill Thomas
Hill William
Himilan Adam
Hines John
Hitchcock John
Hitchcok Samuel
Hix Joseph
Hofford Elijah
Hofford Jesse
Hogan John
Holcomb Beriah
Holcomb Mathew
Holdridge Amasa
Holdridge John
Holdridge Richard
Hole James
Holkens James
Hollenbeeck Jacob
Holmes Obadiah
Holmes Stephen
Holms Daniel
Holms Ezekiah
Holms John
Holms Thomas
Holtzer John
Hope Thomas
Hopkins Noah
Hopper John
Hopper Peter
Horan Phanten
Hornebeak Ephereham
Horsford Joseph
Horton Christopher
Horton Isaac
Horton Thomas
Horton William
Hoser Thomas
Hosford Joseph
Hoskins Thomas
Hoskins William
Hosmer John
Hotskiss William
Hough John
Houghboom Jacob
Houns Zepheniah
House Anthony
House Henry
House Laphariah
Housworth Michael
Howe John
Howe Zephaniah
Howell George
Howell Lemuel
Howell Seth
Howes Zephaniah
Howley Zadak
Hoyt Ceaser
Hudler Nicholas
Hughson Nathaniel
Hull Seth
Hull William
Humphries Alexander
Humphry James
Humphry John
Hunt David
Hunt Joshua
Hunt Prince
Hunt William
Hunter James
Hunthley Thomas
Huntley Bethuel
Hurd Elijah
Hurly James
Hutly Thomas
Hutsal Nicholas
Huyks Joseph
Hyatt Abraham
Hyatt Alphen
Hyatt Alpheus
Hyatt Alvan
Hyatt Henry
Hyatt Minah
Innes Peter
Irwin John
Ivorey Jacobus
Ivorey James
Jabine John
Jabwain John
Jackson Francis
Jackson Micael
Jackson Thomas
Jackson William
Jacobs John
James Ebenezer
James William
Jansing Robert
Jaquist John
Jeffriss John
Jett Michael
Jinkins Philip
Jinson Robert
Joce David
Johns Jacob
Johns Samuel
Johnson Daniel
Johnson Elisha
Johnson James
Johnson Justus
Johnson Moses
Johnson Peter
Johnson Prince
Johnson Richar
Johnson Thomas
Johnson William
Johnston Josiah
Johnston Robert
Joice David
Jones David
Jones Ebenezer
Jones Evan
Jones Ezekiel
Jones Ezra
Jones Griffin
Jones Ivens
Jones John
Jones Joseph
Jones Peter
Jones Ruben
Jones Samuel
Jones Seth
Jones Thomas
Jore David
Joyce James
Jupter Silas
Kably Michael
Kader Adam
Kader John
Kanneday John
Kartwright Henry
Katcham Joseph
Keating Robert
Keddar Stephan
Keeler Frederick
Keeth John
Kelley Robert
Kelly Barny
Kelly Coenrod
Kelly Edmund
Kelly John
Kelly Joshua
Kelly Moris
Kelly Peter
Kelly Silvinus
Kelsey Benjamin
Kelsey Ebenezer
Kelson Phineas
Kennady James
Kent Isaac
Kenyon William
Kershaw John
Kertrem Jesse
Ketchem Ephm
Ketchem John
Killey Silveney
Kind William
King John
King Philip
King Reuben
King William
Kinnaday John
Kinner Jonathan
Kinney Charles
Kinney James
Kinny Roger
Kinsham Frederick
Kinyon William
Kipp Abraham
Kipp Amos
Kipp James
Kipp Moses
Kirn Michael
Kirn William
Kisard Richard
Kitcham Abraham
Kitcham Joseph
Knapp Benjamin
Knapp Caleb
Knapp Daniel
Knapp Isaac
Knapp James
Knapping Jeremiah
Knickabocker Andrew
Kniffen Amos
Knight William
Knights Lucias
Knikaboker Herman
Knoutz John
Koel Henry

Kole Philip
Konklin Joseph
Koole Teunis
Krane William
Kress John
Krom Christopher
Krook William
Krous Jacob
Kyser Edward
Kyser Joseph
Kinkade William
Lacey Philip
Lain John
Lakely John B.
Lalefferty Stephen
Lamb Arthur
Lamb John
Lamb Pomp
Lambert David
Lambert John
Lambertson Simon
Lane Jeremiah
Lane John
Lane William
Langdon Benjamin
Langin William
Lannee Philip
Larabee Elias
Lavett John
Lawder Edward
Lawn George
Lawrance George S.
Lawrence Benjamin
Lawrence Jacob
Lawson Christopher
Lawyer Christopher
Layer Christopher
Layton William
Learey Cadey
Leary John
Leather William
Leck Johan Hangerick
Lee Daniel
Lee Ephraim
Lee William
Lenny Philip
Lent Abram
Lent Elias
Lent Henry
Lent Jacob
Leonard Edward
Lepper John
Lester John
Le Strange Samuel
Letty William
Levy Jacob
Lewis James
Lewis Jesse
Lewis Leonard
Lewis Nathan
Lewis Richard
Lewis William
Light John
Light Lemuel
Like Henry
Linch William
Lindon James
Linney Philip
Lint Elias
Lister John
Livingston Jacob
Loader Daniel
Loather William
Lobby John
Loder Samuel
Lofberry Isaac
Loins Hosea
Lomus Jacob
Loofborrow Isaac
Lord Benjamin
Lord Timothy
Lossey Jacob
Lothorp Icabod
Louchee Jacob
Loucks Peter
Lousbarry John
Love Michael
Lovette John
Lovjoy Nathan
Low John
Lowry John
Luca John
Ludlum Daniel
Ludlum John
Lummess Write
Lusk John
Lutz Coonradt
Lyons David
Lyons Hosea
Lyons Michael
Lyonson William
Mad Calf William
M—ah Josiah
Mahu Peter
Malay James
Mallory Jonathan N.
Man Michael
Manning Stephen
Manrose Elijah
Manross Jesse
Mantanyia Peter
Marble Ephraim
Marian Francis
Marling Isaac
Marly John
Marshall Robert
Martin Alexander
Martin Thomas
Martling Isaac
Marvin Mathew
Masson Thomas
Masters Daniel
Masthers James
Mastin Daniel
Mathers James
Matherson August
Matthews James
Maxim Adonijah
May Daniel
May Hendrick
Mayhew Peter
Mead Jehiel
Mead Nathan
Meaher Ichabod
Meddock John
Meggs Seth
Megriger Daniel
Melcher Paulis
Menrony Florens
Merchall Robert
Merewise Jacob
Merrian Francis
Merritt Jeremiah
Mervin Mathew
Messer William
Metcalf William
Methers James
Michel Edward
Michel George
Milden Daniel
Mildridge Thomas
Miller Benjamin
Miller David
Miller Elisha
Miller Jacob
Miller James
Miller John
Miller Josiah
Mills Andrew
Mills Samuel
Milton John
Mingo Marting
Minks John
Mitchel Ensign
Mitchel James
Mitchel Joseph
Mitchell Martin
Mitchell Richard
Mitchell Samuel
Mitchil David
Moffet William
Moke Gerardus
Molatt Ishmil
Molloy John
Monday James
Mondon John
Monger Joseph
Montayne Peter
Montgomery Hugh
Montgomery James
Moon Matthew
Moony William
Moor Charles
Moor Zebulon
Moore Charles
Moore Thomas
Moorley Abner
Moot Henry
Moot Noah
More John
Morewise Jacob
Morgan Joseph
Morgan William
Morloy James
Morrele Isaac
Morrell Robert
Morrill John
Morris John
Morris Matthew
Morrisson David
Moss David
Mott Isaac
Mott Noah
Mount Henry
Mtt Soon John
Mudg Abraham
Mullen William
Mullerner Moses
Mullin John
Mullin William
Mumford James
Munro Alexander
Munrose Elijah
Murdock Moses
Murray Isaac
Murray Nathan
Murray William
Mute William
Myer Moses
Myers David
McAllister William
McAntiere Alexander
McArthur John
Mc bane Giles
McBride William
McCalley Alexander
McCarney Stephen
McCartee Phelex
McCarty Isaac
McCarty James
McCarty John
McCharlesworth John

McCine David
McClean John
McClean Neal
McClosky Peter
McClure William
McCollum John
McCoomick John
McCoy Daniel
McCray John
McDaniel John
McDaniel Michael
McDaniel Randle
McDanold Ronald
McDole John
McDonald James
McDonald John
McDonald Michael
McDonald Peter
McDonall Patrick
McDugle Daniel
McEvers Daniel
McFall Pawl
McFarling Hosier
Mc farling William
McGinny James
McGlaughlin Neal
McGomery John
McGowen Jeremiah
McGraw James
McGregory Daniel
McGunney James
McIntyer Alexander
McKarney Stephen
McKeal Adam
McKee William
McKelle Adam
McKenny Charles
McKenny James
McKenny John
McKerney Stephen
McKillip Archibald
McKillip Daniel
McKim John
McLeal Charles
McLean John
McMannus Robert
McMaster James
McMiching John
McMurdy James
McNamee Charles
McNeal Adam
McNeil John
McPeak Dennis
McRenemee Charles
McSine Daniel
Naidler Nicholas
Narnil John
Neas George
Nebor Michael
Neeby Michael
Newcom John
Newcomb James
Newcomb Kinner
Newcomb Thomas
Newkerk Myndert
Newman Joseph
Newton William
Nicholas John
Nicholas Thomas
Nicholls Stephen
Nichols Asa
Nichols Thomas
Nichorson Thomas
Nickells Stephen
Nickerson Archibald
Nickerson Thomas
Nickolls John
Night William
Noble Gabriel
Nois William
Norstrand John
Norton George
Norton Isaac
Norton William
Norve Lewis
Nothingham Thomas
Noty Jacob
Nowel Lewis
Nowell Thomas
Nunk Henry
Oakly John
Oathout, Tilman
Obrien John
Occerman Elijah
Odel William
Ogden David
Ogdon John
Oliver Drew
Olmsted Nehemiah
Olmstead John
Omberman Cornelius
O'Niel John
Oosterhoudt Cornelius
Orr Daniel
Orvis Gersham
Orvis Waighstill
Osburn Nathaniel
Osterhout Gilbert
Osterhout Henry
Ostrander Adam
Ousterhout Peter
Outhout Silvester
Owen Abel
Owen Mowberry
Owens Isaac
Owens Moses
Oxten John
Padder John
Padrick John
Pain Daniel
Palmer Jonathan
Palmitear John
Palmitier Joseph
Pangbourn William
Pangburn John
Papping Daniel
Par Matthias
Pardy Silas
Parish Cyprian
Parker Ebenezer
Parker Edward
Parker James
Parker Samuel
Parks John
Parry John
Parsons Elisha
Parsonus James
Patterson Hezekiah
Patterson John
Pattison Michael
Pavy John
Payner Peter
Peck John
Pedder John
Peeler Jacob
Peirce Joseph
Pellam Francis
Pemberton Thomas
Penear Peter
Penny Jonathan
Perigo Usual
Perry William
Peters John
Peterson Barnabas
Petterson John
Pettet Samuel
Pew Abraham
Pew Francis
Pew Henry
Pew John
Phelps Ebenezer
Phelps Israel
Phenix Matthew
Philiph David
Philiph Joshua
Philips Samuel
Philps Ebenezer
Pichtol Henry
Pike John
Pinear Peter
Pitcher Jonathan
Pixley John
Pixly Squire
Plapper Christian
Plaugh Niceholes
Plough Dennis
Plum Stephen
Plummer Ezra
Pocknett John
Pocknot John
Poinear Peter
Pollard Thomas
Polman Salter
Post Conelius
Post Henry
Potter Isaac
Potter Samuel
Powell Elisha
Powell Sam
Powell Stephen
Powell Thomas
Powers Charles
Pratt Chalker
Pratt William
Preston Jonathan
Price James
Prichard Thomas
Prince Kemble
Prior Abner
Pritchard Eleanathan
Pritchard Isaac
Proston Isaac
Pudney James
Pudney Thorn
Pulaman Salter
Pulis John
Pullman Salter
Pumpshin Daniel
Putman William
Putnam Jonas
Putney James
Quawkenboss Jacob
Quick Cornelius
Quick Jacob
Quinn Thomas
Rabby Michael
Rady James
Ramond Seth
Ramson Henry
Ramson Jacob
Ramson James
Randel Henry
Randel John
Randels Joseph
Rano Symon
Ransom Jacob
Ransom James
Rapp George
Ray Isaac
Ray James
Rayley James
Read Brian

Read William
Readey James
Realey James
Redman John
Reed Brian
Reed John
Reed Joseph
Reed Nathaniel
Rennells James
Reno Simeon
Reuben Moses
Rexford Samuel
Reyder John
Reynolds Eliphalet
Reynolds John
Reynolds Joseph
Rhodes John
Rhodes Joseph
Ribley Michael
Rich Henry
Richard Gilbert
Richard Philip
Richards Ezra
Richardson Bezilla
Riche Henry
Richman John
Richmond Benjamin
Richmond John
Rickey Jeremiah
Rider John
Riggs Daniel
Righley Joseph
Riley Sylvester
Risten William
Ritter Moses
Roach William
Roads Joseph
Robards Caleb
Robarts Jonathan
Robarts Warren
Roberson John
Roberson Robert
Roberts James
Robins Daniel
Robinson Edmund
Robinson George
Robinson Issacher
Robinson James
Robinson Stephen
Robinson William
Robley Michael
Rock Hezekiah
Rock Samuel
Rocks William
Roe Lyman
Roomer Benjamin
Roosa Aaron
Roosa Abraham
Roosa Jacob
Root Joseph
Rosa Jacob
Rose Abraham
Rose Andrew
Rose Jacob
Rose James
Rose John
Rose Peter
Ross John
Ross Joseph
Row Antonio
Rowley Daniel
Royal Peter
Rudulph Henry
Ruff Adam
Rugar John
Runnel Able
Runnell Eliphalet
Runnells Stephen
Runnels Eliphalet
Runnolds Timothy
Runo Simeon
Russell James
Russell William
Russle Jonathan
Russle Thomas
Ryan John
Ryder John
Sackett Benjamin
Saddler John
Sammons Cornelius
Sammons Ephrehan
Sammons George
Sampson Isaac
Sanders John
Sanders Robert
Sandford Daniel
Sandford John
Saunders John
Sawyer Jonathan
Saxton Ebenezer
Scaitts James
Schaits James
Scheyer Jacob
Schoomaker Henry
Schriver Jacob
Schutt Frederick
Schutt Timothy
Scilkirck James
Scott Edward
Scott James
Scott John
Scott Timothy
Scott William
Scuitts James
Sculthorp John
Sealy Joseph
Sedore John
Seeds George
Seemore Abraham
Seers Moses
Seeton Willard
Sellers Michael
Semore Abraham
Serine James
Serjantson William
Sertain James
Service Philip
Service Richard
Servis Richard
Seton Willard
Sevis Francis
Seymor Thomas
Shafer George
Shall George
Shance Christian
Shannan Robert
Shants Christian
Sharewood Neamiah
Sharp Hendrick
Shatler John
Shavalier John
Shaw David
Shaw Ichabod
Shaw James
Shaw Michael
Shaw Richard
Shaw Rubin
Shaw William
Shearman Michael
Sheer Abraham
Sheerman Jesse
Shehan Maurice
Shennon Thomas
Shepherd Isaac
Sherewood Abraham
Sherewood Nathan
Sherwood M——
Shiping William
Shippen William
Shoecraft John
Shoemaker Daniel
Shomaker Henry
Shorwood Nathan
Shouthard John
Shove Frederick
Shucraft John
Sikles Zacharias
Silkirk James
Silsby David
Simmons John
Simmons Michael
Simons Joshua
Simons Martin
Simpkins Jeremiah
Simson John
Sitz Nicholas
Sixby John
Sixby Nicholas
Skaits James
Skinner Isaac
Skinner Josiah
Skinner Thomas
Skutt Frederick
Slate Ezlk
Slippey David
Sloan Stephen
Slouter John
Slover Isaac
Slowter Andrew
Slowter Ephraim
Slowter Evert
Slowter John
Slutt Peter
Small Benjamin
Smallee Thomas
Smally Isaiah
Smily Thomas
Smith Archibald
Smith Baltzer
Smith Benjamin
Smith Caleb
Smith Christopher
Smith David
Smith Ebert B
Smith Elihu
Smith Ezekiel
Smith George
Smith Gersham
Smith Henry
Smith Isaac
Smith James
Smith Jered
Smith Jesse
Smith John
Smith Joseph
Smith Lemuel
Smith Moses
Smith Peter
Smith Richard
Smith Samuel
Smith Senior
Smith Shorten
Smith Solomon
Smith William
Smyth Elijah
Smyth Richard
Snedecker Moses
Snedicar James
Sniduar James
Sniffen Amos
Sniffen Nehemiah
Snow John

Snowden John
Sohake Jonathan
Solyer Zacheus
Soucer Henry
Southard Harvey
Southard Henry
Southerd John
Southerland William
Spece John
Speed George
Spencer Asa
Spencer David
Spencer Jabez
Spencer John
Spencer Samuel
Spicor Jacob
Spiers Joseph
Spilsbery Jacob
Sprague John
Sprigs Lazarus
Spring Ephraim
Spring Henry
Springstead Casparis
Springsted Abraham
Springsted Harmaumes
Springsteen Christopher
Springsteen George
Squirell Jacob
Staats Silvester
Stagg John
Stanbery Elijah
Stanciel William
Standford John
Stanford Daniel
Stansbury William
Stanton Benjamin
Stark Amos
Steel James
Steel John
Steenberg Peter
Stenbarreger Theodore
Stephen Nathan
Stephens Hendrick
Stephens Nathaniel
Sternbergh David
Stevens John
Stevenson John
Steves Philip
Stewart John
Sthephens Henry
Stilefen John
Stillwell Thomas
Stilwell James
Stine William
Stinebrinner David
Stivers Philip
Stives Caleb
St. John Tedious
St. Laurence George
Stocker William
Stoner John
Stoner Nicholas
Storms John
Stratton William
Strawbridge Absolom
Streat Samuel
Stringham Henry
Stump John
Sturdeman Samuel
Stursburgh David
Sucanox Daniel
Succanox Peter
Sullivan Dennis
Summors Hugh
Surgeson William
Surs Francis
Suthard Henry
Sutler John
Sweep Jacob
Sweet Reuben
Sweet Samuel
Swift John
Symen Martin
Symkins Jeremiah
Symons Ephraim
Symons Willitt
Syrine James
Tabor Thomas
Talliday John
Talmage Joseph
Tapping Daniel
Tatcher Samuel
Taylor Edward
Taylor John
Teatsworth Thomas
Templar Thomas
Ten Eyck John
Ten Eyck Joseph
Tharp Richard
Thomas James
Thomas John
Thomas William
Thompson Benjamin
Thompson James
Thompson John
Thompson Timothy
Thomson Daniel
Thomson Elias
Thomson Joshua
Thomson Stanley
Thomson William
Thomus Henry
Thorrington James
Thump Frederick
Tice John
Tiemans Jonathan
Timberman Henry
Titsworth Thomas
Titus Jonathan
Tobias John
Todd Adam
Todd John
Todd Thadeous
Tode Adam
Tompkins Nathaniel
Touttell Joel
Towey David
Townsond Samuel
Trautt Michael
Traverse Jacob
Traves Uriah
Travis Abraham
Travis Scott
Treeman Jonathan
Treet Richard
Tremins Abner
Trewelliger John
Trewileger Jacob
Trewillagar Ary Van Etten
Trimier Michael
Trout Adam
Trowbridge Absalom
Truewilleger James
Tubbs Cyrus
Tuck John
Tucker Joshua
Tulva Thomas
Tumans Peter
Turnar Peter
Turner William
Tuthill William
Tutle Solomon
Tuttle Abner
Tylar Ezra
Underdunk Titus
Upright Michael
Utter Gilbart
Utter Isaac
Vacter Nicholas
Valentine Obadiah
Vallance Zachariah
Vallean Stephen
Vany Vinson
Varnill John
Varron John
Vaughhan William
Veley Andrew G
Venus John
Venute Charles
Vermiller Peter
Verritty Gilbert
Vincent Joseph
Virnute Charles
Volingtine Richard
Volkingburgh Francis
Vredenburgh Thomas
Vulvia Thomas
Van Cleack Henry
Van Cleack Peter
Vandavore John
Van de bogort Mindert
Van De Burgh Mathew
Van Demarker John
Van demerk Cornelius
Vandermark David
Vandermark Zachariah
Vandihider Adam
Van Gelder Mathew
Van Gilder Isaac
Van Gordes John I.
Van Hoosen Garret
Van Hoozan Jacob
Van Horn John
Van Kleek Henry
Van Ness Cornelius
Vannetten Jacobus
Van Nornam Isaac
Van North John
Vannute Charles
Van Oman Isaac
Vansaunt John
Van Sice Joseph
Vantosels Cornelius
Van Tyne Isaac
Van Vlack George
Van Volkingburgh Francis
Van Vordenbargh Thomas
Waggoner Henry
Waldrom John
Waldrum Joseph
Waldrum William
Wales Timothy
Walker Edward
Walker Israel
Walker John
Walker Justus
Walker Matthias
Walker Samuel
Wall Patrick
Walles James
Walner Abram
Wandell John
Wanute Charles
Wapshear Simon
Ward Abijah
Ward James
Ward Robert
Ward Thomas
Ward Zadock
Warden Thomas
Wareing Michael
Waring Benjamin

Warner Edmond
Warner William
Warren Francis
Warren John
Warren Nathaniel
Warren William
Washborn Abel
Waterman Henry
Waterman James H
Waterman John
Waterman Samuel
Watkins Benjamin
Watson Richard
Waymire Fredrick
Weaver David
Weaver John
Webb John
Webb Nathaniel
Webb Samuel
Webster Daniel
Webster Thomas
Weckham Stephen
Wedge Benjamin
Weed Abijah
Weed Ezra
Weeks Abraham
Weeks James
Weeks Melatiah
Weesmiller Henry
Welch John
Welsh Edward
Wendell Harmanus
Wentworth John
West Jacob
West John
Westervelt David
Wever John
Weyemiller Hendrick
Wheeler Amos
Wheeler Daniel
Wheeler Joshua
Wheeler Peter
Wheeler Samuel
Wheeler Timothy
Wheelor John
Wheler William
Wheller Richard
Whiley Edward
Whipple Nathan
White Anthony
White Ephraim
White Henry
White John
White Paul
White Peter
White Philip
White William
Whitehead John
Whitehead William
Whitford Joseph
Whitham Joseph
Whitney Ezekiel
Whitney Jacob
Whittemore Cornelius
Whittmore Benjamin
Whyley Simeon
Wickham Stephen
Wilber Ichabod
Wilber Josiah
Wilbur Jacob
Wilbur Joseph
Wildy Edward
Wilkelow John
Wilkerson Joseph
Wilkerson Samuel
Willard Abel
Willcox Aron
Willcox John
Willer Amos
Willess Thomas
Willey Edward
Williams Charles
Williams Francis
Williams John
Williams Thomas
Williamson James
Willkox John
Willmot John
Willsey Isaac
Willson Abraham
Willson Jacob
Willson John
Willson Thomas
Willson William
Willy Samuel
Wilson Archibald
Wilson Samuel
Winchell John
Winters John
Winthrop William
Wire Jerimiah
Wisenfelts George
Wissenfels John
Wolf Hendrick
Wolf James
Wolf Samuel
Wood Jacob
Wood James
Wood John
Wood Joseph
Wood William
Woodmore Cornelius
Woodward Benedict
Woolcutt Justus
Wordan Nathan
Worden Thomas
Worry John
Wright Barrick
Wright Ephram
Wright John
Wright Uriah
Wygant Tibias
Yale Nathaniel
Yarington William
Yates John
Yauness John
Yewmans Eleazer
Yewmans Jeremiah
Yones John
Youmans Jeremiah
Young John
Younkin George
Zamens Ephreham
Zellers Michael

3d Regiment.

COLONEL JAMES CLINTON
COLONEL PETER GANSEVORT
LIEUTENANT COLONEL JAMES BRUYN
MAJOR ROBERT COCHRAN
MAJOR JAMES ROSEKRANCE
ADJUTANT CHRISTOPHER HUTTON
ADJUTANT GEORGE SYTZ
QUARTER MASTER THOMAS WILLIAMS, JUNR.
PAY MASTER JEREMIAH VAN RENSSELAER
SURGEON HUNLOKE WOODRUFF
SURGEON'S MATE JOHN ELLIOT, JUNR.

CAPT. AARON AORSON
" ANDREW BILLINGS
" LEONARD BLEEKER
" JACOBUS S. BRUYN
" EZRA BUELL
" EZEKIEL COOPER
" DANIEL DENTON
" THOMAS DE WITT
" LEWIS DUBOYS
" I. GREGG
" JAMES GREGG
" JOHN GRENELL
" DANIEL GRIFFING
" ELIAS HASBROUCK
" JOHN HULBERT
" ROBERT JOHNSTON
" GEORGE LIGHT
" JOHN NICOLSON
" ABRAHAM SWARTWOUT
" HENRY TEABOUT
" ELIAS VAN BUNSCHOTEN
LIEUT. JOSIAH BAGLEY
" JOHN BALL
" PETER DEBOIS BEVIER
" BENJAMIN BOGARDUS
" ISAAC BOGART
" PRENTICE BOWEN
" WILLIAM COLEBREATH
" PHILIP CONINE
" NATHANIEL CONKLIN
" HENRY DEFENDORFF
" BELTHAZER DEHART
" GEORGE DENNISON
" GEORGE I. DENNISTON
" DAVID DUBOIS
LIEUT. WILLIAM HAVENS
" GEORGE HAMILTON JACKSON
" CORNELIUS T. JANSEN
" ALEXANDER KETCHAM
" PETER KOGGEN
" ANDREW LAWRENCE
" SAMUEL LEWIS
" GILBERT R. LIVINGSTON
" GEORGE LYTZE
" WILLIAM MARTIN
" BENJAMIN MARVIN
" THOMAS MCCLELLAN
" NATHANIEL NORTON
" THOMAS OSTRANDER
" ALBERT PAWLING
" SAMUEL SMITH
" GARRET STAATS
" LEVI STOCKWELL
" WILLIAM TAPP
" HENRY VANDERBURG
" NANNING VANDERHYDEN
" THOMAS WARNER
" JOHN WELCH
" MOSES YEOMANS
ENSIGN AMENT ALDERT
" JOHN BURHANCE
" ALEXANDER CLINTON
" DOUW FONDA
" DOUW I. FONDA
" BENJAMIN HERRING
" GARRIT G. LANSING
" PETER MAGEE
" JOSEPH MORRILL
" MATTHEW POTAN
" JOHN SPOOR

Hon.d Sir

[illegible] a just sense of [illegible] has hitherto so conspicuously been [illegible] to [illegible] the Third New York Regiment [illegible]

We congratulate you that those Characteristics which so eminently point out the Gentleman and Soldier, have by your [illegible] been deservedly noticed by our Bleeding Country.

Altho we rejoice at your Promotion yet we cannot but regret the loss of so worthy a Friend.

That the prosperity which has crowned your Conduct with Victory, may still be continued is the sincere Wish and Prayer of

Hon.d Sir

Your Honor's Most Obedient
and Very Hble Servants

Fort Schuyler 12th October 1777

[illegible] Capt.
Thos DeWitt Capt.
Cornls T. Jansen Capt.
Leond Bleecker Capt.
Henry [illegible] Lieut.
John Bell Lieut.
Philip Conyne Lieut.
John Welch Lieut.
Harmanus [illegible] Lieut.
Isaac Bogert Lieut.
[illegible] Lieut.
George Sytez Adjt.
Prentice Bowen Lieut.

To
The Honorable Brig. Genl.
Gansevoort

TESTIMONIAL FROM OFFICERS OF THE 3D LINE TO COLONEL PETER GANSEVOORT UPON PROMOTION TO BRIG. GENERAL.

Jo^s Rensselaer B.M.

[illegible]

John Elliot P.M.

Gerrit Staats Lieut

Thomas Warner Lieut

Benj Bogardus Lieut

Thomas Ostrander Lieut

Williams Junr Q.M.

Wm Colbath Ensign

Christopher Hutton Ensign

Josiah Bagley Ensign

Samuel Lewis Ensign

Ebert Amant Ensign

ENLISTED MEN.

Abbey Lemuel
Abbey Samuel
Acker Albert
Acker Conrad
Ackerman David
Ackerman Edar
Ackerson Benjamin
Ackerson John
Ackerson Thomas
Ackley Joel
Adams Ephraim
Adams Stephen
Adams William
Adamy Henry
Ade Lester
Adley Peter
Alderman Ephraim
Allen Thomas
Allison John Jr
Allison John Sr
Allison Peter
Allison Richard
Allison Thomas
Alone Christian
Ambler Nathaniel
Ammermon Obadiah
Anderson Ezekiel
Anderson George
Anderson William
Andrews Benjamin
Anning Daniel
Anthony Francis
Anthony George
Anthony John
Anthony Peter
Apart John
Armstrong John
Artwick Lawrence
Ash Henry
Ashley Aaron
Atkins Henry
Austin David
Avrey Humphrey
Babbet Reuben
Babcock David
Bagley David
Bailey Joseph
Bailey Wilkey
Baily Leonard
Bakehorn Jacob
Bakehorn Jeremiah
Baker Bartholomew
Baker Daniel
Baker Ichabod
Baker John
Baker Joseph
Baker Pars
Baker Thomas
Balding Jesse
Ballas Elezer
Banchraft John
Banker John
Banker Thomas
Banks Benjamin
Baptist John
Bardu Elias
Barker Stephen
Barkhoff Frederick
Barnes Henry
Barnes Stephen
Barnhum Samuel
Barns James
Barret Michael
Barrett William
Barrey Charles
Barton Rober
Barton Robert
Barwolf Christian
Bass Henry
Basset Cornelius
Basset Joseph
Bates Joseph
Batman William
Batnar Paul
Bearvert John
Bedle Moses
Beedle John
Beegle Thomas
Beekman John
Beenns Stephem
Begle Moses
Beidle John
Belknap William
Benjamin Daniel
Bennet —— s
Bennett Charles
Bennett Henry
Bennett Jeremiah
Benson Thomas
Berdan John
Berry Charles
Berry James
Berton George
Berwart John
Beurum John
Bickford James
Bishop John
Bishop Levi
Black John
Blacker John
Blancher William
Blanck Cornelius
Blauvalt Abram
Blekwell Gerret
Blowers Ephraim
Blowers George
Bogard Martha
Bogardus Lewis
Bogart John
Bohall Paul
Bont Thomas
Bony William
Booth Henry
Bordon John
Boreman James
Bound Rodman
Bourk Edmond
Bourk John
Bovie Nicholas
Bower Jeremiah
Boyce James
Boyce John
Boyd Robert
Bradley Cornelius
Bradley Richard
Brady George
Brady Richard
Brannen Abraham
Brannon Timothy
Brant Christian
Brass John
Bray William
Brenck Peter
Brewster Benjamin
Brewster William
Briggs John
Brink Robert
Brisbee James
Brocket Moses
Bromley Simon
Brondow Frederick
Brown Charles Fred
Brown Daniel
Brown David
Brown Henry
Brown Isaac
Brown John
Brown John F.
Brown Jonathan
Brown Peter
Brown Richard
Brown Robert
Brown Samuel
Brown Thomas Clark
Brown William
Bryant John
Bryant Melancthon
Bryent Thomas
Buckstaff Peter
Buis James
Bulson Cornelius
Bunce Edmund
Bunce Jesse
Bunskolen Solomon
Buoy William
Burch Philip
Burch Sabins
Burden John
Burgess Michael
Burgun Oliver
Burhans Edward
Burhans John
Burhans Samuel
Burjes Peter
Burk Edmund
Burk John
Burkdorf John
Burke Edmond
Burke John
Burns John
Burrell Zachariah
Burris John
Burroughs John
Burton George
Bushell Joseph
Buskirk Garret
Butler Richard
Butnar Paul
Buyce James
Buyer Godfrey
Buyford Henry
Cable Andrew
Cain Edward
Cain John
Caldwell William
Calf John
Callam Reuben
Cameran Hugh
Campbell Duncan
Cambell Kenneth
Canfield Timothy
Canter Jonas
Carll Lemuel
Carman Abraham
Carmical Blakney
Carmichel Peter
Carpenter Moses
Carpenter Samuel
Carr Norris
Carsad Richard
Cartell John
Casady Luke
Case George
Case Joseph
Cashaday Nicholas
Casler Joseph
Cassells Eliphalet
Cavenough John

Cavin Thomas
Cazard Richard
Certain James
Chaddock Nathaniel
Chaddock Sylvanus
Chambers Francis
Chambers Henry
Chambers Jacobus
Chapel Benjamin
Chase George
Chase John
Chase Robert
Chasee Stephen
Chatfield Lewis
Chatfield William
Chickens Thomas
Christman Nicholas
Chulwell Thomas
Clanchy Daniel
Clansy Daniel
Clark Anthony
Clark Jeremiah
Clark John
Clarke Benjamin
Clarwater Jeremiah
Clemens John
Clement Nicholas
Clerk Benjamin
Clerk Martin
Cline Franses
Clinton Joseph
Clock Jonathan
Closs John
Coad William
Codgdon John
Coe John D.
Cole Francis
Cole Garet
Cole Thomas
Collins James
Collins Joseph
Collins William
Colman Timothy
Commadine Nicholas
Conckling John
Conckling Selah
Conckling Thomas
Conckling Timothy
Conden Philip
Condon David
Cone John
Conet John
Conklin Joseph
Conklin Nathaniel
Conklin Samuel
Conklin Silvanus
Conkling David
Conkling Jacob
Conkling Jonathan
Conkling Thomas
Connoway Cornelius
Connaway John
Conolice John
Conro Darling
Constable Garret
Cook Burnit
Cook George
Cook Jonathan
Cook Samuel
Cook Thomas
Coonet John
Cooper Abram
Cooper John
Cooper John, Jr.
Cooper John C.
Cooper Zebulon, Jr.
Cordwise George
Cormical Blackney
Cornwall Caleb
Cornwall Joseph
Cornwell Silvanus
Corrigal John
Corter John
Corwin Jonathan
Corwin Nathan
Corwin Thomas
Cousins Mathew
Cowdrey Benjamin
Cowen James
Crambary Francis
Crandell Luke
Creamer John
Creaton Thomas
Crekenborne Johannis
Crispell Anthony
Cristy John
Crossman Abner
Crossman Simeon
Crosshar Samuel
Cunningham Charles
Curry Samuel
Curtis John
Curtis George F.
Darby Asa
Darby John
Davenport Thomas
David Henry
Davin Richard
Davis Chapman
Davis Gilbard
Davis John
Davis Matthew
Davis Nathan
Davis Samuel
Davis William
Dawson Daniel
Dawson Richard
Dayton Samuel
Dayton Samuel, Jr.
Dean Edward
Dean Joseph
Dean Samuel
Debois Jacobus
Debois Johannis
De Bois John I.
De Clark Abraham
Deforest Henry
Dejo Hugh
Delamarter John
Delamater John
Demont Joseph
Dempsey Mark
Dempster John
Denn Thomas
Dennis John
Denny Samuel
Deratt John
Devan Cornelius
De Vaults Peter
Devaults Stephen
Devee Henry
Devee William
Devenport Thomas
De Witt Benjamin
Dewitt Jacob
Deyo Hugh
Deyo Hugh H.
Dickerson Jeremiah
Dillinge John
Dobb John
Dobbins Thomas
Dodge Allex'r
Dodge Henry
Dodge Zachariah
Dods Zachariah
Doherty Thomas
Douden John
Doughty Isaac
Douglass William
Dowlar George
Downs James
Dreyer Frederick
Driskell Cornelius
Dumont John
Dunlap James
Dunlap Thomas
Dunn Stephen
Dunnivan Anthony
Dupee Abraham
Eager James
Eagins Joshua
Early Samuel
Easton Henry
Edes Joseph
Edgarly John
Eggs Samuel
Elleback Emanuel
Ellen Jesse
Elliot Francis
Elliot John
Elliot John Jr.
Ellon Jesse
Ellot Archabel
Elmendorph Petrus
Elmendorph Petrus Jr.
Elsworth Peter
Elting Thomas
Emica John G.
English Joshua
English Samuel
Ennis Henry
Ennist Cornelius
Erwin James
Evans Joseph
Everhart John
Everhile John P.
Everstine Francis
Fairchild Jesse
Farrington David
Fausdick Samuel
Fero Andris
Ferran Cornelle
Ferreigh John
Ferry Omer
Fersha Dennis
Fetzerman Barnet
Field James
Finch Charles
Finton Peter
Fitzerman Barna
Fletcher James
Fling Henry
Flynn John
Fokes Robert
Foot Johan Caspar
Forbes Alexander
Force David
Foren James
Forguson Robert
Fosdick Samuel
Foster Daniel
Foster James
Foster Thomas
Fothergill Hugh
Fountain John
Fowler Jabez
Fowles James
France Coonradt
Frayer Thomas
Frazier John
Frear Solomon, Jr.
Frederick John

Freeland John
French Coonradt
Friday Coonradt
Fryer Robert
Fulton Francis
Fulton William
Funna Anthony
Furman Gabriel
Furne Francis
Gadge John
Gahan John
Gail John
Gain Francis
Gains Christain
Gake Samuel
Gall John
Gardineer Samuel
Gardiner Andrew
Gardiner Jeremiah
Garnet John
Garrell John
Garrison Abraham
Garrot Benjamin
Garvey David
Gates John
Gattes David
Gee Thomas
Geege John
Gelston William
Geraghty Bartholomew
Gibson Andrew
Giers Benjamin
Gifford William
Gilbert Samuel
Gildersleaves Philip
Gildersleeve Finch
Gildersleeve Richard
Gillaspy James
Gillaspy James J
Gillaspy William
Gillaspy William Jr.
Gilmore Robert
Glen Robert
Glenn George
Goldsmith William
Goodcourage John
Gould John
Grace James
Graham Andrew
Gray John
Gray Robert
Green William
Gregg Thomas
Griffes James
Griffing James
Grimsly William
Grite William
Groseman Frederick
Grote William
Grummon Joseph
Haburn William
Hadley Bishop
Haight Abraham
Haight Thomas
Hall John
Hallet Moses
Halsey Matthew
Halsey Matthew Jr.
Halsey William Rogers
Haman Daniel
Haman John F.
Hamilton William
Hand Daniel
Handen John
Hannes James
Happle Adam
Hardenbergh Henderick
Hardenbergh Leonard
Harder Adam
Harlow Robart
Harriot Thomas
Harris George Jr.
Harriss Silas
Hart Andrew
Hart Gilbert
Hart Thomas
Harter Adam
Harvey William
Hasbrouck John Jr.
Hatch Timothy
Hatton Jacob
Haven Isaac
Havens Daniel
Havens Joseph
Haycock John
Hebbard Abel
Hedges Elias
Height Abraham
Hellit Francis
Hender Frederick
Henderson Elisha
Henderson Patrick
Henry Michael
Herrald Henry
Herteel John
Hevington William
Hewit Benjamin
Heyer Alexander
Hickey John
Hicks Jacob
Hide Thomas
Hievnard Hendrick
Higby Daniel
Higgans Jonathan
Higher Garrit
Hile Coonrad
Hill David
Hill Eliphelet
Hill Henry
Hill John
Hill Nicholas
Hoffman David
Hoghtaling William
Holbert Aaron
Holley Benjamin
Home Casper
Hone William
Honeywell John
Hooper Jacob R.
Hopkins Stephen A.
Hopp Abraham
Hopping Henry
Hopping Joseph
Horton Isaac
House John
Houser Andrew
Houstman George
Houxly James
How John
Howard James
Howel Samuel
Howell Aaron
Howell Edward
Howell Lemuel
Howell Stephen
Hubbard Rosel
Hudson John
Huff Robert
Huffner Hendrick
Huggans James
Huit Daniel
Hulbert Aaron
Hull Nathaniel Jr.
Hull Samuel
Hully Arthur
Hulser John
Hungerforth Daniel
Hunt Benjamin
Hunt Guilead
Hunter Jonathan
Hunter Thomas
Hurley Arthur
Hurley James
Hutson John Jr.
Huxley John
Hyer Alexander
Hyer Garret
Hyet Joseph
Hyle Coonrad
Hyne Hartman
Hynes Hendrick
Isaacs Isaac
Jackson Archibald
Jackson Francis
Jagger Abraham
Jansen Frederick
Jeffrey John
Jenkin Ennis
Jennings Elnathan
Jessup Zebulon
Jinnings Hazakiah
Jinnings Jonathan
Johnson Edward
Johnson Daniel
Johnson John
Johnston Daniel
Jones David
Jones Elicom
Jones Jeremiah
Jones Joseph
Jones Nathaniel
Jones Seth
Jones Shadrick
Jones Thomas
Jones William
Kallam Reuben
Karr Mark
Kater James
Keator Petrus
Keator Wilhelmus
Keener Christian
Keisbergh Christian
Kellam Reuben
Kelley Patrick
Kelley Robert
Kelley Thomas
Kellion Coonradt
Kelly John
Kelsey Benjamin
Kenny John
Kent Thomas
Ketcham Daniel
Ketcham Philip
Keyser Abraham
King Aaron
King Jeremiah
King Joel
King John
King Jonathan
Kinney Jese
Kinny Charles
Kip Mathew
Kip Moses
Kirk Joseph
Kitcham John
Kitcham Samuel
Klaerwater Daniel
Knapp Benjamin
Knapp Elijah
Knapp Jeremiah
Knapp William
Knapping Jeremiah

Koile David
Kortreght Silvester
Krack Godlieb
Krom Benjamin, Jr.
Kysinger Philip
Ladd Joseph
Lafter John
Lalancet John
Lambert Abraham
Lambart David
Lambert Moses
Lambert John
Lampyer Francis
Langdon Ananias
Lansing Evert
Laport John
Laroy John, Jr.
Lattamore Thomas
Lawrence Benjamin
Lawson George
Lawyer William
Leach John
Leaster Michael
Lee James
Lee Thomas
Leek Abraham
Lees Martin
Lemmon Alexander
Lennington Thomas
Lennox Samuel
Lent Harculous
Lent Moses
Leonard Henry
Leonard Robert
Lepling John
Lewis Lockart
Lewis Peter
Lewis Richard
Lewis Thomas
Lewis Zadock
Lighthall James
Lighthall Lancaster
Limbaker John
Little Peter
Little William
Littlejohn John
Loader Daniel
Lockert Lewis
Loins Michael
Looper Abraham
Looper Amos
Loper David
Losey Paul
Losing Peter
Lossing Lowrence
Loucks Hendrick
Louden William
Louks Hendrick
Lourey Alexander
Loux Nicholas
Love Davis
Lovely Francis
Low Jacob G.
Lowcey Paul
Lowdon William
Lowman Peter
Loyal Edward
Lucy Eleazer
Ludlam George
Ludlam Stephen
Ludlum Daniel
Lusk Francis
Luther John
Lutner James
Lyon Asa
Lyon John
Lyon Joseph
Mackey Thomas
Madden Owen
Mahan Patrick
Mahaune Cain
Maines Mathew
Maker Nathaniel
Maker Solomon
Mallow Thomas
Mane Matthew
Mantanye Jacobus
Manuel Isaac
Marsten James
Marvin Elihew
Marvin Matthew
Marvin Moses
Marvin Seath
Mason James
Masten Daniel
Masten James
Mathers John
Mathews Peter
Matleg Caleb
Matleg Daniel
Matlock Caleb
Maxwell Cornelius
Maxwell William
Mayberry Richard
Maybus Leonard
Meeker John
Meeker Nathaniel
Meeker Solomon
Megere James
Melcher Paul
Mellow Thomas
Mence Christopher, Jr.
Merrick Seth
Merricle Samuel
Mershall William
Middagh George
Miers Jacob
Miles John
Miller David
Miller Henry
Miller Jacob
Miller John, Jr.
Miller Levi
Miller Ludwick
Miller Nathan
Miller Peter
Miller Zephaniah
Miller William
Mills David
Mills Nathaniel
Milspaugh Mathias
Minick Barnhart
Minick Hendrick
Minie Christopher, junr.
Minnen Robert
Minroo George
Mitchell Robert
Mixer Daniel
Moloy William
Monrow Alexander
Montcrief Charles
Moor Frederick
Moor John
Moor Robert
Moor Samuel
Moore Thomas
Morcraft William
Morewise Jacob
Morgin David
Morris Edmond
Morrison Daniel
Morrison Richard
Morrison Thomas
Morrow Patrick
Mosher John
Mosier Hugh
Mosure Ruben
Mott Henry
Mott Jacob
Mott Joseph
Mott Samuel
Mott Thomas
Mowris Daniel
Mulholand James
Mullon John
Murphey Peter
Murray Bartley
Murray James
Murray William
Mute William
Myers Frederick
Myrick Seth
McAnanny John
McAuley Robert
McBride James
McBride John
McCart James
McCarty Dennis
McClanning John
McClean John
McConnelly Hugh
McCord William
McCormick James
McCormick Thomas
McCoy Alexander
McCoy James
McCutcheon Thomas
McDaniel James
McDaniel John
McDermot Cornelius
McDonald Alexander
McDonald Daniel
McDonald Donald
McDougal Alexander
McEwan Duncan
McFarland John
McGinnis John
McGlaghlin William
McGown Archibald
McGraw Alexander
McGuin Abrm
McGuire Abraham
McGuire James
McIntire Phineas
McIntosh John
McKenzie John
McKenzie Neal
McKim John
McKown James
McKown John
McLaughlin William
McMaster Alexander
McMichael John
McNeal Henry
McNeal John
McQuin Philip
McVay John
Nangle Frederick
Nelson Allen
Nelson Caleb
Nemiah John Henry
Nevels John
Newbergh John
Newman William
Newton William
Nichols Simon
Nicolls Robert
Nicols Joseph
Nicolson Jonathan
Nicolson Thomas
Noble Cornelius
Norris Isaac

North John
Northrop Ebenezer S. T.
Nortrap Moses
Nostrant Isaac
Nostrant John
Nostrant Luke
Nottingham William
Nyx Cornelius
Oakes Ephraim
Oakes John
Obrient John
O'Connoley James
Odle Tomkins
Ohlen Henry G.
Oldham John
Olendorph Leonard
Oliphant William
Oliver Thomas
Olmendurff Leonard
Oneal John
Orr Baltis
Orsborn Ezekel
Osborn Aaron
Osborn Cornelius
Osborn Josiah
Osterhout Isaac
Osterhout Peter
Ostrander Peter William
Owens Daniel
Owens Thomas
Owens Uriah
Paddock Levy
Pain Jonathan
Pain Paul
Painter Edward
Palfreman William
Palmateer Isaac
Palpeman William
Parker Daniel
Parker Edward
Parker Timothy
Parkhoff Frederick
Parks Ebenezer
Parks Jonah
Parks Timothy
Parks William
Parshel James
Parson Isaac
Patterson James
Patterson John
Patterson William
Pease Nathaniel
Peirson Isaac
Peirson John
Pells Henry
Peltz Hendrick
Peltz Henry
Peresonias Jacobus
Perkhoff Frederick
Perkoff Hendrick
Perksmith Englars
Pershase Joseph
Peters John
Peters Simon
Phenix Robert
Phillips William
Pillgret Hendrick
Pillow John
Pinkney Jonathan
Pinton Peter
Piny Edward
Piper Lewis
Pitt Abraham
Pittman John
Pixly Eli
Platto Thomas
Plough Jochiam
Plough Samuel
Plumsted Nathaniel
Post Cornelius
Post Richard
Powlson Michael
Pratt Chalker
Pratt John
Preston Benjamin
Preston Othaniel
Price Adam
Price Benjamin
Price Robert
Prince Joseph
Prindle Joseph
Prouth Degory
Putney Joseph
Quackenboss Benjamin
Queen Christopher
Quigley George
Rahea Denie
Ralje David
Randell Henry
Ranger Samuel
Rannels Abijah
Ray William
Read James
Record Wilmot
Reed Garret
Reed Samuel
Reeves Daniel
Rendal Henry
Renne Coral
Rennix William
Rergtmire Conradt
Reynolds John
Reynolds Michael
Rice Samuel
Richardson Alexander
Rider George
Riely Charles
Riley John
Rilya David
Rinder Christian
Ripenbergh Adam
Risdale William
Roads Noah
Roberts Warren
Robinson Andrew
Robinson George
Robinson James
Robinson John
Robinson Richard
Rocaster John
Rodgers Samuel
Rogers James, Jr.
Rogers Stephen
Romer William
Romine John
Roos Lemuel
Roosa Jacob
Root George
Rosa Aaron
Rosa Aldert
Rose Albert
Rose Thomas
Ross John
Rotheart George J.
Rouse Thomas
Rowley Seth
Rowley Thomas
Ruland Thomas
Rumler Thomas
Rump Henry
Ruskill Marlain
Russell Joseph
Russell Oliver
Rutan Peter
Ryan Patrick
Ryan Robert
Ryley Patrick
Rynard John
Rynder Christian
Rynder Christopher
S——— Ephriham
Sammons Matthew
Sandford Benjamin
Sapin Thomas (Sassin)
Sayre James
Sayre Joshua
Schreeder John Joachim
Schultz John
Scott Andrew
Scott John
Scott Timothy
Scott William
Scriber Christian
Scriber Peter
Scudder Alexander
Scudder Edmund
Seaberry John
Seaman Daniel
Seaman Micha
Seamans Ephraim
Seamans Isaac
Searles Thomas
Secor Isaac
Secor James
Seely Silvanus
Seevey Joseph
Semall Anthony
Serals Thomas
Seyley Coenradt
Shades Adam
Sharriner Lodwick
Shatter Hussey
Shaw John
Shawl John
Shay John
Shearwood James
Sheels James
Sheffield Robert
Shell Christian
Shell Christopher
Shell George
Sherlocke John
Sherriden Richard
Sherril Abraham
Sherril Jeremiah
Sherrow James
Sherwood Elijah
Sherwood Seymour
Shields Daniel
Shields James
Shift George
Shires Jacob
Shirts Peter
Shirts Samuel
Shoecraft Joho.
Short Jacob
Shriver Lodewick
Shultz John
Shurky Thomas
Sickels Abraham
Simkins Gideon
Simons Moses
Simwell Anthony
Skiffington John
Slaughter Isaac
Slead Joseph
Slone Thomas
Sluyter Jacob
Sly Samuel
Slyter James
Smider Christejan
Smith Alexander

Smith Archibald
Smith Daniel
Smith David
Smith Duncan
Smith George
Smith Hezekiah
Smith Hugh
Smith Isaac
Smith Jeremiah
Smith Joel
Smith John
Smith Josiah
Smith Nathaniel
Smith Peter
Smith Petrus, Jr.
Smith Solomon
Smith Thaddeus
Smith Wait
Sommers Hugh
Sox Jacob
Sparling John
Speer John
Speigler Frederick
Spensor Joseph
Spensor Mathias
Spiegler Hendrick
Staats Silvester
Stag Jasper
Stagg John
Stalker William
Stanbury Elijah
Star Eli
Starling Levy
Steenbergh Abraham
Steeples Nathan
Stephen Samuel
Stephens Abraham
Stephens John
Stephens Reilef
Stephenson Samuel
Sterling Levi
Stevens Eliphelet
Stevens John
Stevens Samuel
Stewart Samuel
Still James
Stilwill James
Stimas Isaac
Stimwell Anthony
Stitt James
St. Johns Noah
Stodgden Robert
Stokes Alexander
Storer Nehemiah
Stout James
Strickling Samuel
Stuart John
Stump Charles

Sturges Isaac
Sullivan Dennis
Sullivan John
Sumurch Henry
Sutherland Daniel
Sutherland James
Sutler Samuel
Swan Peter
Swartwout Cornelius
Sweeny Roger
Talladay John
Tallerday Stephen
Talmage Elisha
Tammond Peter
Tarry Daniel
Tarry David
Taylor Alexander
Taylor Thomas
Teachout William
Temount Joseph
Tenure James
Ter Bush John
Terry Samuel
Terwelleger Benjamin
Terwelleger James
Thomas John
Thompson Elias
Thompson John
Thompson Joshua
Thomson Benjamin
Thorp Thomas, Sr.
Thorp Thomas, Jr.
Tisdell William
Tisdit William
Tobin Edward
Todd Jonathan
Toll Roger
Tomkins Abraham
Tompkins Thomas
Tompson John
Tone Andrew
Tool Roger
Topping Daniel
Town Timothy
Townshand Richard
Trall Abel
Troop George
Tubee John
Trull John
Truman Jonathau
Tuley John
Turner Alexander
Turner John
Turner Richard
Tuthil Azariah
Tuttle Henry
Tuttle Stephen
Twisle John

Umphrey Evins
Umphrey John
Upright George
Upright Nathan
Utest John
Vader Samuel
Vail Jeremiah
Vail John
Vail Micah
Vail Peter
Valentine Joseph
Valentine Peter
Varner Henry
Varriken Johannes
Vary George
Vaults Peter
Veal John
Veeder Samuel
Verling Andrew M.
Vessels Joseph
Vonck William
Vradenburg William
Van Ambergh Abraham
Van Amboro Abraham
Van Atta John
Van Benscoter Elias
Van Blarcum James
Van Bunhagele, John C. Benj.
Vancamp Abram
Van Cleef Lawrence
Vandemark Cornelius
VanDen Bogart Esoyas
Vandenburgh Jacob
Van Der Burgh Henry
Van Der Burgh Jacob
Van Derhyden Adam
Vanderhyden Derrick
Van Derhyden Gershom
Vandervoort James
Van Der Warken Martin
Van Deusen Abraham
Van devoort James
Van Every David
Van Gasbeek Thomas
Van hour Rineas
Van Kleak James
Van Kleeck Moses
Van Loan Peter
Van Nosdal Cornelius
Van Nosdall John
Van Ordan Charles
Vansail Egbert
Van Schaak Anthony
Van Sickle Ferdinand
Van Sise John
Van Sise Joseph
Van Stenburgh Jeremiah

Vantine Isaac
Van Wagoner John
Wade Bernard
Waddle William
Waggerman Emanuel
Waggerman George
Waiter Thomas
Walby Roger
Wallace James
Wallace John
Walter Coonradt
Wandle John
Ward Daniel
Ward Thomas
Warden Nathan
Waring Benjamin
Warnor Martin
Warren Edward
Warren Francis
Wass John
Watkins Elijah
Watson Joseph
Watson Richard
Watson William
Way John
Weasels Joseph
Weathersline John
Weaver Christian
Weaver Henry
Weaver Johannis
Weaver Richard
Webb Daniel
Weed David
Weeks Andrew
Weeks Jacob
Weeks Jonathan
Weeks Obêdiah
Weken Conrad
Welch John
Welch Richard
Welch Thomas
Welden Robert
Weldon Jeremiah
Wells John
Wells Peter
Wesell Joseph
Weychouer Jacob
Weyfenback Hendrick
Weyherner Jacob
Weyschouer Jacob
Wharry David
Wharry Evins
Whay John
Whiley John
White Joseph
White Thomas
Whitham William
Whitman John

Whitter Ezra
Wilbur Esau
Wiggins Thomas
Wiley John
Wilkinson Robert
Willer Charles
Willes James
Willes Thomas
Willett Francis
Williams Abraham
Williams Arthur
Williams Ebenezer
Williams George
Williams John
Williams Robert
Williams Solomon
Williamson John
Willis John
Willis Thomas
Wills John
Wilsie William
Wilson John
Wilson Robert
Wilson Thomas
Winchester Amariah
Windover John
Wise Gutlip
Witmozier Henry
Witt Christopher
Wood Eliphelet
Wood Gilbert
Wood John
Wood Jonathan
Wood Joseph
Wood Samuel
Wood Silas
Wood Thomas
Wood Timothy
Woodworth Joshua
Wooley Jared
Worden Nathan
Wordenton Mathew
Wright Abraham
Wright Edward
Wright John
Wright Samuel
Wybert Frederick
Wynins William
Yarington William
Yates James
Yengle John F.
Yeomans Isaac
Yeoman Moses
Yoemens Thomas
Youmans William
Young Daniel
Young Isaac
Youngs Israel
Youngs John
Youngs Nathan
Zagart Christian
Zanno Frederick
Zeaster Michael
Zenner Frederick

4th Regiment.

COLONEL JAMES HOLMES
COLONEL HENRY B. LIVINGSTON
LIEUTENANT COLONEL PIERRE REGNIER
LIEUTENANT COLONEL FREDERICK WEISSENFELS
MAJOR BENJAMIN LEDYARD
MAJOR JOSEPH McCRACKEN
ADJUTANT PETER SACKET
ADJUTANT SAMUEL TALLMADGE (ENSIGN)
ADJUTANT JOHN TUTHILL
QUARTER MASTER NEMEMIAH CARPENTER
QUARTER MASTER GELSTON
QUARTER MASTER JOB MULFORD
QUARTER MASTER PETER VONK
PAYMASTER JOHN FRANKS
CHAPLAIN JOHN P. TESTARD
SURGEON CALEB SWEET
SURGEON JOHN FRANCIS VACHE

CAPT. JOSEPH BENEDICT
" JOHN DAVIS
" EDWARD DUNSCOMB
" SILAS GRAY
" RUFUS HERRICK
" AMBROSE HORTON
" WILLIAM JACKSON
" BENJAMIN MARVIN
" DANIEL MILLS
" NATHANIEL NORTON
" DAVID PALMER
" JONATHAN PEARSEE
" JONATHAN PERRY
" JONATHAN PLATT
" REEVE
" DANIEL ROE
" JAMES ROSEKRANS
" SAMUEL SACKET
" ISRAEL SMITH
" NATHAN STRONG
" JONATHAN TITUS
" BENJAMIN WALKER
" NATHANIEL WOODARD
LIEUT. WILLIAM B. ALGER
" JAMES BARRETT
" CORNELIUS BECKER
" BENJAMIN
LIEUT. LEONARD BLEECKER
" GOULD BOUGHTEN
" HENRY BREWSTER
" BRUSH
" MANNING BULL
" EDWARD CONKLIN
" SYLVANUS CONKLING
" WILLIAM CRANE
" DAVID DAN
" DANIEL E. DENISTON
" JAMES DOW
" PETER ELSWORTH
" THEDOSIOUS FOWLER
" CHARLES GRAHAM
" WILLIAM HAVENS
" THOMAS HUNT
" ELIJAH HUNTER
" ABRAHAM HYATT
" JOHN LAWRENCE
" THOMAS LEE
" JOHN LLOYD
" WILLIAM MATTHEWMAN
" MILES OAKLEY
" ISAAC PADDOCK
" SAMUEL TREDWELL PELL
" ABRAHAM RIKER
" ISAAC A. ROSA

A LETTER FROM GENERAL BENEDICT ARNOLD.

Army, you will accept my congratulatory Compliment
on the Occasion.

Howe with his principal part of
the Army are on board Ship, the last acc.
was the 4th Inst. he was in the Offing & uncer-
tained. Burgoyne, I hear this Minute is
retreating to Ty — I make no doubt our
Army which is near Fifteen thousand will cut
off the retreat

Adieu & Believe me to be
Dr Colonel
Yours Sincerely
B Arnold

Colonel Ganzevoort

LIEUT. SAYER
" GEORGE SMITH
" ISAAC SPRINGER
" GILBERT STRANG
" JACOB THOMAS
" JESSE THOMPSON
" DANIEL TOPPING
" WILLIAM TROOP
" ROBERT TROUP
" AZARIAH TUTHILL
" JOHN VAN ANTWERP
" PETER VAN BUNSCHOTEN
" RUDOLPH VAN HOEVENBARGH
LIEUT. ISAAC VANWART
" ROSWELL WILCOCKS
" YOUNGS
ENSIGN JOHN BARR
" CALEB BRUISTER
" SIMON CREGIER (CRYGIER)
" SAMUEL DODGE
" JOSEPH FROILICK
" STEPHEN GRIFFIN
" JOSEPH MORRILL
" JOHN PUNDERSON
" EPHRAIM WOODRUFF

ENLISTED MEN.

Acker Henry
Acker Jacob
Adams Daniel
Adams Ebenezer
Adams James
Adams Jesse
Adams Major
Adoms Samuel
Adurns Thomas
Allen Samuel
Allison Richard
Allport John
Ambler Benjamin
Ambler Stephen
Ammerman Cornelius
Anderson James
Andress Joseph
Anson James
Anthoney Simon
Antone John
Armstrong Jonathan
Ashford Nathaniel
Ashley William
Aston Benoni
Atkins Robert
Atwater John
Austin Holmes
Austin Lockwood
Avery Nehemiah
Avout Philip
Aymes Francis
Backcus Jacob
Bailey Elias
Baker Anthony
Baker Benjamin
Baker Elijah
Baker Henry
Baker John
Baker Joshua
Baker Pierce
Balding Jehial
Balding Nathaniel
Baley Jonathan
Baley Leonard
Ball Samuel
Banker Jacob
Banker William
Baptist John
Barber Reuben
Baremore Edward
Barkens William
Barker Jonathan
Barlow Nathan
Barnhart David
Barnhart Jeremiah
Barns Glean
Barns John
Barns Peter
Barrows James
Barry Charles
Bartley Andrew
Barto John
Bartoe Morris
Basely Cornelius
Bassett William
Bayless Richard
Bayley Daniel
Beaty Hugh
Bebee Benorger
Becker Peter
Beckwith Silas
Beedle William
Beel Matthew
Bellamy Silas
Benedict Ambrose
Benjamin David
Benjamin Stephen
Bennadict Benjamin
Bennadict Nathan
Bennadict Peter
Bennet James
Bennet William
Bennett Jacob
Bennett Timothy
Benschoten Elias
Bentley William
Bergordus Peter
Berrnard Samuel
Berry Charles
Berry Jabez
Berry James
Berry John
Bertley Andrew
Betson Thomas
Betts Nehemiah
Bingham Abisha
Bishop Ebenezer
Black David
Black Richard
Black William
Blank Jasper
Blaze Christopher
Blendberry Elijah
Bodley Andrew
Bogardus Henry
Bogg John
Bogurdus Nung.
Boice James
Boiles James
Boncher William
Bond John
Boughton Moses
Boughton Simeon
Bourne William
Bouten Samuel
Bouton Joseph
Bouton Joseph, Jr.
Bower
Bowers Isaac
Bowers James
Bowman Bacchus
Bowne Rodman
Brady John
Bragame John
Brainerd Ruben
Braney Lowring
Braut John
Brant William
Brewer Jeremiah
Brewland Johiel
Briggs Jacob
Briggs Jeremiah
Brock Robert
Brooks Daniel
Brooks Jediah
Brooks John
Brooks Robert
Brooks Thomas
Brown David
Brown Deliv'ce
Brown Eliphelet
Brown Hubbard
Brown John
Brown Joseph
Brown Samuel
Brown Stephen
Brown William
Brown Zephaniah
Brundage Nathan
Brunson Samuel
Brush Selah
Brush Simeon F.
Brustier Daniell
Bruton Arthur
Bryon Thomas
Buchannan Samuel
Buckingham Stephen
Buckleman Henry
Budd John
Budin Francis
Bump Joseph
Bunday Jeremiah
Bunker William
Burch Jonathan
Burch Henry
Burd Jeremiah
Burdick Elisha
Burges Stephen

Burgess Archibold
Burhans Fjerrick
Burhans John
Burhans Thirh
Burhans Yerick
Burkstaff David
Burnet Ebenezer
Burnet Squire
Burnham William
Burns David
Burns Edward
Burr Daniell
Burrance John
Burrit William
Burrows James
Burrows Samuel
Bush Simon T.
Bussing John
Bustee Peter
Camby James
Cankhert Henry
Cammeron Alexander
Camp Asa
Campbell Andrew
Campbell Jacob
Campbell James
Campbell John
Canaday John
Canady James
Canfield Amon
Canfield Daniel
Carby Richard
Carll
Carney Barny
Carney William
Carny Thomas
Carpenter James
Carr Anthony
Carr James
Carrey John
Carrion Green
Case Ichabod
Casey James
Cashin William
Cato
Cavins Partrick
Chapman Daniel
Chappel Benjamin
Chappel Benjamin, Jr.
Charlesworth John Miles
Chase Isaac
Chatterton James
Cherry John
Chesley John
Chevalier John
Chinander John
Christen Peter
Cisco Dick
Clackson George
Clark Barnabas
Clark Cornelius
Clark David
Clark Ephraim
Clark James
Clark John
Clark Joseph, Jr.
Clark Peter
Clarke Joshua
Clements John
Clift Joseph
Close Christopher
Coats Joseph
Coe Benjamin
Cole Aaron
Cole Abraham
Cole Barnabas
Cole Oliver
Cole William
Coleman Samuel
Collins Edward
Collins John
Colly Henry
Colver Joseph
Colvin James
Conden Philip
Conington Joseph
Conkling Daniel
Conkling Edward
Conkling Nathan
Conkling William
Conkright Henry
Conn William
Conner Joseph
Connerly Dennis
Connoly James
Connor James
Connor John
Connor Patrick
Connor Timothy
Constable Garret
Converse Samuel
Cook
Cook Alexander
Cook Darias
Cook George
Cook Moses
Cook Nathan
Cook Obadiah
Coon Jacob
Coon Peter
Cooper David
Cooper John
Copinger Walter
Coppenger John
Corkangs Eli
Cornell Caleb
Cornwall Caleb
Cornwell Thomas
Cortright Henry
Corwine Edward
Corwine Gersham
Cossington John
Cottrell Richard
Couchoover William
Couray Michael
Cowan Isaac
Cox John
Cox Simon
Cozard Richard
Craft Nathaniel
Craig John
Crane Josiah
Crannell Isaac
Crawford John
Crawford Thomas
Cregear John
Crissler John
Cristie William
Cronch James
Cronk Hendrick
Cronk Timothy
Crosby Enock
Crosby Isaac
Crosby Thomas
Crosman Dan
Cross John
Crossman Daniel
Crowfot Nehemiah
Cummers Jonathan
Cunningham Archibald
Cunningham Henry
Cunningham John
Cunningham Shubal
Curaw Michael
Curby John
Cure William
Curry Elijah
Curry Michael
Cursor Tunis
Curtis Niard
Curtis Solomon
Curwin Edward
Curwin Gersham
Cuzard Richard
Daggett Mahew
Dale Richard
Daley John
Dalton Walter
Dan Abijah
Dan Jonathan
Danavan Peter
Daniels John
Dannolds John
David Isaac
Davids William
Davies Chapman
Davies Joseph
Davis Caleb
Davis Henry
Davis John
Davis Joseph
Davis Joshua
Davis Patrick
Davis Peter
Davis Richard
Davis Thomas
Davison John
Dawson John
Day Aaron
Day Isaac
Day Jonathan
Day Lewis
Dayley John
Dayton Bennet
Dayton Samuel
Dayton Samuel, Jr.
D'Bushe Anthony
Dean Abram
Deaton Frederick
Decker Jacobus
Decker James B.
Decker John
Decker Jon'th
Decker Michael
Decker Yerry
Deen Isaac
Deen John
Deen William
De Frees Reuben
Delaney Dennis
Demerest John
Demerest Nicholas
Demorest John
Demott Peter
Deniereft Nicholas
Dennis Mydert
Dennison Thomas
Denniss Miner
Denny Peter
Depont Bosteon
Depue George
Derby Thomas
Desert John
Dew Francis
D'Frees Ebenezer
Dick Henry
Dick Thomas
Dickerson Abraham
Dickerson Benjamin
Dickerson David
Dickerson Jeduthan
Dickerson John

Dickson Andrew
Dickson Gabriel
Dickson Nathan
Dickson Richard
Dickson William
Dieson John
Dieson Nathan
Dimond Jonathan
Dodge Samuel, Jr.
Dodge Stephen
Dole John M.
Dollaway Andrew
Dolph Jonathan
Donnalds John
Dose Richard
Doty John
Dougherty Mark
Doughty Elias
Doughty George
Dowd Isaac
Downing Andrew
Doxey Stephen
Doyle Hugh
Doyle John
Drake Benoni
Drean Patrick
Drenning Hamilton
Duall Samuel
Ducher Adam
Duff Peter
Duguid John
Dunbar William
Duncan Thomas
Dunk Henry
Dunmore Caesar
Dunnavun Peter
Dunnivan John
Dupont Bosteon
Duran Francis
Dutcher Bornt
Dutcher John
Dwire Simon
Eaddy James
Earl John
Easton Henry
Eastwood Benjamin
Edgit George
Edwards David
Egberts John
Elker Emmor
Elliot John
Elliot John, Jr.
Elliott Archibald
Ellis John
Ellison Isaac
Ellison Richard
Elsworth Ezekel
Ennis Peter
Elsworth John
English John
Ennis Peter
Ephram Ebenezer
Epton Benjamin
Erwin John
Esmond Isiah
Esmond James
Essmond John
Evalt Philip
Evens William
Everit Francis
Every Nehemiah
Fairly William
Fansher John
Fardon Samuel
Farrier Thomas
Fegan Timothy
Ferbush Simon
Ferdon Thomas
Ferdone Samuel
Ferguson Samuel
Ferris John
Ferris Jonah
Ferris Joseph
Ferris Ludowick
Ferris Samuel
Fichett Abraham
Filer Thomas
Finch Eliatham
Finch Elnathan
Finch William
Finton Amos
Fish Ebner
Fisher James
Fitch James
Fitzgerald Christr. Miller
Flemming Patrick
Fletcher Lawrence
Flinn John
Flood Cilas
Forbush Alexander
Ford William
Forgison Jeremiah
Forsey Josh.
Fosburgh Peter
Fosdick Samuel
Foster John
Foster Nathaniel
Foster Vincent
Foster William
Fountain Stephen
Fowler Philip
Foy Edward
Fralick John
Francis John
Franke Michel
Franke Peter
Frasier Jeremiah
Frayer Simon
Fredenbergh James
Freeman Nathaniel
Freeman Robert
Fross Stephen
Frye Benjamin
Fuller Josiah
Fulve Thomas
Furdon Thomas
Furman Samuel
Galasby James
Gantly Patrick
Gardon Andrew
Gardner Jesse
Garrisson Abraham
Garrisson Peter
Gates Nathaniel
Gee David
Gee Ezekiel
Geers Benjamin
Gibbons John
Gibson John
Gibson Robert
Gillcrist John
Gillcrist William
Gillet Joseph
Glover Thomas
Gold William
Golden Isaiah
Golden Thomas
Goldsmith Ezra
Goldsmith John
Goodspeed Hosia
Goodwin George
Gordon William
Gorman Richard
Gosper John
Gosper Peter
Graham Alexander
Graham John
Granger John
Graves Josiah
Graves Seldon
Gray Benjamin
Gray James
Gray Samuel
Greatman John
Green Ebenezer
Green James
Greer David
Gregeer John
Gregory Jehiel
Gregory John
Grey Robert
Griffen Barney
Griffin Benjamin
Grinnel Amasa
Grumman Ephraim
Guin Michael
Guy Edward
Guyre Luke
Haight Jager
Hains Joseph
Hains Saunders
Halenbeek Abraham
Hall Isaac
Hall James
Hallet Jonathan
Halsey Abraham
Halsey Ethan
Halsey Job
Halsey Stephen
Halsey Thomas
Hambleton John
Hammon Chason
Hammon Isaac
Hand Joseph
Hanley James
Hanmore Jabez
Hannah James
Hannevan Rice
Hanries William
Happer John
Hardy David
Harmancy John
Harner Nicholas
Harper William
Harris Abijah
Harris Cilas
Harris David
Harris Evans
Harris Moses
Harris William
Harris Zach
Hartshorne John
Harvey David
Hatt Frederick
Haukins Samuel
Hawkins David
Hawkins Noah
Hawkins Zachariah
Hawkins Zopher
Haynes Joseph
Hazard James
Heartness Andrew
Hedges Nathan
Helmer John
Henderson Alexander
Hennesey John
Henry David
Hermance John
Hermans Edward
Hermansee Edward
Herrick Amos
Herrick Samuel

Herrick William
Herrington John
Hicks Jacob
Higby Samuel
Higgins Moses
High Benjamin
Hike John
Hill Asse
Hill Thomas
Hill William
Himes Joseph
Hinkley Thomas
Hissam John
Hitchcock John
Hodges Joseph
Hoff Bastian
Hoff Henry H.
Hoff William
Hogarty Bernard
Hoit Job
Hoit Silvanus
Holloway Joseph
Holly John
Holly Samuel
Holmes Asa
Holmes Becker
Holmes Daniel, Jr.
Holmes James
Holmes John
Holmes Nathan
Holmes Thomas
Homan John
Hooker John
Hopkins Eli
Hopkins James
Hopper John
Hopper Samuel
Horsford Ithamer
Horton David
Horton Frederick
Hosport Samuel
House Jacob
House Zachariah
How Libeous
Howe John
Howe Silas
Howell
Howell George
Howell Jehiel
Howell Seth
Hoyt Thomas, Jr.
Hubbard
Hubbard John
Hubbard Ezekiel
Huber Jacob
Hubert John
Hudman Charles
Hudson
Huff William
Huffman John
Hufman Gabriel
Hughes John
Hughson William
Humphrey John
Humphrey Samuel
Hunt David
Hunt Solomon
Hunt Theophilus
Hunter Benjamin
Hunter Ezekiel
Hunter Jonathan
Huson William
Hutchings Gabriel
Hyatt Abraham
Hymes Joseph
Hyser Henry
Impson Elias
Impson Robart
Indian Thomas
Ingalls Elihu
English John
Israel Aaron
Jacklin Samuel
Jackson Thomas
Jamerson William
James Ebenezer
James Richard
James Richard
Jane Jotham
Jarman David
Jarvis Nathaniel
Jarvis Thomas
Jay David
Jay John
Jeffries John
Jeyne William
Jillet Joseph
Johns Silas
Johns Thomas
Johnson David
Johnson Isaac
Johnson James
Johnson John
Johnson Joseph
Johnson Samuel
Johnson Uriah
Johnson William
Johnston Benjamin
Johnston Samuel
Jones David
Jones Evans
Jones Jacob
Jones James
Jones John
Jones Squire
Jones Thomas
Joy Samuel
June Stephen
Kader Adam
Kader John
Keaffer William
Keder Stephen
Keefe Arthur
Keefer William
Keeler David
Keeler Ebenezer
Kelley Dennis
Kelley Isaac
Kelley Robert
Kelly Maurice
Kenner Jonathan
Kenney Jese
Kenny Charles
Ketcham John
Ketcham Samuel
Keynon Robert
Kiff John
Kilsey John
King William
Kinney Charles
Kinney Elijah
Kuffen James
Ladoo John
Ladow John
Lamb Isaac
Lamb Joshua
Lambert Cornelius
Lambert Joseph
Lane Jeremiah
Lansing John
Laraby Elisha
Lashier Abraham
Latham John
Lawrence John
Lawrence Uriah
Leawrance Richard
Lee James
Lee Japath
Lee Seth
Lee William
Lent Hendrick
Lent Jacob
Leonard David
Leonard Edward
Lepper John
Leveraga Samuel
Leverage William
Levey Jacob
Lewis Henry
Lewis Jabez
Lewis Samuel
Lhommedieu Mulford
Light John
Light Lemuel
Liley John
Linch John
Linch Laurence
Lines Hosea
Link Henry
Liscomb Isaac
Liscomb Samuel
Little William
Livingston Dick
Livingston Richard
Lloyd James
Loanis John
Lock John
Lockwood Azariah
Lockwood Hezekiah
Lockwood Israel
Lockwood Jonathan
Lockwood Nathan
Lockwood Reuben
Lodovick Peter
Loeson Laurance
Longworth Isaac
Looper James
Loper Abraham
Love John
Love William
Lovejoy Andrew
Lovelis George
Lovelis Jeremiah
Lownsberry Nathaniel
Lowree William
Ludlum Daniel
Ludlum John
Lufberry Jonathan
Lupton
Lusk Jacob
Lusk Michael
Lusk William
Lwinas Herry
Mabee Tobias
Macaulay Charles
Mackrill Richard
Mahane Patrick
Mahone James
Mahony Cornelius
Main Robert
Makraback Dyke
Maloy John
Mapes John
Marchant Ablo
Marks Aholiab
Marr James
Marray Warren
Marsh Benjamin
Marshal Amon
Marshall James
Martin James
Martin Archibald

Martin James
Martin Michael
Martin Samuel
Marling Deliverance
Marvin Stephan
Mason Francis
Mason Thomas
Masson Francis
Masters Jonathan
Mattison Aaron
Matthews Henry
Mattison Aaron
Mead David
Meaker Daniel
Medler Christian
Medler Christopher
Meeker Uzual
Meed Ezekeel
Meesy Benjamin
Merrill Joseph
Merrit Ebenezer
Merrit Luke
Merry Benjamin
Metzger John
Midler Christ'r
Millar John
Miller George
Miller Benjamin
Miller Frederick
Miller Georgo
Miller Jack
Miller Jesse
Miller John
Miller Justus
Miller Lewis
Miller Peleg
Miller Peter
Miller William
Miller Zephaniah
Mills Andrew
Mills James
Mingos Haronimus
Minks John
Mires John
Mitchel George
Mitchel Samuel
Mitchel William
Mitchell James
Money William
Moody James
Moody John
Mooney William
Moore Frederick
Moore John
Moore Joseph
Moore Robert
Moore Thomas
More Martin
More Robert
More Thomas
Moreign Alex
Morpeth William
Morrel James
Morrel Jesse
Morrel John
Morrell William
Morris Edward
Morris Robert
Morrison Duncan
Morse John
Mosher John
Moss David
Moulton Cato
Moulton Josiah
Moulton William
Mount Thomas
Mow James
Mucklow Joseph
Mulford Samuel
Mulliner Moses
Munday James
Munn Benjamin
Munroe Peter
Murfe John
Murn Muhel (Michel)
Murphy Daniel
Murphy James
Myer Christ'r Grind't
Myers David
Myers Zach
McCaffety James
McCarty Dennis
McCauley Charles
McCharlesworth John
McClain John
McClarien David
McClean Neal
McClow Joseph
McColister William
McCollem John
McCollum Malcom
McCracken John
McCullough Andrew
McDaniel John
McDole John
McDonald John
McDonald Michael
McDowal William
McDowel John
McElley John
McEntach William
McEvers John
McFairley William
McFall David
McGilles Hugh
McGilori Fergus
McGowin Duncan
McGready James
McIntosh William
McKee Michael
McKiel Adam
McLain Hugh
McMannus William
McMicken Ebenezer
McNeal Charles
McNeil Thomas
McOlister Alexander
McPherson Lawrence
McWhorster John
Nail Henry
Neal Henry
Neder John
Neilson Thomas
Nelson Thomas
Newman Abraham
Newman Jeremiah
Newman Joshua
Nichols James
Nickols Isaac
Nicols Simon
Nipper John
Nogert John
Norstrandt James
Norton Abel
Norton Calvin
Norton George
Norton Sible
Nostrander James
Nostrant George
Notingham Lewis
Nucom Thomas
O'Brien James
O'Brion Paul
Ogden David
Ogden John
Ogden Jonathan
Ogilsvie John
Ogstrander Peter
Olden Daniel
Onderdunck Abraham
O'Neal Thomas
Orr William
Orsor Abraham
Orsor Edward
Osborn Abraham
Ostrander James
Osborne Henry
Osterout Gilbert
Ostrander Henry
Owen Moses
Owens Ameziah
Ostrander Peter
Owens Elisha
Owens Terrence
Pain Silas
Palmer Amaziah
Palmer Isaac
Palmer James
Palmer Jonathan
Palmer Silas
Palmiteir John
Pangburn John
Pangburn William
Pardy Nathaniel
Parent Nathaniel
Park John
Park Robert
Parker Ebenezer
Parker Joseph
Parks John
Parks William
Parsells Matthew
Parshall James
Parsons Charles
Paul Joseph
Peck Nathan
Peirce Thomas
Peirson
Pell John
Pemderson John
Pendle Jonathan
Pennear Peter
Penney John
Pennoyer Jesse
Penoyer Israel
Penton Amos
Perkins Thomas
Perlee Edmond
Perry David
Pershall James
Persons John
Peterson Simeon
Pettit Abraham
Pettit Daniel
Pettit Samuel
Phillips David
Phillips Jonathan
Pickle John Henry
Pierce Thomas
Pierson
Piggs Richard
Pinyard William
Place Christopher
Place James
Plank Nicholas
Plass Michel
Plaus Peter
Plimley William
Plosser Peter
Plumb Stephen
Pollard Thomas
Polly Hugh

Pond Samuel
Post
Post Samuel
Potter George
Potter William
Poular John
Powel Vinson
Presher Abraham
Presher William
Preston Benjamin
Prim Azariah
Prime Peter
Primm Peter
Prior Abner William
Putman William
Quant Henry
Quinded David
Quinn Thomas
Racket
Racket Noah
Raigins William
Raimond Benjamin
Rainey Jeremiah
Ramis James
Randall Nathaniel
Randle Moses
Randle Seith
Raney John
Ransier George
Ray Charles
Raymond James
Raynor Ichabod
Reader Jacob
Reed George
Reed James
Reed John
Reeve Luther
Reeves Israel
Reives Nathaniel
Reymond Isaac
Renny Jesse
Reynolds Briggs
Reynolds David
Reynolds Ebenezer
Reynolds Eli
Reynolds James
Reynolds John
Reynolds Timothy
Rice Ezekiel
Rice Samuel
Rich Henry
Richards David
Richards John
Riggs Daniel
Ritchie Alexander
Ritchie Isaac
Roader Jacob
Roads Jacob
Roberds Edmun
Roberts Amos
Roberts John
Robertson James
Robins Evans
Robinson Andrew
Robinson James
Robinson Matthias
Robinson Peter
Rockwell Ebenezer
Rodgers Own
Roe John
Roe Silleman
Roe Simon
Rofft Aaron
Rogers John, Sr.
Rogers John, Jr.
Rogers Owen
Rogers William
Romer Benj.
Romer Peter
Roome Benjamin
Roomer Hendrick
Rose Andrew
Rose Jonathan
Rosman Adam
Rosman Henry
Rosman Philip
Ross Aaron
Ross Nathaniel
Ross William
Rossell Thomas
Rough Conrade
Row John
Row Simon
Rowland Phillip
Rowland Thomas
Ruland Jehiel
Rundle David
Runnels Abijah
Runnels Joseph
Russell Jonathan
Russigue Abraham
Sage Allen
Sagor John
Salmon
Salyer Zaccheus
Sanderson James
Sandford Daniel
Sandford John
Sattally Richard
Saxton Gilbert
Sayrs Nathaniel
Scantling Jeremiah
Scates James
Schouten Henry
Schouten John
Schriver Jacob N.
Schut Frederick
Schut James
Schut Tennis
Schofield Samuel
Schofield Silas
Schofield Smith
Scott Alexander
Scott Elijah
Scott Henry
Scott James
Scott John
Scott William
Scriver Christian
Scriver Henry
Scutt William
Sealey Joseph
Seaman Moses
Seaton Rufus
Seeds George
Seers Joseph
Seward John
Shannon Robert
Shatton David
Shaw John
Shaw Michael
Shaw Peleg
Shea Philip
Shear Lodiwick
Shelp Joseph
Sherwood Micajah
Shevalier John
Sibbio Thomas
Sickler Coonradt
Sickler Mitthias
Sicknar Jacob
Simmons Caleb
Simmons John
Simmons Joshua
Simmons Samuel
Sinnott Patrick
Sisco Dick
Sisco Philip
Sitzer Barant
Size Gilbert V.
Slason Stephen
Slosson Amos
Sly William
Smally Timothy
Smith Benjamin
Smith Caleb
Smith David
Smith Ebner B.
Smith Ezekiel
Smith Gersham
Smith Gideon
Smith Isaac
Smith James
Smith John
Smith Joseph
Smith Josiah
Smith Moses
Smith Nathan
Smith Nathaniel
Smith Obediah
Smith Samuel
Smith Solomon
Smith Thaddeus
Smith William
Snadiker Moses
Snowden John
Snyder Peter
Southerland James
Speed George
Speed Henry
Spicer Jacob
Sprage Alexander
Spring Nathaniel
Springer Isaac
Springston Jacob
Squirrell Jacob
Stagg Adam
Stagg John
Standish Amos
Stanley Daniel
Staples Nathan
Stebins Lewis
Steen William
Steenborgh Peter
Steeples Nathan
Stephans Jessee
Stephens John
Stephens Justice
Stephens Thomas
Stewart John
Still James
Still John
Stitt John
St. Lawrence George
Stone Asa
Stone David
Storms Abraham
Stratten Samuel
Stringham Henry
Strong John
Strong William
Stuard John
Sturdifent Jonathan
Suckinut John
Suffrin George
Suitt William
Sullivan James
Swan Robert
Swartwout Henry
Swartwout John
Swartwout William
Sweed William

Sweet Amos
Sweet Benoni
Sweet George
Sweet John
Sweet John, Jr.
Sweet Nathan
Sweet Robert
Swift Ambrose
Talmage Joseph
Tarrent Thomas
Tattenton Jeptha
Taylor Jasper
Taylor Joseph
Taylor Oliver
Taylor William
Teatter John
Terbush Simon
Terry Elijah
Terry James
Terry Samuel
Thomas John
Thomas Richard
Thompson Benjamin
Thompson Elias
Thompson James
Thompson John
Thompson Richard
Thompson William
Thomson Zebulon
Thorp Peter
Tice John
Tice Joseph
Tinkler Henry
Titus Isaac
Titus James
Titus Jonathan
Tompkins Edward
Tompkins Nathaniel
Tool John
Topping Daniel
Town Jacob
Townsend Absolom
Toy Samuel
Traver Francis
Traver Nicholas
Travess Jacob
Travess Silvanus
Travis Robert
Trim Azariah
Trowbridge James
Tubbs Stephen
Tubee John
Tucker John
Tucker Joshua
Tucker Samuel
Tum David
Tuman David
Tuman Peter
Tuman Peter, Jr.
Turner Joseph
Turrel Jones
Tuthill James
Tuttle Moses
Tyler Shublo
Unter Josiah
Upton Benjamin
Utley Ase
Utter Joseph
Utter William
Vail Thomas
Vallentine Gab'r
Valts Coonrod
Vanna Vincent
Vanoore Philip
Venier Peter
Vise Daniel
Voh Peter
Vonck Henry
Vredenburgh James
Vanarter James
Van Benscoten Elias
Vandebogart John
Van Debogart Minard
Van DeBogart Myndert
Vandervort Jacob
Vandevour John
Vandusen Peter
Van Etten Peter
Van Gelder Isaac
Vanhoosen Rinier
Van Horn John
Van Houten John
Van North John
Van Size Gilbert
Vantassell Isaac
Van tassell John
Van Volkenborgh Francis
Van Wicklen Fredrick
Vanworma Cornelius
Wade Elia
Wait Christopher
Walker Edward
Walker Mathew
Walker Matthias
Wall John
Wallace Benjamin
Wallice Uriah
Waner Killean
Ward Abijah
Ward Jadoc
Ward Robert
Ward Zedock
Warden Bernard
Waring Newman
Warner Martin
Warson Thomas
Washburn Joel
Waterbury Ely
Watkins William
Watson Thomas
Watson William
Wattaker Edward
Wattles William
Weaver John
Webb Ebenezer
Webb Silvanus
Webster Joseph
Weed Abijah
Weed Gilbert
Weed John Drew
Weed Nathan
Weeks James
Weeks John
Weeks Jonathan, Jr.
Weeks Macejah
Weiss Daniel
Welch Elijah
Welch Ephraim
Welch Henry
Welch Isaac
Welch James
Welch John
Welch Joseph
Welch Luke
Welch Thomas
Welch William
Wells Calvin
Wells Elijah
Wells William
Wentworth James
West Ase
West Jacob
West Joseph
West William
Westfall Levi
Whaley Samuel
Whaley Timothy
Wheeler James
Wheeler John
Wheeler Thomas
Whipple Nathan
White Ephraim
White George
White Henry
White John
White Samuel Curran
White Stephen
White Thomas
Whitehead Aaron
Whitehead Isaiah
Whitehead William
Wiggins William
Whitman John
Whitney Jacob
Wickham Stephen
Wicks James
Wicks Jonathan
Wildley Edward
Wiley Edward
Wilkinson Robert
Wilks Willis
Williams Aaron
Williams Abiah
Williams Adam
Williams Charles
Williams David
Williams John
Williams Peter
Williamson James
Willis Abraham
Willis David
Wilson John
Winass Silas
Wilson Michael
Wilson Nathaniel
Wilson Samuel
Wiltice Joseph
Winchall Samuel
Winchell James
Witteker Edward
Wood Jacob
Wood John
Wood Matthew
Wood Nathan
Wood Samuel
Wood William
Wood Zopher
Woodruff David
Woodruff Jeremiah
Woodruff Joshua
Woodruff William
Word Abijah
Worden Darious
Worden James
Wordin Shubel
Worpeth William
Wright John
Wyer Jeremiah
Yarrington William
Youmans Eleazer
Youmans Jonas
Youmens Jones
Young Isaac
Young John
Young Thomas
Yurks Harmanus
Zedmond Bartho'w

5th Regiment.

COLONEL LEWIS DUBOYS
LIEUTENANT COLONEL JAMES S. BRUYN
LIEUTENANT COLONEL MARINUS WILLETT
MAJOR SAMUEL LOGAN
ADJUTANT JAMES BETTS
QUARTER MASTER NEHEMIAH CARPENTER
QUARTER MASTER JAMES JOHNSTON
PAY MASTER SAMUEL TOWNSEND
CHAPLAIN JOHN GANO
SURGEON SAMUEL COOKE
SURGEON'S MATE EBENEZER HUTCHINSON
SURGEON'S MATE ROBERT MORRISEN

CAPT. PHILIP DUBOYS BEVIER
" DAVID DUBOIS
" HENRY S. DUBOIS
" HENRY GODWIN
" SILAS GRAY
" JOHN F. HAMTRAMIK
" JOHN HAMTRAMCK
" AMOS HUTCHINGS
" JOHN JOHNSTON
" THOMAS LEE
" JAMES ROSAKRANS
" JACOB ROSEKRANS
" JAMES STEWART
" HENRY H. VANDERBURGH
LIEUT. DANIEL BIRDSALL
" THOMAS BRINCKLE
" JOHN BURNIT
" MICHAEL CONNOLLY
" HENRY DODGE
" SAMUEL DODGE, JR.
LIEUT. JOHN FURMAN
" SAMUEL INGLISH (ENGLISH)
" PATTIN JACKSON
" DANIEL LAWRANCE
" EBENEZER MOTT
" ALEXANDER MCARTHER
" JOHN MCCLAUGHREY
" THOMAS NICHOLSON
" HENRY PAWLING
" SOLOMON PEMBLETON
" HENRY SWARTOUT
" HENRY I. VAN DER BURGH
" HENRY W. VAN DER BURGH
ENSIGN BANKAR
" ASAHEL BERRY
" FRANCIS HANMER
" ABRAHAM LEGET
" BARTHOLMEW VAN DER BURGH
" EDWARD WEAVER

ENLISTED MEN.

Abebin John
Aberson Stephen
Abritt John
Ackler Jacob
Ackor Cornelius
Adams Ephrem
Addoms Peleg
Aggins James
Aires Thomas
Akerson Cornelius
Albertson Stephen
Albright John
Alderson Stephen
Aldridge Jacob
Allin Jasper
Allson John
Amberman James
Amerman Obadiah
Anderson Joseph
Andrews Joab
Arkens John
Arston Holmes
Austen Holmes
Avary Nicholas
Avery Richard
Babcock Abraham
Babcock Elisha
Babcock John
Bailys Jonathan
Baker Samuel
Baker William
Bancker Nathaniel
Barkins William
Barlow Jonas
Barnam Samuel
Barriger Walter
Barritt John
Barry Elisha
Bartlit Lemuel
Bartow Jonas
Battersby John
Bayles Jonathan
Beam William
Beard William
Beeck Amos
Benedic Ambrose
Bently William
Berkins William

Schohary 28th April 1779

To the Treasurer of the State of New York }

Sir

you will much oblige us the Subscribers if you will pay unto Colo. Lewis Dubois the sum of one Hundred and eighty Pounds due each of us agreeable to an act past by the Assembly of said State being Officers of the Fifth New York Battalion Commanded by Colo. Lewis Dubois

Jas. Rosekrans Capt.

Philipp D. B. Bevier Capt.

James Stewart Cappt.

H. Hamtramck Capt.

H. V. D. Burgh Lieut.

Henry Dodge Lieut.

Dan. Birdsall Lieut.

Henry I. Vandenburgh Ensign

Ebenr. Hutchinson Surgn. Mate

SIGNATURES OF OFFICERS OF THE 5TH LINE.

A return of the Commissioned Officers [illegible] of the 5th Battalion of Continental Troops raised under the direction of the State of New York commanded by Lewis Du Bois [illegible] of the [illegible] of the said State [illegible] for the payment of the balance of the [illegible] Officers of [illegible] mentioned. April 27th 1779

Colonel	Lewis Du Bois
Captain	Jonathan Johnson
D°	Philip Du Bois Bevier
D°	James Stewart
D°	John Hamtramck
D°	Peter Johnston
Capt. Lieutenant	Henry Du Bois
1. D°	Henry H. Vanderburgh
D°	Henry Dodge
D°	Michael Conolly
D°	Daniel Birdsall
D°	Samuel English
[illegible] D°	James Betts
[illegible] Ensign	
D°	Henry I. Vanderburgh
Ensign	Thomas Hammond
D°	James Johnston
D°	Bartholomew Vanderburgh
Surgeon	Samuel Cooke
Surgeon Mate	George Hutchinson

I do hereby Certify that the above to be a true return of the Commissioned Officers Surgeon and Surgeons Mate of the 5th Battalion of Troops raised under the direction of the State of New York actually serving agreeable to the late arrangement and establishment of the Army and not prisoners with the Enemy

Lewis Du Bois Col°

State of New York ss. I do hereby certify that I have examined the above return of Commissioned Officers, Surgeon and Surgeons Mate of the 5th Continental Battalion raised under the direction of this State whereof Lewis Du Bois Esquire is Colonel, actually serving agreeable to the late arrangement of the Army and not prisoners with the Enemy amounting to nineteen, and I do approve of the same. Given at Poughkeepsie this 27th day of April 1779

[illegible]

RETURN OF OFFICERS OF THE 5TH LINE.

Berry Elisha
Bertlet Lemuel
Betts James, Jr.
Bevins Crispamur
Bevins David
Bevins Francis
Bishop Ezekiel
Bishop James
Bishop William
Blancher William
Blaws John
Bloomer William
Blosom Sol'n
Boge John
Boid Daniel
Boid Samuel
Bolton George
Bonker Bethuel
Bonker John
Bonker Nathaniel
Bonker Solomon
Bonker William
Bonkers Lawrence
Boutton Joseph
Bowers Joel
Boyce Thomas
Boyd George
Boyd Robert
Boyde Samuel
Branen Adam
Branen Reuben
Briant Matthew
Briggs Jeremiah
Brink Adam
Brocket Moses
Brockway Russell
Broker Walter
Brooks Joseph
Brown John
Brush Eliakim
Buckbe Josiah
Bunday Jeremiah
Buoyd Daniel
Burdge Michael
Burdick Elisha
Burgee Michael
Burhans Samuel
Burnett Ebenezer
Buttles Sebra
Cain John
Caldwell Arthur
Campbell George
Canit Cunradt
Carden James
Carely Joseph
Carley John
Carn Mathias
Carr William

Carrigan Daniel
Carrigan William
Casner Michael
Cass Joseph
Chace Caleb
Chamberlain John
Chandler Jonathan
Channy Richard
Chapman Lemuel
Chatfield Jonathan
Chedestar Benjamin
Cheshier Nehemiah
Cheshley John
Chesser Nehemiah
Chrispell Thomas
Christey John
Christian Peter
Chyser Nehemiah
Clark Benjamin
Clark John
Clark Martin
Clark William
Clarwater John
Clarwattor Martinus
Clay Thomas
Cline Jacob
Cline John
Clinton John
Cocksure Joseph
Coe Philip
Coennight Cunradt
Coil Thomas
Coleman John
Colp John
Combes John
Concklin John
Concklin Samuel
Concklin Thomas
Coningham Moses
Conite Conrad
Connelly Henry
Counight Conrad
Connolly Henry
Cook Isaac
Cook Jacob
Cook Samuel
Cook William
Cooke David
Cooke Thomas
Coombe John
Coombe Peter
Coombes Samuel
Cooper Abraham
Cooper Richard
Cornelias John
Cornwale Joseph
Corren Samuel
Cosgrove John

Cost Martin
Couren Samuel
Cox Thomas
Craw Ebenezer
Crawford Asia
Crawford Thomas
Crispell Thomas
Croft Jacob
Crosby Lemuel
Crullin Jeremiah
Crum Hermanus
Crum Jacob
Crumb John
Cullin Jeremiah
Culp John
Cummins Ebenezer
Cumpton Cbadiah
Cunningham Moses
Curren Samuel
Curtis Ebenezar
Cutting Francis
Daily James
Daker Christopher
Daker Martinus
Dalency Abraham
Damm Frederick
Danford Prince
Dannelson Isaac
Darlin Ezra
Darling John
Davis David
Davis Hezekiah
Davis Jacob
Davis John
Davis Samuel
Decker Christopher
Decker Martin
Deknight Jos'h
Delamarter John
Delevan Frs
Demark Gisbert V.
Denilson Isaac
Denton Amos
Deority William
Depuie Elias
Diamond Moses
Diamond William
Dibble Hezekiah
Dickenson Lewis
Dickenson Versal
Dikeson Gideon
Dillimater John
Dimick Daniel
Dimon William
Dodge Richard
Donalson Isaac
Doty Daniel
Douglas William

Douty James
Dow Volker
Drake Francis
Dubois Nathaniel
Duglas William
Dunford Wells
Dunn Jeremiah
Durgeon Patrick
Eackley Jacob
Eaton Ephraim
Eazor James
Edwards David
Edwards Gilbert
Eggbert Daniel
Elicer John
Ellis Jacob
Ellis Joseph
Ellison John
Factor John
Fairin John
Fardon Abraham
Felix Philip
Ferdon John
Fergeson James
Ferrin John
Filex Philip
Filmore Silas
Finn Thomas
Fish Sebra
Fitzgerallaid Thomas
Fitzgibbons James
Fitzseaman Barnard
Flannigan Daniel
Fluno John
Flyn John
Forgason Samuel
Forrest Robert
Foster Gilbert
Foster Jerem
Foster William
Fowler Michael
Freazer Lewis
Frier John
Fullin John
Furlongh Cornelius
Galasby James
Ganes Francis
Gardineer Andries
Gardner Samuel
Garrison Abraham
Garrison Samuel
Gates John
Gearderman Henry
Gee John
Gee Moses
Gibbins John
Gillaspy Robert
Gilmore Daniel

Givans Samuel
Glason Joseph
Gleen Caleb
Godwin David
Goldin William
Golligan Charles
Gones Griffin
Gones Joseph
Goodspead Gideon
Goodwin Abraham
Goolden Lewis
Gosline Samuel
Gragg Hezekiah
Graham Zachariah
Gray John
Gray Samuel
Grayham John
Greadey Thomas
Greeg David
Green Sutten
Gregg Hezekiah
Grifeth Jeremiah
Griffin Benjamin
Griffin Joshua
Guardner James
Guilbert Seth
Gwen Michael
Hack George
Hackerson William
Hallet William
Hallett George
Hallett Solomon
Hallick Jonathan
Halmore Philip
Hanbaragh Abraham
Hanes John
Hankely Thomas
Hankerson William
Hanky Henry
Hannoh James
Hartwell Thomas
Harty Christopher
Harwood John
Hassbrook George
Hauss Simon
Havens Peter
Hawhey Richard
Hearter Christopher
Hendereks Wansor
Hendrikson John
Hennekey Manuel
Hesom John
Hews Henry
Hews William
Higby Elnathan
Higgins Samuel
Hill Joshua
Hinkley Thomas
Hipp Abraham
Hoisel Nathaniel
Holester Nathaniel
Holet George
Holley John
Hollister Nathaniel
Holloway James
Holmes Peter
Holms Jesse
Hoper Samuel
Hopper Peter
Hornbeck Henry
Hortain Silas
Hosuer John
House Henry
Howal Lemuel
Howel Samuel
Howkey Henry
Howse Henry
Huchins Ebinezar
Hughs William
Hull Samuel
Humphre Alexander
Humphrey James
Humphrey Samuel
Hunt David
Hunt John
Hunt Joshua
Hunter Ezekiel
Hunter James
Hunton John
Hutchinson Ebenezer
Ingram Thomas
Ireland Amos
Jackson Robert
Jackson William
James John
Jee John
Jenkings Thomas
Jewett Caleb
Johnes Seth
Johns Griffin
Johnson Abraham
Johnson Alexander
Johnson John
Johnson Joseph
Johnson Michael
Johnson Prince
Johnston Daniel
Johnston John
Jones Joseph
Jones Robert
Jones Thomas
Joory John
Joory William
Juit Caleb
Keef Con
Keeller James
Keesley Paul
Keller James
Kelley James
Kelly Joshua
Kemble Isaac
Kempton Obadiah
Kendrick Thomas
Kennedy Dennis
Kent Thomas
Kepp Abraham
Keyser John
Kiepp Conn
Kieseer Andrew
Kiesley Paul
Kinsley James
Kirberger Philip
Kiser John
Kizer Andrew
Knaap Aaron
Kniffen Amos
Kniffin Nehemiah
Kniver William
Kolb John
Konover Godfry
Kroat John
Lain William
Lake Joshua
Lander Daniel
Lander Ebenezer
Lane William
Langdon Samuel
Laraway Isaac
Latemor Benjamin
Lates Jems
Lattimore Roger
Lawrance Isaac
Lawrance Jacob
Lawrence Benjamin
Lawrence William, Junr.
Lenington Thomas
Lent Enos
Lent Isaac
Leonard Silas
Letts Evert
Levan Francis
Lewis Henry
Lockwood John
Lockwood Josiah
Lodar Daniel
Longyear Andries
Longyear Jacob
Lounsbury John
Lovitt John
Lucey Eleazer
Lust Francis
Lutter Cuff
Mackey William
Mappes Stephen
Markel James
Markes George
Marks Holiab
Marsh Thomas
Marshall Robert
Marthis Peter
Mash Thomas
Mastis Joseph
Maston Joseph
Matany James
Mathews Justus
Mathews Peter
Matthews John
Menema Benjamin
Mericale Jacob
Merkle James
Merrit John
Metcalf William
Michelvany Phillip
Milagen Robert
Milard John
Miligan Robert
Millar Elisha
Millard Henry
Miller John
Mills Johnam
Minama Benjamin
Mineael Jacob
Mitchall James
Mitchell Joseph
Moncref Charles
Montanyee James
Montieth James
Moonay William
Mooney Absolom
Moor John
Moore Jacob
Mordoch Archibald
More John
Morewise Jacob
Morgan Joseph
Moris Archibald
Morrison Daniel
Morrow Patrick
Morry Patrick
Mott John
Muckelvany Philip
Mullan William
Mungomery John
Munteith James
Murfy Edward
McAfee John
McAnany John
McArthur John
McArthur Thomas
McCarty John
McCarty Thomas
McClannon John

McClean John
McClure Moses
McCollester Walter
McCorn Edward
McDermot Francis
McDonald James
McDonald John
McDonald Thomas
McDugal Dugle
McGraw James
McIntosh John
McKee John
McKeny Michael
McKey Joseph
McKey William
McKinsley James
McKown Duncan
McKown James
McLean John
McNeal John
McVany Philip
Negroe William
Neilson William
Nelson Thomas
Nelson William
Newcomb Kinner
Newman Jonathan
Nicholls John
Nichols Stephen
Niver William
Norton Silas
Nowell Lemuel
Nukemb Kenner
Numan Jonathan
Oakey Abraham
Oakley Jonathan
Oliphant William
Olive Love
Orr Daniel
Osben Daniel
Osborn Casar
Osterhout Peter
Ostrander Henry
Otter Nathan
Outhouse Israel
Owens David
Pake John
Palmerton Thomas
Paresonus James
Parker Elisha
Paronnus James
Paterson Thomas
Paterson William
Patks Jonah
Patks William
Patrick Robert
Patterson James
Paul William
Paulding Henry
Paulis John
Peek John
Pembrook William
Penney Jonathan
Pepper John
Personus James
Peterson Alexander
Pewlis John
Phenix Robert
Philips David
Philips Joshua
Plank Henry
Plough Henry
Plumb Samuel
Post Zebulon
Pudney James
Prague Seth
Prebell Joseph
Preyer Jasper
Priam Michal
Pribbell Joseph
Price John
Pride James
Prime Michael
Pryer Jasper
Pudney James
Puller John
Pullis John
Purdy David
Quan Ephraim
Quick Abraham
Race Ephraim
Rainy Jeremiah
Ramsen Henry
Ramsey Jonas
Ramson James
Randle Mathias
Ransom Henry
Ransom Jacob
Rea Benjamin
Read John
Reeder Joseph
Rhoades John
Rhodes Cornelius
Richard Philip
Richards Gilbert
Richardson Alexander
Richey John
Richmond Josiah
Ricker Jeremiah
Riding Timothy
Ried John
Rieston William
Rillaman Jacob
Rippley John
Ristin William
Ritter Jacob
Ritterman Jacob
Roase Jonathan
Robertson Daniel
Robertson James
Robeson George
Robeson Robert
Robinson Alexander
Robinson Benjamin
Robison Thomas
Ronols John
Roose Jacob
Roose Jonathan
Rosakvance Caeser
Rosekrance Depue
Rosekrans James
Ross Charles
Rubenger Philip
Rultrege Jacob
Rumsey Jonas
Rundle Able
Ruple William
Rusell Thomas
Russell Hugh
Russell James
Russell William
Ruston William
Rylie Silvester
Samson Isaac
Sandford William
Satterly John
Schoonmaker Henry
Schoonmaker Coffey
Scouton Henry
Scudder John
Seaman Ephraim
Seamor Abraham
Sears Francis
Secars John
Serine Jacob
Shapher George
Sharkey Thomas
Shaw James
Shaw Moses
Shaw Reuben
Shaw Solomon
Shay Martin
Shear Abraham
Sherve Andries
Sherwood Nehemiah
Shirkey Thomas
Simmons Ephraim
Simmons Ezekiel
Simmons Isaac
Simpson James
Sinkins Jeremiah
Size Abram
Skinnor Jonathan
Slaven James
Slick Stephen
Slocan Jonathan
Slouyter Evert
Slouyter John
Slutt Abraham
Slutt Marvel
Slutt William
Sluyter Evert
Slyter John
Smawly Thomas
Smedus John
Smith Abner
Smith Abraham
Smith David, Jr.
Smith David, Sr.
Smith Henry
Smith James
Smith Jesse
Smith John
Smith Joseph
Smith Lem Mosier
Smith Reuben
Smith Samuel
Smith Stephen
Smith Thomas
Snyder Peter
Soll William
Southerd John
Speenbergh Joseph
Sprage Seth
Springsted George
Springsted Harmanus
Springsted Isaac
Springsteel William
Springston John
Spunbergh Joseph
Stalk Seth
Stanly John
Stanly Thomas
Stansbury Elijah
Steak Stephen
Steel Daniel
Steel John
Stell James
Stephen Richard
Stephens John
St. John ———
Stolker Seth
Storms John
Straight Henry
Straight William
Street Abraham
Stump John
Suthard John
Sutlif John
Sweep Jacob
Sweete Robert
Swinton Henry

Swiss Jacob
Talliday Stephen
Taloday Solomon
Talowday John
Taphap Peter
Tapper Nathan
Tar Boss Isaack
Taylor Elijah
Teknight Jos'h
Tellent Edward
Teller James T.
Tenigar George
Tenyke Joseph
Ter Bush Cornelius
Ter Bush Isaac
Terwillegar Jacobus
Thayer John
Thomas George
Thomas James
Thomas John
Thompson Elias
Thompson James
Thomson Arch'l
Thonsen Sam
Thorington James
Thorn Benjamin
Thorn Obadiah
Thornton James
Tillton Peter
Tinagar George
Tinker Joshua
Titus James
Tobious Jacob
Toffet Peter
Tomilson Benjamin
Tompkins Edmond
Tompkins Elijah
Tonge George
Tonsen Sam'l
Tophop Peter
Topper Nathan
Townsbury John
Townsend Absalom
Traverse Abraham
Traverse Scott
Trewilliger William
Tryon John
Tucker Joshua
Tupper Nathan
Turner Francis
Tyne Francis V.
Ulter Nathan
Underdunck Titus
Utter Isaac, Sr.
Uutter Gilbert
Vactor John
Vallary John
Vaney Vincent
Vasborough Samuel
Vasburgh Jacob
Vasburgh Lawrence
Venote Joseph
Veny Vincent
Vermiller Peter
Vanasdol Jacobus
Van Asdoll John
Vanate Joseph
Vandel John
Van Demarken Gysbert
Vanderbarak Cornelius
Van Der Mark Cornelius
Van De Water Augustines
Van Gelder Jacob
Van Gelder Matthew
Van Huson Garret
Van Hyning Andrew
Vannort Joseph
Van Nosdall John
Vanosdal Jacobus
Van Tine Francis
Van Tine Isaac
Van Tine John
Vantine Robert
Waddle Rob't
Walcott William
Walker Samuel
Wall James
Wandle John
Ward Josiah
Warren Edward
Wasson James
Watson Levi
Weaver William
Webber Ichabod
Weedd Samuel
Weeker Obediah
Weeks Malatiah
Weldin James
Wells John
Wells Peter
Wells Thomas
Welsh Edward
Welsh John
Wemiah Frederick
Wendall John
West Jacob
West John
Western John
Wever Johanniele
Whaly Benjamin
Wharry David
Wheler Stephen
Wheller Samuel
Wheller Timothy
Wheller William
Whelor Stephen
White Peter
Whitehead John
Whitehead William
Wilboe Jacob
Wilkinson Thomas
Willes William
William Richard
William Wheeler
Williams Ebenezer
Williams Isaac
Williams Wynerd
Willis John
Willis Thomas
Williss William
Wills Peter
Willson Abraham
Willson John
Wilsey Henry
Wimore Frederick
Winchester Danford
Wollcott William
Wood James
Wood Timothy
Woodard John
Woolsey Henry
Worner Edward
Wright Abraham
Wriston William
Wryton William
Yearns Epharim
Yomans Benjamin
Yomans John
Yomans Stephen
Youmans Isaac
Young John
Youngs Henry

Additional Regiment.

COLONEL JAMES LIVINGSTON

LIEUTENANT COLONEL RICHARD LIVINGSTON

PAY MASTER JOHN P. D. TEN EYCK

CAPT. DIRCK HANSON
" TIMOTHY HUGHES
" ABRAHAM LIVINGSTON
" AUGUSTIN LOSEAUX
" JAMES ROBICHAUX
" PETER VAN RENSSELAER
" ROBERT WRIGHT
LIEUT. WILLIAM BELKNAP
LIEUT. JOHN BLACKLEY
" ISAAC NICHOLS
" THOMAS NICOLSON
" PETER J. VOSBURGH
" WILLIAM WALLACE
" ANTHONY WELP
ENSIGN JOHN GATES

ENLISTED MEN.

Anderson James
Belford Anthony (Beford)
Bouy William
Brock Francis
Brock Nathaniel
Brown Nathaniel
Burns John
Canuter John
Clark Joseph
Conden Phillip
Conely Dennis
Falconer William
Flinn John
Frazier John
Garvy David
Gilbert John
Gould Thomas
Griffiths Howel
Harold Henry
Horn Phanten
Hyett Henry
Ketcham David
Lawader William
Lewis Isaac
Little Benjamin
Loder William
Lord Benjamin
Lord Jonathan
Loyal Edward
Ludlow William
Moore William
Morewise Jacob
Murphy Peter
McCord Alexander
McDonald Peter
Newel Edward
Nicolson Andrew
Oharra Cain
Powel Thomas
Powers James
Ready John
Robinson John
Silkirk James
Smith John
Springer William
Steel Joseph
Stener Nicholas
Thompson John
Thompson Thomas
Ward Thomas
Welch William
White Peter
Williams James
Willmot John

Artillery Regiment.

COLONEL JOHN LAMB

MAJOR SEBASTIAN BAUMAN

ADJUTANT JAMES BRADFORD

PAY MASTER ISAAC GUION

CAPT.	THOMAS THEODORE BLISS	CAPT.	JOSEPH THOMAS
"	JONATHAN BROWN	"	THOMAS THOMPSON
"	JOHN DOUGHTY (Brigade Insp.)	"	ROBERT WALKER
"	GEORGE FLEMING	"	JEREMIAH WOOL
"	JAMES LEES	CAPT. LIEUT.	ISAIAH WOOL
"	SAMUEL LOCKWOOD	LIEUT.	CALEB BREWSTER
"	SAMUEL MANSFIELD	"	JOHN BURNSIDES
"	THOMAS MATCHIN	"	WILLIAM CEBRA
"	ANDREW MOODY	"	JAMES GILES
"	GERSHOM MOTT	"	OLIVER LAURENCE
"	ANDREW PORTER	"	GEORGE LEAYCRAFT
"	JACOB REED	"	PETER NESTEL
"	JOSEPH SAVAGE	"	WILLIAM STRAHAN
"	JONAS SIMOND	"	ALEXANDER THOMPSON
"	WILLIAM STEVENS	"	JOHN WALDON
"	CORNELIUS SWARTWOUT	"	HENRY A. WILLIAMS

ENLISTED MEN.

Arvin James
Ashfield John
Ashton Joseph
Badgerow Francis
Bailes James
Bailey John
Bard Robert
Beard Robert
Bennett Jacob
Berwick Marmaduke
Berwick Robart
Betters John
Bon Barnes
Bon Joseph
Brocket Moses
Brower Daniel
Brown James
Bunn Barnes
Bunn Joshua
Campbell Daniel
Carpenter George
Clark Anthony
Clark Martin
Connor John
Cook Michael
Cox John Luke
Crawford Thomas
Curtiss Andrew
Dalzell George
Davis Hugh
Day Thomas
Dean Joseph
Deane John
Devo Francis
De Witt John
Done Thomas
Fenton Peter
Fisher Bartholomew
Fisher John
Garigues John
Gaus Stephen
Goble Joseph
Goe Thomas
Graves Joseph
Green Morris
Harwood Thomas
Hayes Samuel
Hean Frederick
Hesse Henry
Heusted Nathaniel
Holland Shelly
Houck Henry
Houston Nathaniel
Irvin James
Johnson John
Johnson William
Keaughy Matthew
Kelly John
Kenny John
Kerney Thomas
King Adam
Kitchel Matthew
Lewis Charles
Lockwood Silas
Loger Christopher
Martin John
Mason James
Mason John
Meales Matthew
Mielon Francis
Mitchell David
Morrison Thomas
McClue William
McCullough John
McCune Richard
McLean Allen
Nestall Peter
Newton Peter
Nistle Peter
Norris James
Oliver Thomas
Patton James
Paxton Edward
Peed Daniel
Pell Philip
Phraner William
Pillford William
Poalk John
Poole William
Powell William
Raymond Francis
Relay Henry
Roef Michael
Rollins William
Roop Michael
Russell Solomon
Seely Lewis
Sharp Thomas
Shelly William
Smith John
Spranger Henry
Steymest Gasper (Casper)
Sutton Thomas
Telfor William
Torry David
Vanderooh Benjamin
Vix Jacob
Welsh Richard
Wilson Isaac
Winter Thomas
Wirth Christopher
Withwall William

Capt. Alexander Hamilton's Train of Provincial Artillery.

CAPT. ALEXANDER HAMILTON
CAPT. LIEUT. JAMES MOORE
LIEUT. JOHN BANE
LIEUT. JAMES GILLILAND
" MARTIN JOHNSON

ENLISTED MEN

Barber Robert
Barry Lawrence
Bowers Michael
Brooks Joseph
Brown Joseph
Burrage Robert
Cairns John
Campbell Andrew
Chamberlin Uriah
Child Joseph
Crawford Uriah
Deasy James
Delaney Thomas
Dely Henry
Farguson Lawrence
Finton Robert
Forbes James
Gallaway James
Garland George
Gilbert William I.
Griffiths John
Hackett William
Haight Joseph
Hammond John
Harwood Thomas
Henry James
Hervey John
Hyer John
Johnson Isaac
Johnson Martin
King Adam
King Jacob
Lawler Martin
Lewis Thomas
Lilly James
Lockhart William
Magee James
Martin John
Mason Joseph
Miller David
McGeers James
McKinny John
Norris Stephen
Oharro Mathew
Pilling John
Putt John Christopher
Remsen Aris
Robins Aaron
Robins Valentine
Ryan Lewis
Ryan Thomas
Saler John
Sawers Isaac
Scott William
Smith Samuel
Stakes John
Taylor Richard
Taylor Thomas
Thompson Thomas
Thurston Samuel
Wan Lawrence
Wood John

Green Mountain Boys.

These muster rolls are spoken of as "Major Brown's Detachment," and that detachment is spoken of as in "General Arnold's Regiment." (The only mention of General Arnold found in our records).

The fact that, as a matter of history, the "Green Mountain Boys" were at Quebec in 1776; the fact that this detachment was also at Quebec in 1776; the fact that two of the officers on these rolls — Captain and Commissary Elijah Babcock and Captain Robert Cochran — are identical in name and rank with those on a list handed to the Provincial Congress of New York by Ethan Allen and Seth Warner, on July 4, 1775, as officers for the Green Mountain Boys, and the further fact that none of the men are recorded in any other place, or with any other organization, justifies the belief that the soldiers on its rolls herewith were a part of that historic band.

OFFICERS.

COLONEL ETHAN ALLEN

COLONEL SETH WARNER

MAJOR JOHN BROWN

ADJUTANT WILLIAM SATTERLEE

QUARTER MASTER SAMUEL McCLUND

CAPT. AND COM.	ELIJAH BABCOCK	LIEUT.	JAMES GOOLD
CAPT.	GIDEON BROWNSON	"	EBENEZER HYDE
"	ROBERT COCHRAN	"	DAVID PIXLEY
"	GOODRICH	"	ELISHAMA TOZER
"	CHARLES NELSON	"	EBENEZER WALBRIDGE
LIEUT.	PALMERLY ALLEN	"	SETH WHEELER

ENLISTED MEN.

Abbot William
Alden Felix
Allen Abrahan
Allen Amos
Allen Samuel
Ames David
Andress Jeremiah
Andrews Moses
Averil Ebenezer
Averill Robert
Barker Alexander
Barkley Robert
Barlow Samuel
Beach Samuel
Beamen Jery
Beder John
Begar Alexander
Beltheh Stephen
Bennet Isaac
Bennet Nathan
Bheartwick John
Bishop Enos
Black Primas
Blackmon Epheram,
Blanchard Abner
Blanchard Azriel
Blodget Elijah
Boggess Thomas
Brown John
Buck Isaac
Burk Jonathan
Burris John
Burris Matthew
Burroughs Matthew
Cannada John
Capee George
Capern Thomas
Carley Abraham
Caswell Eliphalet
Chadock Jonas
Chamberlin Joseph
Chambers Henry
Chipman Jessey
Church John
Clark Isaac
Clark Jessey
Clarke James
Cobb John
Cochran Samuel
Colter Joseph
Comstock Aaron
Connely John
Corbit Eldad
Cross John
Cross Uriah
Curtis David
Curtis Timothy
David Abel
Davis Abel
Dernim Asa
Dernim Reubin
Dickey Elias
Doud Jesse
Dressen Jonathan
Drew Samuel
Dunlap Samuel
Eastman Nathaniel
Eives Jonah
Erwine David
Fellows William
Fitch Jonathan
Flood Moses
Flood Timothy
Foot Jennor
Freeman Elias
Freeman John

Freeman Moody
French John
Fuller Elijah
Garvin Epheram
Gibson James
Gilbert Elisha
Goodcourage John
Gordon Alexander
Grapes Phillpo
Gray John
Griswell Benjamin
Halet John
Hand Ira
Hand Oliver
Hardy James
Hasleton John
Hastens Jonathan
Hawley Ichabod
Haws Edward
Heart John
Heath Benjamin
Henderson David
Heniman Leonard
Heniman Moses
Holmes Orsamus
House Jonathan
Hulburt William
Huntington Jery
Huntley Benjamin
Hutchins Asa
Jewet Jedediah
Johnson Jehial
Jonston Edin

Jonston John
Jurdon Jonathan
Kelley Abraham
Kelley John
Kellog Joseph
Kellom Samuel
Kentfield George
King Thomas
Klein Adonijah
Lapish John
Lee Jonathan
Libbey Joseph
Locheron John
London
Luttington John
Luttington Moses
Magrager Duncan
Malery David
Mallarce Nathaniel
Messer Abiel
Michel Samuel
Millege John
Miller Robert
Moores Ezra
Moss Timothy
McConnel Jonathan
Nayson Benjamin
Nayson Edward
Olcott William
Olford Alexander
Ovits James
Owen Daniel
Owen Silvanus

Pain Francis
Parker Amasa
Pasavile John
Patee Zephniah
Patterson George
Paul Robert
Philbrook Eliphalet
Piper Thomas
Powers Nicholas
Prindle Joel
Prose Benjamin
Putnam Asaph
Putnam Ephron
Quin Michel
Renolds John
Richards Edward
Richardson Jonathan
Ripney John
Robertson John
Rowe Abner
Rowley Samuel
Rush George
Sanborn John
Saxston George
Serjeant Samuel
Shavalee Joseph
Simpson William
Smith Abraham
Smith Benjamin Young
Smith Eliphelet
Smith John
Spencer Jesse

Spring Thomas
Squires James
Stannard Libeus
Sterling Archibald
Steven Isaac
Stevens John
Stickney Ezekiel
Stockwell Jacob
Stow Seth
Stuart Samuel
Sturges David
Styles Eli
Sullingham Henry
Thomas John
Thurstininlis Ward
Turner Nicholas
Umpsted Israel
Vine Ebenezer
Vine Robert
Vine Solomon
Vangelder John
Wakley Stephen
Walker Jonathan
Wallis Samuel
Waters John
Watkins Daniel
Welch David
Wells James
Whiston John
Wiley David
Willen Amos
Young Joseph

Privateers.

SCHOONER "GENERAL PUTNAM" (FORMERLY THE "BETSEY.")

CAPTAIN THOMAS GREGIER
1ST LIEUT. THOMAS QUIGLEY
2D LIEUT. DAVID WALKER
MASTER ELEAKIM LITTELL
SURGEON JOHN BOYD

SLOOP "MONTGOMERY."

CAPTAIN WILLIAM ROGERS
1ST LIEUT. THEUNIS THEW
2D LIEUT. JOHN LEAYCRAFT

SLOOP "SCHUYLER."

CAPTAIN JAMES SMITH

FRIGATE "CONGRESS."

CAPTAIN THOMAS GRENELL
" WILLIAM ROGERS
LT. OF MARINES VICTOR BICKER, JR.
CAPTAIN WILLIAM MERCIER

ENLISTED MEN.

Allen Ebenezer
Anthony Benjamin
Armstrong Jonathan
Baker Lionel S.
Baker Lionel S., Jr.
Barkiss Thomas
Barres Timothy
Basset Henry
Beebe Eliphelet
Bell William
Bricket John
Bryan Henry
Burns Timothy
Burress James
Butler Thomas
Cambell Archible
Chichester James
Conklang Ebenezer
Conklin Richard
Conkling Titus
Cook James
Damerell Peter
Darcy Augustine
Davis Josiah
Davis Ebenezer
Donaldson Frederick
Donaldson Souevin
Donaldson Subbrine
Dorsey Augustus
French Cornelius
Fritchet Isaac
Ghit Abraham
Gildersleeve Richard
Goodale Jonathan
Griffis John
Griffith John
Hardy John
Hazen Ezekiel
Hencock Thomas
Hyeat Abraham
Jackson John
Jamison Robert
Kellay Robert
Ketcham Solomond
Knight Burchard
Knight Richard
Lahy Morgan
Latley Morgan
Laurance Nathaniel
Leayted William
Lomberd Thomas
Markins Thomas
May Elias
Morrell Benjamin
Morrell Jacob
McDonald Alexander
McDonald Duncom
McGray John
Negro Andrew
Noblit John
Parcels John
Parsons Zachariah
Platt Daniel
Purkinss Thomas
Purkiss Thomas
Radley William
Reeve Elias
Reeve Elisha
Richard John
Roberds Elias
Rogers Jacob
Rogers Joshua
Ruland Thomas
Shaards Thomas
Shelle George
Shells George
Shine John
Shourds Joseph
Simmonds Solomond
Steele Thomas
Stelle Thomas
Still Thomas
Tarbosh Isaac
Taylor John
TerBoss Isaac
Thayer John
Thines John
Thomas John
Tolkenton Joseph
Trail John
Turner Samuel
Waer Joseph
Waistcoat
Weekes Isaac
Weeks Ebenetus
Westcott Jabez
White James
Willasey William
Woodruff Benjamin
Wood Eliphelet
Wyer John

THE LEVIES.

COLONEL JOHN HARPER
MAJOR JOHN CHIPMAN
MAJOR JAMES M. HUGHES
ADJUTANT JOHN BATEMAN
QUARTER MASTER BARENT ROSEBOOM
QUARTER MASTER BARENT TEN EYCK
PAY MASTER ISAAC PARIS
SURGEON WILLIAM PETRIE

CAPT. LOTHROP ALLEN
" ISAAC BOGERT
" JOSHUA DRAKE
" JOSEPH HARRISON
" JONATHAN LAWRENCE, JR.
" GERRITT PUTNAM
" WALTER VROOMAN
LIEUT. ALBERTUS BECKER
" THOMAS BRADSHAW
" EZRA BUELL
" JOHN DUNHAM
" CORNELIUS ECKERSON
LIEUT. JOSEPH HARPER
" RICHARD LAWRENCE
" GEORGE PASSAGE
" OTHNIEL PHILIPS
" MATTHEW POTAN
" VICTOR PUTNAM
" SETH SHERWOOD
" PETER B. TEN BROECK
" PETER VAN BERGEN
" SOLOMON WOODWORTH
" JAMES YULE (YUYLE)

ADDITIONAL NAME ON STATE TREASURER'S PAY BOOK
ENSIGN THOMAS BOYCE

ENLISTED MEN

Acker George
Ackerman John
Ackervon George
Allen Henry
Allis John
Allison Samuel
Ambler Nathaniel
Ansom James
Archey Annanis
Arsha Annanias
Atwood Jonathan
Aylworth Isaac (see Elsworth)
Babark John
Babcock John
Babcock Nehemiah
Babick Nighimie
Ballard Benoni
Banker James
Barnes Samuel
Barns Nathaniel
Barred Peter
Barrington Lewis
Barry William
Baum Frederick
Bell Matthew
Bellinger Christian
Benedick Elias
Benidick Oliver
Bernom Levi
Berry William
Bertley Joseph (see Bartlett)
Bicker Henry
Billings Increse
Billins Ineris
Blamely William
Bogardus James
Bollman John
Bollon Alexander
Bolton Alexander
Bolton John
Bolton Samuel
Boolman John
Bosliver Paul
Boste Henry Julius
Bowdish John
Bowen Timothy
Brannon Abraham
Branon Abraham (see Brandon)
Brockway Gideon
Brower Eldrick
Buckley Andrew
Burchard Nathaniel (see Burcher)
Burgess Stephen
Burhans Therck
Burley Elijah
Bursey Elijah (see Bussey)
Burst Jacob
Burst Jacob I.
Bush Henry
Bush John
Bushanie Carrick
Buzzie Jonathan
Caine Thomas
Ceaton Isaac
Camp Asa
Campbell John
Care Teunis
Carker Jacob
Carpenter Thomas
Carpner Thomas
Carson William
Carter John
Carter William
Carty Solomon (see Curtis)
Chapman Samuel
Chapman Edward
Chatfield Cornelius
Christman John
Clark John
Clark Samuel
Cleveland Samuel
Clemments Philip
Cole John
Coleman Andrew

Collins James
Collins William
Coltman William
Colver Joseph
Conklin John
Conklin Joseph (see Josiah)
Connore James
Cooper Elijah
Cooper Henry
Cooper John
Coplant Samuel Sun
Coplin Samuel
Cornelius John
Cost Martin
Crim Henry
Crisman John
Cross Daniel
Cross John
Cross Ruben
Culley Matthew
Cummings Josiah
Cuper Henry
Darling John
Darrow Jedidiah
Davy Adam
Day Aaron
Day Jonathan
Day Lewis
Debie Adam
De Graff Jesse
De Groff Jesse
De Harsh Philip (see De Narsh)
De Lavign Francis (see Levine)
De Long John
Demott John
Deveraux Joseph
Dickson Robert
Dixon Robert
Dodge Andrew
Dratt John
Dunbar Robert
Dunham John
Dunn Phineas
Dunnim Charles (see Dunham)
Dunnivan Daniel
Dutcher Henry
Dygart Severinus
Dygerd Safrenes
Eastwood John
Ecker George
Eckler Leonard
Edwards William
Eightler John
Ekleman Jacob
Ellis John
Elson David (see Ellison)
Embler Nathaniel
Farnham Asa
Felter Peter
Fetter Peter
Fidler Godfrey
Fiedler Gottfried
Flamsted William
Flansburgh William
Fleming Asa
Folmer Christian
Frank Henry
Frase Isaac
Fuller Daniel
Gardinier Tunis
Garmen James
Gault Story
Gautt John (see Goart)
Germaine James
Ghospead Joseph
Gleson Joel
Golding Benjamin
Goff Oliver
Gooff Joseph
Graham John
Gray James
Green Ebenezar
Griffis James (see Griffen)
Hackman Thomas
Hadley Isaac
Hagedorn Samuel
Hammond Paul
Hanrillor Silas
Harper Archibald
Harrington John
Harris David
Harris Thomas
Harrow Robert (see Herring)
Hatch William
Haugudom Samuel
Hawkins Stephen
Heath Simeon
Helmes John
Hennion John
Henry Hugh
Hewitt James
Highly Seth
Hill Amos
Hilssinger John
Hoard David
Hogeboom Peter
Holiday Henry
Holmes John
Horsford Samuel
House Cornelius
Houser Henry
House Jesse
House Peter
Howel Jesse
Hoyer Peter
Hubbard William
Hubble Ethamour
Humphris John
Hunt David
Hursie Thomas
Hyer Peter
Hyser John
Ikler Johannis
Isden John
Jackson Lyman
Johnson Benjamin
Jones Isaac
Keeler Isiah
Kelley Elenezar
Kelly Henry
Ketchum Joel
Kidder Stephen
Killsey Ebenezer
Kiner William
King Ruben
Kisner William
Kittle Adam
Klein William
Knap James
Knapp Silas
Kronkheit John
Ladine John
Ladoo John
Larraby Elias
Lattimore Francis
Lewis James
Leahy William
Leak William
Leeson Joel
Lefoy Abraham
Lehigh William
Lent Herculas
Lepper Frederick
Lerner Philip
Lettimore Daniel
Levine Francis
Loff David
Long William
Lovejoy Andrew
Loyd William
Luner Philip
Lusk Jacob
Lusk Michael
Lusk William
Lyon Nathaniel
Magee John
Man James
Marks Jesse
Martin Robert
McCauley Charles
McCaulley Robert
McColm John
McMannis William
McNitt John
Mearanas Thomas
Menn James
Mervin Malkica
Middle Christian
Midler Christopher
Miller Jacobus
Miller James
Miller Zadoc
Mitchel Robert
Modlan James (see McClallen)
Monrose Jesse
Moon Matthew
Moran William
Moss Timon
Moss Simon
Murphy Timothy
Murray Nicholas
Murray Peter
Murray William
Myall Joseph
Myers David
Nestell George
Newkirk Jacob
Newcomb James
Newkerk John
Niles Nathan
Norton William
Nottingham Lewis
Oarchard Thomas
Omsted Aron
Orchard Edward
Order Peter V.
Ostrander Adam
Owens Elisha
Parker Robert
Patchin Samuel
Pease Abner
Perry David
Peters Simon
Peterson Peter
Phanton James
Phelps Ebenezer (see Philips)
Philips Jacobus
Philipse James
Phillips Isaac
Piearce John
Pitcher Godlip
Pool William
Porch Andrew
Post Cornelius
Potter Roland

Power Moses
Preston William
Price William
Prusnar Christian
Putnam David
Quant Frederick
Randell Joseph
Read Alphias
Reghmyre Johanis
Renex Andrew
Resacker John P.
Rice David
Rickert Jacob
Riley John
Riley Philip
Roberts Ezekiel
Roberts John
Robinson Jesse
Rockwell Simeon
Rockwell Symon
Romer James
Rose James
Rosliver Paul
Rowley Seth
Russell James
Sackett Benjamin
Sackett John
Sanlam Moses
Schoolcraft Johannis
Scot Benjamin
Scott Thomas
Scranton Merchan
Scribner John
Scutt Solomon, Junr.
Shall John
Secaur Jonas
Seger Evart
Servis John
Sharp Andrew
Sharp Peter
Shaver Adam
Shaw Henry
Shaw Jacob
Shay Malcom
Shepherd James
Sherror James
Sherwood James
Shutts Abraham
Simons James
Slils Amasa (see Stils)
Smith Garret
Smith John
Smith Joseph
Smith Nicholas
Smith Polly Carp
Speed George
Sprague Alexander
Stalker William
Stark Nathan
Starkweather Roger
Starring George
Start Nathan
Start William
Steel Thomas
Stenbergh Peter
Storm Thomas
Strong Robert
Stuart Oliver
Suard Jedediah
Sueldes Jacob (see Soultis)
Sweet James
Swett James
Tancill Daniel (see Densil)
Tanner Benjamin
Taylor Jasper
Tenner Gedion
Thomas Jacob
Thomas Peter
Thorn Zadok
Tice John
Trinker Gullup
Trull John
Truwax Isaac
Tuffs Zachariah
Valkenburgh Joghem
Valentine Alexander
Valentine Peter
Veader Peter
Virgen Abijah
Virgil Abijah
Vosburgh Peter
Van Benthuysen Mark
Van Camp Moses
Vandanburgh Daniel
Van der Bogart Johannis (see John)
Van Dusen Aron
Van Dyck Cornelius
Van Dyck Peter
Van Horn John
Van Houten John
Van Sickler Reynear
Van Wagoner Andrew
Van Yeveren Garret (see Van Ieveren)
Van Zickler Bynier
Ward Zadok
Warden Barnerd
Weed Phineas
Weed William
Wells James
Wertham Warren
Wheeler John
Wholebur John (see Willeber)
Williams Gilbert
Williamson John
Willis William
Wilmer John (see Willman)
Wilsiey James
Wilson William
Willson Silas
Wincel John (see Winshell)
Winchal Penctial
Winne Kelian
Witbeck Samuel
Woodworth Reuben
Wright Robert
Yat James (see Yeat)
Young Jeremiah
Young John
Zitser George

The Levies — (Continued).

COLONEL FREDERICK WEISSENFELS
MAJOR THOMAS DE WITT
MAJOR SAMUEL LOGAN
ADJUTANT PETER WELSH
QUARTER MASTER EDWARD CONNER
QUARTER MASTER EBENEZER MOTT
QUARTER MASTER PETER WELSH
PAY MASTER JOHN VAN DOZER
SURGEON HENRY BUCK
SURGEON PETER VAN DER LYN
SURGEON'S MATE JOHN YOUNG

CAPT. PRENTICE BOWEN
" HENRY BREWSTER, JR
" HENRY DODGE
" HENRY GOODWIN
" JOHN L. HARDENBURGH
" JOHN HORNBECK
" THOMAS HUNT
" GILBERT J. LIVINGSTON
" HENRY PAWLING
" DANIEL SHEPHARD
" ANDREW THOMPSON
" ABRAHAM WESTFALL
" ANDREW WHITE (PAY MASTER)
LIEUT. BUNSCHOTEN (PETER)
" CORNELIUS DU BOYS
LIEUT. JOHN ELLSWORTH
" FINCH GILDERSLEEVE
" JONATHAN T. JANSEN
" JAMES JOHNSON
" MCARTHUR
" JAMES MYER
" WILLIAM NOTTINGHAM
" JOHN OSTRANDER
" ALDERT ROOSA
" CHARLES STUART, JR.
" AZARIAH TUTHILL
" THEODORUS VAN WYCK
" JONAH WEEKS
" SAMUEL YOUNGS

ADDITIONAL NAMES ON STATE TREASURER'S PAY BOOKS

LIEUT. JOHN BARR
" JOHN FINCH
" GEORGE HARSON
LIEUT. JOHN PUNDERSON
" GEORGE P. WEISSENFELS

ENLISTED MEN

Ackerman Casparaus
Ackerman James
Adames Deliverance
Addams Major
Adsit Martin
Ager James
Aherd Jacob
Akard Jacob
Albeen Nathan
Aldridge Benjamin
Alexander Rufus
Aller John
Ambler Enos
Ambler Nathan
Anderson John
Annet Henry
Armstrong John
Austin Lockwood
Avery Nehemiah
Babcock Amos
Babcock John
Backer John
Bailey John
Bailey Samuel
Baker Jessy
Baker John
Baker Richard
Baker William
Balard Caleb
Baldwin Aaron
Baly Richart
Bardge Jonathan
Barlow Joseph
Barnes Gilliam
Barnes John
Barnet Nathaniel
Barns Glean
Barr Daniel
Barret John
Bartlet Haines
Bartlet Jacob
Bartley Jacob
Bassett Cesar
Bates Justus
Beard John
Becker John
Beekman Benjamin
Belknap Thomas
Benedict Azariah
Benedik Tom
Benjamin Cyrus
Bennet John
Berber Alisha
Berber Joseph
Beringer Jacob
Bernard Simon
Berringhas David
Berry Samuel
Besemer Michael
Bevier Andries
Bevier David
Bevier David, Junr.
Birch Josiah
"Black Walter" (colored)

Blanchard Justus
Blawvelt Cornelius
Bogardus Jacobus
Boice Hendrick
Bonker Solomon
Bowington John
Boyd Nathaniel
Boyles Walter
Brannon Reuben
"Brave Boy" (Colored)
Brennen Michael
Bresin John
Brewster Jesse
Brinck John
Broadhead Henry
Brooks George
Brower Aaron
Brower Cornelius
Brower George
Brower Henry
Brower Jeremiah
Brower William
Brown Deliverance (see Bebrown)
Brown Elisha
Brown James
Brown James H.
Brown Samuel
Brundage Sollimon
Brush David
Brush Isaiah
Buckingham William
Burges John
Burgess James
Burhans Jacob
Burr Daniel
Butts William
Byington David
Calkins Ely
Camber John
Camble Archibald (see Campbell)
Camble James
Cameron David
Campbell John
Canfield Ebenezer
Cannon Arnot
Carehart Jacob
Carhaday Nicholas
Carmer Samuel
Carnel Henry
Carner Andrew
Carpenter Barnard
Catterling Nathaniel
Cee Moses
Cepinosa Anthony
Chanders Isaac
Chard Hugh
Chrispell Abraham
Claerwater John
Clark Benjamin
Clark John
Close Henry
Close Peter
Cochran Samuel
Cohoon Heman
Cole Cornelius
Cole Reuben
Colegrove Francis
Collins John
Colwell Arthur
Conckling John
Conklin Jacob
Conkling Abraham
Conare William
Connolly John
Constable Gerret
Conway Michael
Cook Darius
Cook David
Cook Henry
Cook Job
Cook Nathan
Coon Peter
Cooper Gerrit
Coovert John
Cornelison Michael
Coulter John
Covert James
Cowings Isaac
Coxwell Francis
Crans Christopher
Crawford James
Creed Aston
Crissy William
Cropsy Henry
Crosby Ebenezer
Crosby Richard
Cross William
Cry John
Cummins Daniel
Cunningham Benjamin
Cuper Henry
Currie Elijah
Curtis Ezra
David John
Davis Nathan
Davis Samuel
Davis William
Dea Cass Thomas
Dealy Samuel
Dean Ebenezer
Dean James
Dean Reuben
Decker Cornelius
Deforege Reuben
DeGrove William
Degrushie Elias
Delaney Dennis
Delano Thomas
Delavan Daniel
De Lavigne Francis
Demick Samuel
Deo Hugh
Derbishire Daniel
Derbishire James
Derbyshire David
Derly Philip
Devie Isaac
Devoo Anthony
De Witt Jacob
De Witt John L.
De Witt Peter, Junr.
De Witt William
Dimmuck Samuel
Dobbins Hugh
Dodge Daniel
Dolleway Andrew
Dolittle Hopkins
Donnovan Daniel
Doty Elias
Douglass James
Downy John
Doxy Stephen
Draper John
Drew Oliver
Du Bois Cornelius
Dubois John
Dubois Martin
Dubois Matthew
Duley Philip
Dumond Cornelius
Dunlap Thomas
Durling Benjamin
Dutcher Abraham
Dutcher David
Dutcher Henry
Dusenbury William
Dyer James
Eager James
Edwards John
Eigener Jacobus
Elliot Christopher
Elliott Thomas
Ellis Christopher
Ellison Jeremiah
Elmendorph Petrus
Elsworth John
English George
Ennest William
Ennis Peter
Ferdon Samuel
Ferguson Enos
Ferguson Jeremiah
Ferris Benjamin
Finch Elnathan
Finch Philip
Fontaman Frederick
Forgerson Gilbert
Forsbag John
Fowler George
Fowler Nehemiah
France Adam
Franklin Nathaniel
Furman Samuel
Gardinier James
Gardenir George
Garrison Abraham
Garison Jacob
Garrison John
Garrison Joseph
Garrison Peter
Garvey Francis
Gay John
German James
Gerrison Jacob
Gifford John
Gildersleeve Joseph
Gilford Benjamin
Gillespey James
Graham John
Griffin John
Glasby David
Graham Jacobus
Graham James
Gray Jonathan
Green Isaac
Green Jehial
Green John
Green Joseph
Green Peter
Green Samuel
Gunsalon Samuel
Hagaman Nicholas
Hager William
Haight Joseph
Hait Minnah
Hall Benjamin
Hall Boston
Hall Robert
Halleet William
Hallet Jeffery
Halley Robin
Halmer James
Hammel Nathaniel
Hanfield David
Hanna James D.
Hanmore David
Hansen William
Hardenbergh Cornelius
Hardifant Zur
Harington Alexander

Harris Squire
Harris Thomas
Hatch Solomon
Hay Nathaniel
Heevens Justice
Hennicum Elisha
Herdenbergh Lewis
Hergoman Nicholas
Herrick Elijah
Herrick Jonathan
Hicks John
Hines James
Hodge Israel
Hoghtaling William
Holly William
Holmes Anthony
Holmes James
Holt William
Holtslandery Adam
Homan John
Homan Joshua
Hood John
Horton Thomas
Hosier Thomas
Hoskier Lawrence
House Seth
Howe Timothy
Hoyt Elijah
Hubbard Prince
Hubbil Richard
Hubbill Gershom
Hughan John
Hunt Aaron
Hunter Ebenezer
Huskins Asel
Hutchins Jacob
Hyme Cornelius
Ingerson John
Ingraham Justus
Irwin James
Ives Grigery
Jackson James
Jameson Thomas
Jane John
Jansen Thomas
Jansen Thomas, Junr.
Jarvis Francis
Jecocks Gershom
Jenkins Ezekiel
Jennings Stephen
Jersey Richard
Johnson Josiah
Johnson Richard
Johnson Thomas
Jones Isaac
Jonson Daniel
June Abraham
June John

Jursey Richard
Keator Gideon
Keeler John
Kelly Dinnis
Kelly Isaac
Kelly Sylvanus
Kelsey John
Keslor Peter
Kip Igness
Kitcher John
Knapp Shadrick
Koch John Henry
Lake Joshua
Lamphier John
Lane Daniel
Lane Jeremiah
Lane Joshua
Lane Samuel
Lane William
Lassing George
Lattimore Roger
Laurence Alexander
Lawrence Samuel
Lawson Lawrence
Lawyer Adam
Lee Jonathan
Legg Samuel
Lenared Robert
Lent Jacob
Le Roy Henry
Letts David
Lewes Galop
Linsey States
Liskum Samuel
Litts John
Lloyd Elisha
Lockwood John
Lockwood Moses
Loden Pettit
Loder Pettit
Lossing Matthew
Low John
Lucky Robert
Luddington William
Lukky Jeffy
Lyke Hendrick
Matthews Peter
Middagh Daniel
Midgley Joseph
Miller Alexander
Miller George
Miller Peter
Miller Samuel
Miller William
Milligan Robert
Mingas David
Minthorn Nathaniel
Mires William

Monall James
Montanye Peter
Moore Martin
Moore Thomas
Moore William
Mopps Frederick
Morgan Seth
Morris William
Morse Rufus
Mosher Cornelius
Moss Charlie
Murdough Lackey
Murphy Thomas
Mutz Johannes
Myer David
Myer Henry
Myer William
Myers David
Mahoney James
Maines Charles
Mapes Henry
Mapes Henry, Junr.
Marrigut Jacob
Marshall Henry
Martin Thomas
Masstin Thomas
McCann Cornelius
McCay John
McClarning John
McClintock John
McCluer William
McCormick James
McCoy Daniel
McCraney William
McDaniel Daniel
McDonald James
McDugle Alexander
McEuen Cornelius
McHurter James
McKee Thomas
McKenzie Alexander
McLaning John
McMunn William
McNameo William
McSweeney Daniel
Mead Marshel
Meed Lewis
Nap Joseph (see Knap)
Neirn James
Nelson Absalom
Nelson James
Newkirk Isaac
Newman William
Nicmeyer John Henry
Noble Lyman
Nol Christian
Northrup Eli
O'Bradley Daniel

Odell Jonathan
Odle Richard
O'Ferrol Michael
Ogden Joseph
Olcutt Isaac
Oostorhout Aldert
Oosterhoudt Hendricus
Oosterhoudt Tounis
Osterhout Jonathan
Otterman James
Outerman James
Owens Amasa
Owen John D.
Owens Thaddeus
Paddock Daniel
Palmer Henry
Palmer Solomon
Parish Ephraim
Parve Jonathan
Patterson James
Pawn Chance
Pearce Jonathan
Pembrook William
Penny John
Parigo Uzal
Perry John
Perry Samuel
Phillips Isaac
Phillips James
Pine Timothy
Plough Henry, Junr.
Plugh Hendrick
Plumley Jonathan
Polden William
Pond Chance
Post Martin, Junr.
Pots Martin, Junr.
Prince Richard
Prose Abraham
Ranson Barezillia
Ransom James
Reeve Daniel
Rennals John
Renshout John
Reynolds Stephen
Rice Isaac
Rice John
Richard Nathaniel
Richards Ezra
Richmond John
Riddle John
Rile James
Rinders James
Rinders John
Roach William
Robb Aaron
Robbins Lewis
Roberson Lewes

Roberts James
Robinson Lewis
Robison James
Rock William
Rockwell Enos
Roff Christopher
Rogers Joseph
Rogers William
Romer Aaron
Rosa Abraham
Rosa Dirck
Rowley Subil
Rumsey Jonas
Runo Simon
Sampson George
Schoonmaker Hezekiah
Schoonmaker Isaac
Schoonmaker Peter
Schut Christian
Scofield Henry
Scott Archibald
Shadler John
Shaw Joshua
Shearer Robert
Sheldon William
Shepherd Benjamin
Sherwood Moses
Shippard Jonathan
Shoecraft John
Shoefelt John
Shoffer John
Shuts Frederick
Sidney James
Sidway James
Skeldin William
Sleight Abraham
Sleight John
Slouter William
Slover Isaac
Sluyter Cornelius
Sluyter Daniel
Smith Alpheus
Smith Doctor
Smith Isaac
Smith James
Smith John
Smith Lemuel
Smith Peter
Smith Thomas
Smith Thomas, Junr.
Smith William
Smith Zacharias
Smyth Thomas
Snedeker James
Sneyder John
Snider John
Snoden Francis
Sooloy Coonradt
Southard Henry
Southerland Gurline
Sparks George
Sparks Robert
Spicer Jeremiah
Spaningbergh Jacob
Spragge Benjamin
Spraig John
Squier Ichabod
Stafford Richard
Starr Aaron
Stars Moses
Steenbergh Abraham
Stenebrander David
Stephens Justice
Stinard Drake
Stinard Oglisbery D.
Stirdavan Isaack
Stonebrander David
Strong Joel
Strong Joseph
Sturges Abraham
Sullivan Michael
Suthard Henry
Sutharland Gurline
Sutherland Israel
Swartwout Samuel
Swezey Joseph
Tailor Jeremiah
Tankus Isaac
Tappen Matthew
Taylor Ebenezer
Teater John
Ter Bush William
Terilleger William
Terry Benjamin
Terwilleger Cornelius
Terwilliger Josiah
Terwilliger Tunes
Thompson Jack or Swartwout Jack (Colored)
Tobius John
Trim Ezra
Truesdell Jesse, Junr.
Trumbull James
Trusdell Thomas
Turner Jacob
Tuttel John
Tuttle Daniel
Vael Joseph
Vail John
Veal John
Vernooy Abraham
Vinegar Samuel
Vines Jeremiah
Vredenburgh Thomas
Van Amber Joseph
Van Ass Solomon
Van Cleef Isaac
Van Cleift Gerritt
Van Cleift Joseph
Vandenbogard Mindard
Van De Bogart James
Vendervort John
Van De Waters Adolph
Van De Waters Harmanus
Van De Werken Martin
Van Fleet Joshauay
Van Kleeck Michael
Van Kleek George
Van Kleek James
Vannaker Nathaniel
Van Nostrandt John
Van Scoy Jonething
Van Scoy Samuel
Van Steenbergh Benjamin
Van Steenburgh Peter
Van Stervelt John
Van Stienbergh John
Vantasel Isaac
Van Waggoner Garret
Van Zile Abraham
Wade Joseph
Waddle Robert
Waldron Joseph
Waldron William
Wallace John
Ward Jesiass
Ward Joshua
Ward Josiah
Wardell Eliakim
Warner Thomas
Warren Mordica
Waterbury James
Way John
Webb Joseph
Webb William
Weed Charles
Weed John
Weeks James
Weelar John
Weissmiler Jeremiah
Wells Joseph
Wells Samuel
Westervelt John
Westfalls Levi
Whigham Robert
Whitaker Edward
White John
White Solomon (Colored)
Whitlock Thaddeus
Whitney David
Wickson David
Wiggins William
Wilde Thomas
Wilkelow Jacob
Wilkison Thomas
Willbur Gideon
William Elias
Williams Abraham
Williams Daniel
Williams Uriah
Willson Andrew
Willson William
Winans John
Winfield Abram
Winfield Jacob
Winfield Simon
Wird John
Wixson John
Woldorf Henry
Wolf Simon
Wollf John
Wood Alexander
Wood Allickzander
Wood Vincent
Worden George
Wreick James
Wyatt Joseph
Wynkoop Cornelius
Young John
Yuall John
Yune Abraham

The Levies—(Continued).

COLONEL WILLIAM MALCOLM

MAJOR ELIAS VAN BUNSCHOTEN

ADJUTANT JOSEPH HASBROUCK, JR.

ADJUTANT ISAAC REQUA

QUARTER MASTER ALEXANDER STEWART

SURGEON'S MATE PETER OSBORN

CAPT. JAMES BLAKSLEE
" ELIJAH BOSTWICK
" MOSES CANTINE
" DANIEL DELAVAN
" JOSHUA DRAKE
" JACOB LANSING
" JONATHAN LAWRENCE, JR.
" GILBERT J. LIVINGSTON
" MAGEE
" MILLER
" CHRISTOPHER MULLER
" THOMAS MCKINSTRY
" ADIEL SHERWOOD
LIEUT. CORNELIUS ACKERSON
" CORNELIUS ADRIANCE
" CORNELIUS BALDWIN
LIEUT. JOHN BOLTON
" ELIAS DELONG
" ZACHARIAH GIBSON
" JOSEPH JOY
" RICHARD LAWRENCE
" JOHN I. LOW
" JEREMIAH MULLER
" WILLIAM NOTTINGHAM
" JOHN OSTRANDER
" JOSEPH REQUA
" JONAS RICE
" EZEKIEL ROBERTS
" DANIEL SACKETT
" PETER B. TEN BROECK
" SAMUEL UTLEY

ADDITIONAL NAME ON STATE TREASURER'S PAY BOOKS:

LIEUT. JACOB VERMILIA

ENLISTED MEN

Abrams John
Acker Francis
Ackerman John
Adair William
Adams Gilbert
Allen David
Allen James
Allen Samuel
Amberman Aurt
Anderson John
Andrews John
Andries Jacob
Anson James
Anthony Richard
Antis William
Archer James
Arnol William
Ausgood Nathaniel
Ayres Phelix
Ayres Thomas
Babcock Benjamin
Bacon James
Badcock David
Bailey Moses
Bailey Timothy
Baily Richard
Baker Bartholomew
Baker Conrad
Baker John
Baker Judah
Baker Thomas
Ball John
Barber William
Barkman John
Barnes Jacob
Barnet Alexander
Barret William
Bartley Abraham
Beatly Abram
Beckes Elijah
Beebe Constant
Beekman Henry
Beekman John
Bell John
Bell Robert
Bell William
Benjamin Daniel
Bonnet Benjamin
Bennett William
Benson John
Bently Joseph
Berger Jacob
Berges Wilhelmes
Biles George
Black Henry
Black Jack
Black Robert
Blackman Joel
Blakesley James
Blakslee Nathaniel
Blawvelt Cornelius
Blawvelt Isaac
Blowers Samuel
Bogart Cornelius
Bogert Jacob
Boing Peleg
Bont Ephriam
Bradner Benoni
Briggs Caspares
Brinck Peter
Brinck Solomon
Broadstreat John
Brooks Jeremiah
Brower Eldrick
Brown Jeremiah
Brown John
Brown Lackey
Brown Malchi
Brown Samuel
Brown William
Buel Siras
Bulice Peter
Bur Daniel
Burcham Henry
Burdick Gideon
Burgant Lambert
Burgarth Lambert
Burgess Stephen
Burhans Abraham
Burlison Fearnot
Burns William
Burris Charles
But Daniel
Butler Joseph
Cace Zenes (see Case)
Cadmen Joseph

Campbell John
Campbell Robert
Canton David
Carner Andries
Carningham John
Carr James
Case William
Cass William
Casswell David
Cawline Joseph
Chamberlain Gordon
Chase Robert
Chism Peter
Chithster Nathan
Christ Abraham
Church James
Clark Samuel
Clearwater Matthew
Clow John Gotlip (see Clowes)
Cloyde Daniel
Clute John B.
Coal Moses
Codmer Ishmael
Codner George
Codney William
Cohoone Elexander
Coldwell John
Cole Henry
Coleman James
Compton David
Concklin Nathan
Condradt Henry
Conklin Henry
Conklin John
Conklin Matthias
Conner William
Cook Zebulon
Cool Peter
Cooper Ede
Cooper Henry
Cooper John
Cordigal Abraham
Cordman Joseph
Cornelius John
Cornwell William
Cotterell Abis
Cowden John
Cowen William
Crafford Thomas
Crane James
Craven John
Crist Christian
Crist Daniel
Crist Matthew
Crou Peter
Cry John
Cudberth Benjamin
Cunningham John
Curington Enough
Curniston David
Curtus Naniad (see Raniad)
Dains Abraham
Daley Samuel
Darling Samuel
Darrow Amarias
Darrs Jeptha
Davies Jeptha
Davis John
Davis Joseph
Davis William
Davison Barnabas
Daws Jeptha
Day Aron
Dayton John
Decker Francis
De Lancy Abraham
Delaney Abraham
Delimarter Benjamin
Demsey Thomas
Dennis John
Deveraux Joseph
Dickison Judathan
Dinnings Ezra
Dixon Andrew
Dixon Thomas
Dodge Andrew
Dolittle Timothy
Doty Isaac
Doty Shadewick
Dubois David
Dubois Jacob
Ducy Samuel
Dunbar Amos
Dunham Samuel
Dunning David
Durgey Fidias
Dykman William
Earls Daniel
Edwards Thomas
Eivs Phelise
Elder Joseph
Ellison James
Ellison Jeremiah
Ellison Samuel
Ellison Thomas
Engals George
Evans Joseph
Everitt Jacob
Everitt John
Felter Peter
Fish Abner
Fish William
Fitch Elisha
Fleeman Solomon
Flemin Forton (see Porten, Fortune)
Flin Thomas
Fogus Christian
Foot Simeon
Foster John
Foster Jonathan
Francis John
Freel Peter
French John
French Samuel
Fuller Benjamin
Funck Christian
Funck Jacob
Gage Alden
Gardiner Isaac
Gardiner Samuel
Garrison Joseph
Gates Samuel
Gault Alexander
Gearvey Francis
Gibbs David
Gibbs Isaac
Gifford Joseph
Gilberts Jesper
Giles Samuel
Gill William
Gilson Zachariah
Goff Boswell
Gold Elijah
Goodhue Joseph
Goold Pearl
Gernea Benjamin
Goss Oliver
Gould Jesse
Gould William
Graft Philip
Graham William
Graves Josiah
Green James
Green John
Greer Joseph
Grenie Benjamin
Griffen Joseph
Griffin Ebenezer
Griffin Joseph
Griswold David
Guy John
Guy Timothy
Hadley Isaac
Hadley Joseph
Hagaman Nicholas
Hall Christian
Hall William
Halleck Jeffrey
Hanmore Jabis
Hanton Rufus
Harden Joseph
Harrington John
Harris Eliphalet
Harris William
Havens Thomas
Hay William
Hayet Elias
Hazard Joshua
Head Joseph
Heath Winslow
Heathway Jon'a
Heirs Phelix
Hender Joseph
Henderson Alexander
Hendrickson John
Hennion John
Henry Robert
Herrick Joseph
Herris Henry (see Harris)
Herron Eliot
High William
Hobart Joseph
Hochtaling John
Hodge Daniel
Hodge John
Hodgeson George
Hoghtaling John
Hoghtaling Tennis
Hollister Smith
Hollobard Jesse
Holmes Jeddediah
Homer Joshua
Hopkins Robert
Horton Jeremiah
Horton Samuel
House Cornelius
Hover Philex
Howard Enos
Howes Seth (see House)
Hubberd Joseph
Hudler Solomon
Hudson Richard
Hugan John
Humphrey Emry
Hunt Daniel
Hunter Moses
Hutt John
Huyck Nicholas
Hyatt Elias
Hyms Frederick
Irvine Henry
Jackson John
Jacobie Bastian
Jermin James
Jimison Thomas
Johnson John
Johnson Peter
Jones Abraham
Jones Isaac

Jones Jonas
Jones Joseph
Jones William
Joy Amos
June Abraham
Kent Thomas
King Jacob
King John
Knap Benjamin
Knap Ephraim
Koomer Aaron
Krum Benjamin
La faver Noah
Landus Ebenezer
Langdon Benjamin
Lathrop Ebenezer
Lathrop Lebbus
Lawrence George
Lawson Matthew
Lee Jonathan
Leeman Archibald
Lefoy Abraham
Leggitt Lue
Lemon Archabald
Lemon John
Leroy Daniel
Leroy Robert
Letts Abraham
Lewis Isaac
Lewis James
Linerd Henry
Lint Elias
Little Stephen
Little William
Litts Abraham
Livingston Richard
Lothrop Lebious
Luckey James
Lucks Johannis
Luddington Elisha
Luff Nicholas
Luicks Abraham
Luick Andrew
Luicks Johannis
Lull Nathen
Lummes Andrew
Lyons Amaziah
Maaterstock John
Maclos William
Magee John
Magey Peter
Mandovel Mathew
Mapes Henry
Mapes James
Marsh Samuel
Martin Thomas
Masters William
Maybee Peter

Mead Eli
Mead Isaac
Meebe Peter
Mege Peter
Merrit Abraham
Merrit Amos
Merrit Ebenezer
Millard Nathaniel
Miller Amos
Miller Henry
Miller John
Millet Jonathan
Milor Samuel
Milspaugh Cristian
Mires John
Montanye John
Montonya John
Moor John
Moore Joseph
Mores Hezekiah
Morgan David
Morris Duncan
Morris Ebenezer
Morrison Adward
Morrison Duncan
Morrison Hugh
Morrison Jonathan
Moser Joseph
Moses Joseph
Moss Isaac
Mott Jacob
Mount Samuel
Muller Amos
Murphy Thomas
Mynderse Abraham
Mynderse Harman
McCarty Hugh
McCoy James
McCoy John
McDaniel Cornelius
McDonold Edward
McEune Cornelius
McFarling Andrew
McGee James
McInsbry Thomas
McKee Thomas
McNutt Alexander
McPherson Daniel
McRobert John
McWilliams James
Nelson Absolom
Newkirk Mindert
Nichols Jonas
Nickles William
Nimham Isaac
Notingham Thomas
Nowe Lewis
Odle Jonathan

Onderdonk Isaac
Onderdonk Thomas
Osterhout Henry
Ostrander Henry
Ostrander John
Overpaw John
Ovett Isaac
Palmer John
Pareols Peter
Parks Daniel
Parks Oliver
Paroch Peter
Parsons Peter
Partial John
Patterson Asay
Peets Michel
Penfield Isaac
Penil Moses
Perkney Lewis
Persell Peter
Perslow Henry
Phelps Elijah
Philip David
Philips David
Pike Jarvis
Philhama Jurden
Pinfield Isaac
Pinkne Lewis
Pitt Ephraim
Plough Henry
Pollard David
Pool William
Porch Andrew
Prince Kimbell
Quackenbos James
Radly Jacob
Radly John
Rannels Benjamin
Ray Raysal
Read Frederick
Read Leonard
Reed Frederick
Reed Leonard
Reeves Nathaniel
Ressman Henry
Rice Jonas
Rice Samuel
Rice Seth
Richmond Josiah
Rider William
Rightenbergh Addam
Rines John
Rindas John
Rinders John
Ripinbalk Adam
Riser Isaac
Rises John
Robberts John W.

Robert John M.
Robertson James
Robins Daniel
Robinson Charles
Robinson Ezra
Robinson Jesse
Robinson Peter
Robison Hector
Rogen Michael
Roger Michael
Rogers Daniel
Rogers Michael
Rogers Rubin
Romer Aaron
Roose James
Rosa Abraham
Rosa John
Rose James
Rosman Henery
Rowland John
Rowley Jabish
Rumsey Jesse
Runnels Benjamin
Runnels John
Runnels Silas
Rynarde John
Rynder James
Rynders Jacob
Safford Jonathan
Salbury Gedion
Saterly Joseph
Scanlon Matthias
Schanklin Jeremiah
Schoolcraft Peter
Schoonhover Thomas
Schoonmaker Edward
Scofield Abner
Scott Alexander
Scott John
Scott William
Scutt Solomon
Seabree John
Seabury John, Junr.
Sears Alliten
Sears John
Sebrew John
Seward John
Sharp John
Sharp John, Jr.
Shaver Adam
Shaw Henry
Shell Adam
Sherwood Daniel
Sheut John
Shower Adam
Shulp John
Shurt John
Shurts John

Simmons John (see Seamons)
Simmons Reuben
Simpson Robert
Skinner John
Slouter Willam
Slut John
Sluyter Cornelius
Smally Rubin
Smith Daniel
Smith Garret
Smith Henry
Smith James
Smith John
Smith Prusia
Smith Samuel
Smith Solomon
Snyder William
Snyder Willis
Spananburgh Jacob
Speed Henry
Spreag John
Stanton Benjamin
Stanton Rufus
Starns William
Stevens David
Stevens Elijah
Stevens Solomon
Stevens Stephen
Stevens William
Steward John
Steward Solomon
Stewart Samuel
Still Robert
Stocom William
Stoddard John
Stone Selvester
Stoneburner David
Stoner Henry
Stopplebean Peter
Storms Isaac
Strader Jost
Sutling Ambres
Swart Benjamin
Swart William
Taulmon Jacob
Taulman Peter
Taulman William
Taylor James
Teil Andrew
Terneure James
Terry Benjamin
Thomas Caleb
Thomas Ephraim
Tice John
Tigner Jonathan
Tirl Andrew
Tornure James
Trout Adam
Valentine Peter
Valleau Stephen
Viele Johanes
Vredenburgh Abraham
Van Benschoten Harman
Van Bura George
Van Buren George
Van Burgh John (see Vandeburgh)
Van Bury George
Van Dalsen James
Van Dalson John
Vandenburgh Abraham
Van Derbelt Dirk
Van Houton Abraham
Van Houten John
Vanatten Aron
Van Neder Henry
Van Noder Peter
Van Schaick Roger
Van Sicklen Cornelius
Van Sickler Cornelius
Van Stenbergh John
Van Tassel Cornelius
Van Tuye John
Van Urder Hendrick
Van Urder Peter
Van Valer James
Van Valkenburgh Gershom
Van Valkenburg Thomas
Van Valkenburgh Harma
Van Voarhast John
Vanzandt John
Walsworth Gilbert
Ward Josiah
Ward Moses
Warner Ebenezer
Warren Benjamin
Way John
Webb Joseph
Webers John
Webster Milo
Welds Calven
Well Joshua
Wells James
Wentworth James
Westervelt Casparus
Whitcom John
Whitcomb Ezra
White William
Willard Abel
Williams Gilbert
Williams Job
Williams Nathan
Willis William
Wilson John
Wilthouse Aaron
Wilthouse John
Witney David
Wixon David
Wood Isaac
Wood Jacob
Wood James
Wood John
Wood Moses
Wood Robert
Wood Timothy
Woodard Ephraim
Wooding Rubin
Woodward Ephraim
Woolcut Justis
Yorus Benjamin
Younge George

The Levies—(Continued).

COLONEL LEWIS DUBOIS
LIEUTENANT COLONEL BRINTON PAINE
MAJOR JAMES M. HUGHES
ADJUTANT HUGH McCONNELL
QUARTER MASTER JOHN BRADNER
PAY MASTER DANIEL GANO (CAPT.)
SURGEON HENRY BUCK
SURGEON'S MATE SAMUEL ALLEN

CAPT. JOHN BRADBICK
" JOHN BURNETT
" COLBE CHAMBERLAIN
" MARK DE MONT
" HENRY DODGE
" BENJAMIN DUBOIS
" JOHN M. FOGHT
" THOMAS LEE
" JOHN McBRIDE
" THOMAS McKINSTRY
" McQUOW
" JOHN ROLB

CAPT. BENJAMIN STEVENSON
LIEUT. JAMES BETTS
" JACOB BOCKEE
" JAMES BUTTERFIELD
" JOHN COPPERNOLL
" ADAM HELMER
" JAMES OAKLEY
" JACOB PECK
" JAMES PECK
" JOHN VANDERBURGH
" SIMON J. VROOMAN
" WILLIAM WALLACE

ADDITIONAL NAMES ON STATE TREASURER'S PAY BOOK.

LIEUT. EDMUND DUVALL
LIEUT. HENRY VANDERBURGH

ENLISTED MEN

Adam Peter
Adams Peter
Adriance Theodorus
Adsit Benjamin
Akins Stephen
Allen Reuben
Allen Samuel
Allison Isaac
Arnot Cornelius
Armstrong George
Bader Francis
Bailey Daniel
Bairmore Michael
Baker William
Barch Rudolf
Barr John
Beater Jacob
Beckwith David
Bellinger Adam P.
Benjamin Cyrus
Benjamin Jonathan
Bennet Jeremiah
Bishop John
Biskney Francis
Bissell John
Blaesdell Levi
Bloomerone Abraham
Bocrum William
Bogardus Lewis
Bogart Gilbert
Bouman Abraham
Bradner John
Brooks George
Brooks William
Brown Hezekiah
Brown Jonathan
Brown Noah, Junr.
Brown Samuel
Buchiet John
Bump Sathuel
Burch Hezekiah
Burch Iaiah
Burch Jesse
Burling Benjamin
Burlington Joel
Burton Gilbert
Campbell Robertson
Campbell William
Canfield James
Careley John
Carman John
Carney Barnabas
Carter Jabez
Carvender Joseph
Cashin William
Chase Benjamin
Church Jonathan
Churchill James
Clapsadle William
Clark William
Claver Nehemiah
Cleland William
Cline Jacob
Cole John
Concklin Samuel
Connell Benjamin
Cook Solomon
Cosler Joseph
Cowley Jonathan
Crook Coonrod
Crosby Reuben
Crover George
Culver Daniel
Cummins Jacob
Cummins John
Curtis James
Cutler Nathaniel
Cyeserton Manassa
Dalery Jeremiah
Darley Robert
Darling Benjamin
Davis Benjamin
Davison Alverson
Dealeway Jeremiah
Decker Jacob
Demoutt John
Dermott James
Dewel Benjamin
Dewel Emanuel
Dewit William
Drake Joshua
Dunbar William
Durgen Pattrick
Dymoot Dalrick
Edee Joshua
Edesell Joseph
Engle George
Engle William
English Robert
Etch Jacob
Evans Amos
Evans William
Faden John
Felling Philip
Ferguson William
Fetterly John
Forbus Henry
Fowler Daniel
Fox George
Franck Henrich
Freeman Elijah
Fuller Daniel

T. C. Leutze, photo. R. L. Adams, artist.

FORT HUNTER,

(ERECTED IN 1712)

Showing Queen Anne's Chapel in center and parsonage at extreme left.

Fullmore Christopher
Gale John
Galsschus Claus
Garlinghouse John
Garrit Benjamin
Ginson Richard
Graham George
Grant Peter
Green Caleb
Green Isaac
Griffin John
Hall Robert
Hammill Nathaniel
Hamilton James
Handley Mathew
Hans James
Hanson Arthur
Harris Joshua
Harrits Jonathan
Hart James
Hartman Adam
Hatch Joseph
Hatch Oliver
Hawk Frederick
Head Briton
Heberd Prime
Helmer Adam
Hess George
Hester Lawrence
Hewitt Joseph
Hewitt Samuel
Higney Joseph
Hill Nathaniel
Hills John
Hinckley Elkanah
Hock Rudolph
Hoff John
Holdren Daniel
Holenbeck Jacob
Holmes Daniel
Hoover Isaac
Horton William
Hothalin James
How John
Howard William
Howell Josiah
Hubberd Reuben
Hunter James
Irwin Robert
Jewit Alpheus
Johnson John
Johnson Samuel
Johnston William
Jones Richard
Jost
Lake John
Lamphier John
Lane William
Lansing Everent W.
Lappius Daniel
Laughlin James
Letts David
Lewis John
Lowery John
Lua William
Lutts Coonrod
Martin Archibald
Martin Thomas
Massy Andrew
Mead Israel
Mercy Andrew
Miles Benjamin
Millage Thomas
Millet Felix
Milligan Robert
Mills John
Miluan Robert
Moores Thomas
Morehouse Reuben
Morehouse Thomas
Morris John
Morse Josiah
Mosher Abner
Motts Joseph
Myer Lewis
Myer Peter
Myers Abraham
Myers John
Myers Lodewick
McClockin Joseph
McColley Hugh
McConnil Hugh
McCowan Duncan
McEwen Duncan
McGown Robert
McMaster James
McRoy Epraim
McWhorton James
McWhorter Thomas
Nostrandt George
Oakman Presoine
Omsted Gideon
Oosterhoudt Gysbrt
Overbagh Jeremiah
Owen Solomon
Owens Isaac
Panter Jacob
Parmerton Abijah
Parshal James
Pease Asa
Pelham Elisha
Pellenger Adam
Pelham Eli
Perry David
Phillips Samuel
Pipar Elder
Prat William
Price Timothy
Purdy Josiah
Ralphin George
Randle Matthias
Relyea John
Reynolds Shubal
Reynolds Stephen
Richard Edward
Richardson William
Rickman Abraham
Robertson Nathaniel
Robins Elijah
Rock William
Roes John
Rogers Moses
Rood Ezra
Rosa Adert
Ross William
Russel Rowlins
Salisbury Lawrence
Salkill Isaac
Scheit Peter
Schonover Benjamin
Schonover James
Scott James
Scribner Aaron
Scribner Jonathan
Scribner Zadock
Seabury Cornelius
Sears Selah
Seeley John
Seloover Isaac
Sessee Abraham
Shail Peter
Shaw Ezra
Silsby David
Simon John
Simpson Petter
Sits John
Slight Henry
Smith James
Smith John
Smith Joseph
Smith Ludlow
Smith Richard
Smith Thomas
Smith William
Snyder Cornelius
Soper Timothy
Spicer Jeremiah
Spragge Benjamin
Sprague Gideon
Stagg John
Stark Henry
Starks John
Stighter Adam
Stone Daniel
Stunter Ebenezer
Sufelt Christopher
Sutherland William
Targasor Benjamin
Taylor Jeremiah
Taylor Stephen
Taylor William
Terry Usbany
Tees John
Terwillegar Tunis
Terwilliger Abraham, Jr.
Thomas Richard
Thompson William
Thorington Thomas
Thorn Jacob
Tilwillegar James
Tingue John
Tippet Thomas
Titus Phillip
Totten Daniel
Twaghinans John
Vickery Ichabod
Von Netten James
Van Aulstine Derrick
Vandebogart John
Vanderworker Hermanus
Van De Water Adolph
Van Etten Jacobus
Van Every Jacob
Vansize Hanyost
Walbort Tobias
Walker John
Walsz Jacob
Walsz Kunrad
Weaver George
Webster Oliver
Wells David
Wells Gershom
Whaley Timothy
Wheeler Ira
White Nicholas
Willcox David
Williams Pompy
Wilkinson David
Wills Jesse
Winegar Samuel
Wood Job
Wood Solomon
Wood Timothy
Woolgert Joseph
Woolsee Sammon
Wright Edmund
Yongs Alexander
York Aaron
Young Henry
Young Richard
Young Zacharias

The Levies—(Continued.)

COLONEL MORRIS GRAHAM
LIEUTENANT COLONEL BENJAMIN BIRDSALL
LIEUTENANT COLONEL HENRY LIVINGSTON
MAJOR ANDREW HILL
MAJOR MELANCTON LLOYD WOOLSEY
ADJUTANT THEODORUS BAILEY
ADJUTANT JELLIS A. FONDA
ADJUTANT JOHN OSTRANDER
QUARTER MASTER DAVID HUNT
QUARTER MASTER EDEN HUNT
PAY MASTER JAMES MAGEE (CAPTAIN)
SURGEON PETER OSBORN

CAPT. ELIJAH BOSTWICK
" LEMUEL CONKLIN
" JOHN HERMANSEE
" SILAS HUESTED
" JACOB JOHN LANSING
" MALCOMB
" CHRISTOPHER MULLER
" WILLIAM PEARCE
" REQUA
" JOHN M. SACKETT
" ADIEL SHERWOOD
" ISRAEL VEAL
" DANIEL WILLIAMS

CAPT. JAMES WILSON
" JOHN WILSON
LIEUT. WILLIAM BLOODGOOD
" JOHN CALENDER
" MICHAEL DYCKMAN
" ANDREW P. HEERMANSEE
" JACOB HOCHSTRASSER
" JACOB J. HURMANCE
" DANIEL LEROY
" ROBERT H. LIVINGSTON
" JEREMIAH MULLER
" JOHN ODLE

ADDITIONAL NAMES ON STATE TREASURER'S PAY BOOK

LIEUT. GEORGE HARSEN
LIEUT. JACOB H. HEERMANSEE

ENLISTED MEN

Abrams John
Adams Noah
Alser Amiel
Anders William, Junr.
Anderson John
Andreas John
Andrews Isaac
Andries Jacob
Antis William
Atkins Willaim
Ayres Thomas
Babcock Benjamin
Babcock David
Bacon James
Bailey David
Bailey Richard
Bailey Timothy
Baker Conrad
Baker Thomas
Baker Storm
Barber William
Barkman John
Barner Joseph
Barnes Jacob
Barnes James
Barnhart Christopher
Barnhurst Christopher
Bartholimew Dewalt
Becker Adam
Becker Philip
Becker Storm
Becker William
Beebe Constant
Beekman Henry
Bell John
Bell Robert
Benchotten Herman
Bennet Joseph
Berger William
Birkman John
Black Henry
"Black Jack"
Black Robert
Blackman Joel
Blackmore Joel
Bloodgood William
Blyn Simonn
Bont Ephraim
Boyd Peleg
Brannon Abraham
Briggs Stephen
Brink Peter
Brink Solomon
Brooks Jeremiah
Brown Cornelius
Brown John
Brown Samuel
Bugarth Lambert
Burgarth Lamber
Burhans Abraham
Burr Daniel
Burris Charles
Bussing John
Bussing William
Cadman Joseph
Cady David
Calender John
Cameron David
Campble William
Canady Henry
Cansa James
Cantine Moses
Carolina Joseph
Carpenter Uriah
Case William
Chapman Amos

Chapman Heerman
Chard Bears
Chism Peter
Church James
Church Samuel
Clarwater Matthew
Clary Luke
Clous John Gotlip
Cloyd Daniel
Clute John
Clute John P.
Coats Zebulon
Codman Joseph
Codney William
Codwiss Christopher
Cohoone Alexander
Cole Henry
Cole Moses
Coleman John
Conklin Matthew
Connelly Jacob
Conradt Henry
Cook James
Cook Zebulon
Cool Peter
Cooper Eden
Cooper Obadiah
Coopper John
Cotral Abis
Covenhoven Francis
Covenhoven William
Crane James
Crapo Peter
Crist Abraham
Crist Christian
Crist Matthew
Crou Peter
Cry John
Cudberth Benjamin
Culiy David
Cunningham John
Curby John
Currington Enoch
Curtis Joel
Curtis Joseph
Daniels Jacob
Darling Samuel
Darrow Amasias
Darrow Ammerias
Darrow Daniel
Davis John
Davies John
Davies Joseph
Davies William
Day John
Dayton John
Decker Francis
DeCline Leonard
DeCullier James
Degolder John
DeGraff Jesse
Delong Elias
Dickerson Judathan
Dodge Daniel
Dolittle Timothy
Doty Isaac
Doty Shadwick
Doughty Isaac
Dubois Jacob
Dunbar Amos
Earle Joseph
Elsworth John
Evans Joseph
Everouth John
Felbush Jesse
Fish William
Fisk William
Flack James
Fogus Christian
Foster John
Francis John
Frayer John
French John
French Joseph
Fryer John F.
Funk Christopher
Gardinier Samuel
Gates Simon
Gault Alexander
Gibson David
Gilbert John W.
Gold Elijah
Goodhew Joseph
Goss Oliver
Gould Elijah
Gould William
Graft Philip
Graves Nodiah
Graves Timothy
Gray Thomas
Green James
Green Silas
Griffen William
Griffith W.
Griswould David
Griswould Miles
Groat John
Groot Hezekiah
Gurman Benjamin
Hadley Joseph
Hagodorn John
Hagedorn Samuel
Hagerman William
Hagaman W.
Hall Benijah (see Benjamin)
Hall Christopher
Hall William
Hampaugh Peter
Harns William
Harrington Abraham
Harrington Isaac
Harrington John
Harrington Zachariah
Harris Elphalet
Harris Noah
Harsin George
Havens Thomas
Heath Stephen
Hendrickson John
Herring Solomon
Hickman Michael
Hilton Jonathan
Hiltzinger Michael
Hinkley Gershom
Hodge Daniel
Hodgeson George
Hoghtaling John
Hoghtaling Teunis
Hollabard Jesse
Hollister Samuel
Hollister Smith
Homer Joshua
Homes Jedediah
Hopping David
Horton Samuel
Hover Philex
Howard Enos
Huberson Benjamin
Hudson George
Hughan John
Hugom John
Huick Nicholas
Hukman Michael
Hunt Daniel
Hutchinson Benjamin
Hutt John
Huyck Nicholas
Hyms Frederick
Ingles George
Irvine Henry
Isdawy James
Jacobie Bastian
Johnson Elijah
Johnsou Shubal
Johnson Peter
Jonck Jacob
Jones William
Joy Amos
Joy Joseph
Kempel John
King John
Krum Benjamin
Lamont Archy
Landus Ebenezer
Larned Henry
Lawyer Lambert
Leaman Archibald
Lee Jonathan
Lee William
Lefever Noah
Legget Lue
Lemon Archibald
Lemon John
Lewis Christopher
Lewis Hendrick
Lewis Jacob
Lewis Reuben
Little Stephen
Little William
Livingston Richard
Lothrop Ebenezer
Louck Henry
Low John
Luce Israel
Ludington Elisha
Luiks Abraham
Luiks Andrew
Luiks Johannis
Lull Nathan
Lumas Andrew
Lummes Andrew
Luyck John
Lyons Amaziah
Maffett John
Mandevile Matthew
Mann Solomon
Mapes Henry
Mapes James
March Marchus
Marselus Alexander
Marsh Samuel
Mayall Joseph
Mayfield John
Mead Eli
Mead Isaac
Merrit Jeremiah
Merritt Ebenezer
Miles William
Miller Christopher
Miller Henry
Miller Jeremiah
Miller John
Mindersick Frederick
Modevel Matthew
Moffat John
Moloy Thomas
Monies John
Montanye John
Moore Ephraim
Moores Hezekiah
Morrell William

Morris Ebenezer
Morrison Adward
Morrison Edward
Moshier Nicholas
Mosuce Nicholas
Moot Robert
Mott Joseph
Mott Robert
Mount Samuel
Mudge Ebenezer
Murfey Thomas
Myers John
Mynderse Frederick
Mynderse Herman
Myndersenck Frederick
Mynheer John
McCay James
McCoy James
McCoy John
McDonald Edward
McEwen Cornelius
McIntosh Andrew
McIntosh John
McIntosh John, Junr.
McKee Thomas
McKennie Joseph
McKinney Joseph
Nelson Absolom
Nichols John
Nichols Thomas
Nichols William
Norton Stephen
Notingham Thomas
Osborn Peter
Ostrander Henry
Ostrander William
Palmer Amasiah
Palmer John
Parcells Peter
Parks Timothy
Partridge John
Patterson Asa
Pawling Cornelius
Peak Garret
Penfield Isaac
Perslow Henry
Philip David
Pike Jarvis
Pinfeild Isaac
Plum John
Plum John M.
Pratt Robert
Price David
Prince Kemple
Proper Peter
Quick Abraham
Radly Jacob
Radly John
Rawley Jabez
Renard William
Reply Hezekiah
Rice William
Richmond Abijah
Richmond James
Rider John
Rider William
Robberts John
Roberts John
Robertson William
Robins Daniel
Robins Ezra
Robins Timothy
Robinson Ezra
Robinson Hector
Robinson Peter
Robinson William
Rogers Michael
Rogers Reuben
Romer Aaron
Romney John
Rosa John
Rossman Henry
Rowland John
Rowley Jabish
Rubison William
Rumney John
Rumsey Jesse
Rynard John
Rynders John
Rynders William
Salisbury Gideon
Salisbury Joseph
Salyea Henry
Saunders Wait
Saxton Gershom
Scantling Jeremiah
Schaick Jonathan
Schoolcraft Peter
Schoonmaker Edward
Scott William
Seward John
Shader Jost
Shaver Adam
Shaver John
Shell Adam
Shiels James
Shoefelt William
Shuffalt William
Shuffalts John
Shurts John
Shutts John
Skinner Solomon
Slater James
Slocum William
Slowter Cornelius
Smally Ruben
Smith Daniel
Smith James
Smith Michael
Smith Nicholas
Smith Peter
Smith Richard
Smith Samuel
Snyder William
Speed Henry
Spinenbergh Jacob
Spitcer Aaron (see Spitzer)
Springsteen Jeremiah
Stafford Jonathan
Stalker William
Stansel Nicholas
St. Anthony
Stephens William
Stevens David
Steward John
Still Robert
Stopplebean Peter
Strader Jost
Stuart John
Stubrack Barant
Sturdevant Isaac
Sullivan David
Swart Benjamin
Talman Jacob
Taylor James
Taylor Joseph
Teal Andrew
Terry Benjamin
Terry Norton
Thomas Caleb
Thomkins Lawrence
Thompson John
Tigner Jonathan
Tinneger George
Tolbush Jesse
Tollman Thomas
Treat Woodbridge
Tripp Anthony
Truesdale Thomas
Trusdall William
Valentine Richard
Valleau Stephen
Vermillie Jacob
Victory John
Vischer Bastian H.
Vredenburgh Abraham
Vredinburgh William
Vredenburgh Peter
Van Aernam Abraham
Vanaton Aaron
Van Banchoten Heerman
Van Buren George
Vanderbergh John
Vanderbilt D K
Van Houten Abraham
Van Ness David
Vanorden Henry
Vanorden Peter
Van Tassel Abraham
Vantile John, Junr.
Van Tuyl John
Van Valkenburgh Gershom
Van Valkenburgh Harmu
Van Valkenburgh John
Van Valkenburgh Lucas
Van Vradenburgh Peter
Van Zandt John
Wadsworth John
Waggonet Hermonias
Wait George
Walcott Justice
Waldron William
Wallace Benjamin
Walsworth G.
Wanson John
Ward Charles
Ward Christopher
Ward Josiah
Wares Christopher
Wason James
Wason John
Wasson James
Waters David
Webbers John
Wentworth James
Westfall Abraham
Westhead Edward
Whitcom John
Whitcomb Ezra
Whitcomb John
White William
Wilkie Augustus
Williams David
Williams Thomas
Williams William
Williamson James
Wilson Jesse
Wilson John
Wilthouse John
Winters John
Wixon David
Wolfe Anthony
Wood James
Wooding Rubin
Woodward Ephraim
Woolcot Justice
Woolsey M.
Wynances John
Young George
Youngs William

The Levies — (Continued).

COLONEL ALBERT PAWLING
MAJOR THOMAS DEWITT
MAJOR ELIAS VAN BUNSCHOTEN
ADJUTANT CORNELIUS DUBOIS
ADJUTANT JOHN ELSWORTH
QUARTER MASTER EDWARD CONNOR
PAY MASTER JOHN VAN DEUSEN
SURGEON JOHN SMEDES
SURGEON PETER VAN DER LYN

CAPT. JOHN BURNET
" CHRISTOPHER CODWIS
" LEVI DEWITT
" WILLIAM FAULKNER
" JOHN A. HERDENBORGH
" ROBERT HUNTER
" JONATHAN LAWRENCE
" GILBERT J. LIVINGSTON
" ONDERDONK
" HENRY PAWLING
" JONATHAN PEARSEE
" RICHARD SACKETT
" ABRAHAM VAN AKEN
" DERICK WESBROOK
" ABRAHAM WESTFALL
" DANIEL WILLIAMS
" ROBERT WOOD
LIEUT. CORNELIUS ACKERMAN
" TIMOTHY COLEMAN
LIEUT. JOHN J. DUBOIS
" MICHAEL DYCKMAN
" JOHN ENGLISH
" JOHN L. HARDENBERGH
" MARTIN HOMMEL
" JOSHUA T. JANSEN
" RICHARD LAWRENCE
" JOHN MCBRIDE
" WILLIAM MOSIER
" WILLIAM NOTTINGHAM
" JAMES OAKLEY
" JOHN OSTRANDER
" THOMAS OSTRANDER
" ALDERT ROOSA
" HENDRICUS TEERPENNING
" NATHANIEL TUCKER
" HENRY VAN HOEVENBERGH
" MOSES YEOMANS
ENSIGN DANIEL FRAIR

ENLISTED MEN.

Acker Henry
Ackerman John
Ackerson Cornelius
Adriance Theodorus
Agins James
Airs Felix
Albertson Richard
Allen Abenezer
Aller John
Allison Isaac
Allison Samuel
Alsdarph Philip
Amberman Dirck
Anderson George
Anderson John
Andrews John
Ansou James
Anthony John
Armstrong Archibald
Arnel William
Arnold William
Aspenno Anthony
Averet Timothy
Averts Timothy
Avery Henry
Avery Nehemiah
Ayers Thomas
Baily Moses
Baker Coenradt
Baker Judah
Baker Richard
Baker William
Ball William
Ballard John
Bames William
Bames William, Junr.
Bamp Sherry
Bancker Frederick
Barber Elisha
Barber Joseph
Bark George
Barnes William
Barnes William, Jr.
Barnet John
Barns John
Baroon Anthony
Barret John
Barrick George
Barrow Daniel
Bartlet Levi
Bartley Jacob
Base Daniel
Bass Daniel
Bassemer John
Basset Ceasar
Bayard John
Beam William
Bedford Cornelius
Bedford Jonas
Benjamins David
Bennet Mitchel
Berger Jacob
Berger Wouter
Besemer Michael
Bevier Coenradt
Bishop John
Bishop Levi
Bishup John
Black Abraham
Black Lewis
Bloom Oaky
Bloomer Joseph
Bocrum Nicholas
Bocrum William
Bodley William
Boerum Nicholas
Boerum William
Bogue John
Bohannar James
Bouton Samuel

Bouton Timothy
Bovies David
Bowker Silas
Bowker Silas, Junr.
Bradlee Nathan
Bradly Ephraim
Bradly Nathaniel
Bramor Anthony
Braur Robert
Brawm Eldrick
Brink Adam
Brink Cornelius
Brink Cornelius, Junr.
Brink Jacob, Junr.
Brink John
Brink John C.
Brinkerhoff Henry
Brodhead Henry
Brodhead William
Brook Thomas
Brooks John
Brooks Mickel
Brower Eldrick
Brower Henry
Brower Teunes
Brown Asa
Brown Henry
Brown John
Brown Malachi
Brown Moses
Brown Peter
Brown Samuel
Brown Zephaniah
Bruce Robert
Brush David
Brush Eliakim
Bruton Arthur
Budd Frederick
Bunker Solomon
Bunker Thomas
Burger Zachariah
Burgus James
Burhance Terrick
Burhans Cherck
Burhans Isaac
Burhans John
Burhans Therk
Burl Thomas
Burl Zachariah
Burnett John
Burns Edward
Burns William
Burt Christopher
Burwell James
Bush Henry
Bush Peter
Butler John
Byard John

Callagham Thomas
Calwell Arthur
Camble James
Camble John
Cammel William
Cantfield Amos
Cantine John, Junr.
Card Hugh
Carner Andrew
Carney Barnabas
Carpenter Nehemiah
Carpenter Nicolaes
Carte William
Carter Luke
Case Enos
Case William
Case Zenos
Cassady Nicholas
Catterlon Nathaniel
Cawin Daniel
Chamber Cornelius
Chamberland Jacob
Chambers Jacobus
Chambers John
Chambers Joseph
Chapman Daniel
Chapman Stephen
Chapman Uriah
Chase Ebenezer
Chase Gedeliah
Chatfield Caleb
Chatterdon Nathaniel
Chris Matthew
Chrispel John
Christ Thomas
Christian Cornelius
Church John
Churchell Jonas
Churchell William
Claerwater John
Claerwater Matthew
Claerwater Petrus
Clark John
Clark Samuel
Clawter John
Cleland William
Clerk John
Coddington Benjamin
Coddington Levi
Cole Simon P.
Collamar Ebenezar
Collin William
Collins John
Colwall Arture
Combs Michel
Concklin John
Concklin Samuel
Coningham William

Connon Peter
Connor Daniel
Connor James
Connor William
Conway Cornelius
Conway John
Cook Benjamin
Cook David
Cook Dines
Cook Durias
Cook Nathan
Cool Simon P.
Coon John
Coone John
Cooper Henry
Cooper James
Cooper John
Coragell Abraham
Cornelius John
Cornell Benjamin
Corregle Abraham
Cottenden Levi
Courgell Abraham
Cowen Thomas
Cox Benjamin
Cox John B.
Cox William
Craft Thomas
Crandall Luke
Crandle Luce
Crane James
Crane William
Crandle Luce
Cree Joseph
Crispel Abraham
Crispel Elisha
Crispel Hendrick
Crispel Jacob
Crispel John, Junr.
Crist Matthias
Critsinger John
Croft James
Cronk Timothy
Crosby Enoch
Crossman Michael
Crover George
Crowel Joel
Crumb Benjamin
Crumb John
Cuddeback Peter
Culp Johannis
Cunningham Abel
Cunningham Henry
Cunningham James
Cunnigham John
Cunningham William
Curen Portrick
Curtis Jeptha

Daily Robert
Dains Abraham
Dalway Andrew
Darby George
Daton Frederick
Davis Andrew
Davis Benjamin
Davis Daniel
Davis Frederick
Davis Samuel
Davis Valentine
Davis William
Davis William, Junr.
Day Jonathan
Dean Abraham
Deane Samuel
Decker John
Decker John, Junr.
Decker Moses
Decker Noah
Decker Uriah
Decker Urias
Degroot Joseph
Delameter John
Delana Dennis
Delaney Dennis
Demond Isaac
Demond Peter
Dempsey Thomas
Denton Joseph
Depare Andries
Depuy John
Deveny Archibald
Devis Andrew
Devour Abraham
Dewitt Abraham
Dewitt Cornelius
Dewitt Cornelius D.
Dewitt Jacob
De Witt Jacobus
Dewitt James
Dewitt John, Junr.
De Witt Levi
Dewitt Tony
Dewitt William
Dickson Andrew
Dimick Samuel
Dingah Elijah
Divany Archibald
Divine Archibald
Dixon Hezekiah
Docker Jacob
Dodge Stephen
Dolson Jacob
Dolway Jeremiah
Dowty Elias
Doxy Stephen
Drake Gilbert

Draper John
Dubois David, Junr.
Dubois Gerrit
Dubois Isaac
Dubois John
Dumond Cornelius
Dumond Egenas
Dumond Isaac
Dumond Peter
Dunbar Amos
Dunbar William
Dunlap William
Dunneven Daniel
Dunning David
Dutcher Barnes
Dutcher Henry
Dutcher Rockliff
Dutcher Rulef
Dykman Benjamin
Eckert Henry
Eganor John
Eggenaar Johannis
Eggenaer Jacobus
Elit David
Ellison Isaac
Ellison Samuel
Ellot Thomas
Elsworth John
Elsworth Henry
Emrich John
Emrich Peter
Emrich Pitter
English George
English William
Ennis Cornelius
Ennis Peter
Ennis William
Ennist James
Ensley Simeon
Ettinge Thomas
Everitt Jacob
Everts Ambrus
Everts Timothy
Every Henry
Every Nehemiah
Eygenaar John
Farguson Guilbert
Faulkner John
Faulkner William
Fawster Samuel
Fawter Samuel
Felter Peter
Ferguson Gilbert
Ferress John
Ferris Alexander
Ferris Ezra
Ferris Gedion
Ferris James
Ferris John
Ferris Samuel
Ferris Sylvenus
Fice John
Fierce Jonathan
Fieris Coonradt
Fiero Abraham
Fiero Peter
Finch Fawster
Finch Reuben
Finch Samuel
Finn Ezra
Flim David
Flinn David
Flyn Philip
Fogurson John
Folknear John
Foot John
Ford Asher
Ford Esha
Forgason Gilbert
Foster Benjamin
Foster Samuel
Fouler Joseph
Fowler Moris
Fox Oliver
Fox Samuel
Frair Isaac
France John
Frances William
Franklin George
Frans Adam
Frasher John
Freer John
Freer Peter
Frim Ezra
Fuller David
Fullerton William
Gains Josiah
Galasby David
Galasby John
Gale John
Gardner Samuel
Garlinghouse Joseph
Garmain James
Garnse Samuel
Garrison John
Garrison Jonas
Garvey Frances
Gauf Asel
Gilbert Jesse
Godfray David
Goff John
Gold Walter
Goodspeed Isaac
Graham James
Graham Zachariah
Graton Crora
Greaves Thomas
Green Peter
Greenwall Daniel
Gregory Benjamin
Griffin John
Groenvout Daniel
Gunsales Manuel
Haasbrook George
Hadeley Mosses
Hadly Isaac
Haite Abijah
Hall Benijah, Junr.
Hall Benjamin
Hall Boston
Hall John
Hall Robert
Hallock Joseph
Hallock Moses
Hallock Thomas
Hallot William
Hallsted Richard
Hallsted Samuel
Halmes Jeremiah
Handay Manassa
Hanmer Geabes
Hanmore Jabash
Hanmore Moses
Hannions John
Hardenbergh Jacob
Hardon Thomas
Harp Abraham
Harp Henry
Harris Thomas
Hart William
Hausbruck Joshua
Hawkens Stephen
Hawking Thomas
Hawkins Thomas
Haws William
Hays Jesse
Hays Nathaniel
Head Briton
Heaton William
Hedgee Evert
Hedger Evert
Hedgers Samuel
Heermanse Edward
Height Richard
Helm Daniel
Henderson Bamp
Hennion John
Herring Hercules
Herrington Reuben
Herris Henry
Herris Noah
Hicks John
Higby Jacob
Hill Nathan
Hillhouse John
Hines James
Hocks Jonathan
Hodge Ralph
Hodges Israel
Holmes John
Holstead Thomas
Homans John
Homer Francis
Hommel Abraham
Hommel Hermanus
Hood John
Hoornbeek Benjamin
Hoornbeck Cornelius
Hoornbeck Ephraim
Hopkins Thomas
Hopper John
Horton Samuel
Hoskis Bennony
House Cornelius
House William
Howel Isaiah
Hummel Abraham
Hunter John
Hunter Robert
Hurton William
Hutchens Essel
Hutchins Asa
Hutchins Ezekiel
Hutton William
Hyatt Eleven
Hyatt Elias
Hyne Philip
Hynpagh Peter
Ingles George
Inson Richard
Ives Ephraim
Jack Esquire
Jackling Freman
Jackson Hannibal
Jay Augustus
Jayne Matthias
Jean Matthew
Jermaine James
Jinson Richard
Johnson Andrew
Johnson Andrew, Junr.
Johnson Benjamin (colored)
Johnson Jacob
Johnston William
Jones Asa
Jones Benjamin
Jones David
Jones Isaac
Jones James
Jones Jeremiah
Jones Simeon

Jordan Michael
Josillin Zebediah
Karr William
Keator Cornelius
Keator John
Keator William
Kelley Patrick
Kelly Isaac
Ketcham John
Kickfer William
Killam Silas
Killey David
Killey Dennis
King William
Kittle Henry
Klyn John
Knap Nathaniel
Konstable Gerrit
Kostable William
Krom Henry
Krom Simon
Krom Simon C.
Krum Benjamin
Krum John
Krum William
Kuykendall William
Lain William
Laine Samuel
Lake John
Lake Joshua
Langendyck Cornelius
Langyear William
Lanson John
Lanson William
Lawfavour John
Lawrence Joseph
Lawson George
Lawson Matthew
Lawson Samuel
Lattemore Rogers
Leasure Samuel
Lee Zepthe
Lefoy Abraham
Legget William
Leinson John
Leinson William
Lent Hercules
Lent James
Lewis Felix
Lewis Gilbert
Lewis Jabesh
Lewis James
Lewis Robert
Light Josiah
Linch Lawrence
Lines Michel
Lint Isaac
Lions Abel
Lions Barny
Little Frances
Litts David
Lockwood Isaac
Lockwood Moses
Lockwood Timothy
London Edon
Lonts John
Louie Albert
Loun John
Low John
Lucky George
Lucky Samuel
Luke John
Lutts Coenradt
Lyons Abel
Mack Johannis
Mackey Alexander
Mackey Jesse
Mackey John
Madris James
Magie John
Malony John
Mapes Bethuel
Mapes Henry
Mapes Stephen
Marcle Johannis
Mark Johannis
Markle John
Martin Archibald
Martial James
Masten Daniel
Masten Joseph
Masters Dannial
Maston Matthew
Matthew James
Mead Ebenezer
Mead Joseph
Mead Marshall
Mead Mortiat
Mead Moses
Means Charles
Merckle Jacob
Merkle John
Merriman Titus
Merrit Ebenezer
Meyr Abraham
Meyr Teunes
Meyrs Abraham, Junr.
Meyrs Henry
Michels Joseph
Milburn John
Miller Abraham
Miller Arra
Miller Ezra
Miller George
Miller Jacobus
Miller John
Miller Joseph
Mills Jonathan
Mills Samuel
Mills Solomon
Minnin Thomas
Mitchell Joseph
Money Absalom
Money John
Montanie Peter
Montanier Peter
Moore Daniel
Moore Thomas
More Daniel
More Thomas
Morrel John
Morris John
Morris Robert
Morrison Robert
Mosher Seth
Mosure Abner
Mountanie Peter
Mowris Petrus
Mowris Samuel
Mullen Patrick
Muller John
Murphy Robert
Murphy Thomas
Myer Jacob
Myer John
Myer Peter
Myer Philip
Myer William
Myers Abraham
Myers Benjamin
Myers Jacob
Myers John
Myers Philip
Myers William
McCallan Thomas
McCann James
McClane John
McCloud Alexander
McClure William
McCollagham Thomas
McCollan, Thomas
McCollum James
McCrany William
McCollom James
McDannel Daniel
McDonald Daniel
McFitzgerald Christopher
McGee John
McGee Samuel
McGuire Daniel
McGuire Hugh
McKloud Alexander
McMaster John
McMickel John
McName William
McNamel John
McNarne William
McNeally Patrick
McSwainy Daniel
McWherter James
Nairon James
Nathan Reace
Nearing James (see Vearing)
Nelson John
Newkerk Benjamin
Newkerk Isaac
Newkerk Jacob
Newkerk John
Newman Jonathan
Nicolaes John
Niven William
Niver William
Northroup Eli
Nostrand George
Nothingham Thomas
Oaheley Thomas
Oakley Thomas
O'Bradly Daniel
Obrien Morgon
Ochmoody Jacobus
Oddle Abiather
Odle Jonathan
O'Ferl Michel
Oldfield George
Oliver Thomas
Oosterhoudt Ezekiel
Opherl Michel
Osborn John
Osterhoudt Tounis
Osterhout Elias
Osterhout Ezekiel
Osterhout Henry
Osterhout Peter
Osterhout Teunes, Junr.
Ostrander Jacobus
Ostrander Moss
Ostrander Teunes
Ostrant Aldert
Ottarris William.
Otter John
Oumerman Derick
Ousterhout Hermanus
Owens Benjamin
Owens David
Owens John
Pain Ceazar
Palmatier William
Palmer Aaron
Palmerton Thomas
Palmeteer John
Pargret Samuel

Parker James
Parks Samuel
Parrish John
Parshal David
Pass Jonathan
Patterson Ezecal
Patterson Israel
Patterson James
Pattison Michel
Pattison Thomas
Pawling John
Peltze Evert
Penbrook William
Penear John
Peresonus Jacobus
Pergret Samuel
Peterson John
Phelps David
Philips Samuel
Plass Freeman
Ploegh Hendrick
Polhamus Daniel
Pool William
Popple William
Porch Andrew
Post Cornelius
Post Hendrick
Post Henry
Post Isaac
Post Jacobus
Post Martin
Post Samuel
Presler Abraham
Pudney James
Purdy John
Quick George
Quick Jacob
Quick John
Ransom Henry
Ransom Harry
Ray Daniel
Raymonts Sands
Read Samuel
Read William
Reed James
Regnaw Isaac
Relyea John
Relyea Simeon
Relyea Simon
Reton Peter
Reves Elisha
Rice John
Richard Nathaniel
Richards Exrah
Ritenbergh George
Robbison Isaac
Robbison William
Roberson Jesse
Robertson John
Robinson William
Robison James
Rodgers James
Roff Aaron
Rogers James
Rogers John
Rogers Joseph
Romer Aaron
Romsey Jesse
Roosa Abraham
Roosa Aldert
Roosa Evert
Roosa Jacob
Roosa Johannis
Roosa John
Roosa Richard
Roosa William
Roosekrans Jacobus
Rordon Pordick
Rose Jacob
Rose James
Rose Richard
Rosekrans Cornelius
Rosekrans Dirck
Ross Aron
Ross Finly
Rote Christian
Rowland Luke
Rumsey Jesse
Rumsey Nathan
Rundel Elnathan
Rundle Abraham
Rundle David
Rundle Syras
Ryan John
Ryder Benjamin
Ryder John
Rynus John
Sacket Prime
Sackett Richard
Sadlor John
Sammons Cornelius
Sammons Jacob
Sammons Thomas
Saxton John
Schoonmaker John
Schoonmaker Martin
Schutt Christian
Schutt Frederick
Schutt Solomon
Scoffield Ceazar
Scoffield Moses
Scofield Elisha
Scoonover Joseph
Scutt Solomon
Secaus Jonas
Secor Jonas
Sergeant Jame
Shampineday Andrew
Sharer Robert
Shaver John
Shaw James
Shields William
Shiely Coenradt
Shoecraft Jacob
Shoecraft John
Short Henry
Short John
Short Peter
Shulp John
Shuls John
Shultz John
Shurter Casparus
Sillisbury John
Silsby Elijah
Simmins John
Simmons Benjamin
Simmons Cornelius
Simmons Enoch
Simons John
Skoonmaker John E.
Slator David
Slator John
Slator William
Sleighter John
Slint Harculas
Slutt John
Sluyter Abraham
Sluyter Nicholas
Sluyter William
Smedes John
Smith Gerritt
Smith James
Smith Jeremiah
Smith John
Smith Jonas
Smith Joseph
Smith Timothy
Smith Zacheriah
Snyder Abraham
Snyder Christian
Snyder Elias
Snyder George
Snyder Henry
Snyder Jacob
Soleven John
Southard Henry
Southard John
Spanenbergh Jacob
Spark Robert
Sparks Abraham
Sparks Robert
Sparling John
Squoral Daniel
Squrrel Daniel
Stagg Adam
Stagh Benjamin
Stanley Joseph
Staples Nathan
Stater David
St. Clair George
Stephens John
Steward Charles
Stewart John
Sticks John
Stillwill James
Stingro Solomon
St. John Adam
St. John Joseph
St. Johns Joseph
Stockbridge John
Stone John
Storm Abraham
Strong John
Stryker Abraham
Stuart John
Sturdivent David
Sulevan John
Sulliven William
Sumans Jacob
Suthard John
Sutton William
Swaar Jacob
Swart William
Swartwout Cornelius
Swoonover Benjamin
Taning Henry
Tannor Zophar
Tarring Henry
Tarpenning Jacob
Taylor Elijah
Taylor Ely
Taylor Henry
Teerpeny Abraham
Teerpenning Jacob
Teerpenning Lawrence
Tennor Zophar
Ter Bush Henry
Ter Bush Joseph
Terry Benjamin
Terwileger James P.
Terwileger Martin
Terwileger Wilhelmes
Terwilleger Aaron V.
Terwilleger Abraham
Terwilleger Jacobus
Terwilleger Peter V.
Tharp Matthew
Thompkins Lawrence
Thompson Abijah
Thompson Jedediah
Thompson Jediah
Thompson Jesiah

Thompson Joel
Thompson Joshua
Thompson Obijah
Thomson Thomas
Thornton William
Thurston Jason
Tibbles Robert
Tibbles Solomon
Tice Henry
Tice John
Tillsey Job
Tillton Peter
Tilson Timothy
Tip William
Tompkins Jonathan
Tonkry Nicholas
Toundsend Garerdus
Travis Philip
Travis Salvenus
Trawilligar James P.
Triddle Esquire
Trim Ezra
Trumper Nicholas
Trusdle Samuel
Turk John
Tuttle James
Twaghtman John
Tyler Charles
Tyler William
Umberman Dirck
Upright George
Valentine Peter
Vearing James (see Nearing)
Venwer Martin
Vocke Gudfry
Vocke Henry
Vurgin John
Van Aken Natnan
Van Amburgh Jeremiah
Van Anker Nathan
Van Asdell John
Van Auken Elias
Van Benschoten Jacob
Van Bunschoten Solomon
Van Cleaf Michel
Van Cleak Michael
Van Clerk Michael
Van Debogart John
Van De Bogart Peter
Van De Hoef Matthias
Vandemark Ezekiel
Van Der Hoof Mathias
Vandemark Solomon
Van Demerk Jacob
Vandemerke John
Vanden Merk George
Van Denmerk Joseph
Vanderhoof Matthew
Van Dermerk Ezekiel
Vangalder Andrew
Van Garden Jacobus
Van Gerder Andries
Van Heenbergh Abraham
Van Hoevenbergh Eggo
Van Houten John
Van Kamp Abraham
Vankay Carnales
Van Keuren Philip
Van Keuren Tjerck
Van Kleeck Michael B.
Van Leuven Christian
Van Leuven Zachariah
Vanorder Peter
Van Osdell John
Van Pelt John
Van Scorte Abraham
Van Steenbergh John
Van Steenbergh Peter
Van Urden Peter
Van Wagene Daniel
Van Wagenen Jonathan
Van Wart John
Van Wort Goret
Waggonor Tobias
Waily Thomas
Waley Thomas
Wandle Henry
Ward Josiah
Ward Solomon
Ward Thomas C.
Ward William
Waterbury James
Weed Jonathan
Weeks James
Weeks Obediah
Weisenfelt George
Welch William
Weldon James
Wells Prince
Wellsworth Gilbert
Wenigar Samuel
Wentfield Simon
Wesbrook Abraham
Westfall Levi
Weston Joseph
Wheat Amos
Wheeler Timothy
White John
White Nathan
White Tone
Whitney Jacob
Whitney Justus
Whitney Seth
Whony Daniel
Whorry Daniel
Whorry John
Wicks Phinehas
Wiley Thomas
Willcox Isaac
Willems Dage
Williams Abraham
Williams Gilbert
Williams James
Williams John
Williams Reace
Williams William
Willis Henry
Willis James
Willis John
Willis Thomas
Wilson John
Winegar Samuel
Winfield Abraham
Winfield Elias
Winfield Simon
Winkells John
Winn Peter
Winne John
Winney John
Winney Peter
Winniger Samuel
Wispler John
Wittaker Edward
Wood John
Wood Jonah
Wood Jonas
Wood William
Woodworth Daniel
Woolcot William
Woolf Peter
Worden Barnard
Wyley Thomas
Yeaple Hanicle
Yeaple Jacob
York John
Young George

The Levies — (Continued).

COLONEL MARINUS WILLETT
LIEUTENANT COLONEL JOHN McKINSTRY
MAJOR ANDREW FINK, JR. (MAJOR OF BRIGADE)
MAJOR LYMAN HITCHCOCK (MUSTER MASTER)
MAJOR JOSIAH THROOP
MAJOR ELIAS VAN BUNSCHOTEN
ADJUTANT JELLES A. FONDA
ADJUTANT PLINY MOORE
QUARTER MASTER JOHN FONDEY
QUARTER MASTER MATTHEW TROTTER
QUARTER MASTER JACOB WINNEY
PAY MASTER ABRAHAM TEN EYCK
SURGEON CALVIN DELANO
SURGEON WILLIAM PETRY
SURGEON'S MATE GEORGE FAUGH
SURGEON'S MATE MOSES WILLARD
CHAPLAIN JOHN DANIEL GROS

CAPT. JAMES CANNON
" PHILIPP CONINE, JR.
" BENJAMIN DUBOIS
" HOLTHAM DUNHAM
" PETER ELSWORTH
" PETER B. FEARCE (TEARCE)
" ABRAHAM FONDA
" FRANCIS
" ABNER FRENCH
" SILAS GRAY
" LAWRENCE GROS
" AARON HALE
" JOSEPH HARRISON
" NATHANIEL HENRY
" ABRAHAM LIVINGSTON
" ELIHU MARSHALL
" SIMEON NEWELL
" JOHN PERCY
" GERRIT PUTNAM
" JOSIAH SKINNER
" THOMAS SKINNER
" JOSEPH VAN INGEN
" PETER VAN RENSSELAER
" ANTHONY WELP
" ABRAHAM WESTFALL
" STEPHEN WHITE

CAPT. JOB WRIGHT
" GUY YOUNG
LIEUT. WILLIAM BLOODGOOD
" JACOB BOKEE
" BENANIWELL DEUEL
" DUTTON
" EPHRAIM EATON
" NATHANIEL FORD
" BARTEL HENDRICKS
" JACOB HOCHSTRASSER, JR.
" CHRISTOPHER HUTTON
" TIMOTHY HUTTON
" PETER LOOP, JR.
" JOHN LOW
" WILLIAM MOORE
" GERRIT NUKERK
" GEORGE PASSAGE
" VICTOR PUTNAM
" JOSIAH RICHARDSON
" SALKILD ISAAC
" JACOB SAMMONS
" JOHN SHAW
" JOHN SPENCER
" JOHN THORNTON
" WILLIAM VAN ARNUM
" PETER VAN BERGEN

LIEUT. ISAAC VAN VALKENBURGH
" VROOMAN SIMON J.
" RICHARD RANDOLPH WILLSON
LIEUT. WILLIAM WILLSON
" SOLOMON WOODWORTH

ADDITIONAL NAMES ON STATE TREASURER'S PAY BOOKS

CAPT. JOEL GILLETT
LIEUT. STORM A. BECKER
" RICHARD BINGHAM
" DUNCAN CAMPBELL
" GIDEON COWLES
" JOHN FRIMPER
" JONATHAN HILTON
LIEUT. JESSE HUBBELL
" JOHN HUDSON
" WITTER JOHNSON
" OLIVER NEWELL
" CHRISTIAN PEAK
" JOHN C. SHAFER
" JOHN WATSON

Captain, Major, Lieutenant Colonel, Colonel and Acting Brigadier General Marinus Willett was a gallant officer. He held many commands and his promotions were rapid. In 1775–6 he was a Captain in Colonel Alexander McDougal's Regiment, 1st N. Y. Line. On April 27th, 1776, the Provincial Congress recommended him to the Continental Congress for Major of the same Regiment. In November of the same year he was recommended for Lieutenant Colonel of the 3rd Line, and in July, 1780, he was made Lieutenant Colonel Commandant of the 5th Regiment of the Line.

In 1781, as Lieutenant Colonel, he commanded a Regiment of Levies, and in 1782 was made full Colonel of still another Regiment of Levies. After the death of General Nicholas Herkimer, Colonel Willett commanded the Tryon Co. Militia as Acting Brigadier General, and in the battles of Johnstown and Caughnawaga defeated the enemy most signally.

ENLISTED MEN

Adams Elijah
Adamy Peter
Adkins William
Agers Henry Julius
Albert White
Allen Henry
Allen William
Aller Jacob
Allison Samuel
Alter Jacob
Amberman Derick
Ammerman Derick
Anthony George
Arewax Jacob A.
Armstrong John
Arnold Abram
Arnold David
Atwell Paul
Avery Abel
Babcock Benjamin
Backer Phillip
Bagley David
Bailey David
Bailey Timothy
Baker Albert
Baker Albert, Junr.
Baker Andrew
Baker Barrant
Baker David
Baker Samuel
Baker William
Baldwin Alexander
Baldwin Hezekiah
Balse Andreas (see Basly)
Bamm Friterick
Banks David
Banter Hellebrant
Bareup Andrew
Barker Philip
Barnar Simon
Barnhard Harmanus
Barnum Israel
Barritt Bartholomew
Barritt Jonathan
Barstow Job
Bartholomew Dualt
Battle Joseph
Bauck William
Bearworth John
Beaty Samuel
Becker Barnett
Beebe Peter
Beecraft Thomas
Be Gordis Nening
Bendick Frances
Benedict Uriah
Benjamin Breach
Benjamin Brush
Benjamin Ebenezer
Bennet Owen
Bennet Simon
Bernhet Herman
Berry David
Bersey Winning
Bertholemay Theobalt
Bervert John
Bester Joab
Betty Samuel
Beyer Fratz
Bidwell Daniel
Bishop John
Blacius Lawrence (see Blaus)
Blacus Lawrence (see Blesucs)
Blaus Lawrence (see Blacius)
Bloemendale Jacob
Bloomingdall Jacob
Bogardus Hendrick
Bogardus Nanning
Bomehover George
Bonesteel Henry
Bonny John
Booke William, Junr.
Booldman John, Junr.
Boom Frederick
Borks Christian
Borst Christian
Borst Johanis
Boston Negro
Bottles Joseph
Bouchall Hopper
Boughhall Hooper
Boyer John, Junr.
Bradt Storme
Brakemen Jacob
Braner Reuben
Brant Edward
Brantner Anthony

Bratt Storm
Breem John
Breemer Lodewick
Brewer John
Brewer William
Broomhower George
Brown Edward
Brown Dorcs
Brown John
Brown Ned
Brown Perias
Brown Tunis (colored)
Brown William
Buckley Andrew
Buell Jonathan
Bullick Charles
Bullock Charles
Bulman John
Buly Benjamin
Bunshead Frederick
Bunstead Frederick
Burck John
Burdick Gideon
Burk Aronor
Burk George
Burk Henry
Burnk George
Bush John
Bush John
Bust Jhon
Buysbow Andrew
Byer Francis
Byker Henry
Cabeneer John
Cady David
Caine John
Calver David
Cambell John (see Camble)
Camble John (see Cambell)
Campbell John
Campbell Thomas
Cannan James
Carpenter Benjamin
Carpenter Warren
Carr John
Carr William
Carsin William
Carter John
Carts John
Casler Henry
Casler John
Casler Nicholas
Casseler Thomas
Casselman John
Casselman Peter
Casslar John
Cassler Adom
Cassler Thomas
Cassoner William
Caton Thomas
Caveneer John
Chapman Amos
Chapman Ezekiel
Chapman Herman
Chapman Noah
Child Solomon
Chiles Solomon
Christman Nicholas
Church Medad
Cisner William
Clapsadle William
Clark Waters
Clark William
Clause George
Claver Nicholas
Claves Nicholas
Cleightman Frederick
Cline Hennery
Clinton John
Clough George
Clowy George
Clute Garret
Clute Garret D.
Clyne Henry
Cole John
Cole Peter
Cole Simon Peter
Cole William
Coleve Oliver
Coll John
Colver David
Colver Josiah
Combs Barnard
Combs Barnet
Commings Thomas
Commins Phillip
Cone Ichabod
Cone Jacobud
Conklen Isick
Conklin Ephraim
Conly Jacob
Cook Joseph
Cooly James
Cost Martin
Cotton Nathaniel
Covell David
Cowls Oliver
Crandel Martinus
Crandle William
Cranker John
Crawford Joseph
Crannel Martin
Crippen Ichabod
Crisman Nicholas
Crofford Joseph
Crooks John
Crossard John
Crosset John (see James)
Crowley William
Crukes John
Culp John
Culver Joshua
Cunnel William
Cuphin Egbert
Curbey John
Curtis Allantis
Curtis Asahel
Curtis Jotham
Curtis Thomas
Dack Henry
Dale William
Dallaway John
Danels Thomas
Dannals Jacob
Dark John
Darro George, Junr.
Darrow Ammirus
Darrow Daniel
Darrow George
Darrow Jedidiah
Daudge Daniel
Davis Amos
Davis John
Day Aaron
Day Lewis
De Bevoise Charles
Debocker John
Deck Henry
Decker Jacob
Dedrick Frederick
Dedrick Thode
Degolan James
Degolin Joseph
Dekyn Leonar
Delamater Henry
Delamatter Benjamin
De Line Ryer
Delond David
Delong David
Delong Joseph
Demair John
Deniston William
Deuce Henery
Deven Henry
Devereux Theodorus
Devew Henry
Devoe Henry
Dibble Hezekiah
Dickerson James
Dickeson Gideon
Dickson James
Dickson Richard
Dilliwere John
Dimesa Gerret
Dingman Samuel
Dixon Gideon
Dodge Daniel
Dole William
Donnel John
Doty Isaac
Douglass Jonathan
Downen Cornelius
Downing Cornelius
Dox Peter
Doxley Klark
Driselmon Christian
Dubois Charles
Ducker Jacobus
Dunham John
Dusler Marcus
Eagars Julies
Eaker Nicoless
Earcher Edward
Eatick George
Eaton James
Ecker Nicholas
Edick Conrat
Edwards Abel
Edwards Samuel
Ellis John
Ellison David
Elsworth John
Engles James
Engrum Humphrey (see Ingham)
Esselstyn Jacob
Eveson John
Evins Samuel
Faling Lips
Faling Philip
Farguson James
Farris Aron
Felbush Jesse
Ferguson Caleb
Ferguson Hezekiah
Ferris Aaron
Filmore Richard
Fine Reuben
Flanburgh Antony
Flander Henry
Flander Jacob
Flansburgh Matthew
Flemeing Asa
Flicker John
Flipsen Hermennes
Flounsburgh Anthony
Folts Conrad
Fonda John
Fonk William
Foot John
Foot Simeon
Forgason James

Forstor Watson
Fort John
Foster John
Fowler Mayers
Fowler Morris
Fox Benjamin
Fox Peter
Fradenburg Abraham
Fraer Peter
Frailenbury Abr'm
Frank Andrew
Fratinbury Abraham
Freeman Jonas
French Anesel
Frisbee John
Fry George
Fryer Peter
Fuller Daniel
Fuller Isaac
Fuller Josiah
Fuller Varsel
Fulmer Christopher
Fulmore Christian
Funk William
Ganse Benjamin
Garret James
Garvey Thomas
Gause Benjamin
Gibson John
Gile Hennery
Gipson John
Goes Mathies
Goose Mathisi
Goose Nicholas
Graft Philip
Granger John
Green Ebenezer
Greggs Evert
Grime Henderick
Grime Henry
Grippen Egbert
Groat Abraham
Groesbeck Jacob
Groot Abraham
Groot Andrew
Grot Andrus
Guile Daniel
Guiles Henry
Gurshie Edward
Hackney George
Hagedorn Adam
Hagedorn Bartholomew
Hagedorn John
Hager Henry
Hager Joseph (see Nagar)
Haker Jesse
Hakes Jesse
Hall Benjamin
Hall Isaac
Hall William
Hallenbeack Henry, Junr.
Hallenbeck Garret
Hallenbeck Isaac
Hambleton William
Hamilton William
Hammen John C.
Hanby John
Handley John
Hankey John J.
Hannes Jacob
Hannis James
Harkeman George
Harman John Christopher
Harms Jacob
Harrington Isaac
Harrington William
Harrison Peter
Harson Haramnius
Harson Harman
Harson Peter
Harver Christian
Hary Phillip
Hass John
Hatch James
Hatch Matthew
Haugedorn John
Haugedorn Samuel
Haulenbeke Garrit
Haus Hendrick
Hausman John
Haven Christian
Havens Benjamin
Havens Darius
Havens Thomas
Hawley James
Hawley Zadok
Haws John
Heath James
Heath Josiah
Hebzenger Michael
Hebzinger John
Heecock Guiles
Heermance John
Hendericks Peter
Hendricks Peter
Herkimer George
Hermans John
Herrick Daniel
Herrington Isaac
Herrington William
Hervey Phillips
Hess John
Heysser John
Hgaboom James
Hichcox Giles
Hicks Joseph
Hids Daniel
Higgins Enoch
Hill Reuben
Hills Asa
Hillsinger John
Hillsinger Michael
Himlin Adom
Hines Daniel
Hines George
Histead Thaddeus
Hitchcock Zenos
Hobbs Samuel
Hodgson George
Hogoboom Jacob
Hogoboom James
Holdridge Amasa
Holdridge Amesiah
Holly Zadock
Holmes Rozel
Holms Jedediah
Holms Roswell
Holubake Isack
Holsted Ezekiel
Hoos Nicholas
Hopkins Thomas
Hople George
Hopper John
Horton William
Hough Zephaniah
House George
House Henry
Houseman John
How David
How Jesse
How Samuel
Howard Enos
Howard Jesse
Howber Felix
Howes Samuel
Howley James
Hubbard Samuel
Hubbart John
Hubberd John
Hubble Ithamer
Hudson William
Hull Isaac
Hunter James
Hunter John
Huntly Solomon
Husted Thaddeus
Hutchson William
Hyser John
Indian Anthony
Indian Nicholas
Ingels James
Ingham Humphrey (see Engrum)
Ingram Humpry
Ittig Goerg
Jackson Ebenezer
Jainkens Anthony
Jakeway Asael
Jenkins Anthony
Jerome Jason
Johnson Benjamin
Johnson Derick
Johnson John
Johnson Philip
Johnson Samuel
Johnston Benjamin
Johnston John
Johnston Phillip
Jones Harmanus
Jones Richard
Jones William
Jonk Jacob
Kanedy Henry
Kasler John
Kasselman Johannis
Kelly Henry
Kelse John
Kenny Amous
Kesler John
Kessler Adam
Ketchum Benjamin
Ketchum Joel
Ketchum Nathaniel
Ketts George
Kill Christopher
King Leonard
King Thomas
Kinney Amos
Kipple George
Kitman Edward
Kittle Adam
Kittle Jocham
Kitts George
Klukman Frederick
Knapp Henry
Knapp William
Knox Frederick
Kolb John
Koll John
Lain Alexander
Lake William
Lally John
Lambert Peter
Lamon George
Lancaster Samuel
Lance John
Lane Alexander
Lansing John
Lansingh Evert
Lard William
Larraway Jacob
Laughaday John

Laughre John
Laveway Jacob
Lawrence Peter
Leifheat John
Lent Henry
Leonard Elijah
Lewes Ebuniser
Lewis Ebenezer
Libble Thomas
Lighthart Barnabas
Lint Henry
Livingston Richard
Loman George
Lonas John
Lonis John
Lord John
Lord Joseph
Lord Timothy
Lovejoy Daniel
Lovel John
Low John
Lummis Ezekiel
Lusk Jacob
Lusk Michael
Lusk William
Lyfhidt John
Lyons Nathaniel
Mabb John
Makefee William
Malat Richard
Maloon John
Marshel Simeon
Martin Amasa
Mason John
Matherwson Warren
Matteson Warren
Mattice George
Mayer Lewis
Meer John
Meinger Timthy
Miler Peter
Miles William
Miller Andrew
Miller Eleazer
Miller George
Miller James
Miller Peter
Miller William
Mob John
Mobs Peirs
Moles Peeres
Molloy Thomas
Monger Timothy
Montgomerie John
Montgomery John
Moor Peres
Moor Peter
Moore Jacob
More Thomas
Morris Nicholas
Morrison Nicholas
Morroy James
Mors Joshua
Moshier Thomas
Moss Josiah
Mower George
Mower Peter
Moyer David
Mudge Ebenezer
Mulley Thomas
Murray Alexander
Murry James
Myer Lodewick
Myers Frederick
Myers John
McAntier Thomas
McChesney Samuel
McCollister Archable
McDole George
McDowel George
McGee George
McGee William
McGill John
McGurfy Edward
McGurfy Robert
McGurshic Robert
McKeen Samuel
McKnot Jimmie
McMaster Robert
McMichel Ebenezer
McMickle Ebenezer
McNut James
McVane Daniel
McVey Daniel
McWiams John
McWilliams John
Nagar Joseph (see Hagar)
Name Abraham
Nestel Richard
Nestle George
Newkirk Thomas
Newton Benjamin
Nicholls Silas
Nickals John
Nier Casper
Noor Peres
Oakley Jonathan
O'Briant Cornelius
Olman Frederick
Omens Daniel
Orchard Thomas
Orcher Edward
Orendorf Daniel
Orsher Onies
Overbagh John, Junr.
Overpagh John
Pace Henry
Paddock John
Paine John
Palmer Amoziah
Parker Elisha
Parker Robert
Parker Ruben
Patrick James
Patrick Matthew
Paulay Benjamin
Payer John
Payne John
Peak Chris
Pease Abner
Pease Asa
Peek Christopher
Peelor Jacob
Perry David
Peter Godlip
Peters Simeon
Peters Simon
Peterson John
Pettit John
Peulay Benjamin
Phelps Amous
Philips Abner
Philips Amos
Philips Isaac
Philips Jacob
Philips Philip
Plum John
Price George
Prime John
Primer Ludwig
Prince Negro (colored)
Pudney Thorn
Purchase Taberd
Putnam David
Puxley Crark
Quinby Stephen
Quimbey Stephen
Radley Jacob
Randal Nathaniel
Randell Benjamin
Randle Matthew
Randle Matthias
Raspol Frederick
Rattenam George
Rattle Joseph
Ray William
Ray Zacherius
Ray Zacheus
Read John
Reais Daniel
Redwood Prince
Reman John
Remaw John
Rexford Ensign
Rexford Joseph
Rexford Joseph, Junr.
Richards John
Richardson George
Richardson Isaac
Richarson James
Richarson William
Richmond Benjamin
Richmond Silas
Richmond Silvester
Richtmeyer Johannes
Rightmier John
Rightmire Henry
Rihes Henry, Jr.
Rinehart William
Ripley Asa
Ripley Piram
Ritchauson James
Robbens James
Robberds John
Robbins Charles
Roberson Charles
Roberts John
Robertson Jeremiah
Robins Jube
Robinson Hector
Robinson Jeremiah
Rockefeller William
Rogers George
Rogers Jacob
Roop John
Roop Peter
Rosa Storme
Rose Jacob
Rosed Storm
Rottinower George
Rowlee Jabish
Rowley Aron
Rowley Aaron, Junr.
Rowley Samuel
Rowley Samuel Ham
Rowley Seth
Rude Eli
Ruff Jonathan
Rumney John
Rumney John G.
Russel James
Russell Benjamin
Russman Conradt
Ryan Duncan
Ryker Henry
Rynhard William
Salbury Joseph
Salspury Gideon
Saltmarsh William
Saltmask William
Sanders John
Sanders Wat

Sauders Wat, Junr.
Saunders John
Savage Joel
Sayer Lambert
Scarbory William
Schall George
Schall John
Schank William
Scheneman Hendrick
Scheneman Henry
Schermehorn John
Scheyler John
Schmit Anton
Schmit Henrick
Schoolcraft Peter
Schoolcraft Pitter
Scribner Thomas
Schulgraft John
Schultze William
Schutt William
Schutt William, Junr.
Schuyler David
Schuyler David, Junr.
Schuyler Dirck
Schuyler John
Schuyler John Jost
Scott Cornelias
Scott Henry
Scribner Thaddeus
Scribner Thomas
Seeber John
Seeber John W.
Semister John
Senn Aaron
Shafer
Shafer John Conrad
Shall Hendrick
Shall Henry
Shattuck Thomas
Shaver John
Shaw
Shaw Comfort
Shaw Ebenezer
Shaw Jacob
Shaw William
Sheffield Nathan
Shepard James
Sherman Jenkins
Shifflebean Jacob
Shiltenberger Casparus
Shiltenburger Casper
Shoefelt Christopher
Sholl John
Shoolcraft John
Shoot William, Junr.
Show Jacob
Shults Henry
Shults William
Shute William
Shuts Abraham
Simonds Joshua
Simonds Joshua, Junr.
Simons John
Simons John (see Smor Josams)
Sits George
Skiltenberger Casparus
Skinner Jonathan
Skinner Micah
Skinner Michael
Slbury Joseph
Smith Adam
Smith Anthony
Smith Ezekiel
Smith Henry
Smith James
Smith John
Smith John Connat
Smith Joseph
Smith Nicholas
Smith Philip
Smith Thomas
Smith William
Smor Josams (see Simons John)
Sole William
Sparbeck Conradt
Spaulding Nehemiah
Speed Henry
Spencer Truman
Spickerman Philip
Spike Daniel
Spoon John
Sprague Alexander
Stalker John
Stephen John
Stephens Isaac
Stephens John
Stevens Isaac
Stewart James
Steward John
Steward Robert
Stewart John
Stolker John
Stopplebeen Jacob
Storm David
Stormes David
Strobeck Adam
Strong John
Stuart John
Suits George
Suits Peter
Sults Henry
Suts Peter P.
Swayer Lammert
Taber William
Tacker John
Talman Thomas
Tancill Danyel
Tanner Jacob
Tansel Daniel
Tanall Nicholas
Tarbox Job
Tarbush Isaac
Tartle Joseph
Tawner Jacob
Taylor Friend
Taylor Jasper
Taylor Johannis
Taylor Joseph
Taylor Samuel
Taylor Thomas
Teal John
Ten Eyck Barrent
Teneyck Gurney
Ter Bosh Isaac
Thomas Beriah
Thomas Buriel
Thompson Jack
Titus Philip
Tollman Thomas
Tortle Joseph
Townsen James
Trewax Abraham
Trewax Jacob
Trewax Jacob A.
Trim Walter
Tripp Job
Trisselman Christian
Troll John
Truax John
Trumble Judah
Tryon William
Tubbs Cyrus
Turner Lemuel
Tusler Marks
Tussler John
Tymoson Garret
Ullendorf Daniel
Ulman Frederick
Utley Jarmiah
Valentine James
Valentine Stephen
Vedder Peter
Verty Thomas
Vestry Thomas
Vols Conrad
Von Schleik Gorg
Vroman Adam
Vroman Peter
Van Alstyne Cornelius
Van Alstyne John
Van Aps Samuel
Van Arnem William
Van Atter James
Van Camp Moses
Van Deboe Jacob
Vandebol Jacob
Van Deburgh Daniel
Van Derhider David
Van Derhider Gershom
Van Der Wark John
Van Der Werken Henry
Vandeuse Aaron
Vandeuse William
Van Dusen Aaron
Van Dyck David
Van Dyck Jacob
Van Ess John
Van Hoosen Rynier
Van Ieven Thomas
Vannetta Jacobus
Van Nist Janeson
Van Nist Jeranmus
Van Nist John
Van Schaack Nicholes
Van Sicker Rynier
Van Sikle David
Van Slycke George
Van Sycklar David
Van Valkenburgh George
Van Valkenburgh Harmanus
Van Valkenburgh Henry
Van Valkenburgh Joachim
Van Valkenburgh Joachim, Senior
Van Valkenburgh Leanor
Van Valker George
Van Vurman Cornelius
Van Worman Cornelius
Van Wormer Matthew
Van Yevern Thomas
Wagenner Michael
Wagoner George
Wagonnit Hermanis
Wallebure John
Walradt Adolphus
Walter George
Warren Nathaniel
Wart John
Wassou James
Wasson John
Waterman Elisha
Waterman Samuel
Watkins Edmund
Watson Jepson
Watson William
Watson Zephthah
Wauson John
Weat Nathaniel
Weaver David

Webster Peletiah
Weever David
Welch Rozzel
Welch Thomas
Wells Abraham
Wells Philip
Welsh Thomas
Wemp Aron (see Wemple)
Wemple Aron (see Wemp)
Wentworth James
Wentworth Shuble
Werts John
Wheeler Abraham
Wheeler John
Wheever Nicholas
Whing Benjamin
Whing Daniel
White James
White John
White Nathaniel
White Perregreen
White Stephen
White Stephen, Junr.
White William
Whitehead Thomas
Whilbers John
Whitman Benjamin
Whitmore Christopher
Wilcocks Nathan
Wilcox Jeremiah
Wilcox Nathan
Wilcox Nathaniel
Wilcox Salvenus
Wiles John
Willer Amos
Williams Elias
Williams John
Williams William
Willson James
Willson Jesse
Willson John
Wiltsey John
Winne Johannis
Winney John
Winter John
Winters John
Winterscale Barnaby
Wintworth James
Witmer Christopher
Wolf Samuel
Wolsh Rosel
Wood Barnabas
Wood James
Wood Robert
Wood Samuel
Wood Thomas
Wood William
Woodard Ephraim
Woodbeck Samuel
Woolsey Nathan
Wormwood John
Woss Gerrit
Woss Jacob
Wright David
Wright Jacob
Wyat Nathaniel
Yager Hendrick
Yatt James
Yett James
Young Henry
Young John
Young Peter
Young Peter, Junr.
Young William
Yucker John
Yuger Johannes
Yunger Henrick

ALBANY COUNTY MILITIA.

COLONEL ABRAHAM CUYLER
COLONEL JACOB LANSING, JR.
MAJOR JOHN PRICE
MAJOR HARMANUS WANDELL
ADJUTANT HENRY VAN VEGHTEN
QUARTER MASTER GERRIT RYCKMAN

CAPT. ISAAC DE FOREST
" GARRET GROESBECK
" WILLIAM HUNN
" JACOB T. LANSING
" NICHOLAS MARSELIUS
" JACOB ROSEBOOM
" ABRAHAM YATES
LIEUT. NICHOLAS BLEECKER
" JOHN CUDERKIRK
" CONRADT GANSEVOORT
" WILLIAM GROESBECK
" HENRY HOGAN
LIEUT. THOMAS HUN
" ISAAC LANSING
" JOHN SCOTT
" ABRAHAM SCHUYLER
" GERRIT VAN SCHAICK
" JOHN A. WENDELL
ENSIGN WILLIAM BLOODGOOD
" JOHN BOGART
" JOHN FONDA, JR.
" JACOB HOGHSTRASSER
" ABRAHAM A. LANSING

ENLISTED MEN

Bentheunn I. V.
Brooks Jonathan
Campbell Archibald
Croser John
Davis John
Douw Peter W.
Eights M.
Ellis John
Evertsen Barnabas
Fonda Jacobus
Fryer Isaac
Green James
Hansen Benjamin
Harsen Francis
Hilton Jacob R.
Hilton Jonathan
Hoggstrasser Jacob
Hoogkirk M.
Hunn Thomas
Hyer William
Lansing Henry
Marselis John
Myers John
Nisbey Christopher
Peterson Isaac
Pruyn Christopher
Pruyn Jacob
Pruyn Reynier
Redliff John
Ryckman Garret
Schuyler Dirk
Van Gowan Ryener
Van Sante Rybeart
Van Wie William
Wandelaer John D.
Wermer Cornelius
Wilkinsin John

A LETTER FROM COLONEL PETER GANSEVOORT.

[illegible] of Capt [illegible] Beat
Jacobus Phillips
the 27 of April 1780
Major Henry Van Rensselaer
Jacobus Phillips Capt
Jeremiah Muller Lieu
George Phillips Ensign
Stephen Muller Ser
Jacob Muller
Jeremiah Muller
Johannis Muller
Cornelius Muller
Jeremiah C. Muller
[illegible] Sunday
[illegible]
[illegible]
George [illegible]
Adam [illegible]
Simon [illegible]
William Phillips
David Phillips
[illegible]
Adam Phillips
Johannis Shuldt
George Davis
George Landt
William Davis
Johannis Sharp
Peter New
Christian Phillips
Peter Van Broeck
[illegible] Smith Serj
Hendrick Shuldt Jun
Jacob Conklin
Frances Emrick
Adam Emrick
Hendrick Oostrander
Johannis Landt
Johannis Landt Junr
Simon Muller
Abraham Muller
Wilhelmus Phillips

Jacob Phillips
Nicolaas Marten
Jacob Stuppelbean
Jacob Stuppelbean Junt
Valentine Stuppelbean
Michal Stuppelbean
Adam Shave
Jacobus Oostrander
Cornelius Oostrander
Hendrick Oostrander
Adolus Dingmans
Hendrick Dingmans
Johannis Dingmans Ser
William Dingmans
Frank Smith
[illegible] Patrick No. 4
Hendrick Yager
Johannis Salsberry
William Pike Serj
William Phillips Ju
Hendrick Phillips
[illegible] Phillips
Hendrick Phillips
Johannis Moule
Jacob Moule
[illegible] Graudt
Hendrick Kaudt
Andries Kaudt
Emrath Kaudt
Jacob Gaull No. 3
Antoney Mollis
William Reed
John Reed
John Stead Junr
Peter Barger
Samuel Kaltenbeach
Godfree Shoemaker
Hendrick Shoemaker
Whinant Mantle
Frances Mantle
David Darling
Peter Darling
John Grautt
Wilhelmus Grautt

SPECIMEN OF "CLASS" OR "BEAT" ROLL.

Albany County Militia — (Continued).

COLONEL ABRAHAM WEMPLE
MAJOR ABRAHAM SWITS
MAJOR MYNDERT M. WEMPLE
ADJUTANT JOHN VAN DRUSSEN
QUARTER MASTER GERRITT G. LANSING
QUARTER MASTER MYDERT WEMPLE

Capt. Thomas B. Bancker
" Jellis Fonda
" John Mynderse
" Abraham Oothout
" Jacob Schermerhorn
" John Van Petten
" Gerrit S. Veeder
" Jesse Van Slyck
" Abraham Van Eps (Company exempts)
" Thomas Wasson
Lieut. Nicholas Barheydt
" Jellis A. Fonda
" William Moore
" Jacobus Peek
" John Roseboom
" Jacob Sullivan
" John Thornton
Lieut. Daniel Toll
" Gerritt S. Veeder, Jr.
" Philip Vedder
" Arent S. Vedder
" Francis Vedder
" Walter Vroman
" Lawrence Vrooman
" Andries Van Petten
" Cornelius A. Van Slyck
" Philip D. Van Vorst
" Myndert A. Wemple
" Jellis Yates
" Nicholas Yates
Ensign Teunis Swart
" Abraham J. Traux
" Cornelius Z. Van Santvoord
" Myndert R. Wemple

Additional Names on State Treasurer's Pay Books.

Lieut. Robert Alexander
" Robert McMichael
" John B. Vrooman
Ensign Alexander Crawford
" Fram'r Schermerhorn

ENLISTED MEN.

Alexander Alexandee
Alexander Robert
Alexander Sandy
Alison William
Ament Evert
Arkson Gerret
Atlass Lent
Aylworth Abraham
Baker Garrit
Balie Jacob
Barheydt Cornelius
Barheydt Jacob
Barheydt John
Barheydt Lewis
Barhout Cornelius
Barhout John
Barhydt Tunes
Barhyt James
Barop John
Barope Andrew
Barope Thomas
Bartley Daniel
Bartlie Micel
Basteanse John
Basteyan John
Bastien John
Bayrop John
Beath Jelles
Beath Roberth
Beath Thomas
Becker Gerret
Berherdt Lewis
Berhydt Tunes
Bersleder Jacob
Bertie Mykel
Bete Thomas
Beth Jelles
Beth Robert
Betts Robert R.
Boice Abraham
Boice James
Bond Richard
Bot Samuel S.
Bovie Abraham
Bovie Isaac
Bovie Israel
Bovee Nicholas
Bowman Frederick
Boyce Abraham
Bradford James
Bradt Anthony D.
Bradt Aphrieam
Bradt Arent A.
Bradt Arent S.
Bradt Aron
Bradt Aaron A.
Bradt Charles
Bradt Cornelius
Bradt Elias
Bradt Ephraim
Bradt Gerret
Bradt Jacobus
Bradt Jacobus A.
Bradt Jacobus S.
Bradt John
Bradt John S.
Bradt Mindart
Bradt Samuel
Bradt Samuel S.
Bragham John
Braghom Joseph
Braghom Symon
Brat Arent S.
Brath Aphreim
Braun Abraham
Breat Antony
Brewer Henry
Broadford James
Broghom John
Broghom Symon

Brouwen Hendrick
Brower Ritchart
Brown Abraham
Burns Arent
Burns David
Buys Abraham
Buys James
Cain Barrent
Caine Peter William
Caine Warrant
Campbell Daniel
Canaday John, Junr.
Carl Henry
Carl William
Cartright Henry, Junr.
Cartright John
Carty Henry, Junr.
Cassedo John
Catlet Thomas
Caurl Henry
Caurl John
Caurl William
Celder Abraham
Cessler Thomas
Challon Allexander
Channel John
Channel Thomas
Channon Alexander
Channon Robert
Channon Thomas
Charlo John
Charlo William
Charloe Handrick
Charloe Handrick, Jr.
Charls Henry
Charls Tobias
Christeanse Asswerus
Christianse Isaac
Cilker William
Cittle Daniel
Cittle David
Cittle John
Clark Henry A.
Clark Matthew
Clement Arent
Clement Eldert
Clement Johannes
Clement John
Clement Peter
Clut Jacob
Clut John F.
Clute Bartholomew
Clute Daniel
Clute Frederick
Clute Jacob
Clute Jacob P.
Clute John
Clute John B.
Clute John Curtis
Clute Isaac
Clute Peter
Clute Petrus
Combs John
Commens John
Condey Adam
Connor Simon
Consale Manuel
Consalus David
Consaul David
Consaul Manual
Corl John
Corneel Wessel
Cornue Daniel
Cornue Wassel
Covle William
Craneford Joseph
Crawford John
Crawford Joseph
Cristeionse Isaac
Cronshorn John
Cummings John
Cunde Adam
Cuyler John
Daves Abraham
Davis Abraham
Davis John
De Evart John
De Garmo Thewes
Degelen James
Degeler James, Junr.
Degollian Joseph
De Graaf Jesse D.
De Graf Connels
De Graff Abraham
De Graff Andrew
De Graff Jesse
De Graff John
De Graff John N.
De Graff John N., Junr.
De Graff Simon
De Graff William
Degrauf Symon
De Grave John N.
De Gullia James
De Gullia James, Junr.
De Gullie Joseph
Dellemont Abraham
Dellemont Hendrick
Dilleno Hendrik
Dorn Abraham
Dorne John
Douw Abraham
Duncan John, Junr.
Eemqie John
Elkson Samuel
Ellice James
Elsworth Abraham
Ement Eldert
Ennie William
Ensil Bertram
Erkson Garret
Erkson Henry
Erkson William
Falbush Andrew
Falbush Jonas
Farlies Caleb
Farly Caleb
Feldhousen John
Fermain John
Ferman John
Flansbury William
Folger Benjamin
Folger Thomas
Folgier Thomas
Fonda Jelles P.
Fort John
Fort John D.
Foulger Thomas
Frank David
Fransway John
French David
Gardner William
Glen Isack
Glen Jacob
Glen John
Glen John S.
Gorden Charles
Gorden Robert
Gorder William
Gordon Joseph
Gordon William
Grag Andrew
Grag James
Gregg Andrew
Groat Abraham
Groat Abraham C.
Groat Andrew
Groat Cornelius
Groat Simon
Groot Amos
Groot Simon
Groot Simon C.
Grot Abraham
Grot Abraham A.
Grot Cornelius
Grote Abraham C.
Hackney George
Hagadorn Harmanus
Hall John
Hall John W.
Hall Nicholas
Hall William
Hanna Alexander
Hannon Alexander
Hare Peter
Harnel Samuel
Harner Samuel
Hars Peter
Harsey William
Harsford John
Hase Dockter
Heddrington Joseph
Hedget Abraham
Hedrengton Joseph
Helmer Henyost
Hendrick Peter
Henry John
Hoopole George
Horsford John
House John George
House Peter
Hughan John
Hydenburgh Sybrant
Jettle Ezra
Jonsing Abraham
Kaneday John
Kaneday Samuel
Kannady Alexander
Kannel John C.
Kees John
Kelder Abraham
Kennedy John
Kennedy Samuel
Kinsley Joseph
Lambert John
Lansing Abraham G.
Lansing Cornelius
Lansing John C.
Lansing John G.
Lansing Gerrit
Lansingh John
Lansingh John C.
Lewes William
Lewis John
Lighthall Abraham
Lighthall Abraham W.
Lighthall George
Lighthall Nicholas
Littel Thomas
Little David
Littlejohn Duncan
Lonpart Jacob
Lonsing Abraham
Luypart Jacob
Lythall Abraham
Lythall Abraham W.
Lythall William
Lytle David
Maap John
Mab Robert
Mabee Cornelius
Mabee John

Mabee John, Junr.
Mabee Peter
Mabie Albert
Mabie Arent
Mabie Cornelius
Mabie John
Mabie John J.
Mabie Patrick
Mabie Peter
Mabis Aron
Maby Cornelius
Mailes Charles
Main William
Mannen Edward
Mannon John
Marcle Dirk
Markle Matthew
Marrikell William
Marseles John
Marselis Ahaswerus
Marsellus John
Marselus Gilrt
Martin Charles
Maseles John
Masten Robert
Mayston Robert
Meals Charles
Mebie Juiter
Meebie Albert
Melb John
Mercer Alexander
Mercker William
Merical Dirick
Merseles Egsbert
Merseles Henry
Merselius Arent
Merselius Gysbert
Merselius John
Merselous Hendrick
Merselous John
Merselus Alexander
Mils Chris
Mitchals Hugh
Moass John
Moor James
Moore John
Moore William
Morrell Thomas
Muller Jacob, Junr.
Mulray John
Murry John
Myndorse John
Mynderse John R.
Mynderse Laurence
Mynderse Harmen
McBane John
McCallome James
McCanel Alexander
McCartes John
McCarty John
McCarty William
McCew James
McCnut Samuel
McColm James
McDarmont James
McDarmouth James
McDermid James
McDougall Duncan
McEarley John
McFarlin Andrew
McFarlind Andrew
McFerling John
McGenoris Robert
McGinnis Robert
McIntyre William
McKie Samuel
McMarlin William
McMartin William
McMichael Alexander
McMichael Daniel
McMichall James
McMichen Peter
McMickel James
McMickl Danil
McNutt Samuel
McQuean James
McQuier James
Nanning John
Neally Matthew
Neard Christopher
Neiger John
Nixon Josse
Ogden John
Ouderkerk Arent
Passage George
Passage George, Junr.
Patterson Thomas
Patteson Oliver
Peak Jesse
Peck Arent
Peck Cornelius
Peck Daniel
Peck Henry
Peck Jacobus
Peck James J.
Peck Jesse
Peck John
Peck Lewes
Peckburn John
Peeck Arent
Peeck Christopher
Peeck Cornelius
Peeck Cornelius C.
Peeck Harmanus
Peeck Harmanus H.
Peeck Harmanus J.
Peeck Henry H.
Peeck Jacobus
Peeck Jacobus H.
Peeck John
Peeck John J.
Peeck Joseph
Peeck Lewis
Peek Christopher
Peek Daniel
Peek Jacobus Vedder
Peek James J.
Peek Joseph
Peek Lewis
Peeke John J.
Peterson Harmanus
Peterson Herman
Petterson Charles
Petterson Oliver
Petterson Thomas
Philips Thomas
Pruyn Samuel
Putman Aaron
Putman Arent
Putman Arent L.
Putman Aron L.
Putman Cornelius
Putman Cornelius I.
Putman John
Quack Gradus
Quackenbos Genardous
Quackenbos John
Reis John
Reldert Jakop
Renx Anddro
Reyley Jacobus
Rise John
Robison John
Rosa Isaac
Rosa John T.
Rose Elias
Rose John
Ryckman Cournelus
Rykman Cornelius
Rylie Jacobus
Rylie Philip
Rynex Andrew
Rynex John
Rynis John
Rynix Richard
Sacie David
Sanders John
Sawer James
Scanger Thomas
Schemhorn Garret
Schermerhoorn Simen
Schermerhorn Andrew
Schermerhorn Andries
Schermerhorn Aurent
Schermerhorn Barnardus
Schermerhorn Bartholomew
Schermerhorn Henry, J.
Schermerhorn Jacob
Schermerhorn Jacob J.
Schermerhorn John
Schermerhorn John J.
Schermerhorn Nicholas
Schermerhorn Reijer
Schermerhorn Richard
Schermerhorn Ryer
Schermerhorn Rykert
Schermerhorn Symon
Schuyler Reuben
Seacy Wilhelmus
Shallon Alexander
Shannon John
Shannon William
Shelling Alexander
Shellow Alexander
Shennon Thomas
Shutes Christian
Sickel Phylip F'c
Simonds Reuben
Smealle John
Smeth John
Smilie John
Smith Adam
Smith Robert
Speck Abraham
Speck Tobyas
Speek Tobias
Spitcher Gerrit
Spitser Arent
Spitser Aron
Spitser Gerret
Staley George
Staly Jacob
Standly John
Stealee George
Stealy Henry
Steeley Matthew
Steers Peter
Stenerd Daniel
Stevens John
Steward Daniel
Steward David
Steward George
Steward James
Steward John
Stewart Daniel
Stewart John
Steylee Jacob
Steylee Matthew
Stirs Peer
St. John Tedius
Stuart James

Susie Abraham
Susie David
Sullivan Charles
Sullivan Jacob
Swart Jacobus
Swart James
Swart Nicholaas
Swits Henry
Swits Jacob
Swits Jabob, Junr.
Swits Jacob A.
Swits Jacob J.
Swords Thomas
Symons Ruben
Tall Charles
Taus Davis
Tauses David
Taylor Solomon
Taylor Walter
Teller Jacobus
Teller John, Junr.
Teller William
Ten Eyck Jacob
Ten Eyck Myndert S.
Ter Willigen Solomon
Terwilliger Isaac
Terwilliger Jacobus
Terwilliger Solomon
Thaneday John
Thompson John
Thomson John
Thomson Peter
Thorn Samuel
Thornton James
Thornton Thomas
Times Michel
Toll Charles
Toll John
Tortle Selmon
Truax Abraham
Truax Abraham J.
Truax Abraham P.
Truax Caleb
Truax John
Truax John P.
Trumbull John
Turnbull John
Turs Peurs
Turtell Israel
Tutle Ezra
Tuttle Ezerial
Tuttle Solomon
Tyms Michael
Vadder Peter H.
Vagner Andrew
Veader Cornelius
Veader Nicholas
Veader Peter S.
Veader Thelmes
Vealy Philip
Vedder Albert
Vedder Albert A.
Vedder Alexander
Vedder Arent
Vedder Arent A.
Vedder Arent T.
Vedder Barrent
Vedder Cornelius
Vedder Francis
Vedder Frederick
Vedder Harmanis
Vedder John
Vedder John B.
Vedder Nicholas
Vedder Nicoleas
Vedder Peter
Vedder Seymon H.
Vedder Simon
Veder Nicolas
Veder Halimis
Veder Wilhilmus
Veeder Barent
Veeder Cornelius
Veeder Gerret
Veeder Gerret S.
Veeder Helmus S.
Veeder John
Veeder John B.
Veeder Nicolas
Veeder Peter H.
Veeder Peter S.
Veeder Peter T.
Veeder Simon B.
Veeder Simon H.
Veeder Wilhelmus
Vilen Phillip
Visger John
Visger John, Junr.
Visher John, Junr.
Vlack John
Vreene Alexander
Vrooman Adam
Vrooman Adam H.
Vrooman Adam S.
Vrooman Arent
Vrooman Aron
Vrooman David
Vrooman Hendrick
Vrooman Henry
Vrooman Jacob A.
Vrooman Jacob I.
Vrooman Jacob J.
Vrooman John B.
Vrooman John J.
Vrooman John T.
Vrooman Simon
Vrooman Simon J.
Van Antwerp Garret
Van Antwerp Peter
Van Antwerp Peter A.
Van Antwerp Simon
Van Antwerp Simon J.
Van Antwerpe John
Van Benthuysen Peter
Van De Bogert Joseph
Van De Bogert Nicholas
Van De Graff Abraham N.
Van De Graff John
Van Derhyden Daniel
Van Derhyden David
Van Derhyder Daniel
Van Derhyder David
Van Der Valgen Petrus
Van Der Volger Cornelius
Van Dresen Peter
Van Driesen Peter
Van Duyck Cornelius H.
Van Dyck Cornelius
Van Dyck Cornelius N.
Van Dyck Henry
Van Dyck Henry H.
Van Dyck Henry I.
Van Eps John
Van Eps John B.
Van Eps John J.
Van Fran Richard
Van Guyseling Peter
Van Guysling Cornelius
Van Guysling Jacob
Van Ingan John Vicher
Van Inge John
Van Ingen Joseph
Van Leph William
Van Nes Gerret
Van Patten Frederick D.
Van Pette Adam
Van Pette Frederick
Van Pette Frederick D.
Van Pette Jan
Van Pette Nicolas
Van Petto Philip
Van Petten Adam
Van Petten Arent N.
Van Petten Fradrick
Van Petten Frederick
Van Petten Frederick S.
Van Petten Hendrik
Van Petten Henry
Van Petten Nicholas
Van Petten Nicholas A.
Van Petten Nicholas H.
Van Petten Nicholas R.
Van Petten Nicholas S.
Van Petten Philip
Van Petten Simon
Van Petten Simon F.
Van Pitten Andrew
Van Schaick Gerret
Van Sice Abraham
Van Sice Cornelius
Van Sice Gysbert
Van Sice Isaac
Van Sice Jacobus
Van Sice John
Van Slyck Aaron
Van Slyck Adrian
Van Slyck Andrew
Van Slyck Anthony
Van Slyck Cornelius
Van Slyck Cornelius A.
Van Slyck Cornelius P.
Van Slyck Harmanus
Van Slyck Harmanus N.
Van Slyck Peter
Van Veeder Peter
Van Vlak Benjamin
Van Voghter Anthony
Van Vorst Jellis
Van Vorst John D.
Van Vorst Peter
Van Vranken Dirk
Van Vranken Maus
Van Vranken Maus M.
Van Vranken Nicholas
Van Vranken Nicolas N.
Van Vranken Richard
Van Vranken Rykert
Wagenman Michel
Wagner Michael
Wagner Nicolas
Waller Robert
Wallrad
Walrat Jacob
Wandner Richard
Wandry John B.
Ward Christopher
Warner Richard
Wassalse Harman
Watson Alexander
Weaton Robert
Weaton Ruben
Weist Coonrad
Weller Frederick
Weller Robert
Wemple John
Wemple John J.
Wemple John T.
Wemple Mindert R.
Wemple Myndert
Wendell Ahasuerus
Wendle John B.
Wessel Arent

Wesselse Arent
Wesselse Aron
West Coonrad
Whiley John
White William
Wiely John
Willeger Solomon T.
Williams Cornelius
Williams Jacob
Windelby John B.
Wood John
Yanter Henry
Yates Abraham
Yates Abraham J.
Yates John
Yates Nicolas
Yeats Abraham
Young Calvin
Young Fred
Young Frederick
Young Seth
Younter Henry

Albany County Militia — (Continued).

COLONEL PHILIP P. SCHUYLER

LIEUTENANT COLONEL BARENT I. STAATS

MAJOR ABRAHAM D. FONDA

ADJUTANT JOHN P. QUACKENBOSS

QUARTER MASTER CHRISTOPHER LANSING

CAPT. JOHN GROOT
" JARIVAN HOGAN
" ——— HOOKS
" JACOB J. LANSING
" LEVINIS F. LANSINGH
" HENRY OSTROM
" TEUNIS A. SLINGERLAND
" JACOB VAN ARNUM
" JOHN A. VAN WIE
" BASTIAN T. VICHER
" ABRAHAM VEEDER
LIEUT. JOHN AKER
" MATTHEW FLANSBURGH
" WILLIAM FLANSBURGH
" GERRITT R. GERRITSEE
" WENDEL HILDENBRAND
" EPHRAIM HUDSON
LIEUT. TIMOTHY HUTTON
" JACOB LANSING
" JOHN LEONARD
" BARENT MEYNDERSE
" PETER S. SCHUYLER
" ISAAC V. VAN AERNAN
" ISAAC VAN ARNUM
" LEVI VAN AUKEN
" GERRIT VAN DEN BERGH, JR.
" GEORGE WAGONER
" JACOB WEEVER
" LEVINUS WINNE
" CHRISTIAN A. YATES
ENSIGN ADAM DEITS
" DIRK HEEMSTRAAT
" WILLIAM TILLMAN
" JOHN VAN ARNUM

ADDITIONAL NAMES ON STATE TREASURER'S PAY BOOKS.

MAJOR JOHN PRICE

CAPT. DERICK VAN ARNUM
LIEUT. DERICK DE FOREST
" HENRY OSTANDER
" JACOB SCHERMERHORN
" EDWARD THOMAS
LIEUT. TEUNIS VAN DE BERGH
" AUREY VAN WIE
ENSIGN JOHN SHAVER
" JOHN H. VAN WIE

ENLISTED MEN.

Algate Thomas
Allet William
Angus James
Arnold Elisha
Anthony Israel
Anthony John
Aonhoudt Christean
Appel Hennrich
Arnhoudt John
Arrenson
Backer Lowick
Backer Philip
Balner Caunnuad
Bancker Garret
Banks Arthur
Bard Francis
Bartt John
Bauch Nicolas
Bauman Andrus
Beard Francis
Beaver Edward
Becker Adam
Becker Gerret
Becker Henry
Becker John
Bell Stephen
Bender Christian
Berkley Michael
Bever Thomes
Bevins Benjamin
Bevits Benjamin
Bishop Joseph
Bloomendall John
Bogeart Christopher
Boger Peter
Bonkle John
Boom Abraham
Bovis Ride
Bowman Andrew
Bradt Adrian
Bradt Daniel A.
Bradt Gerret
Bradt Hendrick
Bradt John
Bradt Peter
Bramblee William
Bratt John T.
Brower John
Browers Richard
Browne Richard
Bruier Richard
Bulman Jacob
Bulsen Gerardus
Bulsen Henry
Bulsen John
Bulsin Benjamin
Burger John
Burnside John
Burnside William
Calwell John
Cammel Harmanus
Carman Frederick
Carr Joseph
Carr William
Casbert John
Chestney John
Chestney William
Church Jacob
Clase John
Claver Nicholas
Clute Fradrick
Clute Gradus

Clute Jacob
Clute John
Clute Nicholas
Clyne Nicholas
Coenie William
Collance Cornelius
Cooper Obediah
Corking Ese
Corsbort John
Coss Cunrat
Cougneed Peter
Covenhoven Samuel
Craney Philip
Crannel Martha
Crannel Nicholas
Crannell William Winslow
Crannell Martin
Cullan Cornelius
Cunniger John
Cuyler Abraham
Daner Moses
Dannals Jacob
De Forest Dirck
De Forest Jesse
Delap John
Delong David
De Voe John
Dewever Abraham
Douglas John
Dygert George
Dygert William, Junr.
Ecker Dennis
Effner Joseph
Ellicks Frederick
Erchard Edward
Everse John
Eversy Evert
Evertsen Evert
Faro Chritien
Faro Henry
Faro Patris
Featherly John
Feddely Philip
Flansburgh David
Flansburgh Denal
Flansburgh John
Flansburgh Peter
Fonda Jacob D.
Foster Jacop
Fradenbergh Isaac
France Cristiffel
France Jacop
Frasner Lefvenes
Frat John
Frats Casper
Frats Nicholas
Frederick Matthew
Freeman John
Friet Michel
Fryer John
Gardinier Hendrick
Gauns Frederick
Goewey Andrew
Goewey Barent
Goewey Garret
Goowey Solomon
Grass Mikele
Groat John
Groesbeeck John
Groesbeck Anthony
Groesbeck Gilbert
Groesbeck Gysbert
Groesbeck Peter W.
Groot Abraham
Groot Derick
Groot Isaac
Gunsal Peter
Gunsalis John
Guree Philip
Hallenbeck Jacob
Hamilton James
Hanse Jacob
Harbeck John
Heamstreadt Dirck
Heemstraet Jacob
Heemstraet John
Heemstrat Isaac
Heemstrat Philip
Heermans Israel
Heldenbrand Wendel
Hemstraat William
Heverlin John
Hickman John
Hilten Peter
Hockstrasser Baltis
Hockstrasser Jacob
Hockstrasser Paul
Hogeboom John
Hogeboom Samuel
Hoghtaling Storm
Horn John
Hoyer George Frederick
Huick Henry
Hundermont Henry
Huppol France
Jacobson Evert
Jenkins John
Johnson George
Johnson John
Johnson William
Jolly James
Kane William
Kerker Henry
Kerker Jacob
Kerner Frederick
Kerner Jacob
Klein Joseph
Lagrang Isaac
Lagrange Christian
Lagrange Jacob
Lansing Christopher
Lansing Henry J.
Lansing Jacob I.
Lansingh Jacob H.
Lansingh Jacob J.
Laraway Isaac
Laraway Levinus
Latta William
Leekwa Lodewick
Leelman Jacob
Leverse Douw
Leverse Mattew
Leversy Lebinis
Levey Michael
Lewis Robert
Little Henry
Little John
Long Adam
Loop Coenrad
Lotteridge William
Luke Solomon
Machisne Henry
Machisne Joseph
Mackey Alexander
Maersel Gerret M.
Man Jacob
Mareel Michael
Marinus George
Marinus Jeremiah
Marinus William
Markel Michael
Matcher Lodewick
Meyer Percival
Miller Jacob
Miller Jeremiah
Miller John
Miller Samuel
Milwain Thomas
Minchal Isaac
Minkler Esaaccoh
Mitchel John M.
Moak Jacob
Moak John
Morrell John
Muir William
Muller Jacob
Muller John
Murphy John
Murry Thomas
Myers Andries
Myers Philip
Mysener John
McAdam Hugh
McChasney Hugh
McChesney John
McChesney Joseph
McGee John
McHisnay Joseph
Newman Charles
Newman Henry
Nicoll Francis
O'Brian Levis (see Lodowick)
Ochenback Peter
Oliver John
Olver John
Onck Jacob
Onger Frederick
Oothout Henry
Oothout Volkert
Orlep Williu
Orlog William
Orlogh Frederick
Orlope Fradrick
Orlope Henry
Ostrander Teunis
Ostrom John
Ostrom Ruliph
Oudercark Isac
Ouderkerk Jacob
Ouderkerk John
Ouderkerk Peter
Ouderkerk Peter P.
Ouderkirk Tackle
Oudeskerk Andrew
Outnhok John
Oxburger John
Page Samuel
Painter Philip
Pall James
Parkele Jacob
Parker Jacob
Parkle Jacob
Parkly Michael
Pass Christopher
Pass Lodwick
Passinger Andrew
Peers Christian
Pells Gerret
Peterson John
Phero Christopher
Philips James
Philips John
Philips Joseph
Platt Alaxander
Pouhall Adam
Post Richard
Quack Frederick
Quack Isaac
Quack Jacob
Quackenbos Adrian
Quackenbush Garret

Quackenbuss Peter
Quanth Fradrick
Radley John
Radliff Peter
Raff Cristiffel
Rankel John C.
Reeder John
Reese George
Reese Philip
Relyea Peter
Remsy Hendrick
Restyne John
Reyla Jacob
Roff Frederick
Roff John
Roman Peter
Rose John
Ross John
Rouble Hendrick
Rucel John
Ruff John
Runcel Handric
Runchal John
Ruso Frederick
Saltes James
Salts Benjamin
Scharp Coenrad
Scheefer John
Scheefer Peter
Schiley William (see Shelly)
Schnyder Lutwig
Schoolcraft John
Schoolcraft John, Jr.
Schoolcraft Lawrence
Schuyler Peter
Schuyler Philip
Schuyler Reuben
Scraper George
Seeger John S.
Seeger Peter
Severs John
Shaver Jost
Shaver Peter
Shaw John
Shell Philip
Shelly William (see Schilly)
Shuck Zacherias
Shutter Jacob
Simson Henry
Sitterling Henry
Sitterling Jacob
Sitterling John
Sitterly Jacob
Sixbee John
Slater Robert
Slingerland Isaac
Slingerland Jacob
Slingerland Peter
Smith John
Smith John, Junr.
Smith Martis
Smith Wilhelmus
Snyder William
Sommon Nicholas
Soud John
Sparback Martinus
Spawn Jocham
Springer Benjamin
Springer Dennis
Stansel Nicholas
Still Francis
Stoop Francis
Summers Nicholas
Swart George
Syber Jacob
Syble Jacob
Syble Martinus
Taylor James
Taylor Joseph
Teachout Jacob
Tid Samuel
Tilleback Hendrick
Tillman John, Junr.
Tilman Derick
Tingue John
Tisler George
Toll Simon
Truax Abraham
Truax Christian
Truax Isaac
Truax Isaac, Junr.
Truax John
Tucker William
Tymer Peter
Valkenburgh Jacob
Veeder Abraham, Capt.
Veeder Lucas W.
Venolinda Petris
Verplanck Abraham
Vicar John
Vichter Andries
Vine John
Vischer Gerret
Vlaat Henry
Volok John
Voorhuse John
Vosburgh Abraham
Vosburgh Garret
Vosburgh Jacob
Vredenburgh Isaac
Vroman Adam
Vroman Cornelius
Vrooman Arent
Vrooman Hanry
Vrooman Isaac A.
Vrooman Jacob
Vrooman Nicholas
Van Acker John
Van Aernam Abraham G.
Van Aernam Johannis
Van Aernem Jacob
Van Aernem Johen W.
Van Alen John
Van Arnam Abraham
Van Arnem Evert
Van Arnem William
Van Auken Henry
Van Auken Levy
Vande Lende Peter
Van Den Berger Cornelius
Vandenbergh Abraham
Van Denbergh Burger
Van Denbergh Cornelius
Van Den Bergh Cornelius W.
Van Den Bergh Evert
Van Denbergh John
Van Denbergh Levinus
Van Denbergh Winant
Vandenbergh Winant E.
Vanderzee Albert
Vanderzee Albertus
Vanderzee Cornelis
Van Deusen Arent
Van Duesen Matthew
Van Dyck David
Vanetten William
Van Ness John
Van Olenda Jacob
Van Patten Nicoless
Van Pette John
Van Petten Frederick
Van Petten Peter
Van Schaick Gerit G.
Van Sice Cornelius
Van Veghten Philip
Van Vlet Auc
Van Wie Casparus
Van Wie Peter
Van Woert John
Van Woert Rutgert
Van Woord John
Van Wort Jacob
Van Zandt John
Wagner Johann
Waldrom Cornelius
Walls Frederick
Walls Teunis
Wands James
Wands John
Ward Andrew
Ward Benjamin
Ward Edward
Ward John
Ward Moses
Ward Richard
Warmer Peter
Warren William
Watson Zelots
Waults Frederick
Weaver John
Weever Hendrick
Welder William
Wells Teunis
Wemple Aaron
Wemple Arent A.
Westfael Petrus
Wilder William
Williams Petrus
Willson William
Winchel
Winne Anthony
Witbeck Casparus
Witbeck John
Witbeck John L.
Witbeck Samuel
Witbeeck Wouter
Witbeck Abraham
Witeman Jacob
Witterker Thomas
Woormer Fradrick
Wormer Arent
Wormwood John
Wyley William
Wynkoop John
Yates John G.
Ylsebee Niecholas (see Ylxbee)
Ylxbee Niecholas (see Ylsebee)
Young Henry

Sketch by R. A. Grider.

UPPER FORT IN SCHOHARIE VALLEY,

Enclosing John Feek's dwelling, afterwards owned by Timothy Murphy.

R. L. Adams, artist.

Sketch by R. A. Grider.

MIDDLE FORT IN SCHOHARIE VALLEY,

Enclosing Johannes Becker's dwelling.

R. L. Adams, artist.

Sketch by R. A. Grider. R. L. Adams, artist.

LOWER FORT IN SCHOHARIE VALLEY.

Enclosing Stone Church.

Sketch by R. A. Grider. R. L. Adams, artist.

FORT KAYSER.

Stone Arabia.

Albany County Militia — (Continued).

COLONEL KILIAN VAN RENSSELAER

LIEUTENANT COLONEL JOHN H. BEECKMAN

MAJOR JACOB C. SCHERMERHORN

MAJOR CORNELIUS VAN BUREN

ADJUTANT JOHN E. LANSING

QUARTER MASTER JACOB STAATS

CAPT. ANTHONY BRIES
" JAMES DENNISON
" JONATHAN NILES
" STEPHEN NILES
" JOHN OSTERHOUT
" DANIEL SCHERMERHORN
" JOHN W SCHERMERHORN
" NICHOLAS STAATS
" LAWRENCE TOWNSEND
" ICHABOD TURNER
" ROBERT WOODWORTH
LIEUT. BETHNEL BARNUM
" OLIVER BENTLEY
" WILLIAM CORNING
" JOEL DEASE
" ZACHARIA HERRINGTON
" ALEXANDER HUBBS
" DAVID HUSTED
" JAMES JONES
" OBEDIAH LANSING
LIEUT. HOSEA MOFFET
" JOHN MOON
" SILAS MOREY
" JONATHAN NILES
" JOHN OSTRANDER
" SETH PERRY
" REUBEN ROWLY
" JACOB SCHERMERHORN
" WILLIAM SEATON
" SAMUEL SHAW
" PHILIP STAATS
" JACOB VAN VALKENBURGH
" HARPERT WHITBECK
ENSIGN EBENEZER JUDD
" JOHN POTTER
" ISAAC SHELDON
" JOHN J. STAATS
" PETER TEN EYCK
" MARTIN VAN BUREN

ENLISTED MEN.

Abrahams Anthony
Acker Jury
Agnew William
Allen John
Andrews Amos
Andris Amos
Armstrong John
Arnold David
Arnold Stephen
Arnold William
Astyer Isaac
Aursen Thomas
Austin Stephen
Auston Isaac
Avery Abel
Aylsworth George
Babcock David
Babcock Elisha
Babcock Enoch
Babcock John
Babcock Silas
Babcock Silas, Junr.
Babett John
Backer Ichabod
Backer John
Badcock Jonathan
Baker David
Baley George
Barber Edward
Barheyd Elisha
Barhite Walter
Barnum Israel
Barnum Jabus
Barnum William
Bartel William
Bartle Andries
Bateman Reuben
Baurhite Jacob
Beats Jesse
Becker Adam
Becraft Abraham
Becroft William
Begal Samuel
Begel John
Bell John
Benn John
Bennem Peter
Bennet Ezra
Bennet Jesse
Bently Benjamin
Bently Joseph
Bently Joshua
Bently Oliver
Bently Samuel
Berry Elisha
Berry Samuel
Bigelow Joseph
Bissle William
Boos Jeremiah
Brain Moses
Bresea Hendrick
Brest William
Briesee William
Briggs Christopher
Bristol Abraham
Bristol Daniel
Bristol John
Bristoll Abraham, Junr.
Broadhook John
Brocks Joshua
Brockway Consider
Brockway Justus
Brockway Richard
Brockway Yestus
Brodhacker Bartley
Bronner Peter
Brotherton John
Brotherton Micasah
Brotherton Zopher
Brown Caleb
Brown Isaac
Brown Jesse
Brown Jonathan
Brown John
Brown Nehemiah
Brown Peter
Brown Robert
Brown Samuel

Brown Thomas
Brown Timothy
Bruce Benjamin
Bump Reuben
Bunt Evert
Bunt Mindert
Bunt Peter
Burguss Thomas
Burwell William
Bush Daniel
Bush John
Butler Jonathan
Butler Zachariah
Cabels Zebulon
Cain Isaiah
Cals Zebulon
Canter John
Carmichael John
Carpenter Jack
Carpenter Samuel
Carpenter Walter
Carr Charls
Case Joseph
Cates Zebulon
Caveneer John
Center Richard
Chapman Josiah
Charmichel John
Chatfield Cornelius
Chesley Simon
Church James
Clark Caleb
Clark Cary
Clark Thomas
Claw Laurance
Clegrove James
Coale Peter
Coats Joseph
Coats Thomas
Cole James
Cole Joseph
Cole Royal
Colgrove James
Coll Moses
Colom Joshua
Comens Ebenezer
Cone Ichabod
Cone John
Conick Jonathan
Connor Alexander
Cook Isaac
Cook Joseph
Cook Levi
Cook Richard
Coon James
Coon Nathan
Cooper Obadiah
Corey Benjamin
Corey John
Crain Edmund
Crandal Luke
Crowley Jonathan
Cudney William
Cummins Philip
Cunniggnas William
Curtice Thomas
Dachsteter Pieter
Daley Ebenezer
Daverix Elisha
Delano Thomas
Deliton Benjamin
Denison Daniel
Denison Ebenezer
Denord Humpfrey
Deveraux Elisha
Deverix Jonathan
Deverixe Joseph
Deveruex Theadeus
Dey Amos
Dickerson Ichabod
Dimons Henry
Dockstader Peter
Doty John
Dow John D. P.
Ducker David
Dumer Abraham
Dye Amos
Dye John
Dymen Abraham
Earing Samuel
Egberts Anthony
Egberts Benjamin
Egberts Martin
Ehring John
Elsworth George
Eltinge Abraham
Eltinge Henry
Eltinge John
Faakes Isaac
Falensby Jacobus
Falensby John
Farrington Robert
Ferguson Benjamin
Ferguson Jermiah
Filkin Henry
Filkins Abraham
Filkins James
Filkins Johanes
Fisk Joseph
Fisk William
Flagelland Joseph
Folmsbee Jacobas
Folmsbey Jeroen
Fonda John
Fose Consider
Fox Consider
Fox William
Freeman John
Frezone John
Fullomsbe John
Gains Francis
Gardenier Henry
Gardinear Nicholas
Gardiner Robert
Gardinier Nicolas H.
Gardner Benjamin
Gardner Benjamin, Junr.
Gardner Bennone
Gardner Howland
Gardner Simeon
Gates Jered
Gates John
Gates Nathan
Gates Nathaniel
Gates Simon
Geyer John George
Ghoes Henry
Gorton Peleg
Gray James
Green Ambrose
Green Daniel
Green David
Greene Obadiah
Greenfield Archibald
Greenfield Bethuel
Greenfield James
Greenfield Benjamin
Greenman Preserved
Griffis Abner
Gyer John
Hacks James
Hakes Nathan
Halcomb Beriah
Halenbeck Casper
Hall Benoni
Hall Gardner
Hall George
Hall George William
Hall Gustner
Hull Peter
Hall Rowland
Hall William
Hall Yestus
Hamblin Samuel
Handerson John
Hanks Benjamin
Hanks John
Hansen Dirck
Harrington William
Harrington Zachariah
Harrintan Benjamin
Harrintan James
Harris Ahaze
Harris Benjamin
Harris Ephraim
Harris Ezekiel
Harris James
Harris John
Harris Joseph
Harris Nicholas
Hase Nathan
Haus Benjamin
Henckley Gersham
Henry Ephraim
Herdick Peter
Herdick William
Herdick William, Junr.
Hergher Gothlick
Herington John
Herrick Johannus
Herrington Abraham
Herrington Benjamin
Herrington Isaac
Herrington James
Herrington Nathaniel
Hewit Edmund
Hewit James
Hewit Oliver
Hicks George
Hicks Thomas
Hill Ebenezer
Hill Samuel
Hinckley Gershom, Junr.
Hindersass John Georg
Hinkley Paul
Hoard David
Hoard George
Hoard Isaac
Hoard Nathan
Hoard Samuel
Hoard Simeon
Hobusen Henry
Hocksey Frederick
Hocksey William
Hoems Solomon
Hogeboom Dirck
Hogg John
Holland James
Hollenbeck Michel
Holmes Abraham
Homes Abraham
Honckley Gershom
Hoose Peter
Hopkins Frederick
Hopkins Noah
Horton Lemuel
Horton Levy
Houck William J.
Howard Benjamin
Howard Janthon
Howard John
Howard Josiah

Howard Nathan
Hoyt John
Hunter Jonathan
Huyck Hanry
Huyck Hendrick
Huyck Nicholas
Huyck William
Hyms Solomon
Ingels James
Ingels Samuel
Janse Roelif
Joens William
Jones Amos
Jones Henry
Jones James
Jones Roger
Joslen William
Keeffe Daniel
Kerker Yedlock
Kilsey Ebenezer
Kittel John
Kittle Nicholas
Knap Ebenezer
Knap Henry
Knoulton Elijah
Knowlton Ephraim
Knowlton Robert
Lamb David
Lamphear Amos
Landers Jabez
Landers Jesse
Lansen William
Laurence William
Lawrence John
Letese James, Junr.
Levy John
Lewis John
Littar James
Little Stephen
Lobdele Sylvanus
Loce Peter (see Loesey)
Lodawick Henry
Lodewick John
Loesey Peter (see Locee)
Low John
Lower Casper
Lower Michael
Lumis Daniel
Magee John
Malleson Timothy
Malloy Thomas
Maloy John
Mane Henry
Mane Jeremiah
Manger Lawrence
Manyer Laurence
Marinus George
Marinus Jeremiah
Marinus Jury
Marinus William
Mark Isaac
Marks Comfort
Marks Ebenezer
Marks Joseph
Martin James
Michel Nicholaos
Mickel Jurian
Middleton Benjiman
Miers John
Miles Jeremiah
Miller Jeremiah
Miller John
Miner Amos
Mobyor Timothy
Moker Conraud
Moll Isaa
Moll Jecobas
Moll Mindart
Moll Walter
Moon Bennony
Moon Jeremiah
Moon John
Mott Jeremiah
Muller John
Muller Nicolas
Myers Jeremiah
Mynderse Frederick
Myors John
McCalif Nicholas
McGan Peter
McGibbons Peter
McKown James
McMullan Hugh
McMullen Daniel
Nelson Jonathan
Newman Isaac
Newton Abner
Nichals Caleb
Nicholas David
Nichols Benjamin
Nichols Simeon
Nichols Sisson (see Silson)
Nickle Nicholas
Niles Robert
Nolton Abner
Northrup Daniel
Northrup Needham
Northrup Nicholas
Northrupt Joseph
Odeal Jonas
Odel Gersham
Odel Simon
Odell David
Odell William
O'Niel Charls
Ostrander Adam
Ostrander Andrew
Ostrander Gerret
Ostrander Henry
Ostrander Isaac
Ostrander Jonathan
Ostrander Peter
Ovensants Philip
Palmer Gideon
Palmetier Thomas
Pan Moses
Parker Timothy
Partrick Robert
Partrick Robert, Jr.
Pater Elisha
Patrick Matthew
Pearce Levi
Pease Abner
Pease George
Perce Joel
Perie Benjamin
Perry Josiah
Phillips Anthony
Pike Ezra
Pool Anthony
Pool Garit G.
Pool Garret
Pool George Jurian
Pool Henry
Pool James
Pool John
Pool Matthew
Potter Rowland
Price Elijah
Proper James
Proper Peter
Queen Henry
Queen Owen
Race Daniel
Reynolds Henry
Reynolds Joseph
Robenson Benjamin
Robinson Isak
Rogars Joseph
Romien Abraham
Ronald Henry
Ronals Henry
Root Asahel
Rose Ary
Rose Betts
Rose Daniel
Rose John
Rose Nathaniel
Rose Ore
Rose Wiat
Rous Jacob
Rouse Baltus
Rouse Frederick
Rowley Timothy
Ryckman Frederick
Ryckman Gerret
Ryley Sylvester
Sackett Benjamin
Sackett John
Salsbury Harmanus
Salsbury Joseph
Salsbury Laurance
Salsbury Lucas
Salyea Henry
Satin Ease
Schemehorn Jacob H.
Schermehorn Cornelius
Schermehorn Jacob I.
Schermehorn Samuel
Schermerhorn Jacob
Schermerhorn Jacob R.
Schermerhorn Luke
Schermerhorn Philip
Scholl Johan Jost
Seamen Harmenis
Seaton William
Sebie William
Seeger Edward
Sennet Isaac
Seton Willard
Sharp Eliakim
Sharp Solomon
Shaw Anthony
Shaw Comfort
Shaw James M.
Shaw Jeremiah
Shelden George
Shelden William
Shelly John
Sherman Jinker
Shever Hendrick
Sholl John Jost
Shortenburgh Jury Jacob
Shouse Jacob
Shovers Gorge
Shovers William
Shower William
Skinner John
Sliter William
Slyter James
Smith Reuben
Spencer Nicholas
Spoor Henry
Spoor Isaac
Spoor Jeroen
Sprague David
Sprague George
Spring Ephraim
Springsteen Benjamin
Springteen Jacob
Springsteen William
Sprong David

Sprong Epraim
Sprong John
Staats Barent
Staats John
Stall Peter
Stephens Jered
Stephens William
Stewart Eliphlet
Stoul Peter
Sullivan David
Swain John
Sweet Samuel
Sweeting Lewis
Sweeting Nathaniel
Taber Harmen
Taber Havens
Taber Record
Taber Benjamin
Tabor William
Taller Ebeneser
Tanner Abel
Taylor John
Thomas Benjamin
Thomas Israel
Thomas William
Tibbits Jona
Tift Edmond
Tippet Jonathan
Tolmans Thomas
Townsend James
Trim Walter
Turck John
Turk Thomas
Turk Hendrick
Turner Lamuel
Udall John
Udall William
Valentine Benjamin
Valk Isaac
Valk John J.
Valk Matthew
Valkenburgh Dirck
Valkenburgh Jacob
Valkenburgh Jacob N.
Valkenburgh Jacobus
Valkenburgh John
Vallentine Richard
Vinhagen John
Vinhagen Martin
Vinigar Asabel
Vischer John
Vosburgh Matthew
Van Bura Martin B.
Van Buren Abraham
Van Buren Cornelius
Van Buren Harmanus
Van Buren Hendrick
Van Buren John
Van Buren Maas
Van Buren Martin
Van Buren Martin C.
Van Buren Martin P.
Van Buren Peter M.
Van Buren Tobias
Van Buren Tobias H.
Van Buren William
Van Den Bergh Abraham
Van Den Bergh Barent
Vanden Bergh Cornelius
Van Den Bergh Garret T.
Van Den Bergh John
Van Denbergh P.
Vanden Bergh Volkert
Van Der Pool John
Van Derpool Melkert
Van Dobow Jacob
Van Dueson Christopher
Van Dusen Harpert
Van Hoesan Harman
Van Hoesen Mundert
Van Hoesen Rynier
Van Huzon Coonrad
Van Iveren Barent
Van Ostrander John
Van Rensselaer James
Van Salsbury Cornelius
Van Valcenburgh Lambart
Van Valckenburgh Matthew
Van Valkenburgh Abraham
Van Valkenburgh Jochim
Van Valkenburgh Peter
Van Valkenburgh Matthew
Van Valkenburgh Nicholes
Van Veghten Volckert
Wald Joseph
Wandel Garit
Wardon Nathaniel
Wardon Moses
Worner Joseph
Waye Josiah
Wells Ebenezer
Wells Nathaniel
Wendee Garrit
Wenslor Abraham
Wessel Luke
Wessels Andries
West Jonathan
Westcot Joseph
White John
White Nathaniel
Whiteman Benjamin
Whiteman Benoni
Widbeck Abraham
Wiley Primus
Williams John
Willson John
Willson Robert
Winegar Ashbell
Wingerd Peter
Witbeck Harper
Witbeck John
Witbeck Jonathan
Witbeck Martin C.
Witbeck Thomas
Witbeck William
Witebeck Leonard
Witeman George
With Evert
Wood Barney
Wood Job
Woodard Abijah
Woolcot Joseph
Woolcot Justis
Wolcott Luke
Worden William
Wylie John
Wyngaert Peter
Yates Evert
Yoels Thomas
Young John
Young Thomas
Zu Stralsnnd Fillib

Albany County Militia — (Continued).

COLONEL GERRITT G. VAN DEN BERGH
COLONEL HENRY QUACKENBOS
LIEUTENANT COLONEL VOLKERT VEEDER
MAJOR BARENT STAATS
MAJOR COENRAT TEN EYCK

CAPT. GEORGE HOGAN
" PHILIP LUKE
" TEUNIS SLINGERLAND
" JOHN VAN WIE
" ABRAHAM VEEDER
" WILLIAM WINNIE
LIEUT. JOHN DE VOE
" THOMAS ESMAY
LIEUT. WILLIAM FLENSBURGH
" JURIAN HOGAN
" EPHRAIM HUDSON
" JOHN LEONARD
ENSIGN EZRA CLEVELAND
" HENRY SHAFER
" CORNELIUS VAN DER ZEE

ENLISTED MEN.

Aernout Jacob
Albragh John
Allenbrach John
Arnhoudt John
Basinger Andrew
Becker Gerrit
Becker Walter
Bradt Anthony
Bradt Peter B
Bratt Adrian
Burhans John
Conger Reuben
Conger Uzziah
Devoe John
Esmay Thomas
Flansburg Matthew
Flensburg Daniel
Flensburg William
Fuller Gershom
Haswell Joseph
Heller Jacob
Hillebrandt John
Hooghtaling James
Hungerford Elisha
Johnson John
Joost Benjamin
Luke Solomon
Moke Francis
Moke John
Ogenpact Benjamin
Oliver John
Oosterhout Henry
Ostrander Henry
Palmetier John
Pangburn Richard
Pangburn William
Post Benjamin
Schoenmaker John
Shafer Charles
Shaver Hendrick
Salsbury Joseph
Seeger Gerrit I.
Seeger Gerrit S.
Seger John
Taylor James
Taylor Lucas
Viele Jacob
Viele Simon
Van Aernam Isaac
Van Buren Moses
Van Deusen Matthew
Van Etten Benjamin
Van Etten William
Van Wie Andries
Van Wie Gerrit
Van Wie Isaac
Van Wie John H.
Winne David
Wyncoop Evert

Albany County Militia — (Continued).

COLONEL STEPHEN JOHN SCHUYLER
LIEUTENANT COLONEL HENRY K. VAN RENSSELAER
MAJOR FLORIS BANKER
MAJOR JOHN J. FONDA
ADJUTANT JACOB VAN ALSTYN
QUARTER MASTER MATTHEW VAN ALSTYN
SURGEON WILLIAM PETRY
ASSISTANT PAY MASTER JONATHAN BURRALL

CAPT. CALEB BENTLEY
" ISAAC BOGERT
" HENRY DENKER
" ISAAC DE FOREST
" JACOB DE FOREST
" JACOB DE FREEST
" HENRY H. GARDENIER
" LEVI HOKWELL
" DAVID HUSTED
" JAMES HUSTED
" JOHN LANDMAN
" CORNELIUS LANSING
" AUGUSTEN ODELL
" BENJAMIN RANDALL
" GEORGE SCHARP
" SAMUEL SHAW
" CHRISTOPHER TILLMAN

CAPT. ANTHONY VAN SCHAICK (Company exempts)
LIEUT. GEORGE BENINGER
" JOHN CRANNY
" JOHN FONDA
" JOHN P. FONDA
" CHARLES GREENE
" DAVID HUGHSTEAD
" ANDREW MILLER
" JAMES ODLE
" DAVID RANDALL
" JOHN RILEY
" MARTINUS SCHARP
" LODWICK SNYDER
" RYNIER VAN IVEREN
ENSIGN PHILIP HENRICK
" CORNELIUS VAN DEUSEN

ADDITIONAL NAMES ON STATE TREASURER'S PAY BOOKS.

LIEUT. JONAS BALL
" BENJAMIN BLIDTH
" BENJAMIN ELLIOTT
" DANIEL GRAY
" JAMES GRAY
" DANIEL HULL
" HEZEKIAH HULL
" HUGH MCMANUS
" STEPHEN RANDALL
" MATTHEW SCHARP

LIEUT. JONATHAN SEAVER
" NANNING VAN DER HEYDER
" JOHN WILKESON
ENSIGN JOHN CLARK
" JAMES GREEN
" JEREMIAH GRIFFITH
" JAMES PADGET
" THOMAS PALMER
" JOSHUA WARDEN

ENLISTED MEN.

Adams Elijah
Anderson Alexander
Armstrong Robert
Aursen Thomas
Baardt Andries
Baerdt Andries, Junr.
Bailey Elisha
Baker Ebenasar
Baker Elleton
Barber James
Beninger David
Beninger Jacob
Beninger John
Beninger Phillip
Beninger Zachariah
Bennet Owen
Bennit Ephraim
Benson John
Beringer John
Beringer Zacharias
Berkman John
Berringer David
Berringer Jacob
Bloemendal John
Boyd George
Boyde William
Briggs Joseph
Brust Jacob
Brust Matthew
Bumbar Ruben
Burchim Henry
Butler Jonathan
Cammel Henry
Campbel James
Cancker Peter
Canter Jonas
Carner John
Carner Philip
Coenraedt Frederick
Colehamer Andrew

Colehammer Christian
Colehammer George
Concklin John
Coon Abraham
Coon James
Coon Nathan
Coon William
Cooper Christian
Cooper Christopher
Cooper Peter
Cooper William
Crandell Lute
Crennel William
Cuyler Jacob
Deforeest Jesse
De Freest David P.
De Freest John
De Freest Peter
De Freest Phillip
Dick Henry
Dick Nicholas
Dirck Anthony
Dox Samuel
Drum Andrew
Dunbar William
Eastwood John
Eight Abraham
Elmondorph Jacob
Evens James
Evertsen Evert
Feller Jacob
Feller Nicholas
Feller Zacharia
Fonda Douwe
Fonda Isaac
Fonda Jacobus
Frear Hughen
Frolich Jacob
Fisher Christopher
Gasevoort Coenrat
Goewy John
Grauberger Daniel
Greene John
Greene Luke
Griswold Jabes
Habzinger Carl
Haner John
Haner Phillip, Junr.
Haner Wilhelmus
Hansen Benjamin
Harsen Francis
Harwick Phillip
Herway David
Herwey Coenraet
Henneker Emanuel
Henner John
Henselpeck Coenr't
Herwick Coenraat
Herwick Yoost
Heyner Philip, Junr.
Heyner Wilhelmus
Hogel Edward
Hogil Jacob
Hogil Nicholas
Hoogstrasser Jacob
Hull Daniel
Hull Hezekiah
Huntsekker George
Jackson Ephraim
Johnson Thomas
Kanker Peter
Killy John
Kip Benjamin
Krockhyte John
Kuhn Peter
Lansing Cornelius
Lansing Thomas
Lappies William
Leap John
Lent John
Lewis Phineas
Lieverse Levinus
Lones Adam
Lones Bastian
Maley John
Martin Thomas
Marvin Matthew
Mattison David
Marvin Matthew
Meyer Henry
Miller Barent
Miller Herman (see Harmen)
Miller Hendrick
Miller John
Milton Henry
Milton John
Morrison William
Myer Cornelis
Myers Henry
Near Carel
Near Charles
Near John
Neher Charles
Nestle Christian
Norton Christophel
Norton William
Ostrande Hendrick
Ostrande Isaac
Ostrande John
Ostroom Ruloff
Paddock Henry
Paddock Job
Parker Andrew
Peck Abraham
Peeck Gerrit
Perker Andrew
Philip Michael
Plass Henry
Possasy Henry
Pruyn John
Pruyn Rynier
Pugit James
Randal Matthew
Robertson Abraham
Rogers George
Sabin Stephen
Sarls Thomas
Saxton Ebenezer
Schermerhorn Jacob
Scott David
Sharp George
Sharp Peter
Shaver John
Sickles Zacharia
Smith Michael
Smitt Jacob G.
Snyder Gotlib
Snyder Jacob
Springer Jacob
Still John
Strunk Hendrick
Strunk Hendrick, Junr.
Sweet Godfrey
Thomas Israel
Valintine Jacob
Valk Abraham
Veeder John
Visscher Nanning
Vosburgh Myndert
Van Aelsteyn John
Van Aelsteyn Matthew
Van Buren Cornelius
Van Buren Leonard
Vande Bergh Gerrit
Vanden Bergh Gilbert
Vanden Bergh Gysbert
Vanden Bergh Jacob
Van Den Bergh Matthew
Vanden Bergh Matthew C.
Vanden Bergh Rynier
Vanden Bergh Titus
Vanden Bergh Volkert
Vander Heyden John
Van Der Heyden Matthew
Van Deursen Frederick
Van Duusen Hendrick
Van Etten Benjamin
Van Hoesen Henry
Van Ivere Cornelius
Van Ivere Gysbert
Van Ivere Jacob
Van Ivere Martynis
Van Ivere Reynier
Van Iveren Jacob
Van Iveren Martinus
Van Valck Abraham
Walter John
Wendell Jacob H.
Wendell John
Willig Phillip
Willoughby William
Winne Killian
Witbeck Peter
Wool Robert
Yates Joseph
Young Jacob

Albany County Militia — (Continued).

COLONEL ABRAHAM J. VAN ALSTINE
LIEUTENANT COLONEL PHILIP VAN ALSTINE
MAJOR HARMAN VAN BUREN
MAJOR ISAAC GOES
SURGEON EZEKEL THOMAS

CAPT. ——— CHAPMAN
" BURGER CLAW
" AARON OSTRANDER
" JOHN PHILIP
" JOHN SMITH
" GERSHOM TRUESDEL
" ABRAHAM VAN BUREN
" ISAAC P. VAN VALKENBURGH
" EVERT VOSBURGH
" HERMAN VOSBURGH
LIEUT. JONATHAN CHAPMAN
" PETER HUEGENNIN
" FELTER LANDT
" JACOBUS MCNEAL
" JAMES MCNEIL
LIEUT. REUBEN MURRAY
" EDWARD PAINTER
" MATTHIAS TAYLOR
" ABRAHAM VAN ALLEN
" JOHN VAN ALSTYNE
" JOHN J. VAN ALSTYNE
" PETER J. VOSBURGH
" WILLIAM VOSBURGH
" PHILIP WOLFROM
ENSIGN JOHN GOES
" BURGER T. HUYCK
" GEORGE LONG
" HENRY STEVER
" JOHN VAN BUREN
" JACOBUS VAN NESS

ENLISTED MEN

Baches John
Baily Stephen
Baily Timothy
Bawney John
Bell John A. Lem
Bensk Rudolph
Berry William
Berry William, Junr.
Blanchar Abiathar
Blanchard Abraham
Bresee Jellis
Brewer Abraham
Bullis William
Burnham Mashall
Burton Josiah
Calder Hendrick
Canniff William
Carn John
Cecil Richard
Chapman Amos
Chapman Asa
Chapman David
Chapman Ezekiel
Chapman Ezra
Chapman Noah
Claw Andrew
Coenraut Nicholas
Cole Gerard
Cook John
Cornelisan John
Cornelus John
Cramphin Balsan
Crippen Reuben
Crocker Amos
Curtiss David
Curtis Ebenezer
Curtiss Joseph
Davis Dennis
Davis George
Delamattor Benjamin
Delametter Jacob
Deyor Peter
Dingman Casper
Dingman Isaac
Dingman Jacob
Dobs Daniel
Dorn Abraham
Ealon Elijah
Earl Moses
Earl William, Junr.
Eldridge Joseph
Elkinbrach John (see Elkenbragh)
Feely John
Ferguson Jacob
Folmer Zemtus
Fols Conrat
French John
Fuller David
Gardaneer Peter H.
Gardner Godfrey
Goes Derick
Goes Ephraim
Goes John, Junr.
Goes Laurence
Goes Michael
Goes Tobias
Gould Jesse
Graper Ruben
Graves John
Graves Richard
Green Augustus
Gwin Oren
Haak Christopher
Hall Justice
Hamblin Seth
Hamblin Zaccheus
Hancy Fradrick
Hare Daniel
Hark Daniel
Hawk Christopher
Herder John
Herrick George
Hoffman George
Hogan William
Hoyer George
Hrkiman George
Hubbard David
Huguenin David
Humphry Ezra
Huyck Burger D.
Huyck Burger I.
Huyck John A.
Huyck John, Junr.
Ittick George L.
Itting Conrat
Jenkins Anthony
Johnson Isaac
Johnson John
Johnson Peter
Joslin Henry
Kane William
Kelder Hendrick
Kinne Jesse
Kittle John
Kittle Nicholas
Knapp Isaac
Lister Frederick
Luny William
Lusk Jacob
Lusk Michael
Lusk William

Maus John J.
Marsail John
Marshall Enos
Moet Coenradt
Moet Johannis
Miller Casper
Miller Jonathan
Miller John
Mitchel James
Mitchel James, Junr.
Molony John
Montgomery Alexander
Moore John A.
Moot Conrath
Moot Johannis
Morey Elisha
Morey Elisha, Junr.
Morey Samuel
Moshier Jonathan
Mott Henry
Mott Jeremiah
Mudge Michael
Muller John J.
McFail Patrick (see McPhaile)
McMichael James
O'Briant Cornelius
Olthousen Nicholas
O'Neal James
O'Neil John
Paine Daniel
Painter Thomas
Pearsee Isaac
Peersye Isaac
Peterson Benjamin
Peterson Philip
Pew John
Philip Pelnis
Philip Peter
Proper Frederick
Quithot Stephen
Randal Nathaniel
Rees Benjamin
Richmon George
Richmond Conrad
Richmond Simeon
Robertson George
Robinson George
Robison Jeremiah
Root Asahel
Root David
Rowland Samuel
Rowse Coenradt
Ryan Edward
Ryan William
Salisbury Sylvester
Sally John
Sally Thomas
Salsbury John
San Moses
Saunders Isaac
Scharaly Peter
Scharp Jacob
Scharp John
Scharp Laurence P.
Scott John
Scott William
Sebring Lewis
Seley John (see Feeley)
Setler Frederick
Sharp John
Sharp Lawrence
Sharsa Daniel
Shutts John
Sisson Richard
Smith Asa
Smith Christian
Smith John
Smith Joseph
Smith Samuel
Snyder Peter
Snyder Simon
Suthard Thomas
Staats Abraham
Staats Abraham J.
Staats Abraham T.
Staats Jacob
Staats John
Staats John, Junr.
Statts Abraham
Stever Jacob
Stoplebeen Johannes
Thomas Caleb
Thomas Jacob
Trusdeil Hiel
Trusdell Richard
Trusduil Iseel
Utly Jeremiah
Vosburgh Abraham
Vosburgh David
Vosburgh Joachim
Vosburg Matthew
Vosburgh Peter A.
Vosburg William
Vratenburgh John
Vredenbergh John
Van Aelstyn Thomas
Van Alen Abraham
Van Alen Dirck
Van Alen Cornelius
Van Alen Gilbert
Van Alen Henry
Van Alen John E.
Van Alen Peter
Van Alstine Abraham
Van Alstyne Leonard
Van Beuren John
Van Buren Cornelius
Van Buren Ephraim I.
Van Buren Ephraim T.
Van Buren Francis
Van Buren Tobias
Vanderpoel Andrew
Van Derpoel Andries
Vanderpoel Jacobus
Van Deusen Peter
Van Dusen John
Van Hoesen Jacob
Van Hoeson Jacob J.
Van Hoesen John
Van Nass Adam
Van Ness David
Van Slyck Dirick
Van Slyck Peter
Van Valkenburgh Bartholomew
Van Valkenburgh Bartholemew T.
Van Valkenburgh Claudius
Van Valkenburgh Jacob
Van Valkenburgh Jacobus
Van Valkenburgh Joachim
Van Valkenburgh Joachim J.
Van Valkenburgh John
Van Valkenburgh Lambert
Van Valkenburgh Lawrance
Van Valkenburgh Peter I.
Van Valkenburgh Peter J.
Wever George
Wheeler Samuel
White Henry
Whitwood Charles
Whitwood Cornelius
Whitwood Samuel
Wickham Warren
Wilsey Jacob
Wilson Andrew
Wilson Dirick
Wilson Richard
Wiltse Jacob
Wingand James
Wingardt Jacobus
Witbeck Andrew
Witbeck Andrew, Junr.
Witbeck Andris
Wolf George
Wolf Peter
Wolfram John Tice
Wolfrom Mathise
Wolfrem Philip
Wright Arl
Wright Daniel
Wyngart Jacobus
Wynkoop Peter
Yeralewyn John
Young Frederic

Albany County Militia — (Continued).

COLONEL ROBERT VAN RENSSELAER
LIEUTENANT COLONEL HENRY J. VAN RENSSELAER
LIEUTENANT COLONEL ASA WATERMAN
LIEUTENANT COLONEL BARENT I. STAATS
MAJOR RICHARD ESSELTYNE
MAJOR JOHN McKINSTRY
MAJOR HENRY VAN RENSSELAER
ADJUTANT JOHN PENNOYER, JR.
QUARTER MASTER JOHN FISHER

CAPT. EBENEZER CADY
" JOSEPH ELLIOTT
" JONAH GRAVES
" ABNER HAWLEY
" NATHAN HENRICK
" CORNELIUS HOGEBOOM
" MICHAEL HORTON
" CASPER HUYCK
" GIDEON KING
" JEREMIAH JOHANNES MULLER
" JOHN OSTERHOUDT
" JACOB PHILLIP
" WILHELMUS PHILIP
" HENRY PLATNER
" JOHN PRICE
" DIEL ROCKEFELLER
" JACOB VAN ALLEN
" ISAAC VOSBURGH
LIEUT. SAMUEL ALLIN
" THOMAS BROWN
" PETER A. FONDA
" GERRITT GROOSEBECK
" JAMES HOGEBOOM
" RICHARD HOGEBOOM
LIEUT. CHARLES McARTHUR
" DAVID McKINSTRY
" NATHANIEL MIGKELL
" NATHANIEL MILLS
" JOACHIM MULLER
" GEORGE PHILLIPS
" EDWARD REXFORD
" JONATHAN REYNOLDS
" PETER ROCKEFELLER
" NATHANIEL ROWLEY
" CASPARUS SCHULT
" JOHN SCOTT
" (JOSIAH) VAN BEURIN
ENSIGN LEANARD DACKER
" ESA HOLMES
" SIMON LOTHROP
" SAMUEL OLMSTED
" MAURICE ROWLEY
" JOHN SHUTTS
" ADAM TEN BROECK
" MYNDERT VANDEBOGERT
" GERRITT W. VAN SCHAIK
" PETER VAN VALKENBURGH
" JAMES WINGARD

NAMES AS OFFICERS, BUT NO RANK GIVEN:

PETER GROAT
JACOB PHILLIP, JR.
JOHANNIS SHULT
PETER WEISSMAN

ENLISTED MEN

Acker David
Adams Daniel
Adams Noah
Adsit John
Akins Aaron
Akins James
Akins Samuel
Allen Jonathan
Allen Timothy
Alsworth William
Andreas Spira
Andrew Sperry
Anneling John
Aring Samuel
Armerly John
Ashley Peter
Ashton Peter
Atwaters Jeames
Atwaters Benjamin
Atwood Timothy
Austin Peter
Babeck Charles
Baker Andrew
Baker Jonathan
Baker John, Junr.
Baker Samuel
Bamhower Andries
Bantley Samuel
Bantley Thomas
Barker James
Barnet Tyman
Barringer Peter
Barrit Jonathan
Bartle Henry
Bartle John
Bartle Peter
Bartle Peter, Junr.
Bartle Philip
Bartle Philip H.
Bartley John

Bay John
Bayley Asher
Beach Michel
Becker Aarent
Becker Cornelius
Becker John
Beeraft William
Beeroft Jonathan
Begraft Abraham
Begraft George
Begraft Jonathan
Begraft Thomas
Begraft Thomas, Junr.
Benjamin Daniel
Benjamins Ebenzar
Benn George
Bennum Cornelius
Bentin Doctor
Berger Henry
Best Benjamin
Bibbins John
Boent Evert, Junr.
Boent Jacob
Boent Jacob, Junr.
Boent Matties
Boent Mindert
Boent Peter
Boerst Jorst
Boerst Jorst, Junr.
Bonestail David
Bonestail David, Junr.
Bonestail Frederick
Bonestail Peter
Bostwick Edward
Braun Johan Christ
Bresce Cornelius
Bresee Gabriel
Bresee Nicholas
Brooks Joshua, Junr.
Broon Edward
Brown Amos
Brown John
Browen Jurry
Brower Abraham
Brower David
Brower George
Brower Peter
Bryan John
Buebee Constant
Bunt Ephraim
Bunt Peter
Burgart Hendrick
Burgat Hendrick
Burger Peter
Burghart Henry
Burghart Jeremiah
Burnett Peter
Burns Nathan
Bursen Daniel
Bush John
Cable Johan George
Cacoll James
Cadman George
Cady David
Camer Jacob
Campbell John
Caner George
Caring Carel
Carlett William
Carter Jacob
Carter Jacob, Junr.
Carrey Thomas
Carvel John
Casper Petter
Caul Jacob
Cavel Hendrick
Cavel Peter
Cayry Thomas
Champion Job
Chapman Stephen
Chatsy Joseph
Churchill Stephen
Clapper Fredrick
Clapper George
Clapper Henry
Clapper John
Clapper Peter
Clapper William
Clark Abram
Clark David
Clark John
Cleaveland Ezechael
Cleveland Lemuel
Clinchman Christopher
Coal Andrew, Junr.
Cohoon Joseph
Cole Hesparis
Cole Isaac
Cole John
Cole Peter
Colley David
Colley Matthew
Colley Thomas
Colman John
Concklin Jacob
Conklin Isaac
Constaver Phillip David
Conyne Casparus
Cool John
Cool Peter
Cool Peter, Junr.
Cool William
Coon Samuel
Coons Adam
Coons Jacob
Coons John
Coons John, Junr.
Corlett William
Cotton John
Coventry William
Cowle Andres
Cowle Thoda
Cramer Lawrance
Crepes Hendrick
Crousious Christian
Criselar Henry
Criselar John
Crowsioni Johanny
Culley Thomas
Cully David
Cudney William
Cyser John
Dacker Broer
Darling David
Darling Jesup
Danvor Daniel
Darrow Jedidiah
Davis Amos
Davis Daniel
Davis George
Davis Jacobus
Davis William
Day Aron
Deal Laurence
Decker Abraham
Decker Broer
Decker Christopher
Decker George G.
Decker Hendrick
Decker Hendrick B.
Decker Johannis
Decker Jores
Decker Jores J.
Dederick Frederic
Dedrick Christian
Dedrick Johannes
Dedrick Peter
De Lamatter Dirck
De Lamater Gloride
Delamater Jacobus
De Le Matter James
De Lamater Jeremiah
Delamatter Jeremiah J.
Delamater Jeremyes
Deming Daniel
Denions William
Dennis Ezechael
Denneger Mathew
De Pew Elias
Derring Adam
De Yeae Jacobus
De Yeae Jacobus, Junr.
De Yeae Richard
Dicker Francis
Dickson Walter
Didemer George
Didemore John
Dinghmanse William
Dingmansa Dolves P.
Dingmanse Adolfus
Dingmanse Adolfus, Junr.
Dingmanse Andsiel
Dingmanse Hendrick
Dingmanse Johannis
Dingmanse Johannis, Junr.
Dingmanse Peter
Dirck William
Dixson William
D'Lamater Glonde
Docher Jores H.
Doty Isaac
Doty Joseph
Doty Samuel
Dox Peter
Droel John Hendrick
Duff Jonathan
Dutcher Henry
Dutcher Rulef
Dyckman Sampson
Earl Joseph
Eckker David
Edwards Abel
Edwards Samuel
Egers George
Egelston Benjamin
Egins Aaron
Egins James
Elias Jacob
Elling Abraham
Elliot John
Elliot Peter
Ellison David
Ellison William
Elswort Rufis
Elting James
Elting John
Emrich Adam
Emrich Frances
Emrigh Adam
Emrigh Francis
Emrigh George
Emrigh Matties
Enderson Jacob
Enderson John
Enderson Peter
Ergie James
Esselstine Gabriel
Esselstyne Abraham
Esselstyne Andries
Esselstyne Coenradt
Esselstyne Isaac

Esselstyne Jacob
Esselstyne Jacob, Junr.
Esselstyne Richard
Ettinge Abraham
Ettinge John
Everts John
Everts John, Junr.
Evertson Thomas
Fairchild Stephen
Feith Conrath
Ferris Timothy
Filka Stephen
Finger John
Finkle John
Finney Isaac
Fisher Frederick
Flaus Peter
Fonda Abraham
Fonda Cornelius
Fonda Douw
Fonda Jacobus
Fonda Jeremiah
Fonda Lawrence
Fonda Peter A.
Foot John
Fortal John
Fox Jonathan
Frayer Abraham
Frayer Isaac
Frayer John
French John
Frogran John
Fryer Isaac T.
Funday Cornelius
Gaal Jacob
Gardiner James
Gardiner Jeroan
Gardiner William
Garrison John
Gaul Jacob
Good Joseph
Goes Ephraim
Goes Mattise R.
Gordon William
Gott John
Graadt Hendrick
Graadt John
Graadt Wilhelmus
Graadts Peter
Graff Isaac
Grautt Hendrick
Graudt Hyron
Grautt John
Grautt Peter
Grautt Wilhelmus
Graves Noadiah
Graves Seldon
Green Ebenezer
Green Thomas
Green Thomas, Junr.
Green William
Gribdelmyer Christian
Grindlemyer Christopher
Griswold Jabez
Groat John N.
Groat Hendrick
Groat Henry, Junr.
Groat Huron
Groat Hyrone
Groat John
Groat Peter (Officer. No rank given)
Groat Wilhelmus
Haber Johannes
Haddick William
Hagadorn Christopher
Hagedorn John
Hagedorn Jonas
Hagedorn Peter
Hagedorn Joseph
Hale Daniel
Halenbeck Andries
Halenbeck Dirck
Halenbeck Hendrick
Halenbeck Jacob
Halenbeck Jeroan
Halenbeck Matties
Halenbeck Matties, Junr.
Halenbeck John J.
Halenbeck John R.
Halenbeck John W.
Halenbeck John William
Halenbeck Michael
Halenbeck Robert
Halenbeck Samuel
Halenbeck William
Hall Matthew
Hallenback John
Haltsapple Johannis
Haner Christopher
Haner Jacob
Hanner Peter
Harder Adam
Harder Jacob P.
Harder Michal
Harder Peter
Harlow Eliab
Harman Rowse
Harmance Hendrick
Hartick Garrit
Hartick Joneton
Harvy John
Hatch William
Hauver Antren
Haver Andres
Haver Andrew
Haver Christian
Hawkins Daniel
Hawley James
Hawley William
Hawley Zadok
Hayner Peter
Heermanse Hendrick
Hegaman John
Heirmanse Jacob
Heldredg Richard, Junr.
Hellicas Baltus
Hellicas Christian
Hellicas Frederick
Hellicas Lodewick
Helm Jonas
Helm Peter
Helm Peter, Junr.
Helmer Johan Jost
Hendricks John
Hendrye Benjamin
Henry Jacob
Herder Adam
Herder Benjamin
Herder George
Herder Jacob
Herder Jacob, Junr.
Herder Jacob H.
Herder Jacob J.
Herder Jacob P.
Herder John
Herder Jores
Herder Michel
Herder Michel, Junr.
Herder Michael J.
Herder Nicholas
Herder Peter
Herdick Abraham
Herdick Francis, Junr.
Herdick Franck
Herdick Gerrit
Herdick Jacob
Herdick Jacob F.
Herdick Jeroan
Herdick John
Herdick Jonathan
Herdick John F.
Herdick Justice
Herdick Peter
Herdick Peter, Junr.
Herdick William
Herdick William, Junr.
Herdick William L.
Hermance Andres
Hermance Jacob
Hess Michel
Heydenbergh Sybrant
Heydorn Christopher
Heyser Hendrick
Heyser Hendrick, Junr.
Hoff William, Junr.
Hoffman Jacob
Hoffman Johan Nicoll
Hoffman Michel
Hogeboom Bartholomew
Hogeboom Cornelius
Hogeboom Jeremiah
Hogeboom James
Hogeboom Johannis
Hogeboom Peter
Hogeboom Stephen
Hogeboom Tobyas
Houghtaling Dirck
Hoghtaling Jacob
Hoghtaling Henry
Hopp Thomas
Holcomb Zephaniah
Holembick Matthias
Hollenbeck Samual
Holliday Henry
Holmes Asa
Holms Jedediah
Holsappel William
Holsapple Johannis
Holsapple Johannis, Junr.
Holsapple John
Holsapple William
Holtsapple John, Junr.
Horton William
Hough Zephaniah
How Samuel
Howard Enos
Hight Stephen
Higley Daniel
Hilton Jacob W.
Hines Sander
Hnye Charles
Hubbard William
Huffman Augustus
Huffman Jacob
Huguenin David
Huick Marten
Huller Simon
Hultsapple Johannis, Junr.
Hultsapple William
Huston Daniel
Huyck Casper
Huyck Johannis
Jackson Isaac
Jackson James
Jackson Robert
Jacobs John
Jager Hendrick
Jennes David
Jolley Henry
Jorean William
Jubb Negro

Jurdon William
Killey Daniel
Killmore Phillip
Kilmore George
Kilmore Hendrick
King Conrade
King Charles
Kittle John
Kline Anthony
Kline Henry
Kool Gerret
Krath Wilhelmus
Krisler Hendrick
Keble John Jurey
Keble Peter
Kelder Hendrick
Kelder Jost
Kelder William
Kelley Daniel
Kells John
Kells Hendrick
Ketchum Jonathan
Ketchum Stephen
Kettil Daniel
Laap Andries
Laap George
Laap Thomas
Land George
Land Jeremi
Land Jeremiah F.
Landt Frederick
Landt George
Landt Jeremiah
Landt Johannis
Landt Johannis, Junr.
Landt Johannis L.
Landt John, Junr.
Landt Lawrence
Lant Jurry
Larvey Elisha
Larvy William
Lasher John
Lee Ephraim
Lee Israel
Legges James
Legges Tobyas
Legit Tobies
Lemon William
Lewis Abraham
Lewis Peter
Link William
Loomis Andrew
Loop Bastian
Loop Christian
Loop Martin
Loop Peter
Lothrop Josiah
Lott John
Lovejoy Andrew
Lovejoy Benjamin
Ludlow Henry
Ludlow Henry, Junr.
Ludlow William H.
Lych Barent
Madfall Neal
Maier Abraham
Mandiville Matthew
Mannol Docter
Mantle Frances
Mantle Wynant
Marchell Danel
Marhill Daniel
Marte Nicholas
Marten Nicolaes
Martin William
Maul Friedrick
Maul John
Meggs Seth
Meerit Amos
Merrit Stephen
Merrit Thomas
Melius Anthony
Mesick Fite
Mesick Hendrick
Mesick Henry J.
Mesick Jacob J.
Mesick John
Mesick John J.
Mesick Peter
Mesick Peter J.
Mesick Thomas
Meyer Frederick
Michel Henry
Michel Jacob
Michels Anthony
Mighel William
Milham John
Miller Andries
Miller Christopher
Miller Dirck
Miller Frederick
Miller Jacob A.
Miller Jeremiah
Miller Jeremiah C.
Miller Jeremiah J.
Miller Peter
Miller Samuel
Miller Samuel A.
Miller Stephen
Miller William
Miles Anthony
Millet William A.
Mongomry Eshablo
Monnal George
Montgomery Ezekiel
Moon David
Moon Paul
Moon Richard
Moore Paul
Mory Elisha
Morris John
Morris Judg
Morris Nicholas
Morris Richard
Morris Robert
Moul Fraderick
Moul John, Junr.
Moull Jacob
Moull Johannis
Mowal Frederick
Mowel Jacob
Mowal Johannis
Mowal Johannis, Junr.
Mowel John, Junr.
Moyer Fradrick
Moyer Hendrick
Mudge Ebenezer
Muller Christopher
Muller Cornelius
Muller Cornelius C.
Muller Cornelius C. S.
Muller Cornelius H.
Muller Cornelius J.
Muller Cornelius Johannis
Muller Cornelius R.
Muller Cornelius S.
Muller Dirck
Muller Fretireck
Muller Henry
Muller Hessen
Muller Jacob
Muller Jacob, Junr.
Muller Jacob C.
Muller Jeremiah
Muller Jeremiah C.
Muller Jeremiah C. S.
Muller Jeremiah J.
Muller Jeremiah T.
Muller Jeremiah W., Junr.
Muller Jeremy C.
Muller Jocham
Muller Johannis
Muller Johannis C.
Muller Killian
Muller Peter
Muller Stephen
Muller Stephen C.
Muller Stephen H.
Muller Stephen I.
Muller Stephen J.
Muller William
Muller William C.
Mullory Jeremiah Johs
Mun Paulies
Munsee Daniel
Murgethroydt Joseph
Murphey Samuel
Myer Henry
McCall Robert
McCulley Alexander
McDonald
McFale Henry
McFall Robert
McGee James
McGinnis Jacob
McGoraghey John
McMollin Charles
Naile John
Neer Charles
Neer Henry
Neer Jacob
Neer John
New Peter
New Simeon
Nicoll Nicholas
Nooney Thompson
Noyes John
Nuan Frederick
Osterhout John
Oostrander Cornelius
Oostrander Hendrick
Oostrander Jacobus
Ostrande Arent
Ostrande Hendrick
Ostrande Hendrick, Senr.
Ostrande Jacobus
Ostrande Philip
Ostrande Wilhelmus
Ostrander Aron
Ostrander Hendrick
Ostrander Henry, Junr.
Ostrander Wilhelmus
Pabody U. Briggs
Palmer John
Palmer Stephen
Pardee Silas
Patchen Zebulon
Patterson Jacob
Patterson Doctor John
Patrick James
Patrick Thomas
Patterson James
Patterson John
Patterson Richard
Paulding Nehamiah
Payn Daniel
Petterson Benjaman
Phelps John
Philip Adam
Philip Christian
Philip David
Philip George

Philip Hendrick W.
Philip John H.
Philip William
Philip William, Junr.
Philips Adam
Philips Christian
Philips Ebenezer
Phillip Christeana
Phillip Hendrick
Phillip Hendrick H.
Phillip Jacob
Phillip Jacob, Junr. (officer. No rank)
Phillip Jacob H.
Phillip Wilhelmus
Phinney Isaac
Pichtell Jacob
Pichtell Thomas
Pichtell Thomas, Junr.
Pierce John
Pike William
Pitcher Isaac
Plank Michael
Plass Coenradt
Plass Johannis
Platner Hendrick
Platner Jacob
Plunt David
Plunt Henry
Plunt John
Pratt Bill
Pratt Robert
Pratt William
Preston Isaac
Price Timothy
Raadt Andries
Raadt Coenradt
Raadt Hendrick
Raadt Philip
Race Ephraim
Race Henry
Raes Jonathan
Ralf Johannis
Rament William
Rath Coenradt
Raudt Andries
Raudt Hendrick
Raut Adam
Raut Andrew
Raut Conrad
Raut Philip
Raymond William
Ree Daniel
Rees Hendrick
Rees Hendrick, Junr.
Rees John
Rees Jonas
Rees Jonathan
Rees Jonathan, Junr.
Rees Jonathan H.
Rees Jonathan J.
Rees Jonathan W.
Rees Philip
Rees Thomas
Rees William
Relgen Jonathan
Reynolds Lewis
Richardson Joseph
Rifenberger Hendrick
Ring Coenradt
Risedorph Jacob
Roberson John D.
Roberts Peter
Robbins Thomas
Robbins William
Robins Henry
Rocbaugh Robart
Rodman Thoms
Roe Ebenezer
Rogers Othaniel
Rolf John
Rome William
Rooreback Robert
Rorapaugh Robert
Roseboom Barent
Rosman Bastean
Rosman George, Jr.
Rous Harman
Row Hendrick
Row John
Row William
Rowland John, Jr.
Rowley John
Russell Dirck
Russman George
Russman Jurrey
Russman Sebastian
Ryne Lawrence
Rysen John
Salback Jacob
Salback Johannes
Salsberry Johannis
Sarring Amos
Saxton James
Scerrin Amos
Sciem Peter
Scharp Lawrance
Schermerhorn John
Schermerhorn John, Junr.
Schermerhorn William
Schoenmaker Henry
Schoenmaker Hendrick, Junr.
Scholtus Hendrick
Schoudt Coenradt
Schudt Peter
Schult Henrich
Scott James
Scott William
Segar David
Shafer Philip
Sharp Cornelous
Sharp Jacob
Sharp Johannis
Sharp Johannis, Junr.
Sharp Nicholas
Sharts Andres
Sharts Johannes
Sharts Juriah
Sharts Nicholas
Sharts Nicholas, Junr.
Shaver Adam
Shaver Peter
Shaver Phillip
Sheaver Henry
Shephard James
Shephard Jonathan
Shirts Jurry
Shirts Nicholas
Shirts Nicholas, Junr.
Shoemaker Godfree
Shoemaker Hendrick
Sholt Hendrick
Sholt Hendrick, Junr.
Showerman Andres
Shufelt Jeremiah
Shufelt Henry
Shufelt Peter
Shuldt Hendrick
Shuldt Hendrick, Junr.
Shuldt Johannis (named as officer. No rank given)
Shurts Abraham
Shurts David
Shurts Nicholas, Junr.
Shurts Uriah
Shuts Simon
Shuts Abraham
Shuts David
Silkey James
Silvernagel Peter
Simon Jacob
Simson James
Simson Robert
Skinkle Henry I.
Skinkle Henry, Junr.
Skinkle Jacob
Skinkle Jonas
Skinner Josiah
Smart John
Smith Benjamin
Smith Christopher
Smith Coenraedt
Smith Coham Adam
Smith Derick
Smith Dirck
Smith Francis
Smith George
Smith George, Junr.
Smith George A.
Smith George Adam
Smith George P.
Smith Henry
Smith Henry P.
Smith Jacob P.
Smith Jered
Smith Jeremiah
Smith Jeremiah C.
Smith Jerry
Smith Johannis
Smith Johannis C.
Smith John
Smith John G.
Smith John P.
Smith Peter
Smith Peter A.
Smith Peter Adam
Smith Peter Johannis
Smith Philip
Smith Richard
Smith Timothy
Smith Tuenes G.
Smith Tunis
Smith Tunis P.
Smith William
Snook John
Snook Martinus
Snyder Coenradt
Snyder George
Snyder Henry
Snyder Hendrick
Snyder Peter
Snyder Peter, Junr.
Snyder William
Snyder William H.
Sours Peter
Sower Uldrick
Spanord Anthony
Spencer Samuel
Spencer Samuel, Junr.
Spoor Cornelius
Squire Jesse
Stalker Embrew
Stalker John
Stalker Joseph
Stanze William
Stark James
Stever Henry
Stolp Gerlough
Stolp Peter
Stoppelbean George Adam
Stoppelben Faltin

Stopplebean Jacob
Stopplebean Jacob, Junr.
Stopplebeen George A.
Stopplebeen Hendrick
Stopplebeen Hendrick, Junr.
Stopplebeen Michael
Stopplebeen Michel H.
Stopplebeen Nicholas
Stopplebeen Peter
Stopplebeen Valentine
Storm John
Strickland William
Stuppelban Jacob
Stuppelban Nichol
Stupplebau Jacob
Stuppelbean Nichol
Stupplebean Hendrick
Sufelt George
Sufelt George, Junr.
Tallmage John
Talmage Elisha
Teater George
Tedmore John
Ten Broeck Anthony
Ten Broeck Henry L.
Ten Broeck Jeremiah
Ten Broeck John
Ten Broeck John Jeremiah
Ten Broeck Peter
Ten Broeck Peter B.
Ten Broeck Samuel J.
Ten Broeck Samuel Jeremiah
Ten Broeck Samuel John
Ten Eyck Barent
Thompson Alexander
Thompson John
Tickner Benjamin
Tiloman Abraham
Tittemood John
Tittiman Abraham
Toby Seth
Tolley Dyer
Tolley Johan F.
Tram John, Junr.
Treat Teas (see Theaus)
Trier Isaac T.
Tripp Anthony
Trull John
Tunnecliff John
Tunnecliff William
Turner Gilbert
Turner Gysbert
Tuttle William Y.
Utley David
Vallance Zachariah
Vasbarry Peter
Venson Abraham
Vischer Bastian H.
Vonck Peter
Vosburgh Abraham
Vosburgh Dirck
Vosburgh Evart
Vosburgh Isaac
Vosburgh Isaac P.
Vosburgh Jacob
Vosburgh Jacob, Junr.
Vosburgh Jacob D.
Vosburgh Evart
Vosburgh Jacob P.
Vosburgh Jacobus
Vosburgh Peter
Vosburgh Matthew
Vredenburgh Isaac
Vredenburgh Jacobus
Van Alen Adam
Van Alen John
Van Alstyne William
Van Back Nicholas
Van Beuren George
Van Beuren Peter
Van Bregen Peter
Van Deboe Jacob
Van De Bogert Michael
Vandekar Dirrick
Vandekar Joghem
Vandekar Solomon
Van Der Kar Dirck
Van Der Kar Jacob
Van Der Kar Jocham
Van Der Kar Johannis
Van Der Kar Nicholas
Van Deusen Abraham
Van Deusen Adam
Van Deusen Cornelius
Van Deusen Glonde
Van Deusen Glouds
Van Deusen Jacob
Van Deusen Johannis
Van Deusen Johannis J.
Van Deusen John I.
Van Deusen Mattawe M.
Van Deusen Matthew
Van Deusen Robert
Van Deusen Tobyas
Vande Water Michael
Vandusen Barent
Van Dusen Henry
Van Dusen Malacher
Van Dusen Martin
Van Epps Evert
Van Hoesen Abraham
Van Hoesen Albertus
Van Hoesen Burry
Van Hoesen Cornelius J.
Van Hoesen Cornelius N.
Van Hoesen Gerrit G.
Van Hoesen Hendrick
Van Hoesen Jacob
Van Hoesen Jacob, Junr.
Van Hoesen Jacob C.
Van Hoesen Jacob F.
Van Hoesen Jacob I.
Van Hoesen Jacob J.
Van Hoesen Jacob Jacob
Van Hoesen Jacob Jurry
Van Hoesen Jacob L.
Van Hoesen Johannis
Van Hoesen Johannis C.
Van Hoesen Johannis J.
Van Hoesen Johannis Janse
Van Hoesen John
Van Hoesen John Hoes
Van Hoesen John Hoes, Junr.
Van Hoesen John Jacabse
Van Hoesen John Joseph
Van Hoesen John Jurry
Van Hoesen Justice
Van Hoesen Nicholas
Van Hoesen Peter
Van Huesen Cornelius
Van Ness William
Van Ness William, Junr.
Van Rensselaer Henry
Van Rensselaer John R.
Van Renselaer Killyaen
Van Rensselaer Peter
Van Rensselaer Robert
Van Rensselaer William
Van Salsbergh Cornelius
Van Salsbergh Lukas
Van Valkenburgh Abraham
Van Valkenburgh Bartholomew
Van Valkenburgh Bartly
Van Valkenburgh Matties
Van Valkenburgh William
Van Valkencis John
Van Valkeneer Justice
Van Valkeneer Peter
Van Wagenaer Gerrit
Wadsworth John
Wagenaer Carel
Wagenear Jacob
Wagenear John
Wagner Peter
Ward Jacob
Warne Peter
Warne Richard
Warner Peter
Warner Richard
Wattles Samuel
Waymar John
Weager Henry
Weager Jacob
Weager Philip
Wemple Walter V.
Wendell Garrit
West Benjamin
West William
White Benjamin
White John, Junr.
White Jurry
White Peter
White Uriah
White William
Wiessmer Peter (named as officer. No rank given)
Wiessmer Peter, Junr.
Wiley Alexander
Willams Willams
Willcocks Simeon
Willcox Nathaniel
Williams Thomas
Wilsey Cornelius
Wilsey Cornelius, Junr.
Wilsey Henry
Wilsey Jacob
Wilsey Jeames
Wilsey Thomas
Wilton Jacob W.
Wiltse Henry
Wiltse Thomas
Wineradt George
Wise Michel
Witbeck Hendrick
Witbeck Jacob
Witbeck John
Witbeck Lukas
Witbeck Thomas
Witlow John Hartick
Wood James
Wood John
Wood John, Junr.
Wood William
Woodard Asa
Wyat Peter
Yager Hendrick
Yates Peter W.
Yates Robert
Yorker Jacob
Young Calvin
Young Philip
Young William
Zanegall Robert W.

Albany County Militia—(Continued).

COLONEL PETER VAN NESS

MAJOR JACOB FORD

CAPT. BARTHOLOMEW BARRETT
" JONAH GRAVES
" JOSIAH GRAVES
" ABNER HAWLEY
" JOSHUA WHITNEY
LIEUT. BENJAMIN ALLEN
" DANIEL BARNES
" ABNER KELLOGG
" NATHANIEL MEAD
LIEUT. CHARLES MCARTHUR
" DAVID MCKINSTRY
" AMAZIAH PHILLIPS
" JONATHAN PITCHER
" ELEAZER SPENCER
" ABEL WHALEN
" DANIEL WILSON
ENSIGN STEPHEN GRAVES
" PHENIHEAS RICE

ADDITIONAL NAMES ON STATE TREASURER'S PAY BOOKS.

LIEUTENANT COLONEL DAVID PRATT

CAPT. JOSEPH ALLEN TANNER
LIEUT. CALEB CLARK
" THOMAS HATCH
" CHARLES MCKINSTRY
" THOMAS MCKINSTRY
LIEUT. WILL OVE
" JOHN REYNOLDS
ENSIGN JOHN CRIPPEN
" JAMES DELONG

ENLISTED MEN

Ackley James
Adset John
Adsit Samuel
Andreas Ebenezer
Andress Ebenezer
Andrews Elisha
Bagley Asher
Barret Ebenezer
Barret Eleazer
Barrows Ebenezer
——— Benjamin
Blackman Joel
Bont Matthias
Borghordt Lambert
Bower Daniel
Brown Benjamin
Bunhas Charles
Bunt Ephraim
Bunt Matthias
Burgert Hennerey
Burget Johoicam
Cadman John
Cadman Joseph
Carrier Amos
Casterrar John
Castor John
Chaimberlain Benjamin
Chaimberlin Gurden
Childendon Benjamin
Chittendon Benjamin
Cisel Peleg
Cleveland Oliver
Cohoon Joseph
Colver Ebenezer
Crippen John
Crippen Roswel
Culver Ebenezer
Darner Christopher
Darrow Ammerus
Darrow Christopher
Davis Andrew
Day David
Deen Gains
Denison Christopher
Devonport Jonathan
Dibble Henerey
Dolittle Timothy
Doolittle Hackaliah
Dudley Simeon
Earle Benjamin
Elmer ———
Foot Samuel
Foster John
Frask James
Freamon Jonathan
Freeman Daniel
Gardner John
Goff Oliver
Gold Jonathan
Gould Elijah
Gould Jonathan
Graves Increase
Graves Soldon
Green Thomas
Green William
Griswell John
Griswold David
Hacket Joseph
Hall Benijah
Hamblin Jesse
Harris Eliphalet
Hatch Thomas
Hawkins Daniel
Hawley Daniel
Hawley Zadok
Hewit Arthur
Hollister Smith
Horsford Ithamer
House Thomas
Howes Thomas
Huit Arthur
Huntly William
Hurlbert Jesse
Jackson James
Joal Ebenezer
Johnson Thomas
Johnston Abner
Keeney Roger
Ketcham Jesse
Killogh Benjamin
Lawrane Judah M.
Lawrence Joseph
Leanord John
Lee Joel
Liment Archibald, Jr.
Limont John
Lothrop Ebenezer
Lovejoy Andrew
Malleray Samuel
Martin Robert
Meaker Robert
Mirit Amos
Mortain Robert
Mudge Ruben
McArthur John
McKever James
Nicols Eliachim
Palmer John
Palmer Stephen
Palmmer Gilbert
Palmmer James
Palmitier Benjamin

Parks Samuel
Penfield Isaac
Phelps Jonah
Pottor Gideon
Pratt Samuel
Rea Hugh
Reiss Matt
Reynolds Jonathan
Richinson Joseph
Richmond Edward
Robbins Daniel
Robinson Hector
Rodman Joseph
Rodman Thomas
Roldman Joseph
Root Joshua
Root Moses
Root Nicholas
Rowland John
Rowland John, Jr.
Rowley Jabesh
Salsbury —idion
Saxton Ebenezer
Scoot Matt
Shepherd Jonathan
Smith Eli
Smith Elijah
Snyder William
Sole Ebenezer
Spalding John
Spalding Nehemiah
Spalding Samuel
Speer Cornelius
Spencer Amos
Spencer Asa
Spencer David
Spencer Eleazer
Spencer Eliphas
Spencer John
Spencer Matthias
Spencer Phineas
Spencer Samuel
Spencer Tuneas
Stark Amos
Stuart John
Taylor David
Taylor James
Teeckner Benjamin
Thomlinson Lemuel
Tickner Benjamin
Tickner Jonathan
Tilman Jacob
Titus Silas
Tyler Ebenezer
Valcomburgh Johoicam
Vawn Edward
Vawn Richard
Virgin Asa
Van Hoesen Francis
Van Valcomburey George
Walch Thomas
Welch Jonathan
West Samuel
White Johoicam
White William
Wise Samuel
Witmore Reuben
Woodin Rubin
Wrolen John

Albany County Militia — (Continued).

COLONEL MORRIS GRAHAM
COLONEL HENRY LIVINGSTON
MAJOR DIRCK JANSEN
MAJOR SAMUEL TEN BROECK
ADJUTANT PHILIP ROCKEFELLER
QUARTER MASTER CHRISTIAN VAN VALKENBURGH
SURGEON THOMAS THOMPSON

CAPT. JOSEPH ELLIOTT
" ADAM HUSRADT
" CONRAD KLINE
" HENRY PULVER
" DIELL ROCKEFELLER
" DIRCK ROCKEFELLER
" JACOB F. SHAVER
" JOHN SHAVER
" PHILIP SMITH
LIEUT. JOHN BEST
" WILLIAM CASPER
" BARTLE HENDRICKS
" JACOB HAGEDORN
" HENRY IRVINE
" JOHN MCARTHUR
" NICHOLAS POWER
LIEUT. WILLIAM ROCKEFELLER
" JACOB ROSCHMAN
" HARMANES ROSS
" CASPARUS SCHULTZ
" CHARLES SHAVER
" JOHN SHUTS
" JOHANNES STAAT
" JOHANNES STALL
" PETER VAN DE BOGART
" HENRY WILL
ENSIGN LEANARD DACKER
" ASA HOLMES
" PHILIP KNICKERBACKER
" MARX KUN
" COLIN MCDONALD

ADDITIONAL NAMES ON STATE TREASURER'S PAY BOOKS:

LIEUT. WANDEL PULVER
" ADAM SEGENDORPH
ENSIGN JOHN HERDER
ENSIGN BASTIAN LESHER
" JAMES ROBINSON

ENLISTED MEN

Adams Baily
Andon Casper
Angle William
Astin Jacob
Attwood Timothy
Bain Casparues
Baker John
Barganer Peter
Barnet John
Barnet Simon
Bartley Simon
Basseroom John
Batts Johannes
Bearsh John
Becker Jacob
Ben James
Berringer Peter
Best Benjamin
Best Hendrick
Best Peter
Biest William
Bitser Wilhelmus
Blass Michael
Blass Peter M.
Blass William
Bless Hendrick
Bownen Hendrick
Bower Nicholas, Junr.
Bruiree Johannis N.
Bruise John F.
By Phenber Jacobus
Cain Paul H.
Campbell John
Campbell Martin
Capes Martin
Casper Christian
Casper Christopher
Cleevland Lemuel
Cline Anthony
Clum Adam
Clum Adam, Junr.
Clum Hendrick
Coale Johannis
Coale Peter
Coens William
Coitrs John, Junr.
Cole Isaac
Cole John
Cole Peter
Comb Samuel, Junr.
Concklin Elisha
Concklin-John
Conradt Johannes
Coombe Samuel
Coon Adam
Coons Peter
Coons Philip
Cork John, Junr.
Corol Michael
Cotman Conradt
Crammer William
Cun Samuel
Cund Hendrick
Cunn Adam
Cunx William
Cunx William H.
Currey William
Curry John
Dacker John C.
Danels Thomis
Dannilly William
Decker Abraham

Decker Benjamin
Decker Conradt
Decker George
Decker Isaac
Decker Jacob
Decker Jacob C.
Decker John
Decker Lawrence I.
Delamater Abraham
Dick Henry
Dick Paulus
Dicker Charles C.
Diness Philip
Diness Yerry
Dings Jacob
Dings John
Dings Stutfle
Dolph John
Donnolly William
Dougherty Cornelius
Dounatty William
Douy Cornelius
Dubois Abraham
Dunsbach Philip
Egelston Benjamin
Elkenbraugh Jacob
Elkenbrugh Philip
Elliott Michael
Engell George
Erkenbergh Fite
Fox Jonathan
Frasier William
Frits William
Funck Christian
Funck Jacob
Funck Peter
Gardner James
Gardner John
Gobobe John
Graves Bort
Haber Johannos
Hagadom Jacob
Hagedoom William
Hagedorn William
Halter Michael
Halter Peter
Halter John
Halter John, Junr.
Hatter John
Hatter Michael
Hatter Peter
Haver Christian
Haver Johannis
Haver Peter
Heiser Petrus
Herder John
Herder Michel
Herder Petrus
Herder Philip
Heyser Henry
Heyser Jacob, Junr.
Heyser Jacob, Senr.
Heyser Peter
Hofs William
Horck John, Junr.
Houshapple Zacharias
Houward Adam
Hunt Palathia
Hus Casper
Hyck Abraham
Hyck John B.
Imik Johannis
Jacobs Bastian
Janes David
Jorgh Michael
Kain Paul H.
Keephart Caleb
Kline Jacob
Kline Peter
Lape Thomas
Lape Jurry
Lasher Conradt B.
Lasher G. B.
Lasher Garret
Lasher Garret, Junr.
Lasher Johannis
Lasher Johannis J.
Lasher Johannis, Junr.
Lasher Philip
Lasher William
Laubay Carl
Laubay Jacob
Lawrence John
Lawrence Peter
Lemnery Solomon
Lesher Bastian
Loomis John
Lynch Peter
Mayer Johannis
Merky Max
Meyer Friderick
Miller Jonas
Miller Matthew
Minklar Jacob
Moor Peter
Moor Philip
Mower Barent
McArthur Arthur
McArthur John P.
McClean Hector
McIntire John
MacFall Hendrick
MacFall Neal
MacFall Patrick
McFall Robert
McGill John
Nash John
Needen John
Nott John
Ostrander Benjamin
Ostrander John
Parish John
Parve Daniel
Petrie Conrad C.
Petri Cunrath
Phillips Christian, Junr.
Phillips Christopher
Phillips Christopher, Junr.
Phillips John
Phillips Peter
Plass Peter
Plass Peter M.
Polver Jacob
Post William, Junr.
Pulver Wandel
Purden Edward
Quackenbos Daniel
Quackenbos Garret
Race Benjamin
Race Ephraim
Radclift John
Rath Adam
Renolds Lusia
Ringsdorph Phillip
Risdorf George
Robertson James
Robinson James
Rockefeller Diell, Junr.
Rockefeller Simeon
Rose Andrew A.
Rosman Samuel
Rossman Adam
Roth Adam
Russ Hermanus
Russ Samuel
Ruth Adam
Ruyans Philip
Ryfenbergh Adam
Salback Jacob
Salback Johannis
Salback Philip
Salbagh Thomas
Schmit Petrus
Schmit Zacherias
Schnnyder Ludwig
Schut Isaac
Schut Solomon
Schut William
Scutt William
Sebo Harry
Shefter Johannis
Shefter Nicholas
Segendorph Adam
Sharp Peter
Shaver John
Shaver Peter
Shiffer Johannis
Shipperly Barnet
Sholtis Philip
Sholts Barent
Shudes Henry
Shultis Barent
Shultis Davis
Shultis Henry
Shuts Adam
Shuts Johannes W.
Shuts Peter
Simon Battis
Simons William
Sipperly Barnet
Sisam John
Skuts John A.
Slos John
Smith James
Smith Johannis
Smith Joseph
Smith Peter
Smith Philar
Smith Samuel
Smith Zachariah
Snook Conrad
Snyder Conrad
Snyder Conrad, Junr.
Snyder George
Snyder Samuel
Snyder William
Spickerm Philip
Spickerman John
Spilman Conrad
Stahl Johann Henrich
State Benjamin
Stimon Baltis
Strader Jost
Stribel Ulrich
Temple James
Ten Brook Wessel
Ten Eyck Abraham
Ten Eyck Jacob
Ten Eyck John B.
Ten Eyck John, Junr.
Thomas Johannis
Thompson Abisha
Thompson George
Trater Joseph
Trever Peterus
Tunsback Philip
Turner Gilbert
Valkenburgh Christian
Vonck Christian
Vonck Jacob
Vonck Peter
Vosburgh Jacob

Vosburgh Peter
Vosburgh Lawrence
Van De Bogart Arent
Van De Bogart James
Van De Bogen Peter
Van De Bogart Michael
VandeWaters Hynis
Van De Waters Michael
Van Dusen George
Van Dusen Robert
Washburn John
Washburn Martinus
Waters Michael
Weeks Andrew
Whitimast Zachariah
Whitman Izra
Whitmore Stutfel
Widbeck Jacob
Wiest John
Will Chistian
Will Christopher
Will Herik
Willas Henry
Witeree Phillip
Witmore Philip
Yager Philip
Yager Wandle
Young Zacharias
Yunck William
Yunck Zachariah
Zeber Petrus
Zimmerman Henry
Zent Wissell

Albany County Militia — (Continued).

COLONEL ANTHONY VAN BERGEN

LIEUTENANT COLONEL CORNELIUS DUBOIS

PAY MASTER BENJAMIN DUBOIS (CAPTAIN)

CAPT. THOMAS HOUGHTALING
" MYNDERT VAN SCHAICK
" JOHN A. WHITBECK
LIEUT. ANTHONY ABEEL
" ABRAM OVERPAGH
LIEUT. JOHN PERSONS
" FRANCIS SALISBURY
" WESSEL SALISBURY
" JACOB VAN VEGHTEN
ENSIGN JAMES BOGARDUS

ADDITIONAL NAMES ON STATE TREASURER'S PAY BOOKS:

LIEUT. JOCHEM TRYON
" HENRY VAN BERGEN
ENSIGN PETER BRONK
ENSIGN CHRISTIAN MEYER
" JOHN C. SCHACK
" PETER VAN BERGEN

Albany County Militia — (Continued).

COLONEL JACOBUS VAN SCHOONHOVEN
LIEUTENANT COLONEL JAMES GORDON
MAJOR ANDREW MITCHELL
MAJOR EZEKIEL TAYLOR
ADJUTANT JOSEPH COOK
ADJUTANT DAVID RUMSEY (CAPTAIN)
QUARTER MASTER SIMON FORT
QUARTER MASTER HUGH PEOPLES
SURGEON JOHN CUERDEN

CAPT. BENJAMIN AYLSWORTH
" TYRANNIS COLLINS
" THOMAS HICKS
" ELIAS STEENBERGH
" JOSHUA TAYLOR
" JOHN VAN DEN BERGH
" NANNING VISCHER
" STEPHEN WHITE
LIEUT. HENDRICK BONTER
" THOMAS BROWN
" JOHN COREY
" STEPHEN SHERWOOD
" SAMUEL TEN BROECK
LIEUT. NICHOLAS VANDERKAR
" JOHN VAN VRANCKEN
" NICHOLAS VAN VRANCKEN
" NATHANIEL WEED
" EPENETUS WHITE
" BENJAMIN WOOD
ENSIGN CALEB BENEDICT
" CHRISTIAN BONTER
" MICHAEL DE GROFF
" SAMUEL DOX
" NATHAN RAYMOND
" MAAS VAN VRANCKEN
" WILLIAM WALDERON

ENLISTED MEN

Adams Edward
Armstrong Daniel
Arnol John
Arson Thomas
Ashley Alden
Baily Timothy
Ball Flamon
Ball John
Ball Stephen
Banter John
Barbeck James
Barber Solomon
Barne Samuel
Barnes Benoni
Barnes James
Barns Thomas
Barns William
Barnum Thomas
Barter Joseph
Bealy Timothy
Benedict Elias
BenedictElisha
Benedict Elisha, Junr.
Benedict Felix
Benedict Ryer
Benedict Uriah
Betteys Jeremiah
Betteys William
Bigford Samuel
Bourn William
Bogardus Scheboleth
Bohanner Robert (see Mahannan)
Boskerk Martin
Bradshaw William
Bratt Aaront
Bratt Dirck
Bravon Thomas
Brewer Jery
Brooks Joseph
Brown Valintine
Bruer Jeremiah
Bruss Jeremiah
Bryant John
Buchanan Ebenezer
Buckingham Ebenezer
Burk John
Cabel John
Callogg Eliphalet
Camble Harmanus
Cannel Christian
Canniff Isaac
Carey John
Chambers Daniel
Chard Barce
Chatman Josiah
Chestney John
Christee John
Christiaan Cornelius
Christianse Cornelius
Chrtiyonse Cornelius
Cilberth John
Clinton John
Clute Dirick
Clute Gerardus
Clute Gerardas, Junr.
Clute Gerret
Clute Gerret D.
Clute Jacob
Clute Jacob G.
Cole Azor
Cole John
Collins Manasah
Concklin James
Concklin Thomas
Conlin Jacob
Connel John
Conner John
Cook John
Corpe Joseph
Corpe Nathaniel
Crawford John
Craydenwiser Henry
Creamer Christopher
Creamer Hendrick
Creamer Jury
Creps Peter
Crydenwiser Henry

Cunee John
Cuner John
Cunie Ephraim
Curdon John
Dais John
Davis John
DeGroat Elias
DeGroat Henry
DeGroat Nicholas
Degraff Abraham
Degroff Michael (see Degrave)
Degroff Simon
Delong Daniel
Delong David
Delong Ezekiel
Demilt Isaac
Devoe Dirick
Devoe Isaac, Junr.
Devoe John
Devoe John R.
Devoe Martinus
Devoe Samuel
Devoe William
Devoct Abraham
Doppe Johannis
Doty Philip
Douglass Jonathan
Dox Isaac
Dox John
Drett John
Drett John, Junr.
Dunning Jesse
Efner Henry
Efner John
Efner Wilhelmus
Eldred Robert
Eldridge Robert
Elsworth George
Evans Ebenezer
Evens Nathan
Fairchild Matthew
Falmer John
Fitch John
Flynn John
Fonda Isaac H.
Fonda Isaac I.
Fonda John H.
Forgison Peter
Fort Daniel
Fort Nicholas
Forth Nicholas, Junr.
Foster William
Fowlar John
Fracikle Philip
Fraisier John
Frayzer John
Fulington James
Fullerton James
Fullmer Jacob
Fulmer Johannis
Fulwieser Abraham
Gardner George
Garremo Samuel
Goreham Jabez
Green Daniel
Gregory Uriah
Grigg John
Griggs
Griggs Evert
Griggs John
Griggs Simon
Griswould John
Groom James
Grooms David
Grooms William
Groot Claus
Groot Cornelius
Groot Derick A.
Groot Derick C.
Groot Jesse
Groot Nicholas
Griggs Abraham
Griggs Simon
Haens James
Hagedorn Henry
Hagedorn Peter
Hagerman Adrian
Hagerman Nicholas
Hall Levy
Halstead Timothy
Hart Nicholas
Hatt Jacob
Hawkins
Hawkins Arthur
Heagley Seth
Heemstrat David
Heemstrat Dirick
Hiat Roger
Hicks Samuel
Higby Flemin
Higby John
Higby Lewis
Hollister Josiah
Hollister Lazarus
Holmes Caleb
Hooper John
Hooper Stephen
How David
How Isaac
How Jesse
Hubble Abijah
Hubbell Jabez
Hull David
Hunter David
Isdle John
James Henry
James Nathaniel
Jengins Edmon
Jennings Jesse
Jinnin Edmund
Kellogg Azor
Kellogg Eliphalet, Junr.
Kanedy John
Kanedy Thomas
Kennedy George
Kennedy Robert
Kennedy Thomas
Lake Benjamin
Lansing Henry
Lansing Isaac
Lansingh Garrit T.
Lattemore Francis
Lattemore John
Laverse Anthony
Leverse Levenus
Luik George
Mab John
Mab Thomas
Mahannan Robert (see Bohanner)
Main William
Mastin George
Maston George
Matthews Clark
Mead Zachariah
Merrick Stephen
Middlebrook Michael
Miller Christopher
Miller Jacob
Miller James
Miller Jeremiah
Miller John
Miller Joshua
Mirick Abel
Mitchel Robert
Moe Abraham
Moe Husted
Moe Jacob
Moon Jacob
Moon William
Morehouse George
Mosier Joseph
Mourehouse Joseph
Muckle John
Munn Israel
Murry James
McChesney John
McClean Cornelius
McCoy Charls
McCoy William
McCray Samuel
McCready David
McCrear Samuel
McCue Samuel
McDonalds Michael
McIntosh John
McKnight John
McKnight Thomas
McNeil Archibald
McNeil William
Names Abraham
Nash Azor
Nash John
Nash Samuel
Nesler Conrad
Nesler John
Northrop Wilson
Northrop Thadeus
Nothrup Thadeus
Novell James
Olmsted Daniel
Owen Epenetus
Owens Abernatus
Page Samuel
Palmer Amaziah
Palmer Beriah
Palmerton Joshua
Palmeter Joshua
Palmeteer William
Palmetier Isaac
Patchin Jabez
Patchin Samuel
Patchin Squire
Patchin Zachariah
Patterson Adam
Peirson John
Pearse James
Pearse John
Pearse Richard
Peebles Hugh
Philmore Sirus
Prevoct Reech
Prevost Alexander
Putman John
Quackenbush Jacob
Quackinbush Gradus
Reeve William
Rhen William
Rice William
Roff Philip
Root Asa
Root Stephen
Rose John
Rossel Rosel
Rue Joseph, Junr.
Rumney John G.
Rumsey David
Saupers David
Schaaf Henrich
Schonter Hugh
Schoonhoven James

Schouten Darrick
Schouter Jacob
Schouter Johanis
Schut
Schutt Alexander
Scott James
Scranton Marchen
Scribner Aaron
Scribner Thadeus
Sears Sunderland
Seeley John
Seeley Stephen
Seely Nehemiah
Seever Sunderland
Sharp Philip
Shear Matthias
Shere John
Shere Peter
Sherred James
Sherwood James
Shouten Jacob
Shuter William
Sign John
Sines John
Siney Peter (see Sinix)
Sinix Peter (see Siney)
Smith Abijah
Smith Benijah
Smith Elias
Smith Elijah
Smith Henry
Smith John
Smith Lewis
Smith Moses
Snodye William
Soopers David
Sprag Elisha
Sprage Ebenezer, Junr.
Sprage John
Sprague Elijah
Sprague John
Steenbergh James
Steenbergh John
Steenbergh Peter
Sutton James
Taylor John
Teachout Isaac
Teathout Jacob
Teathout Nicholaes
Teathout William
Thalhimer Peter
Todd Robert
Tooper William
Traver Francis
Tymensia Aldert
Vallentine Gabriel
Vedder Corset
Vedder Harman
Vedder Harmanus
Vedder Jacob
Vensen John
Vischer Eldert
Vincent Jeremiah
Vischer Teunis
Van Aelstine Daniel
Van Camp Simeon
VanDenBergh Cornelius
VandenBergh Gerrit
VandenBergh Neeklaes
VanDenBergh Nicholas C.
VanDenBergh Peter
VanDenBergh Rutgert
VanDenKar Abraham
VanDenKar Arent
VanDenKar Derick
VanDenKar Hendrick
VandenKar Nicholas
VanDerhyden Abraham
VanDenWorker Albert
VanDenWerken Barent
VanDenWerken Francis
VanDenWerken Gradus
VanDenWerken John J.
Vanderwerken John
VanDeWerke John A.
Van Ness Cherck
Van Ness William
Van O'Linde Daniel
Van Schaick Goose
Van Schoonhoven Hendrick
Van Vleck Tunis
Van Vranken Abraham
Van Vranken Adam
Van Vrancken Claus
Van Vranken Cornelius
Van Vranken Dirick
Van Vrancken Evert
Van Vranken Gerrit
Van Vrancke Jacob
Van Vranken Isaac
Van Vrancken James
Van Vrancken John
Van Vranken Nicholas
Van Vranken Rykert
Van Vranken Samuel
Van Vranken Wouh
Wait Oliver
Walderon Evert
Walderon Gerit
Walderon Peter
Ward William
Watrous Edward A.
Way Daniel
Way David
Weaver Edward
Weaver Josias
Weed Bill
Weed Phineas
Weed William
Weight Abner
Welden Timothy
Wellden Abraham
White Epenetus
White John
White Jonas
White Nathaniel
Wilde William
Williams David
Williams Fradrick
Williams John
Williamson William
Wilsee Jacob
Wilsee John
Witey William
Wood Elijah
Wood Enoch
Wood John
Wooding Timity
Wooley Daniel
Wooley Jonathan
Wyley Stephen
Young John

Albany County Militia — (Continued).

COLONEL JOHN McCREA
COLONEL CORNELIUS VAN VEGHTEN
MAJOR DANIEL DICKINSON
MAJOR JACOB G. VAN SCHAICK
ADJUTANT ELISHA ANDRUS
QUARTER MASTER MICHAEL BEADLE

CAPT. HOLTON DUNHAM
" MICHAEL DUNNING
" JOHN THOMPSON
" PETER VAN WORT
" PETER WINNIE
" EPHRAIM WOODWORTH
LIEUT. ASHBEL ANDRUSS
" ABEL BELNAP
" STEPHEN BENEDICT
" JOHN DAVIS
" ISAAC DOTY
" HEZEKIAH DUNHAM
" BENJAMIN GUILE
" PHILIPP ROGERS, JR.
LIEUT. SAMUEL SHELDON
" JAMES STORM
" JOSHUA WHEELER
ENSIGN ISAAC D. FONDA
" WILLIAM GREEN
" NATHANIEL GROMMON
" RICHARD HILTON
" JOHN HUNTER
" JOHN MAHONEY
" JOSEPH ROW
" BENJAMIN SHELDON
" GERRITT VAN BUREN
" REUBEN WRIGHT

ADDITIONAL NAMES ON STATE TREASURER'S PAY BOOKS.

LIEUT. JABEZ GAGE
ENSIGN JACOB D. FONDA

ENLISTED MEN.

Abbet David
Abeel James
Abeel William
Ackerman David
Ackerman Isaac
Ackerman James
Ackerman Robert
Airl Nathaniel
Albert White (see White Albert)
Allen James
Andress John
Andress Nathan
Andrus Ephraim
Andrus John, Junr.
Andrus Joseph
Andrus Nathaniel
Andruss Ashbel, Junr.
Andruss Deliverance
Andruss Titus
Anthony Richard
Anthony Stephen
Archer David
Armstrong John
Armstrong Thomas
Arnold Abemelick
Arnold John
Ashman Samuel
Austin Phinehas
Babcock Job
Babcock Jonathan
Badcock Nehemiah
Baker Edey
Baldwin Alexander
Banter John
Barber Simeon
Barden Abraham
Beadle Daniel
Beadle Joseph
Beadle Michael
Beadle Thomas, Junr.
Beadlestone Henry
Beams Jeremiah
Becker Peter
Bedle Thomas
Beltar John
Bemus William
Bennet Bildad
Benson Elihu
Benson Job
Benson John
Bently Benedict
Bently Thomas
Bidwell Daniel
Bidwell David, Junr.
Bidwell Jacob
Bise William
Bitcler Henery
Black William
Blanding John
Bowdish Henery
Bowdish Gideon
Bowler Simeon
Bradshaw William
Briggs Abraham
Brisbee Samuel
Brisben James
Brisbin William
Benson Bildad
Brown Benjamin
Brown Joel
Brown Luther
Brownell Benjamin
Bryan Samuel, Junr.
Buck John
Buck Peregreen
Burden Abraham
Burllinggame Silas
Bush Benjamin
Button Elezer
Cady Zebulon
Calvert John
Campbell Daniel
Campbell Samuel
Campbell Solomon
Cans Joseph
Carpenter Barnet
Carpenter Barney
Carpenter Benjamin
Carpenter John
Carpenter Warren
Carr Joseph
Case Alexander
Case Joseph
Coffin Bartlet
Collins Elber
Conklin Nathaniel
Couton Simeon
Chamberlin Joseph
Chapman Ezekiel

Chapman Noah
Chapman Samuel
Chatfield Jesse
Chidester Daniel
Chidester Nathan
Child Increase
Christionse Cornelius
Clapp Lemuel
Clement Peter
Clute Ephrama
Clute Evert
Clute Gradus
Cobb Ebenezer
Cole Abraham
Collins Benjamin
Collins William
Colvert James
Colvert John
Comstock Peter
Conklen Samuel
Conkling John
Cook Nathaniel
Coon Jeremiah
Cooper William
Coppe Nathaniel
Cornell Paul
Corps Nathaniel
Crandall Jeremiah
Crawford John
Crowel James
Culvert James
Cuningham James
Daly David
Daly Samuel
Davis Ebenezer
Davis John
Davis John, 3rd
Davis Nathan
Dean Henry
Dean Jabez
Dennis Humphrey
Dennis William
Devoe Jacob
Dickenson Zebulon
Dickerson Joseph
Dickerson Zebulon
Dickinson Joseph
Dickinson Samuel
Dumbolton John
Dun Henry
Dunham Elijah
Dunham Hezekiah
Dunham Samuel
Dunham Silvenus
Dunham Solomon
Dunning Ebenezer
Dunning James
Dunning Jesse
Dunning Lewis
Dunning Linus
Dutcher John
Dutcher John D.
Dwelly Abner
Dwelly Abner, Junr.
Dyer Ezra
Eddy Zephiniah
Edmond Robert
Edmond Samuel
Edmonds Matthew
Edwards Abel
Edwards Timothy
Fellows John
Flyn Patrick
Finel Edward
Finch Samuel
Fish Abner
Fish Benjamin
Fish Ephraim
Fish Joshua
Fish Pardon
Fisher Henry
Ford Asher
Ford Thomas
Ford William
Foster Jonathan
Foster Thomas
Foster William
Freeman Elijah
Freeman Elisha
Freeman Gideon
Freeman James
Freeman Stephen
Frisbe William
Fuller Nathaniel
Fuller Varsel
Fullington Alexander
Gage Jabish
Gage Jesse
Gates Stephen
Gay Timothy
Gay William
Gecocks Thomas
Gifford William
Gregory David
Gregory Reuben
Griggs Simon
Grommon John
Griffith William
Guile Amos
Guile Daniel
Guy Timothy
Hagerty William
Hairns John
Halbert White
Hall Sylvester
Hammond Benjamin
Hammond Jonathan
Hammond Paul
Hammond William
Harsha Hugh
Hart Isaac
Hart Jeremy
Hasel Conrad
Hasel Counwast
Havens John
Havens Peleg
Hawk George
Hawkins Adone
Hawkins Edward
Herrington Nathaniel
Hewit Asa
Hibbert Elisha
Higgins Thomas
Hilton Jonathan
Hilton Peter
Hilton Richard
Hitchcock Stephen
Holmes Caleb
Holms Samuel
Hooper Stephen
Howard Jesse
Hubbell Nehamiah
Hull David
Hull Eliphalet
Hull Seth
Hull Setton
Hunt Thomas
Hunt George
Hunter John
Hunter Samuel
Hunter Robert
Huper Stephen
Hurst Thomas
Husted Edward
Hutton Jonathan
Ingensle Daniel
Ingersoll Daniel
Ingersoll Jesse
Ingersoll Philip
Inman Abraham
Inman Benjamin
Inman Ezekiel
Inman Michael
Jackson Andrew
Jakedays George
James Henry
James Robert
Jaqueways George
Jefferies Thomas
Jefferson Thomas
Johnson John
Johnston Peter
Jones Stephen
Jordan Peter
Keeler Isaac
Keeler Isaiah
Koon Jeremiah
Kose Daniel
Knowlton John
Laing John
Lampher Levi
Lansing Garret
Lansing Garret G.
Laranes Gideon
Lawrence Gideon
Lent Abraham
Lent Hendrick
Lent Jacob
Lightheart Barney
Lilly Abner
Mahauney Gacob
Mahoney Jacob
Manserd Simeon
Mansfield Thomas
Marshall Abraham
Marshall Simeon
Marvins Jared
Merrick Thomas
Mervin Gerard
Millard Robert
Millerd Edy
Millerd Eleazer
Millerd Jadidiah
Millerd Nathaniel
Milligan Robert
Mills Timothy
Mires Stephen
Mirick Thomas
Moony Thomas
Moore Alpheas
Moore Charles
Moore Gideon
Moor Hose
Moore Phinheas
Moore Reuben
Moorey Gideon
Morey Thomas
Mosher David
Moss Simeon
Mulligan Robert
Munger Benjamin
Munger Philip
Munger Samuel
Munger Timothy
McBride John
McBride John, Junr.
McCarthy Moses
McCouchan Andrew
McGee William
McKillip William
Neilson John
Newell Asa

Newell Ebenezer
Newland Israel
Newland Joseph
Newland Rial
Newman Benjaman
Norten Samuel
Norton James
Norton William
O'Ferrel Amherst
Palmer John
Palmer Othniel
Palmer Jerard
Palmer Tand
Parke Jehiel
Parke Daniel
Parks Amasiah
Parsons Henry
Patrick Ebenezer
Patrick Robert
Patrick William
Patrick William, Junr.
Patrick Joshua
Patten Jonahan
Pattson Thomas
Pebe Simeon
Perkins Christopher
Perkins Oliver
Persons Henry
Pery John
Peters Matthew
Pettes Matthew
Pharis Levi
Phelps Elisha
Phillips Shadrick
Potten Rowland
Potter Allen
Potter Jonathan
Potter Nathaniel
Potter Simeon
Potter Thomas
Prince Jonathan
Prindle Joel
Purchase Thomas
Purdy Ebenezer
Randle Elias
Rankle John
Ray John
Ray Roswell
Ray Zachariah
Raynolds George
Reagle Daniel
Redder Evert D.
Reed Elias
Reeve William
Reis John
Reis John, Junr.
Reynolds Benoni
Reynolds Elias
Reynolds George
Reynolds John
Rice John
Rice John, Junr.
Richmond Benjamin
Ridder George
Riddle George
Roads John
Roads William
Robards Ezekiel
Robards Purchase
Robards William
Robenson Isachar
Roberts Isaac
Robertson Robert
Robins, William
Robinson Charles
Robison Charles
Rockwell Simeon
Rods William
Rogers Daniel
Rogers Jacob
Rogers Joseph
Ronnels Elias
Ronnels Thomas
Root Asa
Root Denison
Root Stephen
Ross Benjamin
Ross Daniel
Ruger Frances
Ruger Joseph
Ruger Moses
Ryan Christopher
Sasson Thomas
Saxton Gershom
Sayles Ahab
Sayles Ezekiel
Sayles Jacob
Sayles John
Sayles Mordoui
Sayles Silvanus
Sayles Stephen
Scidmore Abner
Scidmore Hoppar
Scidmore John
Scidmore Solomon
Sea Abraham
Sea David
Sea Harmanus
Sears Abraham
Sears Samuel
Sealey Joseph
Sexton Garshen
Seymour William
Sheffield Christopher
Sheffield Nathan
Sheldon Benjamin
Sheldon John
Sheldon Samuel
Shephard Nathaniel
Sherman Henry
Shipman Timothy
Slocum Elezer
Slocum Joseph
Smith Daniel
Smith Elisha
Smith Thomas
Snider Mark
Spike Daniel
Springer Richard
Stafford Amos
Stafford Samuel
Staklen Ebenezer
Stevens Ebenezer
Stevens Joseph
Stevens Peter
Stevens Samuel
Stewart Samuel
Stiltes Isrell
Stiles Reuben
Storm David
Storm Isaac
Storm Isaac, Junr.
Storm James
Strang Gabriel
Strickland Ebenezer
Strong Gabril
Sudmore Zopher
Taylor Israel
Tifft Stanton
Thompson John
Thornton John
Tombs James
Toms James
Toms John
Toms Stephen
Trip Thomas
Tripp Caleb
Tripp David
Tripp Everett
Tripp Job
Tripp Peleg
Tripp William
Tuttle Abijah
Tuttle Jabez
Tuttle John
Tuttle Mizah
Tyler Shubel
Valintine Peter
Vandelinda Daniel
Vandelindar Gerardus
Vandenbergh Wynant
Vanderwarker Isaac
Vanderwarker Marta
Vinhagen Martin
Vroman William
Van Amburgh Matthew
Van Arnum Abraham
Van Buren Hendrick
Van Buren Martin
Van Clike Dirick
Van Den Bergh Garret
Van Dick Dirick
Van Hasen Matthew
Van Hyning Henry
Van Schaick Hendrick
Walls Tunis
Washburn Daniel
Washburn Joel
Watson Cyprian
Watson James
Watts Thomas
Weatherhead Edmund
Webster Elihu
Weeks Daniel
Weeks William
Welch Daniel
Wells James
Wendel Abraham
Wetsel Christian
Wheler Ephraim
Wheler Joshua
Whipple Erick
Whipple Esek
White Albert (see Albert White)
White Rufus
White James
Whitehead Thomas
Whitehock Stephen
Wicks Wiliam
Willcocks Tyle
Willcox Francis
Willcox Gilbert
Willcox Tyler
Willes Ezekiel
Willes Hezekiah
Willes Reuben
Willes Thomas
Williams John
Williams Joseph
Williams Robert
Williams William
Williams William, Junr.
Willse James
Wiltsey James
Wiltsey John
Wiltsey Gardus
Woodbeck Thomas
Woodworth Amos
Woodworth Reuben
Wright Reuben
Young Daniel

Albany County Militia — (Continued).

COLONEL JOHN KNICKERBACKER
COLONEL PETER YATES
LIEUTENANT COLONEL JOHN VAN RENSSELAER
ADJUTANT JACOB VAN VALKENBERGH

CAPT. JOHN ABBET
" GERRITT TUNNES BRADT
" THOMAS BROWN
" MATTHEW DE GARMO
" JAMES HADLOCK
" DANIEL HOBBLE
" HENDRICK MANDEVILLE
" CORNELIUS VANDENBURGH
" HENRY VAN DER HOFF
" CORNELIUS WILTSE
" JACOB YATES
" PETER YATES
LIEUT. JOEL ABBOTT
" WILLIAM BRACE
" JOHN B. BRATT
" MATTHEW BREWER
" RICHARD DAVENPORT
" JACOB DE GARNO
" ELDART FONDA
LIEUT. NATHANIEL FORD
" JACOB FORT
" JOSEPH HALLSTEAD
" JACOB HAULENBECK
" IGNAS KIP
" PETER MARTIN
" JOHN PALMER
" NATHANIEL ROWLEY
" JESSE TOLL
" JOHN VAN ANTWERP
" ABNER VAN NAME
" JACOB VAN NASS
" JACOB VAN WORMER
ENSIGN JOSEPH GIFFORD
" SIMON VANDERCOOK
" SIMEON VAN DAROSH
" DERICK T. VAN VEGHTEN
" JOHN VAN WORMER

ADDITIONAL NAMES ON STATE TREASURER'S PAY BOOKS

QR. MS. STEPHEN VIELE
LIEUT. HENRY BRACE
" JOHN HARDEN
LIEUT. JOHN VAN WORMER
" GAMALIEL WELLS

ENLISTED MEN

Acker Solomon
Adams John
Adkins Thomas
Agan James
Agan John
Aller Abraham
Aller John
Aller Peter
Anthony Bartholomew
Anthony Ellabart
Antony Borthmeues
Armstrong Nathan
Arnold
Arnold Ebenezer
Arnold Elisha
Asten William
Attlar Abraham
Babcock Joshua
Bacon Abel
Bacon Penuel
Bacon Phinehas
Bacon Winthrop
Bacor Herrington
Bagges James
Baker John
Baker Lemuel
Barnet Moses
Barnhart Frederick
Barnhart Jost
Bartel Increas
Bartholomew Philip
Basset Seth
Bates William
Bayelas John
Benedict Aaron
Benedict Isaac
Benedict James
Benedict Joseph
Beniway John
Bennet Amos
Bennet Banger
Bennet Jonathan
Bennet Richard
Bennet Robeson
Bennet Robinson
Bennet William
Bennidick Aaron
Benson Abel
Benson Elias
Benson Elnathan
Benson Joel
Benway John
Benway Peter
Bernhert Frudarick
Bernhert Henry
Bernhert Joseph
Besset Seth
Bethewel
Beyce Tohide
Bikker Nicholas
Blair John, Junr.
Blakesley James
Bleecker John J.
Blowers Abiel
Bouse Jonathan
Bouse Nicholas
Bovee Jacob
Bovee Jacob, Jr.
Bovee Peter
Bovie John
Bowdish John
Boyce Jehoiada
Boyce Millerd
Bratt Daniel
Bratt Nicholas
Brice Henry
Brown Charles
Brown David
Brown Henry
Brown Hezekiah

Brown Jonathan
Brues Henry
Bump Ichabod
Bump James
Bump Jezebud
Bunda Elijah
Bunda Nathaniel
Bunda Simeon
Bunday Ashble
Bundy Elisha
Bundy Simeon
Burroughs Benjamin
Burroughs James
Burtch Richard
Buschart Conrad
Bush Conratt
Bush Guilbard
Bush John
Cadey Zebulon
Caldwell Robert
Camp Nicholas
Carey Lemuel
Carey Seth
Carpenter Jeremiah
Carpenter Josiah
Case James
Chace Lemuel
Champ Nicholas
Chappell Samuel
Chard Abraham
Chase Abraham
Cheney William
Chezel John
Chitteson Elisha
Ciberly Barent
Clark Israel
Clark John
Clark Jonathan
Coal John
Cole James
Cole John
Coll James
Comenengs Josiah
Commins Francis
Commins Isaiah
Commons Josiah
Connell Edward
Cook Henry F.
Coone William
Couey John
Couly John
Covell James
Covey John
Cox John
Crandle Samuel
Crawbarrak Peter
Crittenton Zebulon
Cronk Cornelius
Cronk Francis
Cronk Stephen
Cronkheit Cornelius
Cronkhite Abraham
Cronkhite Aury
Cronkhite James
Cronkhite Stephen
Cronkhite Tunes
Cross Daniel
Cuttinton Jediah
Darrow James
Daught John
Davenport Peter
Degarimo Matthew
Delano Nathan
Delong Jacob
Delong Nicholas
Demaray Samuel
Demoray David
Demoray Davis
Demoree Nicholas
Denton Nathaniel
Devenport Jacob
Dewitt Benjamin
Dewy Isaiah
Doty Jacob
Doty Ormond
Doty Peter
Douglas Thomas
Downson Ichabod
Dunham Elijah
Dunham Ephraim
Dunham Charles
Dunning Ephraim
Dutcher John
Dutcher Lawrence
Dyer Ezra
Earl David
Eastwood Benjamin
Eastwood Benjamin, Junr.
Eastwood Daniel
Eastwood Nathaniel
Echard Solomon
Eckert Peter
Eckert Peter, Junr.
Eckert Solomon
Elliot Daniel
Engrum Humphrey
Evins Samuel
Eycleshymer Peter
Fake Gorg
Finch Ebenezer
Fish Abraham
Fisher Abraham
Fisher Adam
Fisher Christian
Fisher George
Fisher Jacob
Fisher Jeremiah
Follet John
Fonda Abraham
Fonda Eldart
Ford Jacob
Ford John
Ford John James
Fort Abraham
Fort Abraham J.
Fort John
Fort John Isaac
Fort John J. B.
Fort Lewis
Fowler Levy
Fox Nathaniel
Fradenburce John
Francisco Abraham
Francisco Cornelous
Francisco Derick
Francisco Dick
Francisco Henry
Francisco Jeremiah
Francisco John
Francisco John J.
Francisco Levy
Francisco Michael
Francisco Richard
Francisco Thomas
Fredenburgh Abraham
Freeman Isaac
Frier Nicholas
Fuller Daniel
Fuller Jonathan
Fuller Timothy
Gallipser William
Gallup Rufus
Gallup William
Garrison Abraham
Garrison John
Gifford Benjamin
Gifford Gershom
Gifford Giddon
Giles Gilbert
Gillet Beriah
Glass William
Goesbeck Nicholas W.
Golding Benjamin
Golding Jesse
Graves Russel
Grawborgar Peter
Greer Chard
Griffeth Aaron
Griswold David
Griswold Jabez
Griswold Josiah
Griswould Ephraim
Groesbeck Herman
Groesbeck Nicholas
Groesbeck Nicholas W.
Groesbeck Peter
Groesbeck Peter, Junr.
Groesbeck Peter W.
Groff John
Grommon Jacob
Groot Derick
Grousbeck Peter
Growsback Daniel
Grusback Nicholauser, Jr.
Grusebake Nicholis
Grusebeck Hugh
Grusebeck Jacob
Grusebeck William
Guernsey William
Hadlack Samuel
Hadlock Jonathan
Halenbeck Henry
Haling William
Hall William
Hallen William
Hallenbeck Daniel, Junr.
Halley Daniel
Halley Joseph
Halsted Thomas
Handerson Edward
Hanyon Garret
Harden John
Harold William
Hayle Francis
Haynes Pardon
Helling William, Junr.
Henderson Edward
Henewell Rice
Heninger Henry V.
Henney Charls
Hicks Daniel
Hicks Thomas
Hill John
Hill John, Junr.
Hill William
Hix William
Hodges Benjamin
Hodges Ezekiel
Hodges Ezekiel, Junr.
Hodges Isaac
Hodges John
Hodlat Samuel
Hogale Abraham
Hogel John
Hogges Daniel
Hogins Benjamin
Hogle Frencis
Holley Daniel
Holsted Ezekiel
Holsted Thomas
Honeywell Rice
Hooper William

Hopkins Joel
Hornback Deniel
Hose John
House John
Howard Matthew
Hubbil Matthew
Hubble Daniel
Hubble Ithemer
Huble Jonathan
Humphry Evans
Humphry James
Hunt Amasa
Hunt Emery
Huss John
Husting James
Huston James
Huyck Peter
Hynis Benjamin
Ingram Humphrey, Junr.
Isacks Samuel
Ively John
Jadwin Joseph
Johnson John
Johnson Josiah
Kannedy Josiah
Karr Jonathan
Ketcham Daniel
Ketcham Jonas
Ketcham Samuel
Ketchum Abijah
Ketchum James
Kiff John
Kip Lodewick
Kitchum Daniel
Kittchim William
Klein Joseph
Kogh Hezekiah
Lake Garet
Lamb John
Lampmen Peter
Lamser Isaac
Lanard Isaac
Lanard Thomas
Lang Joseph D.
Langunan Abraham
Latham David
Lee John
Lempmen Abrm.
Lennard Isack
Lennard Tomes
Lansing Henry
Lent Abraham
Lent Philip
Lenuell Robert
Lomis Jacob
Lomis Job
Loveless Benjamin
Loveless Elisha
Loveless Jeremiah
Lucas John
Luke James
Lyon George
Lyones James
Mace William
Manderis Hendrick
Mandeville John
Marrick Abel
Marroy William
Marsh Ephraim
Marsh John
Marsh William
Marshel Elihu
Marthis Henry
Martin Henry
Martin Jeremiah
Martin Joseph
Martin Nathan
Martin Peter
Martin Thomas
Mash John
Mash William
Masters William
Matthew Henery
May John William
Mead Nehemiah
Mead Noah
Meads Joseph
Mendeveil John
Merrel Morris
Merrill Moses
Merrit Moses
Mervin John
Millard Stephen
Milliman John, Junr.
Monrow Nathan
Mullory William
Mumford Robson
Munro Samuel
Munson Titus
Murpey Thomas
McClave William
McGowan James
McKay William
McNeal Neal
Near George
Nelson John
Newcomb James
Nicklison Israel
Nickoll Asa
Nokes John
Nye Seth
Oakley Stephen
Odel Gershom
Oderkerk Frederick
Okeley Stephen
Oller Peter
Omsted Gidian
Ostrander Abraham
Ostrander John
Ostrander Johntise
Ostrander Peter
Overocker Adam
Overocker George
Overocker Jacob
Overocker Michel
Paddok Job
Paddock Levi
Page Amos
Palmer David
Palmer Fenner
Palmer Garsham
Palmer Nathan
Palmer Nathaniel
Paree David
Parker Caleb
Parker Jonathan
Parse Benjamin
Patterson Robert
Pattis William
Pattson William
Pearce Levi
Perce David
Perry Absalom
Peter Felix
Pierce Benjamin
Pierce David
Pierce Norris
Porter Felix
Powell Jonathan
Powell Richard
Powell Thomas
Powell William
Price John
Price John, Junr.
Price Jonathan
Price Samuel
Purdy Peter
Quackenbus Harman
Quackenbush Gose
Rager Gabral
Ramer Frederick
Raniser Christian
Ray William
Rehern Joseph
Renler Lawrence
Reynolds Jeremiah
Riar George
Rice John
Rice Seth
Richerdson Isaac
Richardson James
Richenson James
Richenson William
Richeson Thomas
Rickard Conrod
Rickart John
Robins Evens
Roman Peter
Root Josiah
Rose Benjamin
Rose Cornelius
Rose John
Rosefalt Jacob
Rouse Jacob
Rouse John
Rouse Jonathan
Rouse Nicholas
Rowland Oliver
Rowland Samuel
Ruger Gideon
Ryon John
Samboorn Nathaniel
Sammons Jacob
Scheley Martin
Schryer Nicholas
Scot Stephen
Scott Benjamin
Scott Thomas
Scribner Abel
Scribner Abel, Junr.
Scribner John
Scribner Samuel
Scribner Zadok
Scutt Abraham
Seal John
Sealy Matthew
Seperley Barned
Sharp John
Sharp Peter
Shaw Comfort
Shaw Daniel
Shaw Nathaniel
Shearer William
Shearman Caleb
Shele Martin
Shepard Israel
Shepard William
Sipperley Jacob
Sisson John
Slatry Patrick
Slauter Patrick
Slip William
Sly Elisha
Sly John
Smith Benjamin
Smith Simeon
Smith William
Sneider Johannes
Snyder Christopher
Snyder Jacob
Snyder John
Sordam Samuel

Spaulding Elijah
Stark Asel
Stark Christopher
Stark Christopher, Junr.
Start Asahel
Start Christopher
Start William
Stephens James
Stephens William
Stilwill John
Stilwill Samuel
Stinson William
Strovel John
Supphen Abraham
Surdam Samuel
Sweet Amos
Sweet William
Teachout Jacob
Tensler James
Thompson Israel
Tibbit George
Tinseller John
Tinslar John
Toll Charles H.
Toll Jesse
Toll Simon
Tusslar John
Tyler Samuel
Vele Tunas
Velie Cyprian
Viele Abraham
Viele John
Viele John T.
Viele Lewis
Viele Lodervecus
Viele Peter
Viele Stephen
Vinigar Adam
Vissdue Eldert
Voorhees Caret
Vradenburgh Jacobes
Vradenburgh John
Vroman Adam
Vrudenburgh Abr'm
Van Allen Henry
Van Allen Manuel
Van Antwerp Lewis
Van Antwerp Simon
Van Arnon Lewis
Van Arnum Luke
Van Buren Marthen
Van Buskerk Peter
Vancark Peter
Vandenbergh Philip
Vandenbergh Winant C.
Van Der Cook Cournelius
Van Der Cook Michel
Vanderhof Jacob
Van Derhoof Gilbard
Van Derhook Isaac
Van Der Werken Martin
Van Groesbeck Johans
Van Grosbeck Wouter
Van Hyning Hendrick
Van Name Aaron
Van Nest Jacob
Van Nest John
Van Nest Soromer
Van Norton Henry
Vansent John
Van Sirdam Samuel
Van Sordam Andris
Van Sordam Lowrana
Van Sordam Tunis
Van Vactan James
Van Vaghten Herman
Van Valkenburgh Jacob
Van Vorees Garritt
Van Wormer Henry
Van Wormer John
Wait Benjamin
Wait John
Wait William
Walderon Cornelius
Walderon Gerit
Walderum Garret
Waldo John, Junr.
Waldo John, Senior
Wallis Elijah
Wallis Elisha
Wallis Nathaniel
Wallis Nehemiah
Wallis Timothy
Wandell John
Weatherwax Alexander
Weatherwax David
Weatherwax Martin
Weatherwax Peter
Wederwax Alexander
Weeb Jonethan
Weeler Jonathan
Wells George
West Willrston
Wetzel George
Wheeler Jonathan
Wheeler Richard
Whitford Caleb
Wightman Edward
Wilfort Goleps
Wilkins Obadiah
Williams Asher
Williams Azael
Williams John
Williams Thomas
Williams Thomas F.
Williams Thomas P.
Williamson James
Willsen Ebenezer
Wiltse Francis
Wiltse Martin
Winchel
Winchel Jeremiah
Winne Gerret
Wintworth Alpheus
Witerley William
Witherwax Johannes
Withford Ciltip
Wittick Abraham
Wood Nathaniel
Wool James
Wright Alexander
Wuller Jonethen
Yates Abraham
Yates James
Yeats Peter
York Daniel
Young David
Young John
Young Manuel
Younglove Samuel

Albany County Militia — (Continued).

COLONEL PETER VROMAN
LIEUTENANT COLONEL PETER ZIELE
MAJOR JOST BECKER
MAJOR THOMAS EKESEN, JR.
ADJUTANT LAWRENCE SCHOOLCRAFT
QUARTER MASTER PETER BALL
QUARTER MASTER JACOB WINNEY

CAPT. STORM BECKER
" CHRISTIAN BROWN
" WILLIAM DEITZ
" ALEXANDER HARPER
" JACOB HEGER
" DIRK MILLER
" GEORGE RICHTMYER
" CHRISTIAN STUBRACH
" TEUNIS VROMAN
LIEUT. HENRY BORST
" JACOB BORST
" JOHN BAUCK
" JOHN DIETZ
" CORNELIUS FEECK
" PETER HEAGER
" JOHANNES J. LAWYER
LIEUT. JOHN MYERS
" JACOB SNYDER
" PETER SNYDER
" PETER SNYDER, JR.
" JOHN THORNTON
" EPHRAIM VROMAN
" MARTIN VROMAN
" MARTINUS ZIELE
ENSIGN ISAAC BECKER
" JOHN L. BELLINGER
" JOHN BROWN
" JOHN ENDERS
" JACOB LAWYER
" PETER SWART
" PETER VAN ANTWERP
" NICHOLAS WARNER

ENLISTED MEN.

Acker George
Ackerson Thomas
Backer Albartus
Ball Matthew
Baker Johannis
Barnes Joseph
Barnhart Philip
Bartholomew Tabald
Bauch Christian
Bauch Cornelius
Bauch David
Bauch Henrich
Bauch Jacob
Bauch John
Bauch Nicholas
Bauch Peter
Bauch Thomas
Bauch William W.
Bauck Johannes
Bauck Lawrence
Bauck Nicholas W.
Bauck William
Beacker George
Becker Abraham
Becker Adam
Becker Albartus
Becker Bill
Becker Coenraed
Becker David
Becker Fredrick
Becker Garrit
Becker George
Becker Harmanus
Becker Hendrick
Becker Jacob
Becker Johannes
Becker Johannis K.
Becker John A.
Becker John Alb.
Becker John Gert
Becker John J.
Becker Nicholas
Becker Storm
Becker Storm A.
Becker William
Beik Martines
Beiker John P.
Beker Abraham
Belinger Johannest
Bellinger Marcus
Bellinger Marcus, Junr.
Bereamp Benjamin
Berg Abraham
Bergh Philip
Bevam Benjamin
Boon Richard
Borst Jacob
Borst Johannes
Borst John, Junr.
Borst Joost
Borst Joseph J.
Borst Peter
Borst Philip
Borst Martines
Brant Michel
Brantner Anthony
Brewer Peter
Brown Adam
Brown Adam, Junr.
Brown John
Brown Migel
Brown Joseph
Bruer Peter
Burst Peter
Burst Philip
Burst Martines
Borst Baltus
Borst Jost
Borst Migel
Bost John
Braun William
Cachey Hugh
Cadogan Barne
Caghey Andrew
Caghey Andris
Caghey Hugh
Cannady John
Christian
Coenrad Henry
Coenrad Henry, Jr.
Coleman Thomas
Cornelisen Cornelius
Cortney William
Cowley Jonathan
Cramer Charles
Criscoll Jacob

Daley Nathan
Dannea Lewis
Dietz Johnn Jost
Dietz William
Dominick John
Ecker Jost
Eckerson Cornelius
Eckerson John
Eckerson Teunis
Eckerson Tunis, Jr.
Egars Julius
Enders Jacob
Enders Johannes
Enders Peter
Enders William
Evans Joseph
Fakes Piter
Falk Jacobus
Feeck Jacob
Feeck Nicholas
Feek Johanes
Ferguson John
Finck Peter
Finck William
Forster George
Forster Jacob
Frymer George
Frymer Johannes
Frymier David
Frymier John
Frymier Michael
Gerlock Nicholas
Granatier Jacob
Granatier John
Grans Michael
Hagar Handrick
Hagar Joseph
Hagedorn Adam
Hagedorn Bartholomew
Hagedorn Dirck
Hagedorn Samuel
Hager John
Hagetorn John
Hatzel George
Hauck Henrich
Heager Peter
Heger Adam
Henry William
Herron James
Herron James, Jr.
Herron Robert
Hills Christopher
Hills George
Hilsinger Jacob
Hilsinger John
Hilsinger Michael
Hilsinger Peter
Hilts Steffel, Junr.
Hiltsinger Michal
Hitzman Hendrick
Hoftrasser Jacob
Howell Vanson
Huiver Felix
Humphrey Benjamin
Humphrey John
Humphry James
Humphry John
Ingolt Johannes
Janson Hendrick
Jansen Johannis
Jansen Joseph
Jessey Juas
Kanidy John
Kayser Abraham
Kayser Johannes
King Leonard
Kniskern Hendrick P.
Kniskern Henry
Knieskern Jacob
Knieskern Johannes
Kniskern Peter
Kniskern Tunis
Koenig Johannis
Koenig Migel
Koenig Stoffel
Koening Leonard
Krieler Baltus
Kriselor John
Krisler John
Lamb William
Lawyer Abraham
Laucks Andreas
Lawyer David
Lawyer Jacob
Lawyer Johannes L.
Lawyer Lambert
Lawyer Lawrence
Lawyer Nicholas
Lawyer Peter
Leek William
Long Nicholas
Loucks Jeremiah
Low John
Mahalean Hugh
Mann Jacob
Mann Peter, Junr.
Mann William
Marinas Jerremy
Mattice Abraham
Mattice Coenraed
Mattice Elias
Mattice Frederick
Mattice George
Mattice Henrich
Mattice John
Mattice John Junr.
Mattice John H.
Mattice Joost
Mattice Nicholas
Mattice Nicholas F.
Merckel Jacob
Merckel John
Merckel Philip
Merckel Nicholas
Mercker Henrich
Merenis George
Morrow James
Muller Dirik
Munie Jacob
Murphy Timothy
McCoy John
McCoy John, 1st.
McCoy John, 2nd.
McKay John, 1st.
McKay John, 2nd.
McKee Samuel
McLout Alexander
Nitzley Gerret
Nott John
Otto Frantz
Otto Gottlieb
Pain John
Pasolee Gya
Patchin Isaac
Batterson Thomas
Perree Daniel
Price Daniel
Reinhardt George
Reinhardt Mattice
Reinhardt William
Resne John
Richter John
Richter Nicholas
Richtmeyer Christian
Richtmeyer Jacob
Richtmeyer Jonn George
Rickart George
Rickert Johannes
Rickert Marcus
Rickert Nicholas
Right John
Right Thomas
Ritter Andrene
Ritter Christian
Ritter John
Ronyon Samuel
Rorick Bearney
Rorigh Kasper
Roth Thomas
Salge Henrich
Schaefer Johannis T,
Schaefer Lampert
Schaefer Marckus, Junr.
Schafer Adam
Schafer Jacob
Schafer Johannes
Schafer John
Schefer Christian
Schefer Debald
Schefer Denes
Schefer Hendrick
Schefer John
Schefer Joost
Schefer Peter
Schefer Peter, Junr.
Schefer Marcus
Schefer Tenes, Junr.
Schell, Christian
Schell Jacob F.
Schell Jost
Scholman George
Schoolcraft Jacob
Schoolcraft William
Schneyder Lutwig
Schulcrafft Peter
Schuyler John
Schuyler Simon
Shaver Henry
Shell Adam
Shelmidine Richard
Sidney Peter
Singer ———
Sitney William
Sitnich Jost
Sitnig Henrich
Slaughter Nicholas
Sluyder Nicholas
Snyder George
Snyder Henry
Snyder Jacob, Junr.
Snyder John
Snyder John, Junr.
Snyder Philip
Snyder William
Sternberg Jacob
Sternbergh David
Sternberger Abraham
Sternberger Lambert
Sternberger Lambert, Junr.
Strubach Barend
Stynbrenner Benjamin
Sutherly Ankis
Swart Lawrence
Swart Thunes
Tenery Sever
Thornton Thomas
Tufts Zachariah
Turner James
Valck John
Valconburgh Joacum
Valkenburgh Adam
Valkenburgh Joost

Vroman Adam
Vroman Adam J.
Vroman Barent
Vroman Bartholomew
Vroman Isaac, Junr.
Vroman Johan
Vroman Jonas
Vroman Martinas
Vroman Peter
Vroman Peter A.
Vroman Peter C.
Vroman Peter J.
Vroman Simon
Vrooman Samuel
Van Allen Philip
Van Antwarp John
Van Antwarp Peter
Van Bremer Thomas
Van Denbergh Daniel
Van Dyck Cornelius
Van Dyck Jacob
Van Dyck John
Van Gelten Antreas
Van Lone Jacobus
Van Sice Joseph
Van Sisen Joseph
Van Slyck Peter
Van Valkenburgh Harmanus
Waldaway Henry
Weaver Christian
Weaver Henry
Webber Christian
Wenn John
Werner Christopher
Werner George
Werner George, Junr.
Werner Joost
Werner Joost, Junr.
Werth Henrich
Werth Johannes
Wever Henry, Junr.
Wholebur John, Junr.
Wileber John
Williams Elias
Winn John
Young William
Zart John
Zeck Nicholas
Zeh David
Zeh Jost
Ziegraft Jacob
Ziellie Peter, Junr.
Zimer William
Zimmer Adam
Zimmer George
Zimmer Jacob
Zimmer Peter

Albany County Militia — (Continued).

COLONEL JOHN BLAIR
COLONEL LEWIS VAN WOERT
MAJOR JAMES ASHTON
ADJUTANT JOHN McCLONG
ADJUTANT JOSEPH YOUNGLOVE
QUARTER MASTER JOSEPH YOUNGLOVE

CAPT. WILLIAM BROWN
" CORNELIUS DOTY
" GEORGE GILMORE
" ELIAS GOLDEN
" SAMUEL HODGES
" JOHN McKILLIP
" JOHN PATTIS
" JOHN PETTIT
" JOSEPH WELLS
" JOHN WHITESIDE
" WILLIAM WOODWORTH
LIEUT. JAMES BOLTON
" ADMIRAL BURTCH
" SAMUEL CLARK
" JONATHAN FRENCH
LIEUT. DANIEL HEATH
" WILLIAM POWELL
" NATHAN SMITH
" ANDREW THOMSON
" BENJAMIN TIFFANY
" GERRITT VAN NASS
" THOMAS WHITESIDE
" GERSHOM WOODWORTH
" ABRAHAM WRIGHT
ENSIGN SOLOMON KING
" HENRY LOOP
" JAMES MORRISON
" ISAAC PERINE
" ARCHIBALD ROBINSON
" HUGH THOMPSON

ADDITIONAL NAMES ON STATE TREASURER'S PAY BOOKS.

LIEUT. JOAB GREEN
ENSIGN RICHARD ROBINSON

ENLISTED MEN.

Allen Caleb
Allen David
Allen James
Allen John
Allen Stephen
Allis William
Almey Johen
Armstrong Nathan
Ashton Thomas
Astin Parvis
Aston Johen
Aurner Richard
Austin Davis
Austin John
Babcock Johen
Backer John
Backor Martin
Baker David
Baker Martines
Baker Peter
Bane Benjamin
Barber James
Bartt Henry
Beach Thomas
Beavon Jacob
Beebe Nathaniel
Bell Martin
Belmore Stephen
Bennet Jonathan
Berry Bowlen
Berry Ephraim
Bills Elisha
Black James
Black Robert
Blaer Johen
Blair Robert
Blake James
Blower William
Blowers Charles
Blowers Samuel
Boice Benjamin
Boice Henry
Bolton Alexander
Botchen Peter
Bowman Robert
Boyce Millerd
Brace Robert
Bratt John
Brayton Joseph
Brayton Matthew
Brewer Elias
Briggs Josiah
Bright Johenson
Britman Johnson
Brower Elias
Brown David
Brown Samuel
Browning Blackmon
Bruar Hanrey
Buchanan Patrick
Buck Amos
Bump Aaron
Bump Moses
Bur Aaron
Burch Amas
Burch Beverley
Burch Ichabod
Burch Richard
Burch Thomes
Burt Henry, Junr.
Burtch Beverly
Burtch Jenelus
Buscek Marting
Bushark Martin
Buskark Dirick
Buskark John
Butten Peter
Buttey Zebulon
Caldwell Joseph
Canada Thomas
Canady James
Carey Seth
Chase Daniel
Chase Phinehas
Chase Samuel
Clarey Luke
Clark John
Clobright Christopher
Cole Barnabas
Collins John
Collins Julius
Colter James

Conner John
Cook Ichabud
Cooper John
Cooper William
Core Johen
Corey Jonathan
Cornel Joseph
Cotnel Heber
Cottell Eber
Coudin James
Coudin James S.
Coulter Alexander
Coulter James
Covell James
Covell Jonathan
Covell Joseph
Cowan Alexander
Cowan James
Cowan Robert
Cowan William
Crosman Daniel
Crowel Seth
Culver Bezaliel
Culver Nathan
Dack Charles
Dantum William
Datter Benjamin
Davis Squire
Deake Charles
Deake Charles, Junr.
Deming Samuel
Dennis Samuel
Dounlap John
Dunham Joseph
Dunlap William
Dutcher Solomon
Earll Daniel, Junr.
Earll Robert
Easterwood Abel
Edgar William
Edie James
Eldred James
Eldred Thomas
Eldridge James
Eldridge Thomas
Ellis Daniel
Ellis William
Esvet David
Fisher Amos
Fisher William
Foort Daniel
Forde Thomas
Fort Johen
Fort Peter
Forth Daniel
Fowler George
Fowler Isaac
Fowler Johen
Fowler Morrel
French David
Fuller John
Gaffin Jemes
Galaway Thomas
Giffert Gedion
Gillmore George
Gillmore James
Gilmore William
Golden Elias
Golden John
Goldihe William
Gould William Deak
Gray David
Gray Hugh
Gray William
Green Bowen
Green John
Green Thomas
Greene Job
Grene Benjamin
Grene Jeremiah
Groat Henry A.
Groat Henry D.
Haeth Aleyh
Hall Burges
Hall Thomas
Hammond William
Hannan William
Harman William
Harren Ellet
Harren Johen
Hart Daniel
Hathaway John
Hay William
Heath Daniel
Heath Daniel, Junr.
Heath Elijah
Heath Joseph
Heath Samuel
Heath Simeon
Heath Stephen
Heath Timothy
Heath Windslow
Henry Joseph
Herman Lemuel
Hill Thomas
Hodge Solomon
Hodges Curtis
Hodges Daniel
Hodges Joshua
Hodges Samuel
Hogel Cornelius
Hogel Peter
Hoges Carter
Hoges Daniel
Hoges Ezekiel
Hoges Isaac
Holland John
Hond Thomas
Hosken Joseph
Houghtaling Jacob
Hunt Elven
Hunt Thomas
Hurly Elisha
Irvine James
Irwin James
Jaquez Thoma
Johnson Edon
Johnson William
Keittle Benjeman
King Hezekiah
King Israel
Lake Abram
Lake Christopher
Lake Henry
Lake Henry, Junr.
Lake Nicholas
Lake Nicholas, Junr.
Lampkin Thomas
Lastwood Abel
Lewis Christopher
Lewis Robert
Lewis Ruben
Locke Nicholas
Locke Nicholas, Junr.
Loop Martin
Lucas David
Lucas Nathaniel
Luke Clary
Magee James
Manley John
Mead Aron
Menter Robert
Meser John
Millar James
Millar Robert
Miller John
Mires John
Moger Nicholas
Morel Jonathan
Morrel John
Morrison James
Morrison John
Morrison Samuel
Mosher Daniel
Mosher Hezekiah
Mosher Jabez
Mosher Jabez, Junr.
Mosher Nicholas
Moshier David
Mushet William
McAuley William
McChenry John
McClaughry Richard
McDonald Edward
McKie James
McKilip Thomas
McWaters James
Nobles John
Norton David
Norton Joneton
Odel Jonas
Omsted Judson
Onderlee Johen
Oviatt Isaac
Palmer Jeremiah
Paterson Robert
Paterson William
Patterson Adam
Pattson Adam
Perry Aaron
Perry John
Perry Rowlen
Peters Andrew
Peters Joseph
Pettes Asa (see Petteye)
Petteye Asa (see Pettes)
Pettit Micajah
Phelps Timothy
Philips Francis
Pickla Clark
Porter Elijah
Potter Samuel
Pottice Assa
Powel William
Powers John
Preston David
Preston John
Preston Samuel
Preston William
Prince David
Prince Job
Quckanbus Tuenes
Rice David
Rickely Clark
Robertson Archibald
Robertson William
Robinson William
Rodgers Hugh
Rodgers James
Rolo James
Rolo Walter
Rose John
Ross John
Ross Walter
Rotch James
Roth Benjamin
Roughling James
Rutty Zebulon
Santesal Aberham
Schoolcraft Adam
Schoolcraft Christian
Schoolcraft Christopher

Schoulcraft Cobus
Schoten Johen
Scott John
Scott Steven
Scribner Abel
Scribner Samuel
Seeley David
Seeley Ebenezer
Seelye David
Sefridge Edward
Selfridge John
Selfridge Oliver
Serdam Tuneis
Shaaff William
Shaf Henry
Shaf William
Shaff John
Shairman Batchelor
Shairman Shubael
Shan Joseph
Sharman Shubel
Sharp Andrew
Sharp Cornelius
Sharp Johen
Sharp Peter
Sharp Richard
Shauff John
Shaw Daniel
Shearman Back
Shearman Batchelor
Shepman Ezekiel
Sherman Johen
Sherman Lemuel
Shipman Daniel
Shipman Elisha
Shrman Henry
Skelly Alexander
Skelly Welyoum
Small James
Smit Benjamin
Smith Caleb
Smith Henry
Smith Roggerd
Spalden Ellijha
Sprague Gibson
Sprague Solomon
Steel Thomas
Stephens William
Stevens Matthew
Stewart James
Still Thomas
Stock Godfrey
Summers Robert
Sweet David
Symers Robert
Tallman Jonathan
Tallman William
Tanner Joseph
Taruble Judah
Telfer George
Terry Nathaniel
Thomas Robert
Thomson William
Toot Daniel
Trable Judah
Valintine Joseph
Valintine Stephen
Vallantine Alexandar
Volentine John
Vollentine Joseph
Vanduse Abraham
Van Duzer Abraham
Van Duzer John
Van Sandam Anthony
Van Tassell Abraham
Van Tessel Cornelius
Vantessel Hanrey
Wadsworth Elisha
Waldo David
Waldo Jonathan
Waldo Joneton, Junr.
Wallis Benjamin
Ward Alihu
Ward Joneton
Warner James
Waters James M.
Webb Johen
Weir John
Weir Robert
Welch Henry
Weller Amos
Wells Austin
Wells Daniel
Wells Edmon, Junr.
Wells Henry
Wells Shelar
Wells Timothy
Welsh Morto
Weltch Murty
West Benjamin
Whaling James
Wheeler Jacob
Wheeler Samuel
Whiteside Detten
Whiteside Thomas
Whitsid Edward
Wier James
Wilcox David
Willar Amos
Wilson Nathan
Wilson Samuel
Wing Benjamin
Wing David
Woodard Joseph
Woodworth Caleb
Woodworth Gershom
Woodworth Josiah
Woolsworth William
Worden Nathaniel
Wright Caleb
Wright Samuel
Younglove David

Albany County Militia—(Continued).

COLONEL WILLIAM B. WHITING
LIEUTENANT COLONEL ASA WATERMAN
MAJOR MARTIN BEEBE
ADJUTANT JONATHAN WARNER
QUARTER MASTER ANDREW HUNTER
QUARTER MASTER JOHN WATERMAN
SURGEON PATRICK HAMILTON

CAPT. ELIJAH BOSTWICK
" EBENEZER CADY
" JOHN DAVIS
" ELISHA GILBERT
" DANIEL HERRICK
" AARON KELLOGG
" GIDEON KING
" ISAAC PEABODY (see Vol. 6—pg. 90).
CAPT. JOHN SALISBURY
" JACOB VOSBURGH
LIEUT. SAMUEL BAILEY
" WILLIAM HOLLENBACH
" THOMAS HURLBURT
" MOSES JONES
" EZRA MURRAY
" EDWARD WHEELER

ADDITIONAL NAMES ON STATE TREASURER'S PAY BOOKS.

LIEUT. PETER BARKER
" EBENEZER BENJAMIN
" JOHN CALENDER
" ASAHEL GRAY
" NATHAN HERRICK
" EZRA LEE
" JAMES PHELPS
" SAMUEL REXFORD
" REUBEN ROWLEY
" ELIJAH SKINNER
" POLICARPUS SMITH
" SAMUEL THOMPSON
LIEUT. JOSIAH WARNER
" WILLIAM WARNER
ENSIGN BENJAMIN ANDRUS
" ELIJAH CADY
" NATHANIEL COLVER
" SAMUEL DARBY
" ASA DOTY
" BENJAMIN FORD
" JEREMIAH HUBBARD
" SAMUEL JONES
" SAMUEL RUSSELL
" HENRY WALTER

ENLISTED MEN

Beebe Hosea
Chapman Jonathan
Chapman Samuel
Foster William
Graves John
Hamlin Peras
Jackson Thophilas
Orton Thomas
Root David
Volentine Stephen

Albany County Militia — (Continued).

INDEPENDENT COMPANY.

CAPTAIN PETRUS VAN GAASBECK

ENLISTED MEN

Bartell Philip A.
Berringer Petrus
Best Benjamin
Best Johannis, Jr.
Best Jury, Jr.
Best Peter
Best Wilh's
Blass Hendrick P.
Blass Michael
Blass William
Combs Samuel, Jr.
Decker Andries
Decker Benjamin
Decker Jacobus
Decker James
Decker James B're
Decker Leonard
Dick Paul
Finger Coenraedt
Freer Simon
Ham Jacob
Hendricks Bartell
Hop Thomas
Meyer Fredrick
Miller Jacob
Post Samuel
Post Wilhelmis
Power Jacob, Jr.
Power Nicholas, Jr.
Proper Fredrick, Jr.
Rosman Coenraedt I.
Shaver Peter
Shuts Ian
Shuts Johannis H.
Smith William H.
Snyder Lodewyck
Spikeman Frederick
Stael Hendrick, Jr.
Stael Johannis
Stiever John
Vader Samuel
Vonck Jacob
Van De Water August
Wheeler William

CHARLOTTE COUNTY MILITIA.

COLONEL JOHN WILLIAMS (DOCTOR)

MAJOR THOMAS ARMSTRONG

MAJOR ALEXANDER WEBSTER

ADJUTANT REUBEN TURNER

QUARTER MASTER JOSHUA CONKEY

SURGEON JOHN WILLIAMS

CAPT. JOHN ARMSTRONG
" JOHN HAMILTON
" EDWARD LONG
" ALEXANDER MCNITT
" NEHEMIAH SEELY
" SETH SHERWOOD
CAPT. ELISHAMA TOZER
" JAMES WILSON
LIEUT. JOHN MUNSON
" ICHABOD PARKER
" JOHN PATTISON
" DUNCAN SHAW

ADDITIONAL NAMES ON STATE TREASURER'S PAY BOOKS:

QUARTER MASTER A. FULLER

SURGEON THOMAS CLARK

CAPT. SILAS CHILDS
" JOHN THOMAS
" JAMES WILLSON
LIEUT. PAUL AVARILL
" THOMAS BOGES
" THOMAS BRADSHAW
" DANIEL BRUNDAGE
" SAMUEL BUELL
" ASA COOK
" ASAPH COOL
" EPHRAIM FULLER
" JOHN MARTIN
" DANIEL MCCLEARY
LIEUT. GEORGE MCKNIGHT
" JAMES MOORE
" SAMUEL SHERWOOD
" ALEXANDER SIMPSON
" ROBERT STEWART
" ALEXANDER TURNER
ENSIGN BENJAMIN BAKER
" SAMUEL CROSSET
" WILLIAM LITTLE
" ALEXANDER MCNEES
" JAMES MORRISON
" JAMES STEWART

ENLISTED MEN

Armstrong James
Armstrong John
Armstrong Robert, Junr.
Barber Jonathan
Beatty John
Blackley David
Blackley John
Boyd John
Boyd Thomas
Cady Luther
Chambers John
Clark John
Cleaveland Benjamin
Crighton Robert
Crookshanks George
Croset Samuel
Easton George
Edgar David
Evens John
Foster Abraham
Foster John
Fowler George
Getty Robert
Graham William
Gray Isaac
Gray Nathaniel
Grayams William
Grayham John
Grimes John
Gutrey John
Hamilton John
Hanna John
Harris Moses
Harsha John
Henderson Alexander
Hopkins David
Hopkins Isaac
Hopkins James
Hopkins Robert
Hopkins Samuel
Hoy Richard
Hunsdon Allen
Hunsdon John
Hunter John
Jerrel Samuel
Lamen Franses
Law John
Long Edward
Lyon Samuel
Lytle Isaac
Lytle Robert
Lytle William
Martin John
Matterson Daniel
Mattison Daniel
Moncrief William
Moor James
Munson Nathaniel
McArter Robert
McCarter John
McClaughry Matthew
McCleary Daniel
McClothery Matthew
McCoy William

McCraken Joseph
McFarland James
McFarland John
McFarland William
McGinnis Peter
McMichel John
McNight George
McNitt David
McNitt Daniel
McNitt John
McNorsh Alexander
McWethy Silas
Nelson Joseph
Page William
Ramag John
Roge William
Rogers James
Rogers Hughes
Rogers William
Rowen John
Rumage John
Savage James
Sherwood Newman
Simpson Andrew
Simson Alexandor
Smith William
Steel John
Stevenson James
Stewart Alexander
Stewart James
Stuart David
Stuart Robert
Thompson William
Tombs David
Tombs Joseph
Turner Alexander
Wallace John
Webb John
Webster Alexander
Wheedon David
Williams Lewis
Williams Thomas
Williams Samuel
Wilson Samuel
Wilson James
Wilson Robert
Wright Jacob

CUMBERLAND COUNTY MILITIA.

COLONEL WILLIAM WILLIAMS
MAJOR WILLIAM SHATTUCK

CAPT. ASA RICE
" STEPHEN SHEPARDSON
CAPT. DAVID STOWELL

ADDITIONAL NAMES ON STATE TREASURER'S PAY BOOKS.

LIEUT. SIMEON EDWARDS
LIEUT. TIMOTHY ROOT

Cumberland County Militia — (Continued).

(CAPTAIN HATCH'S COMPANY OF MINUTE MEN.)

MAJOR JOAB HOISINGTON

CAPT. JOSEPH HATCH
LIEUT. AMOS CHAMBERLAIN
LIEUT. ELKANAH DAY
" SIMEON STEVENS

MINUTE MEN.

Abby Jacob
Abby John
Abner Thomas
Averill Samuel
Balding Elijah
Baldwin Elijah
Baldwin Seth
Bard John
Barnet Benjamin
Barton Henry
Baxter William
Belding Seth
Bell William
Brown John
Carpenter Uriah
Carr Robert
Chaffee Calvin
Chamberlain Ashur
Chamberlain Joel
Chapley William
Cone Lemuel
Crofford James
Crook Charles
Curtiss Samuel
Darbe Simeon
Davies Abel
Davis Abel, Junr.
Devino Thomas
Dickerson Abraham
Easton Bildad
Eaton Samuel
Ellet John
Foste Antoney
French John
Fuller Jonathan
Gould Moses
Gould Nehemiah
Hadley Jonathan
Hadley Samuel
Hardy Robert
Hasimen Moses
Heath Jesse
Horriman Moses
Herriman Philip
Hickson James
Hogins Daniel
Huntriss James
Hutchinson John
Johnson John
Kelley Moses
Kitredge Nathaniel
Miller Robert
Mills John
Moore Ezra
Moore Fairbank
Moore Fairbank, Junr.
Moore William
Morse John
McLauton James
Osband John
Owen Sylvanus
Page Jacob
Parker Elijah
Parker Timothy
Parkhurst Phineas
Percival Stephen
Phippan Joseph
Poast Eldad, Junr.
Pratt Josiah
Ranny Daniel
Robinson Nathan
Savage Thomas
Serjeant Timothy
Silleway Hezekiah
Skales John
Smith John
Spring Thomas
Stevens Elias
Stevens John
Stevens Otho
Toney Anthony
Waterman Elijah
Webster Ephraim
White Nicholas
Willard Joseph
Williamsonn James
Wise John
Wright Abner

DUTCHESS COUNTY MILITIA.

COLONEL ABRAHAM BRINKERHOFF

LIEUTENANT COLONEL JACOB GRIFFEN

MAJOR ANDREW HILL

MAJOR RICHARD VAN WYCK

ADJUTANT JACOB BRINKERHOFF

QUARTER MASTER URIAH HILL

QUARTER MASTER WILLIAM GOSELINE

QUARTER MASTER ISAAC SEBRING

QUARTER MASTER CORNELIUS VAN WYCK

CAPT. GEORGE BRINKERHOFF
" GEORGE G. BRINKERHOFF
" JOHN G. BRINKERHOFF
" NICHOLAS BROWER
" JOSEPH HORTON
" ABRAHAM LENT
" JOHN SCHUTT
" THOMAS STORM
" EVERT W. SWART
" JAMES R. SWARTWOUT
" JOHN VAN BUNSCHOTEN
" MATTHEW VAN BUNSCHOTEN
" ISAAC VAN WYCK
LIEUT. CORNELIUS ADRIANCE
" ROBERT BRETT
" JOHN COOPER
" JOHANNES DEWITT
" CHRISTIAN DUBOIS
" STEPHEN OSBORNE
" BENJAMIN ROSEKRANS
LIEUT. JACOBUS SCAUTT
" ABRAHAM SCHULTZ
" WILLIAM SWARTWOUT
" ROBERT TODD
" BARENT VAN CLEACK (KLEECK)
" ISAAC VAN CLEEF
" ABRAHAM VAN WYCK
" FRANCIS WAY
" JOHANNES WILTSIE
ENSIGN MOSES BARBER
" JACOB BISSE
" LAWRENCE HAFF
" CHARLES HOFFMAN
" ABRAHAM HOGELAND
" ABRAHAM LADUE
" DANIEL SCHENCK
" JACOB S. SWARTWOUT
" JACOBUS SWARTWOUT
" JAMES R. SWARTWOUT

ENLISTED MEN

Ackarman John
Adriance Cornelius
Adriance George
Adriance Isaac
Adriance John
Adriance Ram, Junr.
Adriance Rem
Adriance Theodorus
Aldyck John
Algatt William
Algelt John
Algelt William
Altgelt William
Ammerman Albert
Annin Daniel
Annin James
Appelge Coenrad
Appilye
Applee Coenradt
Atgelt John
Avery John
Backer Jacob
Bailey John
Bailey Nathan
Bailey Sutton
Baker James
Baker Jesse
Baker Peter
Baker Thomas
Baker William
Baldwin Joseph
Barber John
Barber Moses
Barber Stephen
Barker John
Barker Samuel
Barkins David
Barnard Thomas
Barnes Solomon
Barnes William
Barns John
Bates Stephen
Bedel Jesse
Bedle Jesse
Beedle John
Bell Henry
Bell John
Benjamin Chester
Bennet Joseph
Berkins David
Bernard Thomas
Berry Nicholas
Berry Peter
Bigbey Christopher
Bise Simon
Biship Levi

State of New York

In Senate March 2d 1778.

The Senate being informed that the Hides which the Convention of this State some time ago put into the hands of Messrs. Matthew Cantine and John Anthony at Marbletown to be tanned and dressed by them for the use of this State, or some considerable part of them are prepared for working up into Shoes. —

Resolved, if the honorable House of Assembly concur herein, That Colonel Peter T. Curtenius the Commissary appointed to procure Cloathing for the Troops raised under the Direction of this State, take the said Quantity of Leather into his Care and cause the same to be made up into Shoes with all possible Dispatch, to be delivered by him or his Order into the Cloathing Store of this State; And that Mr. Curtenius be & he hereby is authorized to give Exemptions from Militia Duty to such Shoemakers, their Journeymen and Apprentices as he shall employ in making the said Shoes, to avail them respectively no longer than during the Time they shall necessarily be in the said Employ.

Ordered that Mr. [illegible] carry a Copy of the aforegoing Resolution to the Hon.ble

EXEMPTIONS FOR SHOE MAKING.

Octr 24th 1776

Mr Yates & Co — C Dr

Date	Item	£	s	d
	To 6 dinners		12	
	To Wine		8	
	To toddy		3	
	To Cyder		3	
25	To dinner for 7		14	
	To Wine		16	
	To toddy & Cyder		4	
	To supper for 6		9	
	To Wine		8	
	To toddy & Cyder		6	
	To Waiter Supr & Cyder		1	6
26	To dinner for 13	1	6	
	To Wine	1	12	
	To toddy & Cyder		10	
28	To Mr Dunnes Breakfast		1	6
	To 8 dinners		16	
	To toddy & Cyder		3	
	To Wine		16	
	To Servt Dinr &c		1	3
	To toddy		1	
29	To toddy		2	
	To Wine		8	
	To toddy		1	6
30	To toddy		6	
	To 5 at dinner		10	
	To Wine		16	
	To Cyder		1	
	To Servt Dinner &c		1	6
31	To 9 dinners		18	
	To Wine 6 Bottles & Bowl	2	9	
	To toddy & Cyder		3	
	To Servt Dinner &c		1	6
Novr 1.	To 6 dinners		12	
	To Wine		16	
	To Cyder		1	
	To toddy		5	
	To Servt Dinner &c		1	6
2	To 13 dinners	1	6	
	To Wine	2		
	To Cider & Toddy		4	
	To Sangoree		12	
	To Servt Dinner &c		1	6
		£ 21	9	9

Carried up

EXTRACT FROM A "RECKONING" OF THE "COMMITTEE OF SAFETY."

Bishop Caleb
Bishop Joshua
Bisse Jacob
Bloom Benjamin
Bloom Sylvester
Bocker Adolph
Boerum Hendrick
Boerum Nicholas
Boerum William
Bogardus Cornelius
Bogardus Francis
Bogardus Mathew
Bogardus Peter
Bogardus Shibboleth
Bogart Daniel
Bogart Ort
Bogart Peter
Boice Henry
Boice Simon
Bomp Joseph
Boncker Nathaniel
Boncker Stephen
Bower Daniel
Bown Joseph
Brandage James
Brannah James
Brett Francis R.
Brett Rambout
Brett Robert
Brett Theodorus
Brewer Charles
Briggs Caleb
Brinckerho Abraham J.
Brinckerhoff Abraham
Brinckerhoff Abraham J. or I.
Brinckerhoff Daniel
Brinckerhoff Derick J.
Brinckerhoff Dirck
Brinckerhoff Dirck, Junr.
Brinckerhoff Dirck T.
Brinckerhoff George
Brinckerhoff Henry
Brinckerhoff Isaac
Brinckerhoff Jacob
Brinckerhoff John S.
Brock Francis
Brooks William
Brower Daniel
Brower David
Brower Garret
Brower William
Brown Aron
Brown Jacob
Brown James
Brown Samuel
Brown Stephen
Bruck
Bruer Wilam
Brumfield James
Brush
Budd John
Bump Jacob
Burhans Peter
Burlyson Ferenot
Burnet Isaac
Burroughs James
Bush John
Bush Peter
Bush Zachariah
Bussing Abraham
Butcher Robert
Byce Henry
Canfield Daniel
Canfield James
Canfield Titus
Canniff John
Canniff Levi
Carman John
Carman Thomas
Carpenter Henry
Cary John
Cary Joseph
Chatfield William
Churchill Edward
Churchill Isaac
Churchill Jacob
Churchill John
Churchill Jonas
Churchill Joseph
Clapp John
Clark Samuel
Clarke Matthew
Cleyland William
Cochran William
Coffin John
Cole Aron
Cole Jacob
Coly Aron
Comfort Richard
Compton John
Concklin Elias
Concklin John
Concklin Lawrence
Concklin Matthew
Concklin William
Connor James
Connor John
Connover Benjamin
Cook John
Cook William
Coons Philip
Cooper Cornelius
Cooper Cornelius J.
Cooper Jacob
Cooper John
Cooper Minderd
Cooper Obadiah
Cooper Obadiah J. or I.
Coopman Jacob
Coopper Doct
Coopper Obadiah
Corker John Rynas
Cornell John
Cornwell Clement
Cornwell Silvester
Covenhoven Adrian
Covert John
Covint John
Cowenhoven Benjamin
Cowinhoverd Adrian
Craft Thomas
Crandel Abraham
Crawford William
Crinck Abraham
Cronck Abraham
Cronck Lawrence
Cronk Valam
Cuer Nathaniel
Cuer Samuel
Cuer William
Culver Dennis
Cure Matthew
Currie Archibald
Currie John
Cushman William
Dannels James
Darlon Jacobus
Dates John
Datin Corrinbary
David Henry
Davis John
Davison James
Dayton Hezekiah
Dean Stephen
Debois Christian
Deets John
Degraff Moses
Degraff Simeon
Degrutia Elias
Delamater William
Delaway Jeremiah
Demilt Garret (see Demitt)
Demilt Isaac
Demitt Garret (see Demilt)
Depue Peter
Devine Asher
Devoort Samuel
Dewitt John
Dewitt Peter
Dickinson John H.
Diness Mynard
Dolloway Jeremiah
Donalds James
Doxey Stephen
Dubois Cornelius
Dubois Gideon
Dubois Jacob
Dubois Koert
Dubois Peter
DuBois Teunis
Dubois Thomas
Duboys Jacob T.
Durtwater Daniel
Duryce Abraham, Jr.
Duryee Charles
Duryer Abraham
Dutcher Barnt
Dutcher David
Dycker David
Eldred William
Ellis Henry
Elsworth Ahasserus
Elsworth Alexander
Emans Jacobus
Enness James
Every John
Farington Joseph
Farrel Daniel
Fawlor Austin
Ferhone John
Ferrington Joseph
Fitchout John
Flegler Zachariah
Flowers Benjamin
Flynn Patrick
Forbes John
Forguson Samuel
Fowlar Joseph
Garrison Reuben
Gault Matthew
Gauslin William
Gee Jno.
Gerow Benjamin
Gerow Daniel
Gildersleeve James
Gildersleeve Joseph
Gildersleeve Nathaniel
Giles William
Goddfellow William
Golnack Michael
Goodfellow William
Gorsline Samuel
Gorsline William
Gosling Samuel
Gosling William
Green Ezekiel
Green Gilbert
Green Isaac
Green James
Green James, Jr.
Green Jeremiah

Green John
Green Joseph
Green Joseph, Junr.
Green Joseph, Senr.
Green Stephen
Griffin Cornelius
Griffin Isaac
Griffin Jacob
Griffin John
Griffin Joseph
Griffin Joshua
Griffin Peter
Gue Isaac
Gulnack Jacob
Gulneck Michael
Haasner Jacob
Hageman Francis
Hageman Jeremiah
Hageman Peter
Haines John
Hair Amos
Hallett R.
Halstead Thomas
Halstead William
Halsted Josiah
Haltsead Thomas
Hames John F.
Hanly Matthew
Hanson Aurt
Hanson John
Hardenbergh Dirck
Hardenbergh Garret
Harris Minderd
Harsincise Isaac
Hart Michal
Hasbrook Jacob
Haskins William
Hasner Jacob
Hayburn John
Hawk John Baron
Heeremans Henry
Heermans John
Hegamen Peter
Heliker John
Hicks John
Hicks Joshua
Higbee Flemming
Higbee Lemuel
Higby Flimmewill
Higby Lemuel
Hill
Hilton Joseph
Hodge Abraham
Hoffman Daniel
Hogaboom Bartholomew
Hogan Edward
Hoghtalen John
Holmes Isaac
Holmes William
Homes William
Honson John
Hoogeboom Bartholomew
Hoogland Derick
Hoogland William
Hoogtalen John
Horsuer Jacob
Horton Gilbert
Horton Joseph
Horton Joseph P.
Horton Joshua
Horton Matthias, Junr.
Horton Peter
Hosher Stephen
Howard Joseph
Huff Angel
Huff Lawrence
Huffman Daniel
Hughson Gabriel
Hughson John
Hughson William
Hulst Peter
Humfrey Henry
Hutchings Jacob
Hutchins, Benjamin
Hyer Walter
Innes James
Innis Peter
Isaac Burnet
Jackson Joseph
Jarepenning John
Jarow Daniel
Jarowe Benjamin
Jewell Abraham
Jewell George
Jewell John
Jerwillinger Jerean
Johnson James
Johnson Thomas
Johnston Robert
Jones David
Kappelye Isaac
Kelly William
Kennedy Henry
Kerrilly Daniel
Kershon Isaac
Ketcham Titus
King William
Kip John
Kipp Abraham
Klump Zachariah
Knapp Shadrack
Kniffen Jonathan
Kniver Jacob
Kronk James
Ladeau Daniel
Ladeu Nathaniel
Ladeu Oliver
Ladew Abraham
Ladua William
Ladue Peter
Lane Gilbert
Lane Gilbert, Junr.
Lane Jacob
Lane Jesse
Lane Joseph
Lane Joshua
Lane William
Lane William, Junr.
Langdon Jonathan
Lany William, Junr.
Larry Jno.
Lattemore Thomas
Lattin Ambrose
Lawrence John
Lean Joseph
Leavy John
Ledeau William, Senr.
Ledue Daniel
Lee Jonathan
Leghtatn John
Lent Abraham, Junr.
Lequiere Abraham
Leroy Francis
Leroy Peter
Leroy Simon
Lerye William
Light William
Light Woolsey
Linderbeck John
Lisk Benjamin
Losee Abraham
Losee Abraham L.
Losee Jacob
Losee John A.
Losee Simeon
Low Jno.
Low John
Luckey Samuel
Ludenton Steapen
Ludington Stephen
Luord Josiah
Luyster Dirck
Luyster Peter
Lyster Garret
MacCrady James
Major James
Mannery William
Marcius C.
Marston Aurt
Marten Aert
Marten Peter
Martense Adrian
Martin Ezekiah
Martin Gershom
Martin Jeremiah
Martin Thomas
Masten Aert
Mastin Ezechiel
Maxfield James
Mead David
Meddagh Aurt
Medew Lewis
Meed Jeremiah
Meger William
Menema John
Meritt Joseph
Mestin Aurt
Meyer Abraham
Meyer James
Meyer Peter
Middagh Aurt
Middagh James
Miels Bennajah
Miels Noah
Miles John
Miles Noah
Miller Ezra
Miller James
Miller Philip
Mills Benajah
Mills Robert
Mogar Caleb
Moger William
Monfoort Albert
Monfoort Domenicus
Monfoort Elbert, Junr.
Monfoort John
Monfoort John C.
Monfoort Peter
Monfort Elbert
Monfort John P.
Monger William
Monson George
Montanye Benjamin
Morse Joseph
Mortisa Adriaan
Munfort Adrian
Myer Abraham
Myer Adolph
Myer Jacob
Myer John
Myer John Dikman
Myer John, Junr.
Myer Peter
Myer William
Myers Abraham
McBride John
McCaby Edward
McCredy James
McCudgeon Robert
McKaby Dennis
McKeeby Darius

McKeeby William
McKeely Edward
McKelly William
McManness Michael
McNeal Henry
Naddue Lewis
Neally Samuel
Neeley Rolette
Neepes, Abraham
Nelson Paul
Nettleton Amos
Newton Charles
Nifer Jacob
Noortstrant John
Noortstrant Peter
Norstrand Cornelius
Norstrand Jacobus
Norton Peter
Nostrand George
Odilda William
Oestrande Cornelis
Ogden Benjamin
Ogden Joseph
Osbern Richard
Osborn Doct
Osborn James
Osborn Peter
Osborn Richard
Osborn Samuel
Ostram John, Junr.
Ostrander Cornelius
Ostrander Henry
Ostrom John
Outwater Daniel
Paddock Peter
Palen Hendrick
Palen Peter
Paling Peter
Palm Hendrick
Palmetier Petrus
Pardon Thomas
Parker Joseph
Parker Nathaniel
Pating Hennery
Patterson Abijah
Peck Joseph
Peck Oliver
Petet Ebenezer
Pettit David
Philips James
Philips Ralph, Junr.
Philips Roelof
Philips William
Philips William C.
Phillips Abraham
Phillips David
Phillips Henry
Phillips Jacobus
Pierce Richard
Pine, Philip
Pine Robert
Pine Silvanus
Pine Thomas
Pollock William
Pollom Tice
Post Joseph
Potten Danel
Pudney Cornelius
Pudney Francis
Pudney John
Pullick John
Pullick William
Purdy Elisha
Purdy Gilbert
Purdy Joseph
Purdy Nathaniel
Quan John
Rantsier Andrew
Rapalgeo John
Rapelsee Isaac
Rayer Daniel
Raynor Daniel
Reynolds Andrew
Right Daniel
Robinson Jonas
Roe Benjamin
Roe Daniel
Roe David
Rogers Joseph
Rogers Micah
Rogers Michael
Rogers Platt
Rogers Robert
Rogers Uriah
Roll Henry
Romer John
Rosekrans Benjamin
Rosekrans John
Rosekrans Peter
Rosekrans Thomas
Roukrans Dirck
Rowland Marvin
Rowlin Mervin
Runnels Andrew
Ryce Peter
Rycel Peter
Ryder Caleb
Ryer Tunis
Ryndass John
Ryness Abraham
Ryness Andrew
Ryness John
Sackett Ananias
Santon William
Schenck Daniel
Schenck Philip
Schenck Roeloff
Schounhover Peter
Schouten Cornelius
Schouten Ephraim
Schouten John
Schouten Simon
Schouten William
Schouter Cornelius
Schutt Abraham
Schutt James
Schutt John, Junr.
Schutt Joseph
Schutt Stephen
Schutt Teunis
Scofield Silvanus
Scot Walter
Scouten Andrew
Scouten Andris
Scouten Ephraim
Scouten Johannes
Scouten John
Scouten Simon
Scouten William
Scutt Dennis
Scutt Joseph
Sebring Cornelius
Sebring Isaac
Secord Isaac
Secord Josiah
Seton Heskieh
Shaff Frederick
Shear Abraham
Sherer James
Shevling John
Shults Christopher
Shute Aron
Sickles John, Junr.
Skutt Teunis
Slack William
Sleight Abraham
Sleight John
Slight Abraham, Junr.
Sloot John
Smith Isaac
Smith Jacob
Smith John
Smith Joseph
Smith Joseph, Junr.
Smith Joshua
Smith Martin
Smith Maurice
Smith Morris
Smith Richard
Smith Sylvester
Smith William
Snider George
Snider Moses
Sodom John
Soden John
Somendyke Jacob
Somerndike William
Somes Nathaniel
Somes Richard
Somes Stephen
Southard Gilbert
Southard Henry
Southard Isaac
Southard John
Southard John, Junr.
Southard Richard
Southard Thomas
Southerd Jones
Spence John
Spencer John
Stanton William
Storm Isaac
Storm John
Sutton Joseph
Swartwout Cornelius
Swartwort James
Swartwout John
Swartwout Richard
Swartwout Samuel
Swartwout Thomas
Tallman Timothy
Tanner Zopher
Tarpennye John
Taylor Stephen
Teller Oliver
Terbosh Abraham
TerBush Luke
Tercoss William
Terhone John
Terhune Daniel
Terpanning John
Terwilger Juryan
Thatcher Stephen
Theal Joseph
Thomas Johnson
Thompson Ezra
Thorn Gershom
Thurston Benjamin
Thurston James
Totten Daniel
Traverse Nathaniel
Tremper Michael
Turhune Abraham
Turhune John
Turner Alexander
Turner Ellick
Vail Isaac
Vail Jesse
Vandle James
Vermilier Benjamin
Vermilya John
Vermuly David

Vermuly Gerardus
Vervalin Daniel
Vervalin Jermiah
Vervalin John
Vervalin Moses
Vestervals John
Voorhis Jerom
Van Amburgh Abraham
Van Banech Jacob
Van Benchoten James
Van Bomal Christopher
Van Bomel Peter
Van Bonnel Christoffel
Van Bosnel Peter
Vanbumble Stuffil
Van Bumbler Peter
Van Bunschoten Jacob
Van Bunschoten Teunis
Van Bunschoten Tunis, Jr.
Vanclackren Marinus T.
Van Cleef Michael
Van Cleck Boltis B.
Van Cots John
Van Cott Daniel
Van Crob Abraham
Vancuran Casparus
Vandeburgh Abram
Van Der Bilt Aart
Van Derbilt P.
Vandervoort Jacobus
Vandervoort John
Van Der Voort Samuel
Vander Water John
Vande Water Adolph
Vandewater Harman
Van Dewater James
Vandewort Peter
Van Duwnter John
Vand Water James
Vandworter Jacobus
Van Erway Jacob
Van Every Edde
Van Every Jacob
Van Flack Henry
Van Kerse John
Van Keuren Matthew
Van Kleack Barrant B.
Van Kleeck Baltus
Van Kleeck Barent A.
Van Kleeck Barnard C.
Van Kleeck Barnet
Van Kleeck Michael
Van Kuren Caspowres
Van Leyse I.
Van Norstrant John
Van Nortstrant Cornelus
Van Siclen John
Van Steenberger Cornelius
Van Steenbergh Cornelius
Vantassel Henry
Vantassil Jacob
Van Tassill John
Vantiers William
Vantine Abraham
Vantine Cornelius
Van Tine William
Van Valen Daniel
Van Valen Jeremiah
Van Valen John
Van Valer Moses
Van Velen Ede
Van Veler Daniel
Van Vlack Barent
Van Vlack John H.
Van Vlack Merinus
Van Vleck John
Van Vleck Merine
Van Vleckren Abraham
Van Vleckren George
Van Vleckren Henry
Van Vleckren Marinus T.
Vanvleckren Marinus
Van Voorhees Stephen
Van Voorheis Jeronimus
Van Voorhis Abraham
Van Voorhis Jacob
Van Voorhis Jeromus
Van Voorhis John
Van Voorhis Zachariah
Van Wey Cornelius
Van Wyck Abraham
Van Wyck Cornelius
Van Wyck John
Van Wyck John B.
Van Wyck Theodorus
Waldron Benjamin
Waldron Daniel
Waldron David
Waldron John
Waldron John P.
Waldron Peter
Ward Daniel
Ward James
Ward William
Washburn Isaac
Waters John
Watts John
Way Frederick
Way George
Way Gideon
Way James
Way John
Way Joost
Webard John
Weed John
Wenn William
Westervalt Albert
Westervalt John
Westervelt Elbert
Westervelt George
Westervelt Jacobus
Westervelt John
Wibard John
Wille James
Wilsee William
Wiltse Cornelius
Wiltse Joseph
Wiltse Peter
Wiltsee Hendrick
Wiltsey Geradus
Wiltsie William
Wiltzee Harmery
Winn Johnson
Winn Joseph
Winslow Samuel
Wood Isaac
Wood Jesse
Wood John
Wood Joseph
Wood Solomon
Wood Thomas
Wool Joseph
Worshbourn Isaac
Wright Daniel
Wright Daniel, Junr.
Wright John
Wright Thomas
Wyckoff John
Yeomans John
Yerks John
Young Abraham
Young John
Zachrider Moses

Dutchess County Militia—(Continued).

COLONEL JOHN FIELD
COLONEL ANDREW MOREHOUSE
MAJOR JONATHAN PADDOCK
MAJOR ISAAC TALLMAN
ADJUTANT SOLOMON CRANE
QUARTER MASTER REUBEN CROSBY
SURGEON JOSEPH CRANE, JR.

CAPT. AZOR BARNUM
" WILLIAM CALKIN
" WILLIAM CHAMBERLAIN
" PETER COON
" JOSEPH DYKEMAN
" DAVID HECOCK
" JAMES MARTEN
" WILLIAM PEARCE
" WILLIAM PINE
" ICHABOD WARD

LIEUT. JOSHUA CROSBY
" DANIEL DOANE
" ELIJAH OAKLEY
" URIAH PARRISH
" EDWARD PENNY
" THOMAS SEARS
" VALENTINE WHEELER
" LUKE WOOLCUT
ENSIGN NATHAN GREEN

ADDITIONAL NAMES ON STATE TREASURER'S PAY BOOKS.

LIEUT. JOSEPH CHANDLER
" ASA HAINES

ENSIGN BENJAMIN SLOCUM

ENLISTED MEN.

Anow William
Ashby Anthony
Baker Elisha
Baldwin David
Barleson Joel
Barnum Eliakum
Barnum Jonah
Barnum Noah
Barnum Stephen
Benedict Ebenezer
Benedict Stephen
Benit Amasa
Bennet Amacy
Benson William
Birdsall Elemwill (see Elemuel)
Birdsall Thomas
Birlisson Joel
Bishnite Frances
Bradshaw John
Brewster Pelatiah
Brewster Pell
Brown Israel
Brown Moses
Bruster Samuel
Bumpus James
Burch George
Burch Josiah, Junr.
Burch Josiah, Senr.
Burch Silas
Burjes Thomas
Burkler Jabez
Burlasand Joel
Burleson Joel
Burling Gilead
Burtch Benjamin
Cable Platt
Calkin Elias
Campbell Robert
Cannon Abraham
Carle John
Carter Jabez
Chamberlain John
Chapman Enoch
Chapman Thomas
Chase Bary
Chase Seth
Chase Thomas
Clark John
Clinton William
Closson Wilber
Closson William
Cockshuer Jonas
Cole Benjamin
Cole Sylvenus
Concklin John
Cook Moses, Jr.
Cook Moses, Senr.
Coon Jacob
Coon John
Cornwell David
Covey Joseph
Covey Walter
Crandle Jeremiah
Crane Ira
Crane William
Croker Timothy
Crosby Abner
Crosby David, Junr.
Crosby Elemuel
Crosby Elezer
Crosby Eli
Crosby James
Crosby John
Crosby Joseph
Crosby Josiah
Crosby Lemuel
Crosby Moses
Crosby Obadiah
Crosby Reuben
Crosby Samuel
Davis Paul
Dean Elijah
Delmarter Marting
Doane Elnathan
Dyckman Benjamin
Ellis Elijah
Ellis Thomas
Ellwell Ezra
Elwell Jabez
Elwell John
Elwell Tabis, Junr.
Evans Thomas, Senr.
Evens Thomas
Evens Thomas, Junr.
Ferris Justus
Field Jesse
Foster David
Foster James
Foster John

Foster Samuel
Foster Seth
Fox Oliver, Junr.
Franklin Nathaniel
Fuller Jesse
Gage Alden
Gage Anthony
Gage Justus
Gage Mark
Gage Moses
Gage Silvanus
Gay Jason
Gilchrist Samuel
Gilchrist Thomas
Goodshead Abner
Gray Samuel
Grean John
Green Caleb
Green Isaac
Green Jeams
Griffith Done
Hains Asa
Hall Benaijah
Hall Benjamin
Hall Jesse
Hall John
Hall Martin
Hall Morten
Hall Samuel
Hayden Alpheus
Hazard Samuel
Heaveland John
Hecock Noah
Hecocks John
Hempsted Nathaniel
Heuman Zachariah
Heverland John
Higgins Thomas, Junr.
Hinckley Elkanah
Hinckley Reuben
Hinkley Josiah
Hoecce Tademas
Holladay John
Hollaway Joseph
Holley Joseph
Holliday John
Holliday Simeon
Holms Joseph
Honeyall Mathias
Hopkins Berry
Hopkins John
How Garret
Hunewill Mathew
Hunt Thomas
Johnston Joseph
Jones Ebenezer
Jones Elias
Jones Ephraim
Jones Isaac
Jones Joseph
Jones Levy
Jones Nehemiah
Jones Samuel
Jones Thomas
Kelley David
Kelley Shoubel
Kelly Jonathan
Kelly Reuben
Kelly Sylvenus
Kent Moses
Ketcham Daniel
Killey Reuben
Killey Silvenus
King Caleb
King Myrick
King Nathaniel
Kline John
Lockwood Henry
Lockwood Solomon
Lindsay David
Lincoln Isaiah
Marks Holiab
Marsee Andrew
Marsh Elnathan
Mash Elnathan
Mash John
Massy Andrew
Merick Benjamin
Merjerson Thomas
Mills Benijah
Mills William C.
Mirit Gilburt
Morehouse Stephen
Morrell Abraham
Mosh John
Moshier Johial
Moshoell Isaac
Mott Jacob
Mott Joseph
Mott Thomas
Mott William, Junr.
Murch George
Murch William
Myrrick Benjamin
Nash David
Nicholsone James
Nickerson James
Nickerson Thomas
Nickerson Thomas, Junr.
Notter William
Nubery Joseph
Oates James
Olmstead Ebenezer
Osborn Ezekiel
Osterhout Gideon
Paddock Nathan
Palmer Nickelous
Palmer William
Penney Ammiel
Penney John
Penney William
Perkins Elijah
Perry Samuel
Perry Simeon
Petson Andrew
Philips Joseph
Philips Joshua
Pitcher Benjamin
Ragon Thomas
Raymond Uriah
Reed Jacob
Richardson Isaac
Rider Christopher
Rider David
Rider John
Rider Simeon
Rider Simeon, Junr.
Rinnalds David
Roberts Benjamin
Robert Benjamin, Junr.
Rockwell Stephen
Runnels David
Russel Roland
Ryder Zenous
Sabens Billings
Sackett John
Sampson Abner
Sealy William
Sears Benjamin
Sears Enoch
Sears Peter
Sears Seth
Sears Seth, Junr.
Sears Stephen
Shaw Ichabod
Sherman Darius
Slocum Benjamin
Slocum George
Smith Alpheus
Smith Jonathan
Smith Joseph
Snider Samuel
Snow William
Spenser Samuel
Stark Aamos
Stark Aaron
Stark John
Starke Henry
Start Aaron
Stevens Thomas
St. John Thomas
Stone David
Stow William
Termillear Phillip
Thomas Thomas
Thompson Daniel
Thompson Thomas
Thornton Thomas
Townsend Isaac
Townsend John
Townsend Solomon
Tubbs Benajah
Twitchel Benoni
Utter Aamos
Utter Ebenezer
Vickrey Thomas
Wairing John
Webb Noah
Weed John
Wickson Elijah
Wickson Elijah, Junr.
Wikson Ebenezer
Willcocks Rosel
Willis Charles
Willis Thomas
Wilson John
Winger Hendrick
Winger Samuel
Wixson Elijah
Wixson Isaac
Wooster William
Wright Edmund
Young Elkany
Young Shaw
Youngs Samuel

Dutchess County Militia — (Continued).

COLONEL JOHN FREAR

CAPT. ISAAC CONKLIN
" ——— HAGEMAN
" ELIJAH HERRICK
" ——— KILSEY
" ——— LOW
" DAVID OSTRAND
" SAMUEL SMITH
" LUKE STOUTENBURGH

CAPT. ——— STRAIGHT
" BERNARDUS SWARTHOUSE
" HUGH VAN KLEEK
" JOHN VAN KLEEK
LIEUT. ABRAHAM FORT
" JONAS WEEKS
ENSIGN ALEXANDER FURMAN
" (REUBEN) SPENCER

Dutchess County Militia — (Continued).

COLONEL WILLIAM HUMFREY
COLONEL JAMES VANDEBURGH
MAJOR BENJAMIN BIRDSALL
MAJOR WILLIAM CLERK
ADJUTANT JOHN BUDD
ADJUTANT JEREMIAH CLERK
QUARTER MASTER HENRY BAILEY
QUARTER MASTER JAMES ELLSWORTH

CAPT. CALEB BENTLEY
" JOHN BOYD
" JOSIAH BURTON
" JOSHUA CHAMPLIN
" WILLIAM CLARK
" JOHN CLUM
" JONATHAN DENNIS
" ABRAHAM HARTWILL
" DAVID HECOCK
" JOB MEAD
" JOSEPH RURNIDS
" JOHN SCUT
" BARARDUS SWARTWOUT
" IS. VAIL
" FRANCIS WEST
" VALENTINE WHEELER
LIEUT. STEPHEN AKINS
" SILAS ANSON
" TABOR BENTLEY
LIEUT. TILLING BENTLEY
" JACOB BLATNER
" JOSEPH CHANDLER
" ANDREW HEERMANCE
" JACOB J. HEERMANCE
" ALI HOUGHLAND
" DANIEL HULE
" JAMES HUMFREY
" PETER MAGEE
" ——— MCCLEES
" ROGER MOREY, JR.
" THEOPH SWEET
" BRT. VAN KLEECK
" MOSES VAN VRANKA
" SOLOMON WHEELER
" GILBERT WORDING
ENSIGN DAVID TRUSDAL
" ABRAHAM VAN CURAH
" PETER VAN VALKINBURGH

ENLISTED MEN.

Abbet David
Acker Adam
Adams Ebenezer
Allin Thomas
Alsworth William
Ames I.
Anen
Asseltine Jacob
Atwearter Benjamin
Audriance J.
Aulandorph Christian
Babcock David
Babcock Enoch
Babcock John
Babcock John (1)
Babcock John (3)
Backer John
Bailey Elias
Bailey Elisha
Baker Elnathan
Baker J.
Baker Jonathan
Baker William
Ballim Matthew
Bannam James
Barger
Barkman George
Barnum Bethuel
Barnum William
Barringar Conradt
Barringar William
Bartlee Abraham
Bartlee Jacob
Bartlett Jacob
Bayley S.
Beckett Sylos
Bell Robert
Benjamin Cyres
Bennet Timothy
Bentley Joseph
Bently John
Benton Moses
Berry Nicholas
Berry P.
Bigraft George
Bigraft Jonathan
Billings Increase
Billings John
Birdsall Daniel
Birdsall Jeremiah
Bishop
Borgordis
Bosehonce Isaac
Bouker Thomas
Brenkroff
Brewer D.
Brewer V.
Brill Solomon
Brinkorff I.
Brown Jonathan
Brown Peter
Brown Zepheniah
Brumfield J.
Bruster Peltias
Buck Zadock
Budd Undril
Bugbee George
Bump I.
Bump Joseph
Bunbler P'h
Bunschoten Solomon
Bunt Leasero
Burley Elijah
Cady Elisha
Cahoon Ben
Carle Andrew

Carley John
Carley Peter
Carman Andrew
Cary Stephen
Cash Jonathan
Celey William
Chadwick William
Chahart Jacob
Champlin Thomas
Champlin William
Chapman Josiah
Chase Berry
Chavilear Peter
Christian Cornelius
Clark J. P.
Coberstine John
Cole Benjamin
Cole Jacob
Cole Moses
Coller Norres
Colerell Henry
Coltman William
Conroo Darling
Conroo William
Coock I.
Coock W.
Cook Jere
Cook John
Cook Mathew
Coon Abraham
Cooper William
Corkins Joel
Cornell Benjamin
Cornell John
Cornell Lewis
Cornell Samuel
Cornwill Caleb
Cornwill Sylvan's
Corwill Benjam
Cott D.
Crankite Frederick
Crankite Herculus
Crankite John
Cranfoot James
Creed Austin
Crook William
Crosby Eliezer
Crosby Obediah
Cudbuth William
Cunningham John
Curry Elisha
Daggitt Mayhue
Dannels J.
Darling Peter
David I.
Davis George
Davis Squire
Davison Alverson
Davison Daniel
Debons Math'w
Delong Richard
Demsey Thomas
Denney Charles
Devow John
Dewkine I.
Dickson I. Hanse
Dimond Math'w
Dodg—— I.
Douty Elias
Dowing I.
Downing Andrew
Doxey Thomas
Draper John
Draper Joseph
Dumon Cornelius
Dutcher D
Dutcher Simon
Eda Joshua
Egail Jo'n
Eldred William
Ellott Christian
Elwell Jabez
Ennis P.
Estrus Benjamin
Evans John
Everit Clear
Evins Amos
Evins Oliver
Fillow En
Fillow Finus
Finch Comfort
Fish Joseph
Flinn David
Fonda Cornelius
Forbus John
Forbush William
Force Benjamin
Forgerson Gilb't
Forgerson Jeremiah
Foster Seth
Fox Jonathan
Frech John
Frier Peter
Frior Simeon
Gage Elihu
Gage Moses
Gale Noh
Gardner Simeon
Gowel I.
Gowel T.
Gibson John
Gideon Joseph
Gilbert Ep'm
Gilbert Thad
Gillitt Barny
Gones Seth (see Jones)
Gooden Robert
Goodfeller W.
Goodwin I.
Green Caleb
Green E.
Greves Thomas
Grey John
Griffin Barney
Griffith Solomon
Hale John
Hall Benjamin
Hall Gideon
Hamlin Epraim
Hanes I.
Haner John
Hangadoren John
Hannaburgh Christyaun
Haping David
Harrick Joseph
Harrington William
Harris Noah
Hartwill Ebenezer
Hassiem John
Hatch Cradius
Heermance Jacob
Helmes John
Hendrickson Jacob
Henry Elick
Heracer Emanuel
Herrick Isriel
Hewit Edmond
Hewit Gidion
Hicks Nathaniel
Hicks W.
Hoard Isaac
Hodge K.
Hoffman Patrus
Hoghtailing Abraham
Holmes Alkany
Holmes Ben
Holmes John
Houssinger Frank
Horton D.
Hosher Thomas
Houck William
Howard Jonathan
Howlin Obediah
Hudson Asa
Huff I.
Hulin John
Hull Justus
Humfrey Thomas
Hutchens A.
Hutchings Jacob
Irish Benjamin
Irish Isaac
Jaycocks Thomas
Jinkins Jerry
Johnson Alexander
Johnson Joseph
Johnson Nehemiah
Johnstones I.
Jones Isaac
Jones Nathan
Jones Robert
Jones Roger
Jones Rufus
Jones Seth (see Gones)
Judard H.
Kelly Jonathan
Kime Lourance
King Hezekiah
King Nathaniel
Kip
Kipp Frank
Knognard John
Kool Isaac
Koons Adam
Koonts Nicholas
Lake Henrey
Lake Stephen
Lamb Daniel
Lamb David
Lane J.
Lane John
Lanson Garrit
Lant Jurry
Laroy John
Lawrence Isaac
Lawrence Oliver
Lawrence Richard
Lawsin Mathew
Lawsin Peter
Lean John
Lerue I.
Levy Jacob
Lewis Felix
Lewis Gil
Linn Aaron
Loop Peter, Jr.
Losie Francis
Luis Grawdus
Luke John
Lus Michal
Lus William
Marchant Abel
Marchel Benjamin
Marta David
Martin Elemuel
Mason Fransis
Mathews Justice
Mayhue Ebenezer
Mayhue Levi
Mead King
Mead Zebulin
Miller Jacob

Moon John
Moor Nicholas
Moore Poulis
Moran William
Mordock Zimri
Mott Jacob
Muller Stephen
Mumford P.
Myer Benjamin
Myer Henrey
Mackeny I.
McCreedy Charles
McCreedy James
McKiney Joseph
McLees James
McLoes Peter
McNeel Henry
Near Charles
Nelson Frank
Neutun John
Newill Joseph
Newman Joshua
Nichols Silas
Norton Richard
Noxon Benjamin
O'Cane Edward
Odell Gershom
Odell Jonas
Odle Abiather
Okla Thomas
Olmsted Elijah
Orborn John
Orsborn Corn'l
Ostrander Henrey
Ostrum Gilbert
Owen Anenias
Owens Robert
Pack I.
Paddock Peter
Padock Henry
Palmer Sylvanus
Patterson Ab'm
Pelts Evert
Perce John
Pettitt Jacob
Phillip Adam
Phillip Christyan
Plass Hendrick
Post J.
Potter Rowland
Prope George

Prust Martin
Randel I.
Reesoner David
Reise Jonas
Reynolds Era
Riccord George
Richardson Isaac
Richardson William
Rines I.
Robinson Andrew
Robinson Steph'n
Rogers Ezekiel
Rolitts John
Romer Aron
Rosacrance I.
Row D.
Rowleo Daniel
Rowley Nathan
Rumm George
Runnels I.
Ryder John
Ryley Phillip
Sabins Joshua
Sage Solah
Sarmerhorn Cornelius
Saxton Ebenezer
Schoulen
Schouten E.
Schryver Bartle
Seberry John
Sharks Thomas
Sharts David
Shaw Benjamin
Shede George
Sheer William
Shephierd Israel
Shoff Andrew
Shuter Samuel
Shuts Ab'm
Shuttis John
Sickler Coonrod
Sickler George
Sickler Mathias
Simmons John
Sitcher Andrew
Slaght T.
Slut John
Smith Daniel
Smith Ephraim
Smith Ezekiel
Smith Henry

Smith John
Smith Phillip
Smith Thomas
Soper Bart'n
Soper Henry
Soper Timothy
Sorver Peter
Sparker Andrew
Spencer Abner
Spencer Jabus
Spencer James
Spencer Rufus
Spencer William
Springer John
Stanton Thomas
Stark Aaron
Stark Nathan
Steed Richard
Stinebergh Grandus
Stockholm D.
Stone David
Stubbelbane Michal
Swartout T.
Sweet Amos
Swider M.
Swortout C.
Swortout I.
Talor Gamal
Talor John
Tamph Fredrick
Tanner
Taylor Gamalial
Taylor Joseph
Thompson Thomas
Thompson John
Thorington Thomas
Thorn Benjamin
Toboys C.
Tolks John
Tommes Benjamin
Torboss L.
Tott James
Townsend Able
Turhoon I.
Tyler John
Umphey William
Ureo John
Valentine Benjamin
Veley Peter
Vermillia B.
Vessher Christopher

Vincent Philip
Vradenburgh Abraham
Vradenburgh Peter
Van Cleak John
Van Cott John
Vanderhoof Jacob
Vanderhyder Abraham
Vandevort John
Vandevort S.
Van Dusan John
Van Dusan London
Van Loan Peter
Van Luvan, Zacharias
Van Natte Isaac
Van Slyck Tunas
Van Tasel J.
Vanvlack H.
Van Valkenburgh Peter
Van Voris I.
Van Wicke
Van Wogner John
Walker John
Ward David
Ward Eben
Warner Richard
Warren Samuel
Weeks William
Weiley William
Welch Thomas
Weller Amos
Weller William
Wells Silas
Welsee Abraham
Welsey I.
West Daniel
West Elijah
Whiper I.
Whipple Nath
Whitcomb Simon
White John
White Solomon
Whitmarch Ezra
Wickson Elijah
Wilcox John
Wilcox Stephen
Willey Thomas
Willkason Jon
Wistiveltt James
Wolven William
Wood Silas
Young Benjamin

Dutchess County Militia—(Continued).

COLONEL MORRIS GRAHAM

COLONEL ROSWELL HOPKINS

LIEUTENANT COLONEL JACOB GRIFFIN

MAJOR PETER FELL

MAJOR JONATHAN LANDON

MAJOR BRINTON PAINE

ADJUTANT JOHN GRAHAM

ADJUTANT DAVID HUNT

ADJUTANT DANIEL SHEPHERD

QUARTER MASTER JOHN ELSE

QUARTER MASTER NATHAN FISH

QUARTER MASTER EZRA PAYNE

QUARTER MASTER ABRAHAM VAN WART

PAY MASTER EDMUND PERLEE

SURGEON WILLIAM ADAMS

SURGEON ROSWELL HOPKINS, Jr.

Capt. Sybert Acker
" John Barnes
" Azor Barnum
" John Bell
" John Bradbick
" George Brinkerhoff
" Charles Brodhead
" Moses Cantine
" Colbe Chamberlain
" John Drake
" Andries Heermans
" Elijah Herrick
" Henry Humfrey
" John Klum
" George Lane
" Daniel Martin
" William Pearce
" William Radclift
" John Rouse
" Richard Sackett
" Frederick Strait
" Smith Sutherland
" James Tallmadge
" Elijah Townsend
" John Van Benschoten
" David Van Ness
" Samuel Waters
" Noah Wheeler
" Daniel Williams

Lieut. Stephen Adsit
" Frederick Benner
" John Berry
" Phillipp Bowne
" Wright Carpenter
" Samuel Crandle
" Daniel Delavan
" Christian Dubois
" Abner Gillett
" Abraham Smith Hadden
" Phillipph Harimanse
" Andries Harmans
" Joel Haskins
" John Heermanse
" Stephen Haight
" Adam Helmer
" Abram Hogeland
" Solomon Hopkins
" Stephen Hunt
" Elihu Ingalls
" William Martine
" William Mattemen
" ——— Mead
" James Moore
" Francis Nelson
" Elijah Park
" Jonas Parks
" Bezaleel Rudd
" Abraham Schultz

LIEUT. JOHN SMITH
" FREDERICK STEVENSON
" WILLIAM SWARTWOUT
" TEUNIS TALMAN
" ISAAC TOWNSEND
" JACOB TRIMPER

LIEUT. RESOLVENT VAN HOUTON
" WRIGHT WHITE
" ZOPHAR WICKES
" ROBERT WOOD
ENSIGN WILLIAM BECKER
" JOHN MORE

ENLISTED MEN.

Abbett David
Abboth Abiel
Abler James
Acker Abraham
Ackerman Arie
Ackerman John
Adair William
Adams John
Adams Major
Adsit George
Adsit Silas
Aldridge Jonathan
Allen Asa
Allen Caleb
Allen Jonathan
Allendorph Hendrick
Allsworth Thomas
Ambler Charles
Ambler James
Andres George
Annes Peter
Anson James
Armstrong Benjamin
Armstrong Gabril
Armstrong Robert
Arnold Peleg
Asten Robert
Aston Martin
Aulomdorph Henderick
Ausor Nicholas
Austin Robert
Babcock James
Backer John
Badeau Jacob
Bader Michael
Baker Jesse
Baker Joshua
Baker Judah
Baker Richard
Bailey Elias
Banker Stephen
Barber Nathan
Barber Reuben
Barber Solomon
Barber Thomas
Barker James
Barnhard Henry
Barnum Noah

Barns Jacob
Barringer Conradt
Barringer David
Barringer William
Barton Gilbert
Bartow John
Bates Daniel
Bates Hickey
Bayley Samuel
Beaty John
Becker John
Beecher Nathan
Bell Jacob
Bell William R.
Bell William W
Benner Hendrick, Junr.
Berger John
Beringer Jacob, Junr.
Berry Jabez
Berry John
Berry Peter
Berry Samuel
Betts Gideon
Bishop John
Blaau Henry
Blauvelt Cornelius
Blauvelt Isaac
Bockee Jacob
Bogardus Egbert
Bogardus Henry
Bogardus Peter
Bogart Hendrick
Bogart Jacob
Bonasteal Nicholas
Bonker Stephen
Bonnell Jonathan
Booth Isaiah
Bouton Moses
Boyce John
Boyd Robert
Boyd Samuel
Bradshaw William
Brower William
Brewster John
Brickell George
Briggs Casparus
Briggs Lawrence
Brinckerhoff Daniel

Brinckerhoff Isaac
Brinckerhoff John S.
Brink Cornelius C
Brinkerhoff John
Broadwell Moses
Brodhead Samuel
Brooks John
Brower Samuel
Brower William
Brown Cornelius
Brown Deliverance
Brown James
Brown James H.
Brown John
Brown Noah
Brown Noah, Junr.
Brown Peter
Brown Stephen
Brown Tower
Bruce Robert
Bruster David
Buck Israel
Buck Israel, Junr
Buckhout John
Buel Samuel
Bugbe Samuel
Bugbee John
Buill John
Bullis Peter
Bun John
Bunschoten John
Burel Jesse
Burgh Jonathan
Burley Ebenezer
Burling
Burlinson Fearnot
Burlinson Joel
Burlsona Grover
Burns Edward
Burtis James
Bush Peter
Bush Tryertar
Butler Stephen
Byce Abraham
Byce John
Byington Nathaniel
Cable Platt
Cakbel Plat

Calkins Eli
Calkins John
Calkins Moses
Camberlin Thomas
Camble Daniel
Campbell James
Campbell Robert
Canfield Aaron
Canfield Amos
Canfield Titus
Canniff Levi
Carle John
Carlee Jonathan
Carpender Clark
Carson Samuel
Carter John
Carver Barnabes
Cash David
Casher William
Castle Daniel
Castle Lemuel
Chambers Thomas
Champanois Harman
Chandler Jonathan
Chapman Samuel
Chapman Stephen
Chapman Thomas
Charpanard Simon
Chase Elijah
Chase Gedaliah
Chase Richard
Chase Robert
Christman John
Church Medad
Churchill Edward
Clapp Joseph
Clark John
Clark Othaniel
Clason Wilber
Clawater Jacob
Clement Charles
Clement James
Close Caesar
Closson Wilber
Cocktel Timothy
Coe Samuel
Coenhoven William
Cohler Leonard

Cokler Leonard
Colbreath Thomas
Cole Abraham
Cole Joseph
Collard Abraham
Collins Solomon
Collins William
Colly Matthew
Colwell James
Cone Benjamin (colored)
Conel
Conklin Abraham
Conklin John
Conklin Matthew
Conklin Nathan
Conkling Jacob
Conly Charles
Conner Patrick
Conory John
Conroy John
Converse James
Cook Darius
Cook James
Cook Job
Cook John
Cook Simeon
Cooke Benjamin
Cooke Samuel
Cooper Cornelius
Cooper Garret
Cooper Jacob
Cooper Nicholas
Cornell James
Cornwell Clement
Cott John
Cowen Isaac
Craft Caleb
Craig Francis
Craw John
Crawford Nathan
Crompton John
Cronk Abraham
Crosby Lemuel
Crosby Samuel
Crouch David
Cuch Phillip
Cudbuth Benjamin
Cuff William
Cumfort Josiah
Cunnin John
Cunningham James
Cunningham John
Curry Charles
Cushman William
Dagaettjun Mayhugh
Dagget Mahu
Dannells Thomas
Daten Cornelius
Daton Cornbary
Daton Jonah
Daton Joseph
Davids William
Davies Nathan
Deal George
Dean John
Deboise Peter
Debuy Peter
Decker Reuben
Declark James
Decoine Edward
De Graff Moses
Degrove William
Delamatter Jacob
Demmon Samuel
Denemark Stoffel
Denham Samuel
Deniston John
Denney Charls
Denney Richard
Denton Isaac
Depue Abraham
De Pue Peter
Derue William
Deuce William
Devoe William
Dewit John
Dicker Ephraim
Diel Samuel
Dill John
Dimmick Samuel
Dimmick Shubell
Disbey Andrew
Disbrow Andrew
Dixson Thaddeus
Dodge Stephen
Dolf John
Dolloway Jeremiah
Douey Samuel
Dowling Andrew
Drake William
Dubois Cornelius
Dubois Jacob
Dubois Jacob J.
Duel Wilber
Dun Coenradt
Duncan John
Dunham Joseph
Dusenbery Charles
Dutcher Abraham
Dutcher Jacob
Dutcher John
Edinger Christopher
Elmondorph Samuel
Elseworth Philip
Esters Benjamin
Fairchild Amos
Fairchild Oliver
Fanbramer Peter
Farnell Danel
Ferguson John
Feriss John
Feriss Silvanus
Ferris Seth
Ferris William
Ferrell Daniel
Field Jesse
Field Nathan
Fields Thomas
Finch Amos
Finch Comfort
Finch Elithan
Finch Gilbert
Finch John
Finch Jonathan
Finch Philip
Finch Silvanus
Finch Syc.
Finchout Aurent
Finchout Cornelius
Finton Amos
Fish Joseph
Fish Levi
Fish Moses
Fish Pardon
Fish Seabury
Fisher Daniel
Fisher Daniel, Junr.
Fisher Jacob
Flagler David
Flagler John
Flanders James
Foot John
Foot Samuel
Forbosh Abraham
Forbus Samuel
Ford James
Forgeson John
Forster Joseph
Foster Thomas
Fowler Caleb
Fowler Caleb, Junr.
Fox Xenophon
Franklin Benjamin
Frantz Jacob
Frederick Charles
Fuller David
Furman Cato
Furman Samuel
Fyler Sensor
Gage Mark
Gale Samuel
Gambell Allexander
Ganong Marcus
Gardner David
Garret Benjamin
Garrett Isaack
Gatty John
Gaul Stephen
Gay Daniel
Geaty Robert
Gedawale Elisha
Gegory Rusel
Geray Allexander
Germain David
German James
Germond Peter
Gero Daniel
Gifford Elisha
Gifford Samuel
Gilcrease Thomas
Gildersleeve Joseph
Gillaspy George
Gillaspy James
Gillaspy William
Gillet Charles
Gillit Barnabas
Gootchins John
Gold Elijah
Golnack Michal
Goodrich Elisha
Gordon Cornelius
Gorum Jeams
Gould Elijah
Graham James
Graham Jonathan
Gray Jeduthun
Greek James
Green Caleb
Green Ezekiel
Green Henry
Green Joseph
Green Samuel
Green Tobias
Grefes Thomas
Gregory Joshua
Gregory Roswell
Griffin John
Griffen Joseph
Griffen Peter
Griffin Micheal
Grigeory R.
Guin Michel
Gulneck Michael
Haborn John
Hadley George
Hadley William
Haff Jacob
Haff John
Haight Samuel
Haight Samuel, Junr.
Haines Samuel
Hall John

Hallister Elisha
Hanna William
Hansen Jacob
Hardenburgh Derick
Harper Godfrey
Harris Joseph
Harris Squire
Harris William
Hase John
Havenner John
Hawkins James
Hawkins Samuel
Hawley Henry
Hobard Reuben
Heermana Andries
Heermana John
Heermance Andrew C.
Heermance Evens
Heermance Evert
Heermance John
Helmer John
Helmer Peter
Heltz Lawrence
Henry Robert
Hermans Simen
Herrick Jonathan
Herrington James
Herrington John
Hess Christian
Hess Christopher
Hibbard Reuben
Hicks Benjamin
Higgins Ebenezer
Higgins Joseph
Hill Isaac
Hill John
Hill William
Hiltz Laurence
Hinkley Elkanah
Hinman Zachariah
Hiser Martinus
Hitchis Benjamin
Hoffman Daniel
Hoffman Jacobus
Hoffman Nicholas
Hogaboom Bartholama
Hogan Edward
Hogan Path
Hogins Edward
Holems John
Holkins Samuel
Holley Henry
Holmes Elkanah
Holmes James
Holmes Joseph
Holmes Nathan
Hopkins Benjamin
Hopkins Fredrick
Horton David
Horton George
Horton Joseph
Horton Peleg
Horton Samuel
House John
How John
How Thomas
Howard Joseph
Howard Richard
Howel Frederick
Howel William
Howes John
Howes Thomas
Hoy William
Hoyt Abijah
Hoyt Enoch
Hubbard Ezekiel
Huffman Daniel
Hume William
Humfrey William
Humphreys James
Hunsdon John
Husted Peter
Hutchens Benjamin
Hutchons Absalom
Hutton John
Hyatt Eben
Hyatt Elias
Idare William
Ittig Coenradt
Ittig George
Jackson George
Jacobs Abraham
Jacobs Cornelius
Jakways Daniel
Jansen Benjamin
Jero Daniel
Jewel Ezekiel
Jewell George
Jewell Herman
Jewitt John
Johnson James
Johnson John
Johnson Josiah
Johnson Paul
Johnson Robert
Johnson Samuel
Johnson Thomas
Johnson Timothy
Johnston Robert
Jones Isaac
Jones Levi
Jones Ransom
Joslin Anthony
Julaf Zachariah
Keator Benjamin F.
Keator John
Keator William
Keeler Ezra
Kellee Jeremiah
Kelley Jonathan
Keltz Coenradt
Kenney Henery
Kern John
Kershaw John
Kesler Nicholas
Kickam Solomon
Kill Christopher
Killey Jaramiah
Kilpatrick Samuel
Kimmans John
Kip Abraham
Kip Abraham R.
Kip Aurent
Kip Igness
Kip John
Kip Petrus
Kip Racliph
Kirkun Solomon
Klyne Jacob
Knapp Jeremiah
Knapp Joel
Knapp Nathaniel
Knickebacker John
Knickebacker Lawrence
Kniffen John
Koch Andrew
Kohler Leonard
Kolb John
Kole Jacob P.
Kole Simon P.
Kool Abraham
Kool Elias
Kool Jacob
Kool Simon
Kremer John
Krum Peter
Ladue William
Lamb David
Lamb Johial
Lamberts Cornelius
Lane Joseph
Lane Thomas
Lane William
Langin Benjam
Lanphier John
Laquire Abraham
Larcy John
Larrey J.
Lason Joseph
Lasure Samuel
Lawrence Samuel
Learry John
Lee Jonathan
Legget William
Leonard Robert
Lepper Fredrick
Lesher Conradt
Levy Henderick
Lewis Hendrick
Lewis James
Lewis Lewis
Linderman Cornelius
Linnington Timothy
Little James
Lockard David
Locknut John
Lockwood Daniel
Lockwood David
Lockwood Ebenezer
Losee John
Losee John A.
Loux William
Loveless Elisha
Loveless Joshua
Lucas Israel
Luddington Elisha
Ludenton Elisha, Junr.
Luquer Abraham
Luther Eseek
Lyttle William
Machan Robart
Machoney James
Maffet John
Maffite John
Maher Levy
Marchant Abel
Markell Henry
Marshall William
Marshill Josiah
Marta David
Martin John
Martin Robert
Martin Roledt
Masten Ezekiel
Mayer Henry
Mayer John
Mayer Joseph
Maxsam Benjamin
Mead Ezekiel
Mead Isaiah
Mead Marshal
Meashurcall Cornelius
Melangdon Benjamin
Menoma John
Merrick Benjamin
Merriman Titus
Merrit Ebnezer
Merritt Luke
Mestan Ezekiel
Meyer Benjamin
Middagh Art
Middledough Aert

Miels Noah
Mildun Daniel
Miller Christyaun
Miller David
Miller Henderick
Miller John
Miller William
Mills James
Mills John
Mingo William
Minner James
Moe Abraham
Money Absolum
Monfoort Peter
Monfoort Peter, Junr.
Mongomire Elijah
Mooney Absalom
Moor Jacob
Moor Phillip
Moore John
Moore Martin
Mopes Fredrick
More Abraham
Morehouse Isaac
Morehouse Stephen
Morris Elijah
Morris John
Morris Peter
Mosier William
Mott William
Mouer Henderick
Moul Jacob, Junr.
Mount Andrew
Mountain Andrew
Mumford James
Munrow Justice
Murphy Thomas
Myer Abraham
Myer Benjamin
Myles Benajah
Myles John
McCabe Benjamin
McCoy Daniel
McCreary Robert
McCutchen Robert
McDonald Cornelius
McDonald John
McDonnals Thomas
McGuire Hugh
McKiel John
McKlennen Andrew
McKue James
McNight Robert
McNitt Alexander
McPherson Daniel
Nairn James
Neer Charles
Neer Jost
Neer Zacharies
Nelson Absolum
Nelson M.
Nelson Paul
Newcomb Daniel
Newcomb James
Newcomb Thomas
Newel Joseph
Newnon Zebulun
Nickerson Isachar
Nickerson Joshua
Nickerson Justia
Nogard John
Nooney Zebulon
Nootnagle Frederick
Northrop Stephen
Norton Peter
Nostragel Frederick
Oakley Cornelius
Odle Aaron
Ogden Richard
Olmsted Ebenezer
Onderdonk Garret
Onderdonk Thomas
Orchard John
Orim Robert
Orsor Nicholas
Osborn Peter
Ostrander Jacobus
Ostrom Gilbert
Otterson Andrew
Paine Ichabod, Junr.
Paine Samuel
Palmer Benjamin
Palmer James
Palmer Jesse
Palmer John
Palmer Joseph
Palmer Nicholas
Pangnut John
Pardoe Thomas
Pardy Samuel
Parish Daniel
Park Joseph
Parker Joseph
Parker Nathaniel
Parks Nathaniel
Parks Samuel
Parrish Azariah
Parrish Cypria
Parrish Daniel
Pattison Michael
Paul James
Paulding John
Pawling Henry
Peck Joseph
Pelham Elisha
Pellam Franses
Pellum Abijah
Penfold William
Penny John
Penoyer Amos
Perry James
Perry John
Perry Obadiah
Perry Samuel
Petcher Peter
Peters John
Pettit David
Phelps Abner
Phelps David
Phenton Amos
Phillips David
Phullick David
Pifer Adam
Pike Ezra
Pike Jarvis
Pike Jesse
Pine Thomas
Pink Jacob
Platt Caleb
Platt Eliphalet
Plymit Benoni
Polhemus Theodorus
Pollock William
Post Wilhalmis
Powell Abraham
Price Ebenezer
Pullock William
Punderson John
Purdy James
Purdy Jonathan
Purdy Josiah
Purdy Samuel
Purdy Stephen
Quackinbush Abraham
Randals Hugh
Ray Isaac
Ray Zachariah
Read David
Reanolds Jacob
Reed James
Reed Samuel
Reed Simon
Reguaw Abraham
Rema Jacob
Reynolds Abijah
Reynolds Benoni
Reynolds Caleb
Reynolds David
Reynolds Elias
Reynolds Ezra
Reynolds Joel
Reynolds Shubel
Rhaad Richard
Rhodes Richard
Rhyne Timothy
Riall Peter
Richard Moses
Richards Jacob
Richards Moses, Junr.
Richter Henderick
Rider Christopher
Rip Rulef
Robins Ebenezer
Robinson Ebenezer
Robison Ebenezer
Rockwil Enos
Roe Benjamin
Roe William
Rogers Platt
Rogers Reuben
Romer Henry
Romer James
Roola Jacob, Jr.
Roosa Aldert
Roosa John
Rose James
Rosekrans Thomas
Rosekrons John
Rowley Weeks
Rundle Abraham
Runnels Ezra
Runnels Joseph
Rusel James
Rycel Peter
Rysedorph George
Salkeld Isaac
Sammon Cornelius
Sauffield John
Sayers Benjamin
Schermerhorn Cornelius
Schofield Henry
Schofield Smith
Schoonmaker John
Schouten Cornelius
Schouten John
Schouten Simon
Schultz Abraham
Schutt Joseph
Schutt Stephen
Scott John
Scott Thomas
Scott William
Scryver Albartus
Scutt Abraham
Scutt Joseph
Scutt Stephen
Seacord Andrew
Seacraft William
Seaman Jacob
Seaman John
Seaman Willett
Sears Stephen

Sedore Isaac
See David
Seelee Lodwick
Seely James
Seely Sylvanus
Selvester John
Servine James
Servis John
Shampinway Hormay
Sharwood Abraham
Shavellar William
Shaw James
Shaw John
Shaw Joshua
Shay V.
Shea Lodowick
Shear Lodewick
Shearman William
Sherman William
Sherwood Isaac
Sherwood Lucam
Sherwood Samuel
Sherwood Thomas
Shidler John
Shoemaker Christopher
Shomper Horrima
Shorter John
Shults Jacob
Simma Willet
Simmons Aaron
Simons Insolo
Simons Willet
Simpkins Reuben
Simpson Andrew
Simpson John
Sinkin Reuben
Situtsell Michel
Slason Amos
Slason Ebenezer
Sleight Abraham
Slight Abraham, Junr.
Small Isaac
Small James
Smith Abraham
Smith Alpheous
Smith Asa
Smith Daniel
Smith Garret
Smith Isaac
Smith Israel
Smith James
Smith John
Smith Joseph
Smith Joshua
Smith Martin
Smith Michael
Smith Philip
Smith Samuel
Smith Stephen
Smith Thomas
Smith Zackerias
Sniffen Shubel
Sniffin James
Sniffin John
Snyder John
Sodon John
Somerndike Jacob
Sonamet Isaac
Soper Burtis
Southard John
Southard Richard
Spalding Oliver
Sparks Robert
Spencer John
Spicer Jeremiah
Springsteen James
Springsteen Samuel
Stagg John
Stanton William
Start Nathan
Stauts Peter
Stauts Philip
Stebbins Lewis
Steenberg Cornelius
Stephend Timothy
Stevens Edward
Stevens John
Stevens Peter
Steverson Frederick
Stewart Thomas
Stockam Reuben
Stokum Jonathan
Stokum William
Storm Abraham
Storms Closs
Stuart John
Sturdefant Jonathan
Sturdivent David
Surine James
Suthard John
Suthard Jonas
Suthard Richard
Sutherland Joseph
Sutherland Solomon
Swart Isaac
Swinnerton James
Talman Abraham
Talman Douwe
Tarbill Salvanus
Tater John
Tayler John
Taylor Oliver
Teller Oliver
Terpanning John
Terwilleger Abr'm
Terwilleger James Phenix
Terwilleger Matthew
Teunis John
Tharston Josiah
Thomas Beriah
Thomas John
Thomas Thomas
Thompson Caleb
Thompson Joel
Thompson Joseph
Thomson James, Junr.
Thomson James, Sr.
Thomson Richard
Thomson Samuel
Tobias John
Townsend Charles
Townsend James
Townsend Zephaniah
Trapp James
Travis William
Trim Ezra
Tul Henderick
Tunis Peter
Turner Alexander
Turner Stephen
Twitchell Benoni
Vail John
Varnel Daniel
Veal George
Veal John
Verber John
Vermillier David
Vermillier Isaac
Vermilya David
Vickrey Ichabod
Vom Brocklin James
Voorhis Jeromus
Vorchase Abraham
Vradenburgh Abraham
Vradenburgh Jacob
Vradenburgh William
Van Benthuysin Abraham
VanBomel Peter
Van Camp Isaac
Van Cleef Garret
Van Cock Boltis R.
Vandeburgh John
Vandemark Solomon
Vanderbilt Derick
Vanderdunch Garret
Vanderdunch Thomas
Vander Vort Garret
Vandewater Adolph
Van Dewater Herman
Vandewater Jacobus
Van Dewater Joseph
Van Etten Jacobus
Vanflacken Alxander
Van Houten Abraham
Van Houten John
Van Houten John R.
Van Keuren Matthew
Van Kleek Baltus
Van North John
Vanocker Peter
Van Orden Andrew
Van Orden Henry
Vanosdol James
Vanscoy Abel
Van Scoy Henry
Vansickle Peter
Van Steenbergh Cornelius
Van Steenbergh Gradus
Vantasel Benjamin
Van Tassel Cornelius
Van Tassel Isaac
Van Tassel John
Van Tassel Stephen
Van Vleckren Abraham
Van Voorhis Abraham
Van Voorhis Daniel
Vanvoorhis Henry
Van Voorhis Jeromus
Van Vradenburgh Petrus
Van Wagenen Barrant
Van Wagenen Garret
Van Wart Garret
Van Wart William
Vanwort Benjamin
Van Wyck John
Van Wyck John B.
Van Wyck Theodorus
Wade Morris
Waggoner George
Waisemillar Hendrick
Walalter Benjamin
Walbridge Elijah
Waldorph Hendrick
Waldradt Adolph
Walron Simeon
Walsh Samuel
Ward Israel
Ward Joshua
Waren Theodorus
Warman Phinas
Waring Michael
Warters Benjamin
Wasfallo Gilbart
Waters Cornelius
Waters Isaac
Way Frederick
Way John
Weaver Adam
Weaver George
Weaver George M.
Weaver Jacob
Webb David

Webber Oliver
Webber William
Webbers Isaac
Weed Gideon
Weed Jonathan
Weeks Nathaniel
Welch David
Westervalt George
Wes'fall Abraham
Westfall Benjamin
Westfall Gilbert (see Gilbert)
Westfall Levi
Wheaton Benjamin
Wheaton Isaac
Wheeler Ezra
Whily Matthew
Whitaker Abraham
Whitcom Simon
White John
White Nathaniel
Whitney Ezekel
Wickes Silas
Wickham Benjamin
Wickham Benjamin, Junr.
Wickham Daniel
Wickson Ebenezer
Wilbert John
Wilcox Isaac
Wilde Bartholomew
Wile Nathan
Wilkinson John
Wilkison Thomas
Willcox Aaron
Williams David
Williams Stephen
Williams Thomas
Williams Warren
Williamson Nicholas
Willson Amos
Wilson Andrew
Wilson John
Wiltse Cornelius
Wiltse William
Wiltsee Matthew
Winans Silas
Winegar Henry
Winslow Samuel
Winston Joseph
Winter Moses
Withbeck Harmon
Wolson Simeon
Wood Henry
Wood Jesse
Wood John
Wood Samuel
Wood Solomon
Wood Thomas
Woods Eli
Woods Jotham
Woolsey Nathan
Word Israel
Workman Phineas
Worth Richard
Wright Joseph
Yarns Nathan
Yeomans Jonas
Yerks Aaron
Young Abraham
Young Benjamin
Young Elkanah
Young Garret
Young John
Young John Christian
Young Jonas
Young Robert
Young Thomas
Youngs John

Dutchess County Militia — (Continued).

COLONEL HENRY LUDENTON
LIEUTENANT COLONEL REUBEN FERRIS
MAJOR EBENEZER ROBINSON
MAJOR —— WYCKOFF
ADJUTANT ELIJAH TOWNSEND
QUARTER MASTER ELEZER BAKER

CAPT. EDMUND BAKER
" NOAH BOUTON
" —— CALKEN
" JOHN CRANE
" —— DUSENBURY
" —— HAIGHT
" ALEXANDER KIDD
" ISRAEL KNAPP
" GEORGE LANE
" DAVID MARICK
" HEZEKIAH MEAD
" JOEL MEAD
" —— MORTON
" JOSHUA MYRICK
" —— PIERCE
" RICHARD SACKETT
" NATHANIEL SCRIBNER
" —— WARD
" DAVID WATERBURY
" —— WINNE
LIEUT. JONAS AUSER
" JOHN BERRY
LIEUT. CHARLES CULLIN
" TIMOTHY DELEVAN
" —— ELLIOTT
" ELLIJAH FULLER
" JOSIAH GREGORY
" SOLOMON HOPKINS
" DAVID PORTER
" JOHN ROBINSON
" THOMAS RUSSEL
" ELLIAH SEARS
" DAVID SMITH
" ISAAC TOWNSEND
" ISRAEL VAIL
" ABRAM VAN WERT
" DANIL WILLEE
ENSIGN JOSIAH BAKER
" WILLIAM CALKIN
" JAMES EGELSTON
" JOSEPH GREGORY
" CALEB HAZEN
" JACOB MEAD

ADDITIONAL NAMES ON STATE'S TREASURER'S PAY BOOKS.

QUARTER MASTER THOMAS LEWIS

LIEUT. JOHN DRAKE
" JOHN HALL
" JOHN MCLEAN
LIEUT. JOSEPH PERRY
" HENRY WILTSE
ENSIGN ZEBEDEE KELLY

ENLISTED MEN.

Acker Abram
Adams Gilbert
Adams John
Adams William
Addems John
Addems Major
Addems Thomas
Adriance George
Aliet Elijah J.
Angevine Joseph
Anim Azra
Armstrong Gabriel
Armstrong Jacob
Armstrong Jacob, Junr.
Armstrong John
Arnold Peleg
Arnold Seymour
Astin Joab
Astin John
Astin Smith
Astin Robert
Auser Abram
Austin Job
Austin Robert
Austin Smith
Auston John
Baker Joshua
Baker Stephen
Baldwin Elisha
Baldwin Henry
Baldwin James
Baley Elias
Ballard Caleb
Ballard Peleg
Ballard Tracy
Baly Joseph
Banker Nicolas
Barber Samuel
Barber Stephen
Barger Peter
Barit John
Barret Isaac, Junr.
Barret Samuel
Barret William

Barrett Isaac
Barrett Justus
Barton Andrew
Barton Elisha
Barton Gilbert
Bartow Andrus
Basby Oliver
Baset Edmund
Bashford James
Bayley Peleg
Begal Stephen
Benjamin Darius
Benjamin Elijah
Bemy Samuel
Bennet Isiah
Berry Jabez
Berry Jabez, Junr.
Berry Samuel
Beyea Isaac
Bice John
Binton Samuel
Birdsall John
Bisbey Oliver
Blackman Ephraim
Bolding Elisha
Bolding Henry
Bolding James
Bonker Jacob
Bostwick John
Boughten Samuel
[illegible] Isaac
Brewer Henderick
Brooks William
Brown Cornelius
Brown Deliverance
Brown Ebenezer
Brown Josiah
Bruce Robert
Brundage Jeremiah
Brundage John
Bruster John
Bruster Samuel
Buckbee Sylvester
Buckhout John
Buckley Jabez
Bugbee Ezekiel
Bugbee Silvester
Bulkley Jabez
Burdick Amos
Burdick Caleb
Byinton Samuel
Byinton Solomon
Calwell James
Calwell William
Cambell James
Carey John
Carle Jonas
Carley John

Carly Abert
Carver Barnabas
Carver Timothy
Caton Isaac
Caytom Isaac
Certain James
Chadwick Comfort
Charlick Henry
Chase Jabez
Chase John
Chase Judah
Chase Obadiah
Chase Robert
Christian Charles
Christian George
Christian John
Christian Richard, Junr.
Christian Ritchard
Christian William
Clason William
Closson William
Colberth Thomas
Colberth Thomas G.
Cole Daniel
Cole Ebenezer
Cole Elisha
Cole Elisha, Junr.
Cole Joseph
Cole Reuben
Colly John
Colwell Joseph
Conklin Nathan
Conklin Samuel
Cornelius Ever
Cornwell Daniel
Covart Silvenus
Covey Walter
Cowen Isaac
Cowin David
Crab John
Craft Caleb
Craft Charles
Crane Samuel
Crosby Enoch
Crosby Solomon
Crosby Thody
Culbreth Thomas
Cushman Consider
Daily Lawrence
Dakin Elisha
Dakin Johnson
Dan Thadus
Daniels James
Dann William
Davis Albert
Davis John
Davis Samuel
Davis William

Dean Benjamin
Dean Caleb
Dean Ezekiel
Dean John
Dean Joseph
Delanay Abram
Delevan Timothy, Junr.
Delivan Abraham
Demerce David
Deusenberry Moses
Deusenbery William
Deyenbeg Jarvis
Dian Joseph
Dickson James
Dickson Theodorous
Dimmick Shubel
Dinjah Elijah
Disbrow Andrew
Disbrow David
Disbrow Nathan
Disbrow Nathan, Junr.
Dixson James
Domnee David
Doten William
Downer Israel
Drake John
Drew Gilbert
Drew Isaac
Drew Samuel
Drow William
Dusenbury Charles
Dusenbury Jarvis
Dutcher Abram
Dutcher Jacob
Dykeman Hezekiah
Eakly Benjamin
Edy Joshua
Egelston James
Ellwell Jabez
Elsworth John
Evans Samuel
Evens Thomas
Everitt George
Everitt Isaac
Ferguson John
Ferguson Thomas
Ferris Ezra
Ferris Jonathan
Finch Jonathan
Finch Nathaniel
Finch Reuben
Finch Silvanus
Finiche Reuben
Fish Nathan
Fisher Nathaniel
Forgason John
Forgason Thomis, Junr.
Forman Joseph

Fostor David
Frost David
Fuller David
Fuller Isaac
Fuller Robert
Furman Joseph
Furman Samuel
Gage Ebenezer
Gage Moses
Gage Nathaniel
Ganog Markus
Ganong Isaac
Ganong John
Ganoung Jacob
Ganung Reuben
Gaul Stephen
Gifford Elisha
Gifford Samuel
Golding Amoss
Goodfellow William
Gorney John
Green Thomas
Gregory Daniel
Gregory Ezra
Gregory Joshua
Gregory Rusel
Gregory Samuel
Gregory Thomas
Gregory Timothy
Griffet Lazarus
Griffeth Wiliam
Griffith Joshua
Hadley Moses
Hadley William
Hadley William, Junr.
Hager Robert
Hager Thomas
Haight Samuel
Hall
Hall Elisha
Hall John
Hall Thomas
Hambler Benjamin
Hankkey Richard
Harris William
Hasen Aron
Haul Elisha
Hawkins James
Hawkins Joseph
Hawkins Samuel
Hays William
Hazelton David
Hazen Caleb
Hazen Eleazer
Hazen Moses
Heazeltine David
Heazelton Daniel
Hedger Joseph

Heger Robert
Higgins Ebenezer
Hill Thomas
Hill William
Holley Daniel
Holmes David
Holmes Joseph
Hopkins Ely
Hopkins Isaiah
Hopkins Jeremiah
Hopkins Jonathan
Hopkins Jonathan, Junr.
Hopkins Joseph
Hopkins Thatcher
Hopkins Thomas
Horten Thomas
Horton Thomas, Junr.
How Jesse
How John
Howes Daniel
Howes Job
Howes Moodey, Junr.
Hughson Jeremiah
Hunt Jesse
Huson Aron
Huson Robert
Hyatt Alvan
Hyatt Elias
Hyatt Minan
Hyatt Sminah
Hyatt Stephen
Jean John
Jedd Jonathan
Jenkins Nathaniel
Jenkins Samuel
Jenkins Solomon
Johnston Thomas
Jones Amos
Jones Ananias
Jones Nehemiah
Jones William
June Ezra
Kane John
Keiff Andrew
Keley Jonathan A.
Kelley John
Kelley Judah
Kelley Silvanus
Kerley Albert
Kickem Solomon
Killey John
Killey Judah
Killey Silvenus
Killey Zebedee
King Barzilla
King Bazley
King David
King Heman
King Homan, Junr.
King Obadiah
King Stephen
Kircum Solomon
Knap Gabriel
Knapp Benjamin
Knapp Dannel
Kniffen Amos
Kniffen Samuel
Knott Nathaniel
Lake Stephen
Lambert Cornelius
Lane Nathan
Langdon Benjamin
Lasher Samuel
Lawdue Ambres
Leddoo Ambros
Leonard Robert
Light Henry
Lockwood Ebenezer
Lockwood Peter
Lorens Isaac
Loveless William
Ludinton Comfort
Lupuye John
Maybee Peter
MacIntyre Jaims
Maconth Arlen
Mahoon James
Maibe Tobias
Maker Solomon
Mane Sebeus
Maner Salvus
Marchous Elijah
Marick Isaac
Martine James
Martine Samuel
Mason Jerred
Mazer Abraham
Mead Abner
Mead Bille
Mead Eli
Mead Isaac
Mead James
Mead Moses
Merick John
Merrick Isaac
Merrick Seth
Miller Ebenetus
Millerd Solomon
Mills Titus
Moes William
More William
Moris Eliga
Morse William
Morten Samuel
Myrick John
Myrick Seth
McCabe Benjamin
McCale Benjamin
McCormick Maxel
McFadden James
McLean John
McShosen Peter
McTassel Peter
Nelson Absalom
Nelson Elijah
Newman Jeremiah
Newman Joseph
Nickerson Aron
Nickerson Issachar
Nickerson Thomas
Nickerson Uriah
Norris Ezra
Nott Nathanael
Oakley Robert
Oakley Timothy
Odal John
Odall Amors
Odel Amos
Odell Isaac
Odell John
Odle Isaac
Ogden Benjamin
Osborn Denvis
Owens Jesse
Paddock David
Paddock Judah
Paddock Peter
Paddock Seth
Paddock Stephen
Parce Daniel
Park John
Parrish Daniel
Parrish Silas
Parse Daniel
Paulding John
Peace Isaac
Pearce Isaac
Pell Philip
Pelton Phillip
Perse Isaac
Petton Philip
Pinfold William
Pinkney Frederick
Pinkney Isariel
Pinkney Jonathan
Pinkney Luis
Piper Isaac
Platt John
Platt Richard
Porter David
Post Hennery
Price Ebenezer
Price James
Purday James
Ransier George
Raymond Eben
Raymond Ebenezar
Raymond Thadeus
Raynolds Moses
Read Jacob
Reed Fredrick
Reed John
Reed Samuel
Requa James
Requa James, Junr.
Requa Joseph
Rewel James
Rhead Jacob
Rhoad Richard
Rhoades Isaac
Rhoads Isaac, Junr.
Rhodes John
Rhodes Richard
Rice Edward
Rice Samuel
Richards David
Richards Ezra
Richards Moses
Richards Thomas
Rider John
Rill Samuel
Robenson Asakar
Roberts Peter
Robinson Issachar
Robinson Peter
Rods John
Roe William
Romer Henry
Rorcom Solomon
Runald Moses
Russel James
Russel Robert
Russel John
Rush John
Sackett John
Sackett Solomon
Sampson George
Sarne Jolel
Scofield Ezre
Scribner Nathaniel
Scutt Peter
Sears Willard
Shaddick Comfor
Shadrik Comfort
Sharpenard Simon
Shaw
Shaw Joshua
Sherwood William
Simkins John
Simkins John, Junr.
Simkins Robard
Simkins Robert

Simmons Jonathan
Simons Aron
Simpkins John
Sirrine Isaac
Sloot Isaac
Sloot John
Slut Isaac
Slut John
Small James
Small James, Junr.
Smally James
Smally Zachariah
Smith Abraham
Smith Asa
Smith Bennajah
Smith David
Smith Edward
Smith Elisha
Smith Gideon
Smith Gilbert
Smith James
Smith Jeremiah
Smith Jesse
Smith John
Smith Nehemiah
Smith Phillip
Smith Richard
Smith Samuel
Smith Seth
Smith Solomon
Smith Thomas
Sniffen Sam, Junr.
Sniffin Amos
Soddore Frederick
Soddore Isaac
Sorine Charles
Sorine Israel
Sprage Elijah
Sprage Jaben
Sprage John
Spraguo Jeremiah
Spreg Jeremiah
Stats John
Steward George
Stirdevent Richard
Storm James
Swift Isaiah
Tannors John
Taylor Daniel
Terry Samuel
Tiler Ezekial
Tomkins Cornelius
Tomkins Cornelius, Junr.
Tomkins James
Tomkins Jeremiah
Tomkins Stephen
Tounesend Levi
Townsend Amos
Townsend Charles
Townsend Charles, Junr.
Townsend Daniel
Townsend Daniel 3d
Townsend Eber
Townsend Isaac
Townsend James
Townsend John
Townsend Zephaniah
Travis George
Travis James
Travis Titus
Travis William
Tucker Samuel
Turner Elisha
Turner John
Turner Nathan
Turner Stephen
Utter William
Vail John
Veal John
Vermilyea John
Vermilya William
Vanpett Henry
Vanpett John
VanScoy Abel
Van Scoy Jacob
Van Wert William
Walter Daniel
Ward Finnes
Waring Thaddeus
Waterbury David
Waterbury Enos
Weeks Jonathan
Weeks Stephen
Whaley James
White Stephen
Willcox Stephen
Williams Ichabod
Williams Thomas
Wilsie Daniel
Wilson Daniel
Wilson Thomas
Wiman Jeduthan
Wixsom Daniel
Wixsom John
Wood Israel
Wood John
Wooden John
Wright William
Wright Zebulon
Yarnes Nathan
Young John

Dutchess County Militia — (Continued).

ASSOCIATED EXEMPTS.

COLONEL ZEPHANIAH PLATT

LIEUTENANT COLONEL RUFUS HERRICK

MAJOR ABRAHAM SCHENCK

ADJUTANT WILLIAM SMITH (also Major of Brigade)

QUARTER MASTER JACOBUS SLEGHT

CAPT. ANDREW BILLINGS
" ISAAC BLOOM
" JOHN BRODHEAD
" MOSES JONES
" ROGER KINNE
" THOMAS LEE
" ABRAHAM SWARTWOUT
" ——— VAN DUSEN
" CORNELIUS VAN SANTVOORDT
LIEUT. DAVID BALDWIN
LIEUT. WILLIAM BOERUM
" PETER A. FONDA
" GARARDUS HARDENBROOK, JR.
" JAMES HUGHY
" ELIHU MARSHALL
" DANIEL RAPALJE
" OAK SUIDAM
ENSIGN THOMAS COLE
" ASHAEL TAQUA (JAQUA)

ENLISTED MEN.

Abby Samuel
Alesbury Nathaniel
Alloon Christian
Anderson George
Archabald John
Austin David
Avery Abel
Avez Abel
Baker Joseph
Baker Phineas
Bakman John J.
Barns Richard
Baroon Anthony
Beckman John J.
Bedford John
Bedford Jonas
Beekman John J.
Bender John
Benjamin Cyrus
Benjamin Ebenezer
Benjamins Ebenezer, Junr.
Benner Frederick
Bigraft Thomas
Black John
Blain James
Blaw James
Blaw John
Blom Jonas
Boerum William
Bogardus Peter
Bogardus Peter C.
Bogart Hendricus
Bonstil Philip
Brewer Garrete
Brewer Jeremiah
Brinck Hendricus
Brink John J.
Brooks Reuben
Brown John
Brush Ebenezer
Burhans Cornelius
Caktz Ebenezer
Cambell Daniel
Cambell Thomas
Cannada James
Carman John
Carter Ebenezer
Carther Alexander
Casey Willett
Casey William
Chamberlin Judah
Chase Jabez
Chooper James
Chotper James
Coles Benjamin
Cook Simeon
Cool William
Cooper James
Crispel Anthony
Degrote Isaac
Degrote Peter
Deming John
Dennison Alexander
Dennison James
Devenport Gerrit
Devin Oliver
Devo John
Devol John
Drew Elijah
DuBois Cornelius
Dunkan John
Edmonds Samuel
Edmonds Samuel, Junr.
Elliott Christopher
Every Abel
Fowler William
Fran Elias
Frans Wilhelmus
Fredenbergh Matthew
Freeman Robert
Gallow John
Galridge Michael
Gibson William
Glean Anthony
Gollow John
Goodgoin William
Goodrich Michael
Gott Story, Junr.
Gregg William
Grigs Jeremiah
Hagaman Joseph
Hagg John
Hanmer Robert
Harins George
Harsin George
Harwood John
Harwood Thomas
Henderson Thomas
Henrey Jesse
Herrick Joseph
Herrick Stephen
Heward Edward
Hochstrasser Jacob, Junr.
Hodge Isaac
Holmes Joseph
Howard Edward
Hume William
Jackson Lemon
Jackson Richard
Jaicocks Frances
Janson Johannis J.
Jennis Samuel
Johns Abraham
Johnson John
Jones John
Jones Steven
Keator Jacob T.
Kimbouk Fradrik
Kinne Jesse
Konstable John
Kortright Abraham
Krom Dirck
Lae Joseph
Lane Joseph

Lawrance Andrew T.
Lee Jonathan
Lee Joseph
Lee William
Leran John
Lockwood Amos
Loe William
Loop Christopher
Lorensay Nathan
Lovejoy Mathew
Lovejoy Nathaniel
Lovett John
Lutts John
Magee Samuel
Mance Christopher
Masten Daniel
Masters Danniel
May Daniel
Meggey Samuel
Ments Christopher
Merritt John
Mertz Christopher
Mufflin James
Muller John
Myers Michal
McClees Peter
McGough James
McNeal John
Nap Jonathan
Nellson Francis
Nellson Reuben
Newkerk Myndert
Newkirk Adam
Nollister Benjamin
Nottingham Stephen
Nukerck Hendrick
Null John
Odell James
Osterout Peter
Patterson Michael
Pattison Michael, Junr.
Peny David
Perkins Zophar
Plought William Helimus
Preston Othniel
Price Robert
Ramsey James
Ransom Joseph
Reed John
Rhine Richard
Ribbons David
Right Soloman
Robbins David
Roosa Peter
Rosekrans Zacharius
Row Michael
Rowland Robert
Rumsey James
Ryndert John
Saxton Noble
Schenk Peter A.
Schneyder George
Schoonmaker Samuel
Sckenk Peter
Seely Samuel
Sickner Albartus
Simmons Joseph
Sipher William
Smalley Reuben
Smart
Smart George
Smith Daniel
Smith Daniel, Junr.
Smith Joseph
Smith Nehemiah
Smith William
Snyder Andrew
Snyder Christopher
Spallow John
Spotty William
Stauts Peter
Stephus Matthew
Steymets William
St. John Samuel
Tappen John
Taylor Joseph
Teers Jacob
Terry Omer
Terry William
Tilson Peleg
Titus James
Tompkins Abraham
Townsend Amas
Trimble John
Tyce Joseph K.
Valentine Joseph
Vredenburgh Matthew
Van De Bogert Myndert
Van Deusen John
Van Dusen Matthew
Van Duzer Isaac
Van Hoevenbergh Henry
Van Keuren Tjerck
Van Kleek James
Vantine John
Van Wagenen Benjamin
Van Wagenen Jacob
Van Wagenen Petrus
Van Waggoner Daniel
Waldrom William
Wallace James
Warner Richard
Warren Stephen
Way Thomas
Weaver Edward
Weaver Henry
White Peter
Wickham Jonathan
Wickhams J.
Wide Benjamin
Williams Ebenezer
Wines Jeremiah
Winfield Isaac
Woodward Ephram
Yeomans Francis

Dutchess County Militia — (Continued).

ASSOCIATED EXEMPTS.

CAPTAIN ABRAHAM SCHENCK

ENLISTED MEN.

Allen John
Brett George
Brisby James
Brooks Reuben
Byvanck William
Carpenter Increase
Chamberlain John
Cole Isaac
Compton Obadiah
Conckline Lemuel
Conner Hugh
Cooper James
Dates Peter
Dodge Samuel
Doughty David
Gantz Francis
Gilstone John
Harsin George
Hatting Robert
Hendrickson Stephen
Lawrence Andrew
Lawrence Augustine
Lawrence John
Lefferts Isaac
Livingston Gilbert
Mott Henry
McBane John
Nerveelen Gideon
Newcombe Daniel
Newcombe Zacheus
Peck George
Robinson Thomas
Spranger Charles
Titus Zebulon
Weeks James
Williams John

Dutchess County Militia — (Continued).

REGIMENT OF MINUTE MEN.

COLONEL JACOBUS SWARTWOUT

CAPT. STEPHEN DURYEE
" HENRY GOODWIN
" GEORGE LANE
" COMFORT LUDINGTON
" WILLIAM MOTT
" WILLIAM PERCE
" ABRAHAM SCHENCK
" BERNARDUS SWARTWOUT
" ISRAEL VEAL
" CORNELIUS VAN WYCK
LIEUT. HENRY BAILEY
" JOHN BERRY
" NATHANIEL BUTLER
" WILLIAM COLKIN
" JONATHAN CRANE
LIEUT. BENJAMIN ELLIOT
" JOSEPH GARRISON
" ABRAHAM HIAT
" JACOB HORTON
" JOHN LANGDON
" ANDREW LAWRANCE
" JOHN MANROW
" HENRY MOTT
" THOMAS OSTRANDER
" CHARLES PLATT
" NATHANIEL SMITH
" ISAAC TOWNSEND
" PETER VAN BUNSCHOTEN
" JOHN T. VAN KLEAK

ENLISTED MEN.

Adoms Jesse
Adreanse Thead
Akerby Benjamin
Allen Jorge
Anderson ———eth
Appleyee Coonraad
Ashbe Zebulon
Askin William
Aslen Abm.
Aubley William
Badcock ———eph
Bailey Daniel
Bailey Ebenezer
Bailey Elias
Bakor Eleazer
Baker Elisha
Baker Joshua
Baker Francis
Ball Elephalet
Barker Richard
Barkins —avid
Barnes Henry
Barnhard ———
Barns Will
Barse Zebulen
Bartley ———hall Pels
Baxter Thomas
Bell Henry
Bennet Elihu
Benny John
Bently Joseph
Berger Andrew
Berry ———
Beugus Thomas
Billings John
Birdall Jacob
Bishop Joshua
Bishop Livy
Boga——— Peter
Bogardus Lewis
Bolt Moses
Bonker Dolf
Boyd ———mes
Boyington Solomon
Bozworth Hezekiah
Bradley Nathan
Branah James
Brill Jacob, Jr.
Brinckerhoff Hen
Brisbend James
Brock William
Brower Charles
Brower Hindrick
Brower Lazareth
Brower Rodolphus
Brown Stephen
Brumsfield James
Brustead William
Bunschout Elias C.
Burbanks Noah
Burch David
Burch Jeremiah
Burch Silas
Burdsill Jacob
Burges, Thomos
Burlonon Fearnot
Burnet Isaac
Burnett Peter
Byington Solomon
Camfield James
Carl Joseph
Carman ———
Carman John
Champenois Daniel
Champlin ———
Champlin Joshua, Jr.
Chapman Enoch
Chapman Samuel
Chase Seth
Christian Zechariah
Christie John
Clapp Benjamin
Clark Joshua
Clark Stephen
Cole Andrew
Colkens Eli
Conner John
Cornell Samuel
Cornwell Sylvenus
Corsa Abrah
Corsa Isaac
Courtright John
Craft Caleb
Crane Ira
Croft Jacob
Crowfoot William
Crumwell Aac
Currer Elijah
Curtis Andrew
Dart Hozell
Davids John
Davis David
Davison James
Davison John
Dean Stephen
Degrote John
Dervoort Sam L.
Dimmick Shubal
Disbrow David
Dodge Will
Dollaway Jerem
Dollaway William
Downen Cornelius
Doxey Amos
Draper John
Draper Joseph
Drew William
Dunekin John
Dutcher David
Edams Joseah

Ede Joshua
Edget John
Egelston James
Elderkin James
Eldige Jonathan
Eldridge Elisha
Eldridge Michael
Ellembatz Eman'l
Elliott Abn.
Elwell Ezra
Elwell Jabes, Jr.
Emegh Jeremiah
Evens John
Evens Thomas
Fairchild Nathaniel
Fetch Jerry
Fileow Enoch
Fileow Phineas
Finch Ruben
Force Timothy
Forgason Abram
Forguson Samuel
Foster David
Foster John
Foster Thomas
Fowler Austin
Fowler Isaac
Frear —raham, Jr.
Frear Thomas
Frost Thomas, Jr.
Frost William
Fuller Isaac
Fullmore Jasper
Garrison Abraham
Gedeons Joseph
Gee John
Gielwack, Michel
Gifford Samuel
Gifford William
Goldin Rob
Goodfellow Will
Griffen Isaac
Griffen William
Grigory Daniel
Grigory Josiah
Halsted Thomas
Halsted Will
Harris Peter
Harriss Mendt
Hawkins James
Hawkins Samuel
Hayburn John
Heacock John
Hempstead Nathaniel
Henkly Josiah
Hervy Peter
Heuckly Isaac
Hicks Jacob
Hicks Nathaniel
Higbee William
Hill Antiney
Hill —bert
Hitchcock Joseph
Hoeg Nathan
Hoff Abraham
Hoffman Charles
Hopkins Thacher
Howe William
Howes Moody
Hoyt Michael
Hubbard Joseph
Huff Gamaliel
Huling Walter
Hunt Jessee
Hunt William
Hutchings John
Hyott Steve
Ingersol —pheus
Jewet John
Johnson James
Johnson Sabin
Jones Jeremiah
Jones —lias
Jones Nathan
Jorden John
Judd Ebenezer
Keating Isaac
Keeler Ezra, Jr.
Kelly Shubel
King Jacob
King Richard
Kipp Henry
Kipp Matthew
Kipp Peter
Kirkem Seth
Koonts Nicholas, Jr.
Kniffin Amos
Laine Jacob
Lake Benjamin
Lamb Joseph
Lane
Latson James, Jr.
Laughlin Hugh
Lawrance John
Lawson Isaac
Leggett Abraham
Lent Ab'm
Lent Abraham A.
Lent James
Lent Peter
Lewis Thomas
Lossen And
Lossen Richard
Lossing Peter Q.
Loveless Joseph
Ludington Stephen
Lyons James
Malties ——m'l
Manrow Justice
Maston Ezekiel
Mathews Justice
Merrick Done
Merritt David
Miles John
Miles Noah
Miller Godfrey
Miller John
Miller Solomon
Mitchell George
Moe Isaac
Morehouse John
Morehouse Samuel
Morehouse Stephen
Morey Lotrip
Morfort Peter
Morgain James
Morgan Reuben
Morison —bald
Morse Phil
Moure David
Murray James
McCavy Edward
McChucking Thomas
McColm ——mes
McCreedy James, Jr.
McCullough And
McCutchen Rob
McGragor —union
McLoud Alexander
McNeil ——ry
Nelson Paul
Nichels Epraim
Nickerson Eliphalet
Nickerson Mulfort
Nicolls Thomas
Nikeson Thomas
Noortshant Peter
Noortstrant George
Nostrant Johanes
Outs James
Ockerman Casparus
Olmstead Ebenezer
Ornes George
Osborn Peter
Ouslin Thom
Parker Nathaniel
Parks Andrew
Parks John
Parks John ye 2^d
Parrash Azariah
Peacock
Peet Abraham
Pelse ——hn
Pelse ——oen
Perce William, Jr.
Persons Moses
Philipse Hen
Pindle Jonathan
Plugh —lhamus
Point
Polhamus ——dan
Polmeteer Peter
Pooler Joseph
Post Absolom
Potter Gilbert
Potter Samuel
Pudney Francis
Purdy Abraham
Rainey John
Recorde Wetmore
Reed Aaron
Reed —ohn
Reynolds ——hardson
Reynolds Jesse
Rhynhart Johanes
Richards James
Robbards Benjamin
Roberts Peter
Robinson Andrew
Robinson John
Robinson Jones
Robinson Lewis
Robison Andrew
Roe Benjamin, Jr.
Romer ———, Jr.
Romyne ———as
Roschrans Peter
Runals David
Runells James
Runnells Jonathan
Rush Fredrick
Rynders James
Sabin Elijah
Saminds Jacob
Sarls Nathaniel
Saunders John
Schonover Peter
Schonter Andrew
Scott Timothy
Serhorve John
Shapprong Jan
Shared William
Shaw Daniel
Shaw James
Shear Henry B.
Shear Lodwich
Sherwood Nathan
Shutt Fradrick
Shutt Simes
Sickle Fard C.
Sickler George
Simkins Daniel

Slack ——ile
Slecht Ab
Smallee James
Smith David
Smith Eph
Smith John
Smith John, Jr.
Smith Joseph, Jr.
Smith Joshua
Smith Nemiah
Smith Samson
Smith William
Snedeker James
Snedeker John
Snider Isaac
Snyder ——hn
Soatpard Benjamin
Somes Nathaniel
Storm Jacob
Strickland Samuel
Surrine Charles
Swartout Jacobus C.
Swartwout Cornelius
Sweet John
Sweet Robert
Talmen ——kim
Tanner John
Taylor Gamiliel
Taylor John
Ter Boss Simon
Terbus Peter
Teunis John
Thomas Daniel
Thompson Thomas
Thorn ——horn
Totten ——mes
Townend Joseph
Townsend Daniel
Townsend James
Travis Abrm.
Travis Silvanus
Tripp Othenial
Underwood Hen
Utter Amos
Varmiliah John
Vasdawl Disak
Virmilyan William
Van Cleck Bardard P.
Van De Burg ———
Van Deburgh Henry I.
Van De Burgh Stephen
Van Der Bogert Peter
Van Der Vort Paul
Van Devaters Jacobus
Van Devaters James
Van Stern Bergh Simeon
Van Tassel John
Van Vlorken Benjamin
Van Wagenar John
Wagoner Tobias
Wait Christopher
Ward Daniel
Ward Samuel
Warcing Thadeus
Waron Tedes
Way Giddeon
Weaver Edward
Weaver Peter
Weaver William
Webb Henry
Weddle Robert
Weeks Abraham
Weeks Micajah
Western John
Westervelt Benjamin
Westervett Caspauras C
White Daniel
Whitney Josiah
Wickson Solomon
Wilis Reuben
Willcocks Stephen
Willcox Barnabas
Willis Thomas
Williss Hen
Wilsee Grandus
Winstead Charles
Wood ——eph
Wood Solomon
Wood Timothy
Woodard Ephraim
Woodard Samuel
Woodon John
Worden Shuble
Woster William
Wright Daniel
Wright Gabriel, Jr.
Wright John
Wright Thomas
Yarnes Reuben
Yeomans John
Yeomans Jonas
Young Jacob

Dutchess County Militia — (Continued).

COOPER'S RANGERS.

CAPT. EZEKIEL COOPER
LIEUT. JASPER FULMORE
LIEUT. MARTIN RAY

ENLISTED MEN

Ammerman Dirick
Baily John
Bakehorn Jacob
Bogg John
Boyce Hendrick
Boyce James
Bunt Lodewick
Clink Frederick
Cooper James
Curry Samuel
Darling John
Davison John
Delong Jonas
Depew Abraham
Depew Peter
Doty Jacob
Ferguson James
Ferguson Jeromiah
Frayer Thomas
Hart James
Hicks Jacob
Hinckom Eliga
Honse Tunis
Horton Matthias
Hurly James
Jackson Hyland
Jackson James
Jackson Robert
Kinscom Elisha
Knifer Jacob
Lemon John
Lent Hercules
Lent Moses
Lovejoy Andrew
Lovejoy Nathan
Mandigo Jeremiah
Medlar Aure
Messenger Andrew
Nichols Isaac
Norris Henry
Norton Abel
Norton Sebe
Scott James
Sickler Matthias
Simpson Garret
Smith Deliverance
Smith Israel
Smith Philip
Spencer Amos
Stark James
Steenbark Peter
Stork James
Straghan John
Taylor Gamaliel
Vermillia Benjamin
Vorce David
Van Hooson Francis
Van Kleek Jeremiah
Van Steenbergh Peter
Van Valkenburgh Levi
Welding Jeremiah
Wheeler William
Williams Richard
Willis Henry
Wilsey William
Wood Isaac

ORANGE COUNTY MILITIA.

COLONEL JESSE WOODHULL

LIEUTENANT COLONEL ELIHU MARVIN

CAPT. BREWSTER HENRY
" THOMAS HORTON

LIEUT. JOSEPH CONKLING

ENLISTED MEN

Ayres William
Benjamin John
Benjamin Silas, Junr.
Benjamin Silas, Senr.
Brown Jeremiah
Budd William
Carpenter Jesse
Carpenter John
Carpenter Joseph
Fuller Jedediah
Goble Benjamin
Goble Joseph
Gragge Hughah
Hallcock David
Hobart Peter
Horton Thomas
Horton Tuthill
Haull James
Haull Silas
Horton William
Howel Paul
Manna Barnabas
McVaughn Benjamin
Night Nicholas
Pierson Howel
Runnels William
Thompson William
Youngs Abraham

Orange County Militia — (Continued).

COLONEL ANN HAWK HAY

LIEUTENANT COLONEL GILBERT COOPER

MAJOR JOHN SMITH

MAJOR JOHN L. SMITH

ADJUTANT JAMES D. CLARK

QUARTER MASTER JOSEPH JOHNSON

SURGEON JOHN FERRAND

CAPT. GARRET ACKERSON
" JOHANNES BELL
" AURIE BLAUVELT
" JOHANNES BLAUVELT
" JOSEPH CRANE
" JOHN GARDNER
" JOHN HOGENKAMP
" JOHN M. HOGENKAMP
" JACOB ONDERDONCK
" WILLIAM SICKELS
" AURY SMITH
" HENRY TENURE
" ANDREW THOMPSON
LIEUT. RICHARD ACKER
" CORNELIUS BLAUVELT
" THOMAS BLAUVELT
" MATTHIAS CONKLIN
" HENRY ESLER
LIEUT. WILLIAM GARHAM
" WILLIAM GRAHAM
" DANIEL ONDERDONCK
" ANDRIS ONDERDUNCK
" ROGER OSBORN
" JACOB SICKLES
" JOHN SITCHER
" THEUNIS TAULMAN
" DRICK VAN DER BELT
" PAUL VAN DER VOORT
" RESOLVENT T. VAN HOUTEN
" WALTER VAN ORDER
" JOHN WALDRON
ENSIGN JOHN COE
" WILLIAM CONKLIN
" JOHN MYERS
" ALBERT SMITH

ADDITIONAL NAME ON STATE TREASURER'S PAY BOOKS.

LIEUT. JACOB SICKELSON

ENLISTED MEN.

Accarsen Thomis
Accorson John
Acker David
Acker Derrick
Acker Jacops
Ackerman Eda
Ackerman John
Ackerson Abraham
Ackerson David
Ackerson Jacob
Allison Isaac
Allison Jeremiah
Allison John
Allison Joseph
Allison Joseph B.
Allison Matthew
Allison Peter
Allison Samuel
Allison Thomas
Allison William
Ammerman Aurt
Archer Jacob
Arden Jacob
Armstrong Robert
Babcock James
Babcock Job
Babcock Job E.
Babcock Thomas
Backman John
Baker Thomas
Barmore Henry
Barns Jacob Vanostrant
Barwick Robert
Bate James
Beekman John
Bell Hendrick
Bell Wellem
Bell Wellem, Senr.
Bell William
Bensen Johannes
Bensen John
Berray Isaac
Bill William
Birchel Jeremiah
Bird Samuel
Blancher Anthony
Blanvot Hermones
Blasvielt Herramanes
Blauvalt John H
Blauvelt Abraham
Blauvelt Abraham D.
Blauvelt Adam
Blauvelt Cornelius
Blauvelt Cornelius I.
Blauvelt Daniel
Blauvelt Daneil A.
Blauvelt Garret
Blauvelt Garret Isaac
Blauvelt Garrit J.
Blauvelt Gerret G.
Blauvelt Harmanes
Blauvelt Hendreck
Blauvelt Hendrick A.
Blauvelt Isaac
Blauvelt Isaac G.
Blauvelt Isaac H.
Blauvelt Jacob
Blauvelt Jacobus
Blauvelt Jacobus J.
Blauvelt Johanes
Blauvelt Johanes D.
Blauvelt Johannis G.
Blauvelt Johannis J.
Blauvelt John
Blauvelt John G.
Blauvelt John J.
Blauvelt Joseph
Blauvelt Joseph J.
Blauvelt Peter
Blauvelt Richard
Blawvalt Thunis
Blawvelt Frederick
Blawvelt Nuric
Bogart Johanes
Bogert David
Bogert Gysbert
Bogert Jacob
Bogort John

Bollson John
Bolson Anthony
Bolson Cornelius
Bolsom John
Brewer Aury
Brewer Isaac
Bridggs John
Briggs Henry
Briggs Jasper
Briggs John
Briggs Lawrence
Briggs Matthias
Broadwell Henry
Brooks John
Brouwer Samuel
Brower Abraham
Brower Isaac
Brower Uldrick
Bruce Robert
Brush Robert
Bulson Cornelius
Burchell Jeremiah
Burges Michael
Burgess Archer
Burgis John
Burns David
Butler Isaac
Butler Israel
Butler Joseph
Caine Edward D.
Cammel Albert
Cammel Luke
Cammel Stephen
Campbell Adam
Campbell Luck
Campbell Robert
Campbell Stephen
Campbell Wiam
Cankelen Willem
Canniff James
Cargile Henry
Carloughs Nicholas
Clark Daniel A.
Clark Jacobes D.
Clark James A.
Clark Joseph D.
Clark Michael D.
Coe Benjamin
Coe Daniel
Coe Daniel, Junr.
Coe Daniel S.
Coe Halsted
Coe Isaac
Coe John D.
Coe John S.
Coe Jonas
Coe Matthew
Coe Matthew, Junr.
Coe Matthew D.
Coe Samuel
Coe William
Cohoon David
Cohoon Joseph
Coin Edward D
Cokalect Daniel
Cole Abraham
Cole Andries
Cole Isaac
Coleman John
Collord Abraham
Collorot Abraham
Concklin Ezekiel
Concklin David
Concklin Henry
Concklin John
Concklin Nicholas N.
Concklin Nicholas W.
Concklin Stephen
Conckling Abraham
Conckling Aron
Conckling Gabriel
Conckling Isaac
Conckling John
Conckling John L.
Conckling Joseph H.
Conckling Lewis
Conckling Matthies
Conckling Michael
Conckling Nicolas
Conckling Nicolas W.
Conckling Stephen
Conckling Thomas
Conklin Aaron
Conklin Gabriel
Conklin Isaac
Conklin John
Conklin Joseph
Conklin Joseph J
Conklin Lewis
Conklin Michael
Conklin John
Conklin Stephen
Cooper Abram
Cooper Albert
Cooper Cornelius
Cooper Eda
Cooper Garret
Cooper Gilbert
Cooper Hendrick
Cooper John
Cooper Joseph
Cooper Tunes
Cooper Wolvert
Cornelison John
Cornelison Michael
Cornwell William
Corwine Gilbird
Couter John
Cox John
Crane John
Cregier Thomas
Crom William
Crouter John
Crow Joshua
Crowler John
Crum Richard
Crumb John
Crumb Peter
Crumb William
Cuckleatt Daniel
Culson Alexander
Cuper Henry
Cure Walter
Curren Gilbert
Davison M.
Deal Jacob
Debaun David
DeClark Jacobus
Degraw Cornelius
Degraw John
Degraw Luke
Degraw William
Demarest David
Demarest Jacobus
Demarest Johannes
Demarest Petrus
Demerest James
De Pew Peter
Depue Cornelius
Depue John
Deronde Abraham
Deronde Hendrick
Deronde Henry
Deronde Henry C
Deronde Henry I
Deronde Jacob
Deronde Tobias
Dikins Richard
Dikins Thomos
Dimerest Peter
Doty Adam, Jr.
Dunbar Amos
Dutcher Isaac
Dutcher Peter
Dyckens Richard
Dyckens Thomas
Dyckman Abraham
Eckersen Dirk
Edwords James
Ekerson Derick
Eltergee Michael
Emmens James
Emmit Tunis
Evermore John
Felter John
Felter Peter
Felter William
Ferguson John
Ferguson Thomas
Forgason Thomas
Forgison Gabriel
Forgison John
Fowler Gilbert
Fowler Lewis
Fredenburgh Peter
Fredrick Abram
Fredrick Henry
Fredrick Robert
Furman Benjamin
Furman Ralf
Furshie John
Ganyon Abraham
Gardner James
Garrison Abraham
Garrison Abraham, Junr.
Garrison Joseph
Garrison Peter
Gerow Benjamin
Goetches Abraham
Goetscheus John
Goetschius Abraham
Gornee Benjamin
Gornee Elias
Gornee Isaiah
Gornee John
Gornee Stephen
Gornee Stephen, Jr.
Gornee Stephen, Sr.
Goutches Joseph
Graass Jeob
Graham John
Green Patrick
Gross Jacob
Gross Peter
Gumee Francis
Gurnee Elias
Gurnee Francis
Gurnee Isaiah
Gurnee John
Gurnee John J.
Gurnee Stephen, Junr.
Gutches Abm
Gutches Joseph
Hadley Fredick
Hadley George
Hadley Isaac
Hadley Stephen
Hallsted Jacob
Hallsted Henry
Hallsted John
Hallsted Timothy
Hannah William

Hansua Jacob
Hansy Jacob
Harring Abram
Hause William
Hayston Joseph
Heirs Phelix
Hendrickson Hendrick
Hendrickson Jecobus
Hendrickson John
Herman Joseph
Herring Isaac
Hillaman Nicholas
Heckle Robert
Hogenkamp, Gysbert
Hoghland William
Holdron Andries
Holland John
Holland Thomas
Holstead Edward
Holsted Edmond
Hoogland John
Hoppen Rinard
Hopper Paul
Horton James
House Cornelius
House John
House Richard
House Rinard, Junr.
House Rinard, Senr.
Houser Henry
Howard Richard
Huff Gershom
Huffman Harmanes
Hunt Gilbert
Hunt Gilliad
Hunt Joseph
Hunt Ruben
Hunt Samuel
Hutchings Amos
Hutson John
Hutton John
Immons James
Iseman John
Jennyks Hendrick
Jerfers Edward
Jersey Peter
Jinkings Arie
John Peter
Johnson Gisbert
Johnson John
Johnson John, Junr.
Johnson Thomas
Johnston John
Jones Benjamin
Jones Edward
Jones Isaac
Jones Jacob
Jones John
Jones Jonas
Jones Joseph
Jones William
Jonson Shepherd
Juruill Franses
Kahoon Samuel
Kelly Carpenter
Kelly Daniel
Kelly Dennis
Kelly Thomas
Kerhoon Samuel
Kieslar Philip
Kiesler R.
King Arie
King Jacob
King Walter
Kislor Hermanus
Knap Benjamin
Knap James
Knap Jared
Knap Jeremiah
Knap Jonas
Knap Joseph
Knap Lebbeus
Knap Samuel
Knapp Abel
Knapp Silas
Kniffin Jacob
Krum Peter
Kuypert Theunis
Lamb Alexender
Lamb Jacob
Lamb Martin
Lamb Pomp
Lane Henry
Lawrence David
Lawrence George
Leaycraft William
Lefoy Thomas
Lent Jacob
Lent John
Lewis James
Linkleten James
Linklettor James
Lowry Tobias
Lynch James
Lyons Samuel
Mabe John
Mabee Jeremiah
Mabee John Peter
Mabie Abraham
Mabie Casparus
Mabie Cornelius
Mabie Peter
Mabie Peter Charles
Mabie Yoast
Magee John
Man George
Martine John
Marvin Elihu
Mathews Samuel
Maybie Jesper
Mead Joel
Meeks Joseph
Mefoy James
Megee John
Mekes Joseph
Meyer Jacob
Mier Cornelius
Montanye John
Morgan David
Morris David
Mott Charls
Mott Jacob
Mott Mordica
Mott Salvenas
Mountain Andrew
Myer Abraham
Myer Daniel
Myer Garret
Myer Jeams
Myers Andrew
Myers John
McCarter Peter
Nostand Thomas
Oblenis Henry
Oblenis Peter
O'Brien John
Ockerman Deavid
Odle Nathaniel
Onderdonck Abraham
Onderdonck Adrayon
Onderdonck Adriance
Onderdonck Albert
Onderdonck Andris
Onderdonck Aron
Onderdonck Garrit
Onderdonck Isaac
Onderdonck James
Onderdonck Thomas
Onderdonk Henry
Onderdunck John
Osborn Benjamin
Osborn John
Osborn William
Palmer Jonathan
Parker Isaac
Parker Jacob
Parker John
Parker Peter
Parsel William
Parsell Johanes
Parsell John
Paul James
Paulding Cornelius
Paulding Garret
Perrie Johannis
Perry Jacobus
Perry Urin
Persell Jacob
Persell Paul
Phillips Eli
Phillips Daniel
Phillips Gilbert
Pierson James
Polasker Anthony
Polhamus Abraham
Polhemus Aurt
Polhemus Jhon
Post Abraham
Post Daniel
Post Isaac
Post Isaac Abraham
Post John
Poulhamus Handrick
Poulhamus Theodorus
Quackenboos Riner
Quackenbos Reynard
Quackenbos Rynar
Quackenboss Abram
Quackinbush James
Ramsen Abraham
Ramsen Aurt
Ramsen Garret
Ramson George
Read Peter
Reader Josiah
Remsen Aurt
Remsen Johannes
Remsen John
Reynolds Abraham
Reynolds Benjamin
Rider Conrad
Rider Josiah
Riker Henry
Robertson Jese
Robins Joseph
Rodgers Justus
Root William
Rose Jacob
Rose John
Rosevelt Joseph
Runnelds Benjamin
Ryker Abraham
Ryker Hendrick
Ryker James
Ryker Matthew
Salsar Mical
Salyer Edward
Salyer William
Sanven Garris
Seaman Calub
Seaman Joseph
Seaman Powlis

Seamons John
Seamons Paul
Secaur Benjimen
Secaur Jacob
Secaur James
Secaur Samuel
Secor Andrew
Secor Benjamin
Secor Daniel
Secor Isaac
Secor Isaac I.
Secor Jacob
Secor James
Secor James E.
Secor Jonas
Secor Samuel
Servant Abraham
Servant Adriaen
Servant Henry
Servant Philip
Servron Abraham
Sharp James
Shaw Patrick
Shay Patrick
Sherwood David
Shourt Adolph
Shourt Lewis
Shourt Hendrick
Shurt Henry
Sickels John
Simmons Paul
Smeth Garret
Smit Abram
Smith Abert
Smith Abraham
Smith Adam
Smith Cornelius
Smith Cornelius C.
Smith David
Smith Edward
Smith Frederick
Smith Garret
Smith Isaac
Smith James
Smith John
Smith John C.
Smith Nathaniel
Smith Peter
Smith Reynard
Smith Reyniere
Smith Samuel
Smith Stephen
Snedker Tunis
Snyder Abraham
Snyder Hendrick
Snyder Hermanes
Snyder Peter
Sprieg Gidion
Springsteel Isaac
Springsteen David
Springsteen Isaac
Springsteen Johanes
Springsteen John
Springsteen Samuel
Springsteen Staughts
Stagg John
Stagg Paul
Stamford David
Stepenson Stephen
Stephens Peter
Stephens Rulif
Stephens Stephen
Stephens Stephen A.
Stephens William
Stevens Albert
Stevens Resolvent
Stevens Stephanes
Steward James
Stewart Charles
Storm Abraham
Stott William
Straut Jacob
Stringham William
Talema Theunis
Talemen Gerrit
Tallman Abraham
Tallman Dowey
Tallman Harmanas
Tallman John
Tallman Peter
Tallman William
Talman Theunis H.
Talman Thomas
Tarneur Woodhul
Tarnur James
Taulman Dowe
Taulman Harmh
Taylor Abner
Taylor Jeams
Taylor John
Taylor Jonathan
Taylor Joshua
Taylor Moses
Taylor William
Teneur Johanneus
Teneyke Hendrick
Tenure John
Tenure Odle
Tunre Woodhull
Tenyke Jacob
Tenyke John
Thew Garret
Thew Gilbert
Thew John
Thiell Jacob
Thompson
Thompson William
Tice John
Tiebout George
Tiebout Henry
Tilt William
Tinkee Coonro
Tinkee Coonrod
Tinkee John
Tinkey Jacob
Tirneir Micheal
Tirnier Hanry
Tonure Lourance
Tonyke Jacob, Junr.
Torneur James
Toun John
Tournend James
Tourneur James
Trimper James
Trumper Thunis
Turnere Lawranc
Tutler Daniel
Underdonck Roulof
Vaber John
Valentine Peter
Vardossen Johannis
Velte Willem
Venala Cornelius
Venhousen John
Vervalan Cornelius
Vervaler James
Vervalin James
Verveelen Jacobus
Vonck Peter
Vorhis Stephen
Van Antwerp Daniel
Van Antwerp John
Van Buskirk Gorge
Van Clec Garrit
Van Cleck Jacobus
Van Cleft Garret
Vandarbeek David
Van Debelt Cornelius
VanDebelt Derick
Vanderbelt Dowah
Vanderbelt James
Vanderbelt John
Vander Voort Barent
VanDervoort Garret
Vandervoort John
VanDervoort John, Sr.
Vandervoort Jonas
Van Der Voort Paul
Vandervoort Peter
Van Dolson Jacobis
Vandyke John
Van Hooutan Derick
Van Houghen John
Van Houten Abraham
Van Houten Charles
Van Houten John
Van Houten Klaas
Van Houten Peter
Van Houten Samuel
Van Houten Thunis
Vanordan Hendrick
Van Ordee Hendrick
Vanorden Andres
Vanorden Jacobus
Van Orden John
Van Order Andreis
Van Order Peter
Van Order Hendrick
Van Sickel Daniel
Wagoner Tobias
Waldrom Jacob
Waldrom James
Waldrom Janis
Waldrom John
Waldron Edward
Waldron John
Walker John
Wallace John
Wanamaker Adolph
Wanamaker Peter
Wandle Jacob
Warrin Theodores
Weggin Tobias
Welch Richard
Wessels Richard
Westervelt Abraham
WesterVelt Casparus
Westervelt Daniel
Westervelt Peter
Whitten Joseph
Wickham Warrin
Williams Gilbert
Williams Josiah
Williamson Jeremiah
Williamson Nicholas
Willon Andrew
Willsey James
Willson Andrew
Willson James
Wilson Albert
Wilson Uriah
Woldrom Jacob
Wood Ebenezer
Wood Henry
Wood Jacob
Wood Joseph
Wood Samuel
Woolsey Jacob
Youmans Samuel
Young Frederick
Zodenpah John
Zuniker Lodowick

Orange County Militia — (Continued).

COLONEL WILLIAM ALLISON

LIEUTENANT COLONEL BENJAMIN TUSTON

MAJOR MOSES HETFIELD

CAPT. SAMUEL COLE
" JOHN JACKSON
" SAMUEL JONES
" MOSES KORTWRIGHT
CAPT. JOHN LITTLE
" DAVID SWAZY
" JOHN WOOD

ENLISTED MEN.

Ballis Richard
Black David
Boyl James
Bradner Benony
Dains Abraham
Dick (colored)
Dickasen John
Doty Isaac
Horton Fradrick
Howel John
Humphry Samuel
Hunter Ezekiel
Lee Seth
Lewis Jabez
Lidel William
McCormick James
McDonald John
Nelson Martin
Reeves James, Jun.
Russel Benjamin
Sheridan Richard
Seeley Thaddeus
Van Tassel John
Wilson David

Orange County Militia — (Continued).

COLONEL JOHN HATHORN
LIEUTENANT COLONEL JOSEPH HASBROUCK
LIEUTENANT COLONEL HENRY WISNER
MAJOR WILLIAM BLANE
MAJOR MOSES PHILLIPS
MAJOR JOHN POPPINO
MAJOR ADRIAN WYNKOOP
ADJUTANT JOHN BARBER
ADJUTANT NATHANIEL FINCH
ADJUTANT GEORGE LUCKEY
QUARTER MASTER JEREMIAH CURTIS
QUARTER MASTER PHILIP KINGSLAND
QUARTER MASTER JOHN J. LOW
CHAPLAIN REV. JOHN CLOSE

CAPT. RICHARD BAILEY
" PETER BERTHOLF
" EVERETT BOGARDUS
" CHARLES BROADHEAD
" STEPHEN CASE
" JACOB CONKELIN
" MATTIS FELTER
" SAMUEL JONES
" JOHN LITTLE
" SETH MARVIN
" CORNELIUS MASTERS
" ANDREW MILLER
" JOHN MINTHORN
" JAMES MCBRIDE
" DAVID MCCAMLY
" ——— NEWKIRK
" JOHN NICOLE
" EBENEZER OWENS
" SILAS PERSON
" JOHN SAYRES
" COLVILL SHEPARD
" ARTHUR SMITH
" BARDOWINE TARPENING
" WILLIAM TILFORD
" ISAIAH VEAL (VAIL)
" CHRISTIVER VAN DUZER
" HENDRICK VAN KEUREN
" SAMUEL WATKINS
" ——— WOODHULL
LIEUT. ALEXANDER BATY
" BENJAMIN COOLEY
" DAVID CRAWFORD
LIEUT. JOSEPH CROFFORT
" JOHN DEBOW
" MARTIN DECKER
" JACOB DENNING
" JAMES DENTON
" HENRY DOBBINS
" THOMAS EAGLES
" JAMES FARNER
" SOLOMON FINCH
" ISAAC FOWLER
" WILLIAM GILLET
" DAVID GUE
" ISAAC HARDENBERGH
" JOSEPH HASBROUCK, JR.
" MARTIN HOMMELL
" JOHN HOWELL
" MATTHEW HUNTER
" ROBERT HUNTER
" JOSEPH JEWELL
" JOHN JOHNSTON
" JACOB LAWRENCE
" EDWARD MCNEAL
" HENRY NEELY
" JOHANNIS NIERSON
" DAVID OSTRANDER
" JONATHAN OWEN
" SILAS ROBISSON
" PETER ROOSA
" HEMAN ROWLEE
" THOMAS SAYRES
" HENRY SMITH
" THOMAS SMITH

LIEUT. JACOB TERWILLEGAR
" GEORGE VANCE
" BENJAMIN VEAL
" FREDERICK WESTBROOK
" JOHN WILKIN
" THOMAS WISNER
" ALEXANDER WOOD
" JOHN WOOD
" JOSEPH WOOD
" JEAMS WRIGHT
ENSIGN JOHN BENEDICT
" HENRY BERTHOLF
" ISAAC BURHANS
" JOHN BURNET
" DANIEL CLARK
ENSIGN WILLIAM CRIST
" MOSES DEPUY
" NATHANIEL DUBOIS
" ELIJAH FENTON
" JONATHAN HALLACK
" RICHARD JOHNSON
" CHARLES KNAPP
" WILLIAM MILLER
" ANDREW NELY
" LEONARD NICOLE
" JACOB ROSECRANSE
" ROBERT THOMPSON
" DANIEL VAIL
" SAMUEL WETHERLOW
" MARTIN WYANS

ENLISTED MEN

Abraham John
Addison William
Acton Morey
Adcock William
Agers Lowrance
Albertson Richard
Albertson Stephen
Albirtson Josh
Aldrich Robert
Aldrige Peter
Alidorp Simon
Allison Harvey
Allison James
Allison Michael
Allison Richard
Alsdarf Philip
Alyea John
Alyea John, Junr.
Alyea Peter
Alyea Samuel
Anderson James
Anderson Joseph
Antony Albert
Appertell Abr'm
Arche Jonathan
Archer Jonathan
Armstrong
Armstrong Archibald
Armstrong David
Armstrong Frances
Armstrong George
Armstrong James
Armstrong John
Armstrong Joseph
Arnit Nathan
Arnout Peter
Ashel James
Askin William
Asten Grif
Atwood Benjamin
Ausburn Abram
Aygor Thomas
Babcock John
Baelys Richard
Baillie John
Baily Joseph
Baily Samuel
Baker Bartholimu
Baker Joseph
Baley Nathan
Baley Richard, Junr.
Baley Silas
Baley Thomas
Baly Archible
Baly Daniel
Baly Nathan, Jr.
Bandol Will
Bank Coin
Banker Frederick
Banker Justus
Bannam James
Barber Nathan
Barckley James
Barckey Thomas
Bard Peter
Bartholf James
Bartholf Stephan
Bartlet Ebennezer
Bartoff Samuel
Barton Gilbert
Barton Roger
Baty John
Bawson Jonathan
Bayham Robert
Bayles Richard
Bayley Daniel
Bayley Nathaniel
Beaneanon James
Bears Timothy
Becker John
Becker Silas
Beeder Christian
Beers John
Belknap David
Belknap Isaac
Belknap Isaac, Junr.
Belknap Jonathan
Bell William
Bellows Jonas
Belmain William
Bemar Adam
Benedict Daniel
Benedict James
Benedict William, Senr.
Benham James
Benjamin Daniel
Benjamin Mac[h]
Benjamin Nathaniel
Benjamin Richard
Benjamin Samuel
Benet Abraham, Junr.
Bennet Jeremiah
Bennet Thaddeus
Bennet Thomas
Bennett Abraham
Bennitt Ephraim
Bennitt Ephraim, Junr.
Bennitt James
Berger Wouter
Bennit Mathew
Berian Peter
Berlick Benjamin
Berry James
Bertholf Crines
Bertholf John
Bertoff James
Bertoloff Stephen
Bevier Ab[m]
Bevier Jonathan
Bickek John
Birchard Nathan
Birdsall Nathaniel
Black James
Black John
Black Robert
Blaen John, Junr.
Blain John Junr.
Blain Thomas
Blar John
Blisard Oliver
Bloom John
Bloomer Gilbert
Bloomer William
Bodine David
Bodine Isaac
Bodine John
Bodine William
Bogart Cornelius
Bogart Henry
Bogart Peter
Bookstower William
Booth Joshua
Borger Robert
Bowen Daniel
Bower Heman
Bower Isaac
Bower Joel
Boyd Robert
Bradley Daniel
Bradner Colvil
Bradner John
Bramer Antony
Brewster Francis
Brewster Nathan
Briggs Joel
Brink Solomon
Brock George
Brockaway Jesse
Brodhead Charles W.
Brondrage Jonathan
Brooks Francis
Brooks John
Brooks John, Jr.
Brown Alexander

Brown Duncin
Brown Ebenezer
Brown Isaac
Brown James
Brown Peter
Brown Richard
Brundige John
Brush David
Brush Jacob
Brush John
Brush Joshua
Bruyn Jacobus
Bruyn William
Bryans James
Buchanan James
Buchannan Robert
Bucingham Solomon
Buckelow George
Buckinham Richard
Budd Benjamin
Budd Fredrick
Buey William
Bull Abrm
Bull Samuel
Bundle Benjamin
Buning Charles
Bunnell Stephen
Burger Wortel
Burk John
Burnet Patrick
Burnet Robert
Burney William
Burns William
Burris Philip
Burroughs Philip
Bursh John
Burt David
Burt James
Burt John
Burt Thomas
Buryan Peter
Butler Abraham
Butler Joseph
Butters Jacob
Buveir Nathaniel
Byran Asa
Cableley Philip
Cachel John
Cahill John
Cain Daniel
Camble Edward
Camble Joshua
Camble Levi
Camble Robert
Camble Samuel
Camble Thomas
Camfield John
Cammle Simon

Campbell Simeon
Camrin Duncin
Caniday John
Canniff Jeremiah
Cantine Benjamin
Car David
Carner Andrew
Carpender Richard
Carpenter Benjamin
Carpenter John
Carpenter Joshua
Carpenter Michel
Carpenter William
Carr John
Carr Richard
Carr William
Carter John
Case Jesse
Case John
Case Joshua
Case William
Casedy Patrick
Celmans Benjamin
Cens John
Cesle Joshua
Cetchem John
Chaimbers Tomas
Chandler Abraham
Chandler David
Chard Hugh
Chatfield Thomas
Chilson Joseph
Chrispel Abraham
Christie Andrew
Cilrey Henry
Cimbergh Matthew
Clark Anthony
Clark Daniel
Clark George
Clark James
Clark Reuben
Clark Richard
Clark Thomas
Clark William
Clarke Henry
Clarke John
Clawwater Jacob
Cleark Aaron
Cleark Richard
Clearwater Jeremiah
Clerk David
Clerk James
Clerk Ruben
Clerk Smith
Clintic Samuel
Clyne Jacob
Coal Bornt
Coble George

Coddington Benjamin
Coddington Jacob
Codington Levy
Coe Moses
Cole Abraham
Cole Benjamin
Cole Cornelius
Cole John
Cole Tobius
Cole William
Coley Nathn.
Coleman Jonh.
Colman Barnabas
Colman Gideon
Colman Samuel
Colman Timothy
Comfort John
Concklin Higgins
Concklin William
Conegim Aron
Conger David
Constable Christhophel
Content Moses
Conway Cornelius
Cook David
Cook William
Coole Barent
Cooley Benjamin
Cooley Isaac
Cooley Jonathan
Cooly Peter
Cooper William
Cope Joseph
Corter Peter
Corter William
Cortwright Abraham
Cory Gabril
Cory John
Cox John
Crage David
Crage John
Craig Adam
Crane James
Crane John
Cranse Henry
Crawford Nathan
Crawford Jonathan
Crawford John
Crawford Robert
Crawford Samuel
Crawford Thomas
Crispel Abraham
Crist Abrm.
Crist Christian
Crist Martinas
Crist Philip
Critsing John
Croffort Robert

Crofort Jonathan
Cronk Henry
Crons Henry
Croosman Nath.
Cropsy Adam
Cropsy Isaac
Cropsy Jacob
Crospey Matthew
Cross David
Cross Joel
Cross Leonard
Crosson David
Crum James
Crum William
Cruver Aron
Culbert John
Culp Jacob
Cumfort Josiah
Cumton Zakirnah
Cuppler William
Cure Walter
Curey William
Currant Silas
Curry Benjamin
Curry Joseph
Curtice Jeremiah
Curtis Joshua
Curwin Jediah
Curwin Joshua
Curwin Phenis
Curwin Silas
Curwin Timothy
Cury Benjamin
Cypher Cistrian
Daley Danl.
Daly John
Darby Berym.
Darby Danl.
Darvin William
Daton Hezekiah
Daton Joseph
Daughety William
David Henry
David John
Davis Benjamin
Davis James
Davis Joseph
Davis Nicolas
Davis Richard
Davis Saml
Davis Thomas
Davis William
Davisson John
Day Barne.
Day Henry
Day Ithamer
Dealls John
Dean Jebediah

Deane George
Debois Samuel
Decay Jacob
Decay Thomas
Decker Abm.
Decker Benjamin
Decker Cornelius
Decker Elias
Decker Ephraim
Decker Fredrick
Decker Gabl.
Decker Gabriel, Senr.
Decker Garrit
Decker Gilbert
Decker Henry
Decker Jacob
Decker John
Decker Jonathan
Decker Joshua
Decker Levy
Decker Peter
Decker Petrus
Deen William
DeGraff Hendrick
DeGroat Jesse
Dekay Thomas Junr.
Dekor John
Delyell William
Demarest David
Demarest David, Junr.
Demarest Peter
Demarest Samuel
Demerelst Cornelus
Demerest Cornelius
Demerest Jacob
Demonis John
Demott Isaac
Dening Ephrim
Denny James
Denoray James
Denton James
Denton Nath.
Denton Nehemiah
Depaw Henry
Depuy Elias
Devenport Robert
Devinport Garret
Devinport John
Devinport Oliver
De Witt G.
DeWitt Garret
DeWitt Jacob
Dewitt John
DeWitt John
DeWitt John A.
DeWitt William
Dial Phillip
Dikesson Am.
Dikesson Andr.
Dikesson Boadhed
Dimoris David
Dimoriss Peter
Dinnis Danll
Dirks John
Dives Robert
Divoe David
Dobbins Daniel
Docker Cornelius
Doerty Thomas
Dolsen Abraham
Dolson Isaac
Dolson John
Domineck George
Dorf J. E., Junr.
Dorkes John
Dorkes Jonathan
Dox James
Drake Joshua
Drew Oliver
Druming John
Dubois Andrew
Dubois Isaac
Dubois James
Dubois John
Dubois Nath
Dubois Wessel
Dubois Wilhelmus
Duff Peter
Duffield John
Dummerist Cornelius
Dumond Egenos
Dunbar Amoss
Dunbleser George
Dunlap William
Dunn John
Dunn Phineas
Dunning David
Durlin Danll
Durya George
Dusenbury William
Eagleston Amos
Eagor William
Ean Ceaser
Ean James
Earl Jonathan
Ears Phillip
Eaton Alexander
Eckert Martinus
Edmondston William
Edsall John
Edsall Philip
Eganar William
Egelston Paliants
Eggener Jacobus
Elder Joseph
Elliot Archible
Ellison Benjamin
Ellisson Isaac
Ellisson John
Ellisson William
Elmendorph Ari. G.
Elmendorph Auriges
Elsworth John
Elsworth William
Elting John
Elvindorph Jacobus
Elyea Elbert
Elyea Joseph
Elyea Samuel
Emirick Wilhelmus
Emrich Peter
Emrich Wilhelmus, Junr.
Ensign James
Erwin Robert
Eumons David
Evins John
Farguson Samuel
Faver Robert
Felmer George
Feltman John
Feltor Gidion
Fener Robert
Fero John Christeian
Fero Peter
Feroes Conroed
Ferrill Matthew
Fiero Peter
Finch David
Finch Heziah
Finch Jabish
Finch James
Finch John
Finly John
Finn Anthony
Finton John
Fisher Alexander
Fitchjirl Jeremiah
Flunams Gidion
Foost John Peter
Forest James
Foresyth William
Forger Jacomiah
Forgonson Daniel
Forguson William
Fowler Stephen
Foy Bartholomew
"Free Jack" (Colored)
Freligh John
Freligh Samuel
Frier John
Fuller David
Fulton Alexander
Fulton David
Fulton Hugh
Gale Able
Gale Abm.
Gale Moses
Gale Richard
Gale Samuel
Gannon Joseph
Ganog William
Garder Samuel
Garner Francis
Garner Silas
Garno James
Garrison Jonas
Garrison William
Genneiag Benjamin
Gennings Isaac
Gesip Ebenezer
Gibson James
Gidney Eleazer
Gidney Joseph
Gilbert Jesse
Giles Charles
Gilles Jacob
Gillaspy George
Gillation Jame
Gillis Daniel
Gilson Samuel
Glaspy Mathew
Goble George
Goble Jacob
Godfrey David
Gossip Jeremiah
Graham James
Graham Thomas
Gray John
Gray Mathan
Greatsinger Jonathan
Green Daniel
Green Richard
Green William
Greer David
Guigge William
Gwings Samuel
Hagerthy John
Hains Henrey
Halbut Thomas
Hall Daniel
Hall James
Hall John
Hall Reuben
Hall Stephen
Hallet Joseph
Hallick Jothem
Hally Noah
Hamilton John
Hammel John
Handmore John
Hanna James
Hanna Samuel

Hannion David
Hanyens David
Happer Cornelius
Harcort John
Harden Thomas
Hardon Samuel
Hardenbergh Lewis
Harford Francis
Harres Jaimes
Harris James
Harris John
Harrison Daniel
Hass Nicholas
Havell David
Hawkins David
Hawkins James
Hawkins Thomas
Haycock Richard
Headley Isaac
Hedger Evert
Hedger John
Hedger William
Heermanse Edward
Heffernen John
Heger Samuel
Helms William
Hemingway Samuel
Henber Frederick
Henderson Robert
Henry John
Herrington John
Higbie James
Hill James
Hodge Samuel
Hodge William
Hoel Jeremiah
Hogan James
Holey Bebasable
Holly Israll
Holly William
Holmes Reuben
Hibee James
Higbee James
Hinds James
Hommel Abraham
Hopper Cornelius
Hopper Edward
Hopper John
Hopper Lambert
Hopper Paul
Horn Phenton
Horse Uriah
Horton Israel
Horton James
Horton Jeremiah
Horton John
Horton Joshua
Horton Zachariah
Horton Zacheus
Houston Joseph
Houston Zebulon
Howard Ezekiel
Howel John
Howel Nathan
Howel Phenis
Howell David
Howell Ezra
Howell George
Howell Gilbirt
Howit John
Huff Henry
Hufman John
Hulbert Peter
Hulse Daniel
Hulse Jacob
Humphrey Charles
Hunter Robert
Inman Ely
Ivery Helmis
Jachen Henuelbd
Jackson Alexander
Jackson Enoch
Jackson George
Jackson Hanibal
Jackson Henry
Jackson James
Jackson William
Jacox Bowras
Jacson Richard
Jane Samuel
Jansen Cornelius
Jay John
Jecocks Bowers
Jennings Benjamin
Jessup Ebenezer
Johnsen Aurter
Johnson Abraham
Johnson John
Johnson Jonathan
Johnson Nich'ls
Johnson Richard, Junr.
Johnson Thomas
Johnson William
Johnson Zaer
Johnston Thomas
Joinen Jonathan
Jones Ambors
Jones Augustus
Jones Cornelius
Jones Nathan
Jones Richard
Jones Robart
Jonsen Dan'tt
Joy Albartus
Kain Adam
Kain Francis
Kain John
Karnaghen Charles
Keafer William
Keating William
Keator Jacob
Keator Jacob N.
Keator John C.
Keator William
Kecth Job
Keffar William
Kelley John
Kelley Michel
Kelley Peter
Kelly Abram
Ketcham Hoel
Ketcham Nathaniel
Ketcham Samuel
Ketchum Azariah
Ketchum Phillip
Keyler Ebenezer
Killey Benjamin
Killey John
Kilpatrick Samuel
Kilse John
Kimble William
King John
King Martin
King Stephen
King William
Kinkade Moses
Kinner James
Kinner John
Kinner John, Junr.
Kirkandle Solomon
Kline Jacob
Klynman Thomas
Knap Charles
Knap Daniel
Knap Joseph
Knap Joshua
Knap Moses
Knap William
Knapp Caleb
Knapp Joseph
Kniffin John
Knock Thomas
Krom Benjamin
Krom William
Kroug Leonard
Kyte John
Lamb James
Lamoureux Joseph
Lamoureux Luke
Lancaster David
Landon James
Lane Solomon
Laroy Simeon
Lattemore Benjamin
Lawless Martin
Lee Seth
Lefever John
Lefever Solomon
Lefver Noach
Lenci Godfree
Leonard Constent
Leonard George
Lerrue Cryner B.
Lerrue Henry
Leveroe Robeard
Leves Hendery
Lewis Benjamin
Lewis Cornelius
Lewis Samuel
Lewis William
Lightbody Gabriel
Lin George
Little James
Little William
Litts Abraham
Lockwood Caleb
Lockwood James
Lonard John
Longwill John
Longyear William
Lotts Conrad
Loudon Samuel
Louw Benjamin
Low Jacob
Low James
Low Peter
Low Samuel
Luckey George
Luckkey Jesse
Lueman John
Luicy John
Lumux Joseph
Lusey John
Lutz Jacob
Lyans James
Lyne Jonas
Mabee Jacob
Mace Gideon
Mackey John
Mackey William
Main William
Major Stevvilas
Mandeville Henry
Maning Benjamin
Many James
Mapes Henry
Mapes James
Mapes Jonah
Mapes William
Marshall Henry
Martin David
Martin Henderick

Martin James
Martin Joseph
Martin Samuel
Martin Thomas
Marvin Uriah
Masten Abr'm
Masten Cornelius
Masten Cornelius B.
Masten Henry
Masten Matthew
Masters Joh's
Masters Joseph
Masters Richard
Mauterstock Jacob
Medock Peter
Meker Silas
Mekimme Isaac
Melborn John
Melborn Robert
Merritt Thomas
Mewttin David
Michels William
Mieler Jacob
Milbourn Andrew
Milchpough Jacob
Miligan John
Miliken Alexander
Millar Jacobus
Millar John
Millen John
Miller Alexander
Miller Andrew
Miller David
Miller Edward
Miller James
Miller John
Miller Joshua
Miller Peter
Miller Zebelin
Mills Jonathan
Milsbaugh Jacob
Milshepough Matthew
Milspagh Benjamin
Milspagh Jacob
Milspah Mathu
Mink Chrs. Junr.
Minthorn Nathaniel
Mitchell John
Moer Robert
Moffet John
Moore Thomas
Moore William
More George
Morehouse Josua
Morgan Thomas
Morisson Daniel
Morphet John
Morrall William
Morris Duncim
Morris John
Morrison William
Morrisson John
Morrison Richard
Mouir John
Mountain Nehemiah
Mulborn John
Munnil James
Murdock James
Myer Eph
Myer Ephraim
Myer Peter L.
Myer William
Myer William, Junr.
Myers Chr'st
Myers John
Myers Michel
McAulay Oliver
McCain William
McCamble David
McCambly David
McCaue Joseph
McCane Robert
McCanen Robert
McCann James
McCannel John
McCay John
McClaghen James
McClaghen Peter
McClaghry John
McClea Hugh
McClouer Joseph
McCluer William
McCollum Matthew
McCollum Samuel
McCollum William
McColm Thomas
McCon John
McConley Philip
McConnck Matthew
McConel John
McConnel Phillip
McConnels Matthew
McCord James
McCord John
McCowen James
McCowen John
McCrane Robert
McCreery Alexander
McCrery John
McCrery Robert
McCuchen Thomas
McCurdey John
McCurdy Archibald
McCurdy Daniel
McCure Duncan
McCutchen John
McCutchen Robert
McDanel James
McDonald James
McDougal Elexander
McDowel Henery
McDowel James
McDowell William
McElwin David
McEnis Daniel
McGorrah John
McGuire Daniel
McHurter Hugh
McHurton Hugh
McKain William
McKay William
McKee Thomas
McKeune Joseph
McKey Alexander
McKong Mathew
McKown Hezekiah
McLaughlen John
McLay William
McLockin William
McLroy Cornelius
McMicle Ebenezer
McMillin William
McMunn John
McNely Henry
McQuier Daniel
McReas Alexander
McSwiney Daniel
McVa Bomabs
McVain Benjamin
McVeagh James
McVeaugh Benjamin
McVey John
McWaters John
McWay Daniel
McWhorter John
McWhorter Thomas
McWilliams John
McWorter James
Neal Josiah
Nely Edword
Nely John
Newberry Edy
Newkirk Jacob
Newkirk Samuel
Newson Robert
Nichold Benjamin
Niels Benjamin
Nicoll William
Nicolson Jon
Nilliken Alexander
Nolton Daniel
NonneBrook Benjamin
Noris James
Noris Shadrac
Odle Jesse
Odle John
Odle Stephen
Oldrige Daniel
Oldrige Robert
Oliver Samuel
Oosterhoudt Exekiel
Oosterhout Kryne
Orsborn Daniel
Orsborn Israel
Ostrander Daniel
Ostrander Henry
Ostrander John
Palmer Jonth'n
Papono John
Papono William
Parker Benjamin
Parlaman Johannis
Parshal David
Parshall John
Paterson Joseph
Patterson Alexander
Peach Jacob
Percy David
Persen Johonnis
Peshamis John
Pifer Adam
Pifer Fedreck
Pilgrum Morris
Pine Josh
Plantiss Andrew
Planton Andrew
Platt George
Plumsted Nathaniel
Polhamus Cornelius
Polly Hugh
Poppino Daniel
Poppino William
Post Garrit
Post Henry
Post Jacobus, Junr.
Post Martin
Posts Garrot
Potter Aron
Potter Edward
Powers James
Pudney James
Putman John
Price Joseph
Pride Peter
Puff John
Puff Peter
Purdy Nathen
Purdy Peter
Purnet Patrick
Quick Benjamin
Quick John
Quick Lewis

Quick Peter
Quick Thomas
Quigly George
Quimly Nathaniel
Qury Alexander
Rainy David
Raner William
Rank Philip
Ranod William
Rauer Samuel
Ray Simon
Raynor William
Raynord William
Reave James
Recol John
Redman David
Reed Moses
Reeder William
Relye Dene
Relyea Simon
Remsen Tunis
Reves Lawrance
Rey Simon
Reynolds David
Rhyne Richard
Ricely David
Richards Benjamin
Richards Eliphelit
Richards Nathan
Riche Eliphelit
Rickey Brice
Rickey John
Rider Benjamin
Ridick Philip
Right David
Rinords Clodius
Roads John
Robbeson Isaiah
Robertson John
Robin (colored)
Robinson John
Robison Andrew
Rockifellow John
Rockwell Jonathan
Rodes Hope
Roe John
Rogers Ananias
Rondale William
Roos Abraham
Roosa John E.
Roosakrans James, Junr.
Roose Evert
Rosa John E.
Rosa Tuns
Rosakras Fredrick
Rosakrause Hen'k
Rose Abraham, Junr.
Rose Abraham, Senr.
Rose Robert
Roth William
Row Nathaniel
Rowley Constant
Rump Cristian
Rumsey David
Rumsey Eria
Rumsey Jonas
Rumsey Moses
Rune James
Ruse Henry
Russle Alexander
Sadler William
Sager Malachiah
Sammons John
Sample Robert
Sanford David
Sanford Ezra
Sanford John
Saterley John
Sayer Daniel
Sayers James
Sayr Benjamin
Sayre Job
Sayre Jonas
Sayre Lewis
Sayre Seley
Sayre Thomas
Scaden Alexander
Scaden Audrew
Scaden William
Schofield Jonathan
Schoonmaker Edward
Schoonmaker Edward E.
Schoonmaker James
Scofield David
Scofield Hezekiah
Scofield Joshua
Scoonover Cor'l
Scot Thades
Scott Alexander
Scott Archibald
Scott Fedrick
Scott Hen
Sears Elnathan
Sears John
Seely Caleb
Seely John
Selden Richard
Selley Samal
Sely Sam'll, Jr.
Sley Sam'll, Sr.
Sely William
Semans Samuel (colored)
Seneapagh Henry
Serjent Nathen
Shaffer John
Sharter John
Shaver John
Shears Andrew
Sheerridan Richard
Shepard John
Shephard Benjamin
Shiers Andrew
Shorter John
Silkworth Thomas
Silkworth William
Silsbe Enos
Silsbe Joseph
Simmons Joseph
Simson John
Simson Peter
Simson Samuel
Sincapagh Jacob
Sinckler John
Sinnot Thomas
Sitd Iasiah
Sitts Joh's
Slaughter John
Sleght John
Sloan William
Slutts Hugo
Slutts Lewis
Sly Conrard
Sly John
Smith Ab'm
Smith Adam
Smith Albertson
Smith Alexander
Smith Caleb
Smith David
Smith Esial
Smith Fedrick
Smith Frances
Smith Henry
Smith Isaac
Smith Jacob
Smith Jacobus
Smith James
Smith Jeremiah
Smith John
Smith Jonas
Smith Jonathan
Smith Joseph
Smith Joshua
Smith Ludlom
Smith Peter
Smith Robert
Smith Samuel
Smith Sealy
Smith Thomas
Smith Tobias
Smith Wallor
Smith Wessels
Smith William
Sneigles Mattias
Snider Cornelius
Snyder Elias
Snyder Henry
Snyder Martyn
Sommon Israel
Sommons Cornls.
Sotherland Hugh
Spagh Philip
Sparks Abraham
Sparks Robert
Spencer Hedley
Sprague Amasa
Sprague Gidean
Sringham James
Stage Abram
Stambergh Elijah
Stanton William
Sted James
Steenbargh John
Steenbergh Abm.
Stennebrenner David
Stephens Jedediah
Stephens John
Stevens David
Stevens Elisha
Stevens Jonathan
Stevens Joseph
Steward Danel.
Steward Silas
Stid William
Still Robert
Stilwel Nicolas
Stiples Nathan
St. John Matthew
Stothisland Hugh
Strainer John
Stratting Robert
Stratton Robert
Stricklin Abm.
Stricklin Jacob
Strong John
Suitt Abm.
Sutton John
Swart Abr.
Swart William
Swarthout Aaron
Swazy David
Swegels Mathew
Taeson James
Tarpenny Peter
Tarpenny Ritchard
Tax Lawrance
Taylor Abram
Taylor Caleb
Taylor Elias
Taylor Nehemiah
Taylor William
Tayn Benjamin

Teagles Jacob
Teed Jacobes
Tenbrook William
Ten Eyck Richard
Terbush Henry
Terpening Levi
Terpenning Abraham
Terpenny Abraham
Terril Mathew
Terry Benjamin
Terwilegar Abram
Terwilegar Coin
Terwilegar Jonathan
Terwilger Ezekiel
Terwilla Benjamin
Terwilla Nathaniel
Terwillager Evert
Terwillager Simon H.
Terwillager Tunis S.
Terwillegar Harm
Terwillegar Peter
Terwilleger Arie
Terwilleger Benjamin
Terwilleger Jacob
Terwilleger Johs.
Terwilleger Teunis
Terwilligar Aura
Terwilligar John
Terwillsgai Peter
Tewileger Simon
Thomas Jno.
Thompson James
Thompson Jonth.
Thorne Alexander
Thurton Chrs't
Tid Josiah
Tilsey Timothy
Tilson Thimoty
Timberson Benjamin
Tobius Fred'k
Todd Joseph
Todd Josh
Todd William
Tom (colored)
Tomkens Feneus
Tomkins John
Tomkins Jonathan
Tomsin Phinis
Tomson John
Tooker Daniel
Torgisson William
Totten Jonas
Totton James
Totton Levy
Totton Thomas
Towman Elisha
Trainer John
Trickey Christopher
Trickey William
Tricky Jarimiah
Trimble John
Trimble William
Trimper John
Trumper George
Turck Jacob
Turck John A.
Turner Cornelius
Turner Hugh
Tuthill James
Tuthill Francis
Tuthill William
Tuttle John
Tuttle Jonathan
Tutton Thomas
Umphry David
Upkins Anthony
Upright Nathan
Vallentine Annanias
Vance James
Vance John
Veal Daniel
Vanall Andrew
Van Brunt Rulef
Vancleaf John
Vandenbegh Mathew
VanDerHoof Jacob
Vanderoef Henry
Vangasbeck John
Van Heusin Mathew
Vanhorn Dan'll
Van Keuren Matthew, Junr.
Vankuren Henry
Vankurer Jacobus
Vannaken Cornelius
Van Luvan Christopher
Vannaken Elisha
Vannaton Levy
Van Steenbergh Benjamin
Van Steenburgh Benjamin, Junr.
Vantassle Nich'l
Van Vagener Andries
Vanvleat James
Van Vlecht George
Van Vliet George
Vanwyan Henry
Wackman Daniel
Walken William
Walker Andrew
Walker Isaac
Waller John
Walling Inman
Wallworth William
Wandle Abraham
Ward Isaac
Ward Joshuah
Ward Munson
Ward Richard
Ward Thomas
Warren John
Warrin Joshua
Warrison Siah
Watenon Hugh
Watkins Ephrim
Watkins Thomas
Waugh Robert
Wawzer Comfort
Webster James
Weeb Charles
Weller Jacob
Weed Colwell
Weeks Sam'el
Welch John
Weldon Francis
Weler David
Welks Nathan
Wellar William
Weller John
Weller Lodawike
Welling John
Welling Thomas
Welling Thomas, Junr.
Wells David
Wells Gershom
Wells James
Welte Jacob
Weorle Jacob
Wesner Albert
Westbrook Samuel
Westbrouck Joel
Westfall Holm
Westlick Samll
Wharry Daniel
Wheeler Nathan
Whitacar Squair
Whitaker Abraham
Whitaker Benjamin
Whitaker Edward
White Cornelius
Whitney Abijah
Whitney Benjamin
Whitney Matthew
Whittentort Jacob
Whory John
Whyggant Michel
Wibb Jonathan
Wiete Samuel
Wiggins Charles
Wiggins Jacob
Wiggins Robert
Wiggins Step'n
Wilkins James
Wilkins John
Wilkins Thomas
Wilkisson Jonathan
Willens Peter
Willens William
Williams Adam
Williams James
Williams Jeremiah
Williams John
Williams Matthew
Williams Samuel
Willims Adam
Willing John
Willis Henry
Willis Thomas
Wilson David
Wilson John
Wilson William
Winans Ichabod
Windfield Abraham
Windfield Elias
Windfield Isaac
Winens Isaac
Winfield Henry
Winfield William
Winner Will
Winter Zakariah
Wisner Albert
Wisner Ase
Wisner David
Wisner Samuel
Wisner Smith
Wisner William
Wollen Addom
Wolsey Henry
Wolsey Noah
Wood
Wood Abner
Wood Amous
Wood Andrew
Wood Daniel
Wood Ezekiel
Wood George
Wood Isral
Wood Job
Wood John
Wood John, Junr.
Wood Jonas
Wood Jonathan
Wood Jones
Wood Moses
Wood Stephen
Wood Stephen, Junr.
Wood Timothy
Wood Vincent
Wood William
Woodhull Jesse
Woodhull Nathaniel
Woodruff John

Wool Jer'm
Woolley John
Woolsey John
Woolsey Jonathan
Worden Elisha
Worden Obediah
Wright Solomon
Write James
Write William
Wssee Benjamin
Wyat Nathaniel
Wyatt David
Wyatt Hezekiah
Wyatt Sam'll
Wygant John
Wyllis Henry
Wynans W.
Wynkoop Cornelius
Wynkoop Johannis, Junr.
Wynkoop John
Yane Samuel
Yeaman John
Young Charles
Young Christ
Youngs Benjamin

Orange County Militia — (Continued).

CAPT. JOHN WOOD'S EXEMPTS.

CAPT. JOHN WOOD
LIEUT. JONATHAN BALEY
" JACOB DUNNING
ENSIGN HADMIAL MOORE
" WILLIAM THOMPSON

ENLISTED MEN.

Arnet Jacob
Barker William
Brinson John
Butler James
Carpenter Samuel
Case Phenias
Clark James
Cole Jacob
Davis John
Davis Joshua
Denton John
Everitt Daniel
Everitt James
Gale Coe
Gale Richard
Grummun Joseph
Jackson George H.
Ludlum William
Waston Epherim
Napp James
Roe Nathaniel
Thompson Jonathan
Veal Gilbert
Wells Jorel
Wood Joseph

Sketch by R. A. Grider. R. L. Adams, artist.

PORTION OF STONE ARABIA BATTLEFIELD,
Col. Brown was slain near the two trees at right.

Sketch by R. A. Grider. R. L. Adams, artist.

BOWLDER MONUMENT
On Stone Arabia Battlefield.

Sketch by R. A. Grider. R. L. Adams, artist.

KLOCK'S FIELD,

Where battle of St. Johnsville occurred. Showing the Adam Klock house, built in 1750.

Sketch by R. A. Grider. R. L. Adams, artist.

CHRISTIE'S RIFT,

Near Upper St. Johnsville, where Johnson crossed and made his escape.

SUFFOLK COUNTY MILITIA.

1st Suffolk County Regiment of Minute Men.

COLONEL JOSIAH SMITH

CAPT. CLARKSON
" BENJAMIN COE
" JOHN DAYTON
" DAVID FITHIAN
" DANIEL HEDGES
" DAVID HOWELL
" JOSIAH HOWELL
" SAMUEL L'HOMMEDIEU
" WILLIAM LUDLAM
" R. MANEE
" EZEKIEL MULFORD
" PETER NOSTRAND
" DAVID PIERSON
" NATHANIEL PLATT
" PAUL REEVE
" WILLIAM ROGERS
" ZEPHANIAH ROGERS
" JOHN SANDFORD
" SELAH STRONG
" THOMAS WEEKS
" JOHN WHITE
" JOHN WICKES
" THOMAS WICKES
LIEUT. JOSHUA BENJAMIN
LIEUT. CALEB BREWSTER
" THOMAS BRUSH
" WILLIAM CLARK
" TIMOTHY CONKLING
" JOHN CORWIN
" JOHN FOSTER
" NATHANIEL HAND
" DAVID HORTON
" NATHANIEL HOWELL
" PAUL JONES
" CARL ISAAC KETCHAM
" EPHRAIM MARSTON
" JOHN MILLER
" ABRAHAM ROSE
" MATTHEW SAYRE
" HENRY SCUDDER
" SAMUEL SMITH
" EDWARD TOPPING
" JOSHUA YOUNGS
ENSIGN BENJAMIN BLATSLEY
" NATHANIEL BREWSTER
" NATHANIEL HUDSON
" NATHANIEL WILLIAMS, JR.

ENLISTED MEN.

Abbet James
Akerly John
Albertson John Parker
Aldrich Jacob, Junr.
Aldridge Joshua
Allen Nathaniel
Armstrong Bishop
Askly John
Bailey Joseph
Baker Daniel
Baker Henry
Baley John
Barnes Jeremiah
Barnes Jonathan
Barrett William
Barts Francis
Basset Cornelius
Bayley John
Bayley Philip
Baylis John
Baylis Nehemiah
Baynels Israel
Beale George
Beale Matthew
Beekwith Phineas
Benjamin Azariah
Benjamin David
Benjamin James
Benjamin Nathan
Benjamin Richard
Benjamin William
Bennet Edward
Bennett Gamaliel
Bennett John
Betts Richard
Biggs Silas
Bishop David
Bishop Enos
Bishop John
Bishop Samuel
Blatsley Daniel
Blidenburgh Daniel
Booth Wheelock
Bower David
Bower Hezekiah
Bower Jeremiah
Bower Zephaniah
Brewster John
Brian James
Brian Lemuel
Brown Caleb
Brown Daniel
Brown David
Brown Henry
Brown Henry, Junr.
Brown Reuben
Brown Richard
Brush Eliphalet
Brush Gilbert
Brush James
Brush Nehemiah
Brush Nehemiah, Junr.
Brush Robert
Bryan Jesse
Bryant Alexander
Buchanan William
Bunce Jesse
Burnett Joseph
Carle Jesse, Junr.
Carll John
Carll Scudd
Carpenter Nehemiah
Case Ichabod
Chatfield Henry
Chichester Eliphalet
Clark Elisha
Clark Stephen
Cleaveland Joseph
Coan Abraham
Conklin Jacob
Conkling Benjamin
Conkling Ezra
Conkling Jacob
Conkling Jeremiah
Conkling John
Conkling Joseph
Conkling Nathaniel
Conkling Samuel

Conkling Silvanus
Conkling William
Conkling William, Junr.
Conklinh Thomas
Conn William
Cook Calvin
Cook John
Cook Jonathan
Cook Nathan
Cook Silas
Cooper Benjamin
Cooper Charles
Cooper David
Cooper Matthew
Corey Isaac
Corwin Gershom
Corwin Jacob
Corwin Jeremiah
Corwin Jonathan
Corwin Joshua
Corwin Nathan
Corwin Nathan, Junr.
Corwin Simeon
Corwin Thomas
Corwithe Caleb
Corwithe Henry
Corwithe John
Crook Benjamin
Dains Paul
Davall Samuel
Davis Daniel
Davis Matthias
Davis Timothy
Davis William
Davison Isaac
Dayton Jacob
Dayton Jeremiah
Dayton Samuel
Denton Benjamin
Dibble Isaiah
Dickerson Abraham
Ditmas Garret
Doming Henry
Downs Peter
Drake Richard
Durree Charles
Edwards Daniel
Edwards David
Edwards Henry
Edwards Isaac
Edwards John
Edwards Silas
Edwards William
Ennis George
Everett George
Fanning Nathaniel
Fleet Alexander
Fordham Stephen
Foster Asa
Foster David Hains
Foster James
Foster Jedediah
Foster John
Foster Wakeman
Foster William
Fowler Richard
Gardiner Jeremiah
Garrard Zopher
Gates William
Gau John
Gear John M.
Gelston Hugh
Gelston William
Gerrard Benjamin
Gerrard John
Gerrard Joseph
Gerrard William
Gildersleeve
Gildersleeve John
Gildersleeve Philip
Gladin George
Goldsmith John
Goldsmith John, Junr.
Goldsmith William
Goodale Joseph
Gould John
Gray David
Griffing John
Griffis James
Guyer Lazarus
Haff Isaac
Haff James
Hallock Daniel
Hallock John
Hallock Peter
Hallock Richard
Hallock William
Hallock Zachariah
Halsey Abraham
Halsey Daniel
Halsey David Fithian
Halsey Ethan
Halsey James
Halsey Job
Halsey Philip
Halsey Silas
Halsey Silvanus
Halsey Stephen
Halsey Thomas
Halsey Timothy
Halsey William
Hand David, Junr.
Hand John, Junr.
Hand Jonathan
Hand Joseph
Hand Josiah
Hand Nathan
Harcus Selah
Harris George
Harris Henry
Harris Stephen
Hart John
Hart Nehemiah
Hart Samuel
Haven Constant
Hawkings Alexander
Hawkings Eleazer
Hawkings Gershom
Hawkings John
Hawkings Jonas
Hawkings Zophar
Hawks John
Hedges Christopher
Hedges Eleazer
Hedges Elihu
Hedges Job
Hedges Jonathan
Hedges Nathan
Hedges Timothy, Junr.
Herrick Micaiah
Hicks Zachariah
Higbee Jonas
Higbie Stephen
Hildreth Joshua
Hildreth Luther
Hill William
Homan Joseph
Homan Phineas
Hopkins Samuel
Hoppin Daniel
Horton Calvin
Howell David
Howell Edmund
Howell Edward
Howell James
Howell Jehiel
Howell John
Howell Jonathan
Howell Matthew
Howell Matthew, Junr.
Howell Moses
Howell William
Hubbard Richard Steers
Hubbard Samuel
Hubbel James
Hubbs Jacobus
Hubbs James
Hudson Ebenezer
Hudson Henry
Hudson John
Hudson John, Junr.
Hudson John Fred.
Hudson Samuel
Huff John
Hulse David
Hulse Richard
Hunt Benjamin
Ireland Joseph
Isaacs Aaron, Junr.
Jackson David
Jackson Richard
Jackson Samuel
Jaggar Abraham
Jagger Jeremiah
Jagger Matthew
Jarvis Joseph
Jarvis Nathaniel
Jarvis Seth
Jayne Robert
Jayne Shadiack
Jennings Silvanus
Jennings Stephen
Jennings Thomas
Jennings Zebulon
Jervis Isaiah
Jessup Isaac
Jessup Zebulon
Johnes Thomas
Jones Benjamin
Jones Elisha
Jones Jeremiah
Jones Obadiah
Jones Thomas
Kellum Jesse
Kellum Obadiah
Kelly Stephen
Ketcham Daniel
Ketcham Jesse
Ketcham John
Ketcham Joshua, Junr.
Ketcham Stephen
King Abraham
King Alexander
King Gilbert
King Samuel
Lewis Samuel
L'Hommedieu Benjamin, Junr.
L'Hommedieu Ephraim
L'Hommedieu Grover
L'Hommedieu Henry
L'Hommedieu Hudson
L'Hommedieu John
L'Hommedieu Mulford
Liscomb Isaac
Lockwood John
Longbottom Jacob
Longbottom Samuel
Loper Abraham
Loper James
Loper John
Ludlam George

Ludlam Jeremiah
Ludlam Parsons
Lupton David
Lyon Henry
Maccolum Malcom
Makes Joseph
Maynor Josiah
Messenger Oventon
Miller David
Miller Ezekiel
Miller Huntting
Miller Joel
Miller Nathan
Miller Peleg
Miller William
Mills Israel
Mills Jedidiah
Mills Jonas, Junr.
Mills William
Monroe David
Moore Henry
Moore Thomas
Morgan John
Mulford David
Mulford Elisha
Mulford John
Mulford Jonathan
Mulford Matthew
Mulford Samuel
Newman William
Nicoll Benjamin, Junr.
Nicoll Robert
Nicolls Stephen
Norris James
Norton George
Nostran Jacobus
Nostran Samuel
Oakes Simon
Osborn Abraham
Osborn Cornelius
Osborn Joseph
Osborn Smith Stratton
Osburn James
Osman Jacob
Osman Jonathan
Oventon James
Oventon John
Overton Joel
Overton Nathaniel
Packin Andrew
Pain John
Pain Silas
Paine Isaac
Parshall James
Parshall John
Parsons Samuel
Patty Ezekiel
Patty James
Payne Paul
Payne Peter
Peas Matthew
Pelletreau John
Perry Edmund
Petty James, Junr.
Pierson Abraham
Pierson Elias
Pierson Isaac
Pierson Job
Pierson John
Pierson Lemuel
Pierson Zachariah
Pike Amasa
Platt Amos
Platt Arthur
Platt Ebenezer
Platt Jeremiah
Post Jeremiah
Ramsons Auris
Raynor Ichabod (see Reigner)
Raynor Joseph
Raynor Josiah
Raynor Stephen
Raynor William
Reeve Ishmael
Reeve James
Reeve Jonathan
Reeve Luther
Reeve Obadiah
Reeve Stephen, Junr.
Reeve William
Reeves Barnabas
Reeves Purr, Junr.
Reeves Purryor
Reynolds Israel (see Baynels)
Rider Jesse
Robijson Edmund
Robinson David
Rogers Abraham
Rogers Abraham, Junr.
Rogers Caleb
Rogers Jarvis
Rogers Job
Rogers Stephen
Rogers Topping
Rogers Topping (see John)
Rogers William
Rolph Benjamin
Rose David
Rose Lemuel
Rugg Silas
Ruland David
Ruland John
Ruland Luke
Ruland Zophar
Rusco David
Rusco Nathaniel
Russell David
Russell Jonathan
Ryder Stephen
Sammis David
Sammis Ebenezer
Sammis Joseph
Sammis Nathaniel
Sammis Philip
Sammis Platt
Sammis Timothy
Sammis William
Sandford Abraham
Sandford Benjamin
Sandford Daniel
Sandford David Howell
Sandford Lewis
Satterly Josiah
Satturly Samuel
Sayre Abraham
Sayre Stephen
Schellenger Isaac
Schellinger Daniel, Junr.
Schellinger Jacob
Scribner Seth
Scudder Timothy, Junr.
Shaddain Henry
Shearman Anthony
Sherrill Daniel
Sherrill Henry
Sill Wessel
Simmons Samuel
Simons Moses
Smalling William
Smith Abner
Smith Arthur
Smith Charles
Smith Daniel
Smith David
Smith Epenetus
Smith Floyd
Smith Gilbert, Junr.
Smith Hezekiah
Smith James
Smith Jeremiah
Smith Jesse
Smith Job
Smith John
Smith Joseph
Smith Josiah
Smith Lemuel, Junr.
Smith Matthew
Smith Nathan
Smith Nathaniel
Smith Noah
Smith Obad
Smith Obadiah
Smith Philip
Smith Peleg
Smith Silas
Smith William
Smyth Sylvester
Soaper Gilbert
Soaper Jesse
Soaper Jonah
Soaper Moses
Solomon Jonathan
Stanbrough Josiah
Stanbrough Thomas
Stephens Thomas
Still William
Stratton Daniel
Stratton John
Stratton Samuel
Stratton Stephen
Strong Selah
Sweasey Daniel
Sweasey Isaac
Sylls Phineas
Talmage Enos
Talmage Joseph
Tanner Benjamin
Tarbel David
Taylor George
Taylor Nathaniel
Taylor William
Terril James
Terry Daniel
Terry Daniel, Junr.
Terry Elijah
Terry James
Terry John
Terry Joseph
Thompson Jonathan
Thompson Zebulon
Titus Timothy
Topping Henry
Topping Jeremiah
Topping Matthew
Topping Silas
Topping Zephaniah
Totten John
Totten Losse
Tredwell Thomas
Turner Henry
Tuthill John
Tuthill Nathan
Tuttle Jonathan
Tuttle Joshua
Udali Nathaniel (see Udell)
Udle Nathaniel
Vail Christopher
Vail John
Vail Platt, Junr.
Vail Samuel

Weed Jehiel
Weeks Jesse
Wells David
Wells Isaac
Wells Isaiah
Wells John Calvin
Wells Joseph
Wells Joshua
Wells Joshua, Junr.
Wells Manley
Wells Nathaniel
Wells Youngs
Wheeler John
Wheeler Thomas
Wheeler William
Wheldon Jonathan
White Ephraim
White Memucan
White Samuel
White Stephen
Whitman Nathaniel
Wick Silvanus
Wickes Samuel
Wicks Josiah
Williams John
Williamson James
Williamson Jedediah
Wilmot Jesse
Wilmot Nathaniel
Wood Epenetus
Wood Epenetus, Junr.
Wood Jeremiah
Wood Jonas
Wood Joseph
Wood Richard
Woodhull Abelenus
Woodhull James
Woodhull John
Woodhull Nathan
Woodruff David
Woodruff Joshua
Woodruff Silas
Woolley Charles
Youngs Nathan

3rd Suffolk County Regiment of Minute Men.

COLONEL THOMAS TERRY.

CAPT. JONATHAN BAYLEY
LIEUT. JOHN TUTHILL
LIEUT. JOSHUA YOUNGS
ENSIGN JAMES REEVE

ENLISTED MEN.

Beebe Lester
Booth Prosper
Brown Daniel
Brown James
Conkling Thomas
Demmon Jonathan
Dickerson Nathaniel
Drake Richard
Gardener James
Glover Ezekial
Glover Joseph
Goldsmith John
Griffing Peter
Havens John
Hemsted Thomas
Horton Benjamin
Horton Calvin
Horton David
Horton James
King Benjamin
King Jeremiah
King John
King Jonathan
Newbury Samuel
Overton Aaron
Pain Benjamin
Prince Thomas
Racket Absalom K.
Racket Noah
Rogers William (see Roghers)
Rogers William
Salmon Jonathan
Salmon Joshua
Tabor Ammon
Tabor Frederick
Terry David
Terry Elijah, Junr.
Terry Thomas
Truman David
Truman Jonathan
Tuthill Christopher
Tuthill David
Tuthill James, Junr.
Vail Benjamin, Junr.
Vail Daniel
Vail Elisha
Vail Jonathan
Vail Thomas
Wells Jonathan
Wiggins David
Wiggins William
Youngs John
Youngs Joseph

Suffolk County Regiment of Minute Men.

COLONEL DAVID MULFORD

CAPT. JOHN DAYTON
" DAVID FITHIAN
" DANIEL HEDGES
" DAVID HOWELL
" JOSIAH HOWELL

CAPT. SAMUEL L'HOMMEDIEU
" WILLIAM ROGERS
" JOHN SANDFORD
" JOHN WHITE

Canajoharry Dist.t July 29.th 1777.

Sir,

As the Time of my Militia now Stationed under your Command at Fort Schuyler will be expired this Week, I beg you not to detain them longer. The County Committee promised them not to stay longer but sixteen Days but I prolonged the Time to three Weeks from Home to home, which I assured them under my hand. They will long for the Time in Regard to their Hay and Wheat Harvest, as their presence at home is most necessary at this Season. I hope therefore, that you'll grant them their Discharge next Thursday, so that they may reach home at the three Weeks End, especially as one hundred and sixty Men Continental Troops are set off to day for Fort Schuyler to reinforce your Garrison. In case of detaining them longer as promised, I really fear, that it will cause a Disturbance and an unwillingness for their future Service, when wanted, and besides they perhaps would desert from their Station, to the dishonor of our County. — I have procured twenty fat Cattle for your Garrison agreeable to your Request, they are ready and waiting for to be drove along under a sufficient guard —

I am always with Resp.t

Sir

Your obed.t humble Serv.t

Nicolas Herckheimer

P.S.

Col.o Weston, as I understood of him is ready and willing to march up with his Men to Fort Schuyler, as soon as you will Require the same, otherwise he is to stay at Fort Dayton

Col.o Peter Gansevoort

Command.t

Fort Schuyler

A LETTER FROM "THE HERO OF ORISKANY," GENERAL NICOLAS HERCKHEIMER

TRYON COUNTY MILITIA.

COLONEL SAMUEL CAMPBELL
COLONEL EBENEZER COX
LIEUTENANT COLONEL SAMUEL CLYDE
MAJOR PETER S. DEYGERT
MAJOR ABRAHAM COPEMAN
ADJUTANT JACOB SEEBER
QUARTER MASTER JOHN PICKARD
SURGEON ADAM FRANK
SURGEON DAVID YOUNGLOVE

CAPT. JOHN BOWMAN
" MATTHEW BROWN
" JACOB DIFFENDORFF
" JOST DEYGERT
" JOSEPH HOUSE
" ADAM LEYP
" JOHN ROOF (RUSS)
" RYNER VAN EVEREN
" NICHOLAS WEYSER
" JAPES WILSON
LIEUT. PETER ADAMY
" ABRAHAM ARNT
" NICHOLAS BARTH
" HENRY BRATE
" CONRAD BRAUN
" GEORGE CONDERMAN
" NICHOLAS DEYGERT
LIEUT. DEDRICK HORNING
" JACOB MATTHEWS
" CHARLES POWELL
" JACOB SCHNEYDER
" JOHN SEEBER
" WILLIAM SEEBER
" HENRY SHRUMLING
" JOHN VAN EVEREN
" HANES WINDECKER
ENSIGN JOHN L. BELLINGER
" JOHN CUNDERMAN
" RICHARD ELLWOOD
" ADAM FLIND
" JACOB HANES
" HENRY MYER
" CORNELIUS VAN EVERY
" HENRY WALWRATH

ADDITIONAL NAMES ON STATE TREASURER'S PAY BOOKS.

LIEUT. ENGLEHARDT WAGENER
ENSIGN JOHN PICKERT
ENSIGN JEREMIAH YOUNG

ENLISTED MEN.

Adamy Peter
Ale Christian
Ale Peter
Apel Henry
Batenauer Jacob
Batenaur George
Bearmour Henry
Becker Henry
Becker Peter
Beellinger Adam
Bell Fredrick
Belleanger Fredrick
Belliner Henrick
Bellinger Adam
Bellinger Philip
Bellinger William
Bendeman Peter
Besner Jacob
Bettinger Martin
Benteman Simmon
Bickerd Henry
Bickerd Isaac
Billing William
Billinger William
Bitelman Peter
Blats George
Bleats George
Boball Adam
Bolier Frederick
Bolt Fillip
Boom Fredrick K
Boss Christian
Bost Christian
Botman Adam
Brate James
Brisenbecker Balser
Broukman Godfret
Bruckeman John
Bruckman Godfrid
Brunner Christian
Bush George
Butcluter John
Buterfield James
Cannan Matthew
Castler Thomas
Christman John
Clapsattle William
Clapsedel George
Clebsater William
Clock Joseph
Cockton Thomas
Cohat Adam
Cohert Adam
Conterman John
Contryman John
Contryman John M
Coon John
Crais George
Cramer Godfred
Cramer Joast

Creamer John
Creamer Joseph
Crimm Jacob
Crisman John
Crosmen Frederick
Crouse Friederick
Crows George
Crum Adam
Crum Jacob
Cuff (colored)
Cunderman Cunrath
Cunderman Frederick
Cunderman John J.
Cunderman Marius
Cuntrman Adam
Cuntryman Cunrad
Curtner Peter
Cypher John
Damuth Richard
Darwind Bindier
Dasler John
Deck Henry
Defendorf Jacob H. R.
Demult Richard
Demuth Dederick
Devery Arent
Devy Adam
Deygert Nichlas
Didenbeck Baltus
Diefendorff H. Jacob
Diefendorff Johannes
Diefendorff John J.
Diefendurff John
Diefendurff John, Jun.
Dietrich Dewald
Dilenbeck Baltus
Dilenbeck Martin
Dinstman Antony
Dinstman Denis
Docksteader John
Dreisselmann Christian
Dunckel Frank
Dunckel Nicholas
Dunckel Peter
Dunckell Garrett
Dunkle George
Dunlap John
Dunlap William
Dus Ler Jacob
Dusler John
Dusler Marx
Dyckert Thabolt
Dygart Sevrinus
Dygert Henry
Dykert Henery
Eatkens William
Eckler Christ Sogel
Eckler Christstofel
Eckler Ernest
Eckler Hanos
Eckler Henry
Eckler Henry, Jun.
Eckler Johannes
Eckler Lenet
Eckler Pitter
Ehl Christian
Ehl Peter
Ehle Anthony
Ehle Harmanus
Ehle John
Ehts Adam
Ehts Christopher
Ehts John Christ.
Ehts William
Elfendorf Debois
Ell John
Ellwood Benjamin
Ellwood Isaac
Elvendorf Tobias
Elwood Peter
Embody Henry
Estter John C
Farbus Nichlas
Faubelo Johnas
Feeble John
Fehling Andreas
Feling Henry
Felling Jacob
Felling Nicholas
Felling Peter
Fetterly John
Fetterly John T.
Fouston John
Flack Peter
Flind Alexander
Flint Alexander
Flint Cornelles
Flint John
Flint Robert
Folkert John
Folyg Peter
Forbush Johnes
Fork Isaac
Forre Adam (see Furry)
Foster John
Foster Moses
Fox Peter
Fox William
Frantz Stoffel
Fretcher Conraed
Fuks Peter
Fun Adam
Furro Rudolph (see Furry)
Galger Isaac
Garlock Adam
Garlock George P.
Garlock Jacob
Garlock Philip
Gelly Thadeus
Gerlack Gorge
Gerlack Han Christian
Gerlach Henry
Gerlock George W.
Givit Fridrick
Givet John J.
Grim Jacob
Haber Jacob
Haberman Jacob
Hack Fredrick
Haffer Jacob
Hake Frederick
Hako Fradrick
Harning Lienert
Haus Adam
Haus Henrick
Haus Peter
Heerway Charles
Helmer John
Helmer John G.
Helmer Joseph
Helmer Jost
Henry Andrew
Hess George
Hess Henry
Heuth Joshua
Heyntz William
Hicky George
Hicky Michal
Himer William
Hines Andrew
Hootmaker Adam
Hoover Jacob
Horning Adam
Horning Dederick
Horning George
Horning John
Horning Lanert
Hous Harman
House George
House Jacob
House John
House Joseph
House Jost C.
House Nicholas
House Peter
Jacob Henry
Johns William
Jordan Adam
Jordan Casper
Jordan Casper L.
Jordan Gasper
Jordan George
Jordan John
Jordan John Peter
Jordan Nicholas
Jorden John P.
Jorden Peter
Jung Jacob
Jung Thommes
Jungijo Jacob
Kellar Jacob
Keller Andras
Keller Andres, Jun.
Keller Felix
Keller Gasper
Keller Jacob R.
Kelly Thomas
Kelmer John
Kerlach Henry
Kesles Thomas
Kessler Peter
Killy Thomas
Kling Ludwig
Knausz Johannes
Knautz John
Knieskern Pitter
Knouts George
Koemer Johannes
Kcrning Adam
Kretsinger Jacob
Lambert George
Lambert Peter
Lambert Peter, Jun.
Lambert Peter, Sen.
Lampert Peter
Lape John
Lappius Daniel
Lentner George
Leeve Phillip
Leipe John L.
Lepert Fredrick
Levey Michael
Leyli Simon
Lint Georg
Lints Gorg
Lipe John
Lipe John, Jun.
Loucks Peter
Loux Jost
Low Lawrence Gras
Lure Philip
Lurzdemann Simon
Mai Henrich
Marten Robert
Mayby David
Mayby Joseph
Mayer H. Henry
Mayer Jacob
Mayer Jacob S.
Meier Matthew
Meyer Henrick
Meyer Henrick S.

Meyer Jacob
Meyer Jacob R.
Meyer Johan Henrick
Meyer Solomon
Mier John
Miler John C.
Miller Conraed
Miller Dionysius
Miller Garret
Miller John
Monck John, Jun.
Monke John
Moone James
Moos Pitner Rufus
Morfey Henry
Moyer David
Moyer John
Murphy Henry
Murphy Thomas
Myer Matthias
Myers Dewel
Myers John
Myre Henry
Myre John
McCartey Dunkon
McCartey John
McFie Alexander
McKillip John
McLonis Jurry
McVagulhen Peeter
Neles Cris John
Neles Rowerd
Neles Willem
Nelles Christian
Nelles George
Nelles Gerry
Nelles Henrick
Nelles Henry
Nelles Henry N.
Nelles John
Nelles William
Nellies Gerry
Nellis Henry
Nellis Jacob
Netherly John
Netherly John H.
Netherly John I.
Nolgert John
Ohn Jacob
Outerman Jacob
Ovendurff Conrad
Paba Ernst
Parsheall James
Pauly Jacob
Phenes Michael
Pickard Cunrad
Pickerd Adolph
Pickerd Nicholas
Pickert Conradt
Pickert George
Pigner Tise
Plets George
Plough Nichlas
Plunes John
Price George
Qollinger Henry
Quackenbos Honter Soct
Quackenboss Isaac
Quakenbush David
Quakenbush Jeremiah
Quakenbush Peter
Quollenger Gosper
Quollinger Andrew
Radenaer Jacob
Radimour Jacob
Ransier George
Ratnower George
Ratnower Jacob
Reasnor James
Reinhartd Willem
Remer Jacob
Remer John
Remer Martin
Revershon John Peter
Ribsomer William
Rice John
Riebsomer Matteys
Riverson John Peter
Rodgers Samuel
Roneons Jonathan
Ronnin John, Jun.
Roof John
Roseel John
Roth John
Ruff John
Runnins John, Jun.
Runnins John, Sen.
Sacknar John
Sander Henrick
Scheat Andony
Schefer Adam
Schiely Martin
Schimmel Francis
Schneck George
Schneider Michael
Schreiber Steffan
Schuyler David
Schuyler Jacob
Schuyler John Jost
Schuyler Nicolas
Schuyler Peter P
Schyler David, Jun.
Scoulen Essias
Scoulen Tosseos
Seaber John W.
Seeber Jacob
Seeber John
Seyber John
Shall Henry
Sheafer Adam
Sheafer Henry
Shelly John
Shimel Dieterich
Shireman George
Shmit Hendrick
Shnyder Gottlib
Simmerman Conratee
Simmerman Henery
Sits Hendrick
Sits John
Sits Nichlos
Sitts Peter
Sitz Baldes
Smidt Philip
Smith Johannes
Smith John
Smith Philip
Snake George
Snyder John
Sober Jacobus
Spalsbeck John
Sparback Martinus
Sparks Pearl
Stansell Nicolas
Steinmetz Philip
Stensell George
Stensell Nicoles
Stensell William
Stephen John
Strawbeck Adam
Stroback Fradrick
Strobeck Jacob
Sullenger Gosper
Suller Andrew
Suller Gosper
Tailor Nathan
Tetterly John H.
Thompson Aaron
Thompson John
Thompson Thomas
Thompson William
Tillenback Martin
Tom (colored)
Tucks Peter
Tulling Henry
Tygert Henry
Ullendorff Daniel
Ulsever Stephen
Ulzhaven Bastian
Uthermark John B.
Uttermark John J.
Van Johannes
Van Allstine Abraham
Vanallstine Abraham C.
Van Allstine Peter
Van Alsten Cornelius C
Van Alstin Harmans
Vanalstine Cornelius
Vanalstine Cornelius J.
Vanalstine John
Vanalstine John G.
Vanalstine John M.
Vanalstine Martin
Vanalstine Martin A.
Vanalstine Martin G.
Vanalstine Philip
Vanalstyn Peter
Van Camp Isaac
Van Campen Cornelius
Van Derwarken Harmanus
Vanderwarker Joshua
Van Derwartin Joshua
Van Eaverak John
Van Everen John
Van Slike George
Van Slyke Garret
Van Slyke John
Wagener Engelhard
Waggoner Isaac
Waggoner Jacob
Wagner George
Wagner Jacob
Wagoner Gorge
Wallart Hannes
Wallrad Georae
Wallrate Adolph
Wallrate Frederick
Wallrate Jacob
Wallse Conraed
Wallse Conraed, Jun.
Wallse Jacob
Walrad Jacob
Walrate Henrick
Walrath George
Walrath Henry
Walrath Jacob
Walrath William
Wals Cunrath
Wals Cunrath, Jun.
Wals Cunrath, Sen.
Warmood Pete
Warmorte Petter
Warmuth John
Wath Jacob
Westerman Peter
Wiele Henry
Wiele Joss Henry
Wilson James
Windecker Fredrick
Windker Nicolas
Winn John
Wohlgemuth John

Wohlgemuth Wiliam
Woldorf Johannes
Wolkemood John
Wollever John
Wollever Nicholas
Woolf Jacob
Wormut John
Wright Jacob
Yates Chris P.
Young Adam
Young Andreas
Young Andrew
Young Christian
Young Christian A.
Young Crist, Jun.
Young Frietrick
Young Godfred
Young Henry
Young Henry P.
Young John
Young Joseph
Young Jost
Young Lodwick
Young Peter
Young Robert
Young Thomas
Zola Casper

Tryon County Militia — (Continued).

COLONEL JACOB KLOCK
LIEUTENANT COLONEL PETTER WAGONER
MAJOR CHRISTIAN WILLIAM FOX
MAJOR CHRISTOPHER FOX
ADJUTANT SAMUEL GRAY
ADJUTANT ANDREW IRVIN
QUARTER MASTER JACOB EAKER
SURGEON JOHANN GORGE VACH

CAPT. JOHN BRADBIG
" SEVERINES COOK
" PETER S. DYGART
" JOHN HASELMAN
" CHRISTIAN HOUSE
" PHILIP HELMER
" JOHN HESSE
" ——— HOOVER
" JOHANES KAYSER
" SEVERINUS KLOCK
" RUDOLPH KOCH
" HENRY MILLER
" NICHOLAS RIGHTER
" JOHANNES RUSS
" JOHN ZILLEY
LIEUT. JOHN ADAMS
" ADAM BELLINGER
" HARMAN BREWER
LIEUT. NICHOLAS COPPERNOLL
" RICHARD COPPERNOLL
" JOHN KOCH
" LODOWICK NELLIS
" ISAAC PARIS
" JOHN SCHALL
" JOHN SUTZ
" JOHN P. SUTZ
" JOHN TIMMERMAN
" HENDRICK TIMMERMAN
" SAMUEL VANETTA
" JOHN VAN SLYCK
ENSIGN GEORGE FEY
" PETER GREMS
" PETER SITZ
" CONRATH TIMMERMAN
" NICHOLAS VAN SLYCK

ADDITIONAL NAMES ON STATE TREASURER'S PAY BOOKS.

LIEUT. JOHN EIGENBROOT
" JOHN FINCK
" WILLIAM FOX
" HENYOST SCHOLL
ENSIGN GEORGE ECKER
" GEORGE WAGONER
" NICHOLAS WALRATH
" FREDERICK ZIMMERMAN

ENLISTED MEN.

Acker Abraham
Adamy Peter
Apply Jacob
Arkson John
Bader Melgert
Bader Michael
Bacchus John
Bagley Andrew
Bailer Joseph
Baker Joseph
Baldsperger Johannes
Balsby Peter
Balsle Andrew
Barder Nicholas
Bates Michael
Baul Samuel
Baum Frederic
Baum Philip
Bayard John
Bayard Valentine
Bayer John
Beacker Henry
Bealer John
Bealor Joseph
Beaum Philip
Becker Henry
Becker Philip
Bellinger Adam
Bellinger Adam P.
Bellinger Friedrich
Beeker Peter
Beeler Jacob
Beely Jacob
Bellinger Henrich
Bellinger Jost
Bellinger Peter
Bicker Corse
Bishelt Charles
Bishet Charles
Bishop Charles
Blessen Lorance
Blesseus Lorents
Bost Andres
Boush George
Braun Christien
Bratt Henry
Bratt Jacobus
Brewer John
Brewer William
Brower William
Brunner Jacob
Bush George
Bush Julius
Buyie John B.
Candon John
Casselman John
Casselman Peter
Cayser Barnerd
Christman Jacob
Calutia Thomas
Christman John
Clapper Christian
Clapsattle Andrew
Clapsattle William

Claus George
Clements Jacob
Coleman Henery
Conningham William
Conterman John
Coppernoll John
Coppernoll William
Crama Jacob
Cramer Andreas
Cranse Jacob
Craus Jost
Crause Jacob
Crim Hendrick
Crounhart George
Crowhart Georg
Cruysler George
Culman Henry
Cuningham Johannis
Cuningham William
Dackson John
David Adam
Davis Joseph
Deacke John
Deacker Hendrick B.
Dellenbag Hendrick
Dellenbag John
DeHarsh Philip
Deavies Jacob
Deygert Peter S.
Deygert Petrus J.
Deygert Rutderph
Deygert Salvinus
Deygert Soeferinus
Deygert Sevrines H.
Dillebagh Martin
Dillenbach Henrich
Dillinbach John
Dockstater Nicolaus
Dum Conradt
Dum Melgert
Dum Nicholas
Dure John
Duslar Jacob
Dusler William
Dygert Henry
Dygert George
Dygert Peter W.
Dygert Seffreanes, Junr.
Dygert Seravinis P.
Dygert William
Dygert William H.
Dygert William, Junr.
Eading Conrad
Eadle George
Eadle Hendrick
Eaker George, Junr.
Eaply Philip
Ecker Abraham
Eckler Henrich
Ecker Johannes
Egenbrode John
Egenbrode Peter
Eher Nicholass
Ehl William
Ehll Michel
Eigenbrade George
Ekar George
Eker Nicholas
Ellwood Isaac
Embie Phillip
Emge Johannes
Emge Johannes, Junr.
Emge Phillip
Emphe John
Empie Adam
Empie Andrew
Empie Frederick
Empie John
Empie John, Junr.
Empie Philip
Engush John
Erichman Gottfried
Erksen John
Faling Jacob
Faling Philip
Feanes Michael
Feather William
Fehling Jacob
Feling John
Fert Jacob
Fey George, Junr.
Filling John
Finch Christian
Finch Hanyost
Finck Andrew
Finck Christian
Finck Hanyost
Finck John
Finck William, Junr.
Fitcher Coenrad
Flander Henry
Flander Jacob
Flander John
Flander Tenus
Fon Stoffil
Foneyea John
Forbush Bartholomew
Fort Andres
Fox Daniel
Fox Joseph
Fox Peter
Fox William
Foy George
Frealing Jacob
Frebach George
Freihtag Johann
Frelich Francis
Frelich Jachiob
Frelich Felte
Frelich Valentine
Freytery J. G.
Fritcher Henry
Frolich Jacob
Fry Jacob
Furneay John
Fykes George
Fykes Philip
Garlock Adom
Garrison John
Gerder Henrich
Gerlag Adam
Gerlag Philip
Gerlack Georg
Gerlock Christian
Gerlock William G.
Getman Christian
Getman George
Getman Johannes
Getman Peter
Getman Thomas
Gettman Frederick
Ginder Henry
Glantz John
Gorofe Henray
Graen John
Graff Christian
Gram John
Grant John
Gray Adam
Gray Andrew
Gray John
Gray Robert
Gray Samuel
Greay Adam
Greay Andreis
Greay John
Greay Robert
Greh Robert
Grembs Hendrick
Grems John
Grems Peter, Junr.
Grey Andrew
Gross Lawrence
Guywitz Frederick
Haeman Peter
Hainer Hendrick
Hallenbolt Andrew
Harkimer Abram
Hart Conradt
Hart Daniel
Hart John
Hause Adam
Hauss George
Hawerman Jacob
Hayney Henry
Heaber John
Headeach Daniel
Heer Casper
Hees Johannes
Heintz Andreas
Hellebolt Andrew
Hellebolt Dennis
Hellebould Tunis
Hellegas Conrad
Hellegas Peter
Hellmer Henrich
Hellmer John
Helmer Adam
Helmer Lenerd
Helmerd Lenerd L.
Helmore John
Helwig John
Heoman Peter
Herkimer Abraham
Herkimer Gerg
Herkimer Nichol
Herring Henry
Hertiss Andreas
Hess Christian
Hess Daniel
Hess Henry
Hess John
Heyney Frederick
Hillts John
Hoeman Peter
Honshield George
House Adam
House Elias
House Fredrick
House Harman
Habner Andrew
Huffnagel Christian
Hutmacher Adam
Hyney George
Janea Christian
Johnston William
Jordan Caspar
Jordan George
Juger Jacob
Juger John
Jung Jacob, Junr.
Jung Lutwig
Kalley George
Kaselman Bertel
Kasselman Johannes
Keaber John
Kearn John
Keasselman Peardle
Keasselman John, Junr.
Kees Henrich
Keiltz Peter
Keller Anderis

Keller Felix
Keller Kasher
Keller Piter
Kelley Thomas
Kelly George
Kern Beades
Kern John
Kern Michael
Kessler Conrath
Kessler Joseph
Kessler Melgert
Keyser Barent
Keyser Hanjost
Keyser Henry
Keyser Michael
Kiles Conrath
Kiley Henrich
Kills Peter
Kils Conrath
Kils Peter
Kilts Adam
Kilts Conrath
Kilts Nichelas
Kilts Peter
Kilts Peter N.
Kilts Philils
Kilts Phillip
Kim George
King John
Klock Adam
Klock George G.
Klock Hendrick
Klock Hendrick J.
Klock Henry, Senr.
Klock Jacob H.
Klock John
Klock Joseph
Klock Jost
Knap William
Koch Beadus
Koch John
Koch Rudolf, Junr.
Kock Caspaurus, Junr.
Koock Rudolf
Kramer John
Krause Lenard
Krays Johannes
Krembs Henry
Kremer Gotfrey
Kreams Hendrick
Krems John
Kretzer Leonard
Kring Johannes
Kring John Louck
Krouse Jost
Kroust Jost
Kuhl Philip
Kurn Carl

Kurne Charley
Kyser Hanyost
Kyser Hendrick
Kyser Michael
Labdon Daniel
Lambert Peter
Lampman Peter
Lasher Garrit
Lasher Gavoet
Lasher John
Laucks Adam
Laucks Adam A.
Laucks George
Laucks Henry W.
Laucks Jacob
Laucks John
Laucks Piter
Laucks William
Laux Conrad
Laux Dietrick
Laux Hendrick
Laux Jacob
Laux Peter
Laver Conrath
Lawer Conrath
Leaning Jacob
Leasher Garnet
Leather Christian
Leather John
Ledder Christian
Ledder John
Lelly Toyn
Lentz Jacob
Lephard John
Lepper Frederick
Lepper Wiand
Leschr Gerred
Lesher John
Long Hendrick
Loucks Henry
Loucks William
Loux Adam
Loux Jacob
Loux William
Lutz George
Lyke John, Senr.
March Stephen
Macknod James
Marinus Abraham
Martin Alexander
Martin Philip
Mayer Dewalt
Merckel Dewalt
Merckel Peter
Merkill Jacob
Merkill Richard
Meyer Deobald
Meyer Deowald

Meyer Johannes
Meyer John
Meyer Theobald
Miller Conrad
Miller Garret
Miller John
Miller Philip
Miller Samuel
Murray Thomas
Myer Jacob
McArder Duncan
McArder John
Nehr
Nelles Andreas
Nelles Gorg
Nelles Henry
Nelles John
Nelles Joseph
Nelles Lodowick
Nelles Peter
Nelles Philibs
Nelles William
Nellis Joseph
Nells George
Nestel Andrew
Nestel George
Nestle Gottlel
Nestel Gottlib
Nestel Henry
Nestel Martin
Nestel Mearty, Junr.
Newman Joseph
Osterroth Friederich
Palsperger John
Peaker Adolt
Peaker Philip
Pellinger Joseph
Peters Joseph
Phenix Michael
Philips James
Pickard Conrad
Pickard Jacobus
Pickert Adolph
Pickerd John
Pitry Hancost
Plantz Johannis
Plapper Christian
Potman Arent
Price John
Putman David
Raisner Jacobus
Rapspel Frederick
Rattenaur Jacob
Read John
Reeder Hendrick
Remesnyder John
Richard Jacob
Richter Nicholas

Rickerd Bartholomew
Rickerd Lodowick
Rickert Jacobus
Rickert Lodowick
Rickert Ludwig
Rikert John
Ritzman Johannes
Rob John
Roller Andrew
Root Christian
Ropp George
Rosekrans Nicholas
Rosecrantz George
Ruff Michael
Rust George
Salbag Hangrist
Saltman John
Saltsman George
Saltsman Henry
Schaffer Henrich
Schaffer John
Schall Georg
Schebber Johannes
Scheffer Jacob
Scheit Peter
Schnel Adam, Junr.
Schnell Adam
Schuldye John, Junr.
Schuldys John
Schuls Henrich
Schuls Jacob
Schultheis Johannes
Schultheiss Georg
Schultz Hendrick
Schultz Jacob
Schultz John
Schulz John
Schupp Nicolaus
Seaker Philip
Seart Jacob
Seeber Conrad
Seeber John
Seelbach Johannes
Serd Jacob
Shaffer John
Shaffer Nicolaus
Shait Peter
Shall Johan Yost
Shaver Bartholomew
Sheffer Jacob
Shiely Mantus
Shill Jacob
Shite Peter
Shittser Hendrick
Shouldis Hendrick
Should George
Shoulds John
Shultis Jacob

Shults Henry
Shultz John
Shultz William
Shutthers Georg
Sietz George
Sits Hendrick
Sits George
Slutz Jhames
Smeath James
Smith Baltus
Smith Baltus S.
Smith Bolzar
Smith George
Smith Henry
Smith James
Smith Matthias
Smith Nicholas
Smith Nicholas, Junr.
Smit Paltes
Smith William
Sneek George
Snell Adam
Snell George
Snell Hanickle
Snell Hanyost
Snell Jacob
Snell John
Snell John F.
Snell John J.
Snell John, Junr.
Snell John P.
Snell Nicholas
Snell Peter
Snell Sefrinus
Snell Thomas Jacob
Spalsperger John
Spanknebel John
Spracher Conreth
Spracher George
Spracher George, Junr.
Spracher John
Spreacher Conrad
Spreacher George
Spreacher George, Junr.
Spreacher John
Spucher George
Spucher George, Junr.
Spucher John
Stall Rudolf
Stam Jacob
Stamm George
Stamm Lawrence
Staring Adam
Staring Jacob
Steak George
Steancle Nicholas
Stenbey Jeremiah
Stencil Nicholas
Stencil William
Stenfell George
Strader Nicholas
Straher John
Straub William
Streeder Nicholas
Streter Nicklas
Strubel Christian
Strubel Christopher.
Sults Peter
Suts Derick
Suts John
Suts Peter
Suts Peter P.
Sutt Peter
Sutz Peter
Sutz Richert
Syphert Godfry
Teed Samuel
Temerman Jacob J.
Temermen Jacob
Tham Adam
Thousler William
Thum Conrath
Thum Nicolas
Tillenbach Heinderick
Tilm Nicholas
Timberman John
Timmerman Adam
Timmerman Christian'
Timmerman Conrath L.
Timmerman Hendrick L.
Timmerman Jacob L.
Timerman Jacob T.
Timmerman John
Timmerman John G.
Timmerman William
Tread Samuel
Tucker George
Tucker Jacob
Tucker Johannis
Tyger George
Tygert Peter S.
Ullenforff Daniel
Utt Francis
Vedder Arnout
Voss Nicolas
Van Alstine Nicholas
Van Alstyne Marten C.
Vanderwerke John
VanDerWerke Thomas
VanDerWerken William
Van Etten Jacobus
Van Lichel Samuel
Van Loon John
Van Slick Adam
Van Slick Copes
Van Slick Nicholas G.
Van Slick Samuel
Van Slick William
Van Slyck John
Van Slyck Nicholas
Van Slyke Adam
Van Slyke Jacobus
Van Slyke Samuel
Van Slyke William
Wabel Hendrick
Wafel Adam (see Wasel)
Wafel George (see Wasel)
Wafel Henry (see Wasel)
Wafel John (see Wasel)
Wafel William (see Wasel)
Wagner Engelhard
Waggoner George
Waggoner Joseph
Waggoner Jost
Walder Adam
Walder George
Walrad Adolph
Walrad Gerhart
Walrad Jacob
Walrad John
Walrad Peter
Wallrath Adam
Wallrath Hannes
Wallrath Henrich
Wallrath Isaac
Wallrath Nicholas
Walrath Adolf
Walrath Friterick
Walrath Henrich
Walrath Henry
Walrath Jacob H.
Wallratt Jacob
Walt Christian
Walter Adam
Walter Christian
Walter George
Waltz Conrad
Waltz George
Walvel Johan Gerg
Warmooth Christian
Warmooth William
Warmouth Nathaniel
Warmouth Peter
Warmouth Peter J.
Warmouth William
Warmud John, Junr.
Warmut Christean
Warmwood Mathias
Warmwood Peter
Wasel Adam (see Wafel)
Wasel George (see Wafel)
Wasel Henry (see Wafel)
Wasel John (see Wafel)
Wasel William (see Wafel)
Wassel Henry
Wassel William
Water George
Weack Sefrnus
Weak John
Weaver Jacob
Weaver Nickalas
Weber Nicolass
Weimer Andrew
Werner Andrew
Werner Charles Alexander
Werner Christian
Werner Elexander
Wessel George
Wessel George W.
Wesser Nicholas
Wester Jacob
Wezer Nicholas
Wick John
Wick Michael
Williams Eliser
Williamson Elizer
Winckel John
Windecker Nicholas
Windeeker Jacob
Windeker Frederick
Winn John
Woleben Nicholas
Wolever Peter
Wormud Mattis
Wormwood John
Wormwood William
Wormer Andrew
Wyles George
Wyner John
Yanney Christian
Yoram Jacob
Yorna Jacob
Young Adam
Young Andrew
Young Christian
Young Gotfried
Young Jacob
Young Jacob, Junr.
Young Lodowick
Young Ludwick
Young Nicholas
Young Richard
Yucher George
Yuker George
Yuker Jacob
Yung Ludwick
Yuran Jacob
Zessinger Nicholas
Zimmerman Christian
Zimmerman Conrad
Zimman Jacob L.

Schoharie creek.

Van Epps' swamp.

By permission of C. P. Teeple, photographer, Fonda, N. Y.

Van Epps' Swamp.

By permission of C. P. Teeple, photographer, Fonda, N. Y.

CONTINUOUS VIEW OF JOHNSON'S ROUTE OF MARCH, ON SOUTH SIDE OF MOHAWK RIVER, FROM SCHOHARIE CREEK TO ABOUT ONE MILE ABOVE VAN EPPS' SWAMP (FULTONVILLE).

By permission of C. P. Teeple.

VIEW OF JOHNSON'S ROUTE OF MARCH FROM VAN EPPS' SWAMP TO WILLOW BASIN, ON SOUTH SIDE OF MOHAWK RIVER.

By permission of C. P. Teeple.

VIEW OF JOHNSON'S ROUTE OF MARCH FROM ANTHONY'S NOSE TO KEATOR'S RIFT, ON SOUTH SIDE OF MOHAWK RIVER.

Tryon County Militia—(Continued).

COLONEL FREDERICK FISHER

(Scalped by the Indians and left for dead at Caughnawaga, October 25, 1781.)

LIEUTENANT COLONEL VOLKERT VEEDER

MAJOR JOHN BLUEN

MAJOR JOHN NUKERK

ADJUTANT PETER CONYN

ADJUTANT JOHN G. LANSINGH, JR.

ADJUTANT GIDEON MARLATT (ENSIGN)

QUARTER MASTER THEODORUS F. ROMINE

QUARTER MASTER ABRAHAM VAN HORN

QUARTER MASTER SIMON VEEDER

SURGEON JOHN GEORGE FOLKE

SURGEON WILLIAM PETRY

CAPT. AMAUNNIEL DEGRAUF
" JOHN FISHER
" JELLIS FONDA
" JACOB GAERDENYER
" DIRIK HOGOBOOM
" JOHN LITTEL
" HARMANUS MABIE
" ISAAC MARSELIS
" DAVID MCMASTER
" GERRIT PUTNAM
" SAMUEL REES
" WILLIAM SNOOK
" ABRAHAM VEEDER
" ANDREW WEMPLE
" JOHN WEMPLE
" ROBERT YATES
" JOSEPH YEOMANS
LIEUT. AMOS BENNET
" BENJAMIN DELINE
" NICKLIS DOCKSTETTER
" CHRIST ERNEST
" WILLIAM HALL
" WILLIAM LARD
" GERRITT NEWKIRK
LIEUT. BENJAMIN OLINE
" JOSOP PRINTUP
" FRANCIS F. PRUYN
" ABRAHAND QUACENBOSH
" MC W. QUACKENBUSH
" VINCENT QUACKENBUSH
" LORENTZ SCHULER
" JOHN SNOOK
" ISAIAS J. SWART
" GARETT S. VAN BRACKLEN
" THOMAS VAN HORN
" PETER VAN OLYNDE
" DERICK VAN VEGHTEN
" HENRY H. VROMAN
" PETER YATES
" PETER YONG
ENSIGN HENRY LEWIS
" RECHRT POTMAN
" FRANCIES PUTMAN
" CONRAD STONE
" GORG STONE
" GARRETT G. VAN BRACKLEN
" PETER VROMAN

ADDITIONAL NAMES ON STATE TREASURER'S PAY BOOKS.

LIEUT. DAVID BEVERLY
" JACOB DINGHARDT
" CHARLES HUBBS
" JAMES MC MASTER
" JOSEPH PRENTISS
" VICTOR PUTNAM
" MYNDERT W. QUACKENBUSH
LIEUT. FRANCIS REYNER
" JEREMIAH SWART
" WILLIAM SWART
" SOLOMON WOODWORTH
ENSIGN THOMAS HARRISON
" EPHRAIM PIERCE
" TEUNIS VAN VAUGHN

ENLISTED MEN

Acker John
Aker Gorge
Albrant Hendrick
Albrant Henry
Algire John
Allen William
Anderson William
Antus Coenrad
Antus John
Any Jacob
Archer Ananias
Baker Adam
Barbat John
Barcly Isaas
Barnhart Charls
Barnhart John
Barhydt Thunis
Barkill Lowis
Barnes Jacob
Barnes John
Barns Aron
Bayor John, Jun.
Billings James
Beakemen Eshemeal
Beddle Benijah
Bell John
Bell Matthew
Bellinger Christian
Bellinger Philip
Berkley Isaes
Berlett John
Berrey Nicholas
Berry William
Beverly David
Beverly Thomas
Bodin John
Bogards Henry
Bogert Henry
Booldman John
Boshart John
Bove Nicholas
Bowman John
Breem John
Brewster John
Brothers John
Bun Jacob
Bun John
Burch Jeremiah
Butler Thomas
Cachey Andrew
Cady Nathalen
Cagal John
Caimon Andrew
Caine John
Caine Peter
Caine Thomas
Calyar Isaac
Campbell John
Campbell Nathaniel
Campel Samul
Cane Samuel
Cannan Andrew
Canner John
Carrall John
Cas Peter
Catman William
Carey William
Chrasse Francis
Chrisse Simon
Clark William
Clemant John
Clement Lambert
Cline Adam
Cloes Reuben
Cobon William
Cochran Andrew
Cock Petter
Cogmer Jacob
Cohenut Jacob
Colun William
Colyar Jacob
Colyer John
Colyer Willim
Comrie James
Connelly Hugh
Conner James
Conradt Joseph
Conyne John
Corsaart David
Cossaart Tracis
Cossote James
Coughvenhover Isaac
Coughvenhover John
Counrad Nicholes
Covenhove Abraham
Covenhoven Isaac
Covenhoven Peter
Cownovan Jacob
Crackenberch Adam
Crackenberch George
Crannell Thomas
Crans Henry
Croll John
Cromert Aaron
Cronkhite Abraham
Crook Christopher Forn
Crossett Benjmin
Crossett John
Crowley Jeremiah
Crummel Herman
Dachsteter John F.
Dachstetter Frederick F.
Dachstetter Markus
Daline Benjamin
Dallimthis James
Dannel John M.
Darrow John
Dasinham John
Daukstetor Fredrick H.
Davis Isaac
Davis James, Jr.
Davis John
Davis Thomas
De Eifix Max
Deline Benjamin
Deline Isick
Deline Ryer
Diefendorff Jacob
Diline Willim
Dingman Gerrit
Dingman Jacob
Dingman Peter
Dingman Samuel
Divis Abraham
Dockstader George A.
Dockstader John H.
Dockstater Henry H.
Dockstator George
Docksteder Adam
Docksteder Haniskel
Docksteder Nicholas H.
Docksteter Leonhart
Dockstetter Henrich
Dockstetter Nicolas
Dopber Robert
Doranberagh John
Doren Alicksander
Dorn David
Dorn John
Doron Jacob
Dorp Mattias
Doucksteter John
Doughstedar Jacob
Doyle Stephen
Dum Richard
Dunham Ebenezer
Dunham John
Dunn James
Dunn John
Eargesengar John
Earnest Jacob
Eaten Elezar
Eaton Ephraim
Eel Nichel
Eliot Jacob
Eliot Andrew
Elliot Joseph
Ellis John
Eman Jacob
Ener Peter
Eney John
England Benjamin
Eny George
Eny Godfret
Ernest Jacob
Eten Efrim
Eten Elezer
Eten James
Eten Tomes
Eversay Adam
Eversen John, Jun.
Farguson Willim
Fars Christian
Ferrel Charles
Fishar Harmanis
Fisher John
Fie George, Jun.
Fine Andrew
Fine Frances
Files John
Fishback Henry
Fithpatrick Peter
Fonda Adam
Fonda John
Forgason Daniel
Forrest Matthew
Fowler James
Frakk Henry
Frank Adam
Frank Albart
Frank Andrew
Frank Henry
Fredreck Jacob
Frederick Peter
Frederick Francis
Fredrick Phillip
French Ebenezer
French Josuf
Frenk Henry
Fuller Abraham
Fuller Isaac
Fuller Michel
Gallenger Henry
Gardenar William
Gardener Martin
Gardinier Martyn J.
Gardinier Matthew
Gardinier Nicholas
Gardinier Nicholas T.
Gardenir Abraham
Garsling Peter
Gerdanell John
Gibson William
Giles John
Goihnet John
Grace Owan M.
Graft Jacob
Grass Phillith

Hagal John
Hagal Magal
Hains John
Hall Jacob
Hall John
Hall Peter
Hall William
Han Jacob
Han Peter
Hanna James
Hanna William
Hansen Ficktor
Hansen Nicholas
Hanson John
Hanson Richard
Hare James
Harpper Archiball
Harrison Harmanis
Harrison Peter
Harrison Tomis
Havinser Toro
Helmer John
Henn Marks
Herring John, Sen.
Hird Leonard
Hoch Georg
Hodges Abraham
Hoff Richard
Hoff Richard, Jun.
Hogoboom Christion
Hogoboom John
Hogoboom Peter
Holdenbergh Abraham
Horn Jams
Horn Mattis
House Jacob
Hubbs Alexander
Hubbs Charles
Hulsbarker Addem
Hunt Timothy
Hutchson Edward
Inxale Joseph
Jones James
Jones Harmanus
Jones Richard
Johnson Andrew
Johnson John
Johnson Robert
Johnson Ruliph
Johnston Witter
Juman David
Jurry John
Kartright Hanry
Keech James
Keech Jorge
Keelman Jacob
Keith Jacob
Kell Nicolas

Keller Jacob
Kelly Peter
Kennedy James
Kenneday Robert
Ketcham Ephraim
Kiley Henry
Kitts John
Kitts John, Jun.
Kline John
Kline Martin
Lacess Samul
Lane Daniel
Lane Jacob
Lannen Rechert
Lapper John
Lawis David
Leets David
Lenardson James
Lenardson John
Lenardson Timothy
Lennes William
Lever John
Lewis Adam
Lewis David, Junr.
Lewis Frederick
Lewis John
Lewis William
Leyd Richard
Leypert Jacob
Liddel John
Lincompetter Mighael
Link John
Linox John
Loyde Daniel
Mabee Peter
Mambt Willem
Manness Hugh M.
Marlat Michael
Marlatt Abraham
Marlatt Gideon
Mason John
Mayer Jacob
Mayer Jacob, Junr.
Marlatt John
Marlatt Thomas
Martin John W.
Martin Peter M.
Martin Philip
Mashel John
Mason Jacob
McArthur Daniel
McArthur Donald
McArthur Duncan
McCallum John
McCollam Findlay
McClumpha Thomas
McCredy William
McDonald James

McDonald Nicholas
McGraw Christopher
McGraw Danel
McGraw Dennis
McGraw John
McGraw William
McKenney Dainnel
McMaster Hugh
McMaster James
McMaster Robert
McMaster Thomas
McNaughton Petar
McRadey William
McTaggert James
Mears Thomas
Melone John
Mets Henry
Meurinus William
Miller Fredrick
Miller Adam
Miller Gorge
Miller James
Miller Jillis
Miller Johan
Milloy Alexander
Montgomry Peter
Montek Willam
Moon Jacob
More Conrad
More John
Mount Joseph
Mount Samuel
Mower Barrant
Mower George
Mower Henry
Murdorph Gorge
Murray David
Musner John
Myers George
Myers Peter
Mave John
Nelley John
Newkirk Abraham
Newkkerk Garret
Newkerk Garrit C.
Nukerck Jacob
Ogden Daniel, Sen.
Ogden David
Panter Ulrich
Pater Francis
Patteson Adam
Percy Ephraim
Peters Joseph
Peters Joseph, Jun.
Pettingell Henry
Pettingell Jacob
Pettengell John
Pettingell Joseph

Pettingell Samuel
Pettingell William
Phileps Abraham
Philes Henry
Philips Henry
Philips Phillip
Philipse James
Philipse Volkert
Phillips Jacob
Phillips John
Phillips Lewis
Phillips William
Phillipsa Harmanis
Phillipsa John
Pickes John
Plank Adam
Plank John
Polmanter Thomas
Polmateer John
Polmateer Willem
Potman Aaren
Potman Adam
Potman George
Potmon Hendrik
Prentes Daniel
Prett John
Prime David
Prime Henry
Prime Petter
Prine Luis
Printup William
Pruime John
Pruyn John
Pruyne Henry
Pyrune Daniel
Putman Cornelys, Jun.
Putman David
Putman Factor
Putman Fredrick
Putman Hanry
Putman Jacobus
Putman John
Putman Lewis
Putman Lodiwik
Putman Victor
Putman William
Quack John
Quack Petar
Quack Willem
Quackinboss Nicholas
Quackenbush Abraham, Jun.
Quackenbush David
Quackenbush Isaac
Quackenbuss John G.
Redy Charles
Reed Conrad
Renins Samul

Richardson Jonathan
Riker Henry
Rinyens Samuel
Roberson Robert
Robeson George
Robison Joseph
Roelofson Abraham
Rogers John
Rogers Samul
Roges Samuel
Rombough Ausmus
Romeyn Theodorus F.
Romien Abraham
Romien Nicholas
Runyans John
Runyens Henry
Rury Henry
Rury William
Ruse Jacob
Salsbury John
Sammons Frederick
Sammons Thomas
Sammore Frederick
Saron Philip
Sarvis Frederick
Sarvis Richart
Scarbury William
Schaffer John
Schoonmaker Thomas
Schot Joseph
Schramling Henry
Schrambling Dewald
Schuler Lorentz
Schuts Joseph
Scoot Joseph
Scott James
Scott Joseph
Semple Hugh
Semple Samuel
Serves Christian
Servies Philip
Serviss George
Servos Christian
Servos John
Shaddack Tomis
Shaddock Jams
Shaffer James
Sharpenstine Jacob
Shasha Abraham
Shasha William
Sheham Butler
Shelp Fredrick
Shew Godfrey
Shew Henry
Shew Jacob
Shew John
Shew Stephen
Shilp Frederick
Shilip Christian
Shinner Tomes
Ship George F.
Shoemaker Thomas
Shoemaker Tomis
Shoemaker Rudolph
Sillebach Christayane
Sillibogh Hincrist
Sillibig John
Simpson Nicholas
Simpson Henry
Sixbarry Adam
Sixbary Cornelus
Sixberry Bangnen
Sixberry Cornelius, Jun.
Skinner John
Slack Martinis
Smith Harmanus
Snook Henry
Snyder Adam
Southwoth Willam
Spencer Jonathan
Spencer Aaron
Spencer Nathan
Spoor Nicolas
Spore John
Stabits Micheal
Stale Gorg
Staley Henry
Stall Joseph
Stalye Roulof
Starn Adam
Starn Philp
Starin Frederick
Starin John
Staring Joseph
Stephens Amasa
Sterman Christiana
Stern Neckliss
Sternberg Christian
Sternbergh Jacob
Sternbergh Joseph
Stine William
Storme Jacob
Strail John
Stuart William
Stung Peter
Swart Benjamin
Swart John
Swart Tunes
Swart Walter
Sylmur Marsster
Tanner Jacob
Terwilliger Hermanus
Terwilliger James
Thelm John
Thompson James
Timmerman Christian
Tims Michael
Tontill Joseph
Tyms Michael
Ulman Burnt
Ulman Johanes
Ulman Leonard
Vadder Isack
Vaghte John
Van Allen Jacob
Van Antwerpen John, Jun.
Van antwerpen John, Sen.
Van alstene Jacob
Van Alstin Gilbert
Van Alstine Abraham
Van Alstine Cornelius
Vanalstine Isaac
Vanalstine John
Vanbrakel Malkert
Van Bralan Gisbert
Van Brackleu Alexander
Van Bracklin Garret G.
Vandelinder Benjamin
Vandeuson Abraham
Van Deusen Harpert
Van Darwark Willim
Van Dewarck Thomis
Vanderwerken Albert
Van Derwerkin Gasper
Van Dewerkin John
Van Duzen Gilbert
Van Duzen Mathu
Van Eps John
Van Geyseling Peter
Van Horn Cornelius
Van Horn Henry
Vanhorn John
Van Husen Albert
Vanolinde Benjamin
Van Olinden Benjamin
Vanolynde Jacob
Van Sice Cornelius
Vansickler Ryneer
Vanslick Nechless
Van Vorst Jelles
Van Wurst Jelles
Vedder Albert
Veeder Abraham
Veeder John J.
Veeder Cornelius
Veeder John
Ven Husen Albert
Venolinde Benjam
Vinter William
Vroman Henry H.
Vroman Simon
Vrooman Henry B.
Vrooman Isaac
Vrooman John J.
Vrooman Peter
Walrath Adolphus
Wampal Cornelius
Wampel Handrick
Wample John
Wample William
Wart Andrew
Wart Matise
Weart John
Weaver Nicholas
Weener Peter
Weks Sammul
Wemple Barent
Wemple John T.
Wemple Myndert
Weser Nicholas
Wile Christian
Wiley Nicholas
Williams Daniel
Willson Aliner
Willson John
Wilson Abner
Wilson Andrew
Wilson Samuel
Wiser John
Witbeke Leonord
Wheeler Isaac
Whiler Henry
White Edward
Wood William
Woodcock Abraham
Woodcock John
Woodcock Peter
Woodworth
Woodworth Selah
Wright David
Yanney Christian
Yanney Henry
Yoran Jacob
Yost Peter
Young George
Young Lodowick
Young William

Tryon County Militia — (Continued).

COLONEL PETER BELLINGER
ADJUTANT GEORGE DEMUTH
QUARTER MASTER PETER BELLINGER, JR.

CAPT. HANS MARK DEMUTH
" FREDERICK FRANK
" FREDERICK GETTMAN
" HENRIG HERDER
" HENRY HUBER
" MICHAEL ITTIG
" JACOB SMALL
" HENRICH STARRING
LIEUT. PATRICK CAMPBELL
" HANNES DEMUTH
LIEUT. TIMOTHY FRANK
" GEORGE HELMER
" JACOB MYER
" JOHN SMITH
" GORG A. WEBER
" PETER WEBER
ENSIGN HANNES BELLINGER
" JOHN MAYER
" JACOB PETRY
" ADAM A. STARRING

ENLISTED MEN.

Ahrendorff Frieterich
Ahrendorff Piter
Ahrentarff Peter
Ahrentorff Gorg
Armstrong Archibald
Armstrong John
Badcock John
Balthaser Breih
Bany Ichabod
Bauman Adam
Bauman Frederick
Bauman Georg A.
Bauman Jacob
Bauman Johannes
Bauman Nicolas
Bauman Stophel
Becker Henrich
Beffer Jacob
Bell G. Henry
Bell Jacob
Bell Nicolaus
Bell Thomas
Bellinger Frederick
Bellinger John
Bellinger Peter
Bellinger Peter B.
Bellinger Peter P.
Bellinger Stoffel
Bendel Catren
Bender Jacob
Benrich Frans
Bercki Jacob
Berckie Peter
Berdrick Frantz
Bersh Lutwig
Bersh Rudolph
Beshar Jacob
Betrer Jacob
Bonny Ichabod
Bouman Adam
Bouman Frederick
Bouman Nicholas
Breidenbucher Balthass
Breidenbue Baldes
Brothack Jacob
Brothak Bartolomay
Brothock John
Burcky Peter, Senr.
Burti Jacob
Byrky Jacob
Byrky Peter
Campbell John
Campbell Ludwig
Camples Patrick
Casler Conrad
Casler Jacob H.
Casler Jacob J.
Casler Jacob Junr.
Casler John
Casler John T.
Casler Nicholas
Casler Peter
Caslor Malger
Chitter John
Chokin Thomas
Christman Frederick
Christman Fritrich
Christman Jacob
Christman John
Christman Nicolaus
Clapsattel Andrew
Clapsattle William
Clements Jacob
Clements Philip
Clenicum John
Cline William
Cochen Thomas
Coken Dome
Colsh John, Junr.
Colsh John, Senr.
Connghem Willem
Corrol George
Cox Fauet
Cox Fesser
Cram Jacob
Crantz Hanry
Cremm Jacob
Cristman Jacob
Cunicum Wiliem
Cunningham John
Dabush Jacob
Dachsteter Georg
Dachsteter John
Dachsteter Piter
Davis
Davis George
Davis John
Davis Peter
Dawie John
Daygert William A.
Deisellman Chrisdian
Demote Marx
Demuth Diterich
Demuth John
Demuth Marx
Dinges Hannes
Dinus Jacob
Dom Melger
Dunuss Jacob
Edie Frederick
Eiseman Stephen
Etig Gorge
Etigle Morse
Eyseman Johannes
Eyseman Steffe
Feelis Jacob
Finster John
Flack Pitter
Flock Peter
Follick Thomas
Folmer Christian
Folmer Conrad
Folmer Thomas
Folmer William
Fols Conrath C.
Fols Georg
Fols Jacob
Fols Melger
Fols Peter
Folts Conrad
Folts Jost
Foltz John Jost
Fox Friederich
Fox John
Frank Henry
Frank John
French Henrich
Fux Hannes
Getman Conrad
Getman Frederick

Gettman Frederik, Junr.
Gettman Petter
Gortner Peter
Harlam Adam
Hartch Adam
Hartman Adam
Hatz Peter
Hayer Georg
Hebrissen Martin
Heller John
Helmer Frederick
Helmer Frederick A.
Helmer Philip
Hendert John
Herchmer Jost
Herckmer Abraham
Herkemer John
Herkimer George
Herkimer Nicholas
Herder John
Herder Lorens
Herder Niklas
Herter Frederick, Junr.
Herter Lawrence
Herter Lorens
Herter Lorens F.
Herter Lorens N.
Herter Lorens P.
Herter Nicolas
Herter Nicolas F.
Herter Philip
Herter Philip F.
Hes Conrat
Hesler Morten
Hess Augustinus
Hess Christian
Hess Conrad
Hess Fridrik
Hess George
Hess John
Hoyer George
Heyer George Frederick
Heyer Peter
Hils Georg
Hils Hannes
Hilt George N.
Hilts John
Hiltz Georg
Hiltz George G.
Hiltz George, Junr.
Hiltz George N.
Hiltz Gotfrid
Hiltz Hannes
Hiltz Laurence
Hiltz Nicolas
Hochstrasser Christian
Hoffstader Christian
Hoyer George
Hoyer Gorg Friederich
Hoyer Peter
Huber John
Hyser Martin
Itig Georg
Itig Marck
Ittig Christian
Ittig Conrath
Ittig Frieterich
Ittig Jacob
Ittig Jacob J.
Karle George
Kast Frederick
Keller Nicolaus
Kelsch John, Junr.
Kelsch John, Senr.
Kesler Hannes
Kesler Nicholas
Kesslar Conrat
Kesslar Jacob John
Kesslar John
Kessler Jacob
Kessler Jacob J
Kessler John P
Kessler Johney
Kessler Joseph
Kessler Melger
Kiltz Georg
Kiltz Laurants
Koch Jost
Krans Michel
Krantz Henrich
Kreim Jacob
Kuran Michael
Kyler Nichlas
Lantz
Leithal Abraham
Lentz Jacob
Lentz John
Lentz John, Junr.
Lentz Peter
Lighthall George
Lighthal Nicholas
Lithall Abraham
Macnod Jeams
Manderback John
Mauyer Nicklas
Mayel Matthias
Mayer Frederick
Mayer Henry
Mayer John
Mayer Joseph
Mayer Mates
Mayer Michel
Mayer Nicolas
Mayer Piter
Meller John
Miller Henrich
Miller Johannis
Miller John, Junr.
Miller John, Senr.
Miller Nicolaus
Miller Fette
Miller Valentine
Millor Hanry
Molter Jacob
Molter Peter
Moyer Frederick
Moyer Hanry
Moyer Joseph
Moyer Margeris
Moyer Peter
Muller John
Multer Jacob
Multer Piter
Munterba Hannes
Myer Josaph
Myer Michel
Myndnbach Johanne.
McNutt James
Nahs James
Nesch Schims
Newkerk Benjamin
Ogt Georg
Ohrendorph Frederick, Junr.
Ohrendorph Frederick, Senr.
Ohrendorph George
Ohrendorph Peter
Osterhout John
Osteroth Johannes
Osterttout John
Pedery Marx
Pedri Ditrich
Peifer Jacob
Pesausie John
Petrey John Marx
Petri Daniel
Petri Jacob
Petri Johannes
Petri Joseph
Petrie Marx
Petry Diterich
Petry John
Petry John M.
Petry Jost
Phyfer Andrew
Phyfer Jacob
Piper Antoore
Piper Jost
Rabold Georg
Rasbach John
Regel Godfray
Remah George
Rickel Christian
Riema Georg
Riema John
Riema John, Senr.
Rigel Frederick
Rima Johannis, Junr.
Rima John, Senr.
Rimer Hannes
Rosekrantz Nicolaus
Ryan John
Schell Christian
Schell Johannes
Schenck Georg
Schieff Georg
Schmid Friedrich
Schmit Adam
Schmit Frederick
Schmit George
Schmit John
Schmit Jost
Schmit Peter
Schumacher John
Schumacher Stoffel
Schut Wiliem
Seimer Isack
Shall Fredrick
Shell John
Shoemaker Christopher
Shoemaker Frederick
Shoemaker Hanjost
Shoemaker John
Shoemaker Jost
Shoemaker Thomas
Shute Frederick
Shute William
Simer Gesom
Smith John
Smith Nicholas
Smith William
Sneck George
Spon Nicklas
Spoon Werner
Stahring Attam, Senr.
Stahring George
Stale Gorge
Staring Adam
Staring Adam J.
Staring Conrat
Staring Henrich
Staring Margred
Staring Nicklas
Staring Peter
Starring Nicholas N.
Starring Nicholas, Senr.
State George
Steal Ditrick
Steale Adam
Stehl Ditterich
Stering Adam

Straubel Stoffel
Strobel Christoph
Tinis Jacob
Tinis John
Usner Peter Gorg
Van Slyck Jacobus
Weaver George
Weaver Nicholas H.
Weaver Nicholas, Junr.
Web Nicolas G.
Weber Frederick
Weber Frederick G.
Weber Frederick, Junr.
Weber George
Weber George F.
Weber George, Junr.
Weber George M.
Weber Jacob
Weber Jacob G.
Weber Jacob J.
Weber Jacob N.
Weber Jacob, Senr.
Weber Johannes
Weber Michel
Weber Nicolas
Weber Nicolas G.
Weber Nicholas H.
Weber Peter
Wederstine Henry
Wents George
Widerstein Henry
Widrig Jacob
Widrig Michael
Witerig Georg
Witrig Conrat
Witterstein Henrich
Wohleben Abraham
Wohleber Abraham
Wohleber Jacob
Wohleber Pitter
Woleben Jacob
Wolff Johannes
Wolleben Peter
Wollerver Abraham
Won Niclas

Tryon County Militia — (Continued).

COLONEL JOHN HARPER

MAJOR JOSEPH HARPER

No enlisted men found.

Tryon County Militia — (Continued).

BATTALION OF MINUTE MEN.

COLONEL SAMUEL CAMPBELL

CAPT. FRANCIS UTT
LIEUT. ADAM LIPE
LIEUT. JACOB MATTHIAS
ENSIGN WILLIAM SUBER

ENLISTED MEN.

Ayle Christian
Ayle Peter
Ayles William
Bellinger William
Bohall Adam
Bydaman Simon
Countreyman Counradt
Countreyman John
Cramer John
Crows George
Dedrick David
Duncle Nicholas
Duncle Peter
Dunkle Gerrit
Endler Michal
Felling Henry John
Felling Henry Nicholas
Felling Peter
Flock John
Harld Henrey
Hickey George
Jones William
Jordan Adam
Jordan Casper
Jordan George
Jordan John
Keller Andrew
Kerlack Adam
Kerlack George
Kesler Thomas
Kessler John
Korey Benjamin
Lapp Daniel
Lipe John
Miller Deonyceons
Netherly John
Netherly John, Junr.
Othermark John B.
Plats George
Schall Hendrick
Schall John
Schall Matthyas
Scrembling Henry
Scremling David
Seeber Jacob
Stansel Nicholas
Steffan John
Truax John
Ulshaver Bastian
Wabadt George
Walradt William
Westerman Peter
While Henry
While Youst Henry
Woulkermouth John
Wourmuth John
Wourmuth Peter
Young Jacob
Young John
Young Peter

Tryon County Militia — (Continued).

ASSOCIATED EXEMPTS.

CAPT. JELLIS FONDA
LIEUT. ZEPHENIAH BATCHELLER
" ABRAHAM GARRASON
ENSIGN SAMSON SAMMON
" ———— LAWRANCE

ENLISTED MEN.

Algyre John
Allin Thomas
Alt Johannis
Anderson Duncan
Ansley Samuel
Antes Jacob
Barmore William
Barry Guilbert R.
Bashan Jacob
Benson Jonathan
Bickle John
Boshart Jacob
Boss Heinrich
Bridelburgh Baltus
Brook Robert
Cameron Angus
Cochnet Jacob
Collins Richard
Conner Edward
Cratchenberger Conrate
Creesy John
Cromel Jacobes
Cromnel James
Crossett Benjamin
Crossett James
Crotchinbrge Conrad
Crowley Jeremiah
Dachstetter Marx
Dachsteter Nicolaus
Dochstader Frederick
Dockstader John H.
Dop David
Dunn Richard
Ecker John
Ensign Lawrance
Eversas Adam (see Everson)
Everson Adam (see Eversas)
Everson John
Fey Jacob
Finck Mattgred
Fonda Adam
Fonda John
Frederick Barent
Frichert Henry
Froman Henry
Fyes George
Fyles George
Graft Jacob
Hall John
Hall William
Hanson Barent
Hanson Richard
Hardle Johannes
Herring John
Hover Johannes
Hower Nicholas
Johnson Andrew
Kelder Henry
Kelder John
Kilts Johannes
Kinkead Crownidge
Kitts Jacob
Krose Moses
Ladde Johannes
Lenardson Timothy
Marlatt Mark
Marseles John
Mason Jeremiah
Michard Henry
Mickle John
Miller Philip
Momtrute Steven
Morgan John
Morger John
Myers Michael
McCollum John
McDonald John
McDonnel John
McGlashen Robert
McGrigor Duncan
McIntire John
McKenny John
McKinney John
McKerque Duncan
McManus Hugh
McMarlinger Duncan
McMarten Duncan
McVain Daniel
Nanes Joseph
Nest Johannes
Perine Daniel
Perine David
Phile George
Philips Abraham
Philips William
Plants John
Platto James
Poter France
Putman Cornelius
Quackenbush David
Remise John
Reyer John
Rickle John
Rightmyer Johannes
Roase James
Robertson John
Ruport Adam
Ruport D.
Rykert Hendrick
Ryer Henry
Sammons Jacob
Schwob Michel
Seeber Henry
Schieb Georg Friderick (see Sheep)
Shanck George
Shaver Nicholas
Shew George
Shew Steven
Shewmaker Hanjost
Shoeman William
Sixberry Cornelius
Smith Arent
Smith Conradt
Smith Cornelius
Smith Daniel
Smith John
Snell Robert
Staring John
Staly Jacob
Stealy Jacob
Stoner Nicholas
Terwillegen Harmanis
Vactor John
Vorbis John
Van Alstine Cornelius A.
Van Alstyne C. V.
Van Antwerp John
Van Bracklen Gysbert
Van Bracklen Nicholas
Vanderwerke Johannis
Vanderwerkin Albert
Vandesen Melgert
Van Deusen Jacobus
Van Deusen Matthew
VanDewarkin Class
Van Dewerken Jacob
VanDewerker Henry
Van Eps Charles
Van Eps Evert
Van Zelen John
Wallace William
Wallrad Johannes
Walters John
Well John
Wemple Barent
Wemple Hendrick
Whitekar Thomas
Wilson John

Tryon County Militia — (Continued).

RANGERS.

CAPT. JOHN WINN
LIEUT. LAWRENCE GROSS
LIEUT. PETER SCHREMLING

ENLISTED MEN.

Adamy Peter
Andrews Lewis
Anthony John
Atkins William
Bellinger Adam
Bratt James
Bush George
Bush William
Christman Nicholas
Cogdon John
Countryman Johannes
Embody Henry
Dingman John
Franck Adam
Freeman Joseph
Fritsher Conradt
Gueenall James
Hamilton James
Hayes Thomas
Heath Josiah
Hellegass Peter
Helmer Godfried
Hornung Burent
House Elias
House George
House Johanjost
House John
Jackson Joseph
Johnston Richard
Kaach John
Kennedy Samuel
Kesslaer Johannes
Kook William
Kremer Johanjost
Kronckhite Abraham
Lampford Peter, Jr.
Lampford Peter, Sr.
Leathers Ezekiel
Lepper Fredrick
Liewry Jacob
Llump Thomas
Mackly Felix
Maybee John
McCollum John
McDonnald John
Nellis Christian
Nellis William
Ogden Daniel
Pickerd John
Price Adam
Reebsamen Francis
Reebsumen Johannes
Roader Jacob
Roorey William
Scotten Josiah
Seger Fredrick
Shillip Christian
Snyder Gonlieb
Snyder Johannes
Stensell Nicholas
Stensell William
Stevens Samuel
Styne Conradt
Timmerman Jacob
Van Der Warke Gershom
Vander Warke James
VanSlyck George
Weaver Jacob
Young Richard

Tryon County Militia—(Continued).

RANGERS.

CAPT. CHRISTIAN GETMAN
LIEUT. JAMES BILLINGTON
LIEUT. JACOB SAMMANS

ENLISTED MEN.

Agin Joshua
Biller Michel
Box John
Brame John
Canton John
Coplin Samuel
Coppernol Adam
Coppernol Richard
Cratzer Leonhart
Crum John
Dop John
Earl William
Empie Jacob
Fishbock Jacob
Flander Hendrick
Flune John
Fralick Felter
Freman Richard
Fry Jacob
Fuller Isaac
Fuller Michel
Getman Thomas
Hails John
Hart Conrad
Hart Daniel
Hawk George
Hodges Abraham
Hoyney Fredrick
Hoyney George
Hulser John
Jenne Christian
Karin William
Kind William
Kring Ludwick
Kufe Johanes
Leather Christian
Leather Johanes
Loux George
Miller Johanes
Mills Cornelius
Phillips Philip
Rickard Jacob
Saltsman George
Saltsman George, Jr.
Shafer Hendrick
Shuell John
Shuell Peter
Smith Bolzer
Smith John
Spankrable Johanes
Storing Jacob
Strader Nicholas
Sutes Johanes
Tusler Jacob
Vrooman Hendrick
Vrooman Minehart
Vananwarp John
Vanderworkin Hendrick
Vanderworkin John
Vanderworkin Martin
Walliser Christian
Williams Nehemiah
Wormwood Christian
Wormwood Johanes

Tryon County Militia — (Continued).

RANGERS.

CAPT. JOHN KASSELMAN
LIEUT. JOHN EMPIE
ENSIGN GEORGE GITTMAN

ENLISTED MEN.

Backer John
Bickerd Adolph
Dusler Jacob
Empie John
Ettigh Coenrad
Fry Jacob
Gittman Peter
Harth Daniel
Haynes George
Hortigh Andrew
House Peter
Kasselman John
Kretzer Leonard
Kulman Henry
Shuell John
Smith Henry
Smith William
Strater Nicholas
Tillenbach Christian
Vander Werke John
Walter Adam
Walter Christian

ULSTER COUNTY MILITIA.

COLONEL JOHANNES SNYDER
MAJOR PHILIP HOOGHTELING
MAJOR ADRIAN WYNKOOP
QUARTER MASTER JOHN J. LOW
SURGEON PETER VAN DER LYN

CAPT. EVERT BOGARDUS
" MATTHEW DEDERICK
" JOHN L. DEWITT
" CHARLES NEWKIRK
" EDWARD SCHOONMAKER
" HENDRICK SCHOONMAKER
" JEREMIAH SNYDER
" PHILIP SWART
" TOBIAS VAN BEUREN
LIEUT. PETER BACKER
" CORNELIS BEEKMAN
" TJERCK BEEKMAN
" ISAAC BURHANS
" PETRUS EYGENAAR
" ABRAHAM HOFFMAN
" MARTIN HOMMEL
" TOBIAS MYER
" PETRUS OSTERHOUDT
" JOHANNIS PERSEN
LIEUT. PETER POST
" JAMES ROE
" OKE SUDAM
" HENRICUS TEERPENNING
" ABRAHAM VAN AKEN
" JOHN VAN DUSEN
" ABRAHAM VAN GAASBEEK
" JACOBUS VAN GAASBEEK
" PETER VAN GAASBEEK
" ANDREW VAN LEUVEN
" EDWARD WHITTAKER
ENSIGN PETER BRINCK, JUNR.
" CORNELIUS BURHANS
" JOHN P. DUMOND
" THEOPHELUS ELSWORTH
" STEPHANUS FIERO
" ANDREW VAN LEWIN
" TOBIAS WYNKOOP, JUNR.

ADDITIONAL NAMES ON STATE TREASURER'S PAY BOOKS.

CAPT. ABRAHAM VAN KEWREN
LIEUT. ABRAHAM FRANKA
LIEUT. ANTHONY FREAR

ENLISTED MEN.

Acker Jacob
Acker Solomon
Ackert Jacob
Ackert Jeremiah
Ackert Martin
Ackert Stephen
Ackmoodia David
Amrick Johannis
Amrick Peter
Arshly Jacob
Artly Jacob
Auchmoudey David
Auker Henry
Auker Mar
Badford Andrew
Badford John
Badford Simeon
Baer Adam
Banschten Salomon
Barger Jacob
Bargher Wilhelimis
Barnes Hans Jury
Barnhart Jeremiah
Barringer Jacob
Barrow Danell
Bear Coffe
Bear Henry
Bear John
Bear Jurrie
Beaver John
Beaver Peter
Beckman Hendrick
Bedford Andrew
Bedford Simon
Beekman Benjamin
Beekman Hendrick
Beekman John, Junr.
Beekman John J.
Beekman Thomas
Berger Jacob
Berger Wilhelmus
Berner Hans Jurry
Bernhart Jeremiah
Besmer Johannis
Bever John
Bever Peter
Biar Adam
Biar John
Black John
Bogardus Nicholas
Bogardus Peter
Bogardus Petrus
Borrow Daniel
Brar Coffey
Brar Henry
Brar Jury
Breadsted Andrew
Breasted
Brett Peter
Briett William
Brinck Cornelius
Brinck Cornelis C.
Brinck Hendrick
Brinck Jacob
Brinck Jacob, Junr.
Brinck John
Brinck John C.
Brinck John J.
Brinck Peter C.
Brink Henry
Brink John Junr.
Brink John A.

Brink John C.
Brink John G.
Brink John T.
Brink Peter
Bristead Andrew
Britt Fredrick
Britt Willem
Bruyer James
Buckman Benjamin
Buckman Hendrick
Buckman John J.
Buckman Thomas
Burhans Abraham
Burhans Abraham, Junr.
Burhans Barent
Burhans Benjamin
Burhans Cornelius
Burhans Corpelius
Burhans Edward
Burhans John
Burhans John, Junr.
Burhans John, Senr.
Burhans John W.
Burhans Jonathan
Burhans Richard
Burhans Samuel
Burhans Thark
Burhans Tjinck
Buyer James
Callor John
Carareych Heronemus
Carnright Aronamis
Carrel Jury
Carrell George
Caruyster Silvaster
Castell William
Castle William
Cater Abraham
Cator John
Chrispel John T.
Chrispell Abraham
Clearwater Jeremiah
Cole John
Colgrove Francis
Cones Causin
Conjes Jacob
Constaple William
Conus Jacob
Cool Peter
Coolgrove Francis
Corns Causin
Corrle Gorg
Cramer Wandal
Crammer Wendell
Crispell Abr[m]
Crispell Jacob
Crispell Petrus J.
Crispell Peterus T.

Crisple Benjamin
Crisple John J.
Critsinger John
Crook Martin
Croos John
Croose Lenord
Cross John
Crum Henry W.
Crum Jacob
Cruyslaar Silvester
Davenport John
Davis John B.
Davis Joseph
Davis Sampson
Davis Samuel
Davis Willem
Davits John B.
Debois James
Debois William
Decker Ephraim
Decker Isaak
Decker Petrus
Dederick Cato
Dederick Gilbert
Dederick John
Dederick Jonathan
Dedrick Harmanus
Dedrick Jacobus
Degraaf Hendrick
Degraaf John
Degraaf William
De Grave Henry
De Grave John
De Grave William
Delafever Coenradt
De Lefever Jonathen
De Lemeter Abrahm
Delamater Abraham A.
Delameter Benjamin
Delameter Cornelis C.
Delameter David
DeLameter John
Delamatter Abraham C.
Delamatter Cornelius
Delemature Cor's J.
Delimater Cornelius I.
Deronde Matthew
Devenport John
De Wett John T.
Dewitt Abraham
Dewitt Cornelis
DeWitt Jacob
Dewitt Jacob J.
De Witt Johannis
Dewitt John
Dewitt John J.
Dewitt Tjerck
DeWitt Tjerck C.

Diederick Harmanus
Dobois James, Junr.
Doyle Charles
Dubois David
DeBois Jacobus
Dubois James
Dubois James, Junr.
Dubois Jeremiah
Dubois Johannes
Dubois John
Dubois John I.
Dubois John J.
Dubois John T.
Dubois Matthew
Dubois Robert
Dubois Willem
Dull Christian
Dumon John, Junr.
Dumond Cornelius
Dumond Cornelius, Junr.
Dumond Egbert
Dumond Igenas
Dumond Isaac
Dumond John
Dumond John, Junr.
Dumond Peter
Dumond Peter, Junr.
Dumont Peter
Dumont Peter, Junr.
Eccor Jeremiah
Eccor Martin
Eccor Solomon, Junr.
Eckerd Stephan
Eckert Henry
Eckert Jacob
Eckert Jeremiah
Eckert Marthinus
Eckert Solomon
Eigeneer Frederick
Eigener Jacob
Eigener Joh's
Eigener John
Eigener Peter, Jr.
Eigener Peter P.
Eigener William
Eigeniar Cor's
Eigenor Jacobus
Eignuir Peter D.
Eligh Jacob
Eligh Johannis
Elling Hendrick
Elling William
Elmendorf Coenradt Edward
Elmendorph Abraham
Elmendorph Benjamin
Elmendorph Coenradt C.
Elmendorph Coenradt W.

Elmendorph Lucas
Elmendorph Lucas, Junr.
Elmendorph Peter, Junr.
Elmendorph Petrus
Eltinge Hendrick
Eltinge John
Eltinge Peter
Eltinge Peter, Junr.
Eltinge William
Elyrah Jacob
Emert Mathew
Emighery Joh's
Emrich Johannis
Emrich Peter
Emrich Wilhelmus
Emrich Wilhelmus, Junr.
Emrigh Wilhelmus, Junr.
Emrugh John
Enveigh Wilhelimus
Ernest Matthew
Ersh Jacob
Etting Peter, Junr.
Ettinge Hendricus
Eygenaar Cornelis
Eygenaar Fredrick
Eygenaar Jacobus
Eygenaar John
Eygenaar Peter
Eygenaar Willem
Eygener Petrus, Junr.
Eygener Peter P.
Falk Johannis
Falk Wilhelmes
Falkenbargh Abr'm
Falkenbargh Joh's
Fanaka Abraham
Felie Johannis
Fellor Joh's
Felrs Joh's
Felten Benjamin
Felten Jacob
Felten Johannis, Junr.
Felton John
Felten Peter
Felten Philip
Felter Jacob
Felter Johannes, Junr.
Felter John
Felter Petrus
Felter Philip
Felton John, Junr.
Felton Peterus
Fernoo Christian, Junr.
Feroo John C.
Feroo Peter
Ferris Counradt
Ferro Stephen
Ferro William

Fiero ——
Fiero Christian
Fiero Christan, Junr.
Fiero Han Christian
Fiero John C.
Fiero Peter
Fiero William
Fieres Coenraedt
Fietsel Johannis
Filton John
Finis Counradt
Firers Coenradt
Firnes Counradt
Foland George
Folk Johannis
Folkenburgh Abraham
Follant Jacob
Follen Jury
Follent Jury
Fosburgh Abr'm
Fowler James
France Adam
France Cornelis
France Jacob
France Jacob, Junr.
France Johannis
France Wilhelmus
Frans Joh's
Frans Wilhelmus
Frans William
Frar Gerrit
Freer Abraham
Freer Benjamin
Freer Garret
Freer Hugo
Freer Jeremiah
Freer Jeremyas
Freer Johannis
Freer Jonathan
Freer Peter
Freer Samuel
Frees Johannis
Freland George
Freligh Hendrick
Freligh Henrick, Junr.
Freligh John
Freligh Samuel
Frier Benjamin
Frier Samuel
Gee Joseph
Gilbert Ephraim
Gilbert Justin
Groen Jacob Marius
Groen Jacob Marius, Junr.
Groen Peter Marius
Groen Sylvester Marius
Groen William Marius
Groone Peter Morris
Groone Saberster Mars
Groone Silvaster M
Groone William Monis
Hanpaugh Peter
Hance Willem
Hardenbergh Lewis
Hardenbergh Peter
Hasbrouck Daniel
Haasbrouck Jacobus
Hasbrouck Jacobus, Junr.
Hasbrouck John
Hasbrouck Jonathan
Hasbrouck Solomon
Hendricks Jacob
Hendricks John
Hendricks Philip
Hendrickson Johannis
Hendrix Jacob
Hendrix Joh's
Hendrixson Jacob
Hendrixson John
Hendrixson Philip
Heermanse Abraham
Heermanse Edward
Heermanse John
Herrington Moses
Hinmans Abr'm
Hodler Solomon
Hommel Abraham
Hommel Hermanus
Hommel Jurrie
Hommel Jurrie, Junr.
Hommel Petrus
Hooghtalin William, Jr.
Hoogtaling Wilhelmus, Junr.
Houghtaling Jeremiah
Houghtaling John
Houghtaling Thomas
Houghtaling Wilhelmas T.
Houghtaling William F.
Houghtaling Willem T.
Huddlor, Salomon
Hudson Jonathan
Huffman Abr'm
Hummel Abraham
Hummel George, Junr.
Hummel Harman
Hummel Harman, Jr.
Hummel Harmanis
Hummel Harmanis, Junr.
Hummel Jurry
Hummel Peter
Humstead Elias
Hymback Peter
Hynpals Peter
Japh Jacob
Japle Jacob
Joung Jeremiah
Jurrie Hans
Karley George
Kattor Abr'm
Keater Abraham
Keater John
Keeler John
Keffer Battije
Keffer Lourance
Keffer William
Keffer William, Jr.
Kellenburgh Isaac, Jr.
Kerlach Nicholas
Kersteed John
Kersteed Wilhelmis
Kiefer Baltis
Kieffar William, Junr.
Kieffer Lowrence
Kieffer William
Kiffer William
Kierstead John
Kierstead Wilhelmus
Kodler Solomon
Krom Benjamin
Krom Henry B.
Krom Jacob
Kroom Hendrick
Kros Johannes
Krous Leonard
Krum Hendrick B.
Krum Hendric W.
Lafever Jonathan
Lamendyck Cor's
Lamendyck John
Langendyck John.
Langendyke Cornelis
Langyan William
Langyare Christian
Lanjaar Christopher
Lanjaar Willem
Larway Peter
Lefever Conrad
Legg John, Junr.
Legg Samuel
Lits Willem
Lomgendyck Cor's
Louck Peter, Jr.
Louw Abraham
Louw Cornelius
Loux Cor's
Loux Peter W.
Low Abr'm
Low Abr'm A.
Low Abraham C.
Low Abraham E.
Low Cor's
Low Frederick
Low Jacobus
Low Johannis
Low John C.
Low Peter
Low Tjerck
Luyks Cornelis
Luyks Peter, Junr.
Luyks Peter W.
MaCleen John
Maderstock Adam
Magee Peter
Magee Peter, Junr.
Magee Samuel
Maris Robert
Markul Johannis
Mars Robert
Marsial John
Marten Joseph
Martin Cor's B.
Martin Joh's B.
Martin Joseph
Masten Abraham
Masten Abraham, Junr.
Masten Abraham A.
Masten Cornelius B.
Masten Cornelius C.
Masten Daniel
Masten Hendrick
Masten Johannis B.
Masten Johannis C.
Masten Johannis E.
Masters Joseph
Mastin Daniel
Materslock Johannis
Materstock Jacob
Materstock Johannis
Materstock Peter
Matterstock Adam
Matterstock John
Mauer Jacob
Menkelar Cor's
Menkial Johannes
Merkel Johannis
Meyer Christiaen
Meyer Peter L.
Mickel John
Minkalar Cornelius
Minkelar Harmanus
Mire Stephen
Morris Robert
Mosten Joseph
Mouries Jacob
Mouries Johannis, Junr.
Mousier Jacob
Myer Abraham
Myer Benjamin
Myer Benjamin, Junr.
Myer Christian
Myer Cornelis

Myer Counright
Myer Ephraim
Myer Hendericus
Myer Henry
Myer Johannis, Junr.
Myer Peter
Myer Peter, Junr.
Myer Peter B.
Myer Peter L.
Myer Peter T.
Myer Stephan
Myer Stephen, Junr.
Myer Thunis
Myer William, Junr.
McCay John
McClean John
McFarling Andrew
McGroone Peter
McKenney Alexander
McKinsy Alexander
Neukeuk Charles
Newkerk Benjamin
Oosterhaude Hendrick
Oosterhoudt Benjamin
Oosterhoudt Jacob
Oosterhoudt Jacobus
Oosterhoudt James
Oosterhoudt John
Oosterhout Joseph
Oosterhoudt Peter
Oosterhoudt Peter, Junr.
Oosterhoudt Petrus
Oosterhoudt Petrus L.
Oosterhoudt Samuel
Oosterhoudt Teunis
Oosterhoudt Willem
Osterhoudt Abraham
Osterhoudt Benjamin
Osterhoudt Edward
Osterhoudt Peter
Osterhout Abraham
Osterhout Samuel
Osterhout William
Osterhoutt Elias
Ostrander Henry
Ostrander James
Ostrander Samuel
Parsel Jeremiah
Patterson Moses
Percal Cornelis
Periall Cor's
Perse Cornelius
Persell Jeremiah
Persen Cornelius
Persen John
Persen John J.
Persen Matthew
Persey Cor's
Perslow Henry
Phenix Abraham
Ploegh Teunis
Plough Hendrick
Plough Henry
Plough Tunis
Polhamus Daniel
Post Abraham
Post Abraham A.
Post Cor's
Post Henry, Junr.
Post Isaac
Post Isaac, Jr.
Post Jacobus
Post John
Post John, Junr.
Post Marte, Junr.
Post Marteynus
Post Martin
Post Martin, Junr.
Post Samuel
Poust Cornelius
Rechtmeyer Hermanus
Rechtmyer Coenrad
Rechtmyer George
Rechtmyer George, Junr.
Rechtmyer Johannis
Rechtmyer Jurry W.
Rechtmyer Peter
Richley Andrew
Richley Jacob
Richtmyer Johannis
Rickle Andrew
Rihley Jacob
Roase John, Jr.
Roosa John, Junr.
Rossell Lodewick
Rost Henry
Rouce Benjamin
Rouw Benjamin
Russel Ludwigh
Salisbury Silvester
Sax Peter
Schapmis William
Schepmoes John
Schepmoes William
Schitt Solomon
Schoemaker Nicolas
Schoemaker Petrus
Schoomaker Samuel
Schoonmaiker Neh's
Schoonmaker David
Schoonmaker Edward
Schoonmaker Edward E.
Schoonmaker Egbert, Junr.
Schoonmaker Egbert C.
Schoonmaker Hisakia
Schoonmaker Johannis
Schoonmaker Johannis, Junr.
Schoonmaker John E.
Schoonmaker Nicholas
Schoonmaker Thark
Schoonmaker Thark, Junr.
Schoonmaker Tjink
Schriver Johannes
Schryber Albertus
Schryber Martinus
Schryber Stephan
Schut Christian
Schut Solomon
Scryer Albertus
Scryer Stephen
Scryver Marten
Scyriver John
Share Andries
Shears Andrew
Shoe Augustus
Short Hendrick
Short Henry
Short Petrus
Shue Augusteane
Sleght Hendricus B.
Sleght Petrus
Sleght Salomon
Sleght Teunis
Smedes Peter B.
Snyder Abraham
Snyder Abraham, Junr.
Snyder Benjamin
Snyder Christian
Snyder Hendricus
Snyder Henry
Snyder Johannes
Snyder Johannis M.
Snyder John
Snyder John, Junr.
Snyder Martinas
Snyder Martyn
Snyder Solomon
Sperling George
Sperling John
Staats Hendrick
Stattas Henry
Steenbargh Thomas G.
Steenbergh Thomas
Stienbergh John
Stoutenburgh Isaac, Junr.
Sulant John
Suyland Johannis
Swart Benjamin
Swart Cornelius
Swart Cornelius, Junr.
Swart Cornelius L.
Swart Petrus
Swart Teunis
Swart Thomas
Swart Tobias
Swart William
Tappen Peter
Tarpenning Willem
Teerpening Gerrit
Teerpening Petrus
Teerpening Simon
Teerpenning Abraham
Teerpenning Jacobus
Teerpenning Jacobus, Junr.
Teerpenning Willem
Tenbroeck John
Ten Eyck Dirck
Ten Eyck Richard
Terpenney Hendrick
Thompson Jonathan
Thompson Mathew, Jr.
Thompson Matthew Edward
Thompson William
Thomson Jonathan
Thomson Matthew, Junr.
Tremper Jacob
Trimper Wilhelmus
Trompor Joh's
Trompor Johannis, Jr.
Trompour Valentino
Trumbouner John
Trumpbour Jacob
Turck Hendrick
Turck Jacob, Junr.
Turck Johannes
Turck Johannis, Junr.
Turk John
Tutsell Joh's
Ulmstead Elias
Valck Johannes
Valk Wilhelmus
Valkenbergh Abraham
Valkenbourgh John
Viele John
Vollant George
Vollant Jurrie
Vosburgh Abraham
Van Aken Benjamin
Van Aken Cato
Van Aken Eliphas
Van Aken Gideon
Van Aken Isaac
Van Aken Peter
VanAken Peter G.
Van Atten John
Van Beuren Philip
Van Beuschoten Solomon
Van Bunsholin Solomon
Van Buren Philip
Van Burin Tobias

Van Etten John
Van Gaasbeck AbrahamW.
Van Gaasbeek John
Van Gaasbeek John, Junr.
Van Gasbeck Abr'm, Jr.
Van Gasbuck Peter
Van Gesbuck John, Jr.
Van Hunbargh John
VanKeuran Cornelius
Van Keuran Cornelius M.
Van Keuran Matthew, Junr.
Van Keuren Abraham
Van Keuren Gerrit
Van Keuren Matthew
Van Keuren Philip
Van Keuren Tjerck
Van Kunn Abr'm
Van Kunn Mathias
Van Leuven Andries
Van Leuven John
Van Leuven John, Junr.
Van Leuwen Zacheriah
Van Schayck Anthony
Van Steenbargh John, Jr.
Van Steenbargh Paulus
Van Steenbargh Peterus
Van Steenbargh Tobias
Van Steenbargh Tobias, Jr.
Van Steenbergh Abraham
Van Steenbergh Benjamin
Van Steenbergh Dirick
Van Steenbergh Henry
Van Steenbergh John
Van Steenbergh Matthew
Van Steenbergh Peter
Van Steenbergh Pontis
Van Steenbergh Poulis
Van Steenbergh Thomas
Van Steenbergh Thomas, Junr.
Van Steenberghn Tobyes
Van Steenberghn Tobyes, Jr.
VanVleit Arie
Van Vliet George
Van Vliet John
Van Vliet Jurry
Van Vliet Tjerck
Van Wagenen Abraham B.
Van Wagenen AbrahamW.
Van Wagenen Benjamin
Van Wagenen Henry
Van Wagenen Jacob, Junr.
Van Wagenen Johannis J.
Van Wagenen Ysack Y.
Van Waggoner ——
Van Waggoner Abr'm W.
Van Waggoner Benjamin
Van Waggoner Henry
Van Waggoner Isaac T.
Van Waggoner Jacob, Jr.
Van Waggoner Joh's I.
Weaver John
Wells Christian
Wells Cornelis
Wells Henry
Wells Jacobus
Wells James
Wels Peter
Wenne Peter A.
Whitaker Edward
Whitaker Edward, Junr.
Whitaker James
Whitaker Philip
Whiteaker Abraham
Whiteaker Abraham, Junr.
Whiteaker Benjamin
Whiteaker Jacobus
Whiteaker Petrus
Whittaker James W.
Whitteker John
Wiest Peter
Wiest Peterus
Wiliker Petrus
Will Christian
Williams John
Windfield Benjamin
Winfield Daniel
Winfield David
Winfield Simon
Winna John
Winne Benjamin
Winne Peter A.
Winne Peter J.
Winnen Arent
Winnen Arent, Junr.
Winnen Cornelis
Winnen Jacobus
Winnen James
Winnen John
Winnen Peter
Winnen Peter, Junr.
Winnen Peter J.
Winnia Arant
Winnia Arant, Jr.
Winnia Benjamin
Winnia Cor's
Winnia Jacobus
Winnia James
Winnia Peter
Winnia Peter, Jr.
Winnia Peter A.
Winnia Peter I.
Winns William
Witecker Jacob
Witiker James I.
Witteker Abraham
Witteker John
Woester George
Wolf Adam
Wolfen John
Wolfent Jeremiah
Wolfent Joh'h
Wolfent John
Wolfet John
Wolff John
Wolven Jeremiah
Wolven Johannis, Junr.
Wolven John
Wolvin Adam
Wolvin Jeremiah
Wolvin Johannes, Jr.
Wolvin Johanes H.
Wolvin John H.
Wynkoop Evert
Wynkoop Hezekiah
Wynkoop John, Junr.
Wynkoop Peter
Wynkoop Willem
Yaple Hannicle
Yaple Jacob
Yeoman Moses
Yeomens Moses
Yepeel Jacob
Yeuple Hannele
York Daniel
Young Abraham
Young Jeremiah
Yourk Moses

Ulster County Militia — (Continued)

COLONEL JAMES McCLAGHRY
LIEUTENANT COLONEL JACOB NEWKIRK
MAJOR MOSES PHILLIPS
ADJUTANT GEORGE DENNISTON
QUARTER MASTER PETER CRANCE
QUARTER MASTER EVINS WHARRY

CAPT. DAVID CRAWFORD
" ABRAHAM CUDDEBACK
" MATTHEW DUBOIS
" MATTISE FELTER
" WILLIAM FAULKNER
" JAMES HUMPHREY
" JOHN HUNTER
" MATTHEW JANSEN
" ANDREW MILLER
" JAMES McBRIDE
" JOHN NEWKIRK
" JOHN NICHOLS
" LEONARD D. NICOLL
" DAVID OSTRANDER
" WILLIAM TILLFORD
" BENJAMIN VAIL
" ISAIAH VAIL
" HENRY VAN KEUREN
" SAMUEL WATKINS
LIEUT. SAMUEL ARTHUR
" JOHN BARBER
" ALEXANDER BEATTY
" JAMES BURNET
" ROBERT COOK
" DAVID CORWIN
" DAVID CURRING
" JOHN DUNNING
" JOHN ENGLISH
LIEUT. JAMES FAULKNER
" STEPHEN HARLOW
" JAMES HUNTER
" WILLIAM JELLET
" JAMES KERNAGHAN
" ALEXANDER KIDD
" SAMUEL KING
" JOHN L. MOFFATT
" DAVID MONNELL
" EDWARD McNEAL
" HENRY NEELY
" MATTHEW NEELY
" JONATHAN OWEN
" WILLIAM ROSA
" ISAAC SHULTZ
" HENRY SMITH
" JOHN WILKINS
" SILAS WOOD
ENSIGN ROBERT BURNET
" EDWARD BURNS
" TIMOTHY COLEMAN
" SAMUEL DUPIE
" ARCHABLE McBRIDE
" ANDREW NEELY
" JOSEPH SEARS
" JOSHUA SEERS
" TUNIS VANORSDALE
" SAMUEL WETHERLO

ADDITIONAL NAME ON STATE TREASURER'S PAY BOOKS.

LIEUT. JAMES McCLAUGHREY

ENLISTED MEN.

Abrahams John
Adams Chestor
Adcock William
Atherston Joel
Badle William
Baily John
Barber John
Barber Thimothy
Barkley Thomas
Barton Elijah
Bayard James
Baylis Nehemiah
Bealy John
Beatty Archibald
Beatty James
Beatty Thomas
Beatty William
Beaty Alexander
Beaty Arthur
Beaty John
Beaty Robert
Belknap Benjamin
Belknap David
Belknap Isaac
Belknap Isaac, Jr.
Belknap Jeduthan
Belknap Jonathan
Belknap Jonathan, Jr.
Belknap Thomas, Jr.
Bell Mathew
Bennet Benjamin
Bennet John
Biram Asa
Black James
Black John
Blizzard Oliver
Bodine Lewiss
Bodle Samuel
Bodle William
Boides Robart, Jr.

Bookstaver Frederick
Bookstaver Jacob, Jr.
Bookstaver Jacob, Sr.
Booth John
Booth Thomas
Boreland Charles
Boreland Thomas
Boyd James
Boyd Robert
Boyd Samuel
Brannen Ruben
Brewster John
Brewster Samuel
Britnow Henry
Brockway Jesse
Brooke Jeremiah
Brooks Jeremiah
Brooks John
Brooks William
Brown Archabald
Brown Duncan
Brown Gilbert
Brown James H.
Brown John
Brown Neal
Brundage William
Brurdish Gilbert
Buchanan Robert
Buhannan Alexander
Buhannan James
Buhannan John
Buhannan Robert
Buice James
Bull Moses
Bunet Benjamin
Burnet John
Burnet Patrick
Burnet Robert
Burnet Thomas
Burns Francis
Burns Robert
Burns William
Buts Jacob
Caldwell James
Calwell William
Camble John
Campbell Levi
Campble Edward
Campble Ezekiel
Canfield John
Cantine Moses
Carman Yoest
Carney Barnabas
Carney Stephen
Carpenter William
Carskaden Thomas
Carter Luke
Case Benjamin
Caulkin Oliver
Chandler Enos
Clark Henry
Clark Jeremiah
Clark John
Clark James
Clark Joseph
Clark Phineas
Clawater Tice
Clemons Daniel
Clerk Henry
Cobb Asa
Coddinton Benjamin
Coddinton William
Codington Joseph
Coleman David
Coleman John
Congo David
Conkling Ananias
Conkling John
Content Benjamin
Content Moses
Cook John
Cook Thomas
Cook William
Corethers John
Cortwright Silvester
Corwin David
Corwin Eli
Cowin Elic
Cox Benjamin
Cox Jeremy
Cox John
Cox Reeves
Cox William
Cox William, Jr.
Crane Benjamin
Crawford Alexander
Crawford James
Crawford John
Crawford Samuel
Crist Abraham
Crist Daniel
Crist David
Crist Henry, Jr.
Crist Henry, Sr.
Crist Matinis
Crist Philip
Crist Stophonis
Crodethers John
Crons Adam
Cross John
Cross Robert
Cuddeback Abra'm, Jr.
Cuddeback Abra'm, Sr.
Cuddeback Abraham A.
Cuddeback Benjamin
Cuddeback James
Cuddeback Peter
Cuddeback William
Currenton Richard
Curtenius Peter, Jr.
Curtice Benejah
Curtice Noah
Curtice Thomas
Curwin Barnabas
Daily Samuel
Daily Samuel, Jr.
Dales John
Daly David
Daly John
Darkeas John
David Henry
Davidson John
Davis John
Davis Pathick
Davis Thomas
Davis William
Dealls John
Dealls William
Dearkis John
Decay Jacob
Decker David
Decker Evert
Decker Isack
Decker Martinas
Defrees James
Den Christopher
Denna Hinnery
Denman Isack
Denn William
Denniston Alexander
Denniston Charles
Denniston James
Denniston John
Denniston William
Denton Isaac
Denton Joseph
Denton Samuel
Depuy Benjamin
Depuy Benjamin, Jun.
Depuy John
Depuy Moses
Devans James
Dick Thomas
Dickarson Benjamin
Dickson Androw
Dill David
Dill John
Docksey James
Donavan Daniel
Douglass James
Douglass William
Douty Benjamin
Doxey James
Drake Joseph
Duffy John
Dunen Samuel
Dunlap James
Dunn George
Dunn William
Durham Andrew
Duryee Jacob K.
Eager John
Eager William
Easten Jeremiah
Eastman Tilten
Edmonstin James
Edmonston William
Elder Joseph
Elis James
Ellison David
Ellott John
Elsworth Henry
English William
Everit Nehemiah
Evret John
Falls William
Faulkner William
Finch James
Finley John
Fitzjerrild Jeremiah
Fowler Stephen
Frashor William
Fuller Jepotha
Fulton Thomas
Gage William
Gale Richard
Gale Moses
Gale Samuel
Galloway John
Garisson Nathaniel
Giles Charles
Gillispie Mathew
Gillispy David
Gillispy John
Godfry David
Godfry David, Jr.
Goldsmith Caleb
Goldsmith Stephen
Golow Christopher
Golow John
Golow Joseph
Green Ebenezer
Green Daniel
Green Israel
Green John
Green John, Jr.
Gumaer Elias
Gumaer Jacob
Gumaer Peter, 2d
Gumar Ezechial
Gunsalis Danial
Gunsalis Manuel

Gunsalis Samuel
Haines Charles
Hains Benjamin
Hains David
Hains John
Hains John B.
Halabut John
Halsey Jabas
Halstead Gershom
Hanesey James
Hanmer John
Hanyon Garret
Harden John
Harlow William
Harris George
Harris John
Harskal Jonathan
Hart Andrew
Hasbrook Cornelius
Hays James
Headin James
Hegerman Thomas
Helms Daniel
Helms Vincent
Hinneris Aron
Holsey Zephaniah
Homan Benjamin
Homan John
Homan Pheneas
Hopkins Garner
Hortin Jacob
Horton David
Horton John
Horton Joseph
Horton Silas
Howell Stephen
Hubart Joseph
Hubbard Joseph
Hulse John
Humphrey David
Humphrey George
Humphrey William
Humphry Charles
Humphry Oliver
Huse John
Hutson Richard
Inglis John
Inglis William
Jackson Silas
Jagger David
Jaques David
Jillett John
Johnson David
Johnson George
Johnston Robert
Johson David
Jones Augustus
Jones Phillip
Keen Jacob
Kelso Henry
Kernaghan Alexander
Kernaghan Charles
Ketcham James
Ketcham Joseph
Ketcham Philip
Kidd James
Kidd Robert
Kilburn James
King Clement
King Nicholas
King Stephen
Kingham Thos.
Knapp Zephaniah
Knox George
Lee Jepthath
Lee Jonathan
Leo Solomon
Leonard Henry
Lewers Williams
Liscomb John
Low James
Low Peter
Lowdy John
Lusk Francis
Mains Francis
Mandevil Cornelius
Mandevil David
Mandevil John
Mapes Henry
Mapes Samuel
Mapes Smith
Mapes William
Marshall David
Martin Charles
Martin John
Mathers Ebenezer
Mathers James
Matthews Amasa
Meloy James
Miller Edward
Miller Elias
Miller John
Milliken Alexander
Milliken Hugh
Milliken James
Millor Ezrah
Mills Daniel
Mills Jacob
Mills Jonathan
Mills John
Milspaugh Adam
Milspaugh Benjamin
Milspaugh Jacob
Milspaugh Jonathan
Milspaugh Philip
Milspaugh Philip, Jr.
Milspaugh Tice
Moffat Samuel
Moffatt William
Moncrief Charles
Monnel James
Moor William
Moore James
Moore Robert
Moore William
More David
More John
More Nathan
More Nathan, Jr.
More William
Morrison Daniel
Morrison James
Morrison John
Mould Christopher
McArter John
McArthur Neal
McCallon Thomas
McCalough Alaugh
McClauglury John
McClean John
McClotham Joseph
McCollam Matt
McConnely John
McCord Andrew
McCord James
McCreary Alexander
McCurdy Archibald
McDawell William
McDonal Alexander
McDowel Thomas
McDowell James
McEnty Michael
McEver Daniel
McGaragh John
McGown John
McKee Thomas
McKessock Thomas
McLoy William
McMaster James
McMichel John
McMillian Mathew
McMunn John
McNeas Clark
Mc Neas George
McNeely David
McNes Daniel
McNish Clark
McSwaney Daniel
Neal Mal'h
Neely Edward
Neely John
Neely John, Jr.
Neely Thomas
Newkirk Adam
Newkirk Hendrick
Newman Scuder
Newston Robbart
Nichols William
Nicholson Daniel
Nicholson Thomas
Nickoll William, Sr.
Nikols Nathan
Nobel Jabes
Obrien John
Oliver David
Oliver Thomas
Outerman Stephen
Overton James
Owen Amasa
Owen David
Owen Eleazer
Owen Jonathan, Jr.
Owen Joshua
Owen Nathaniel
Owen Oliver
Owen Solomon
Owens Amasa
Owens Eleazer
Owin John
Palmer Henry
Park William
Parks Amos
Pars Jonathan
Parshall John
Parshall Jonathan
Patterson James
Patterson Samuel
Patton James
Pelton Gideon
Perry David
Perry John
Polley William
Porter Thomas
Post Zebulon
Potter Aaron
Price John
Puff John
Reed John
Reed Moses
Reeder Charles
Reeve Ely, Jr.
Reeve Nathaniel, Jr.
Rhoads Thomas
Rickey Andrew
Ritenbergh Addam
Ritenbergh Aron
Robert Danel
Roberts Daniel
Robertson Benjamin
Robinson William
Rocefeller j nd'r
Rockefella Christian

Rockefella Henry
Rockefella John
Rockwell Samuel
Roe Samuel
Rogers Moses
Rogers Robert
Rogers Solomon
Rogers William
Roosa Cornelius
Roose Aldert
Roose Jacob
Rosa Evert
Rosa Jacob
Rose Jacob
Rose Samuel
Sanders John
Satan Jonathan
Sayer Stephen
Sayres Stephen
Scates Bartholomy
Scavon Mills
Scott Archibald
Scott James
Scott William
Seely Bezaleel, Jr.
Seely Elijah
Seely Israel
Seely Samuel
Sergeant Nathan
Seybolt John
Seybolt John, Sr.
Shaw William
Shay John
Shea George
Sheerman Henry
Shilp Johonis
Shutter Robert
Siah Indian
Sickels Zachariah
Sicars Benjamin
Siears John
Siers Elethan
Siers Samuel
Simeril Robert
Simmonds Jacob
Simpson Peter
Sinsabok Henry, Senr.
Sinsabok William
Skinner Abner
Slott Cornelius
Slott John
Slott John, Junr.
Slott John, Senr.
Slott Jonas
Sly John
Sly Samuel
Sly William
Smedes Moses
Smiley James
Smith Bastian
Smith David
Smith David, Junr.
Smith George
Smith Jacob
Smith James
Smith Jeremiah
Smith John
Smith Jonathan
Smith Jonathan, Junr.
Smith Joseph
Smith Mathew
Smith Nathan
Smith Samuel
Smith Simon
Smith Stephen
Smith William
Southerland James
Sprague Andrew
Springsted James
Springsteen Henery
Squirrel Jacob
Stag John
Stan'on Rufis
Steel Alexander
Stewart Alexander
Stewart Robert
Stickney James
Stinson William
Stout David
Strickland Eli
Strong John
Stubs William
Swarthout Cornelius
Swarthout Gerad
Swarthout James
Swarthout Philip
Swartwoud Jacobus
Taylor Abraham
Taylor James
Thomas Ephraim
Thomas John
Thomson John
Thorn Obadiah
Thorn Samuel
Tillford Alexander
Totton James
Totton Thomas
Travis Ezekial
Tremper George
Trewilliger Isaac
Trewilliger John
Trewilliger Math
Trimble John
Trumpoor Nicholas
Trumpore Peter
Tucker James
Turner Hugh
Turner John
Tuttle Borzila
Vail Alsop
Vail Josiah
Vail Obediah
Vanburah Court
Vanfleet Daniel
Vaninwagen Cornelius
Vaninwagen Jacob
Van Inwegen David
Van Inwegen Herman
Van Nosdall John
Van Vara Cort
Vanwey Henry
Wair William
Wallace William
Wallice John
Wastbrook Abraham
Wastval Joseph
Watkins Ephraim
Watkins Thomas
Webb Jonathan
Welch John
Welch Thomas
Weller Lod'k
Wesbrook Abra'm
Westbrook Terrie V.
Westlake Samuel
Westlick Benjamin
Westlick George
Whary James
Wheat Amos
Wheat Solomon
Wheelar David
Wheler Gilbert
Whit Geames
White James
White Silas
Wickham William
Wilkins Daniel
Williams Isaac
Williams Jonas
Willing Frederick
Willoughby John
Wilson Andrew
Wilson William
Winter Ezra
Wood Alexander
Wood Benjamin
Wood Daniel
Wood John
Wood Samuel
Wood Silas
Wood William
Woodruff John
Woods Benjamin
Woodward Hezekiah
Woodward Hezekiah, Junr.
Wool Ellis
Wood Robert
Wooley Charles
Wright David
Wright William
Young Benjamin
Young Charles

Ulster County Militia — (Continued).

COLONEL LEVI PAWLING

COLONEL JOHN CANTINE

LIEUTENANT COLONEL JACOB HOORNBEEK

QUARTER MASTER PHILIP HOORNBEECK

QUARTER MASTER JOHN VAN DUSEN

CAPT. ANDREW BEVIER
" JOHN BRINKERHOFF
" FRANCIS BURNS
" MOSES CANTINE
" JACOB CONKLIN
" WILLIAM CROSS
" WILLIAM FAULKNER
" JOHN A. HARDENBERGH
" JOHN HASBROUCK
" BENJAMIN KORTROGHT
" JAMES MILLIKEN
" PELEG RANSOM
" FREDERICK SCHOONMAKER
" JOCHEM SCHOONMAKER
LIEUT. ALEXANDER BEATTY
" RICHARD BRODHEAD
" JOHN DEPUY
" JOHN C. DEWITT
" RUBEN DEWITT
" CORNELIUS DUBOYS
" DANIEL FREER
LIEUT. NICHOLAS HARDENBERGH
" JACOBUS HASBROOCK
" JOSEPH HASBROOK
" JOSIAH HASBROUCK
" JONATHAN HERDENBERGH
" NATHANIEL POTTER
" WILLIAM SWARTWOUT
" JONATHAN TERWILEGER
" ROBERT THOMPSON
" CORNELIUS VAN WAGANEN
" DIRRICK WESBROOK
" FREDERIC WESBROOK
ENSIGN MOSES DEPUY, JR.
" JOHN DEWITT
" LEVI DEYO
" WILLIAM ELSWORTH
" JACOB D. HOORNBEEK
" ROBERT MOLE
" JOHN ROOSA
" PETER SMITH
" JACOBUS SWARTWOUT

ENLISTED MEN.

Achmodey Jacobus
Acker Johannis
Airs William
Aker John
Aldridge Daniel
Aldridge Gilbert
Aldridge Robert
Allen Isaac
Aller John
Anderson William
Annist Corn
Annist Peter
Arnet John
Aston Jeremiah
Atkins David
Baker Bartholomew
Barager Wm. Helimus
Barber William
Barger Wouler
Barley Jonathan
Barlow Nathan
Barret John
Barten Isaac
Bartholamoo John
Beaker Ephraham
Beasmer Michel
Beatty John
Beaty Robert
Beck Nathaniel
Bell William
Benjamin Chester
Benjamin Darius
Benjamin Devyno
Benjamin Uriah
Berrit John
Berry Peter
Besemer Jacobus
Bevier Abraham
Bevier Abraham, Jr.
Bevier Benjamin
Bevier Coenradt
Bevier Cornelius
Bevier Jacob
Bevier Matthew
Bevier Nathaniel
Bevier Petrus
Bevinns David
Bishop James
Bishop John
Black John
Black Robert
Blows John
Bodeley John
Bodel Samuel
Bodley John
Bogardus Petrus
Bogart Cornelius
Braden Thomas
Bradley Daniel
Bray William
Brian James
Bride James
Brink John
Brink Robert
Brodhead Daniel
Brodhead Henry
Brodhead Samual
Brodhead William
Brooks Joseph
Brooks William
Brown George
Brown John
Brown Joseph
Brown Josiah
Brown Peter
Buch Jacobus, Junr.
Bunshoten Jacob
Buoy William
Burge Thomas
Burger Nicolaes

Burger Petrus
Burges Thomas
Burhans Abraham
Burnet Isaac
Burpans Edward
Bush Jacobus
Buswel Zahariah
Buyker Ziles
Cambell Robert
Camble I. Reuben
Camble Rubin
Camble Simeon
Campbell John
Campbell Joshua
Can Abraham
Cantine John
Cantine John, Junr.
Cantine William
Carflow Henry
Carner Andrew
Carson Johanis
Carson Samuel
Cater Wilhalmes
Cavere Miles
Celder Hendrick
Chambers Cornelius
Chambers Jacob
Chambers John
Chambers Joseph
Chambers Thomas
Chenix William
Clark John
Clarwater Thomas
Claurwater Joseph
Clee Hugh
Cley Hugh
Clouse Henry
Clyn Jacob
Clyn Johannis
Coddington Jacob
Cole John
Cole Simon
Colman Israel
Colter John
Comfort Richard
Coningham William
Conklin Seven
Connely Patrick
Conner Jacobus
Conner John
Connor Daniel
Conaway John
Constable John
Content Moses
Conway Cornelius
Cook John
Cope William
Cortragth Henry
Cortreght Jacobus
Cottenton Jonah
Cottonton Josiah
Coudegal Abraham
Cowen Thomas
Cox John
Crane James
Crans Peter
Crawford Robert
Crispell Abraham
Crist David
Crist Martines
Crom John
Croover Aron
Croover George
Cross Noah
Crum Hendrick, Jr.
Crum William, Jr.
Cryspell Benjamin
Currenton Richard
Daily Robert
Dan John
Danaldson Abraham
Davis Andrew
Davis Benjamin
Davis Frederick
Davis Isaac
Davis Jacobus
Davis John
Davis Peter
Davis Richard
Davis William
Deake Josiah
Dealy David
Dean Gidon
Dean Isaac
Dean Jedediah
Decker Benjamin
Decker Frederick
Decker Jacobus
Decker Noah
Decker Ruben
Degair Elias
DeLametter John
Delametter David
De Lemetter Benjamin, Jr.
Denniston James
Deny Nicolas
Deo Hendrick
Deo John
DePew Jachim
DePew Jacob
Depew Moses I.
Depue Benjamin
Depue John, Junr.
Depuy Cornelius
Depuy Cornelius, Junr.
Depuy Ephraim
Depuy Ephraim, Junr.
Depuy Joachim
Depuy Joseph
Depuy Moses
Depuy Simon
Devenpoort Gerrit, Junr.
Devenport Jocobus
Devoe Abraham
Dewitt Andries A.
Dewitt Cornelious
De Witt Egbert, Jr.
Dewitt Jacob I.
De Witt Jacob T.
De Witt Jacob's
De Witt John
Dewitt John I.
Dewitt Jone
Dewitt Peterus
De Witt Stephen
Dewitt Tjerck
Dewitt William
Deyeo Henry
Deyeo John
Deyes Abraham, Junr.
Deyes Ezekial
Deyo Danial
Deyow Ezikeal
Deyo Isaac
Deyo John
Deyo Simon
Deyoy Abraham B.
Dick Thomas
Dickason Joseph
Dickerson Benjamin
Dickson Andrew
Diel Thomas
Dimon Moses
Diver Daniel
Dodge Samuel
Dolson John
Dolson Theunis
Donadson Abraham, Junr.
Dongarms Elias
Donoven Daniel
Douglass John
Doyoo Daniel
Doyoo Levi
Drake Josiah
Drake William
Drew Joshua
Drew Josiah
Drew Oliver
Dubois Andrew
Du Bois Aseph
Dubois Conradth
Dubois Danial
Dubois Daniel, Junr.
Dubois Hendrickus
Dubois Henry
Dubois Isaac
Dubois Jacob
Dubois Jacobus
Dubois John
Dubois Matthewsem
Du Bois Nathaniel
Dubois Wessel
Duboys Jacob
Duffield John
Dugin Christopher
Dumond Johannis, Junr.
Dumond John D.
Dumond John P.
Dumond Peter
Dumont Cornelius
Dunbar Charles
Dunlap William
Dunn Jorimiah
Dunn John
Dunn Thomas, Jr.
Dunn William
Dupuy Brisk
Ecker Solomon
Een Abraham
Elder Joseph
Ellen Jesse
Elmendorph Abraham
Elmendorph Benjamin
Elmendorph Coenradt C.
Elmendorph Coenradt W.
Elmendorph Garrit C.
Elmendorph Jonathan, Jr
Elmendorph Petrus
Elsworth Benjamin
Elsworth Henry
Elsworth John
Elsworth Joseph
Elsworth William
Elsworth William W.
Elting Ab'm
Enderle Peter
Ennerly Petrus
Ennest Cornelious
Ennest Hartman
Ennest Peter
Ennest William
Every Henrey
Feer Stephenes
Fiffer William
Filips Ebenezer
Fitch Samuel
Fowler Samuel
Frair Isaac
Friar Joseph
Friar Powles
Friar Solomon, Jr.
Friar Thom's

Fraklen Bejenen
Frame Jacob
Frame Johannis
Franklair Benjamin
Frare Jacob, Junr.
Freer Jacob J.
Freer Jacob S.
Freer John I.
Freer Paulis
Freer Peter
Fulton William
Geggy John
Gellaspy Matthew
Giddes Hugh
Gilaspy David
Gilaspy George
Gilbert Ebenezer
Gildersleeves Daniel
Ginggy John
Givens James
Goodspead Nathaniel
Graham Daniel
Graham Jacobus
Graham John
Graham Phasso
Graham Robert
Grnham Silvanus
Grahams James
Grahams Jacobus
Grahams Thomas
Gray Abraham
Greatreaks Silvanus
Green Henry
Green Jacob Marius
Green Peter Maurius
Green Sylvester Marius
Greenwalt Daniel
Griffen Benjamin
Griffin John
Griffin Joseph
Griffin Matthew
Guiggy George
Gunsallus Benjamin
Haasbrouck Jonas
Hadley Moses
Haip Hom'y, Jr.
Halstead Josiah
Hamilton William
Hance Henry
Handricks Johannis
Handricks Lawrence
Haner Robert
Hanie Henry
Hannes Henry
Hansbrouck John
Happy George
Hardenbergh Elias
Hardenbergh Jacob, Junr.
Hardenbergh Johannis
Hardenbergh John
Hardenbergh John C.
Harp Henrey
Harp John
Harp Peter
Harret Thomas
Harris George
Harris Henry
Harris James
Hasbrock Jonas
Hasbrook Solomon
Hasbrouck Benjamin
Hasbrouck John, Junr.
Hasbrouck Severyn
Hass Nicholas
Hatman Danial
Headley Moses
Hedger Evert
Hedger Samuel
Heermanse Edward
Hellister William
Helm Daniel
Helm Simon
Helms Daniel
Hendricks Lawrence
Hondrickse Peter
Hendrickson Jacobus
Hendrickson Petrus
Hennis James
Hermanse Abraham
Hermanse Jacob
Herrington Alexander
Hess Nicholas
Hess Robert
Hewit Benjamin
Heyer Hartman
Himes Fradrick
Hoghteeling Thomas
Hoghteeling William
Hollister William
Holsted Joseph
Holsted Josiah
Homan John
Hood William
Hooghteling John
Hoornbeeck Cornelious
Hoornbeek Benjamin, Junr.
Hoornbeck Giedeon
Hoornbeek Isaac
Hoornbeck Jacob, Junr.
Hoornbeek Jacob D.
Hoornbeek Joel
Hoornbeek Johannes
Hoornbeek Lowerens
Hoornbeeck Petrus
Hoornbeek Philip
Hoornbeek Samuel
Hoornbeek Warner
Hornbeck Henry
Hornbeek Cornelius, Junr.
Hornbeek Samuel
Huey James
Hull Nathaniel
Hull Samuel
Humphrey James
Hutchin George
Impson Benjamin
Ireland Thomas
Irwin Jerred
Irwin John
Ivery Henry
Ivory Helmus
Jansen Tunis
Jarman James
Johnson Abraham
Johnson Benjamin
Johnson David
Johnson Isaac
Johnson John
Johnson Jonathan
Johnson Peter
Johnston Elexandrie
Johnston William
Jones Ebinezar
Karner Andrew
Kater Jacob, Jr.
Keator Cornelous
Keator Cornelius, Junr.
Keator John P.
Keator Petrus I.
Keator Samuel
Keator William, Junr.
Keatter William N.
Keel Samuel
Keifer Laurence
Kelder Hendrickes
Kelder Joseph
Keley John
Kelley John
Kelsey John
Kerk Gerrit N.
Keter Jacob
Keter Jacob F.
Keter Petrus
Keter Samuel
Kiersted Wilhelmus
Kilsey Thomas
King Jeremiah
Kirkpatrick Samuel
Kittle Henry
Knox Thomas
Kole Petrus
Kortrecht Lowranse
Kortreght Louwerens, Junr.
Krinn Benjamin G.
Krinn Hendrick B.
Krom Jacob
Krom Jacob D.
Krom John
Krom Reuben
Krom William
Kroom Jacob
Kroom William
Kroum Johannis, Junr.
Krum John G.
Krum Simon
Lafaver Johannis
Lafaver John A.
Lafaver Philip
Lalmatier Abraham
Lamb Samuel
Lane Benjamin
Lapowl Johan's
Laroy Francis
Laroy Simion
Laroy Trop
Lefavour Andries
Lefavour Noah
Lefever Jonathan
Lefever Solomon
Lofevor Matthew
Lefevre John
Lemunyan John, Junr.
Lent Enus
Leroy Francis
Leroy Rop
Leroy Simon
Litts John
Lockwood Isaiah
Lofovor John
Lofovor Matthew
Louw John C.
Low Abraham C.
Low Cornelius
Low Jehue
Low Johannis
Low John
Low John J.
Low Samual
Lyons Thomas
Mack Johannis
Macky John
Makaive Matthew
Marcle Samuel
Markell Benjamin
Marshall Henry
Marshall Jeremiah
Marshall John
Marth Peet
Masten Abraham, Jr.
Masten Cornelius B
Masten Cornelius C.
Maston Johannes B.

Masten John C.
Masten Joseph
Masten Robert
Matt Ezekiel
Mawris Samuel
Megrorty Patrick
Meldown Daneal
Meloy William
Merkel Elias
Merkill Benjamin
Merkle Frederick
Mickle Frederick, jr.
Middagh Abraham
Middagh Claudea
Middagh George
Middagh Joh's
Middagh Martin, jr.
Mildun Daniel
Miller Johannes
Miller Philip
Miller William
Milliken John
Mills David
Millspaugh John
Milspaugh Abraham
Milspaugh Mathias
Milton John
Monrief Charles
More Nathan
Morris Arthur
Mouris Daniel
Mouris Petrus
Mours Samuel, jr.
Muir William
Mulks Benony
Murdough Lecky
Myer James
Myer Peter L.
Myer Samuel
Myer William, Jr.
Myers Michael
McBride Francis
McCay Alexander
McClougen James
McClughen Robert
McCollum Samuel
McConnel John
McCord John
McCreary John
McCreary Robert
McCue James
McDonnel William
McDougall Alexander
McDougle Hugh
McDowl Daniel
McElvannon Barney
McEwen Duncan
McGinnes William
McGlaughlin John
McHenry John
McKee Thomas
McKinsey John
McMaster James
McMullen William
McMunn James
McMunn John
McNay James
McNeal John
McSweney Daniel
Neass Jerry
Neef Jurry
Neely Abraham
Newkerck Matthew, jr.
Newkerk Aron
Newkerk Henry
Newkerk Isaac
Newton George
Nicholson Charles
Nicholson Jonathan
Nottingham Thomas
Nublo Justis
Oar William
O'Brien John
Odle Jonathan
O'Farrel Michal
Oin Abraham
Oosterhoudt Henriecus P.
Oosterhoudt Martines
Oosterhoudt Samuel
Oosterhoudt Teunis
Oosterhout Benjamin
Oosterhout Cornelius
Oosterhout Cornelius, Junr.
Oosterhout Ezekiel
Oosterhout Hendrices
Oosterhout Hendrick
Osterhoudt Henry
Ostrander William
Palmater Michal
Palmeter Abraham
Pamiteer Henrey
Patterson Michel
Patterson Samuel
Patterson William
Pattison William
Pemmet Michal
Perkins Ebenezer
Perkins Goddam
Perkins Jordon
Perry David
Perslow Henry
Peterson Alexander
Petibone Danial
Pettigo Daniel
Polaniteer Peter
Pontimer Henry
Presler John
Pressler Jonathan
Preston John
Pride James
Quick Hendricous
Quick Jacobus
Rabye Dene
Radman Michal
Ramson Jacobus
Rank John
Redigher Hendrick
Reed John
Reider Johannis
Reighter John
Remson Herre
Richard Daniel
Richards Nathaniel
Rider Benjamin
Roads Cornelius
Roberts Daniel
Roberts Gilbert
Roberts John
Robison Josiah
Roe David
Rogers James
Rogers Samuel
Roosa Egbert
Roesa Jacob
Roose Abraham
Rosacran Hendricus
Rosecrane Jacobus
Rosecrans John
Rossa Teunis
Row David
Ruger John
Russel Alexander
Ryder Benjamin
Rylya Denie
Samamins Joseph
Samenons Johanis
Sammon Johannis
Sammons John
Sanders John
Sanmaker Fredrick
Sarjent Wile
Sasson Thomas
Satchwell William
Sax John
Sax Peter
Sayre Joshua
Scapmus Derick
Schepmoes John
Schepmoes William
Schoonmaker Benjamin
Schoonmaker Cornelius
Schoonmaker Daniel
Schoonmaker Isaac
Schoonmaker Jacob
Schoonmaker Jacob Dewitt
Schoonmaker Jochem D.
Schoonmaker Johanis
Schoonmaker John E.
Schoonmaker Lodewyck
Schoonmaker Martin
Schoonmaker Martinus
Schoonmaker Petrus
Schoonmaker Thomas
Schoonmaker Wilhelmus
Scofield James
Sears Nathan
Seiele Coenraet
Semple Robert
Senogh Jacob
Sergeant Robert
Shaw Thomas
Shear Abraham
Shorter Chrispares
Shorter John
Shucraft Jacob
Simon O. O.
Simons Joseph
Sleght Henry B.
Sleght Teunis
Sloat David
Slowter Walter
Sluyter Abraham
Sluyter Cornelious
Sluyter Jacob
Sluyter James
Sluyter John
Sluyter William
Slyter I. Benjamin
Smedis Benjamin B.
Smedis Jacob
Smith Abraham
Smith Henry
Smith Jacob
Smith James
Smith Johannis
Smith John
Smith Jonas, jr.
Smith Peter, jr.
Smith Thomas
Smith Valentine
Smith William
Snyder Christopher
Sparks Jacob
Stanton Benjamin
Stephenson John
Stilway Cornelius
Stinson William
St. John Noah
Stumble Abraham
Swart Cornelius
Swart Isaac

Swart Tobias
Swartwout James R.
Tarwiller Simon
Terwiligar Arry
Terwiliger Tunis
Terwilleger Hans, Jr.
Terwilleger Joseph
Terwilliger Evert
Terwilliger Joshua
Thaxter Benj. F.
Theator Gideon
Thlarwater Joseph
Thomas John
Thompson Aaron
Thompson Andrew
Thompson Archibald
Thompson William
Thounsend Ben
Thrum John
Thuttle Barzile
Tirwilleger Johannis
Tolten James
Tomkins Isaac
Tomkins Jeremiah
Tomkins Jonathan
Tomkins Thomos
Tompkins Lowrance
Tompson Joshua
Tonkins Thomas
Tornuer Jacob
Toursen Samuel, Sr.
Travis Gabril
Trowbridge Ralph
Turner Jacobus, Jr.
Turner William
Tutle Israel
Varner Philip
Vernooy Johannis
Ver Rooy Nathen
Viely John
Van Beuren Philip
Van Blascom James
Vanburen Christopher
Van Curen Ruben
Vandamarck Orry
Vandamark Ezekiel
Vandemark Cornelius
Vandemark Solomon
Vandemerke John
Vandemerke Joseph
Vandemerke Lodewyck
Vandemerken George
Vandemerken John
Van De Merken Joseph
Van Demerker Frederick
Vanderhoff Cornelius
Vandermarke Arie
Vandermarke Fradrick
VanDermarke Jacob
Vandermarke Joseph
Van der merk Ghysbert
Van dermerk Solomon
Vandermerkon Frederick
Van Gaasbeek Abraham
Van Gasbeck Thomas
Vanheng Abram
Vanheran Christopher
Van Ining Abraham
Van Keuren Abraham
Van Keuren Matthew
Van Keuren Mattheus
Van Keuren Tcherick
Vanlauvan Petrus
Vanlauven John
Van Luvan Christopher
Vanluven Andria
Van Steenbergh Abraham
Vansteenbergh Benjamin
Van Steenbergh John
Van Steenbergh Matthew
Van Stienbergh Dirck
Van Stienbergh Tobias
Vanvlack Cornelius
VanVlerkum James
Vanvliet Tennis
Van Waganen Daniel
Van Wagenen Benjamin
Van Wagenen Jacob
Van Wagenen John
Vanwagenen Levi
Van Wagenen Peter
VanWagenen Simon
Wackman Daniel
Waismiller Henry
Walker Justus
Wallace John
Wallas William, Jr.
Wasbrouck Jonathan
Waters Nathaniel
Waugh Robert
Weekman Danial
Weeks Abraham
Weeler William
Weller Fredrick
Wells Jacobus
Wells James
Wells Peter
Wesmiller Jeremiah
Wherry David
Whitaker John
White Silas
Whitney David
Whitney David, Junr.
Whitney Jacob
Wilder Daniel
Williams Abraham
Williams John
Willson Thomas
Wilmiller Henry
Winfield David
Winfield Simon
Winn John
Winne Peter I.
Wismiller Jeremiah
Witney David
Wolsey Daniel
Wolsey Henry
Wood Job
Wood Theophelus
Woods Silas
Woolsey Daniel, Junr.
Wright William
Wynkoop Cornalius
Wynkoop Dirck D.
Wynkoop Tobies
Wynkoop William
Yaple Adam
Yates Thomas
Yelverten Anthony
Yelverton Anthony, Junr
York Johannis
York John
York Petrus
Young Alexander
Young John

Ulster County Militia — (Continued).

HARDENBURGH'S REGIMENT.

This Regiment seems to have had a somewhat torturous career.

On March 13, 1776, the Provincial Congress received a letter from Colonel Abraham Hasbrouck, Major Johannes Snyder and the other officers of the Field and Staff, returning their commissions for "childish reasons," as the proceedings of the Provincial Congress characterized them. On August 3, 1776, Captain Salisbury complained to the same body that Colonel Snyder had ordered that his Troop of Horse be drafted as Foot soldiers. Congress countermanded the order. Soon afterward, charges were preferred against Colonel Snyder, but whether on account of the above action does not appear, nor is the result given.

As he was still in command in 1782, the charges could have had no serious result. As far as can be gathered, the Regiment served at different periods from October 25, 1775, until 1782.

Many changes were made in the officers at a reorganization in February, 1778.

On November 2, 1781, Lieutenant Colonel Elmendorf resigned, but no record is found of who succeeded him.

COLONEL JOHANNES HARDENBURGH
LIEUTENANT COLONEL JONATHAN ELMENDORPH
LIEUTENANT COLONEL JOHANNIS JANSON
MAJOR JOHN GILLESPY
ADJUTANT ABRAHAM SCHOONMAKER
QUARTER MASTER CORNELIUS DUBOIS, JR.
QUARTER MASTER JAMES ROE

CAPT. JOHANNIS BEVIER
" EVERT BOGARDUS
" DANIEL CANTINE
" JACOB CONCKLIN
" WILLIAM CROSS
" ISAAC DAVIS
" MICHAEL DEVOE
" ANDRIES J. DEWITT
" JOHN L. DEWITT
" LUCAS DEWITT
" LEWIS J. DUBOIS
" JOHN ELMENDORPH
" GERARDUS HARDENBERGH
" JACOB HASBROUCK, JUNR.
" PHILLIP HOOGHTELING
" JACOB HOORNBEEK
" JAMES HOUSTON

CAPT. MATTHEW JANSEN
" CORNELIUS MASTEN
" MATTHEW MASTEN
" DAVID OSTRANDER
" SIAH ROBINSON
" JAMES ROBISON
" JACOBUS ROOS
" PETER ROOSA
" EGBERT SCHOONMAKER
" ARTHUR SMITH
" JOHANNIS SNYDER
" ADAM SWART
" PHILIP SWART
" JASON WILKINS
" EDWARD WITAKER
" JACOB WOOD
" JURRY W. WREGHTMIRE

CAPT. ADRIAN WYNKOOP
LIEUT. ANDRIES BEVIER
" JACOBUS S. BRUYN
" ABRAHAM CANTINE
" JOSEPH CRAWFORD
" PETER DECKER
" MATTHEW DEDERICK
" JACOB DELAMATER
" JAMES DENTON
" ELIAS DEPUY
" THOMAS DEWITT
" JOSHUA DUBOIES
" ABRAHAM DUJEY, JUNR.
" CHRISTIAN FIEROE
" JOHN FOSTER
" ISAAC FOWLER
" ANTHONY FREER
" SAMUEL GILLESPY
LIEUT. DAVID GUION
" JOHANNIS A. HARDENBERGH
" NICHOLAS HARDENBURGH
" PETRUS HASBROUCK
" JURRY HUMMEL
" WILLIAM KEITCH
" NATHANIEL KELSEY
" MATTHEW LEFEVER
" SIMEON LEFEVER
" BENJAMIN LOW
" JAMES LYON
" TOBIAS MIRE
" PETRUS MYNDERSY
" JOHN MACARTHUR
" PETRUS OOSTERHOUT
" WILLIAM OSTRANDER
" EBENEZER PERKINS

LIEUT. PETER POST
" PETRUS ROSA
" SYLVESTER SALSBERRY
" FREDERICK SCHOONMAKER, JR.
" PETRUS SCHOONMAKER
" ANNING SMITH
" SAMUEL SWART
" CHRISTOPHER TAPPEN
" JACOB TERWILLIGER
" PETER THOMPSON
" ROBERT THOMPSON
" JOHN VAN BEUREN
" TOBIAS VAN BEUREN
" WILLIAM VANDAMARK
" JACOBUS VAN GASEBEEK
" MATTHEW WYGANT
" CORNELIUS E. WYNKOOP
" EVERT WYNKOOP
ENSIGN SAMUEL BEVIER
" PETRUS BRINCK, JUNR.
" JOHN BROADHEAD, JUNR.
" RICHARD BRODHEAD
" MOSES CANTINE, JUNR.
" METHUSALEM DUBOIES
" NATHANIEL DUBOIS
" PHILLIP HOORNBEEK
" EDWARD LUNSBERRY
" HENDRICUS MIRE
" ROBERT MOUL
" JOHANAS ROBISON
" JACOBUS ROSEKRANTS
" JOHN SLEGHT, JUNR.
" JOHN VAN DEUSEN
" DANIEL WOOLSEY

ADDITIONAL NAMES ON STATE'S TREASURER'S PAY BOOKS.

LIEUT. NATHANIEL HARKER
" JAMES KANE

LIEUT. HENRY VAN WEGAN
ENSIGN REUBEN TOOKS

ENLISTED MEN.

Admins Samuel
Albertson Joseph
Albertson Stephen
Albertson William
Aldrich Gilburth
Alekenbrgh Peter
Allen John
Alsdarf Lowrance
Alsdarf Philip
Alsdorph Jacobus
Alsdorph Johannis
Alsdorph Philip
Alsdurf Jacobes
Anderson William
Anthony Alard
Anthony John
Anthony John, Junr.

Arslen Daniel
Bach Joh's Lorence
Bading Isaac
Baily Thomas
Bain David
Baker Bartholomew
Ball Thomas
Bancker Solomon
Bang Samuel
Banks Justus
Bardine William
Bark George
Barker Isaac
Barkly James
Barman Peter
Barns Stephen
Barrik George

Barthy James
Bartley James
Barwill James
Bealy John
Bedford Jones
Beleger Frederic
Bell Thomas
Bell Thorue
Bell William
Beroon Anthony
Bevier Abraham
Bevier Cornelius
Bevier Daniel
Bevier Jonas
Bevier Nathaniel
Beymer Joh's
Billiger Michael

Binson Peter
Blensham Matthew I.
Blensham Matthew J.
Bloomer William
Bodine Francis
Bodine Isaac
Bodine John
Bodine William
Bonker John
Boons Daniel
Borton Isaac
Borwell James
Bouen Daniel
Bout John
Bowings Daniel
Brannen Addam
Breaden Thomas

Brinck Sollom
Brink Cornelius
Brink John
Brink John, Jr.
Brink Peter
Brink Solomon
Brook Abraham W.
Brown Ebenezer
Brown Edward
Brown Isaack
Brown Jonathan
Brown Jonathan, Junr.
Brown William
Brush Eliakim
Brusie Andries
Bruyn Abraham
Bruyn Cornelius
Bruyn Ebenazer
Bruyn Johannis
Bruyn Safryn
Bruyn Zacheriah
Bull Daniel
Bump Cornelius
Burdin Francis
Burdin William
Burdine John
Burhans Samuel
Burns Charles
Burwell James
Bush Hanory
Cahill Daniel
Caldwell James
Camble John
Camp Eldard
Carman John
Carny Stephen
Carpenter Wight
Case John
Case Joseph
Caviler John
Cerley Israel
Chisom Hendrik
Christice Johan
Claarwater Jeremiah
Clark James
Clarwater Jacob
Clarwater Joseph
Cline Jacob
Cline Jonas
Coldwell John
Cole Cornelius
Cole Johannis
Cole William D.
Coleman Duncken
Coleman Joseph
Colter John
Colwell Jacob
Combs Solomon
Comfort Benjamin
Comfort John, Jr.
Comfort Samuel
Conkling William
Cool Cornelius
Cool Maritie
Cool William
Cornes Solomon
Coulter John
Coulter John, Junr.
Cowen Martin
Cox William
Crage Francis
Cramer Wendle
Crances Henry
Crank Frederick
Crans Cristuphel
Crans Ezekiel
Crans Henry
Crans Phillip
Crawford David
Crawford Jonathan
Crawford Nathan
Crawford Robert
Crawford Samuel
Credit Benjamin
Crestise John
Criswell John
Crofford Samuel
Cronck Fradrick
Cronee Ezekiel
Crons Ezekiel
Crooger Barnest
Crook Conrad
Croover John
Cropsey Henry
Cropsey Matthew
Crosby Thomas
Crover Aron
Crover George
Crover John
Crowford Nathan
Cross Leonard
Cruger Arnest
Crumm Jacob
Cunbergh Matthew
Dacker Elezar
Dailey Robert
Dalls William
Davis John
Days Handrick
Dealls William
Deane Solomon
Decker Abraham
Decker Abraham, Junr.
Decker Ambrick
Decker Benjamin
Decker Benjamin, Junr.
Decker Benjamin J.
Decker Benjamin T.
Decker Elias
Decker Elisha
Decker Elizar
Decker Evert
Decker John G.
Decker Jurry
Decker Manasse
Decker Noah
Decker Peter
Decker Peter, Junr.
Decker Uriah
Decker Wilhelmes
Decker William
Dederick Lucas
DeLefever Coenrad
Demott James
Denniston John
Derlin David
Devenport Robert
Devins Jacobus
Dill David
Dinager George
Divenu Jacobus
Divins Jacobus
Dobins James
Docherty Cornelius
Dolson John
Dougless James
Drake William
Dubois Andries
Dubois Hezekiah
Dubois Jonathan
Dubois Nathaniel
Dubois William
Duboys Aadris
Duffield John
Du Mott Isaac
Dunlap John
Du Witt Jacob
Eaker Steven
Eckert Stephanus
Edmons Samuel
Empson Benjamin
Empson John
English John
Ennis James
Erwen Robert
Farris James
Ferguson Samuel
Forbes William
Forbes William G.
Forcits William
Forgeson Samuel
Forsght William
France Youst
Frayer Jeremiah
Freeman Samuel
Freer John
Frint Jacob
Frons Phillip
Galation James
Garrison Isaac
Gee Andero
Gee Jeremiah
Gee John
Gee Nathaniel
Gillaspy David
Gillespy George
Gillespy James
Gillespy James, Junr
Gillespy John
Goetschus Henrocus
Graham James
Graham Robert
Graham Thomas
Graham Wilyham
Grahams James
Gray Andrew
Gray Benj.
Green John
Green William
Griffice Barne
Gunsalis Samuel
Gunsalus Danel
Gutches Hendricus
Hadger John
Hadly Fredick
Hains Henry
Halett Moses
Hallett George
Hallett William
Hannah Samuel
Harcourt John
Harcourt Nathaniel
Harding James
Harris Alpheus
Harris Jonathan
Hathy Fredrick
Hatley Frederick
Hauter Isaac
Hawkins James
Heady Marcus
Hedger John
Hedger Wilhelmus
Hedgner John
Heemanse Edward
Hendrickson Jacob
Herr David
Herrinton Moses
Hide Henry
Hill George
Hill William
Hofman John
Holester Isaac

Holl John
Hollet Willem
Hollett Moses
Hollister Isaac
Hollister William
Holmes Asa
Homes Reubin
Hoole John
Hornbeek Ephraim
Hosbrock Benjamin
Huffman Nicolas
Hufman John
Hughes Evert
Hughes William
Hull Nathanel
Hull Samuel
Hunter Archebel
Imson Benjamin
Innis James
Irvine William
Irwin Robert
Jacklin Daniel
Jansen Jacobus
Janson Nicholas
Johnson Abraham
Johnsen Richard
Johnston Arthur
Johnston Jacobus
Johnston Ritchard
Jonson John
Kain James
Kane Cornelius
Kauter Isaac
Keyser Ephraim
Kimbarrack Matthew
Kimbary Mathew
King Clayman
King Nicholas
Kirkpatrick Samuel
Kitchen Richard
Kline Jacob
Kline Jonas
Knifin John
Knolton Daniel
Knox Thomas
Kraus Henry
Kyrk William
Lair Adam
Lane George
Lane William
Lattimore Roger
Laughlin James
Lawrence John
Lawrence William
Laybolt Jacob
Lenderman, Cornelius
Lester Allen
Lewis Cornelius

Lewis John
Lewis Ritchard
Lewis Samuel
Lilley John
Linn George
Lister Allon
Litch Rulif
Lits Evart
Lits Rulif
Loomis Timothy
Lotts Conrad
Lovell Alexander
Lovell Jost Minard
Low Jacob
Luts Henry
Lutts John
Luwes Corneles
Mac Dugal Duncan
Mackey Alexander
Mackey Alexander, Junr.
Macord John
Malford David
Mance John
Marshall Jeremiah
Marten John
Masten Abraham
Masten Art
Masten Ezekiel
Masten Jonathan
Masten Matthew
Masters Daniel
Maston John
Matterstock Joh's
Mentz John
Merritt George
Milbourn Andrew
Miller Abraham
Miller Hans
Miller Jacobus
Miller James
Miller John
Miller John, Junr.
Millin Alexander
Mills David
Millspaugh Abraham
Milspaugh Fredrick
Milspaugh Isaac
Milspaugh Mathias
Milspaugh Matthew
Milspough Mattichia
Minthorn John
Mirrit Thomas
Mole Philip, Junr.
Moor Jacob
Moor Martin
Morse Benjamin
Moss Benjamin
Moule Philip

Mullen Michal
Muller Michal
Munford James
Murdogh Lackey
McBorney William
McCay Alexander, Junr.
McCleen John
McClouchan Robert
McClughan Robert
McCollhem Robert
McCullom William
McColm Robert
McColough John
McCord John
McCoughan Robert
McCreery John
McCreery Robert
McCue James
McCurdy John
McDermont Lawrence
McDowal Daniel
McDowell Jonathan
McElvin David
McIlvean David
McIlwain David
McKay John
McKenny Matthew
McLackler John
McLaughlin John
McMullen John
Nainy Samuel
Nicols William
Nox Thomas
O'Bradly Daniel
O'Cain Edward
Odle Jonathan
Opright Malaicah
Oproght George
Osborn Daniel
Osterhoudt Henry
Osterhoudt Peter
Ostrander Christophel
Ostrander Jacob
Ostrander William
Owen John
Owns Benjamin
Palmer William
Palmiteer William
Parsel Jeremiah
Pembrook William
Penny James
Penny John
Penny Stephen
Pensil Peter
Perveer James
Pholps Shadrik
Pifer Hendrick
Pixley Jona

Pixley William
Place William
Plumsted Joseph
Post Abram, Junr.
Potman John
Potter Edward
Purdy William
Putnam Henry
Putnam John
Radiker Henry
Rain James, Junr.
Rainey David
Rainey Samuel
Raljay Denye
Raljay Simon
Rank Cornelius
Rank Philip
Rea Matthew, Junr.
Rea Stephen
Read Stephen
Realya Simon
Reany David
Reighter John
Relyea Dene
Relyea Dene T.
Relyea John
Rekman Harmanes
Richard Nathaniel
Richman Harramanis
Ricknen Harmanus
Roe John
Ronk John
Roof John
Roos Avart
Roos Evert, Junr.
Roos John
Roos Peter A.
Roosa Aldert
Roosa Derick
Roose Evert
Rose John
Rose Evert, Junr.
Rosekrans Hendrick
Rosekrans Hendrick W.
Rosekrans John
Rosekrans Wilhelmes
Rosekrans Wiliam
Rosman Hendrick
Ross Finley
Ross William
Rossell Ludwigh
Rump Christian
Rump Henry
Russel William
Sageman Jacob
Sager Malachy
Sammons Cornelius
Sammons Jacob

Sammons Matthew
Sammons Matthew, Junr.
Sammons Tunis
Scarscadden Robert
Schoonmaker Abraham
Schoonmaker Isaac
Schoonmaker Jacob
Schoonmaker Wilhelmus
Schriver Martin
Schutt Abraham
Schutt H.
Scott James
Scott William
Sears Lawrence
Segor Malacchia
Seneebauch Henery
Sension Adam
Seoos John
Shafer George
Shammons Jacob
Shaver Daniel
Shaw Thomas
Shear Salvinus
Shoecraft Jacob
Shorter John
Sidman Jacob
Sifertis Manassa
Silkworth William
Simmons Jacob
Simmons Sylvanus
Simmons Tunis
Sincebaugh Henry
Sinclair John
Sinkler John
Sinsepough Henry
Skit Hugh
Slaughter Isaac
Slaughter John
Slauter John
Sloot William
Slot William
Smedes Benjamin
Smedes Benjamin B.
Smith Francis
Smith George
Smith John Meribray
Smith Ladlaw
Smith Leege
Smith Ludlom
Smith William
Snider Daniel, Junr.
Snyder Daniel
Snyder Henry
Snyder Jacob
Snyder John
Sommons Matthew
Sparks Abraham
Sparks Jacob
Sparks Robert
Sprage Amasa
Springsteel Joseph
Stalker Seth
Starks Robert
Steenbargh John
Stevenson Hugh
Stitt James
Stitt John
St. John Adam
St. John Noah
St. John Samuel
Storm Jacob
Stowell John
Strickland Abraham
Strickland Jacob
Striker Abraham
Summons Tunis
Swart Abraham
Swart Benjamin
Swart Daniel
Swart Isaac
Swart John
Swingel Harromus
Swingle Cronimus
Taerpanning Lavi
Tampson Archibald
Tarepening Richard
Tarepening Samuel
Tarepenning Lawrance
Tarpening Derrick
Tarpenney Elias
Tarpenny Abraham
Taylsor John
Teerpenning Teunis
Teers Lowrence
Terbos Henry
Terpening Abraham
Terpening John
Terwelgen Petrus Vas
Terwilagar Philip
Terwiliger Hezekiah
Terwiliger John
Terwillager Joseph
Terwilleger Arie V.
Terwilleger Daniel
Terwilleger Isaac, Jr.
Terwilleger James F., Junr.
Terwilleger Jonathan
Terwilleger Matthew
Terwilleger Simon H.
Terwilleger Wilhelmus
Terwilleger Zacharias
Terwilligar Jacobus
Terwilligar Josiah
Terwilligar Peter N.
Terwilliger Abraham
Terwilliger Abraham, Junr
Terwilliger Aroon
Terwilliger Arra
Terwilliger Benjamin
Terwilliger Cornelius, Junr.
Terwilliger Evert
Terwilliger Hendrick
Terwilliger Isaac
Terwilliger Jacob, Junr
Terwilliger James
Terwilliger James F.
Terwilliger Jonas
Terwilliger Peter P.
Terwilliger Petrus
Terwilliger Petrus Vas
Terwilliger Simon
Terwilliger Solomon
Terwilliger Tunis
Terwilliger Tunis C.
Terwilliger William
Thompson Alexander
Thompson Andrew
Thompson Archabald
Thompson Richard
Tice Hen:y
Tirwillegar Henry
Tooker Reuben
Traith John
Trape James
Trapp James
Trumpurt Jacob
Tucker Ruben
Tuttle Israel
Upright George
Upright Malichia
Upright Nathan
Vawn Richard
Viburgs Peter
Vanamburgh Hanry
Vanamburgh Jeremiah
Vancuran Benjamin
Vancuren Levi
VanDelyne Peter
Vandemark Ezekiel
Vandemarken Ezekial
Vandemarken Jacob
Vandenmark Jacob
Vandenmerk Jacob
Vandermerke Wilhelmis
Vangarden Jacobus
Vangarden James
Vangorden James
Van Keuren
Van Keuren Benjamin
Vankeuren Charick
Van Keuren Cornelius
VanKeuren Hazael
VanKeuren Jacobus
VanKeuren Jacobus, Junr.
Van Keuren Levi
Van Keuren Ruben
Vankuren Benjamin
Van Steenbergh John
Van Steenburgh Abraham
Van Wagenen Benjamin I.
Van Wegan Henry
Wackman Henry
Wackman Marcus
Waderwan William
Wagenor Johanis
Wakman Henry
Waller John
Walles William, Junr.
Wallis Hugh
Wallis William
Ward David
Ward Richard
Ward William
Warkman Henry
Warrey John
Washburn John
Wath Nicholas
Watts Nicholas
Weed Samuell
Welch Ephraim
Weller Frederick
Weller John
Westbrook Abraham
Whany John
Wharing James
Whorrey John
Wigant John
Wigens Michal
Wiggan Michael
Wiggons Annon
Williams Adam
Williams John
Williams Richard
Williams William
Wilsey William
Winfield Elias
Winfield Peter
Wintfield Peter
Wintworth John
Wood Abraham
Wood Job
Wood Stephen
Wood Timaty
Woodward Daniel
Workman Henry
Wygant Martin
Yorks Aron
Young Christian
Young Johan Christ

Ulster County Militia — (Continued).

INDEPENDENT COMPANY.

CAPTAIN SAMUEL CLARK

ENLISTED MEN.

Albertson Joseph
Albertson Stephen
Albertson William
Allen Jesper
Armstrong James
Bloomer William
Buckingham Solomon
Clark James
Cropsy Jacob
Degroot Jacob
Degroot Joseph
Denton Nathaniel
Donaghy John
Edwards Gilbert
Fowler Daniel
Givens Samuel
Hollet
Johnson David
Kent Thomas
Kilsey Thomas
Kniffin John
Langley George
Lattemore Rogger
Lester Allen
Mackey Charles
Morrison Robert
Mulliner John
Parks William
Patten James
Pembrook William
Place William
Plumsted James
Price Joseph
Richards Philip
Robinson William
Shay John
Sinnot Thomas
Smith David
Smith David, Sr.
Smith Samuel
Stephenson Hugh
Stilwell John
St. John Noah
Tilton Peter
Ward Isaac
Weed John
Weekes Obadiah
Wool Jeremiah
Woolsey Jonathan
Wuts Solomon

WESTCHESTER COUNTY MILITIA.

COLONEL JOSEPH DRAKE
COLONEL JAMES HAMMAN
MAJOR JONATHAN HORTON
MAJOR JONATHAN H. PAULDING
QUARTER MASTER RICHARD GARRISON

CAPT. JESSE BAKER
" NICHOLAS BERRIEN
" GEORGE COMB
" GILBERT DEAN
" JOSEPH DRAKE
" ISRAEL HONEYWELL
" DANIEL MARTLING
" JONAS ORSOR
" GABRIEL REQUAW
" RICHARD SACKETT
LIEUT. BENJAMIN BROWN
" WILLIAM DAVIS
" DANIEL DEVOE
" NATHAN FISH
" NATHANIEL GARRISON
LIEUT. JONATHAN KNAPP
" HENRY LAMBERT
" HEZEKIAH MILLER
" WILLIAM MOSHER
" ISAAC REQUA
" CORNELIUS VAN TASSELL
" JACOB VAN TASSELL
" JOHN VAN WORT
" WILLIAM WARNER
" DANIEL WILLIAMS
ENSIGN THOMAS BOYCE
" JOHN OAKLEY
" PETER PAULDING
" STEPHEN SHERWOOD
" ISAAC VALENTINE, JR.

ADDITIONAL NAMES ON STATE TREASURER'S PAY BOOKS.

LIEUT. DENNIS LENT
" GERSHOM SHERWOOD
LIEUT. WILLIAM VAIL

ENLISTED MEN.

Aaron Blak
Acker Abraham
Acker Benjamin
Acker Isaac
Acker Jacob
Acker John
Acker Stephen
Acker Sybert
Acker Tobias
Ackerman John
Alair Peter
Allen Samuel
Applebe Elnathan
Archer Benjamin
Archer John
Armstrong Edward
Aster Jonathan
Baker Gilbert
Baker Daniel
Baker John
Baker Moris
Baker William
Baley John
Bancker Nicoles
Banton Samuel
Barrett Samuel
Baxter Lock
Beise Ray
Berrien Cornelius
Berrien George
Bertholf Crines
Bertholf Henry
Bertholf Peter
Bertine John
Besser Teunis
Beylo Jacob
Bice Abraham
Bice James
Bice John
Bice Peter
Bice Thomas
Binker Hendrick
Bishop John
Boice Abraham
Bont Peter
Boughton Timothy
Bout Peter
Brewer Deliverance
Brewer Matthew
Brewer Nazareth
Britt William
Brook Michel B.
Brooks Michael
Brooks —roms
Brower Jacob
Brown Abraham
Brown —bert
Brown Isaac
Brown John
Bruce Robert
Buckhout Jacob
Buckhout Jacob, Jr.
Bugby John
Bugby Thomas
Buice Aaron
Buice Abraham
Buice John
Buill Abraham
Buill Johannas
Buise Peter
Burdet Elethar
Burgess Archer
Burgess Archibald
Burgess James
Burling Ebinezer
Burns Edward
Bussing Henry
Bussing Peter
Bussing Peter, Jr.
Buyl William
Buyse Genie
Buyse Jacob
Buyse William
Byce John
Byse William
Carr Jacob
Chanpenois Andrew
Chanpenois Nommay
Chanpenois Thomas
Chanpenois William
Chapman ——
Chapman Danel
Charpanat Simon
Chatterdon James
Cillet David
Clark Daniel
Clark Isaac
Clark Othaniel
Clark Titus
Conklin Joseph

Cookstone John
Corter Willeom
Courtract John
Covenhoven Edward
Cowen Danunt
Croft ——mes
Cronk Garret
Cronk Harclos
Cuningham Abraham
Cuningham John
Currin Patrick
Cursor Benjamin
Cursor Isaac
Cursor John
Cypher Jacop
Cypher John
Cypher John, Junr.
Daton Joseph
David William
Davids David
Davids Isac
Davids William
Davis William
Dean Isaac
Dean John
Dean Samuel
Dean Thomas
Dee David
Delamater Abraham
Delamater Isaac
Delanoy Abraham
Delevier Hendrick
De Pew Henry
Derevere Hendrick
Dereviere John
Deriver Cornilous
Derivine Henry
Devoe David
Devoe James
De Voe John
Devoe William
Dicerman Joseph
Dickinson Ezekeal
Dingy Eliga
Dodge Nathaniel
Dolem ——
Drake Samuel
Ducker Abraham
Dutcher Abraham
Dutcher John
Dyckman Garret
Eacker Jacob
Edget Joel
Elit David
Embre John
Embre John, Jr.
Embre Joseph, Jr.
Embre Samuel

Fancher John
Farrington Jonas
Ferris John
Ferris Peter
Ferris Samuel
Finch Jonathan
Fish Nathan
Fisher Elijah
Fisher James
Fisher John
Fisher Samuel
Fork Daniel
Forshee James
Forshee John
Forshu William
Fosha John
Foster Reduke
Fowler Joshua
Fowler Marton
Fowler Moses
Frasher John
Frazier William
Gall Stephen
Garrison Dennis
Garrison John
Garrison Tunis
Gilmore Robert
Gravestine Garret
Gravestine John
Green ——
Green Isaac
Green William
Hadley Frederick
Hadley Isaac
Hadley Joseph
Hadley Moses
Hadley Stophen
Haight Reuben
Haight Walter
Hait Abijah
Hait Daniel
Hait Phineas
Hamman James, Jr.
Hammon John
Hammond John
Hammond States
Hanis Moses
Har Abraham
Haris Moses
Haroods ——
Harper George
Harris Edward
Harris William
Hatfield Joshua
Hawks —athan
Hayes Jesse
Hayes Nathaniel
Hedger Thomas

Hegby Jacob
Helker John
Hichcock John
Higday George
Hill James
Hitchcock David
Holmes Jeremiah
Holmes Rubin
Holmes Samuel
Hornbeck Henry
Horton Caleb
Horton John
Horton Thomas
Horton William
How Silvanus
Howell Siles
Hughsted Noah
Humphey Thomas
Hunt Arnold
Hunt Eliab
Hunt Jacob
Hunt Philip
Hunt Robert
Hunt Samuel
Hunt Thomas, Jr.
Hunter John
Hutter William
Hyat Thomas
Hyde Diah
Ingersol John
Israel John
Jackling Truman
Jacobs Cornelius
Jacobs —uha
Jewel John
Johnson Levi
Johnson Samuel
Jones ——
Jones Corneles
Jones —msa
Jouel John
Kanker Nicoles
Keiff Andrew
Knap Joel
Knapp Jonathan
Lafferjea Tunis
Lamberdson Lambert
Lambert Abraham
Lambert Cornelius
Lambert Henry
Lambert Lambert
Lamberth William
Lauser Samuel
Lawrence Isaac
Lawrence Thomas
Lawson Samuel
Learure Samuel
Lefurgy Peter

Legget Ebenezer
Legget Elijah
Legget Gabriel
Legget William
Lent Isaac
Lewis John
Light Josiah
Livurgis Peter
Lounsbury Joseph
Lovebury Jonathan
Lownsbury Joshua
Lyon Esreal
Mainer Stephen
Mangam Daniel
Marshall James
Martine John, Jr.
Martine Samuel
Martling David
Martling Peter
Mead Joseph
Mead Joshua
Mead Marsel
Mead Mortchet
Mead Paschel
Mener A.
Miller Abraham
Miller Ebenetus
Miller Moses
Miller Peter
Miller Samuel
Mills ——on
Miner Albert
Minner James
Mirtine John
Money —lum
Morrill
Morris Abraham
Mouer Alburt
Mullin Richard
McChain John
McCloud Alexander
McCord
McCord Robert
McFarding Gabriel
McFarding James
Naviring —es
Neal William
Nelson John
Newman Jonathan
Newman Platt
Nicols Abram
Northrup Eli
Oakley Caleb
Oakley Isaac
Oakley John
Oakly Myles
O'Brian Morger
Odel Jacob

Odell Isaac
Onsar Abraham
Orcer Elbert
Orser After
Orser Isaac
Orser Solomon
Orsor Niccles
Osbon John
Osborn Danvers
Osburn John
Pain Joseph
Palding John
Palding Joseph
Palmer Aaron
Parsall Devenport
Paulding John
Paulding John, Junr.
Paulding Joseph
Paulding William
Peterson John
Pever Cornelius
Phillips Samuel
Pinkney David
Place Uriah
Plase Freeman
Porday John
Poulding Reoger
Poulding Thomas
Pugley Tolman
Pugsly Toloman
Purday Esrael
Purday James
Purdy Anthony
Purdy Solomon
Rafter William
Ragen Jeremiah
Ransen Henry
Rassque Ab'm
Ratton Willam
Raymond, Sands, Junr.
Rayrdon Patrick
Reed Isaac
Reed James
Repua James
Requa Isaac
Requaw Abraham
Requaw Daniel
Requaw John
Requaw James
Requaw James, Junr.
Requaw James, Senr.
Requaw Joseph
Retong William
Revere Cornelius
Robeson John
Rockwell William
Romer Hendrick
Romer Hendrick, Jr.
Romer James
Roomer Henry
Rull John
Rundel David
Rundel —ham
Rundel —nes
Russell Abraham
Russell John
Russell Timothy
Ryer ——
Ryer Hendrick
Ryer John
Ryer Tunis
Sackett ——
Sands Stephen
Saxton —n
Schofield ——
Schofield —lisa
Scofield Silas
Sedore Isaac
See Abraham
See David
See Isaac
See Isaac, Junr.
See James
See James, Sr.
See John
Sergeants James
Shearwood Isaac
Shearwood Joshua
Sheerman Joseph
Sherewood Moses
Sherewood William
Sherman Adrian
Sherman Jacob
Sherwood Elijah
Sherwood Job
Sherwood Samuel
Sherwood Solomon
Shute Ezekiel
Sice James
Sice Paul
Sice Peter
Sider Stephen
Sidore Coonrod
Sifer Jacob
Sifer John
Siffer John
Siffer John, Senr.
Silbay ———
Simmons Isaac
Simon —nail
Slater David
Smith Isaac
Smith Stephen
Snell Stephen
Soodor Stephen
Standard Richard
Stantin Elijah
Stater —d
Stephens John
Stevenson Frederick
Steves Jerimiah
Steward Gershem
Stingrod —non
Storm Abraham
Storm David
Storm Gorus
Storm John
Storms David
Storms Nicholas
Storms Stotts
Stuart ———
Stuart —arts
Stuart John
Stuart Solomon
Swain James
Syfer Peter
Syper Jeremiah
Sypher John
Tailer Gilbert
Taylor Elijay
Taylor Elnathan
Taylor Henry
Terup James
Tice John
Tippet James
Tippet Thomas
Tompkins Jeremiah
Tompkins Ab'm
Tompkins Elijah
Trusdel Samuel
Tucker —and
Turbush —nry
Turnier John
Tuttil, James
Underhill Nathan
Vahe Godfray
Valentine Jacob
Varden John
Varney —aham
Veach Andrew
Veach John
Veal Abraham
Vearin James
Veel William
Veil William
Vermillia Joshua
Voke Henry
Van Wormer Peter
Van Buer Marten
Vanhouten Peter
Van Norstrand William
Van Osterand William
Vanscoy Cornelius
Vantassel Abraham
VanTassel Cornelious
Van Tassel Cornelius, Jr.
Van Tassel Jacob
Vantassel John
Van Tassel Stephen
Van Tessel David
Vantessel Isaac
Vantessell Peter
Van Wart
Van Wart Abraham
Van Wart Garret
Van Wart Henry
Van Wart Isaac
Van Wart Jacob
Van Wart Jacob, Junr.
Vanwart James
Van Wart John
Vanwart William
Van Wormer Cornelius
Wagenor Tobias
Waldron Isaac
Ward Charles
Ward Daniel
Ward Hezekiah
Ward Nathan
Ward William
Washburn Daniel
Washburn Joseph
Washburn Silas
Webbers Isaac
Weed —athan
Weeks —ames
Weeks Jonathan
Weeks Reuben
Weeks William
West Zephaniah
Weston Joseph
Wheteen Benjamin
Wheteen Luthel
Whitny —itus
Wilday James
Wildey Jacob
Williams
Williams Abraham
Williams David
Williams Daze
Williams John
Williams Marcus
Wood Jonah
Wolsey Daniel
Woolsey Abraham
Yerkis William
Yerks John
Yorks James
Yorks John
Youngs Joseph
Youngs Samuel

Westchester County Militia — (Continued).

COLONEL THOMAS THOMAS
LIEUTENANT COLONEL GILBERT BUDD
MAJOR DAVID HOBBY
MAJOR JESSE TRUESDELL
ADJUTANT WRIGHT CARPENTER
ADJUTANT EDWARD THOMAS
QUARTER MASTER TIMOTHY BRUNDIGE
QUARTER MASTER JAMES McDONALD
QUARTER MASTER WILLIAM MOSHER
QUARTER MASTER NATHANIEL TUCKER
COMMISSARY THEODOSIUS BARTOW

Capt. Noah Bouton
" Benjamin Chapman
" Peter Fleming
" Abijah Gilbert
" Samuel Haight
" ——— Hunter
" Gilbert Lyon
" Josiah Miller
" Marcus Moseman
" Jacobus Purdy
" Richard Sackett
" Benjamin Stevenson
" Moses St. John
" John Thomas

Lieut. Thomas Carpenter
" Jesse Holly
" Caleb Lawrence
" David Lyon
" Silas Miller
" Joseph Miller
" Elijah Scott
" Ebenezer Scofield
" Jacob Travis
" William Wright
Ensign Samuel Banks
" John Falconer
" Eli Tyler
" Abraham Wearing

Additional Names on State Treasurer's Pay Books

Lieut. Isaac Clark
" Jacob Haight
" Gabriel Higgins
" Isaac Miller
" James Miller

Lieut. Hezekiah Miller
" Sands Raymond
Ensign Benjamin Ambler
" Timothy Miller

ENLISTED MEN

Abraham Henry
Additon Ebenezer
Additon William
Ambler Benjamin
Ambler Jeremiah
Anderson Benjamin
Anderson Jermiah
Angavine Gilbert
Archant George
Arden Gideon
Arhart George
Armstrong Edward
Armstrong Isaac

Arnold James
Arnold Jeremiah
Astine Amos
Austin Amos
Baker Daniel
Banks John
Banks Jonathan
Banks Obediah
Barret Abraham
Barret Bethuel
Barret Marcus
Barret Marcus, Senr.
Barrett Reuben

Barrett Samuel
Bea Peter
Benedict Amos
Benedict Benjamin
Benjeman James
Bettis John
Betts Nathan
Bishop Epenetus
Black Isaac
Blew Isaac
Bloodgood Oliver
Bonker Abraham
Borett Bethuel

Bortick Robert
Bortwick Samuel
Bosthewick James
Bostwick James
Bostwick John
Bostwick Robert
Bostwick Samuel
Bostwick Stephen
Bouton Benajah
Bouton Ebenezer
Bouton Ezra
Bouton Joeb
Bouton Samuel

Westchester County Militia — (Continued).

COLONEL THOMAS THOMAS
LIEUTENANT COLONEL GILBERT BUDD
MAJOR DAVID HOBBY
MAJOR JESSE TRUESDELL
ADJUTANT WRIGHT CARPENTER
ADJUTANT EDWARD THOMAS
QUARTER MASTER TIMOTHY BRUNDIGE
QUARTER MASTER JAMES McDONALD
QUARTER MASTER WILLIAM MOSHER
QUARTER MASTER NATHANIEL TUCKER
COMMISSARY THEODOSIUS BARTOW

CAPT. NOAH BOUTON
" BENJAMIN CHAPMAN
" PETER FLEMING
" ABIJAH GILBERT
" SAMUEL HAIGHT
" ——— HUNTER
" GILBERT LYON
" JOSIAH MILLER
" MARCUS MOSEMAN
" JACOBUS PURDY
" RICHARD SACKETT
" BENJAMIN STEVENSON
" MOSES ST. JOHN
" JOHN THOMAS

LIEUT. THOMAS CARPENTER
" JESSE HOLLY
" CALEB LAWRENCE
" DAVID LYON
" SILAS MILLER
" JOSEPH MILLER
" ELIJAH SCOTT
" EBENEZER SCOFIELD
" JACOB TRAVIS
" WILLIAM WRIGHT
ENSIGN SAMUEL BANKS
" JOHN FALCONER
" ELI TYLER
" ABRAHAM WEARING

ADDITIONAL NAMES ON STATE TREASURER'S PAY BOOKS

LIEUT. ISAAC CLARK
" JACOB HAIGHT
" GABRIEL HIGGINS
" ISAAC MILLER
" JAMES MILLER

LIEUT. HEZEKIAH MILLER
" SANDS RAYMOND
ENSIGN BENJAMIN AMBLER
" TIMOTHY MILLER

ENLISTED MEN

Abraham Henry
Additon Ebenezer
Additon William
Ambler Benjamin
Ambler Jeremiah
Anderson Benjamin
Anderson Jermiah
Angavine Gilbert
Archant George
Arden Gideon
Arhart George
Armstrong Edward
Armstrong Isaac

Arnold James
Arnold Jeremiah
Astine Amos
Austin Amos
Baker Daniel
Banks John
Banks Jonathan
Banks Obediah
Barret Abraham
Barret Bethuel
Barret Marcus
Barret Marcus, Senr.
Barrett Reuben

Barrett Samuel
Bea Peter
Benedict Amos
Benedict Benjamin
Benjeman James
Bettis John
Betts Nathan
Bishop Epenetus
Black Isaac
Blew Isaac
Bloodgood Oliver
Bonker Abraham
Borett Bethuel

Bortick Robert
Bortwick Samuel
Bosthewick James
Bostwick James
Bostwick John
Bostwick Robert
Bostwick Samuel
Bostwick Stephen
Bouton Benajah
Bouton Ebenezer
Bouton Ezra
Bouton Joeb
Bouton Samuel

Bridge Salvanus
Briggs Joshua
Brigs Thomas
Brooks Michael
Brower Holsey
Brown Daniel
Brown Deliverance
Brown David
Brown Holsey
Brown John
Brown Joseph
Brown Lawrence
Brown Lebous
Brown Nehemiah
Brown Titus
Brown William
Bruce Robert
Brundago David
Brundage James
Brundage John
Brundage Josiah
Brundage Masten
Brundage Salvenus
Brundge Jeremiah
Brundges Selevans
Brundige Jesse
Brundige Nathaniel
Brush Jesse
Buckbee John
Bugbee John
Bugbee Jonathan
Busbee John
Cabee Stephen
Cambell James
Campell James
Cauengham James
Canfield James
Canfield Nathan
Canfield Nathan, Junr.
Canfield Stephen
Carney Thomas
Carpenter Rufus
Carr Charles
Champenois Andrew
Chapman Benjamin
Chapmen Benjamin
Chapmen John
Charlick Henry
Charlick John
Clapp Benjamin
Clapp Benjamin, Junr.
Clapp Henery B.
Clapp Henry
Clark Caleb
Clark Cornelius
Clark Daniel
Clark David
Clark Henry
Clark Isaac
Clark Isaac Miller
Clark Jacob
Clark James
Clark Joseph
Clark Josiah
Clark Nathan
Clark Silas
Clark Titus
Clarke Nathaniel
Cleen Daniel
Clements Charles
Clements James
Clock Jacob
Close Benjamin
Clyde Benjamin
Comes Solomon
Conkling Ebenezar
Connell Peter
Connery John
Connoly John
Connott Peter
Conway Thomas
Crab Fradrick
Crab Richard
Craft William
Crane Peter
Crawford Robert
Crissey Silvenus
Crissey William
Crissy Ebenezer
Crowford Robert
Cuningham John
Cunningham Abel
Cunningham James
Curby Stephen
Dalton Wiliam
Dan Abraham
Dan Jonathan
Daniels Elijah
Dannels James
Dayton Jonah
Deforest Reuben
Denge Elige
Dengee Emery
Denton Alexander
Denton Daniel
Denton Joseph
Denton William
Depew Abraham
Dibbel Daniel
Dingar Elijah
Dingee Emery
Dingee John
Dingee John, Junr.
Dinger John, Senr.
Dingy Elijah
Dinza John
Dodge Nathaniel
Doe Jonathon
Doesbusteed Daniel
Doge Nathaniel
Donalds John
Donalson Joseph
Drack John
Egbert Abraham
Elliot Robert
Elmore Ichabod
Fairchild James
Fansher John
Feecks Joseph
Feeke Joseph
Feeks Pryer
Feeks Robert
Felter Henry
Ferres Daniel
Ferris John
Ferris Jonah
Ferris Jonathan
Ferris Samuel
Ferris Thomas
Ferriss Silvanaus
Finch Elnathan
Finch Jonathan
Finch Philip
Fisher Abijah
Fisher Elijah
Fisher Gilbert
Fisher Joseph
Fisher Joseph, Junr.
Fix Pryor
Fowler Moses
Franklin James
Frayer Zebulon
Frazier John
Fuller Joseph
Furman Miles
Gale William
Garrett George
Gaulding Zenus
Gilbert Benajah
Gilbert Jacob
Gilchrist Samuel
Gilcrease Samuel
Gillchrist Thomas
Golding Amos
Graham Robert
Graham Tony
Green Abraham
Green Charles
Green John
Gregory Daniel
Gregory Jehiel
Gregory Nehemiah
Gregory Zekiel
Haight Charles
Hail Daniel
Hains David
Hait Jacob
Hait Jonathan
Hait Thaddeus
Hall John
Hall Joseph
Harness Robert
Harper Godfree
Harris Abijah
Harris Ezekiel
Harris Justus
Harris Robert
Harris William
Harris Zebulon
Hatton William
Hawkins Samuel
Hawxhurst Thomas
Hayes James
Hayes Josiah
Hayes Stephen
Hayes Thomas
Hayes Thomas A.
Haynes David
Hays Benjamin
Hays Nathaniel
Hayt Hezekiah
Hayt Jakin
Hayt Jonathan
Hector Fredrick
Heggens Ebenezer
Hellem Robert
Hibbirt Joseph
Hiff Andrew
Higen Eskel (see Higgens Ezekiel)
Higens Eben
Higgens Joseph
Higgins Gabriel
Higgins Moses
Higgins Joseph
Hill James
Hill Joshua
Hobby Jonathan
Hodges James
Hoff William, Jr.
Hoit Ezra
Hoit Phineas
Holister Plesant
Holladay William
Holmer David
Holmes Abijah
Holmes Beacher
Holmes Becker
Holmes James
Holmes Jeremiah
Holmes Jonathan
Holmes Reuben

Ranson Henry
Rasco John
Raymond Enoch
Raymond James
Raymond James, Junr.
Raymond John
Raymond Sands
Raymond Sands, Junr.
Raymond Thomas
Raynolds John
Reeve Andrew
Rerenhout George
Reynolds Jesse
Reynolds Jessop
Reynolds John
Reynolds Jonah
Reynolds Valentine
Rimes Henry
Risle James
Robenson John
Roberts Amos
Robertson John
Robeson John
Rockwell Nathan, Junr.
Rockwell William
Rockwill Benjamin
Rockwill Jobe
Rott Henry
Ruff Henry
Rumsey John
Rundal Jabus
Rundel Charles
Rundell David
Rundell Jesse
Rundle Richard
Rusco John
Ruso Samull
Ruso Thomas
Sacket James
Sackett ——n
Sackett James
Sackett John
Sackett Jones
Sackett Sollomon
Sanders John
Sands Samuel
Sarley James
Sarlls James
Sarlls John
Sarlls Richard
Sarlls Thaddeus
Sarlls William
Sarts John
Saws James
Schofield Enos
Schofield James
Schofield Jesse
Schofield John
Schothman James
Scofield David
Scofield Silas
Scofield Smith
Seaman Isaac
Seely Eli, Junr.
Seely Eli, Senr.
Seely Thadeus
Seley Joseph
Seley Thedas
Sellut Frederick
Semans Willet
Shampenway Andrew
Sherwood Nehemiah
Silkman John
Simmons Moses
Simons Isaac
Slauson Stephen
Slawson Amos
Slawter Gulbert
Smith Benjamin
Smith Caleb
Smith Caleb, Junr.
Smith Daniel
Smith Daniel, Junr.
Smith David
Smith Isaac
Smith James
Smith Jesse
Smith John
Smith Mathew
Smith Maurice
Smith Nathaniel
Smith Noah
Smith Oliver
Smith Philemon
Smith Richard
Smith Stephen
Smith Ward
Sniffen Andrew
Sniffen George
Sniffen James
Sniffen Reuben
Sniffen William
Snyder Jonathan
Sprage John
Stebbins Nehemiah
Stephenson Frederick
Stephenson Wilber
Stewart John
Sticklen John
Sticklen John, Junr.
Stine William
Stins John
St. John Abijah
St. John Moses
Stormes Hank
Strowbridge James
Sutherland Silas
Tanner John
Tayler Henry
Taylor Jonathan
Thomas Edward
Thomas John
Thorn Daniel
Tollerday Zachariah
—— Toney (colored)
Townsend Ephraim
Travis Zebulon
Tucker Robert
Tucker Ruben
Tucker Samuel
Tucker William
Tyler John
Tyler Jonathan
Tyler Simeon
Vincent Joseph
Vorhis Jacob
Vorhis Samuel
Van Dyck Jacob
Vansant Levy
Vantasell John
Van Waggoner Micheal
Vanzant Levi
Wall John
Wardel Eliakim
Wardel Solomon
Wareing Joshua
Waring David
Wascott Abram
Webb Sylvanus
Webb Sysumet
Weed Jonathan
Weeks Daniel
Weeks James
Weeks Jonathan
Weeks Nathaniel
Weeks Simon
Wendell Stephen
Wescot Abram
Wescot Annanias
Westcot Ezra
Westcot John
Westcot Samuel
Wheaton Benjamin
Wheten Benjamin
Whiller Ebenezer
White Jacob
White James
White John
White Stephen
Whitney Silas
Wicks James
Wight John
Willamesso Marcus
Williams Dage
Williams Marcus
Williams Robert
Williams Stephen
Williamson Jams
Williamson Marcus
Williamson William
Willis Maurs
Wood Jacob, Junr.
Wood Joseph
Wood Nathan
Wood Nathaniel
Wood Philip
Wood Stephen
Wood Timothy
Woodward William
Woolsey John
Woolsey John, Junr.
Woolsey Josiah
Word Jonath
Worden George
Worden Gilbert
Worden Joseph
Worden Voluntine
Wright Gilbert
Wright William
Young Joseph

Westchester County Militia — (Continued).

COLONEL PIERRE VAN CORTLANDT
(Elected Lieutenant Governor June, 1778, and resigned)
COLONEL SAMUEL DRAKE
LIEUTENANT COLONEL GILBERT DRAKE
LIEUTENANT COLONEL JOHN HYATT
MAJOR NATHANIEL DELIVAN
MAJOR JOSEPH STRANG
ADJUTANT JOHN COOLEY
ADJUTANT JAMES PENNOYER
QUARTER MASTER JOHN GREGORY
QUARTER MASTER ROBERT LANG
SURGEON ELIAS CORNELIUS
SURGEON EBENEZER WHITE

CAPT. TIMOTHY BENEDICT
" EBENEZER BOYD
" ABRAHAM BUCKHOUT
" ——— CRANK
" SAMUEL DELAVAN
" JASPER DRAKE
" JOHN DRAKE
" BENJAMIN GREEN
" SAMUEL HAIGHT
" ABRAHAM SMITH HEDDON
" JOHN HYATT
" JAMES KRONKHITE
" SAMUEL LAWRENCE
" EPHRAIM LOCKWOOD
" JOSHUA ROGERS
" ——— SCOFIELD
" GIDEON SEELY
" ELI SELY
" EBENEZER SLASON
" HENRY STRANG
" JAMES TELLER
" ——— TRUESDEL
LIEUT. JAMES ARCHER
" CORNELIUS CLARK
" WILLIAM CLARK
" JOHN CUDNEY
" JOSHUA DRAKE
LIEUT. BENJAMIN DYCKMAN
" DAVID FERRIS
" WILLIAM GAILER
" HARMANUS GARDINIER
" ——— HAYES
" EZEKIEL HYATT
" ——— LODER
" DANIEL MARTINE
" ZEPHANIAH MILLS
" JOHN MCCEAL
" EBENEZER PHILLIPS
" JONATHAN PORTER
" ABRAHAM PURDY
" ALVAN PURDY
" SOLOMON PURDY
" AUSTIN REYNOLDS
" EBENEZER SCOFIELD
" ELIJAH SCOTT
" HENRY SLASON
" JOSEPH VAIL
" JACOB VAN TESSELL
ENSIGN ——— BENEDICT
" ELIJAH DRAKE
" PHILIP LECK
" JOHN MCCREARY
" DANIEL WATERBERRY

ADDITIONAL NAMES ON STATE TREASURER'S PAY BOOKS.

LIEUT. DANIEL DELAVAN
" MOSES HEADOW
" JOHN MANDEVILLE
" JOHN C. MILLER
" OBEDIAH PURDY
LIEUT. ABRAHAM TODD
" URIAH WALLACE
ENSIGN JOHN CARMAN
" ISAAC CLARK
" JACOB MCNARMILY

ENLISTED MEN.

Acker Tobias
Adams Amos
Alen Samuel
Ardsehigel Richard
Arther Platt
Ashley Absalom
Aslin Isaac
Aure John
Austen Isaac
Avery Ebenezer
Avery John
Baet Marcus
Bailey Devoe
Baily James
Baly John
Banker Adolf
Barsely James
Barton Caleb
Bartow Elijah
Baset Samuel
Basford William
Batts John
Bayle Jonathan
Bayly Devone
Bedel Samuel
Beeckman Garrard G.
Benedich Jacob
Benedict Timothy
Berry Charles
Betts Gideon
Bevie Isaac
Billew Isaac
Birdsall Dannil
Birdsall Samuel
Birdsell Jacob
Bishop Epenetus
Bishop John
Blatchly Daniel
Bloom Zachariah
Bloomer Abraham
Borden Daniel
Borret Abraham
Boset Jesse
Boshford William
Bostwick John
Bostwick Robert
Bostwick Samuel
Bostwick Stephen
Bottle Thomas
Boughton Calope
Bouton Ezra
Bouton James
Bouton Jehiel
Bouton Joel
Bouton Joseph
Bouton Moses
Bouton Stephen
Bouton Timothy
Boyce John
Brant Philip
Briggs Edward
Briggs Isaac
Briggs Philup
Brock William
Brooks Daniel
Brooks John
Brown Adonijah
Brown Brockwa
Brown David
Brown Eber
Brown Elijah
Brown John
Brown Nathan
Brown Nathaniel
Brown Samuel
Brown Solomon
Brown Timothy
Brown William
Brundage Nathan
Brundige Hezekiah
Brush Elicam
Bryant Jeams
Buice John
Bunce Edmund
Burdjat Conerad
Burgdof Philip
Burgdurf Philip
Burges Archibald
Burwagen Saul
Bush William
Butal Thomas
Cable Samuel
Cadman Daniel
Calman Jaims
Campbell James
Canfield James
Canman Thomas
Cannon Henry
Carles Hennery
Carll David
Carman John
Carvender Joseph
Cats Michal
Catt Michal
Cear Hennery
Chace Thomas
Chalerton Jacob
Chapman Daniel
Chapman Stephen
Chatterton Jonathan
Chatterton Thomas
Chechister Jeremiah
Clark Isaac
Clark Nathan
Clarke James
Clawson Ezra
Clawson Jacob
Clements Aaron
Coley Samuel Brooks
Collard James
Combs Michael
Coucklin Seth
Conklin Jeremiah
Conkling Isaac
Conkling Israel
Conkling John
Conkling Jonathan
Conkling Zophar
Conlin Timothy
Cook Able
Cooley Samuel
Corlmon James
Crawford Robert
Crawford Robert, Junr.
Crofert Ase
Crofort Samuel
Crowfit John
Crissey John
Currey Richard
Currey Stephen
Cyper Ivy
Cypher Jerry
Danolds Eligah
Danslas Elijah
Davis Daniel
Davis Isaac
Davis John
Davis William
Davison Isaac
Dean Ephraim
Dean William
Dean William W.
Degroat Garet
DeGroot States
Dehue John
Delamter Isaac
Denton Alexander
Denton Joseph
Depue Abraham
Depue Hennery
DePue John
Devoe David
Devow Peter
Devowe William
Dibble Jonathan
Dibley Daniel
Dibley Solomon
Dickson Daniel
Dinger John
Dinges Samuel
Done John
Dotton Isaac
Drake
Drake Elijah
Drake Gilbert, Junr.
Drake Jasper
Drake Jeremiah
Drake John
Drake Joseph
Drake Joshua
Drake Josiah
Drake William
Dullunse Abraham
Dusenberry Richard
Dusenbry Jarvis
Dyckman Benjamin
Dyckman Garrett
Dyckman Jacobus
Dyckman William
Elk John
Elliot Robert
Ellit John
Facton Abraham
Fancher Abraham
Fancher David
Farguson John
Felss Coonrod
Fergerson Thomas
Ferris Caleb
Ferris David
Ferris James
Ferris Jonathan
Ferris Joshua
Ferris Richard
Field Benjamin, Junr.
Field Cumfurt
Finch James, Junr.
Finikin Edward
Fonnan Gilbert
Forbes James
Foreman Caleb
Forman Jacob
Formon Gilbert
Fort Silas
Fowle James
Fowle Solomon
Fowler Isaac
Fowler Justus
Fowler Martin
Fowler Reuben
Fowler Solomon
Fuller Elijah
Fuller Joseph
Gailer Robert K.
Gailer William
Garnsey Joseph
Garnsey William
Garrard Elias

Garrard Isaac
Garrisen John
Garrison Dennis
Garrison John
Gaulerd Willi
Gazeley Jame
Gean Shadrick
Gilbert Benajah
Gilbert Jacob
Golden Amos
Goler Samuel
Goler William
Goodman John
Gordinear Horremoni
Gould John
Gray Hezekiah
Gray Robert
Green Andrew
Green Samuel
Gumman Ephraim
Hadden John
Hadden Joseph
Haight Elnathan, Junr.
Haight Benjamin
Haight John
Haight Joseph
Haight Soloman
Hall Caleb
Hall Dan
Hall John
Halsted Michal
Hand Ezecal
Harris Enoch
Harris Justice
Hart Jonathan
Hartford Peter
Hartford Thomas
Hatfield Dannil
Hatfield Joshua
Hawkens Isaac
Haws Pelatiah
Haws Pelatiah, Junr.
Haws Seth
Haws Solomon
Hayse Abraham
Hayse Nathaniel
Hedden John
Helipen Harmen
Henbrown Chrislop
Herder Daniel
Hibner Mikel
Higgens Ebenezer
Higgens Joseph
Hill James
Hill Joshua
Hitt Dennis
Hitt Garard
Hitt Henry
Hitt Jarvard
Holladay William
Holmes Jonathan
Holmes Joseph
Holmes Rhuben
Holmes Samuel
Homand Ebenezer
Horis Ezekiel
Horton Daniel
Horton John
Horton Joseph
Horton Nehemiah
Horton Stephen
Horton William, Junr.
Hows Pilutiah
Hoyt Abraham
Hoyt Enoch
Hoyt Gideon
Hoyt Jacob
Hoyt Jesse
Hoyt Major
Hoyt Silas
Hoyt Silvenus
Hughson Jeremiah
Hults David
Hunt Obiah
Hunt Ward
Hustead Thomas
Husted Jabos
Huton Richard
Hyatt Elias
Hyatt John
Hyatt Solomon
Indien Ceser
Ingdell Jonathan
Ingosal John
Jackson Samuel
Jemmison William
Johnson Timothy
Johnston John
Jones Esquire
Jones George
Jones Isa
Jones John
Jones John, Junr.
Jump Amos
Jump Reuben
Keeler Nathaniel
Keen Henry
Kenedey David
Ketcham John
Kile James
King Jushua
Knapp David
Knapp Joseph
Kniffin Gilbert
Kronck Isaac
Kronckhyt Danniel
Kronkhite James
Laight Lodewick
Lain Jeremiah
Lamb
Lamb Patrick
Lamberdson Lambert
Lane Abraham
Lane Amos
Lane Doxe
Lane Elisha
Lane Joseph
Lane Nathaniel
Lane Peter
Lane Solomon
Lane Stephen
Larnes John
Lascelles Edward
Lawson Isaac
Lawson Lawrence
Lawson Samuel
Leach William
Leaverage Benjamin
Lee Abijah
Lee Dorcas
Lee Enos
Lee John
Lee John, Junr.
Lee William
Leggett Gabriel
Lent Abraham
Lent Albert
Lent Harmones
Lent Henry
Lent Isaac
Lent Jacob
Lent John
Lent John L.
Lent Lug
Lent Matthew
Lent Tobs
Lent Tunis
Lent William
Levines John
Levinus Thomas
Lockwood Hezekiah
Lockwood Jacob
Lockwood Nathan
Lyon Alven
Lyon James
Lyon John
Lyon Samuel
Lyons
Mabey Peter
Magere Joseph
Mandeville John
Marshell Amon
Marvin John
Mathors Joseph
Mead Andrew
Mead Danil
Mead Ebenezer
Mead Ethan
Mead Joseph
Mead Joshua
Mead Libeus
Mead Marshall
Mead Selah
Mead Stephen
Meed William
Meritt Abraham
Miller Abraham
Miller Ebenezer
Miller Ephenetus
Miller Gidion
Miller Isaac
Miller Jacob
Miller James
Miller John
Miller Nathan
Miller William
Mills Israel
Mills John
Mills John, Junr.
Mills Joseph
Mills Titus
Moger Lemuel
Montross James
Moore Marten
Morgan Thomas
Morrel James
Mosman Maseno
Mosman Peter
Mott Joseph
Mott Thomas
Munday Elijah
McCeald Nathan
McCoy John
McDonalds James
McFarthing James
McForlhing Gabriel
McKeel John
McLean Daniel
McLeel John
McNoughty Michael
Neekles Josiah
Neilson John
Nelson John
Newman James
Newman Nathaniel
Newman Peter
Niccols Robert
Nickels William
Nicols Benjamin
Northrup David
Northrup Isaac
Northrup Isaac, Junr.
Northrup Joel
Oakly William
Oaks John
Odell Isaac

Odell Jacob
Odell Jonathan
Odell Nathan
Odell Peter
Odell William
Odle Richard
Osburn John
Page Jonah
Palmer Levi
Pardee David
Pardee Nathaniel
Parent Jacob
Parent Levi
Patta Robert
Peatt James
Pell Roger
Pellem Elisha
Pellem John
Pellem Joseph
Pelton Daniel
Pennoyer Joseph
Perry James, Junr.
Phillips Philip
Phillips Samuel
Pine Samuel
Plan John
Plant John
Pohn William
Post Joseph
Potter Gilbert
Potter Samuel
Preason Abraham
Pugsley Samuel
Purdy Israel
Purdy James
Purdy Joseph
Purdy Samuel
Purdy Silvanus
Purdy Solomon, Junr.
Raymond Thomas
Raynolds Ephraim
Read James
Ren Solomon
Requaw Gabriel
Reynold Benjamin
Reynolds Nathaniel
Rider John
Roff Christopher
Roff Henry
Rogers Daniel
Rogers William
Rognale Gabril
Romer Hendrick
Ruff Samuel
Ruland Benjaman
Ruland John
Ruland Zophar
Runalds Austin
Russel Abraham
Ruton William
Sacket Richard
Sackett Richard, Sr.
Sands John
Sarles Elijah
Sarles Richard
Satterly Samuel
Sawson Isaac
Scudder Jacob
Scudder Nathaniel
Sealey Silvenos
Seaman Henry
Secor Warnar
Sely Thadius
Scofield Amos
Scofield Gedion
Scofield Joseph
Scofield Michel
Scofield Peter
Scofield Smith
Sharrock James
Shaw John
Shearwood Elijah
Shearwood Jobe
Sherwood Joseph, Junr.
Sherwood Joshua
Sherwood Justus
Shock James
Short Joseph
Sillicar Jacob
Simmons Danil
Slason Abraham
Slutt Silus
Smith
Smith Benajah
Smith Daniel
Smith Ebenzor
Smith Eleazor
Smith Isaac
Smith James
Smith Jeremiah
Smith John
Smith Joseph
Smith Joseph, Junr.
Smith Lemuel
Smith Ward
Smith Zebulon
Soliss John
Soper Gilbert
Soper Jesse
Soward Joseph
Spring Samuel
Squires Frank
Standley Garret
Standley Gidion
Stebbins Lewis
Stedwell John
Stevens John
Stevers Jeremiah
St. John Moses
Strang Gilbert
Strang Henry
Strang Jared
Strang John
Strang Joseph, Junr.
Strokam Isaac
Strong Joseph
Sutton Andrew
Sutton John Pell
Sutton Soloman
Sweesy Daniel
Tattel John
Taylor
Taylor Edmon
Taylor Gilbert
Taylor Henry
Taylor John
Taylor Thomas
Teed Charles
Teed William, Junr.
Teller Piere
Terrel Peter
Theall William
Thomson Elias
Thomson Jonathan
Thorn Daniel
Thorn Thomas
Tiel Hendrick
Tillison Niccols
Titus Beniaman
Titus Josiah
Tomkins Silvanus
Tomson Jonathan
Townsend James
Travis Absalom
Travis Daniel
Travis Ezekil
Travis Gabriel
Travis Jonathan
Travis Joseph
Travis Stephen
Traviss Gilbart
Truesdell Samuel
Tucker Jervis
Turner John
Turnor Joshua
Tuttle Abraham
Tyce John
Tylar Jonathan
Underwood William
Vermelya Jacob M.
Vernam Thomas
Viel John
Voght Godfrey
Voght Henry
Vogt Christian Joseph
Volentine Elvin
Vredenburgh Abraham
Vredenburgh Benjamin
Vredenburgh William
Van Scoyt Abram
Vanstine Ellvan
Van Tassel Abraham
Van Tassel Cornelius
Vantassel David
Vantassel Isaac
Vantassel John
Vanvoor Abrem
Van Wart Cobus
Van Wart John
Van Wart William
Van Worman Peter
Van Wormer Peter
Wagger Tobias
Wanger Thomas
Ward Moses
Warden Joseph
Waring David
Waterberry Samuel
Webster Joseph
Weed Jehial
Weeks Absalom
Weeks Gilbert
Weeks Malaki
Weeks Nathaniel
Welch William
West John
Westcott Reuben
Whiliam Joshayh
Whitman John
Whitney Abijah
Wickes Jesse
Wickes Jonathan
Wickes Stephen
Wicks Nathaniel
Wicks Nathaniel, Junr.
Wicks Phineas
Williams Gilbart
Williams Ichabud
Williams Isaac
Williams States
Willimson David
Willimson Jeddediah
Willmanson James
Willson James, Junr.
Wilmot Nathaniel
Wilson John
Wilson Valentine
Wood Caleb
Wood Elexander
Wood Eliphalet
Wood Nathan
Wood Philip
Wood S.
Wood William Scuder
Woolsey John
Wright Jacob
Wright Nivayah

Westchester County Militia — (Continued).

COLONEL THADDEUS CRANE
MAJOR NATHANIEL DELAVAN
ADJUTANT JOHN COOLEY
QUARTER MASTER JACOB GILBERT
SURGEON SAMUEL BARNUM

Capt. Daniel Bouton
" Benjamin Chapman
" Samuel Lawrence
" Samuel Lewis
" Ephraim Lockwood
" Jonathan Loder
" David Pardee
" Ebenezer Scofield
" Jesse Truesdell
Lieut. Ebenezer Avary
" Joseph Benedict
" Benajah Brown
Lieut. Cornelius Crane
" David Fansher
" Joseph Doolittle
" Isaac Keeler
" Daniel Purdy
" Nathaniel Reynolds
" Abraham Smith
" David Smith
Ensign Enoch Benedict
" Jehiel Bouton
" Samuel Lewis
" William Rogers

Additional Names on State Treasurer's Pay Books:

Adjt. Thomas Hunt
Lieut. Benjamin Benedict

ENLISTED MEN.

Aiers Reuben
Alleby Nathan
Allen Samuel
Alvord Belah
Ambler Abraham
Ambler Enos
Ambler John
Anderson James
Armstrong James
Avary Elisha
Avary James
Avary John
Avery Ebenezer
Avery Enoch
Avry Solomon
Ayers Reuben
Ayres Reuben, Junr.
Baily Gilbert
Bartlet George
Barton Joseph
Bates Elisha
Baxter David
Baxter John
Baxter Thomas
Bedient Falmen
Beers Fanton
Benedict Benjamin
Benedict Caleb
Benedict Isaac
Benedict Jacob
Benedict Jonah
Benedict Joseph
Benedict Joseph, Junr.
Benedict Lewis
Benedict Nathan
Benedict Timothy
Benjamin James
Betts Gideon
Betts Nathan
Bishop Andrew
Bishop Epeneus
Bishop Garret
Bishop James
Bishop John
Blackman Ephraim
Bloodgood Oliver
Bloom Stephen
Bloomer Abraham
Bloomer Stephen
Bolt Azariah
Bolt Daniel
Boucks Daniel
Boutan Jehial
Bouten Seth
Bouton Benajah
Bouton Ebenezer
Bouton Elijah
Bouton Ezra
Bouton Gould
Bouton Jesse
Bouton Joel
Bouton John
Bouton Joseph
Bouton Matthew
Bouton Moses
Bouton Nathaniel
Bouton Noah
Bouton Samuel
Bouton Seymour
Bouton Shubeal
Bouton Stephen
Bouton Timothy
Boutton Hiel
Boutton Jesse
Boutton John
Boutton Nathaniel
Boutton Seth
Bready Jesseay
Brigs
Brigs Philip
Brooks John
Brooks Michael
Brown Abraham
Brown Adonijah
Brown Adonijah, Junr.
Brown Amos
Brown Annanias
Brown Benajah
Brown Brockey
Brown Deliverance
Brown Ebenezer
Brown Eber
Brown Eliphalit
Brown Elisha
Brown Enos
Brown Jacob
Brown James
Brown John
Brown John, Junr.
Brown Jonas
Brown Jonathan
Brown Joseph
Brown Joseph, Junr.
Brown Josiah
Brown Nathan
Brown Peter
Brown Reuben
Brown Samuel
Brown Silas
Brown Solomon
Brown William
Brown Elijah

Bruce Robert
Brucks Daniel
Bruice Robert
Brun Edward
Brundage Nathan
Brundige Joseph, Junr.
Brundige Stephen
Brush Gilbert
Buckbee Russel
Burns Edmond
Burns Edward
Callender Samuel
Canada Philip
Canady Philip
Canfield Isaiah
Canfield James
Carpenter James
Carpenter Thomas
Chapman Daniel
Chapman Stephen
Chapmon John
Clark Daniel
Clark Jabez
Clark John
Clark Jonathan
Clarke Daniel
Clarke Ephraim
Close Jabez
Close Jesse
Coldwin James
Coley John
Coley Samuel B.
Collard James
Colvin James
Colyard James
Conklin Jacob
Conkling Jonathan
Connada Philip
Corley John
Crane James
Crane Peter
Crawford Daniel
Crawford Henderson
Crawford John
Crawford Stephen
Crawford William
Cross John
Cross Lemuel
Dalton William
Dan Abraham
Dan Hezekiah
Dan James
Dan James, Junr.
Dan Nathaniel
Dan Samuel
Dan Squier
Defrees Ebenzer
Delavan Daniel
Delevan Timothy
Delivan John
Delivan Nathan
Delivan Stephen
Dibble Jonathan
Dick (Colored)
Dickens Arnold
Dickens Arnold, Junr.
Dickens Moredcai
Dickins Samuel
Dickson Daniel
Dickson John
Dickson Marshel
Dickson Nathan
Dolton William
Dooletle Hopkins
Doolittle Daniel
Doolittle Reuben
Drake Gilbert
Dunkin Daniel
Durand Francis
Falconer John
Fansher Abram
Fansher Daniel
Fansher David
Fansher Elijah
Fansher Elisha
Fansher John
Fansher Joseph
Fansher Nathaniel
Fansher Squire
Fansher William
Feek Benjamin
Feris Peter
Feris Samuel
Ferris Benjamin
Ferris Goold
Ferris James
Ferris John
Ferris Samuel
Finch John
Finny Ward
Flood John
Foshea John
Foster John
Foster Jown W.
Fourey Ward
Frasher John
Frost William
Fuller Elisha
Fuller Jabiz
Fuller Joseph
Fuller Simeon
Garnsey William
Garrisen William
Gaufey William
German David
Gilbert Benajah
Gilbert Jacob
Gornsey William
Gould John
Graham Robert
Green Andrew
Green Benjamin
Green Jehiel
Grummon Ebenezer
Grummon Ephraim
Hait Abijah
Hait Benjamin
Hait Enoch
Hait Gideon
Hait Hezekiah
Hait John
Hait Jonathan
Hait Parson
Hait Silvanus, Junr.
Hallsted Micah
Halsted Michael
Hanford Abraham
Harford Pater
Harper Godfree
Hartford Ephraim
Hartford Peter
Hartford Thomas
Haut Jesse
Havery Reuben, Junr.
Hayes Freegift
Hayes Isaac
Hayes James
Hayes Jesse
Hayes Josiah
Hayes Nathaniel
Hayes Stephen
Hayes Thomas
Hays Abraham
Hays Caleb
Hays Henry
Hays John
Hayt Abel
Hayt Abijah
Hayt Abram
Hayt Caleb
Hayt Jachim
Hayt Nathan
Hayt Rice
Hayt Silas
Hayt Uriah
Hodge James
Hoit Jonathan
Hoit Nathaniel
Holmes John
Houson Eleazer
Hoyer Isaac
Hoyes Thomas
Hoyt Abijah
Hoyt Benjamin
Hoyt Enoch
Hoyt Hezekiah
Hoyt Jachim
Hoyt Jacob
Hoyt Jacob, Jr.
Hoyt Jeremiah
Hoyt Jesse
Hoyt John
Hoyt Person
Hoyt Silas
Hoyt Silvanus
Hubbell Peter
Hughes William
Hull Isaac
Hull Stephen
Hunt Gibourd
Hunt Gilbert
Husted James
Husted Thaddeus
Ingerson John
Ingersull John
Isaacs Samuel
Jane Israel
Janse Abraham
Jarman David
Johns Timothy
Johnson Stephen
Johnson Timothy
Jones Abraham
Jones Ebenezer
Jump Amos
Jump Gilbert
Jump Reuben
Jump William
June Israel
Kanady Joseph
Kanady Wilham
Keeler Aaron
Keeler David
Keeler Jeremiah
Keeler Nathaniel
Keeler Obadiah
Keeler Phinehas
Keeling Adam
Kenady Josep
Knapp Joshua
Knapp Moses
Kniffin Benjamin
Knox Abraham
Knox Joseph
Knox Robart
Krauston Joseph
Lawrance Samuel
Lawrance Samuel, Junr.
Laymor Jesse
Legget William
Lewis Samuel
Lobdell Jacob

Lobdell John
Lockwood Daniel
Lockwood David
Lockwood Ebenezer
Lockwood Hezekiah
Lockwood Jacob
Lockwood Job
Lockwood Joseph, Junr.
Lockwood Nathan
Lockwood Reuben
Lockwood Samuel
Loder John
Loder Pettit
Lounsbury Gideon
Lourd Joel
Lowrey Joel
Lowrey Thomas
Lucas William
Lyon Caleb, Jun
Lyon Noah
Lyons Caleb
Manrow Joseph, Junr.
Manrow Nathan
Marshall Henry
Marshall Joseph
Marshell Amon
Marshell Anthoney
Mead Aaron
Mead Abraham
Mead Andrew
Mead Calvin
Mead Daniel
Mead David
Mead Enoch
Mead Halsey
Mead Henry
Mead Jesse
Mead Jonah
Mead Levi
Mead Marshal
Mead Stephen
Mead Zelek
Meritt John
Merrit Luke
Mershal Amon
Morshal Henry
Miller Henry
Miller John A.
Miller John, Junr.
Miller Josiah
Miller Nathan
Miller Samuel
Moger James
Monrow Seely
Moorhouse Samuel
Mopen James
Morehouse Benjamin
Moses John
Mosher James
Mosher Lemuel
Munro Joseph
Murphy Robert
Natelbery James
Nelson John
Newman Caleb
Newman Isack
Newman James
Newman Jonathan
Newman Peter
Newman Samuel
Nickels Abel
Nickols Gershom
Nickols Jesse
Nickols Thomas
Nickols Thomas, Junr.
Northrop Abijah
Northrup David
Northrup Eli
Northrup Isaac
Northrup Joel
Northrup John
Northrup Stephen
Olmsted Hezekiah
Olmsted James
Olmsted Nathan
Osburn John
Palmer Elisha
Palmer Gideon
Palmer Jesse
Palmer Obadiah
Pardee John
Pardee Nathan
Pardy Samuel
Peatt Jeams
Peatt Lewis
Peck Abijah
Peck Benjamin
Pederick Abijah
Pelham John
Pellam Joseph
Pellum Elisha
Phillips Joseph
Potts David
Potts Thomas
Pratt James
Purdy Abraham
Purdy Daniel
Purdy David
Purdy Deliverance
Purdy Deliverance, Junr.
Purdy John
Purdy Jonathan
Purdy Joseph
Purdy Stephen
Quick John
Radon Partrick
Radtoick John
Randol John
Randolph Benjamin
Ranolds Benjamin
Ranrod Solomon
Raymond James
Raymond Land
Raymond Sands
Raynolds Gilbert
Reseco John
Resquie John
Roynolds Benjamin
Reynolds Gilbert
Reynolds Joshua
Reynolds William
Riggs Daniel
Riggs Josiah
Rockwell Job
Rockwell Nathan
Rockwell Nathan H.
Roff Samuel
Rogers Amos
Rondles Abraham
Rosecrans Dirk
Rovtlit George
Row Seely M.
Ruff Samuel
Rundel Ezra, Junr.
Rundell John
Rusco John
Rusco Noah
Rusco Samuel
Rusco Theophilus
Rusco Thomas
Russ Stephen
Russel John
Ryan Timothy
Ryion Bont
Sarlls Thaddeus
Scofield Amos
Scofield David
Scofield Deliverance
Scofield Elisha
Scofield Elnathan
Scofield Gideon
Scofield Henry
Scofield Jonas
Scofield Joseph
Scofield Josiah
Scofield Michel
Scofield Peter
Scofield Smith
Scofield William
Scribner Zephaniah
Seeley Nathaniel, Junr.
Seely Gideon, Junr.
Seely Nathaniel
Seely Silas
Selleck Darling
Selleck Nathan
Seward Daniel
Seward Stephen
Seymour Jesse
Shay Timothy
Shearman Abial
Shecrman Peter
Sherman Peter
Sherwood Oliver
Sido Henry
Silleek Frederick
Silleck Gershom
Sillick Darbey
Sillick Nathan
Silsbe Israel
Slasen Nathan
Slason Abraham
Slason Amos
Slason Deliverance
Slason Ebenezer
Slason Ebenezer, Junr.
Slason Eleazer
Slason Israel
Slason Jesse
Slason John
Slason Jonathan
Slason Nathan
Slason Samuel
Slason Stephen
Slauson Eleazer
Slauson Eleazer, Junr.
Slauson Israel
Slauson Jesse
Slawson John
Slawson Lamb
Slawson Nathan
Slawson Samuel
Sloson Ebenezer, Junr.
Sloson Jesse
Smith Abraham
Smith Abraham, Junr.
Smith Caleb
Smith Caleb, Junr.
Smith Doctor
Smith Isaac
Smith Isaac, Junr.
Smith Jacob
Smith John
Smith Joshua
Smith Lemuel
Smith Matthew
Smith Nathan
Smith Nathan, Junr.
Smith Nathaniel
Smith Peleg
Smith Reuben
Smith Solomon

Smith Thomas
Stebbins Nehemiah
Stebbins Samuel
Steenrod Ebenezer
Steenrod Solomon
Stevens John
Stevens Moses
Stevens Oliver
Stevens Reuben
Stevens Reuben, Junr.
Stevens Silvanus
Steward Stephen
Stewart Charles
St. John John
Stockham Samuel
Strobridg James
Suard Daniel
Suard John
Sutherland Stephen
Terry Samuel
Titus Benjamin
Titus John
Titus Joseph
Titus Timothy
Todd Abraham, Junr.
Todd Oliver
Tounsend James
Travis Jacob
Trowbridge James
Trusdail Joseph
Trusdell Jesse, Junr.
Trusdell Jonathan
Trusdell Joseph
Trusdell Richard
Tyler Jabes
Tyler James
Quick Andrew
Quick John
Vamoe Daniel
Vandel Abraham
Varnal Daniel
Varnel John
Vanscoy Abraham
Vanscoy Abraham, Junr.
Vanscoy Cornelius
Vanscoy Jonathan
Vanscoy Samuel
Vanscoy Timothy
Wallace Abijah
Wallace Jacob
Wallace James, Junr.
Wallow James
Wandle Abraham
Warring James
Warring Peter
Waterberry Daniel
Waterberry John
Waterberry Samuel
Watt James
Wauser Thomas
Wearing James
Webb John
Weed Alexander
Weed Eli
Weed Gilbert
Weed Jonathan
Weed Nathan
Weeks Nathaniel
Weeks Phinehas
Wheeler Josiah
Whitnee Benjamin
Whitney James
Wickes Nathaniel, Junr.
Wickes Phineas
Wicks Nathaniel
Williams Ichabod
Williams Samuel
Williams Stephen
Wilson Valentine
Wood Benjamin
Wood Hezekiah
Wood Israel
Wood Jacob
Wood Jacob, Junr.
Wood Jared
Wood Jonah
Wood Jonathan
Wood Joseph
Wood Nathaniel

Westchester County Militia — (Continued).

ASSOCIATED EXEMPTS.

LIEUTENANT COLONEL JOSEPH BENEDICT
MAJOR EBENEZER SLASSON
ADJUTANT ENOCH MEAD
QUARTER MASTER JOEL BOUTON
SURGEON BENJAMIN MILLER

CAPT. GOULD BOUGHTON
" JOSEPH OSBURN
" GIDEON SEELY
LIEUT. SAMUEL BOUTON
" SOLOMON CLOSE
LIEUT. MOSES HADDEN
" BENJAMIN JONES
" ZEPHANIAH MILLS
" TITUS REYNOLDS

ENLISTED MEN.

Ambler John
Bedient Nathan
Benedict Joseph
Benedict Peter
Benedict Peter, Junr.
Bishop Epeneos
Bouton Gould
Bouton John
Bouton Noah
Bundell John
Brown Andrew
Brown Deliverance
Brown Eber
Carman Henry
Carman Peter
Chapman Daniel
Clark Cornelius
Crawford Robert
Cross John
Crumpton John
Dan David
Dean Gilbirt
Dean Isaac
Dibbell Daniel
Dibble Jonathan
Dickens Thomas
Dickson John
Duetcher William
Eliot John
Fansher William
Ferris Jonathan
Flood John
Fuller Micajah
Green Benjamin
Hait Jacob
Hait John
Hanford Abraham
Hartford Thomas
Hatfield Abraham
Hawley Ezekiel
Hayes Isaac
Hayt Gideon
Hedding Moses
Hobby Caleb
Holmes Isaac
Holmes John
Hunt Jacob
Hyatt Ezekiel
Ingersoll Josiah
Jacobs Israel
Jones Asa
Jump Amos
Lamb Abraham
Lee Elijah
Leek Phillip
Lent Abraham
Lockwood Joseph
Loder John
Luks P.
Lyon Benjamin
Lyon Samuel
Mead Andrew
Meershell Anthoney
Mekell John
Miller John C.
Miller Josiah
Miller Nathan
Milles James
Mills Josiah
McKeel John
Newman Isaac
Newman James
Newman Nathaniel
Oakley Isaac
Olmsted Nathan
Pinkney Thomas
Pordy Obediah
Potter Peter
Potter Robert
Raymond James, Junr.
Raymond Sands
Reynolds Gilbert
Runolds Nathaniel
Scofield Amos
Selleck Gershom
Sene Abraham
Seymoure Thaddeus
Slason Abraham
Slason Henry
Smith Benjamin
Smith Nathaniel
Stebbins Nehemiah
Stillwell Thomas R.
Taylor Gilbert
Todd Abraham
Titus Benjamin
Titus John
Titus Joseph
Truler Mathaw
Tyler Jonathan
Wandel Abraham
Waterbery David
Weed Gilbert
Weed Jehiel
Wheeler Josiah
Whitmore Pelatiah
Whitne Pelatiah
Whitney Seth
Witney Seth
Wood Benjamin
Wright Benjamin

Westchester County Militia — (Continued).

SEPARATE EXEMPTS.

CAPTAIN JONATHAN HORTON

ENLISTED MEN.

Acker Jacob
Bailey John
Bell William
Bice Abraham
Bice Abraham, Junr.
Bice Jacob
Bice James
Bice Peter
Bice William
Bice Yawnas
Brundage James
Chanpenois Andrew
Cunningham John
Dalton William
Fisher Elijah
Fisher Samuel
Horton Caleb
Owens Jeremiah
Palden John
Purdy Jacob
Purdy Jonathan
See James
Smith James
Syphor John
White Stephen

COLONEL JOHN LASHER'S REGIMENT.

COLONEL JOHN LASHER
LIEUTENANT COLONEL ANDREW STOCKHOLM
MAJOR WILLIAM SMITH LIVINGSTON
ADJUTANT JERONEMUS HOOGLAND
QUARTER MASTER MATTHEW DAVIS

CAPT. JAMES ABEEL
" THEOPHILUS BEEKMAN
" CHARLES DICKENSON
" DAVID DICKSON
" WILLIAM W. GILBERT
" SAMUEL JOHNSON
" WILLIAM LEONARD
" JACQUES RAPALJE
" ABRAHAM VAN DYCK
" VINER VAN ZANDT
" THOMAS WILLCOCKS
" JACOB WRIGHT
LIEUT. JOHN ANTHONY
" JOHN BANCKER
" THOMAS BEEKMAN
LIEUT. HENRY BREEVORT
" EDWARD DUNSCOMB
" JOSEPH FORTIN
" JOHN HARBECK
" JESSEY HICKS
" THOMAS LAWRENCE
" OLIVER MELDEBERGER
" ABRAHAM MESIER
" BENJAMIN NORTH
" ETHAN SICKELS
" FREDERICK STEYMETS
" RALPH T. THURMAN
" ROBERT TROUP
" THOMAS WARNER
" GEORGE YEAMANS

ENLISTED MEN.

Acley John
Apple Anthoney
Beaty John
Burras Benjamin
Burras John
Cambel James
Carmer James
Choen Daniel
Contelyo George
Crolious John
Donelson Frederick
Donelson Jesse
Donelson Joseph
Donelson Soverin
Duglas James
Elsworth John, Junr.
Elsworth John T.
Frilock Joseph
Heyer William
Howser Jacob
Hyer Walter
Johnson William
Kersted James
Longley Thomas
Mandevill David
Markland John
Myers Peter
Peckwill William
Reed John
Rome William
Salmond John
Shaddle David
Snider Simon
Strachan William
Ten Brook William
Ten Eyck Andrew
Van Dalsin Henry
Van Dewater Gerret
Van Hook Isaac
Young Peter

COLONEL JOHN NICHOLSON'S REGIMENT.

COLONEL JOHN NICHOLSON
LIEUTENANT COLONEL JOHN VISCHER
ADJUTANT JOHN BROGDON
CHAPLAIN ISRAEL EVANS
SURGEON JOSEPH MARVIN

CAPT. ELISHA BENEDICT
" EZEKIEL COOPER
" JOHN COPP
" BENJAMIN EVANS
" JOHN GRAHAM
" DIRCK HANSEN
" ROBERT JOHNSTON
" GERSHOM MOTT
LIEUT. WILLIAM BELKNAP
" JOHN BLACKNEY
" FRANCIS BRENDLY
LIEUT. ISAAC GUION
" NATHANIEL HENRY
" ISAAC HUBBLE
" TIMOTHY HUGHES
" JOHN G. LANSING
" DIGBY ODLUM
" WILLIAM MARTIN
" THOMAS MCCLALTEN
" ISAAC NICHOLS
" THOMAS NICHOLSON

ENLISTED MEN.

Hartan Peter
Holmes Asa
Lasan Thomas
Lennington Thomas
Prebble Samuel
Shaw Francis
Weisenfels Charles F.

COLONEL CORNELIUS D. WYNKOOP'S REGIMENT.

COLONEL CORNELIUS D. WYNKOOP

QUARTER MASTER THOMAS WILLIAMS

CAPT. ROBERT McKEAN
" HENRY O'MARA
" JACOB SEEBER
" GERRET S. VEEDER
" HERMAN VOSBURGH
" CORNELIUS VAN SANTVOORT
" SAMUEL VAN VIGHTEN
" JOHN H. WENDELL
LIEUT. JOHN BALL
" DAVID BATES
" ABRAHAM BECKER
" ISAAC BOGART
" ABNER FRENCH
" JOHN HOGHKERK
" JACOB HOUSE
" SOLOMON PENDLETON
LIEUT. JOHN SEEBER
" ABDIAL SHERWOOD
" LEVY STOCKWELL
" JOHN TEN BROECK
" OBADIAH VAUGHAN
" ALBERT VANDERWERKEN
" BARENT S. VAN SALSBURY
" JOHN WELCH
ENSIGN DAVID BECKER
" JOHN DUNN
" DANIEL EVERITT
" ABRAHAM HARDENBERGH
" JOHN OSTRANDER
" WILLIAM SCUDDER
" EPHRAIM SNOW
" SAMUEL WILSON

ENLISTED MEN.

Admay Henry
Anderson David
Anderson Lewis
Anderson Robert
Arkson William
Atkins Samuel
Baker John
Baker William
Barnes Timothy
Bartholemew John
Biggam William
Blair John
Bogardes David
Boom John
Boom Matthias
Bowen Wasel
Brown John
Cadogan John
Calaghan John
Caller John
Campbell Robert
Cane Peter Warren
Casey Robert
Chaddock Thomas
Chalenor Christopher
Cheeck George
Clark Francis
Colley David
Cook John
Cook John, Jr.
Copernoll John
Coplin Samuel
Davis John
De Gollier James
DeGollier James, Jr.
Donaldson James
Donaldson Rt. John
Dunlap John
Ehle William
Ferguson James
Ferguson William
Frazier Duncan
French Peter
Hamilton William
Handley David
Harper Joseph
Harrison Hermanus
Harrison Phillip
Hodges David
Horne Mathias
Hughes Thomas
Hungerford Daniel
Huyler James
Jeffries John
Johnson John
Lacey Hugh
Lansingh Garret
Liddel John
Lighthall John
Linnager John
Lock Nicholas
Maya— Joseph
Midelle John
Miller Jacobus
Mills Alexander
Molby Thomas
McClean John
McCo— Mathias
McCormick John
McGrady Robert
McIntire Barnabus
McKown Robert
McMachan Michael
McMurdays John
Nelson Jonathan
Obrian John
Obrian John, Jr.
Obrian Thomas
Ogston John
Osterman Christian
Otter Isaac
Owens Owen
Philipse John
Pickerd Nicholas
Plugh Dennis
Powel Joseph
Rose John
Runnels Jonathan
Rynax William
Scerberaw William
Schermerhorn Jacob
Shankland Andrew
Shannon George
Shannon Thomas
Skinner Apollos
Skinner Gershom
Smallwood Isaac
Spear Henry F.
Stanley John
Statia William
Steward James
Stiles Moses
Stuart James
Sutherland Hector
Sutton James
Switz Walter
Teed Samuel
Thompson William
Thornton John
Tobin Edward
Truax John
Tuttle Solomon

Veder Aaron
Vrooman Peter
Vanden Bogart Minard
Van Der Bogardes Nicholas
Vanderwerker Thomas
Vannatten Benjamin
Van Sice John
Vansice Joseph
Van Texel Jacob
Van Vorst Jelles
Welch John
Wemple Barent
Wheeler Henry
White David
Wilday Nathaniel
Wilken John David
Wilkie Augustus
Willson William
Wilson Israel
Wood John
Wright Benjamin
Young Frederick

MAJOR JOHN WHEELOCK'S INDEPENDENT COMPANY.

MAJOR JOHN WHEELOCK

CAPT. SAMUEL ASHLEY
" ABEL CURTIS
" SAMUEL PAYNE

LIEUT. JOHN YOUNG
ENSIGN DANIEL WALDO

ENLISTED MEN.

Allen Samuel Griks
Arsworth Amariah
Baron Samuel
Baxter Simon
Bliss Ebenezer
Broughton William
Brown Thomas
Burman Benjamin
Capron Nathan
Caswin Nathaniel
Chamberlin Richard
Chase Benjamin
Closson Nehemiah
Damo Ebenezer
Dark Thomas
Darn Eben
Dart Roger
Dike Samuel
Doolittle Lusius
Gilman Jeremiah
Goodell Titus
Hammond Elijah
Harmon Elijah
Hatch Josiah
Higbee Charles
Hodgkins Joseph
Huntington Asa
Maning Stephen
Matthews Ebenezer
Moredock —sahel
Norback Philip
Ordway John
Osborn Isaac
Osgood Thomas
Petterson Andrew
Plummer David
Ray John
Royse Silas
Rudd Gideon
Skeen John
Stockbridge John
Tibbets Henry
Tilden Charles
Tilden Joel
Tola Josiah
Tooly Josiah
Trescott Jeremiah
Trichy John
Vorback Philip
Willcox John
York William

FONDEY'S PARTY.

ENSIGN JOHN FONDEY, JR.

ENLISTED MEN.

Beeker Peter
Bogart Barnit
Boyd Jonathan
Cluct Frederick
Griffin Alexander
Hilton John
Kip Benjamin
Mulberry Peter
Muller Stephen
Mynderson Frederick
McCloud Alexander
Vosburgh Peter
Vroman Adam
Williamson John
Wilson Andrew
Wood James
Wormer Corn's
Young Christr

BRADT'S RANGERS.

CAPTAIN JOHN A. BRADT

ENLISTED MEN.

Allen John
Barret Walter
Bate Joseph
Bovie John
Bovie Nicholas
Bradt Andrew
Brown Thomas B. L.
Christiaense Ahasuerus
Curtwright Hendrick A.
Early Edward
Gardiner James
Hitsman John
Kain Richard
Kelley Barney
Lansing John S.
Lyne Mathew
Monroe Alexander
Morgan James
McGinnis John
Patterson Adam
Quackenboosh Gerardus
Quackenboosh John G.
Quackenboosh John J.
Shades Adam
Shelley Samuel
Sluyter Nicholas
Smith Conrad
Sparger Edward
Spitzer Gerrit
Ten Eyck John
Thomas James
Thompson Thomas
Vedder John, Junr.
Van Benthuysen Martha
Willson John

REILAY'S RANGERS.

CAPTAIN JOHN REILAY.

ENLISTED MEN.

Benson John
Berringer John
Boomhower George
Herwick Philip
Heyner Philip, Jr.
Huntsicker George
Kelley John
Milton John
Parks Andrew
Van Alstyn Cornelius
Welch Philip

LIST OF PENSIONERS AND APPLICATIONS FOR PENSIONS.

Abeel Garret
Acker Jacob
Adams James
Adams Matthew
Allison Richard
Armstrong Edward
Baldwin Daniel
Banks Obadiah
Barber Silas
Bardt Nicholas
Barnum Joshua (Capt.)
Bartlett John
Baxter John
Bell George H.
Bennet John
Bishop Joshua
Blauveld Abraham
Bovie Nicholas
Bowen Timothy
Boyce Thomas (Ensign)
Boyd Ebenezer (Capt.)
Bradenburg Balthus
Bradt James
Breadbick John (Capt.)
Breidenbacker Balthus
Brewster Henry, Junr. (Lieut.)
Brooks John
Brooks Michael
Brown David (Lieut.)
Brown Nicholas
Buchannan John (Capt.)
Burgess James
Burgess John
Butler John
Buyse Jacob
Cady David
Cadey David, Junr.
Callaghan Edward
Callahan Edward
Canfield Philo
Cannon Matthew
Carpenter Thomas (Lieut.)
Carrigain Gilbert
Case John
Certain James (see Sartin)
Chace John
Charpanard Simon
Commoding Nicholas
Conely James
Cook John
Cooper John
Coppernoll Adam
Corwin Gershom
Courtney Francis
Covenhoven Peter
Crane Thaddeus (Major)
Crawford Thomas
Cruduck William
Crumb John
Cutler Joseph (Ensign)
Dalton Thomas
Davis William
Decamp Matthew
Delong Francis (Lieut.)
Demond Marx (Capt.)
Dickson Marchil
Doit Joseph
Dole James
Dole William
Done Thomas
Donely James
Dougharty John
Dougherty William
Douglass William
Drew William
Duncan Thomas
Dunham Cornelius
Dunkill George
Dunlap Andrew
Dunlap James
Elbertson William
Elwood Isaac
Fansher Squire
Fansher William
Faulkner William (Capt.)
Feagan William
Feeks Robert
Ferris John
Ferris Silvanus
Finch Jonathan
Finchley George
Fisher Frederick (Col.)
Foltz Hanjost
Forbes Alexander
Foster John
Foster William
Fox Christopher (Capt.)
Frank Andrew
Frazier Duncan
Fry John (Brigadier Major)
Gallut James
Gardineer Jacob (Capt.)
Gardenear Samuel
Garrison Richard (Qr. Master)
Geer Bennajah
Gibbs Samuel (Lieut.)
Green Josiah
Green Zachariah
Gregg James (Capt.)
Griffiths Barney
Groteclass Gilbert
Hale Mordica (Surgeon's Mate)
Hall Talmage (Lieut.)
Hamman Stats
Hanford Ozias
Hansel George
Harper Joseph (Lieut. Col.)
Harper William
Harris Joseph
Harris Robert (Lieut.)
Hartman Adam
Havart John
Helmer George (Lieut.)
Helmer John
Henderson William
Hepworth Daniel
Hess Johannes
Higgins Jonathan
Hill Asa
Hilton John
Hines Thomas
Hink John
Hogan Patrick
Holmes John
Hopper Henry
Horsford Jesse
Hunt Eden (Qr. Master)
Hurlbutt Stephen
Ivery James
Jacobs William
James William
Jansen Matthew, Junr. (Capt.)
Jones Samuel
Jordan John
Jordan Nicholas
Jump William
Kearny Thomas
Keeler Isaac (Lieu .)
Kenny Thomas
Ketcham John
King Reuben
King Walter
Knap Abal
Knapp Joseph
Knox George
Koch Johannis
Kolb John
Kough John
Lampman Peter
Lang Robert (Qr.-Master)
Lee John
Lines Michael
Locharty John
Lockwood Moses
Louks William
Lucas William Budd
Lues William
Lyon Thomas (Lt.)
Marshall Mead
Martin Philip
Martine William
Mathers James
Mead Libbeus
Merselles John J.
Mills Alexander
Milspaugh John
Moak Gerardus
Mooney Barnet
Mosher John
Mowris Daniel
Muller Jeremiah C. (Capt.)
Murden John
Murphy Henry
Myers Michael
McCay Alexander
McCracken Joseph (Major)
McDonald Daniel
McDonald Donald
McFall Paul
McGraw James
McKeen Samuel
McKiney Charles

McKinstry John (Capt.)
McMaster Hugh
McNish Alexander
Neely Abraham (Capt.)
Nestle George
Paine Joseph
Parrish Silas
Peek Garret
Peterson Simon
Petrie John
Pickard Adolph
Pickard John (Qr.-Master)
Plumb Stephen
Powell Thomas
Preston Jonathan
Printup Joseph
Purdy Jonathan
Purdy Solomon, Junr.
Quick John
Ransom Joseph
Rasbach Frederick
Rattenaur Jacob
Realey James
Reeve Israel
Reeve James, Junr.
Rehern Joseph
Requa John
Reynolds Benjamin
Reynolds Jonathan
Rice John
Richards Philip
Richardson Robert
Richter Nicolaus
Rightmire Henry
Rima Johannes
Robertson John
Sanders Robert
Sargent William
Scott James
Seber Henry
Seely Silvanus
Sely Thadeus
Sharer James
Shearman Abiel
Smith Benjamin
Smith James
Smith Josiah (Lt.)
Snell Hanyost
Sparks Pearl
Staats Philip (Lt.)
Stensell George
Stevens Daniel
Stewart John
Stillwell James
Strobeck Adam
Sulbach Gerrit
Summers Farrel
Swartwout Cornelius
Sweet Godfrey
Swift John
Talbot Silas (Col.)
Taylor Asa
Taylor John
Telford Alexander
Thomas John
Timmerman Henry (Ensign)
Townsend Daniel
Travis Ezekiel
Travis Jacob (Lt.)
Tyler Asa
Tyler Ebenezer
Vandal Adam
Vincent Joseph
Voit Joseph
Van Nort Jacobus
Van North Joseph
Van Rensselaer Henry K.
Vanwart William
Wagner George
Wallrath Nicolus
Walrath Hendrick
Wandle Daniel
Ward Joseph
Ward Thomas
Warren Gideon (Capt.)
Waysal Nicholas
Welch Edward
Wells James
Welter George
Whelan Edward
White Joseph
White William
Williams Ezekiel
Williams Ichabod
Willson Thomas
Wilson David
Winn John
Wire James
Wolever Abraham
Wood Lemuel
Woodworth Rozuil
Wright Isaiah
Wright Jacob
Yordan Nicholas
Young Godfrie
Younglove Davis
Zimerman Henerich

NAMES OF SUNDRY PERSONS

WHOSE

Service is evidenced by Manuscripts on file in the Comptroller's Office, though not found on the Papers of any of the Regular Organizations.

Abarr Peter
Anderson Thomas
Arnold (Benedict) Gen.
Babbett John
Babcock William
Baldwin Alexander (Capt.)
Baldwin Daniel
Ball Isaac
Barber ——— Col.
Barkem William
Bartow Gilbert
Billeger Michael
Bears John
Beebe Ezre
Benniger Isaac
Bequan Isaac, Adjt.
Bingham Silas
Blass Peter
Boils James
Bothwick Edward
Boughrougs James
Boughton Nathan
Boulton George
Bradley Stephen B., Col.
Brown ——— Col.
Bull Charles
Bull William, Capt. Lt.
Burgoyne ——— Gen.
Cadey Palmer, Lt.
Cady Eliezar
Carpenter Caman
Cary Reuben
Chamberlin Gorden
Chaney Isaac
Chapen Zadoc
Claughry John, Ensign
Coen Mark, Junr.
Coleman Michael
Colver Jonathan
Cooke Simeon
Covell Philip
Covetins Moses
Crane John, Adjt.
Crane John, Col. of artillery,
Cudner John, Lt.
Daily Charles
Danes Abraham
Davenport Jonathan
Decker Gerard
Demarest John
Dickingson Charles
Doty Simeon
Drake James
Dubois Zachariah, Major
Ellison ——— Col.
Ennely Petrus
Evets Milds
Fenno Ephraim, Capt. Lt.
Ferdon Abraham
Fey George
Fish Nicholas, Brigade Major
Flamming Francis
Follard John
Forster John
Frey John, Major of brigade,
Gaile Asa
Gansevoort Peter, Brigadier General
Gardiner Joseph
Garey John
Gates ——— Major Gen.
Gilchrist Adam, Asst. C. G.
Gildersleeve F——, Lt.
Gillikins James
Gilliland James
Glean Oliver, A. Q. M. G.
Gonsales Samuel
Goold Jesse
Graves Jedidiah
Green Levi
Greene Clark
Griffith Nathan
Grossvenor ——— Col. D. A. General,
Haick Nicholas
Halstead Benjamin, Lt.
Hammon James
Hatch Samuel
Hazen Moses, Col.
Heath W., Major General
Herkimer Nicholas, Brigadier General
Hill Lemuel
Hoffmans Aaron
Holdridg Abraham
Hopkins ——— Col.
Hornbeck Cornelius
Hortun Thomas, Capt.
Howley Seth
Huble Ithamar
Huges H., Col. D. L. Gen.
Humphrey Cornelius, Col.
Hunter John, Lt.
Hurt Arthur
Hyle James
Jackson Jesse
Jack Thomas
Jaikson Lyman
Jen David
Johnson ——— Col.
Johnston William, Capt. Lt.
Jones Reuben
Kush James
Lang Robert
Lansing Jacob John, Judge Advocate
Legget Abraham, Ensig
Letts Abram
Livingston William S., Lt. Col.
Lush Stephen, Major
Lyben John
Mangus Mowris
Mapes Israel
Marsh Ephraim, Junr.
Mattoon John
Maxwell Anthony, Lt.
Maynard Israel
Menbeth James
Meyer Moses
Moor Henry
Morrill William
Morris ——— Gen.
Morris Lewis, Brigade Major
Morse Ebenezer F.
Morse Stephen
Mott Ebenezer, Lt.
McClaughry John, Ensign
McDougal Alexander (Major Gen.)
Nash Stephen
Nicholas ——— Col.
Nichols Guisham
Nicoll Isaac, Col.
Noys Nathan
Osterhout Cornelius
Oustrander Henry
Owen Charles
Palfrey William, Pay Master General
Pecavin ——— Col.
Peek Moses
Peet Stephen
Pennear William
Pepoon Silas
Pettie Abel
Phelps Jacob
Phelton Lewis
Pierce John, Pay Master General
Pixley David
Pixley Peter
Poyton James
Prindle Samuel
Pulfer Wendall, Junr.
Putnam (Israel) Gen.
Quin Thomas
Racket Samuel
Rankins James, Junr.
Raymond Seth
Reeves Elisha
Requaw Isaac, Adjt.
Revere John
Reynolds Nathan, Lt.
Reynolds Nathaniel, Junr.

Rice Moses
Roads Isaac
Robarts Ezekiel
Rose —— Major *
Rude William
Rutger Henry, Deputy Muster Master General
Ruse Abraham
Schutt Andries
Schutt Hendrick, Junr.
Schutt Isaac
Schutt Abraham H.
Schutt William
Schuyler Nicholas, Surgeon
Scott —— Gen.
Sexton Ebenezer
Sleauly Benjamin
Slowter Nicholas
Smith William, Lt. Col.
Spencer Oliver, Col.
Stagg John, Lt.
Stillwell John
Street Samuel
Swartwout Cornelius, Capt. Lt.
Swartwout Henry, Ensign
Swartwout Jacobus, Gen.
Swathout Moses
Tallar John William
Taulman P——, Lt.
Taylor Ephraim
Ten Broeck Abraham, Brigadier General
Terbus Isaac
Terwilleger Peter Vas
Thompson Daniel
Thompson —— Ensign
Traverse Gabriel
Turpenny Bowdewin
Tuthill Jeremiah
Variel Joseph
Vosburgh Richard
Vanamburg Joseph
Vanburen Matthew
Van Buren Matthew, Lt.
Van Cleeft William
Vandemark Frederick
Vanderpool Malget
Van Gasbeck Peter, Major
Van Rensselaer Robert, Brig. Gen.
Vansalisbury John
Vansalisbury Joseph
Van Scort —— Col.
Van Vleet Abraham
Van Vleet Daniel
Warner Zebulon
Washburn Robert
Washington George, Gen. Commander-in-chief
Way Bernaman
Webb Samuel B., Gen.
Welding Francis
Wells Michael
Westbrock Yong
Wilbur Joseph
Williams Asa
Williams Daniel (guide)
Winchell Timothy
Wittbeck Peter, Junr.
Wittmarsh Ezra
Wood Uriah
Woodbeck Abraham
Woodbeck Henry
Woodbridge Sahe.
Woolcut Claudius
Woolcut Peter
Worner Abram
Wright Elisha
Write Daniel
Youngs Abymael

* Commanding the Royalist troops in the expedition of October, 1781.

INDEX TO ILLUSTRATIONS.

General Washington's Certificate to the Character of a Scout........................ Frontspiece

OPP. PAGE

Treasurer's Certificate viii
Touching the Ownership of a Slave.......... ix
Table of Militia Pay.......... xii
Map of the Schoharie and Mohawk Valleys, Showing the Route traversed by Colonel Sir John Johnson in his Raid of October, 1780.......... xviii
Account Current with Major General Alexander McDougal and Suite.......... xx
A Parole.......... 1
Appointment of Chaplain Gros.......... 12
Account Current with Major Nicholas Fish.......... 12
Signatures of Officers of the 2d Line.......... 13
A Discharge from General Washington.......... 14
Reverse side of Discharge from General Washington.......... 15
Testimonial from Officers of the 3d Line to Colonel Peter Gansevoort upon Promotion to Brig. General.......... 24, 25
A Letter from General Benedict Arnold.......... 32, 33
Signatures of Officers of the 5th Line.......... 40
Return of Officers of the 5th Line.......... 41
Fort Hunter.......... 62
A Letter from Colonel Peter Gansevoort.......... 80
Specimen of Class or Beat Roll.......... 81
Upper Fort in Schoharie Valley.......... 88
Middle Fort in Schoharie Valley.......... 88
Lower Fort in Schoharie Valley.......... 89
Fort Kayser.......... 89
Exemptions for Shoemaking.......... 132
Extract from a "Reckoning" of the "Committee of Safety".......... 133
Portion of Stone Arabia Battlefield.......... 176
Bowlder Monument.......... 176
Klock's Field.......... 177
Christie's Rift.......... 177
A Letter from "The Hero of Oriskany," General Nicolas Herckheimer.......... 183
Continuous view of Johnson's Route of March, on South Side of Mohawk River, from Schoharie Creek to about one mile above Van Epp's Swamp (Fultonville).......... 190
View of Johnson's Route of March from Van Epp's Swamp to Willow Basin, on South side of Mohawk River.......... 191
View of Johnson's Route of March from Anthony's Nose to Keator's Rift, on South side of Mohawk River.......... 191

INDEX BY ORGANIZATIONS AND COUNTIES.

LINE.

PAGE.
1ST REGIMENT.—Colonel Goose Van Schaick, Lieutenant Colonel Cornelius Van Dyck................ 1
2ND REGIMENT.—Colonel Goose Van Schaick, Colonel Philip Cortland, Lieutenant Colonel Peter Regnier, Lieutenant Colonel Robert Cochran, Lieutenant Colonel Frederick Weissenfels.............. 13
3RD REGIMENT.—Colonel James Clinton, Colonel Peter Gansevoort, Lieutenant Colonel James Bruyn.. 24
4TH REGIMENT.—Colonel James Holmes, Colonel Henry B. Livingston, Lieutenant Colonel Pierre Regnier, Lieutenant Colonel Frederick Weissenfels.................................... 32
5TH REGIMENT.—Colonel Lewis Duboys, Lieutenant Colonel James S. Bruyn, Lieutenant Colonel Marinus Willett.................................... 40
ADDITIONAL BATTALION.—Colonel James Livingston, Lieutenant Colonel Richard Livingston........ 45
ARTILLERY REGIMENT.—Colonel John Lamb.................................... 46
PROVINCIAL TRAIN OF ARTILLERY.—Captain Alexander Hamilton.................................... 47
GREEN MOUNTAIN BOYS.—Colonel Ethan Allen, Colonel Seth Warner.................................... 48
PRIVATEERS.—Armed vessels.................................... 50

LEVIES.

Colonel John Harper.................................... 51
Colonel Frederick Weissenfels.................................... 54
Colonel William Malcom.................................... 58
Colonel Lewis Dubois, Lieutenant Colonel Brinton Paine.................................... 62
Colonel Morris Graham, Lieutenant Colonel Benjamin Birdsall, Lieutenant Colonel Henry Livingston, 64
Colonel Albert Pawling.................................... 67
Colonel Marinus Willett, Lieutenant Colonel John McKinstry.................................... 78

MILITIA.

ALBANY COUNTY.

1ST REGIMENT.—Colonel Abraham Cuyler, Colonel Jacob Lansing, Jr.................................... 80
2ND REGIMENT.—Colonel Abraham Wemple.................................... 81
3RD REGIMENT.—Colonel Philip P. Schuyler, Lieutenant Colonel Barent I. Staats.................................... 86
4TH REGIMENT.—Colonel Kilian Van Rensselaer, Lieutenant Colonel John H. Beeckman.............. 89
5TH REGIMENT.—Colonel Gerrit G. Van den Bergh, Colonel Henry Quackenbos, Lieutenant Colonel Volkert Veeder.................................... 93
6TH REGIMENT.—Colonel Stephen John Schuyler, Lieutenant Colonel Henry K. Van Rensselaer...... 94
7TH REGIMENT.—Colonel Abraham J. Van Alstine, Lieutenant Colonel Van Alstine.................. 96
8TH REGIMENT.—Colonel Robert Van Rensselaer, Lieutenant Colonel Henry J. Van Rensselaer, Lieutenant Colonel Asa Waterman, Lieutenant Colonel Barent I. Staats.......................... 98
9TH REGIMENT.—Colonel Peter Van Ness, Lieutenant Colonel David Pratt.................................... 104
10TH REGIMENT.—Colonel Morris Graham, Colonel Henry Livingston.................................... 106
11TH REGIMENT.—Colonel Anthony Van Bergen, Lieutenant Colonel Cornelius Dubois................ 109
12TH REGIMENT.—Colonel Jacobus Van Schoonhoven, Lieutenant Colonel James Gordon.............. 110
13TH REGIMENT.—Colonel John McCrea, Colonel Cornelius Van Veghten.................................... 113
14TH REGIMENT.—Colonel John Knickerbacker, Colonel Peter Yates, Lieutenant Colonel John Van Rensselaer.................................... 116
15TH REGIMENT.—Colonel Peter Vroman, Lieutenant Colonel Peter Ziele.................................... 120
16TH REGIMENT.—Colonel John Blair, Colonel Lewis Van Woert.................................... 123
17TH REGIMENT.—Colonel William B. Whiting, Lieutenant Colonel Asa Waterman.................. 126
INDEPENDENT COMPANY, Captain Petrus Van Gaasbeck's.................................... 127

CHARLOTTE COUNTY.

PAGE

Colonel Doctor John Williams 128

CUMBERLAND COUNTY.

Colonel William Williams 130
COMPANY OF MINUTE MEN.— Major Joab Hoisington, Captain Joseph Hatch 131

DUTCHESS COUNTY.

2ND REGIMENT.— Colonel Abraham Brinkerhoff, Lieutenant Colonel Jacob Griffen 132
3RD REGIMENT.— Colonel John Field, Colonel Andrew Morehouse 137
4TH REGIMENT.— Colonel John Frear 139
5TH REGIMENT.— Colonel William Humfrey, Colonel James Van Deburgh 140
6TH REGIMENT.— Colonel Morris Graham, Colonel Roswell Hopkins, Lieutenant Colonel Jacob Griffin, 143
7TH REGIMENT — Colonel Henry Ludenton, Lieutenant Colonel Reuben Ferris 150
ASSOCIATED EXEMPTS.— Colonel Zephaniah Platt, Lieutenant Colonel Rufus Herrick 154
ASSOCIATED EXEMPTS.— Captain Abraham Schenck 156
REGIMENT OF MINUTE MEN.— Colonel Jacobus Swartwout 157
RANGERS.— Captain Ezekiel Cooper 160

ORANGE COUNTY.

Colonel Jesse Woodhull, Lieutenant Colonel Elihu Marvin 161
Colonel Ann Hawk Hay, Lieutenant Colonel Gilbert Cooper 162
Colonel William Allison, Lieutenant Colonel Benjamin Tuston 166
Colonel John Hathorn, Lieutenant Colonel Joseph Hasbrouck, Lieutenant Colonel Henry Wisner 167
ASSOCIATED EXEMPTS.— Captain John Wood 176

SUFFOLK COUNTY.

REGIMENT OF MINUTE MEN.— Colonel Josiah Smith 177
REGIMENT OF MINUTE MEN.— Colonel Thomas Terry 181
REGIMENT OF MINUTE MEN.— Colonel David Mulford 182

TRYON COUNTY.

1ST REGIMENT.— Colonel Samuel Campbell, Colonel Ebenezer Cox, Lieutenant Colonel Samuel Clyde .. 183
2ND REGIMENT.— Colonel Jacob Klock, Lieutenant Colonel Petter Waggoner 187
3RD REGIMENT.— Colonel Frederick Fisher, Lieutenant Colonel Volkert Veeder 191
4TH REGIMENT.— Colonel Peter Bellinger 195
5TH REGIMENT.— Colonel John Harper, Major Joseph Harper 198
BATTALION OF MINUTE MEN.— Colonel Samuel Campbell 199
ASSOCIATED EXEMPTS.— Captain Jellis Fonda 200
RANGERS.— Captain John Winn 201
RANGERS.— Captain Christian Getman 202
RANGERS.— Captain John Kasselman 203

ULSTER COUNTY.

1ST REGIMENT.— Colonel Johannes Snyder 204
2ND REGIMENT.— Colonel James McClaghry, Lieutenant Colonel Jacob Newkirk 209
3RD REGIMENT.— Colonel Levi Pawling, Colonel John Cantine, Lieutenant Colonel Jacob Hoornbeek .. 213
4TH REGIMENT.— Colonel Johannes Hardenburgh, Lieutenant Colonel Joanthan Elmendorph, Lieutenant Colonel Johannis Janson 218
INDEPENDENT COMPANY.— Captain Samuel Clark 223

WESTCHESTER COUNTY.

1ST REGIMENT.— Colonel Joseph Drake, Colonel James Hamman 224
2ND REGIMENT.— Colonel Thomas Thomas, Lieutenant Colonel Gilbert Budd 227
3RD REGIMENT.— Colonel Pierre Van Cortlandt, Colonel Samuel Drake, Lieutenant Colonel Gilbert Drake, Lieutenant Colonel John Hyatt 231
4TH REGIMENT.— Colonel Thaddeus Crane 235

PAGE.

ASSOCIATED EXEMPTS.—Lieutenant Colonel Joseph Benedict.......... 239
SEPARATE COMPANY.—Captain Jonathan Horton.......... 240

COLONEL JOHN LASHER—Lieutenant Colonel Andrew Stockholm's Reg't.......... 241
COLONEL JOHN NICHOLSON—Lieutenant Colonel John Vischer's Reg't.......... 242
COLONEL CORNELIUS D. WYNKOOP'S REG'T.......... 243
MAJOR JOHN WHEELOCK'S INDEPENDENT COMPANY.......... 245
ENSIGN JOHN FONDEY, JR.'S PARTY.......... 246
CAPTAIN JOHN A. BRADT'S RANGERS.......... 247
CAPTAIN JOHN REILAY'S RANGERS.......... 248

List of pensioners and applications for pensions.......... 249
Names of sundry persons whose service is evidenced by manuscripts on file in the Comptroller's office, though not found on the papers of any of the regular organizations.......... 251

ALPHABETICAL INDEX TO COMMANDING OFFICERS.

		PAGE.
Allen Ethan Colonel	Green Mountain Boys	48
Allison William Colonel	Orange County	166
Beeckman John H. Lieutenant Colonel	4th Albany	89
Bellinger Peter Colonel	4th Tryon	195
Benedict Joseph Lieutenant Colonel	Exempts (Westchester)	239
Birdsall Benj. Lieutenant Colonel	Levies	64
Blair John Colonel	16th Albany	123
Bradt John A. Captain	Rangers	247
Brinkerhoff Abraham Colonel	2nd Dutchess	132
Bruyn James Lieutenant Colonel	3rd Line	24
Bruyn James S. Lieutenant Colonel	5th Line	40
Budd Gilbert Lieutenant Colonel	2nd Westchester	227
Campbell Samuel Colonel	1st Tryon	183
Campbell Samuel Colonel	Battalion (Tryon)	199
Cantine John Colonel	3rd Ulster	213
Clark Samuel Captain	Independent Company (Ulster)	223
Clinton James Colonel	3rd Line	24
Clyde Samuel Lieutenant Colonel	1st Tryon	183
Cochran Robert Lieutenant Colonel	2nd Line	13
Cooper Ezekiel Captain	Rangers (Dutchess)	160
Cooper Gilbert Lieutenant Colonel	Orange County	162
Cox Ebenezer Colonel	1st Tryon	183
Crane Thaddeus Colonel	4th Westchester	235
Cuyler Abraham Colonel	1st Albany	80
Drake Gilbert Lieutenant Colonel	3rd Westchester	231
Drake Joseph Colonel	1st Westchester	224
Drake Samuel Colonel	3rd Westchester	231
Dubois Cornelius Lieutenant Colonel	11th Albany	109
Dubois Lewis Colonel	Levies	62
Duboys Lewis Colonel	5th Line	40
Elmendorph Jonathan Lieutenant Colonel	4th Ulster	218
Ferris Reuben Lieutenant Colonel	7th Dutchess	150
Field John Colonel	3rd Dutchess	137
Fisher Frederick Colonel	3rd Tryon	191
Fonda Jellis Captain	Exempts (Tryon)	200
Fondey John Jr. Ensign	Fondey's Party	246
Frear John Colonel	4th Dutchess	139
Gansevort Peter Colonel	3rd Line	24
Getman Christian Captain	Rangers (Tryon)	202
Gordon James Lt. Colonel	12th Albany	110
Graham Morris Colonel	Levies	64
Graham Morris Colonel	10th Albany	106
Graham Morris Colonel	6th Dutchess	143
Gregier Thomas Captain	Schooner "Gen. Putnam"	50
Grennell Thomas Captain	Frigate "Congress"	50
Griffen Jacob Lieutenant Colonel	2nd Dutchess	132

		PAGE.
Griffen Jacob Lieutenant Colonel	6th Dutchess	143
Hamilton Alexander Captain	Artillery	47
Hamman James Colonel	1st Westchester	224
Hardenburgh Johannes Colonel	4th Ulster	218
Harper John Colonel	Levies	51
Harper John Colonel	5th Tryon	198
Harper Joseph Major	5th Tryon	198
Hasbrouck Joseph Lieutenant Colonel	Orange County	167
Hathorn John Colonel	Orange County	167
Hatch Joseph Captain	Minute Men (Cumberland)	181
Hay Ann Hawk Colonel	Orange County	162
Herrick Rufus Lieutenant Colonel	Exempts (Dutchess)	154
Hoisington Jacob Major	Minute Men (Cumberland)	181
Holmes James Colonel	4th Line	32
Hoornbeek Jacob Lieutenant Colonel	3rd Ulster	213
Hopkins Roswell Colonel	6th Dutchess	143
Horton Jonathan Captain	Separate Company (Westchester)	240
Humfrey William Colonel	5th Dutchess	140
Hyatt John Lieutenant Colonel	3rd Westchester	231
Kasselman John Captain	Rangers (Tryon)	203
Klock Jacob Colonel	2nd Tryon	187
Knickerbacker John Colonel	14th Albany	116
Janson Johannis Lieutenant Colonel	4th Ulster	218
Lamb John Colonel	Artillery Regiment	46
Lansing Jacob Jr. Colonel	1st Albany	80
Lasher John Colonel	....	241
Livingston Henry Lieutenant Colonel	Levies	64
Livingston Henry Colonel	10th Albany	106
Livingston Henry B. Colonel	4th Line	32
Livingston James Colonel	Additional Battalion	45
Livingston Richard Lieutenant Colonel	Additional battalion	45
Ludenton Henry Colonel	7th Dutchess	150
Malcom William Colonel	Levies	58
Marvin Elihu Lieutenant Colonel	Orange County	161
Mercer William Captain	Frigate "Congress"	50
Morehouse Andrew Colonel	3rd Dutchess	137
Mulford David Colonel	Minute Men (Suffolk Co.)	182
McClaghry James Colonel	2nd Ulster	209
McCrea John Colonel	13th Albany	113
McKinstry John Lieutenant Colonel	Levies	73
Newkirk Jacob Lieutenant Colonel	2nd Ulster	209
Nicholson John Colonel	....	242
Paine Brinton Lieutenant Colonel	Levies	62
Pawling Albert Colonel	Levies	67
Pawling Levi Colonel	3d Ulster	213
Platt Zephaniah Colonel	Exempts (Dutchess)	154
Pratt David Lieutenant Colonel	9th Albany	104
Quackenbos Henry Colonel	5th Albany	93
Regnier Pierre Lieutenant Colonel	4th Line	32
Regnier Peter Lieutenant Colonel	2nd Line	13
Reilay John Captain	Rangers	248
Rogers Wm. Captain	Sloop "Montgomery"	50
Rogers Wm. Captain	Frigate "Congress"	50
Schenck Abraham Captain	Exempts (Dutchess)	156
Schuyler Philip P., Colonel	3rd Albany	86
Schuyler Stephen John Colonel	6th Albany	94
Smith James Captain	Sloop "Schuyler"	50

		PAGE.
Smith Josiah Colonel	Minute Men (Suffolk County)	177
Snyder Johannes Colonel	1st Ulster	204
Staats Barent I., Lieutenant Colonel	3rd Albany	86
Staats Barent I., Lieutenant Colonel	8th Albany	98
Stockholm Andrew Lieutenant Colonel		231
Swartwout Jacobus Colonel	Minute Men (Dutchess)	157
Terry Thomas Colonel	Minute Men (Suffolk)	181
Thomas Thomas Colonel	2nd Westchester	227
Tuston Benjamin Lieutenant Colonel	Orange County	166
Veeder Volkert Lieutenant Colonel	5th Albany	93
Veeder Volkert Lieutenant Colonel	3rd Tryon	191
Vischer John		242
Vroman Peter Colonel	15th Albany	120
Van Alstine Abraham J. Colonel	7th Albany	96
Van Alstine Philip Lieutenant Colonel	7th Albany	96
Van Bergen Anthony Lieutenant Colonel	11th Albany	109
Van Cortland Philip Colonel	2nd Line	13
Van Cortlandt Pierre Colonel	3rd Westchester	231
VanDeburgh James Colonel	5th Dutchess	140
Van den Bergh Gerrit Colonel	5th Albany	93
Van Dyck Cornelius Lieutenant Colonel	1st Line	1
Van Gaasbeck Petrus Captain	Independent Company	127
Van Ness Peter Colonel	9th Albany	104
Van Rensselaer Henry J. Lieutenant Colonel	8th Albany	98
Van Rensselaer Henry K. Lieutenant Colonel	6th Albany	94
Van Rensselaer John Lieutenant Colonel	14th Albany	116
Van Rensselaer Kilian Colonel	4th Albany	89
Van Rensselaer Robert Colonel	8th Albany	98
Van Schaick Goose Colonel	1st Line	1
Van Schaick Goose Colonel	2nd Line	13
Van Schoonhoven Jacobus Colonel	12th Albany	110
Van Veghten Cornelius Colonel	13th Albany	113
Van Woert Lewis Colonel	16th Albany	123
Wagoner Petter Lieutenant Colonel	2nd Tryon	187
Warner Seth Colonel	Green Mountain Boys	48
Waterman Asa Lieutenant Colonel	8th Albany	98
Waterman Asa Lieutenant Colonel	17th Albany	126
Weissenfels Frederick Lieutenant Colonel	2nd Line	13
Weissenfels Frederick Lieutenant Colonel	4th Line	32
Weissenfels Frederick Colonel	Levies	54
Wemple Abraham Colonel	2nd Albany	81
Wheelock John Major	Independent Company	245
Whiting William B. Colonel	17th Albany	126
Willett Marinus Colonel	Levies	73
Willett Marinus Lieutenant Colonel	5th Line	40
Williams Doctor John Colonel	Charlotte County	128
Williams William Colonel	Cumberland County	130
Winn John Captain	Rangers (Tryon)	201
Wisner Henry Lieutenant Colonel	Orange County	167
Wood John Captain	Exempts (Orange)	176
Woodhull Jesse Colonel	Orange	161
Wynkoop Cornelius D. Colonel		243
Yates Peter Colonel	14th Albany	116
Ziele Peter Lieutenant Colonel	15th Albany	120